The Nobel Laureates and their Legacies: A Survey of Contributions to Economic Thought

VOLUME - I

The Nobel Laureates and their Legacies: A Survey of Contributions to Economic Thought

VOLUME - I

Professor B.S.R. Rao

BSP **BS Publications**

An Imprint of **BSP Books Pvt. Ltd.**

4-4-309/316, Giriraj Lane,

Sultan Bazar, Hyderabad - 500 095

The Nobel Laureates and their Legacies: A Survey of Contributions to Economic Thought, Volume I
by **Professor B.S.R. Rao**

Published by

BS Publications
An Imprint of **BSP Books Pvt. Ltd.**
4-4-309/316, Giriraj Lane, Sultan Bazar,
Hyderabad - 500 095
Phone: 040 – 234456 88
e-mail: info@bspbooks.net
www.bspbooks.net

ISBN
Volume I : 978-93-95038-94-2
Volume II : 978-93-95038-82-9

DEDICATED TO

MY PATERNAL GRAND PARENTS

BALANTRAPU RAMAYYA

BALANTRAPU SURAMMA

Dr. C. Rangarajan
Former Chairman, Economic Advisory Council to the PM
Former Governor, Reserve Bank of India

FOREWORD

Prof. BSR Rao has undertaken the painstaking work of bringing together in two volumes a gist of the contributions made by the Nobel Laureates in Economics. The Nobel Award for economics was instituted only in 1969. Economics is a growing science. It is difficult for anyone to be an expert in all the sub disciplines. However, every student and teacher in economics must have some understanding of the developments in every field of economics. All the Nobel Laureates in economics have been well known names in their fields. Their writings have contributed immensely to the development of economics as a discipline. This book will give to every student of economics a brief insight into various developments. For a deeper understanding of the developments in any field, the student however will have to go to the original seminal articles. Prof. Rao instead of going chronologically has grouped the Nobel Laureates in terms of their contributions to the various subfields. This book should serve as an appetizer for further study. Prof. Rao has done a signal service to the students and teachers of economics by bringing out this compendium.

Chennai
November 10, 2014

C. RANGARAJAN

PREFACE

The unstructured and inadequate teaching in our colleges and many universities in our country of even the significant and major developments in economics - both theoretical and empirical – during the later part of the last century puts the Indian students at a disadvantageous position for pursuing advanced studies including the choice of a contemporary relevant topic for research. To partly alleviate the situation a reasonably comprehensive history of modern economic analysis encompassing the major contributions to various branches of the subject is called for. Such a work would facilitate interested students and teachers to update their knowledge and further help who would like to deepen and widen their intellectual base. This would hopefully help in improving the standard of post graduate teaching of economics as also enriching the research work on contemporary economic problems.

The present work is a humble and modest attempt in that direction. It summarizes major contributions of sixty-seven winners of Nobel Memorial Prize for economic sciences during 1969 through 2010. A brief biographical note on each of the winners is provided to make the reader note and appreciate the progress achieved by each of them including in some cases the hardships and privations they had to pass through in order to indicate the difficulties to be faced to reach the top. To enable interested readers make further reading, select bibliography of the work of each Nobel laureate is appended.

The award of a research project – History of Modern Economic Analysis: Contributions to Economics by Nobel Laureates – by the University Grants Commission, New Delhi, provided the initial impetus to this work. I took up the research work, acutely conscious of the daunting task what with the difficulty in collecting vast material and scrutinising it single handed. The project was completed and the draft report submitted to the sponsors in 2005. This has whetted my appetite; encouragement of professional friends made me decide to continue the work with the objective of bringing out a volume spanning the contributions of Laureates up to 2010. This meant revising and updating the earlier work. When I completed the work in 2013, I heaved a sigh of satisfied and delighted relief.

This work has been a long time in writing. I have accumulated debt of gratitude to many persons. However, first I sincerely thank the University Grants Commission that was instrumental in igniting my interest in the work by awarding a research project.

My deepest sense of gratitude is to the members my family who gave unstinted support to my research effort all along, putting up with my neglect of all other activities. I cannot adequately thank my wife, Seshasayi Balantrapu, who cheerfully took care of all family responsibilities, leaving me free to concentrate on my intellectual effort. My two sons and two daughters and their families were quite helpful in the completion of the work.

In writing this book, I have greatly depended on the websites of Noble Foundation such as its Archives. The photographs of the Laureates are given in the work. My sincere thanks to the Foundation. For providing valuable material, I have acknowledged it by specific reference to it at appropriate places. It would not be redundant if I once again express here my gratitude to Nobel Foundation.

Some of the material I have used here was supplied to me by one of my former students, Madhusudan Kalimipalli, currently Associate Professor at Wilfried Laurier University, Waterloo, Ontario, Canada. My profound thanks to him.

Two visits to the USA by me and my wife were very helpful in completing the work. Our stay at Irvine, Dulles, with my younger son, Krishna Balantrapu, was memorable and very fruitful. I was provided by him and my daughter-in-law, Sunita Balantrapu, besides warm and affectionate hospitality, conducive conditions for completing the work. In the second visit, Krishna has helped me improve the computer presentation and in finalising the manuscript for publication.

I have to acknowledge with thanks the help and co-operation of the library, librarian and staff of Ratan Tata Library, Delhi School of Economics, New Delhi of Gokhale Institute of Politics and Economics, Pune, of Jayakar Library, University of Pune, Pune and Library of Department of Economics, Osmania University, Hyderabad. I express my grateful thanks to Ms. N. Srilekha for the computer help in regard to a part of the work.

Last, but not the least, my gratitude to Messrs Nikhil Shah and Anil Shah, Directors of BSP Books Pvt. Ltd., Hyderabad for undertaking the publication of the work and to Mr. Mohit Singha, for introducing them to me.

Professor B. S. R. Rao
Hyderabad.

CONTENTS

VOLUME - I

SECTION - I

MACROECONOMICS

Chapter 1

Milton Friedman

(1912 – 2006)

Chapter 2

Bertil Gotthard Ohlin

(1899 – 1979)

Chapter 5

Sir William Arthur Lewis

(1915 – 1991)

Chapter 6

Lawrence Robert Klein

(1920 – 2013)

Chapter 7

James Tobin

(1918 – 2002)

Chapter 10

Robert Emerson Lucas Jr.

(1937 –)

Chapter 11

Robert Alexander Mundell

(1932 –)

Chapter 12

Finn Erling Kydland & Edward Christian Prescott

(1943 –) & (1940 –)

Chapter 13

Edmund Strother Phelps Jr.

(1933 –)

Chapter 14

Paul Robin Krugman

(1953 –)

Chapter 15

Peter Arthur Diamond, Dale Thomas Mortensen & Christopher Antoniou Pissarides

(1940 –), (1939 – 2014) & (1948 –)

SECTION-II

FINANCIAL ECONOMICS

Chapter 16

Harry Max Markowitz

(1927 –)

Chapter 17

William Forsyth Sharpe

(1934 –)

Chapter 18

Merton Howard Miller

(1923 – 2000)

Chapter 19

Robert C Merton & Myron Samuel Scholes

(1944 –) & (1941 –)

Chapter 21

Jan Tinbergen

(1903 – 1994)

Chapter 22

Wassily Wassilyovich Leontief

(1906 – 1999)

Chapter 23

Leonid Vitaliyevich Kantorovich

(1912 – 1986)

Chapter 24

Tjalling Charles Koopmans

(1910 – 1985)

Chapter 25

Sir John Richard Nicholas Stone

(1913 – 1991)

Chapter 26

Trygve Magnus Haavelmo

(1911 – 1999)

Chapter 27

James Joseph Heckman

(1944 –)

Chapter 28

Daniel Little Mcfadden

(1937 –)

Chapter 29

Clive William John Granger

(1934 – 2009)

Chapter 30

Robert Fry Engle III

(1942 –)

Volume - II

Section - IV

GENERAL EQUILIBRIUM THEORY

Chapter 33

Kenneth Joseph Arrow

(1921 –)

Chapter 34

Gerard Debreu

(1921 – 2004)

Chapter 35

Maurice Allais

(1911 – 2010)

Section-V

MICROECONOMIC THEORY

Chapter 36

George Joseph Stigler

(1911 – 1991)

Chapter 37

James Alexander Mirrlees

(1936 –)

Chapter 38

William Spencer Vickrey

(1914 – 1996)

Chapter 39

George Arthur Akerlof

(1940 –)

Chapter 40

Andrew Michael Spence

(1943 –)

Chapter 41

Joseph Eugene Stiglitz

(1943 –)

Chapter 42

Vernon Lomax Smith

(1927 –)

Chapter 43

Leonid Hurwicz, Eric Stark Maskin & Roger Bruce Myerson

(1917 – 2008), (1950 –) & (1951 –)

Section - VI

INTERDISCIPLINARY RESEARCH

Chapter 48

James McGill Buchanan Jr.

(1919 – 2013)

Chapter 49

Ronald Harry Coase

(1910 – 2013)

Chapter 50

Gary Stanley Becker

(1930 – 2013)

Chapter 51

Robert William Fogel

(1926 – 2013)

Chapter 52

Douglass Cecil North

(1920 –)

Chapter 53

Amartya Sen

(1933 –)

Chapter 54

Daniel Kahneman

(1934 –)

Chapter 55

Oliver Eaton Williamson

(1932 –)

Chapter 56

Elinor Ostrom

(1933 – 2012)

Section - VII

GAME THEORY

Chapter 57

John Forbes Nash, Jr.

(1928 –)

Chapter 58

John Charles Harsanyi

(1920 – 2000)

Chapter 59

Reinhard Selten

(1930 –)

Chapter 60

Thomas Crombie Schelling

(1921 –)

Chapter 61

Robert John Aumann

(1930 –)

INTRODUCTION

The Sveriges Riksbank Prize in economic sciences in memory of Alfred Nobel was instituted by the central bank of Sweden to mark its tercentenary celebration in 1968. The award, based on an economic commitment by the bank in perpetuity, is given by the Royal Swedish Academy of Sciences according to the same principles as for the Nobel Prizes that have been awarded in Physics, Chemistry, Medicine/Physiology, Literature and Peace since 1901. The procedure that is followed for selecting the laureates in Economic Sciences is the same as for the other subjects.

The procedure that is followed for the selection of the laureate(s) is described by Assar Lindbeck. According to him each year the Royal Swedish Academy receives roughly 200-300 nominations, covering about one hundred nominees. The Economics Prize Selection Committee of the Academy (with 5 to 8 members) commission expert studies of the most prominent candidates. The prize committee presents its award proposal to the Social Science Class of the Academy in the form of a report including all solicited expert studies. This forms the basis for the class to suggest a Laureate or a shared prize between two or, at most, three laureates. Finally the entire Academy at its meeting takes the final award decision usually in October every year.

The Royal Academy started awarding the prize in 1969. In the first 42 years (1969 - 2010, the period covered in this work) the laureates totalled sixty seven. It is proposed to attempt a bird's eye view of the type of awards given so far under a rather arbitrary classification, drawing heavily from Lindbeck's article "The Sveriges Riskbank Prize in economic sciences in memory of Alfred Nobel 1969 – 2007; Nobel Prize. Org".

I. General Equilibrium Theory

Paul A. Samuelson (1970)

John R. Hicks, Kenneth J. Arrow (1972)

Gerard Debreu (1983)

Maurice A. Allais (1988)

The economists included in this category have basically studied analytical structure of theoretical economic models, specifying the conditions for consistency, equilibrium, stability and efficiency of the economic system. Their contributions also analysed how equilibrium positions change when changes occur in exogenous factors (comparative static analysis). General equilibrium theory has emerged as a basic approach in theoretical economic analysis as a result of their efforts.

Hicks was awarded the prize for formulating multi-market stability conditions, extending the applicability of static analysis to several periods. Hicks was the first economist to attempt a rigorous dynamic analysis of capital accumulation. Another notable feature of Hicks's work was his anchoring it in microeconomic theories of behaviour of individual households/families and firms which helped the study of consequences of changes in various parameters. He also presented a widely-used and celebrated aggregate general equilibrium model with four markets – commodities, labour, money and credit – the well-known IS-LM model.

Samuelson's work is considered both continuation of the contributions by Hicks as also a break-through, specially in terms of analytical sophistication. It is widely accepted: Samuelson "single-handedly re-wrote considerable parts of central economic theory, microeconomic theory, static and dynamic, partial and general equilibrium theory, as well as welfare economics." Further, using simple mathematical models and employing second-order conditions of maximization procedures, he established important results that are treated now as classical theorems of economics.

Arrow and Debreu used powerful mathematical methods (for example theory of convex sets) to obtain more general results in general equilibrium theory. They were able to define broadly the concept of a good so that they can use it in static equilibrium analysis as well as in inter-temporal analysis, spatial distribution of production and consumption activities and in the analysis of decision-making under uncertainty. Arrow has also formulated well-known "impossibility theorem"- difficulties in deriving social welfare functions from preferences of individuals.

Maurice Allais's work has great similarities with the work of Samuelson and Arrow and Debreu. A particularly interesting aspect of Allais's work is his showing that an economy's path to equilibrium as a process by which competition exhausts all surpluses in firms. He is credited with demonstrating that returns to scale in production result in natural monopolies.

II. Macroeconomics

Milton Friedman (1976)

Franco Modigliani (1985)

James Tobin (1981)

James Meade and Bertil Ohlin (1977)

Robert Mundell (1999)

Lawrence Klein (1980)

Robert E. Lucas (1995)

Robert Solow (1987)

Arthur Lewis and Theodore Schultz (1979)

Finn Kydland and Edward S. Prescott (2004)

Edmund S. Phelps (2006)

Paul Krugman (2008)

Peter Diamond, Dale Mortensen and Christopher Pissarides (2010)

A number of prizes (13 prizes to 18 economists) have been awarded to macroeconomics. It is a branch of economic analysis that seeks to explain the behaviour of the whole national economy in terms of broad aggregates such as private consumption, investment, exports, government expenditure on goods, services etc. Some of the awards, however, were given to contribution in studies relating to some specific sectors.

The prize in 1976 was given to Milton Friedman for his contribution to consumption analysis, monetary history and theory. In his book A Theory of the Consumption Function, he joined together formal consumption theory and empirically applied it to a specific sector of the U.S. economy. His extensive and robust empirical study of monetary history of the U.S together with Anna Schwartz is a prime example of pure empirical research. The study is regarded as a monetary interpretation of macroeconomic fluctuations in the country (U.S.A).

Franco Modigliani who was awarded the prize for 1985 is specially known for two important building blocks, namely, sub models of private consumption and financial sector, in macroeconomic models. His analysis of the consequences for household saving of changes in demography and economic growth in his life-cycle theory of saving (together with Brumberg and Albert Ando) is particularly noteworthy. Together with Merton Miller, he pioneered the field of what has come to be known as corporate finance. The Modigliani-Miller theorem specifies the conditions under which the value of a firm in the stock market is not influenced (or influenced) by the way the firm finances its investment through equity capital or borrowed funds and by its dividend policy.

James Tobin was given the prize (in 1981) for his analysis of "financial markets and their relation to expenditure decisions, employment, production and prices." The award was for his theoretical contributions relating to specific sectors in the national economy. Tobin's approach modelling interactions between financial and real sectors in the economy received wide acceptance and got integrated into macro models of national economies. In this, "Tobin's q" – important role played by the relation between the market value of a capital asset and its reproduction costs – played an important role. Furthermore, Tobin's portfolio model has gained acceptance as a useful analytical tool for analyzing direct effects on product prices of changes in money supply.

James Meade and Bertil Ohlin shared the 1977 prize for their contributions to the theory of international trade and international capital movements. The award is another example of a contribution concerning the sector of foreign transactions. The award to Ohlin is for his development of a theory of international and interregional trade – referred to as Heckscher-Ohlin model – which seeks to explain both the causes and consequences of trade. Ohlin showed that the proportions of available factors of production, namely labour and capital, determine the trade pattern of individual countries. He further demonstrated that international trade tends to equalize the return to these factors among countries. Meade anticipated the theory of "second best" resource allocation by analysing trade policy in a world market with various market distortions. He also pioneered the theory of open-economy macroeconomics and worked on the analysis of the relation between internal and external balance and the relation between targets and instruments of economic policy.

Robert Mundell carried Meade's work further and has laid the foundation for today's theory of open-economy macroeconomics – the so-called Mundell-Fleming model. He is the recipient of 1999 Prize. Mundell is reputed for introducing foreign trade and global capital movements into Hicks's IS-LM model for a closed economy. Taking inspiration from David Hume's work, he showed that the effects of fiscal and monetary policy crucially depend upon international capital mobility. Mundell did creditable work on optimum currency areas, delineating the advantages and disadvantages for countries giving up their monetary sovereignty in favour of common currency.

Robert Klein did important macroeconomic research work for national economies and even regarding interaction among several national economies for which he is given the 1980 award. The prize citation specifically mentions his "creation of econometric models and their application to the analysis of economic fluctuations and economic policies". He employed statitical model simulation for analyzing the effects of economic policies. His contributions to developing forecasting techniques are noteworthy. It is also observed that initially Klein used Keynesian type of macro theories; however, over time they became eclectic and more detailed.

Robert Lucas (who received the 1995 prize) further strengthened macroeconomic model building with particular emphasis on the important role of expectations. He is especially remembered for developing consequences of "rational expectations" among agents. According to him the agents exploit all available information and do not make any systematic expectational mistakes. Lucas showed the way the policies of government and central bank change in response to changes in the economy. He has become well-known for his criticism of traditional macroeconomic estimation – the so-called "Lucas critique" – and ways of obviating the problem.

Robert Solow received the prize in 1987 for his work on the theory of long-term macroeconomic growth by building a simple mathematical model demonstrating how capital accumulation process raises productivity in an economy. The prices of capital and labour determine the capital intensity of production. He is also known for his pioneering work in "growth accounting."

Arthur Lewis and Theodore Schultz shared the 1979 prize for their research on "economic development with particular consideration of the process of developing countries". The award to Lewis particularly mentions his two long-term growth models for developing countries, laying stress upon the consequences of an elastic supply of labour and the determinants of the terms of trade exporting tropical products. In the case of Schultz, the award is for his analysis of the role of investment in human capital for economic development, particularly in agriculture. He made specific reference to the seeming efficiency in the agricultural sector in less developed countries in the context of resource and knowledge constraints in those countries. Lewis analysed the situation in that these countries are characterised by large, stagnant agricultural sector and a dynamic capitalist sector (as almost an economic enclave). Both Lewis and Schultz have not used formalised statistical or econometric techniques.

The award for 2004 was shared by Finn Kydland and Edward Prescott for showing that economic policies are often afflicted with problems of "time consistency." Without prior commitment to a specific policy rule, economic policy makers may find it convenient not to pursue a policy which they initially thought to be the best one. Even when price stability is the desired objective of monetary policy, national economies get caught in high inflation. Kydland and Prescott's research highlighted the need for economic research into the issue of the credibility and feasibility of economic policy. Their work also moved the discussion of economic policy from isolated policy measures to the institutional mechanism of policy making. Another important aspect of their contribution relates to joining together the analysis of short-term economic fluctuations with analysis of long-term economic growth – earlier considered separate fields. They also underlined the role of supply shocks or productivity disturbances in studies of short-term macroeconomic fluctuations in addition to the analysis of economic growth. This insight was integrated by subsequent studies relating to the role of aggregate demand shifts and wage – and price – rigidities while explaining short-term and long-term economic development.

Another prize awardee in macroeconomics was Edmund Phelps (2006). He has provided a number of previous missing pieces to the macroeconomic problem which helped in greater understanding of the relation between short-run and long-run effects of economic policy. Phelps was considered the first economist who challenged successfully the so-called Phillips curve explanation of a stable trade-off between inflation and unemployment. He contended that inflation is affected by the structure and functioning of the labour market.

Phelps demonstrated when changes in the saving rate confer inter-temporal benefits, benefits across all generations. He underlined the key role human capital plays in encouraging economic growth through diffusion of new technology.

Paul Krugman was awarded the 2008 prize for his research in international trade and economic geography. After Second World War, traditional foreign trade theory could not satisfactorily explain the emerged pattern of trade. In 1979 Krugman presented a new model which provided a convincing explanation for the observed foreign trade patterns. He made assumptions of presence of economies of scale in manufacturing industry and also that consumers desire to have product diversity in consumption.

Krugman's award was also for his presentation of a new model of economic geography. He developed a comprehensive theory of location of labour and firms.

The 2010 Nobel Memorial Prize in Economics was awarded jointly to Peter Diamond, Dale Mortensen and Christopher Pissarides for their "analysis of markets with search frictions." The real world markets are quite different from their idealized verison as put forward by classical economists. The real world markets are search and matching markets. From out of the work of the three economists on search and matching theory emerged the Diamond – Mortensen – Pissarides model or DMP model. The DMP model has been found useful to analyse the process of transmission of aggregate shocks to the labour market that would result in fluctuations in unemployment in the economy, job vacancies and employment flows. The theory has been used extensively to study a number of economic issues in consumer theory, inventory theory, financial economics among others.

III. Microeconomic Theory

George Stigler (1982)

James Mirrlees and William Vickrey (1996)

George Akerlof, Michael Spence and Joseph Stiglitz (2001)

Leonid Hurwicz, Roger Myerson and Eric Maskin (2007)

Vernon Smith (2002)

Contributions of researchers in microeconomic theory devoted to decision-making by individual households and firms and allocation of resources among different uses and production sectors received a total of five awards to ten economists.

George Stigler was awarded the prize (in 1982) for his studies of "industrial structures, functioning of markets and causes and effects of public regulation." By analysing how economic regulations are managed by political leaders and public administrators, he showed, for example, that it results in "regulatory capture" – that is, those who are supposed to be regulated dominate the regulators. His contributions to the history of economic analysis is widely recognised and appreciated. Like Friedman, Stigler belonged to positivist tradition, laying particular stress on analytical simplicity and significance of empirical application. He pioneered the field of information economics, bringing information costs specifically into his analysis.

James Mirrlees and William Vickrey shared the prize (in 1996) for their work in information economics with particular focus on consequences of limitations in individuals' information, including information asymmetries among economic agents. Such information asymmetries play an important role in the functioning of markets such as financial markets. Mirrlees did important work on results for taxation of asymmetric information between tax payers and government. Vickrey did valuable work on various types of auctions. His analytical insights have significant impact on developing efficiently – functioning auction of rights to broadcast, airport landing permits, television rights and privatisation of government assets.

A more general theory of asymmetric information was developed by George Akerlof, Michael Spence and Joseph Stiglitz for which they shared the 2001 Prize.

Akerlof studied markets where sellers of products have more information than buyers about product quality. He showed that low quality products may squeeze high-quality products in such markets and that prices of high quality products may suffer as a result. The analysis helps explain, for instance, extremely high borrowing rates in poor countries and the difficulties for broad markets for health care insurance to emerge. Spence and Stiglitz analysed various types of spontaneous adjustment mechanisms in such markets. Spence showed how better informed agents may improve the market outcome by taking costly actions for the purpose of transmitting information to poorly informed agents. Important examples of such 'signalling' are education as a signal of individual in labour markets and dividend payments to signal high profitability of individual firms. Stiglitz however, analyzed the role of 'screening' in markets with asymmetric information. Relevant examples include attempts by insurance companies to partition contracts into risk classes, thus offering different types of contracts among which customers can choose. He has also shown how a number of market phenomena may be explained by the theory of asymmetric information such as unemployment, credit rationing, and share cropping contracts in agricultural sector in some developing countries.

The role of information asymmetries has been further probed by theorists studying alternative allocation mechanisms – Leonid Hurwicz, Roger Myers and Eric Maskin. They shared the 2007 prize.

Hurwicz defined allocation mechanisms as a game in which the participants act as if they send messages to each other, or to a hypothetical "message centre". He also emphasised the importance that an allocation mechanism is "incentive compatible" in the sense that the predicted, or desired, outcome is consistent with all agents' economic incentives to act. Other important roots of the theory of mechanism design are Mirrlees's optimisation analysis and Vickrey's analysis of auction markets, referred to earlier. A number of authors, in particular Myerson and Maskin have generalised and developed the insights of Hurwicz, Mirrlees and Vickrey. Through a calculation algorithm called the "Revelation Principle", they have simplified the analysis of alternative allocation mechanisms. Generally speaking, this mechanism states that the researcher can restrict his attention to a subset of hypothetical mechanisms, denoted "direct mechanisms", that satisfy the condition of incentive compatibility. Myerson has applied the method, for instance, to auction markets and regulation. Since one and the same mechanism in some cases turns out to generate several different equilibria (multiple equilibria) the task remained to develop methods to find an optimum equilibrium. Maskin has developed analytic tools for this purpose, what he calls "implementation theory". He has also classified the importance of monotonocity of the preference ordering among individuals when attempting generation of efficient allocation mechanisms.

Traditionally, economics has been a non-experimental discipline, till the emergence of the work of Vernon Smith who has shared the Prize in 2002 with Daniel Kahneman. To help understand economic behaviour, Smith has developed methods for conducting laboratory experiments in economics. He demonstrated that interaction of sellers and buyers in laboratory experiments often yielded prices that were quite close to market prices predicted by traditional supply-demand theory.

Smith has also developed the theory underlying the auction markets and enriched literature in this regard.

IV. Financial Economics

Harry Markowitz, William Sharpe and Merton Miller (1990)

R. Merton and M.Scholes (1997)

In recent years, financial economics became an important and rapidly growing field. As mentioned earlier, Modigliani and Tobin built vital financial building blocks to macro-economic theory. The real foundations of financial economics were laid in the 1950s and 1960s by Harry Markowitz, Merton Miller and William Sharpe who were jointly awarded the prize in 1990. Markowitz's main contribution was in formulating a micro theory of portfolio management of individual wealth holders. Equilibrium analysis in financial markets was primarily developed by Miller and Sharpe. Miller's main work was in the field of corporate finance (in the beginning, his work was in collaboration with Franco Modigliani). He is credited with underlining the factors that determine share prices in the market and capital costs of firms. Sharpe's pioneering work is in the development of a general theory for the pricing of financial assets in the market.

Subsequently R. Merton and M. Scholes were given the prize (in 1997) for their analysis of price formation of so-called derivative instruments such as options, which are claims on underlying financial instruments including shares and financial assets. (The late F. Black, cooperating with Scholes, was also instrumental for this achievement). These contributions were a necessary condition for the subsequent development of today's huge markets for various types of derivative instruments. These markets have increased the possibility for individual agents to choose appropriate risk levels according to their own preferences, regardless whether they choose low or high exposure to risk.

V. Interdisciplinary Research

James Buchanan (1986)

Gary Becker (1992)

Ronald Coase (1991)

Herbert Simon (1978)

Oliver Williamson and Elinor Ostrom (2009)

Simon Kuznets (1971)

Robert Fogel and Douglass North (1993)

Amartya Sen (1998)

Friedrich Hayek and Gunnar Myrdal (1974)

Daniel Kahneman (2002)

These are economists who have widened the domain of economic analysis to new areas.

J. Buchanan got the prize (1986) for his research on the boundary between economics and political science, or more specifically, "for his development of the contractual and constitutional basis for the theory of economic and political decision-making." This research made him one of the founding fathers of the 'Public Choice' school which analyses the driving forces behind political decisions and tries to endogenise political behaviour in models of national economies. The Public Choice school assumes that politicians are motivated by considerations similar to those explaining the behaviour of other agents, including the striving for personal benefit and a desire for power.

G. Becker had worked on the borderline between economics and sociology, in particular in his research about the family, e.g, he studied the household's role as a combined producer and consumer of goods and services. He had, however, not only analysed the economic behaviour of families – labour supply, consumption, household production and household saving – but also behaviour that has not earlier been considered by economists, such as education, marriage, child birth and divorce. He had both shown how economic considerations influence choice in these areas and analysed "social interaction" between individuals outside the market system, reflected in the prize citation (1992): "for having extended the domain of microeconomic analysis to a wide range of human behaviour and interactions including non-market behaviour." Becker's influence today extends far outside economics, in particular the so-called 'rational choice' school of sociology.

R. Coase (1991 award winner) made important contributions on the borderline between economics, law and organization. In particular, he showed which factors determine the size of firms. He also clarified conditions under which voluntary contracts between private agents can resolve problems with "external effects" of production, important example being pollution. These contributions are reflected in the Prize citation: "for his discovery and clarification of the significance of transaction costs and property rights for the institutional structure and functioning of the economy". Coase's concept of transaction costs has become an important foundation for the theory of contracts and for the whole field of law and economics.

H. Simon's prize citation (1978) refers to his research on "the decision-making process within economic organizations". He challenged some basic building blocks of microeconomic theory, in particular the maximisation principle and the assumption about full ("unbounded") rationality. He argued that the decision-makers are content with a "satisfactory" outcome – satisficing behaviour. This is an important contribution in the field of administrative (management) science.

Oliver Williamson, who shared the 2009 Nobel Prize with Elinor Ostrom has carried further the work of Herbert Simon and Ronald Coase. Accepting Simon's view that human behaviour is boundedly rational and Coase's work on the importance of transaction costs in any study of firm and market organisation, Williamson analysed the issue of economic governance. He has studied the rationale for the existence of markets and hierarchical organizations in, say, resolving conflicts of interest. The resolution of such conflicts crucially depend upon the complexity of transactions and costs of transactions. Williamson is recognised as the founder and chief developer of what has come to be known as 'Transaction Cost Economics'.

Elinor Ostrom who shared the 2009 prize with Williamson, was awarded the prize "for her analysis of economic governance, especially the commons". The contributions of Williamson and Ostrom are complementary. While the former concerns himself with the problem of regulating transactions, Ostrom's focus was on the issue of enforcement of rules. The work of Ostrom, a political scientist, was associated with the new institutional economics. By her work she was responsible for the resurgence of political economy.

S. Kuznets (1971 award winner) made empirical research on the borderline between economics and history; the citation states "for his empirically founded interpretation of economic growth." The award to Kuznets is an example of an award for inductive rather than deductive analysis. His important contributions include the celebrated "Kuznets curve" of the U-shaped relation between GDP and income inequality as well as his findings that the long-run average propensity to consume out of income tends to be constant in time series data whereas it tends to fall in cross-section data. He used very long-term data to identify regularities by characterizing economic growth and the distribution of income in different nations at different times.

The concentration of R. Fogel and D. North (1993) again lie in the boundary between economics and history. The Academy cited them "for having renewed research in economic history by applying economic theory and institutional change." Fogel's main contributions have been to clarify the role of railways for the development of the national economy in the U.S. and the economic role of slavery. By comparing the factual development with a counter-factual benchmark, Fogel has concluded that previous studies of economic-growth in the U.S. had vastly over estimated the importance of railways. He also concluded that slavery was not abolished because of falling profitability of the slave system, but rather because of humanitarian considerations.

North has shed new light on the economic development in Europe and the U.S. before and in connection with the industrial revolution including the roles of sea transport and changes in the pattern of regional specialisation and interregional trade. He has also been a pioneer in analysing the role of institutions (property rights), for economic development as well as the importance of different types of transaction costs. In these fields he developed and applied the ideas of Ronald Coase.

Amartya Sen's (1998) research is on the borderline between economics and philosophy; the citation says: "for his contributions to welfare economics". He scrutinised the philosophical foundations of collective decisions and welfare evaluations, including problems of evaluating the distribution of income and wealth. He has also constructed influential indices to measure income distribution and poverty. Sen has also analysed the determinants and consequences of starvation in a number of less developed countries. These empirical studies of actual famines show that reduced aggregate supplies of food has not always been the most important factor for starvation catastrophes, which, in some cases, have instead been caused by redistribution of income to the disadvantage of the poor.

While the early contributions of Friedrich Hayek and Gunnar Myrdal (award in 1974) in the 1930s related to business cycles and monetary phenomena, their works from early 1940s dealt with the interrelation between economic, social and political processes. Hayek is particularly known for his emphasis on information and incentive content of the price system. He bestowed special attention to individual behaviour, to the institutional framework for economic decisions, especially the political constitution and the legal rules that define contracts and property rights. In addition, he is remembered for his emphasis on the significance of "spontaneous" social order in contrast to planned institutional designs.

Myrdal showed how interaction of economic, political and social forces often generate virtuous circles. He claimed that his methods of analysis of "mutual causation" was a generalisation of Knut Wicksell's "cumulative process in monetary theory." In this context, a reference is to be made to his study of the Negro problem in the United States in his work An American Dilemma which has undoubtedly influenced social science research generally; it was referred to by the U.S. Supreme Court when outlawing segregation. A similar approach was employed by Myrdal in his subsequent work on poverty and economic development in South Asia.

Research in psychology has influenced economic research in recent years which is reflected in the award to Daniel Kahneman (2002) who, in cooperation with Amos Tversky has made significant contribution to decision-making under uncertainty. They developed an alternative theory – Prospect Theory – to the traditional theory of choice under uncertainty. Tversky died in 1996. They have specifically shown how choice of individuals is systematically influenced by their perception of alternatives and by the exact "framing" of these alternatives.

VI. New Methods of Economic Analysis: Econometrics etc.

Jan Tinbergen and Ragnar Frisch (1969)

Trygve Haavelmo (1989)

Leonid Kantorovich and Tjalling Koopmans (1975)

James Heckman and Daniel Mcfadden (2000)

Clive Granger and Robert Engle (2003)

Wassily Leontief (1970)

Richard Stone (1984)

The very first-award in 1969 jointly to Ragnar Frisch and Jan Tinbergen is a case in point. The award to them was for their pioneering work on Econometric Model building. The prize citation says "for having developed and applied dynamic models for the analysis of economic processes." Frisch is credited with developing general methods of dynamic and econometric analysis. Tinbergen had applied them empirically, besides developing rigorous statistical tests to empirically verify alternative business cycle theories. They both developed a formalized theory of the relation between instruments and targets of economic policy – paralleling Meade's analysis of similar issues.

The award to Haavelmo (in 1989) was "for his clarification of the probability theory foundation of econometrics and his analysis of simultaneous economic structures." He showed that complex economic relations, if estimated simultaneously, could lead to avoiding misleading interpretations of partial relations between economic variables.

The 1975 award jointly to Kantorovich and Koopmans was for their methodological contributions in theory. Kantorovich developed the concept of efficient resource use in individual enterprises and for the whole economy. He also showed the theoretical link between resource allocation and the price system. Koopmans, through the development of activity analysis, demonstrated the correspondence between efficiency in production and existence of a system of "accounting prices." Both Kantorovich and Koopmans demonstrated the theoretical possibility of decentralised decision-making in a centrally planned economy being linked to the existence of an efficient price system, including a uniform accounting price of capital for making investment decisions. One can see how this analysis is related to the achievements in general equilibrium theory by Arrow and Debreu. Kantorovich and Koopmans also made vital contributions to the mathematical technique of linear programming.

The breakthrough in econometrics achieved by James Heckman and Daniel Mcfadden, namely development of microeconometrics, was recognised by the award of the prize to them jointly in 2000. Their contributions have importantly facilitated analysis of data relating to large groups of individual agents – households as well as firms.

Heckman had developed methods to obviate biased statistical estimates in situations in which the sample data being analyzed are non-random – the well-known Heckman Correction (the Heckit method). Examples include studies of wage formation and return on education, since individuals who do not work and do not have the type of education that is being studied are outside the sample.

Mcfadden has developed methods for analysing discrete choice by individuals. Prominent examples include choice of profession, occupation, residence and means of transportation.

Conditional logit analysis is a significant contribution by Mcfadden. This method, besides utilising observable facts about individual agents and available alternatives, exploits unobservable differences among individuals and among alternatives. They are represented by random error terms.

The 2003 award jointly to Clive Granger and Robert Engle is in regard to their work (separately and jointly) on analysis of time series data.

Granger had developed and applied new statistical methods based on "cointegration" to differentiate between short-term fluctuations and long-term trends and combine them. This is vital in the case of analysis of "non-stationary" time series. For instance, when temporary disturbances in aggregate production have long-lasting effects; that is, when time series reflect a "stochastic trend." Granger made his contributions partly in association with Engle. Cointegration has now become a central aspect in time series analysis in economics.

Engle is best known for his work involving study of the volatility properties of many time series in economics, for example in financial markets. For this purpose, he applied the concept of ARCH (autoregressive conditional heteroskedasticity). His method is particularly useful in clarifying market developments where turbulent periods marked by large fluctuations are followed by calmer periods, with modest fluctuations.

Wassily Leontief was awarded (1970) the prize for the development of the input-output method or inter-industry analysis. His work highlighted in quantitative form, the interdependencies between different sectors of the economy. The analysis is also found suitable for analysing short-term effects of shocks in one sector on the other sectors of the economy. He not only formulated the method but also applied it to empirical data.

Richard Stone, who received the award for 1984, got it for his "fundamental contributions to the development of systems of national accounts." It is hard to imagine empirical analysis in macroeconomics without comprehensive systems of national accounts. In this regard, a reference has to be made to the earlier work by Ragnar Frisch, Erik Lindahl, Colin Clark and Simon Kuznets. Leontief-style input-output tables also formed a useful component of this type of work.

VII. Game Theory

John Nash, John Harsanyi and Reinhard Selten (1994)

Thomas Schelling and Robert Aumann (2005)

John von Neumann and Oskar Morgenstern pioneered the development of game theory in 1940s. A couple of awards were made to contributors in this area. The award for 1994 was made to John Nash, John Harsanyi and Reinhard Selten "for their pioneering analysis of equilibrium in the theory of non-cooperative games." Nash draws a distinction between cooperative games, in which obligatory agreements can be made, and non-cooperative games, where such agreements are not feasible. He is well known for developing an equilibrium concept for predicting the outcome of non-cooperative games that later came to be known as Nash equilibrium. By providing theoretical foundation for predicting outcomes of games characterised by incomplete information, Harsanyi provided the needed impetus to further development in the field of information economics following the lead of Stigler, Vickrey and Mirrlees.

The concept of Nash equilibrium was refined by Reinhard Selten which was helpful in analysing dynamic strategic interaction among different agents. He applied these refinements in the analyses of markets with a few sellers. Selten's refinements helped in excluding a number of theoretically possible but unstable or irrelevant equilibria.

After a gap of over a decade, the prize for 2005 was awarded in game theory to Robert Aumann and Thomas Schelling, the former for his theoretical work and the later for his work involving important social, political and economic problems. Both of them analysed conflict and cooperation through game-theoretic methods.

Aumann pioneered comprehensive formal analysis of infinitely repeated games, laying stress upon the types of outcomes that can be maintained over time in the context of long-run economic relations. His analysis has many practical applications such as price wars among business firms, and trade wars among nations. Aumann's approach is found useful for understanding the emergence of institutions such as those for wage negotiations and international trade agreements.

Schelling's analysis of strategic commitments has found to be useful in explaining a wide range of phenomena, from competitive strategies of firms to delegation of political decision-making power to administrative agencies. He showed that an agent may strengthen its position in bargaining by openly worsening its own options and that the ability to retaliate can be more useful than the capacity to attack. Schelling also demonstrated how under certain circumstances uncertainty about retaliation strengthens one's position than certainty about retaliation. He is instrumental in making game theory a unifying framework for all social sciences.

VOLUME - I

SECTION - I

MACROECONOMICS

CHAPTER 1

MILTON FRIEDMAN

(1912 – 2006)

Milton Friedman of University of Chicago, Illinois, U.S.A., was awarded the 1976 Prize in Economic Sciences in memory of Alfred Nobel "for his achievements in the fields of consumption analysis, monetary history and theory, and for his demonstration of the complexity of stabilization policy." His name is mainly associated with the renaissance of the role of money in inflation and the revival of interest and understanding of the instrument of monetary policy. He is also credited with being the architect of the Chicago school and with the coining of the now widely used terms "money matters" or "money alone matters." His strong emphasis on money may be contrasted with a narrow interpretation of Keynes's theory that for a long time "almost entirely ignored the significance of money and monetary policy" in the analysis of business cycles and inflation.

Friedman's pioneering attack on the early post-Keynesian one-sidedness (extolling fiscal policy and underestimating the role of monetary policy) goes as far back as the early 1950's. Thanks to Friedman's brilliant espousal of the importance of monetary factors, the macro econometric models of 1970's differed greatly from such models of the preceding two decades. The widespread debate on the theories put forward by Friedman had led to a review of monetary policies followed by central banks of developed countries, particularly the United States. The Royal Academy of Sciences while announcing the award to Friedman observes: "It is very rare for an economist to wield such influence, directly and indirectly, not only on the direction of scientific research but also on actual policies."

Friedman had carried out a number of empirical studies that are both 'original and weighty,' in support of his analysis of the role of money in an economy. By putting forward a new formulation of the theory of the demand for money or liquid resources, he conducted empirical studies of the relationship between increases in money supply and the resultant changes in incomes and prices. His findings on the relevance of the quantity theory of money in explaining developments in the economy were based on the premise that the demand for money is very stable.

Friedman's major work in the field of money is A Monetary History of the United States 1867-1960. This work is widely regarded as one of Friedman's "most profound and also most distinguished" achievements. The award citation specifically mentions: Most outstanding is perhaps his original and energetically pursued study of the crucial role played by the policy of the Federal Reserve System in the U.S. in sparking off the 1929 crisis and in deepening and prolonging the depression that ensued. Critics generally agree that this work of Friedman is a monumental scientific work which will long stimulate the re-examination of the course of events during this epoch.

Friedman's refashioning of the theory of consumption is considered of great interest from purely scientific point of view. He had put forward "permanent income hypothesis" which postulated that what he called 'permanent income' and not year-to-year measured income is the prime determinant of households' total consumption outlay. Friedman drew the "extremely valuable" distinction between temporary and permanent incomes of households. He had argued that a greater part of transitory income is saved than that of the permanent income.

Friedman's studies of lags appearing in all areas of economic policy are another significant contribution. The Nobel award states that it was Friedman who coined the terms "observation lag," "decision-lag" and "effect lag" to express a fundamental problem in regard to effectiveness of a policy that was neglected earlier; that is, the right timing for taking stabilisation measures during a business cycle. He had argued and had shown how changes in money supply could have a destabilising effect because of prolonged effect-lags of varying lengths. On the basis of his studies, Friedman drew a policy conclusion that monetary policy should be simplified and the goal of the monetary policy should be to ensure a long-run stable growth rate of the supply of money.

The Phillips Curve explanation of inflation that there is a permanent trade-off between unemployment and the rate of inflation was questioned by Edmund Phelps and Milton Friedman. However, Friedman was the first to demonstrate that the accepted assumption of a trade-off between unemployment and the rate of inflation was only a temporary phenomenon; no such trade-off exists in the long run. According to him, unemployment below a "structural" level of balance (referred to as "natural" level of unemployment) leads to a cumulative increased rate in prices and nominal wages, primarily due to the destabilising influence exerted by expectations. His hypothesis on the importance of inflationary expectations has strongly influenced the modern thinking regarding the factors determining the structure of wages in an economy.

Friedman was a pioneer among the economists who recommended in the beginning of the 1950s a reorganisation of the then existing international monetary system of fixed exchange rates to a system based on free exchange rates. Besides analysing the theoretical aspects of the problem, he used also empirical studies to evaluate how such a system could be made to work. He strongly opined that the Bretton Woods system characterised by relatively fixed exchange rates was bound to break down sooner or later.

1.1 A BRIEF BIOGRAPHICAL NOTE: MILTON FRIEDMAN

Milton Friedman was born on July 31, 1912 in Brooklyn, New York city. He was the son of a poor immigrant dry goods merchant, who died when Friedman was 15. Milton Friedman graduated (B.A.) at Rutgers University in 1932 and completed his M.A. at Chicago University the following year. Initially, Friedman specialised in Mathematics, intending to become an actuary, and went so far as to take actuarial examinations, "passing several but also failing several." Shortly, however, he became interested in economics. After spending a year under a fellowship at Columbia University in 1933-1934, Friedman returned to Chicago as a research assistant to Henry Schultz to work on demand analysis until 1935, when he joined the staff of the U S National Resources Committee. He worked for the Committee from 1935 to 1937. From 1937, Friedman started his long association with the National Bureau of Economic Research (NBER), New York, which persisted until 1981.

Friedman was, for a brief period in 1940, a visiting professor of Economics at the University of Wisconsin. After a two-year stint (1941-1943) in the division of tax research of the U.S. Treasury, he became Associate Director of the Statistical Research group in the Division of War Research at Columbia University until the end of World War II. Spending a year as Associate Professor at the University of Minnesota, he returned to Chicago as Professor of Economics in 1946, the year in which he received a Ph.D. from Columbia University. At Chicago, he later became Paul Snowdon Russell Distinguished Service Professor of Economics. He retired on January 1, 1977 to take up a position as Senior Research Fellow at the Hoover Institution at Stanford University.

His teachers at Rutgers were Arthur F. Burns and Homer Jones; at Chicago, Frank Knight, Lloyd Mints, Jacob Viner, Henry Schultz and Henry Simons; and at Columbia, Harold Hotelling, J. M. Clark and Wesley C. Mitchell.

Friedman stated in his autobiographical note: "The combination of Chicago and the Bureau [NBER] has been highly productive. At Chicago, I established a 'Workshop in Money and Banking' which has enabled our monetary studies to be cumulative body of work to which many have contributed...our work on monetary history and statistics has been enriched and supplemented by both the empirical studies and theoretical developments that have grown out of Chicago workshop."

Friedman was President of the American Economic Association in 1967. He was conferred numerous honorary degrees. He was economic columnist for Newsweek for a long period (1966-1984). In 1988, he was awarded the Presidential Medal of Freedom and the National Medal of Science. He died at San Francisco, CA, on November 16, 2006.

1.2 A BRIEF SURVEY OF MILTON FRIEDMAN'S MAIN CONTRIBUTIONS

Friedman's work is very vast and covers a wide and large number of fields including microeconomics, macroeconomics, monetary theory and policy, international monetary issues and methodology of economics. Any survey of his work has necessarily to be selective and cannot claim or pretend to be exhaustive even in the fields chosen for the survey. As such, the survey presented here is brief and highly selective, given the self-imposed constraint of space. The present write up on the scientific contributions of Friedman is organised under the following heads.

1. Consumption Function;
2. Monetary Theory and Policy;
3. International Monetary Problems;
4. Microeconomics; and
5. Methodological issues.

1.2.1 CONSUMPTION FUNCTION

J.M. Keynes's central proposition in The General Theory of Employment, Interest, and Money is that in the short run as income of a household increases, other things being equal, its consumption also increases, but less than proportionately. That is, as income rises, consumers tend to save proportionately more and spend proportionately less. He also postulated that this relationship is sufficiently stable to form the basis for the multiplier through which an autonomous expenditure at the macroeconomic level "generated a considerably larger increase in real aggregate demand." Many subsequent empirical works (including that of Simon Kuznets) have demonstrated significant inconsistencies between the patterns of household behaviour from the time series data and from cross section data of household surveys. To resolve such observed inconsistencies, in the early post-Keynesian empirical work, economists like Duesenberry, Modigliani and Brown had introduced modification of the simple linear consumption function. Ms. Dorothy Brady, Ms. Rose Friedman and Tobin also effected modifications in their empirical studies. The modifications suggested that better empirical results were obtained when current income is supplemented with some measure of the previous highest income or consumption or with a wealth variable in explaining consumption expenditures of households.

Friedman argued that people adjusted their consumption with respect to variations in their long-term expected income or "permanent" income and ignored the transitory variations in income. Alan Walters comments: "This basic idea was not new--indeed it can be found in the 18th century writings of Bernoulli-- but Friedman's development showed his genius for simplicity and for the insights of thinking concretely.... The main quality of A Theory of the Consumption Function was the incomparable amassing, organization and interpretation of the evidence."

The permanent income hypothesis at the micro level may be summarised as follows, comprising a behavioural relationship supplemented by two definitions and some assumptions about the mutual independence of the variables that are included.

$$C_p = k(i,w,u)\,Y_p \qquad (1)$$

$$Y = Y_p + Y_t \qquad (2)$$

$$C = C_p + C_t \tag{3}$$

$$\rho(Y_{p,} Y_t) = 0, \overline{Y} = 0 \tag{4}$$

$$\rho(C_{p,} C_t) = 0, \overline{C} = 0 \tag{5}$$

$$\rho(Y_{t,} C_t) = 0 \tag{6}$$

where

Y: Personal disposable income

C: Consumption of non-durables and services plus use-value of consumer durables

ρ: Correlation coefficient

Barred variables represent mean values

C and Y stand for the household's consumption and income;

The subscripts p and t represent their permanent and transitory components. Permanent consumption is described as certain proportion, k, of permanent income, k depending on the rate of interest (i) at which consumers may borrow or lend, w represents the relative importance of property and non-property income, expressed by the ratio of non-human wealth to human wealth, and u the household's rate of time preference.

Equation (4) stands for the assumption that the permanent and transitory components of income and consumption are uncorrelated. Similar assumption is made in regard to the two transitory components.

Thus, Friedman hypothesises that in the system, there exists a stable relation between the two permanent components – permanent consumption and permanent income.

Incidentally, the above formulation of permanent income is a good example of the problem in econometrics of errors in variables. Friedman observed: "The estimation problem is the classical one of 'mutual regression' or regression 'when both variables are subject to error'." Friedman's definition of consumption excludes expenditures on major consumer durables and includes their own use value. Permanent income is measured as an exponentially weighted average of past measured incomes allowing for trend.

The empirical work of Friedman using cross section data yielded relatively low propensities to consume while analyses of aggregate time series gave much higher propensities to consume. Friedman had shown that these apparently conflicting results can be reconciled and can be shown to be consistent when the results are interpreted on the basis of permanent income hypothesis. Walters commends the integrity of Friedman's scholarship, particularly his diligent search to find evidence that would discredit the permanent income hypothesis. Walters further observes: "one of the great contributions of this book [A Theory of the Consumption Function] was to give a new standard for empirical economics generally. Clearly this was how it should be done."

Thygesen of the University of Copenhagen is of the view that "the permanent income hypothesis and the particular choice made by Friedman in defining the empirical counterparts to his theoretical constructs has had a profound impact on empirical work on the consumption function. Its great appeal was due to the rare combination of simplicity with a wide range of testable propositions." Another important impact of Friedman's work was the introduction of the concept of permanent income into many fields of applied economics, such as monetary economics, international trade, transportation and housing.

The verdict, nearly forty years later, is that the permanent income hypothesis has left a "profound mark" on subsequent work in the field of consumer behaviour. Thomas Sargent is of the view that "the basic insight of the permanent income model is that in response to a possibly erratic and unsmooth income stream, consumers would optimally smooth their consumption streams by borrowing and lending or by physically investing."

1.2.2 MONETARY THEORY AND POLICY

Friedman's rise to fame and his attainment of prominence in the economics profession and outside was primarily as a monetary theorist. It is rather difficult to separate the theoretical aspects of Friedman's work from his empirical contributions in the field of monetary economics as the two are quite intertwined in his work. As will be discussed later in the section on methodological issues, Friedman was strongly of the view that for testing economic theory one has to use the implications rather than assumptions. In 1950s many economists, particularly of Keynesian hue, ridiculed the quantity theory of money as a mere tautology. Furthermore, the most important conclusion that had emerged from the Radcliffe Committee Report, 1959, was that the quantity of money was of little or almost no interest since the velocity of circulation of money has practically no limits. The Report expressed the view that the central bank has to watch the rates of interest in the economy rather than the quantity of money for the purpose of evaluating the efficacy of monetary policy.

The quantity theory of money was empirically tested extensively over several critical periods of change by many economists, among whom should be prominently mentioned Irving Fisher, J. M. Keynes and Clark Warburton. However, the methodology they used was considered "murky", the statistics termed "slim" and inter-relationships between data and theory were described as rather "obscure". Since 1950, "intensive" empirical work was undertaken by Friedman and his associates in the Workshop in Money and Banking at the University of Chicago and in the National Bureau of Economic Research (NBER). In Studies in the Quantity Theory of Money, Friedman and his co-authors postulated that the demand for money by individual households is a stable function of its money income (later amended as a function of permanent income or wealth), cost of holding money represented by the rate of interest and the expected rate of inflation. To ultimate wealth holders (individuals and families), the stock of money yields a flow of consumption services while to non-financial business firms it yields a flow of productive services. The theory of demand for money in Friedman's formulation is analogous to the theory of demand for a durable consumer good or capital good. Friedman asserted that the quantity theory was in the first instance a theory of the demand for money. It is not a theory of output, or of money income, or of the price level.

Friedman gave the following equation which expresses the demand for real balances as a function of "real" variables independent of nominal/ monetary values.

$$\frac{M}{P}=f\left(r_b, r_e, \frac{1}{\rho}\frac{dP}{dt}, W, \frac{Y}{\rho}, u\right)$$

where

r_b and r_e are real rates of return on bonds and equities

$\frac{1}{\rho}\frac{dP}{dt}$ is rate of change of price level,

$\frac{Y}{\rho}$ is the real income

W is ratio of income from non-human wealth to income from human wealth; and

u stands for utility determining variables.

Friedman's presentation of the theory of the demand for money in the first essay in the Studies in Quantity Theory is "one of his most widely quoted papers."

The main criticism of Friedman's restatement as presented by Bent Hansen and Don Patinkin was that Friedman's formulation is not in the tradition of quantity theory; it was essentially Keynesian in spirit. It would have been difficult to conceive of it without Keynes. As Alan Walters aptly puts it "Friedman was a closet Keynesian." It is said that Friedman's "Restatement" can be considered as a generalisation of Keynesian monetary theory by enlarging the range of assets beyond long-term securities and money. By including real assets in the demand function for money and transforming it into a portfolio choice, Friedman brought in the role of price expectations in financial behaviour in the tradition of Irving Fisher. The other essays in The Studies, notably Cagan's on hyper-inflation (in which movements in price expectations variable swamp the effect of other determinants) and Selden on Velocity, underscored the importance of examining nominal income and inflation in the context of the demand for money. The seminal contribution the volume made was the need for incorporation of inflationary expectations into the demand for money. The later empirical work attests this point.

Though, the theoretical framework put forward by Friedman received, by and large, general acceptance, the equation employed by Friedman for empirical work of the demand for money consisting of a few variables was less acceptable. Friedman believed that, in practice, the demand for money function to be stable in a small number of variables. He believed that, in practice, the degree of substitutability between money proper and any one of the near-money assets is low. He categorically rejected the Keynesian view of a very high elasticity of demand for money with respect to yield on long-term securities, the so-called liquidity trap. Later, he moved away from this extreme position as, according to him, "no fundamental issues," in either monetary theory or monetary policy hinge on whether the estimated elasticity can for most purposes be approximated by zero or is better approximated by – 0.1 or –0.5 or – 2.0, provided it is seldom capable of being approximated by ∞. The direction of causation remained an unanswered issue in Friedman.

The direction of causation remained an unanswered issue in Friedman's work. Specifically, the crucial issue is: whether prices and output respond to endogenous changes in money supply or whether stock of money is passively accommodating to changes in nominal income or wealth? According to the Chicago Workshop, the answer to such questions should be sought from a careful and diligent research into the history of the monetary process. One important factor which was noted by the Workshop relates to the role played by the exchange rate and the balance of payments. Friedman was clear that a stable growth of money supply was unlikely to be feasible under a fixed exchange rate regime.

Despite the increasing attention devoted to the issue of the balance of payments and the money supply process by the profession, Friedman's main focus in his work was on the examination of the effects of changes in money supply on nominal income, prices and output. In the words of Walters "the main questions were: (a) what was the relative importance of money compared with fiscal variations (the Keynes.vs.Monetarist debate) (b) what was the time pattern of adjustments; and (c) could expansionary financial or fiscal policies affect real output in the short or long run?"

The answers to these three questions that have emerged from Friedman's empirical work are:

Increased deficit has an impact effect on nominal income; it does not last; it soon disappeared. On the other hand, an increased rate of the growth of money stock has a lasting effect in raising the inflation rate, though with a lag.

The lag in the impact of increased growth rate of money and nominal income is long and variable; and in the long run, the increased growth of money stock has no effect on the level of output or its growth rate but only on the inflation rate.

Friedman's important empirical finding is that variations in the rate of growth of money supply has short run real output effect as also price effects; however, in the long run, the only "substantial" effect is on prices in the economy. It appears from a reading of the relevant literature that Friedman's finding in respect of the long run has received wide acceptance of the profession. However, this is not so for his claims in regard to short-run effects – the relative ineffectiveness of fiscal policy as a counter-cyclical policy measure and the large but unpredictable effects of variation in money stock on real output and employment.

Two papers of Friedman with his associates, the first one written in collaboration with David Meiselman ("The Relative Stability of Monetary Velocity and the Investment Multiplier in the United States, 1897-1958") and the second paper co-authored with Anna J. Schwartz ("Money and Business Cycles"), present Friedman's position on the nature of the transmission mechanism from changes in money stock to the market for current output. The conclusions Friedman and his co-authors drew in this regard are considered as subsequent rationalisations, "almost as an afterthought." Critics allege that the processes of monetary transmissions as put forward by Friedman and his associates are "black boxes" with no precise formulation of the way in which money works in the economy in bringing about the effects.

Critics of Friedman's work on money point out the lack of a sound theoretical structure. To meet such criticism, Friedman made an attempt to put forward theoretical underpinnings for his approach to research on money in Milton Friedman's Monetary Framework. In this publication, he gave a basic model comprising seven equations of a closed economy. He asserted that the critical difference between the quantity theory or classical model and the Keynesian model lies in the choice of the last equation. Friedman stated that the classical economists hypothesised that the model determines the general price level and the level of real output was determined by factors such as technology and skills. On the other hand, Keynesians supply an equation that specifies the determination of prices as being influenced by exogenous forces and the level of aggregate demand as a factor determining the output level. Neither economists adhering to the quantity theory approach nor those who belonged to the Keynesian group accepted the simple model contained in the Framework. Furthermore, model was found to be deficient in that it failed to provide a sound basis for the dynamics of adjustment to the long run equilibrium through price, output and interest effects. As Walters appropriately comments: "The transmission mechanism and dynamics remain enshrouded in the gloom of a black box."

Most of Friedman's empirical work relating to money and monetary policy is essentially one enormous research project at the National Bureau of Economic Research (NBER). One topic is the definition of money and determination of the group of financial assets that can be categorised as money. On the issue of definition Friedman adopts a pragmatic attitude. As he was interested in the interrelationship between money and income, the criterion he adopted is the ability of various measures to predict changes in money income or induced expenditures. The two main contenders are the narrow money stock (M1) comprising currency outside commercial banks plus demand deposits with commercial banks after appropriate adjustment for government deposits and inter-bank claims and the broad money stock (M2) consisting of M1 plus time deposits with commercial banks. The broad definition was preferred on the basis of the simple criterion of the correlation in a regression of various measures of income on money. Friedman emphasised the tentative nature of this choice: "...the selection of a specific empirical counterpart to the term money seems to us a matter of convenience for a particular purpose, not a matter of principle. Dogmatism is out of place." On the position of Friedman, Tobin commented:

"We don't know what money is, but whatever it is, its stock should grow steadily at 3 to 4 per cent per year."

As regards the determinants of money stock and its independence of current income, Friedman (jointly with Schwartz) and Cagan have analysed in great detail. They identify the triad of factors as the three "proximate determinants" of the money stock: the stock of high powered money or monetary base, the reserve ratio of the commercial banks and the ratio of currency to bank deposits in the portfolios of the public. The first one represents the behaviour of the central bank or monetary authorities, the second one of the commercial banks and the last and third one of the non-bank public.

It is a considered view of many economists that the NBER volumes co- authored by Friedman and Schwartz (A Monetary History of the United States, 1867-1960; and Monetary Statistics of the United States) present a strong case for the view that high-powered money, which has been the dominant longer-run influence on the money stock, moved basically independently of current income. They also demonstrate that "even in the great contraction of 1929-1933, money was not an endogenous element that adapted largely in a passive way to a decline in commodity markets brought about by other factors." Friedman was of the view that monetary policy was a factor that speeded up the decline in the economic activity in the U.S.: "it [the money stock] fell because the Federal Reserve System forced or permitted a sharp reduction in the monetary base, because it failed to exercise the responsibilities assigned to it in the Federal Reserve Act to provide liquidity to the banking system. The great contraction is tragic testimony to the power of monetary policy – not, as Keynes and so many of his contemporaries believed, evidence of impotence."

Friedman's paper jointly written with David Meiselman (a reference to which has been made earlier) is a frontal attack on the Keynesians. The paper empirically tested simple Keynesian income-expenditure model and the money velocity model in the linear form for the levels and changes in the variables with annual data for a fairly long period, 1897-1958. The authors' conclusion is striking: for every decade except the 1930s and for the period as a whole the money stock was clearly superior to autonomous expenditure in explaining consumption. Friedman stated that the verdict was "strikingly one-sided." It is Thygesen's view that "it is possible to argue in retrospect that this is the single most influential study among Friedman's many publications." To counter Friedman's view, Keynesians built larger and larger econometric models, such as FMP (Federal Reserve Board, Massachusetts Institute of Technology and University of Pennsylvania) model. Likewise, it paved the way for a number of small-scale "monetarist" models such as St. Louis Model.

In his later work on monetary theory and policy, Friedman attempted careful analysis of timing patterns. He devoted considerable attention to the problem of time lags between variations in the money stock and in money or nominal income. On the basis of his empirical work relating to time lags, Friedman drew an important conclusion. It is that "fine tuning" in the form of frequent discretionary changes in M2 designed to keep the economy on course is not possible. As he found that the lags were not merely long but they were seen to be of unpredictable length, the variation in monetary policy as a part of active stabilisation policy is likely to be "inappropriate" to the situation. Despite strong criticism of Friedman's methodology on several points, Friedman's policy advice had remained the same. He was against discretionary monetary policy because of his belief that knowledge of time lags between monetary policy actions and their effects were not sufficiently precise to expect any stabilising role from the discretionary policy. Instead, he championed a "monetary rule" in the form of a steady rate of growth of money stock corresponding roughly to the growth of capacity output. It is to be remarked that perhaps, no aspect of Friedman's writings is more controversial than the "monetary rule" of steady growth in the money stock.

In his presidential address to the American Economic Association which Walters considers the most important and influential paper in macroeconomics in the post-war years, Friedman argued that the view of macroeconomic policy as a trade- off between unemployment and inflation (the Phillips curve approach) is fundamentally flawed. Friedman's argument was that "...there is always a temporary trade-off between inflation and unemployment; there is no permanent trade-off. The temporary trade-off comes not from inflation per se, but from unanticipated inflation." In Walter's words: "The so-called Phillips curve was a short-term temptation rather than a long-term choice." Thus, according to Friedman, the long-run Phillips curve was vertical. Friedman called this level of unemployment as the "natural rate" (a Wicksellian term). The natural level of unemployment, according to Friedman, was determined by the nature of labour markets. Throughout the 1960s, the trade-off between unemployment and inflation appeared more and more illusory – unemployment rose but inflation had shown no abatement; it had, in fact, shown an increase. We could do no better than quote Walters again: "Like Keynes's General Theory, it was one of the very few contributions that changed, both the approach of professional economists and the policies adopted by finance ministers." Friedman contended that attempts at diverging from the "natural" level can only succeed temporarily and at considerable cost in terms of subsequent adjustment. "It [the monetary authority] cannot use its control over nominal quantities to peg a real quantity – the real rate of interest, the rate of unemployment, the level of real national income, the real quantity of money, the rate of growth of real national income or the rate of growth of the real quantity of money."

Thomas Sargent considers that Friedman's Presidential address to the American Economic Association as "the opening shot of 'rational expectations revolution' in macroeconomics.... Subsequent work on the natural-rate hypothesis has strengthened Friedman's original vision. In raising the possibility that the data could be rendered consistent with a dynamic model in competitive equilibrium, Friedman began a re-birth of equilibrium macroeconomics."

Friedman's "The Optimum Quantity of Money," is viewed by many economists as building upon the ideas of Henry Simons and Lloyd Mints regarding Chicago Plan of Banking Reform and is considered important both substantively and methodologically. Thomas Sargent argues that if Friedman's model is modified by formulating that the only taxes available to the government are distortionary ones, "...one discovers a version of Finn Kydland and Edward Prescott's (1970)' time inconsistency' problem."

1.2.3 INTERNATIONAL ECONOMIC PROBLEMS

Friedman's outstanding contribution to the field of international economics was his advocacy of flexible foreign exchange rates. In 1950, when the orthodoxy of fixed exchange rates was well and truly established, Friedman wrote a fairly long essay titled "The Case for Flexible Exchange Rates" during a consultancy for the Economic Cooperation Administration. The essay was later included in his 1953 book, Essays in Positive Economics.

In the paper, Friedman examined the arguments put forward by Nurkse, among others, that flexible exchange rates are likely to encourage destabilising speculation. In reply, Friedman advanced two main arguments.

1. The implication that flexibility in exchange rates would encourage destabilising speculation is that speculators, on the average, would lose money. According to Friedman, this appears to be unlikely.
2. There was no evidence available at that time in favour of this proposition.

Friedman and Schwartz in A Monetary History...showed that the United States' experiences with floating exchange rates between 1862 and 1879 did not encourage speculation of a destabilizing type.

Furthermore, Friedman was of the view that floating dollar is eminently sensible for the U.S. to achieve domestic policy objectives in the backdrop of the fact that 95 per cent of the output produced was for domestic use. He had therefore welcomed the shift in the U.S. economic policy in regard to exchange rates since 1971.

The extent of his understanding of practical problems of international finance is very much evident in his 1969 article titled "The Euro-Dollar Market: Some First Principles." In the article, Friedman developed the analogy of credit creation in a domestic banking system to the operation of the Euro-dollar market.

1.2.4 MICROECONOMICS

In the field of microeconomics, Friedman had made significant contributions. His two papers with L.J. Savage relating to the utility analysis of risk and the measurement of utility based on the work of von Neumann and Morgenstern are particularly noteworthy. The authors, making use of acceptable axioms, showed that choice under conditions of uncertainty could be represented as a process of maximising expected utility. Specifically, the authors stated that the utilities of each of the expected outcomes are weighted by the probability of occurrence of that outcome and the sum gave an index of expected utility. Given the axioms, an individual would maximise the index of expected utility by choosing from the alternative uncertain prospects.

While the basic idea was developed originally by Bernoulli in solving the St. Petersburg Paradox, the contribution of Friedman and Savage lay in discovering new insights and implications with wide-ranging applications. The expected utility hypothesis had attempted at reconciling the wide-spread practice of simultaneously gambling and insuring. In addition, the hypothesis has a "profound effect" on the theory and practice of portfolio selection. It has also offered for the pure economic theorist an attractive proposition that up to an arbitrary linear transformation of origin and scale, utility has to be regarded as a cardinal magnitude. While subsequent work of economists, particularly Maurice Allais threw some doubt about the plausibility of one of the axioms and applicability of the expected utility hypothesis in some specific fields, the hypothesis still forms a cornerstone of all work in choice under conditions of uncertainty. It is commented that these two papers of Friedman (co-authored with Savage) mark "the last contributions of Friedman to the pure theory of statistics and decision-making."

Another outstanding contribution of Friedman to microeconomics concerned his reformulation of Marshallian demand theory as a practical instrument of analysis. This contribution is regarded as "meticulous scholarship" in the history of economic thought. It favoured approaching demand analysis as a positive rather than as a normative discipline.

Friedman in his lectures on price theory at the Graduate School of University of Chicago highlighted the uses and some abuses of the theory of price. His lectures opened up to students "new vistas – such as the theory of human capital – and exciting ways of unravelling puzzles and resolving problems." Walters says: "in his hands, economics had both power and point, and reality and relevance.... Friedman showed how to interpret simple ideas in a most sophisticated way."

1.2.5 METHODOLOGICAL ISSUES

From the very beginning, Friedman made clear his methodological position. In the essay "The Methodology of Positive Economics," he urged using the implications rather than the assumptions as testing ground for economic theory. For judging the usefulness of a theory, the realism of the assumption is not a good criterion. The conformity of assumptions with reality "...promotes misunderstanding about the significance of empirical evidence for economic theory, produces a misdirection of much intellectual effort devoted to the development of positive economics, and impedes the attainment of consensus on tentative hypotheses in positive economics." The prime issue in evaluating the usefulness of the theory, according to Friedman, is whether it yields predictions that are sufficiently accurate for the purpose at hand.

According to Thygesen "The 'as if' hypothesis is essential to an understanding of Friedman's subsequent empirical work, particularly in the field of monetary theory and policy." For example, in choosing between various possible empirical counterparts to the theoretical concepts of money, Friedman was guided by the reliability of the linkages of variations in various empirical constructs to movements in money income and prices rather than by the '<u>a priori</u>' notions of the functions performed by money.

Many economists point out that the possibilities of testing either the assumptions or the implications of economic theory are limited. Friedman's position has been criticized by several economists, one of the prominent among them being Paul Samuelson. Samuelson noted that the distinction between assumptions and implications disappears in a well-developed theoretical structure.

In his recent comments on methodology, Friedman considered himself as working in Marshallian tradition (in contradistinction to the Walrasian tradition) who regarded economic theory as "an engine for the discovery of concrete truth." Friedman shared with Keynes and some of the Keynesian economists, such as Kaldor and Davidson, scepticism towards general equilibrium economics.

Friedman's work on money is a brilliant application of his methodology of positive economics.

1.3 CONCLUDING OBSERVATIONS

In addition to the areas surveyed above, Friedman contributed to a number of other fields. They are revealed in his more popular writings on issues such as public spending, price and rent controls and taxation. The conventional view is that he had been one of the most ardent, most effective and most persuasive advocates of free enterprise and monetarist policies. He was universally regarded as the founder and leading proponent of "Monetarism," an economic doctrine which considers supply of money and changes therein to be the primary determinant of nominal income and prices in the economy. In his appearances in the various media, Friedman had been "a great persuader, his role being critical in promoting such ideas as an all volunteer army, the voucher schemes for education and health, and indexing income tax."

Reverting to the issue of relation between inflation and unemployment, Friedman traced the professional views on the topic during 1950s, 1960s and 1970s and stated that they have gone through two stages and are now (Nobel lecture was in 1976) entering a third. The first stage was the acceptance of a stable trade-off (a stable Phillips Curve). The second was the introduction of inflation expectations, as a variable causing a shift in the short-run Phillips Curve and of the natural rate of unemployment, as determining the location of a vertical long-run Phillips Curve. The third is occasioned by the empirical phenomenon of an apparent positive relation between inflation and unemployment.

Elaborating on them in his Lecture, Friedman remarked that the Phillips Curve hypothesis that there is a stable relation between the level of unemployment and the rate of inflation was adopted by the economics profession with alacrity. It seemed to provide reliable tool for economic policy. He went on further: "As in any science, so long as experience seemed to be consistent with reigning hypothesis it continued to be accepted."

As time passed, it seemed to take larger and longer doses of inflation to keep down the level of unemployment. "Stagflation reared its ugly head." Attempts to patch up the hypothesis did not yield satisfactory results. A radical revision of the hypothesis was needed. The attempts at revision underlined the importance of surprises; that is, differences between anticipated and actual magnitudes. Friedman put forward the idea that natural rate of unemployment at any time is determined by real factors. He asserted that this natural rate would tend to be attained when expectations were, on the average, realised. Thus, the natural rate hypothesis of Friedman and Phelps contains the original Phillips curve hypothesis as a special case and rationalises, say, the phenomenon of stagflation.

Friedman observed that the natural rate hypothesis "in its present form has not proved rich enough to explain a more recent development – a move from stagflation to slumpflation." That is, higher inflation is associated with higher unemployment. This situation may have come about because of events such as oil crisis. A major factor in some countries and a contributing factor in others may be that they are in a "transitional period – this time to be measured by quinquennia or decades, not years. The public has not adapted its attitude or its institutions to a new monetary environment."

Government's macroeconomic policy, specifically relating to inflation and unemployment has responded almost entirely to the force of events: brute experience proved far more potent than the strongest of political or ideological preferences. Friedman then remarked: The importance for humanity of a correct understanding of positive economic science is vividly brought out by a statement made nearly two hundred years ago by Pierre S. du Pont to the French National assembly and he quoted: "....It is necessary to be gracious as to intentions, ...but we do not have to be gracious at all to inconsistent logic or to absurd reasoning. Bad logicians have committed more involuntary crimes than bad men have done intentionally."

To a non-specialist reader, or general public, some of the most interesting publications of Friedman (singly or jointly with his wife Rose Friedman) include Capitalism and Freedom, Free to Choose and Tyranny of the Status Quo.

In Friedman's essay included in the Lives of the Laureates, Friedman stated that he had been enormously impressed by the role that pure chance plays in determining one's life history. He confessed: "By accident, I also took some courses in economics, and that is where the goddess of chance entered the picture, because the Rutgers economics faculty included two extraordinary teachers [Arthur F. Burns and Homer Jones] who had a major impact on my life." He concluded the essay with the following observations: "...my life as an economist has been the source of much pleasure and satisfaction. It is a fascinating discipline. What makes it most fascinating is that its fundamental principles are so simple that they can be written on one page, that anybody can understand, and yet that very few do."

Paul Krugman compares the 20th century economic thought to the history of Christianity in the sixteenth century. He says that until the publication of Keynes's General Theory in 1936, economics was completely dominated, at least in the English-speaking world by 'free-market orthodoxy.' Heresies that occasionally popped up were systematically suppressed. In 1936, Keynes wrote, Classical economics "conquered England as completely as the Holy Inquisition conquered Spain."

However, with the onset of the Great Depression and the failure of Classical economics to provide either explanations or solutions for it, "the challenges to orthodoxy could no longer be contained." Krugman carries the religious analogy further. He continues: "Keynes played the role of Martin Luther, providing the intellectual rigor needed to make hearsay respectable." Keynes argued that free markets could not be relied upon to provide full employment and created "a new rationale for large-scale government intervention in the economy," Krugman observes:

"Keynesianism was a great reformation of economic thought. It was followed, inevitably by a counter-reformation.... If Keynes was Luther, Friedman was Ignatius of Loyola, founder of Jesuits. And like the Jesuits, Friedman's followers have acted as a sort of disciplined army of the faithful spearheading a broad, but incomplete, rollback of Keynesian hearsay. By the century's end, classical economics had regained much though by no means all of its former dominion, and Friedman deserves much of the credit."

Friedman had contributed to the advancement of economics in at least four ways, according to Thygesen. He had reformulated the theory of the consumption function by his permanent income hypothesis. He had initiated an important debate about the scope for discretionary action in monetary and fiscal policy. He had "forced the re-evaluation" of important phases of economic history of the United States through his stupendous and massive work with historical monetary statistics. He revived interest in the methodological issues in economics. Critics talk about Friedman's influence well beyond the academic. His greatest asset is his ability to formulate powerful hypotheses in the simplest terms. His work on money for over thirty years gave direction to the profession that monetary economics is to be interpreted as part of the central corpus of price theory.

Friedman's work is seemingly simple, eschewing complexities, concentrating on essentials; all combined into a lucid exposition. He believed that economics should be viewed as an empirical science. We cannot do better than conclude this essay with Walter's and Sargent's assessments; "In effectiveness, breadth and scope, his only rival among the economists of the 20th century is Keynes."(Walters)

"Many very good researchers continue to pay Milton Friedman of thinking hard about issues that he posed, often in terms that he defined, and using methods that he invented or inspired."(Sargent).

1.4 SELECT BIBLIOGRAPHY OF MILTON FRIEDMAN'S WORKS

1.4.1 BOOKS

1945 (with Simon Kuznets) Income from Independent Professional Practice, NBER, New York.

1953 Essays in Positive Economics, Chicago University Press, Chicago, Ill.

1956 (ed.) Studies in the Quantity Theory of Money, Chicago University Press, Chicago, Ill.

1957 A Theory of Consumption Function, Princeton University Press, Princeton, NJ.

1959 A Program for Monetary Stability, Fordham University Press, New York.

1962 a Capitalism and Freedom, University of Chicago Press, Chicago, Ill.

b Price Theory: A Provisional Text, Aldine Publishing Co., Chicago, Ill.

1963 (with A. J. Schwartz) A Monetary History of the United States,1867-1960, Princeton University Press for NBER, Princeton, NJ.

1967 (with R. V. Roosa) The Balance of Payments: Free versus Floating Exchange Rates, American Enterprise Institute, Washington D.C.

1968 Dollars and Deficits: Inflation, Monetary Policy and the Balance of Payments, Prentice-Hall, Englewood Cliffs, NJ.

1969 The Optimum Quantity of Money and Other Essays, Aldine Publishing Co., Chicago, Ill.

1970 (with A. J .Schwartz) Monetary Statistics of the United States, Columbia University Press for NBER, New York.

1973 Money and Economic Development, Horowitz Lectures of 1972, Praeger, New York.

1976 Price Theory (Revised and Enlarged Version of the 1962 edition), Aldine Publishing Co., Chicago, Ill.

1980 (with R. Friedman) Freedom to Choose, Harcourt, Brace, Jovanovich, New York.

1982 (with A. J. Schwartz) Monetary Trends in the United States and the United Kingdom, University of Chicago Press for the NBER, Chicago, Ill.

1984 (with R.Friedman) Tyranny of the Status Quo, Harcourt, Brace, Jovanovich, New York.

1.4.2 ARTICLES

1948 (with L.J. Savage). "The Utility Analysis of Choices Involving Risk," JPE, Vol. 56, Aug.

1949 "The Marshallian Demand Curve," JPE, Vol. 57, Dec.

1952 (with L .J. Savage) "The Expected Utility Hypothesis and the Measurability of Utility," JPE, Vol.60, Dec.

1963 (With D. Meiselman), "The Relative Stability of Monetary Velocity and the Investment Multiplier in the United States, 1897-1959," in Stabilization Policies, Commission on Money and Credit, Prentice-Hall, Englewood Cliffs, NJ.

1968 "The Role of Monetary Policy," Presidential Address, American Economic Association, AER, Vol.58, Mar.

1977 "Inflation and Unemployment," Nobel Lecture, JPE, Vol.85, No.3.

2004 Friedman's Essay in Lives of the Laureates: Eighteen Nobel Economists, (Eds. W. Breit and B.T. Hirsch) Fourth Edition, The MIT Press, Cambridge, MA.

1.5 WORKS OF OTHERS

Brunner, K and A. H. Meltzer (1972)"Friedman's Monetary Theory," JPE, Vol. 80, Sept/Oct.

Davidson, P. (1972), "A Keynesian View of Friedman's Theoretical Framework for Monetary Analysis," JPE, Vol. 80, Sept/Oct.

Gordon, R.J.(1974), Milton Friedman's Monetary Framework: A Debate with his Critics, Edited and with an Introduction by R. J. Gordon, University of Chicago Press, Chicago, Ill.

Hahn, F. (1971), "Professor Friedman's Views on Money," Economica, New Series, Vol. 38, Feb.

Johnson, H (1971), "The Keynesian Revolution and the Monetarist Counter Revolution," AER, Vol. 61, May.

Patinkin, D (1972),"Friedman on the Quantity Theory and Keynesian Economics," JPE, Vol.80, Sep/Oct.

Thygesen, N. (1977), "The Scientific Contributions of Milton Friedman," ScandJE, Vol.79, No.1.

Tobin, J. (1965), "The Monetary Interpretation of History," AER, Vol. 55, June.

Tobin, J. (1972), "Friedman's Theoretical Framework," JPE, Vol.80, Sept/Oct.

Walters, A. A. (1965), "Professor Friedman on the Demand for Money," JPE, Vol. 63, Oct.

Walters, A. A. (1987) "Milton Friedman," The New Palgrave: A Dictionary of Economics, Macmillan, London.

CHAPTER 2

BERTIL GOTTHARD OHLIN

(1899 – 1979)

The Official Announcement of the Royal Swedish Academy of Sciences says that the Academy has decided that the 1977 Prize in Economic Sciences in memory of Alfred Nobel "shall be shared equally" by Professor Bertil Ohlin, Stockholm, Sweden, and Professor James Meade, Cambridge, U.K., for their "path breaking contributions to the theory of international trade and international capital movements."

Bert Ohlin's classic study, *Interregional and International Trade*, had brought him recognition as founder of the modern theory of international trade. He had delineated in his theory the factors that determine the pattern of a country's foreign trade and the international division of labour. Ohlin had also demonstrated the effects of a country's foreign trade on its allocation of resources, price relations and income distribution in the country. In his work, he had also shown similarities and dissimilarities between intranational (inter-regional) and international trade and the relation between international trade and the location of industries.

James Meade primarily in his major study, *The Theory of International Economic Policy*, had analysed the effects of economic policy on foreign trade and made a deep study of the problem of stabilisation policies in 'open' economies. Open economies are defined as those economies that are greatly dependent on foreign trade. The main focus of his analysis was on identifying the conditions necessary for internal and external balance; that is, balance both in the domestic economy and in external transactions. Meade had also shown why and how a successful stabilisation policy has to take into consideration not only the level of aggregate demand for goods and services but also relations between prices and costs. The award particularly refers as to how these achievements have made Meade the "leading pioneer" in the field of international macroeconomic theory and international economic policy.

The award committee makes specific reference as to how both Ohlin's and Meade's pioneering works attracted a great deal of attention immediately after their publication (1933 and 1951/1955, respectively). Their works have also inspired extensive empirical research on international trade, international capital movements and problems of stabilisation in open economies.

The breadth and significance of Ohlin's and Meade's contributions did not, however, become clear until 1960s and 1970s in conjunction with the growing internationalisation of economic systems. It has become increasingly obvious that problems related to resource allocation, business cycles and income distribution are largely global problems. It implies that foreign trade, international price fluctuations, the international allocation of economic activities and the resources transfer, as well as international payments systems, have become dominant factors in economic analysis and economic policy.

Bert Ohlin's contributions to economic science are surveyed in this chapter while the next chapter covers James Meade's contributions to the subject.

2.1 A BRIEF BIOGRAPHICAL NOTE: BERTIL OHLIN

Ohlin was born into an upper-middle class family in a village (Klippan) in the south of Sweden on 23rd April 1899. He took a degree in mathematics, statistics and economics at the University of Lund, a degree in economics under Eli Heckscher at the Stockholm School of Business Administration in 1919. He obtained an (M.A.) degree under Taussig and Williams at Harvard in 1923 and a Ph.D. degree under Gustav Cassel at the University of Stockholm in 1924.

Ohlin taught at the University of Copenhagen during 1925-1930 and as Heckscher's successor at the Stockholm School of Business Administration.

He was a visiting professor at the University of California at Berkley in 1937 and at Columbia and Oxford in 1947.

In 1931 Ohlin prepared a report on the world depression for the League of Nations and in 1934 prepared a report on unemployment for Swedish Government. Ohlin was a member of the Swedish parliament between 1938 and 1970 and minister of Commerce, 1944-45. He was the Leader of the Swedish Liberal Party from 1944 to 1967.

Bert Ohlin died on 3 August 1979 in Stockholm.

2.2 A SUMMARY OF BERTIL OHLIN'S CONTRIBUTIONS

Ohlin is best known for his modernisation of the theory of international trade. The modernisation was long overdue. The labour theory of value persisted in international trade theory long after it was discarded in general economic theory after 1870. Inspired by his teacher Eli Heckscher, Ohlin set out to modify Cassel's model (Cassel's version of a Walrasian general equilibrium model of a closed economy with perfect mobility of goods and factors and fixed factor endowments of households).

Ohlin's first modification of Cassel's model consisted of visualising an economy composed of regions within which exists perfect factor mobility but there was imperfect factor mobility between regions. In fact, as a first approximation, he assumed that factor mobility was non-existent. Another assumption Ohlin made was that the regions differed solely in their factor endowments but not in their technology or preferences. Finally, he allowed for factor substitution. Let us take a simple case of two factors, two goods and two regions.

If trade takes place between regions, exports would expand a region's demand for its abundant factor and imports would reduce the demand for its scarce factor. As a result of trade, the price of the abundant factor would increase and the price of the scarce factor would decline, encouraging substitution between them in production. In the absence of transportation costs and in the absence of specialisation, Ohlin showed that trade would eventually equalise factor prices in terms of either good between regions. Factor price equalisation would fail if there were more than two factors, two goods or two regions.

Ohlin saw international trade as a special case of inter-regional trade. The pattern of international trade as outlined by Ohlin revealed that a nation tends to export those goods which would be relatively cheap in the absence of trade. This is called the 'weak version' of the Heckscher – Ohlin theorem. We have the strong version of the theorem, if we also suppose that patterns of demand differ little from country to country. In such a case, a country tends to export those commodities requiring relatively large quantities of its relatively abundant factors and import those commodities requiring (if produced at home) relatively large quantities of its scarce factors. When we combine Gottfried Harberler's substitution of opportunity cost for the labour theory of value in the theory of international exchange "this idea conforms international economics to Walrasian general equilibrium theory."

Ohlin's work has brought in many more important changes, extending the reach and generality of international trade theory. It ended the "traditional split" between the theory of inter-regional trade and the theory of international trade. The dependence of the trade theory on the assumption of no international mobility of factors of production has also been ended. Instead, his work provided a theorem identifying the substitute relation between international movements of goods and factors of production. Later research has "consolidated this analysis of the role of factor migration by establishing vigorously the conditions required for trade in goods alone to eliminate international differences in the marginal products of factors."

Richard Caves's comment in this context is worth recalling. "In its operational and empirical context, however, Ohlin's contribution did not displace the earlier Ricardian model...but rather supplied a richer and a more general model resting on different assumptions." In any case, Ohlin's approach emphasised the positive and predictive content of the theory of international trade and shifted the earlier focus on normative issues of gains from trade and commercial policy.

The later writers on trade theory and policy have continued the simplified version on the lines of two-country, two-product two-factor employed by Ohlin in the text, Inter-regional and International Trade. This generally employed simplified model has yielded important theorems on the factor prices and prices of goods (Stolper-Samuelson Theorem) and on the relation between quantities of factors used and quantities of goods produced at given terms of trade (Samuelson-Rybczynski theorem). Critics consider Ohlin's work important in helping make general equilibrium theory useful for studying problems of income distribution and public finance in a closed economy.

For improving the formal structure of Ohlin's model, many economists have made substantial contributions.

2.2.1 THE BASIC FACTOR-PROPORTIONS MODEL

While Heckscher stated that necessary conditions for international trade to take place are differences in relative factor endowments and factor intensities of goods, Ohlin recognised that demand as well as supply factors could cause ex- ante differences in relative product prices.

2.2.2 FACTOR PRICE EQUALISATION THEOREM

Under very restrictive assumptions specified by Samuelson, trade can be shown to equalise prices of physically comparable factors of production even when factor movements across countries do not take place. Ohlin's discussion in his book anticipated a good deal of later work by economists including extension of the theorem; for example, Ohlin's statement that presence of transportation costs and imposition of tariffs prevent equalisation of factor prices. Ohlin also stated that an increase in the number of traded goods strengthens the tendency towards equalisation. This conclusion was later shown by Ohlin to be true in n-dimensional statements of the theorem.

2.2.3 PRICE RESPONSE OF FACTOR SUPPLIES

The basic Heckscher-Ohlin theorem pre-supposed fixed national endowments of factors of production. Yet, according to critics, the general equilibrium framework underlying the work of Ohlin can accommodate variations in factors supply in response to variations in their real prices. The later work relating to variable factor supplies could have profited from a careful reading of Ohlin's original text.

2.2.4 EMPIRICAL VERIFICATION

Ohlin's model is particularly suited for empirical verification. One of the earliest formal testing of Heckscher-Ohlin theorem was by Leontief in his 1953 paper "Domestic Production and Foreign Trade: The American Capital Position Re-examined." The outcome of this test is the famous "Leontief Paradox." Richard Caves remarks: "...all parties would have benefited from a more careful reading of Ohlin. This book places the 'strong' theorem tested by Leontief in the setting of a comprehensive general equilibrium model, and thereby provides a ready check list of reasons why the theorem might fail." There are others who felt that Leontief study could never be an adequate test of the Heckscher-Ohlin theorem, since the conditions under which that theorem was constructed are not present in reality. The inescapable conclusion is that the theorem had not been refuted by Leontief study.

2.3 BERTIL OHLIN'S OTHER CONTRIBUTIONS TO INTERNATIONAL ECONOMICS

In addition to Heckscher-Ohlin model outlined above, Ohlin made a number of other important contributions to international economics, some of which are briefly outlined below.

2.3.1 THEORY OF CAPITAL TRANSFERS

The discussion on capital transfers had, for long, been clouded by preoccupation with the problem of post-war reparations. Ohlin imparted clarity to the discussion on the issue by arguing that a transfer of purchasing power comprises the essence of the initiating disturbance to the economic system. Any variation that has to occur in the lender's terms of trade is determined by the net payments imbalance that subsists consequent on variations in the level of expenditure associated with the change in the incomes of the transferor and transferee.

2.3.2 SOCIAL LEGISLATION AND EFFICIENT EXCHANGE

Ohlin emphasised, in his later contributions, the need to harmonise social legislation and taxation systems when nations form an economic union. He, however, stated that the need for harmonisation was overstated. Ohlin also demonstrated that social legislation can distort the location of activity in an economic union if it induces factor migrations.

2.3.3 REGIONAL AND LOCATIONAL ECONOMICS

Ohlin's ideas had exerted considerable influence on regional and locational economics. The framework that Ohlin employed for the analysis of the effects of regional differences on trade and movement of factors of production complemented the analysis of location and transport costs provided by location theorists like Weber and Losch.

2.3.4 MACROECONOMIC THEORY

Hans Brems makes particular reference to Ohlin's contribution to macroeconomic theory. Ohlin's important work in this field was not completely translated into English. Ohlin was inspired here by Wicksell and Lindahl. Brems observes: "Two years ahead of Keynes, Ohlin used three Keynesian tools, i.e. the propensity to consume, liquidity preference and the multiplier and one non-Keynesian tool, i.e. the accelerator." The feedback mechanism developed by Ohlin works as follows: "If consumption demand is stimulated by exogenous forces, the economy's physical output would rise, generating additional income. Physical consumption rises to the new level of physical output because of the propensity to consume, thus causing a consumption feedback. An investment feedback would be established through the operation of the accelerator which links physical investment to the growth of physical output. The Wicksellian type of cumulative process is generated in Ohlin's system as a result of the operation of the two feedbacks. The process consists of a succession of disequilibria as a result of continuous revision of expectations and plans in the light of new experience. In contrast, Keynes used only one feedback, the consumption feedback, and "telescoped it into an instant equilibrium."

2.4 CONCLUDING OBSERVATIONS

Heckscher-Ohlin model has become an essential part in any text book on international economics. On the appearance of Ohlin's Inter-regional and International Trade in 1933 C. R. Whittlesey of the University of Pennsylvania had this to say: "...by all odds the most important book on international economics that has appeared in recent times." Reviewing the book, James W. Angell wrote: "A signal contribution to the theory of international trade, and one which will interest every student of economic problems." According to Caves "since World War II probably a majority of papers published in the pure theory of international trade have employed the framework of this model." It has also inspired an interesting line of empirical research work with the purpose of verifying its predictions.

The English language writings of Ohlin are considered by critics as marked by "a scrupulous concern both for the rigor in analytical reasoning and the relevance of that reasoning to explain actual phenomena and informing policy." His contributions reflected his concern for the soundness of economic analysis and its readiness to do empirical service.

In his Nobel lecture titled "1933 and 1977 – Some Expansion Policy Problems in Cases of Unbalanced Domestic and International Economic Relations," Ohlin compared two cases of serious international depressions in countries with an essential orientation towards a market economy – in the first half of the 1930s and in the middle of 1970s. In the former case, the recovery started after a few years without the help of much conscious expansionist policy. In contrast, the recovery which started in 1975 and 1976 was somewhat slower and more hesitant than in the earlier case. These two episodes he studied prompted Ohlin to raise the following question: which kind of expansion policy can result in relatively large increase in output and employment and a relatively small degree of inflation? The optimum is determined by a political decision. He then enumerated a number of policy aspects that could alter the optimum position. The policy-makers have to make the "trade off" between the different possible combinations of output and inflation to find a "Pareto Optimum."

After analysing the above problem from the viewpoint of an individual country, Ohlin then diverted his attention to the international economic policy. He identified several additional difficulties and problems created by shifting developments in different countries and their influence on international economic relations and had undertaken a brief interesting analysis.

At the Nobel symposium he made an important personal observation. We conclude the essay with that quote. "It has not been easy to combine scientific work, teaching, journalistic writing and political leadership. All of these types of activity have no doubt suffered from my attempts to do too many things at the same time. However, I have found it all to be a fascinating business."

2.5 SELECT BIBLIOGRAPHY OF BERTIL OHLIN'S WORKS

2.5.1 BOOKS

1933 Interregional and International Trade, Harvard Economic Studies, Harvard University Press, Cambridge, MA.

2.5.2 ARTICLES

1927 "The Plea for Freer Trade," in The Economic Consequences of the League, London.

1928 "Equilibrium in International Trade," QJE, Vol.43, No.1.

1929 "The Reparations Problem: A Discussion: Transfer Difficulties, Real and Imagined," EJ, Vol. 37, Pp.172-183. Reprinted in Readings in the Theory of International Trade, H.S. Ellis and L. Metzler (eds.), Blakiston, Philadelphia and Toronto, 1949.

1937 a "Mechanism and Objectives of Exchange Control," AER, Vol.27, No.1.

b "Some Notes on the Stockholm Theory of Saving and Investment, I and II," EJ, March and June, Reprinted in Readings in Business Cycle Theory, G. Haberler (ed.), Blakiston, Philadelphia and Toronto,1949.

1971 "On Model Construction in International Trade Theory," in Induction, Growth and Trade: Essays in Honour of Roy Harrod, Ellis W.A. et. al. (eds), Clarendon Press, Oxford.

1976 "Some Aspects of the Relations between International Movements of Commodities, Factors of Production and Technology," Nobel Symposium, June 1976. Proceedings published by Macmillan, London, 1977.

1978 "Keynesian Economics and the Stockholm School: A Comment on Don Patinkin's Paper," ScandJE, Vol.80, No.2.

1992 "1933 and 1977 – Some Expansion Policy Problems in Cases of Unbalanced Domestic and International Economic Relations," Nobel Lectures, Economics, 1969-1980, Assar Lindbeck (ed.), World Scientific Publishing Co. Singapore.

2.6 WORKS OF OTHERS

Brems, H. (1978) "What was New in Ohlin's 1933-34 Macroeconomics?" HOPE, Vol.10, No. 3.

Brems, H. (1987) "Ohlin, Bertil, Gotthard" The New Palgrave: A Dictionary of Economics, Macmillan, London.

Caves, R.E. (1978), "Bertil Ohlin's Contribution to Economics," ScandJE, Vol.80, No.2.

Leontief, W.W. (1955) "Domestic Production and Foreign Trade: The American Capital Position Re-examined," Proceedings of American Philosophical Society, Vol.97, No.4.

Samuelson. P. A. (1948), "International Trade and the Equalization of the Factor Prices," EJ, Vol.58, June.

Samuelson, P. A. and Stolper W.F. (1941) "Protection and the Real Wages," RES, Vol.9, No.1, Reprinted in Readings in the Theory of International Trade, H.S. Ellis and L. Metzler (eds.) Blakiston, Philadelphia and Toronto, 1949.

CHAPTER 3

JAMES EDWARD MEADE

(1907 – 1995)

James Edward Meade was awarded the Nobel Memorial Prize in Economics in 1977, jointly with Bertil Ohlin for his work in international economics; in particular, The Theory of International Economic Policy: Volume 1, The Balance of Payments; Volume 2: Trade and Welfare. However, his contributions are not confined to international economics but have spanned the entire discipline of economics. In microeconomics, he had contributed to the fields of abstract welfare theory and theory of imperfect competition. He also made contributions to economic planning and the theory of labour-managed cooperatives. He wrote extensively on areas forming macroeconomics, such as national income accounting, monetary theory, public finance, growth theory and income and wealth distribution. It is proposed to summarise here his notable contributions, with focus on international economics. But before doing that, it is in order to provide a short biographical sketch.

3.1 A BRIEF BIOGRAPHICAL NOTE: JAMES MEADE

James Meade was born on 23 June 1907 and brought up in the city of Bath, Somerset, England. He had his education at Lambrook School and Malvern College. Later, he studied at Oriel College, Oxford University. After graduation in 1930, Meade was elected a Fellow of Hertford College, Oxford, and appointed to a Lectureship in Economics. But his college first sent him to Cambridge University "to learn my subject before I started to teach it. I had the good fortune of being taken into Trinity College, Cambridge... by Dennis Robertson, to whose teaching that year [1930-31] I owe a deep debt of gratitude." Robertson suggested to Meade that he "should set to know" Richard Kahn of King's College. This resulted in the "intellectually most exciting year" of his life.

At Cambridge, Meade spent a formative and creative year making a close friendship with Richard Kahn and becoming a member of the 'Circus' (around Keynes) with Kahn, Piero Sraffa and Joan and Austin Robinson. Meade had described the "workshop style" of the "Circus" meetings. Keynes took no part in the proceedings. After each meeting of the "Circus," Kahn used to report orally to Keynes the subject matter of the discussions. In Meade's own words: "From the point of view of a humble mortal like myself, Keynes seemed to play the role of God in a morality play; he dominated the play but he rarely appeared on the stage. Kahn was the Messenger Angel who brought messages and problems from Keynes to the 'Circus' and went back to Heaven with the result of our deliberations." In this way Meade belonged to, in his own words again, "that group of men and women of the interwar years who fell under the influence of Keynes because we thought that the mass unemployment of those years was both stupid and wicked and because we found in Keynes someone who inspired us with a hopeful answer to the problem. I say that we fell under the influence of Keynes; it would be more accurate to say that we fell under the magic spell of Keynes, and I personally am still under that spell 53 years after it was cast on me and 37 years after the death of the magician." Meade admitted that he abandoned the formula MV=PT for I=S.

From 1931 to 1937, he was a Fellow and Lecturer at Hertford College, Oxford. Though his job was to teach the whole corpus of economic theory, he was especially interested in two subjects – the economics of mass unemployment and international economics. At the end of 1937, he joined the Economic Section of the League of Nations in Geneva as economist and editor of the World Economic Survey and produced two issues for 1937/38 and 1938/39. After the outbreak of World War II, returning from Geneva, he became a member of the Economic section of the British War Cabinet Secretariat where he remained till 1947, while becoming Director in 1946.

In 1947, Meade became a Professor of Commerce at the London School of Economics where Lionel Robbins was "our leader" in the Economics Department. Among his colleagues there, he specifically mentioned A.W.H. Phillips to whom he owed "an immense intellectual debt of gratitude for education in the treatment of dynamic systems."

In 1957, Meade moved from London to the Chair of Political Economy in Cambridge which he held till 1967, when he resigned to become a Senior Research Fellow of Christ's College, Cambridge. The purpose of retiring early was to concentrate on writing. Meade relinquished that Fellowship on retirement age at 1974. Then, he became full-time Chairman of a Committee set up by the Institute for Fiscal Studies to examine the structure of direct taxation in the United Kingdom. Meade continued to engage himself in research work in economics. Meade was credited with having helped to create a sea change in the 1980s in British discussion of incomes policy.

James E. Meade died on December 22, 1995.

3.2 A SUMMARY OF JAMES MEADE'S MAJOR CONTRIBUTIONS

As mentioned earlier, Meade's contributions were in almost all fields of economics. Our survey here would be confined, however, to his contributions falling under the following heads. Out of them, the first one is considered the most important and Nobel award cites it as the contribution for which the award was made.

1. The Theory of International Economic Policy;
   - (a) The Balance of Payments;
   - (b) Trade and Welfare.

2. A Geometry of International Trade;
3. The Theory of Customs Union;
4. The Theory of Flexible Exchange Rates; and
5. The Theory of Economic Growth.

3.2.1 THE THEORY OF INTERNATIONAL ECONOMIC POLICY

Meade's claim to fame for making significant contribution to the development of economic science rests importantly on the two volumes of The Theory of International Economic Policy; the first volume of which was entitled The Balance of Payments and the second volume, Trade and Welfare and the Mathematical Supplements thereto.

(a) ***The Balance of Payments*****:** This volume aims at achieving a synthesis of Keynesian theory with classical theory, specifically with Hicksian general equilibrium theory. Furthermore, Meade had the desire to extend the traditional concern of the balance of payments theory with current account balance to the overall balance by including international capital movements assumed to depend upon incomes and interest rate differentials. Another purpose of Meade in writing the book was to employ the theory resulting out of the synthesis to analyse the interrelationships between two economic policy instruments – management of domestic demand and change in exchange rate-on the one hand and the objectives of macroeconomic policy in an open economy – full employment (internal balance) and a satisfactory position of overall balance of payments or a balanced balance of payments (external balance) on the other.

According to David Vines, in both ways the book broke new ground. At the level of technical analysis, before Meade, most of the investigations into exchange rate change were premised on the assumption of unchanged incomes and Marshallian partial equilibrium concepts using the approach of elasticities. At the level of the theory of economic policy, Meade's prescription for the use of two policy instruments to attain the twin objectives of internal and external balance simultaneously, though familiar to him from his work on Bretton Woods, was truly revolutionary.

In his article in the Economic Journal reviewing Meade's book, Harry Johnson while paying ample tribute to the value of the underlying model, found fault with the treatment of saving in the model. According to Johnson, Meade made an 'indefensible' assumption that the amount of real saving coming from a given real income is independent of the terms of trade.

Johnson was also critical of Meade's taxonomic approach of the theory. It was his view that for the purpose of policy-making, there should be a concrete relation of the theory to specific problems of policy. In contrast, any general model formulated to permit consideration of a large number of possible cases was considered not particularly efficacious. When a policy fails in practice, the problem is not with the adaptation of the basic theory to the details of issues connected with the problem on hand but in the basic understanding of the theory itself.

Harry Johnson, in a later article (1973), was critical of Meade's integration of Keynesian with Hicksian theory. Essentially, Meade's model was a real model in that it ignores the fundamental characteristics of a monetary economy and monetary theory, despite all its appearance of analysing the monetary problem of the balance of payments. Johnson asserted that "the crux of analysis of a monetary economy is the real balance effect, and the associated stock adjustment behaviour by which actual real balances are adjusted to desired levels by price level changes in a closed economy, and international reserve flows in an open economy." Such stock adjustment behaviour was not adequately captured by Meade's model which, Johnson termed, as "fundamentally misconceived." This criticism does not in any way detract from the importance of Meade's achievement in synthesising Keynesian and Hicksian analysis in a policy-oriented model.

(b) ***Trade and Welfare***: The second volume of <u>The Theory of International Economic Policy</u> is called Trade and Welfare in which Meade presented a systematic analysis of arguments for trade and factor controls – an analysis of protection-versus-free trade in movement of both goods and factors of production. Meade, in this volume, made the assumption that internal balance and external balance are maintained by the policies analysed in the first volume, i.e. The Balance of Payments. The focus is on conditions under which interventions in the freedom of international exchange may increase welfare. For this purpose, an all-inclusive definition of welfare was employed (welfare of individual countries, groups within countries and the total global output available for distribution). The analysis was confined to a two-country world.

Harry Johnson identified two major contributions made by Meade to the development of the pure theory of international trade as applied to policy interventions in trade and movements of factors of production. The first and, perhaps, the most fundamental is "a reformulation of the theory of economic welfare." The theory that was developed by Meade is applicable to the theoretical analysis of what is referred to as "distortion cases" – cases in which perfect competition will not produce potential welfare maximisation. At the same time, the theory is operational in the sense of permitting empirical estimation of the quantitative effects of policy changes (referred to as cost- benefit analysis).

The other major contribution of the work as Johnson stated was that "the emphasis on factor movements especially capital movements is highly relevant to current international economic problems. Given subsequent concern...with the 'brain drain', direct foreign investment, and...'the multinational corporation', Meade's inclusion of international factor movements in the main corpus of his theory of international trade represented a distinct improvement over the contemporary tradition of formal trade theory...."

The book – The Theory of International Economic Policy – was marked by a number of important innovations in technical analysis whose influence in economic theory had gone beyond the study of international phenomena. Firstly, his discussion of the meaning of the concepts of optimum population and of optimum savings and of the relationship between the two, broke new ground. Secondly, Meade's invention of the concept of the "theory of second best" showed that a move towards pre-trade position may not improve the society's welfare in the presence of distortions elsewhere in the economy. He applied the methodology of "second best" in his notable work, The Theory of Customs Union. Thirdly, Meade generalised the Marshallian consumers' surplus with all its attendant limitations. Finally, Meade pioneered a new approach to welfare economics. He defined welfare as an appropriately weighted sum of individual welfares. This attempt, according to Johnson, was "a brilliant feat of imagination" taking over the approach from Fleming and reworking it into a powerful general technique for welfare analysis of practical policy problems.

3.2.2 A GEOMETRY OF INTERNATIONAL TRADE

Meade filled an important gap in the technique of geometrical representation of international equilibrium as also of the effects on equilibrium of policy changes such as international transfers and taxes and subsidies on international trade. Meade's technique, while facilitating drawing of welfare conclusion for all possible trade equilibria, allowed the incorporation of induced changes of production allocation.

Using Stolper-Samuelson relation between commodity and factor prices, one can study the effect of trade and changes in trading conditions on earned factor incomes. This exercise, is of limited interest since it was conducted on the unrealistic assumption of identical tastes and factor endowments of individuals needed to obtain unique community indifference curves. For factor earnings to be an interesting problem, what is required is an assumption of differences in tastes of factor owners, or differences in relative factor ownership or both. Critics feel that Meade's attempted real analysis to get predictions regarding the impact of changes in policy on the exchange rate by assuming that each country attempts at stabilising the domestic factor cost price of its exportable good is rather faulty. Instead, Johnson was of the opinion that Meade should have taken as given the quantity of domestic money and analyse the implications of changes in policy on the domestic money price level before working out the required change in the exchange rate for attaining equilibrium.

3.2.3 THE THEORY OF CUSTOMS UNION

Jacob Viner, who provided for the first time the insight of contemporary international trade theory into the customs union, envisaged a simultaneous movement towards free trade among the participating countries and a movement towards protection of producers in participating countries in each other's markets against those in non-participating countries. It involved both trade creation as well as trade diversion, the former being beneficial to global well-being and the latter being harmful to world welfare.

Meade's major contribution to the area of customs union was to formulate the problem in a general equilibrium framework. For this purpose, he incorporated relationships of complementarity and substitutability among goods in both production and consumption. He then examined the possibility of gains and losses from changes in quantities of goods consumed, induced by changes in prices facing the consumers. Meade thus attempted an analysis of welfare implications for all three types of parties involved – members, partners and non-participants – and the world as a whole. The latter is considered an important theoretical advancement.

Harry Johnson commented: "Meade's work on the theory of customs union, and more generally the analysis of Trade and Welfare, is important not only for its own sake but as the point of initiation of subsequent significant developments in general economic theory and in trade theory." The "general theory of second best" has been put forward first in general economic theory by Lipsey and Lancaster. However, it was 'explicit' in the introduction to and contents of Trade and Welfare. Johnson again explained the content and significance of this theory: "Paretian welfare economics specifies a set of marginal equalities and inequalities that must be fulfilled simultaneously for the achievement of a welfare optimum subject to resource constraints; but practical policy problems typically involve the question of moving towards achievement of one of these marginal conditions, under circumstances in which institutional, legal or other artificial constraints prevent the simultaneous fulfilment of other marginal conditions; the general theory of second best asserts that there is no way of telling, in the absence of specific information about relevant parameters, whether such a move will improve or lessen welfare; it also indicates that a partial rather than complete movement towards fulfilment of the Pareto-optimal condition in these circumstances is likely (though not certain) to prove second-best optimal."

In trade theory, the theory of 'second best' applies optimal commercial policy in the presence of domestic distortions, besides to the partial freeing of trade. The exploration into the former problem formed the subject-matter of articles of Bhagwati and Ramaswami as also of Harry Johnson among others.

3.2.4 THE THEORY OF FLEXIBLE EXCHANGE RATES

Meade was a consistent votary of flexible exchange rates. He explored in great detail the welfare effects of speculation under a floating exchange rate regime in his 1950 article in The Review of Economic Studies.

He made a convincing case for flexibility of exchange rates of the currencies of the members of an area such as European Free Trade Area in his 1957 article in The Economic Journal.

In his Nobel lecture, Meade commended the policy of flexible exchange rates. He stated: "The case for use by developed countries of massive import restriction rather than of gradual and moderate changes in exchange rate to look after their balances of payments would, I suspect, evaporate. It is the spectacle of imports competing with the products of domestic industries in which there is already serious unemployment, which is the greatest threat to the freedom of imports into the developed countries. With full employment and price stability at home [attainment of internal balance through the instrumentalities of demand management and wage-fixing], the balance of payments could with much more confidence be left to the mechanism of flexible foreign exchange rates."

3.2.5 THEORY OF ECONOMIC GROWTH

When Meade moved to Cambridge, growth theory was very much in the air. He brought out a useful book A Neo-classical Theory of Economic Growth which covered a number of aspects (for instance, presence of land, which is a fixed factor), accessible and useful to an undergraduate student, presenting in detail the mathematics of a two-sector growth model. He also made "advanced" contributions to growth theory in collaboration with Frank Hahn. But his lasting contribution in this area, according to David Vines, was his 1964 essay, "Efficiency, Equity and the Ownership of Property." Writing in International Encyclopaedia of Social Sciences, Biographical Supplement, Vol.18, Corden and Atkinson have this to say about the book: This "provides a very suggestive account of the forces underlying the accumulation of capital and the relationship between earned and unearned income" and stimulated revival of interest in the subject, at least in the United Kingdom. Meade rated this book as his best book as he put together into a "single synoptic framework" his views on economic growth, on the micro economic role of the price mechanism, on aspects of demography such as size and genetic composition of the population as also on the distributional implications of ownership of property.

3.3 CONCLUDING OBSERVATIONS

It is well known that Meade took up the study of economics in order to help make the world a better place for ordinary people. In this, he stands in the great Cambridge tradition of Marshall, Sidgwick and Keynes. Meade in his 1983 essay had underlined this shared objective as "the decisive factor in binding me so closely to (Keynes)...he had...a passionate desire to devise a better domestic and international society." Meade's conception of a better society was one "combining freedom, efficiency and equity in social affairs." In his Nobel Banquet speech on December 10, 1977, Meade declared: "without some vision of the nature of the good society the whole activity is pointless, and the immortals of the subject – Adam Smith, Wicksell, Keynes, to name only three of my favourite gods - bear witness to this truth." He also described the qualities an economist should possess: "The well-balanced economist is a normal human being with his warm heart on the left, his practical work-a-day hand on the right, and his clear and thoughtful head in the centre. Nowhere today is this combination...more needed than in the development of a decent and effective international economic order, the field in which Professor Bertil Ohlin and I have been so greatly honoured by this award."

In his Nobel Prize lecture, Meade made a specific reference to the deficiencies in the first volume (The Balance of Payments) of the Theory of International Economic Policy, and admitted that the basic analysis in the book was conducted in terms of static macroeconomic equilibrium models rather than in terms of dynamic growing or disequilibrium models. He categorically declared: "...If I were now rewriting that book I could do the underlying analysis not in terms of the reconciliation of the two objectives of external balance and internal balance, but in terms of the reconciliation of the three objectives of equilibrium in the balance of payments, full employment and price stability." In any real world situation now, one would have to take price stability and full employment as separate macroeconomic objectives with wage-fixing arrangements as one of the instruments of policy. Meade was of the view that an effective combination of full employment with the avoidance of inflation to attain internal balance necessarily requires that wage-fixing should take as its main criterion the supply-demand conditions in the labour market. He concluded his prize lecture which is essentially devoted to the topic of international economics with focus on internal balance by saying that one of the really important factors on which the world's health now depends is the "recasting the wage-fixing arrangements in a limited number of developed countries."

As regards evaluation of Meade's contribution to economics we could do no better than summarise the evaluation made by Harry Johnson in his 1973 essay. "Meade has delivered a lifetime of high standard performance in economic theory, characterized in spite of his socialist political views by an unusually high degree of objectivity and scientific detachment in the employment of theory in the clarification and solution of policy problems and theoretical problems arising in the context of policy." His two volumes of The Theory of International Economic Policy together with the related work, The Theory of the Customs Union rank very high. James Meade is credited with much of the development of the theory of commercial policy and optimal trade intervention.

While the first volume – The Balance of Payments – was very influential and had an immediate impact on the profession and the policy-makers in the field, the same cannot be said of the second volume. It had a delayed impact. Further, to a great extent, many of its original ideas were "rediscovered later." Corden and Atkinson remark that both volumes are written in a 'taxonomic' and 'heavy style.' The message often reaches a wider audience "only through the intermediation of more succinct, if less original, writers."

3.4 SELECT BIBLIOGRAPHY OF JAMES MEADE'S WORKS

3.4.1 BOOKS

1936 An Introduction to Economic Analysis and Policy, Oxford University Press, London.

1944 (with J. R. N. Stone) National Income and Expenditure, Oxford University Press, London.

1948 Planning and the Price Mechanism: The Liberal Socialist Solution, George Allen & Unwin, London.

1951 The Theory of International Economic Policy, Vol.I, The Balance of Payments, Oxford University Press, London.

1952 A Geometry of International Trade, George Allen & Unwin, London.

1953 Problems of Economic Union, The Charles R. Walgreen Foundation Lectures, University of Chicago Press, Chicago, Ill.

1955 a The Theory of International Economic Policy, Vol.II: Trade and Welfare, Oxford University Press, London.

b The Theory of Customs Union: The De Vries Lectures, Vol.1, North Holland, Amsterdam.

1958 a The Control of Inflation: Inaugural Lecture, Cambridge University, Cambridge University Press, Cambridge.

b A Neo-Classical Theory of Economic Growth, George Allen& Unwin, London.

1964 Efficiency, Equality and Ownership of Property, George Allen & Unwin, London.

1965 Principles of Political Economy: I, The Stationary Economy, George Allen & Unwin, London.

1968 Principles of Political Economy: II, The Growing Economy, George Allen & Unwin, London.

1970 The Theory of Indicative Planning, Lectures given at the University of Manchester, Manchester University Press, Manchester.

1971 a Principles of Political Economy: III, The Controlled Economy, George Allen & Unwin, London.

b Wages and Prices in a Mixed Economy, The Wincott Memorial Lectures, Institute of Economic Affairs, IEA Occasional Paper, No.35.,London.

1975 The Intelligent Radical's Guide to Economic Policy, George Allen & Unwin, London.

1976 a Principles of Political Economy: IV, The Just Economy, George Allen & Unwin, London.

b (with others) The Structure and Reform of Direct Taxation, George Allen & Unwin, London.

1988, 1990 The Collected Papers of J.Meade, Vols.1-4, S.Howson and D. Moggridge (eds.) Unwin Hyman, London.

3.4.2 ARTICLES

1955 "The Case for Variable Exchange Rates," Three Banks Review, No. 27.

1965 (with F. H. Hahn)"The Rate of Profit in a Growing Economy," EJ, Vol.75, June.

1972 "The Theory of Labour Managed Firms and of Profit Sharing," EJ, Vol.82, March.

1974 "Preference Ordering and Economic Policy," in Economic Theory and Planning: Essays in Honour of A. K. Dasgupta, Ashok Mitra (ed.), London.

1975 "The Keynesian Revolution," in Essays on John Maynard Keynes, M. Keynes (ed.), Macmillan, London

1977 "Nobel Lecture," Nobel Lectures, Economics 1969-1980, Assar Lindbeck (ed.), World Scientific Publishing Co., Singapore, 1992.

1978 "The Meaning of Internal Balance," EJ, Vol.88, No.351.

3.5 WORKS OF OTHERS

Corden W. M. and Atkinson. A. (1979) Meade, James E., in International Encyclopaedia of Social Sciences, Vol.18, Biographical Supplement, D. L. Sills (ed.), Free Press, New York.

Johnson, Harry (1978) "James Meade's Contribution to Economics," ScandJE, Vol.80, No.1.

Vines D.C (1987) "Meade, James. E," The New Palgrave: A Dictionary of Economics, Macmillan, London.

CHAPTER 4

THEODORE WILHAIN SCHULTZ

(1902 – 1998)

Professor Theodore W. Schultz, University of Chicago, U.S.A., shared the 1979 Alfred Nobel Memorial Prize in Economic Sciences with Professor Sir Arthur Lewis. The award was given "for their pioneering work in economic development research, with particular emphasis on the problems of developing countries."

Schultz started his career as an agricultural economist. During the 1930s and 1940s he brought out a series of studies devoted to the analysis of the crisis in American agriculture and later took up for study agricultural issues in various developing countries. His best known works from this period are Agriculture in an Unstable Economy and Production and Welfare of Agriculture. His notable publication on the subject was Transforming Traditional Agriculture. The main feature of his studies in agricultural economics was his penchant to treat the agricultural economy as an integral part of the entire economy. His particular focus in his studies relating to agriculture was on the imbalance between relative poverty in and under-development of agriculture as compared with the higher productivity and higher levels of income in industry and in other urban economic activities. He applied this approach both to industrialised countries and developing nations he had studied.

The Award Committee makes particular reference to the disequilibrium approach he had adopted in his analysis of the development potential of agriculture. Schultz highlighted the gap between traditional production methods and the more effective methods now available, which created necessary conditions for dynamic development. Making use of this approach, Schultz had critically analysed the industrialisation policies pursued by developing countries and their relative neglect of agriculture.

Though Schultz's roots are in agricultural economics, in the late 1950s he began his pursuit of human capital theory. He was a pioneer in the development of the field. He was the first to systematise the analysis of how investments in education can favourably impact the productivity in agriculture as also in the entire economy. Conscious of the limitations of the method, he had as a first approximation, defined and measured the size of educational capital as a sum of accumulated investments in education. The loss of earnings from employment during the periods of study, constituting a kind of opportunity cost, can be taken into account in individual or private context as well as in national context.

In his study of the theory of human capital, on a broad front, Schultz had drawn fresh insights from the writings of his great predecessors, such as Alfred Marshall, Frank Knight and Irving Fisher. He and his students at Chicago had demonstrated that, for a long time, there had been a considerably higher yield on "human capital" than on physical capital in the U.S. economy, which has led to much more rapid expansion of investments in education than other investments.

Schultz had always kept close to economic reality in his work as an economic researcher and as an adviser in various capacities. He had shown great ability to define factors facilitating development which model-building economists tend to neglect. Schultz had also done research in a number of other fields. They include subjects connected with health and disease as essential factors in economic development in the Third World countries as also on population issues in general. His important role in inspiring colleagues and students to undertake quality research is also widely acknowledged.

The award citation particularly underlines the common features in the analyses of development problems by Lewis and Schultz and their complementary nature. At the centre of their research lies economic development, which implies more than the concept of economic growth. Schultz's research work devoted great attention to a number of strategic issues connected with conditions for efficient use of productive resources, such as vocational skills, schooling, research and its application.

Lewis also emphasised the crucial importance of efficiency and development of agriculture to the economic growth in developing countries. In Lewis's analysis, low productivity in agriculture is a causal factor for the poverty of developing countries and a constraint on their growth through effects on terms of trade with developed countries.

Another common feature in Lewis's and Schultz's work is the importance they attached to facts and empirical research. They were both crucially interested in the historical aspects of development in different areas with reference to problems of economic policy. Both economists were deeply concerned with the poverty in the world. Schultz, in his Nobel lecture stated: "Most of the people in the world are poor" and were engaged in finding ways of emerging from underdevelopment. Both Lewis and Schultz were very critical of the agricultural policy as also other economic policies, which have been pursued by developing countries during various stages of development. The citation observes: "Their widespread and profound experience of economic policies and the underlying political system in developing countries makes their presentation of the basic problems vivid and sincere."

Lindbeck observes: "Both Lewis and Schultz were concerned with combining their theoretical reasoning with empirical data, though they used the traditional expository techniques of economic history rather formalized statistical or econometric testing techniques. Schultz emphasized the apparent efficiency in the agricultural sector in less developed countries, considering existing constraints with respect to resources and knowledge available in these countries. Lewis instead focused on the tensions between a large and stagnant agricultural sector, with a low marginal product of labour, and a dynamic industrial ('capitalist') sector, which is sometimes in the nature of an economic enclave."

4.1 A BRIEF BIOGRAPHICAL NOTE: THEODORE SCHULTZ

Theodore Schultz was born in Arlington, South Dakota, U.S.A., on April 30, 1902. The adverse economic events following the First World War turned him towards economics. He learned during his youth how hard it was for farm families to stay solvent. Farm product prices fell sharply and abruptly. After undergraduate studies at South Dakota State College, he received his M.S. in 1928 and Ph.D. in 1930 from the University of Wisconsin. He served on the faculty of Economics at Iowa State College between 1930 and 1943. He was head of the Department of Economics and Sociology there between 1934 and 1943. In 1943, Schultz moved to the University of Chicago, where he became Professor of Economics that year, Chairman of the Department of Economics, 1946-1961 and Charles L. Hutchinson Distinguished Service Professor since 1952 till retirement.

Schultz received many honours and honorary degrees. The honours he received include President, American Economic Association, 1960, Francis A. Walker Medal, American Economic Association, 1972 and Leonard Elmhirst Medal, International Agricultural Economic Association, 1976. He was at some time or the other, Fellow, American Farm Association, American Academy of Arts and Sciences and American Philosophical Society. He received honorary degrees such as LL.D. or D. Sc from South Dakota State College (1959), Michigan State University (1962), University of Illinois and University of Wisconsin (1968). Schultz was a member of Board of Directors of National Bureau of Economic Research from 1949 to 1967 and was its Vice- President in 1958. He was a Trustee of Population Council and Institute of Current World Affairs.

Theodore W. Schultz died on February 26, 1998.

4.2 A BRIEF SURVEY OF THEODORE SCHULTZ'S WORK

While Schultz's contributions essentially pertained to the understanding of economic development, his concern for economic changes that would benefit the world's poor and his serious attempts to foster enlightened economic policies in furtherance of human welfare, his fame mainly rests on his outstanding contribution to agricultural economics and his pioneering work in the field of human capital. As such, it is proposed to summarise here his research effort in these two fields.

1. Agricultural Economics;
2. Human Capital.

4.2.1 AGRICULTURAL ECONOMICS

Schultz had, throughout his life, retained his role as leader in research in agricultural economics. From the start of his academic career, Schultz believed that any economist working in the area of agricultural economics must possess good grounding in general economics. He provided stimulation and encouragement to undertake research and to carry out analysis of the effects of instability in the urban sector upon agriculture. Furthermore, he encouraged researchers to enquire into the effects of contemporary agricultural policies upon "farmers' incentives and behavior and upon distribution of income and wealth in agriculture."

Schultz's work in agricultural economics (in early work as well as in later studies) contained mainly two themes: distortions of incentives and issues concerned with change and uncertainty. He also encouraged his colleagues to work on strategies that could "smooth adjustments in agriculture to economic fluctuations and vagaries of weather. The work which grew out of his leadership in the field threw up policy options in agriculture, such as crop insurance and forward pricing of agricultural products" and a number of studies throwing light on decision-making under uncertainty in agriculture. The studies that had been undertaken by Schultz in the field related to the interdependence of agriculture and rest of the economy in developed countries as well as in developing countries. Mary Jean Bowman observes: "The throttling of agriculture in development policies over much of the Third World has been a steady lament in Schultz's work for three decades."

In his work, Schultz had demonstrated that market prices act as a signalling device to allocation of resources, within and across the sectors of every economy. He had shown that price-depressing marketing arrangements and various taxes had the deleterious effect of distorting agricultural production, besides adversely affecting the general economic development. Schultz had been a strong critic of the programmes of food aid to poorer countries. Schultz's opposition to food aid was based upon his view that it would cause a setback to agricultural advance in the absence of deliberate steps "to minimize indirect perverse effects" on agricultural progress. On the other hand, he had advocated programmes that could raise productivity in farming in developing countries. In order to transform traditional agriculture into a vibrant, dynamic and progressive agriculture, Schultz had assigned a crucial role to education and information. He was convinced that while schooling would be of little economic value in traditional societies, in a society undergoing change, it can be of very great value.

Thomas Balogh who reviewed Transforming Traditional Agriculture in the Economic Journal had said: "...this is an ill-informed and potentially mischievous book on a subject which is among the most vital and most urgent in the world. It is ill informed because Prof. Schultz ignores literature essential if a balanced judgment on the problem on transformation of primitive peasant agricultural production is to be arrived at....Mischievous because he refers only selectively--that too from unpublished doctoral dissertations and odd 'mimeos', ignoring the devastating attack by Prof. Samuelson on the 'Chicago Twist'...."

4.2.2 HUMAN CAPITAL

Mark Blaug has called Schultz "the father of the concept of Human Capital." Mary Jean Bowman, however, feels a more apt title is "the father of the human investment revolution in economic thought." It is widely acknowledged that "Schultz's initial ideas about investment in human beings...have spawned a remarkable diversity of research endeavors; in development economics, agricultural economics, labor economics, economic history, international economics, business economics, urban economics, and 'the new economics of family' (Inclusion in public finance was more obvious and older)."

Schultz, who drew the initial inspiration for the work in this field from Irving Fisher, was clearly against treating capital as homogeneous. He had emphasised in his study of investments in people to the formation of "the ability to deal with disequilibria." Schultz's first major paper in the field was published in 1958. The rapid growth experienced in 1950s by the industrialised countries could not be explained adequately by conventional aggregative models. He rejected the hypothesis that it could be explained by the phenomenon of increasing returns to scale. The residual of unexplained growth by these nations was sought to be explained in different ways by economists. Schultz was the first economist who "turned the spotlight directly on people." He focused on schooling. He began with an inference from plain economics: "...if returns to scale are constant, and if the marginal rate of substitution between labor and capital is unchanged, and if under these circumstances more output is forthcoming, it is the production function that has been altered; that is, production has risen relative to inputs of labor and capital as conceived and measured. We can, however, transpose any gains in output under these conditions back to the input account, and embody them in labor and capital as improvements in quality. This, then, permits us to treat the production function as unchanged and to represent the increases in output as a measure of the improvements in the quality of labor and capital." While encouraging attempts fully to take into account quality in measurement of inputs for analysis of aggregate production functions, Schultz in his work "paired attempts to estimate effects on output with identification of inputs in cost terms."

In a 'fundamental' paper on "Formation of Human Capital," Schultz presented a series of estimates of the cost value of human capital embodied in the labour force that was employed over the period 1929-1957. The cost estimates were supposed to reflect the investment decisions people had made. The estimates were also expected to highlight the importance of investments in the schooling component of human capital as compared with investments in non-human capital over time. Mary Jean Bowman evaluates the importance of this work of Schultz: "...the demonstration of the importance of foregone earnings in estimates of the formation of human capital and Schultz's presentation of the logic for inclusion of foregone earnings in an analysis of human investment decisions was to usher in a whole set of new set of theoretical-empirical developments with wide-ranging application to both market and non-market economies."

Research work on the topic of human capital in developing countries has lent support to "the statistical significance of foregone productive activities (whether on the family farm or in wage employment) for the explanation of school attendance, even for children as young as 8 to 10 years."

In his work on investment in human beings, Schultz had raised questions about differences in the quality of schooling as also the impact of these differences on productivity of workers and distribution of earnings. He argued how changes in quality of education affect economic growth, linking this to his emphasis on investment in R & D as an endogenous variable. Schultz also underlined the need to take a dynamic growth view of distribution effects and equity, both between levels of education and within higher education.

Transforming Traditional Agriculture emphatically argues in favour of the efficiency of farmers in traditional agriculture. Schultz argued that under carefully specified assumptions, "the fully traditional agricultural economy will be a Pareto-optimal economy; farmers are rational men and there have been many years of experience in which to develop the best method of farming...." Schultz would prefer "the brutal methods that work to elegant refinements of little practical utility." He, however, placed special emphasis on the generation of knowledge and capabilities for participation in creative change. Schultz's proposition that schooling and research should be complementary inputs into agricultural development has been widely tested. There is robust empirical support to the hypothesis that there is a positive association between effects of schooling on productivity and on increases in productivity. "Schooling of farm people seems to make a substantial difference to farm productivity when, but only when, applicable new technologies are available."

Mary Jean Bowman sums up the importance of Schultz's work in these words: "...with Schultz's stress on the diseconomic effects of an exaggerated emphasis on industrialization that penalizes rural development, we come out with implications that focus attention on people, research, and the largeness of small things. This is a strongly humanistic perspective in that it speaks for the reasonableness of all men."

4.3 CONCLUDING OBSERVATIONS

Schultz, as we can see, had never stood still. He continuously stressed on incentives, on change and uncertainty and on human potential. In regard to economic progress of nations, he particularly emphasised the improved ability to deal with disequilibria as necessary.

About economists, Schultz, in his Nobel Banquet speech, had this to say: "The more intelligent the people are, the more certain they tend to disagree on matters of social principle and policy, and more acute will be the disagreement." He observed that herein lies the proof, if proof were required, that economists are intelligent. At the same time, he is critical of economists in regard to some aspects: "...they neglect history...they give too little attention to the cultural and social values to please the humanities. Their mathematics does not impress the mathematicians.... The only real friends economists have are impersonal adverse events: inflation, unemployment and hard times."

Schultz's continuing concern for the poor, particularly of developing countries (including India), was vividly brought out in his Nobel lecture. He diagnosed: "The decisive factors of production in improving the welfare of poor people are not space, energy and cropland; the decisive factor is the improvement in population quality." His emphasis of human capital is particularly important. He said that most observers including economists overrate the economic importance of land and greatly underrate the importance of the quality of human agents. He acknowledged the contribution of fellow research scholars in the understanding of the economics of human capital, with special reference to the economics of research, the response of farmers to new and profitable techniques of production, the relationship between production and human welfare and the economics of family.

With respect to understanding the problems of developing countries, Schultz observed that among economists there is a mistaken "presumption that standard economic theory is inadequate...and that a separate economic theory is needed. Models developed for this purpose...were at best intellectual curiosities." It is increasingly realised that standard economic theory is applicable equally "to the scarcity problems that confront low income countries." Another "intellectual mistake" which economists generally commit, according to Schultz, is the neglect of economic history. Classical economists dealt with conditions that were similar to those that prevail in low-income countries today. He specifically referred to the work of Ricardo and Marshall and made a pertinent comment: "In India people live under the Ricardian shadow. Understanding the experience and achievements of poor people over the ages can contribute much to the understanding of the problems and possibilities of low income countries today...than the most detailed and exact knowledge about the surface of the earth, or of ecology, or of tomorrow's technology."

Schultz questioned, as mentioned earlier, the overrated importance of land. Remarking that differences in soil productivity is not useful to explain why people are poor in long-settled parts of the world, he cited the examples of Deccan Plateau in India where the productivity of the rain-fed soils is low, and on the higher productive soils of South India. "What matters most in the case of farmland are the incentives and associated opportunities that farm people have to augment the effective supply of land by means of investments that include the contributions of agricultural research and the improvement of human skills."

As regards the underrating of the quality of human agents, Schultz stated: "While land per se is not a critical factor in being poor, the human agent is: investment in improving population quality can significantly enhance the economic prospects and welfare of the poor people. Child care, home and work experience, the acquisition of information and skills through schooling and in other ways consisting primarily of investment in health and schooling, can improve population quality." In this connection, he remarked that it is now well documented that poor people engaged in agriculture sector do respond to better opportunities. (This has to be appreciated by policy makers, particularly in India!)

He had a word of praise for farmers' wisdom. "Farmers the world over, in dealing with costs, return and risks, are calculating economic agents. Within their small, individual, allocative domain they are fine-tuning entrepreneurs...they [farmers] provide an essential human resource, which is, entrepreneurship.... On most farms there is a second enterprise, the household. Women are also entrepreneurs in allocating their own time and in using farm products and purchased goods in household production.... The allocative roles of farmers and of farm women are important and their economic opportunities really matter." Government cannot perform efficiently the function of farm entrepreneurs, Schultz opined. He also emphasised the essential need for entrepreneurship in research.

Schultz acknowledged the achievements, over time, in improving population quality. Quality in this context consists of various forms of human capital. Approvingly quoting Hicks's statement that capital homogeneity assumption is the disaster of capital theory, Schultz stated in his Nobel lecture "This [homogeneity] assumption is demonstrably inappropriate in analyzing the dynamics of economic growth that is afloat on capital inequalities...because they are the main spring of economic growth." He treated population quality as a scarce resource and hence has economic value and its acquisition entails a cost. Education accounts for much of the improvements in population quality.

Schultz observed that the "Theory of Human Capital" treats everyone's state of health as a stock, that is, as health capital. He, however, expressed the view that part of the quality of the initial stock is inherited and part is acquired. The improvement in health revealed by the longer life span of people in many developing countries has been the key advance in population quality and the favourable economic implications of these increases in life span are pervasive. Longer life spans, according to him, provide additional incentives to acquire more education, as investment in future earnings.

Schultz concluded the Nobel lecture with the following sum up: "The central thrust of this lecture is that population quality and knowledge matter. A goodly number of low-income countries have a positive record in improving population quality and in acquiring useful knowledge. These achievements imply favorable economic prospects, provided they are not dissipated by politics and governmental policies that discriminate against agriculture.... We...have forgotten the wisdom of Alfred Marshall, when he wrote, 'knowledge is the most powerful engine of production; it enables us to subdue nature and satisfy our wants.'"

Before concluding, reference may be made to two glowing tributes paid to Schultz on his death.

D. G. Johnson in Economic Development and Cultural Change titled "In Memoriam T.W." states: "He [Schultz] received the Nobel Prize...for his outstanding contribution to our knowledge of the process of economic development. This contribution rested on two major points."

1 "... that farmers in developing countries, though often illiterate, were rational and made efficient use of their resources."

2 "...his contribution to the understanding of human capital and its role in production."

Marc Nerlove pays the following tribute to Schultz in The Economic Journal:

"Well-reasoned doubts are good for economics. Neither theory, nor data, nor mathematics can fully resolve them.... Economic behaviour is more complex than our thoughts about it; our thoughts, however, are more comprehensive than standard theory; and standard theory is more comprehensive than mathematical economics.... Economics would be better if we would substitute reasoned doubts for our parochial economic doctrines. An obituary should be a celebration of life rather than a dirge to mourn passing. Ted Schultz's life was lived in and through his ideas, and in his life he transformed economics."

4.4 SELECT BIBLIOGRAPHY OF THEODORE SCHULTZ'S WORKS

4.4.1 BOOKS

1943 Redirecting Farm Policy, Macmillan, New York.

1945 Agriculture in an Unstable Economy, Macmillan, New York.

1953 Economic Organization of Agriculture, McGraw-Hill, New York.

1963 The Economic Value of Education, Columbia University Press, New York.

1964 Transforming Traditional Agriculture, Yale University Press, New Haven, Conn.

1968 Economic Growth and Agriculture, McGraw-Hill, New York.

1971 Investment in Human Capital: The Role of Education and of Research, Macmillan, New York.

1972 Human Resources, Fiftieth Anniversary Colloquium, NBER, New York.

4.4.2 ARTICLES

1932 "Diminishing Returns in View of Progress in Agricultural Production," Journal of Farm Economics, Vol.14, No.4.

1933 (With G.W. Snedecor) "Analysis of Variance as an Effective Method of Handling the Time Element in Certain Economic Statistics," JASA, Vol.28, Mar.

1939 "The Theory of Firm and Farm Management Research," Journal of Farm Economics, Vol.21, Aug.

1940 "Capital Rationing, Uncertainty and Farm Tenancy Reform," JPE, Vol.48, June.

1941 "Economic Effects of Agricultural Progress," AER, Vol.30, Feb.

1944 "Two Conditions Necessary for Economic Progress in Agriculture," Canadian Journal of Economics and Political Science, Vol. 10, Aug.

1950 "Reflections on Poverty Within Agriculture," JPE. Vol.43, Feb.

1951 a (with D. R Gadgil et. al.,) Measures for Economic Development of Underdeveloped Countries, U.N. Department of Economic Affairs, New York.

b "Economic Efficiency: Its Meaning, Measurement and Application to Problems," Journal of Farm Economics, Vol. 33, Feb.

1960 "Capital Formation by Education," JPE, Vol.68, Dec.

1961 "Investment in Human Capital," (Presidential Address to American Economic Association), AER, Vol.41, No.1.

1965 "Investing in Poor People: An Economist's View," AER, Vol.45, No.2.

1968 "Human Capital," International Encyclopaedia of the Social Sciences, David L. Sills (ed.) Macmillan Co., and the Free Press, New York.

1975 "The Value of the Ability to Deal with Disequilibria," JEL, Vol. 13, No.3

1980 "Investing in People: The Economics of Population Quality," (Nobel Lecture), University of California Press, Sanfrancisco, Ca.

4.5 WORKS OF OTHERS

Bowman, Mary Jean (1980), "On Theodore W. Schultz's Contributions to Economics," ScandJE, Vol.82,No.1.

Bowman, Mary Jean (1987) "Schultz, Theodore Wilhain," The New Palgrave: A Dictionary of Economics, Macmillan, London.

Lindbeck, A.(2001) "The Sveriges Riksbank Prize" in Economic Sciences in Memory of Alfred Nobel 1969-2007, The Nobel Prize: The First 100 Years, A. W. Levinivitz and N. Ringertz (eds.)Imperial College Press and World Scientific Publishing Co Pvt Ltd.

CHAPTER 5

SIR WILLIAM ARTHUR LEWIS

(1915 – 1991)

The 1979 Alfred Nobel Memorial Prize in Economic Sciences was awarded jointly to Professor Arthur Lewis of Princeton University, U.S.A., and Professor Theodore W. Schultz of University of Chicago, U.S.A., for "their pioneering work in economic development research, with particular emphasis on the problems of developing countries."

In the citation announcing the award, the Royal Swedish Academy of Sciences refers to Arthur Lewis as a leading figure and pioneer in economic research on developing countries. Particular reference is made to his fundamental studies from the middle of 1950s, namely, <u>Economic Development with Unlimited Supplies of Labour</u> and <u>Theory of Economic Growth</u>. The most significant of the other important works of Arthur Lewis, according to the Royal Academy, were <u>Aspects of Tropical Trade</u> (Wicksell Lectures in 1969) and <u>Growth and Fluctuations</u>, 1870-1913.

Lewis devoted his attention to the basic factors responsible for poverty among populations in the developing countries and to the far from satisfactory rate of economic development in those countries. He received wide praise for his two theoretical models, which attempt at describing and explaining the "intrinsic" problem of underdevelopment. Lewis's original premises in these works had undergone many variations and received numerous additions as a consequence of widespread scientific debate generated by his theories. These two models (which are outlined below) have been subjected to extensive empirical verification confirming the "realistic structure and usefulness" of the models.

The dual nature of a developing economy is the prime basis of the first model developed by Lewis. Developing countries are characterised by dual economies of a few urban growth centres surrounded by large areas of traditional agriculture, which engages the labour of a substantial part of the country's population. The former sector – a modern market-oriented sector- engages mainly in production of industrial goods. This sector – market-oriented sector – which provides the impetus for the growth of the economy, expands with the support of unlimited supplies of labour through migration from the agricultural sector. The workers employed in the market-oriented or modern sector accept low wages that correspond to standards of living and conventions in underdeveloped agricultural areas. The profits in the modern or capitalist sector generate increased savings, providing the needed financial capital for expansion.

The focus of the other important model of Lewis, which was in classical tradition, was concerned with the question of determination of the terms of trade of industrial products on one hand and raw materials and tropical products on the other. Lewis classified the countries in the world into two groups – Southern and Northern, poor and rich. He hypothesised that each group produces two types of products, one of which both group of countries produce, that is, food. The other two products the two groups produce were represented by what he called 'coffee' and 'steel'. These two products are traded between the two groups. Lewis demonstrated that, under certain stipulated conditions, the terms of trade between the two groups in regard to the products were determined by the relationship between productivity of labour in agriculture in the developing countries and that in the developed countries. The most important result which Lewis's model obtained was that "lower agricultural productivity in the developing countries as compared with the rich countries is the decisive factor in the real terms of trade between the two groups of countries and determines the long-term development of the terms of trade."

Lewis's work incorporated the main factors responsible for the poverty and development problems in developing countries. The Swedish Academy's announcement of the Prize makes particular reference as to how Lewis's experience as economic advisor and administrator of a financial institution influenced his economic research work. "Lewis is very much the economic historian shedding new light on growth processes and short and long economic cycles in the nucleus of industrialized countries which influenced a periphery of developing countries."

5.1 A SHORT BIOGRAPHICAL SKETCH OF WILLIAM ARTHUR LEWIS

W. Arthur Lewis was born on the island of St. Lucia in the British West Indies on January 23, 1915. After leaving school at the age of 14, he went to work as a clerk in the Civil Service. This job taught him to write, to type, to file and to be organized. He studied at the London School of Economics for a Bachelor of Commerce degree, which offered accounting, business management, commercial law, a little economics and statistics. Lewis stated: "This training has been very helpful in the various administrative jobs I have had to do, its weakness from the standpoint of my subsequent career (which was then inconceivable) was that it lacked mathematics."

Lewis obtained his doctoral degree from London School of Economics in 1940 and taught there for several years after the war. His research work had been mainly in three fields: industrial economics till 1948; history of the world economy since 1870 which he started in 1944 and pursued throughout his life and development economics since about 1950. Lewis got into the history of the world economy because Frederich Hayek, then Acting Chairman of the Department of Economics of London School of Economics (LSE) suggested that he teach a course on "what happened between the wars." Lewis was reported to have replied: "I did not know what happened between the wars; to which Hayek replied that the best way of learning a subject was to teach it." Lewis's first three books were written during the period in which he taught at the LSE. Economic Survey 1919-1939, which began as a course of lectures to the students with some background knowledge of the period, grew into "an overambitious attempt to interpret the inter-war years in the setting of world economic history." Also dating from this period was a collection of essays titled Overhead Costs and Principles of Economic Planning, an early discussion of the subject.

The time Lewis spent at the LSE can be considered as preparatory to his work on development economics, which began after he moved to Manchester University, where he occupied the Stanley Jevons Chair of Political Economy. In the 1950s he was a senior official in the U. N. Agencies. In 1963 he was knighted and was also appointed a University Professor at Princeton University where he was at the Woodrow Wilson School of Public and International Affairs. At the University, he occupied the James Madison Chair of Political Economy. He had also held several important administrative positions in the West Indies. Lewis held many part-time advisory positions with international organisations and governments in developing countries. In 1970, Lewis became the Director of the Caribbean Development Bank.

Lewis's achievements have been recognised by the naming of 'The Arthur Lewis Building' (opened in 2007) at the University of Manchester, where he once lectured.

Sir Arthur Lewis died in Bridgetown, Barbados, on June 15, 1991.

5.2 A BRIEF SUMMARY OF ARTHUR LEWIS'S CONTRIBUTIONS

Ronald Findlay in his evaluation in 1980 of the contributions of Sir Arthur Lewis has put his work in the perspective of the times in which Lewis did his work. He states: "A major concern of economics in our time has been the problem of economic development, the achievement of a sustained increase in per capita incomes of the millions of people living in the so-called Third World. The urgency of this issue has led the economists in the past three decades to return to the "inquiry into the nature and causes of the wealth of nations" that they had abandoned during the previous century for the investigation of the allocation of given resources and the stabilization of employment and income. Among the many distinguished economists who have contributed notably to this recently revived field the pre-eminent figure is Professor W. Arthur Lewis of Princeton University."

The contributions of Lewis to the field of economic development, specifically of developing countries, are summarised under the following heads.

1. Lewis's early research work;
2. Lewis's outstanding contributions to Development Economics in the form of his 1954 article titled "Economic Development with Unlimited Supplies of Labour;"
3. Trade-Development Nexus; and
4. Relationship between Lewis's approach and Neo-classical approach to explaining Modern Economic Growth.

5.2.1 EARLY WORK

The early original research work of Lewis was concerned with the application of the theory of price to problems of industrial organisation and public utilities. A series of studies by him published during the 1940's such as "The Two Part Tariff," "Competition in Retailing" and "Fixed Costs" were put together in a volume entitled Overhead Costs published in 1949. The article on "Two-part Tariff" discussing the issues connected with pricing of electricity services and telephone services provided "a definitive analysis of this scheme." The article on "Competition in Retailing" discussed the important question of the optimal number of retail stores, in terms of balancing scale economies vis-à-vis customer convenience in having a large number of retail outlets from which purchases can be made. According to Findlay, this work of Lewis "anticipates the work done only very recently by Lancaster and others on optimal product variety."

Another early work of Lewis discussed, at an introductory level, the issues involved in economic planning, titled "Principles of Economic Planning." It examined the problems involved in coordinating government intervention and the market in a mixed economy.

5.2.2 ECONOMIC DEVELOPMENT WITH UNLIMITED SUPPLIES OF LABOUR

Lewis's outstanding and most influential contribution in the field of economics is his 1954 paper in Manchester School entitled "Economic Development with Unlimited Supplies of Labour." Critics consider that his subsequent work and a large part of the literature of development economics in 1950s and later as an "extended commentary on the meaning and ramification" of this big idea, which dominated an entire field.

Economists identify basically three alternative approaches to the subject, namely the classical (including Marxian), the Keynesian and the Neo-classical. The classical approach postulates a real wage rate for unskilled workers determined by social conventions. The Keynesians stipulate that aggregate output is constrained by lack of effective demand. To raise the aggregate output, particularly in conditions of depression, the Keynesian prescription is well known--aimed at boosting effective demand. At full employment when both factors of production (labour and capital) are scarce, the rewards to the two factors are determined in the Neo-classical approach on the basis of the principle of marginal productivity. In Lewis's opinion, the neo-classical approach is eminently applicable for developed industrial economies. He considered the classical approach as the most appropriate model for developing countries. Thus, Lewis was closer to the thinking of Sraffa and other Cambridge economists in that the real wages are taken as exogenous for developing countries.

Lewis, in his paper, presented a stylised model in which the typical poor country, characterised by a "dual" economy, is divided into a "traditional" sector and a "modern" sector. The traditional sector comprises peasant agriculture as well as self-employment of various types in urban areas or service occupations, such as domestic servants. The primary objective of economic activity in this sector is to maintain consumption. The modern or "Capitalist" sector consists of commercial farming, plantations, mines and manufacturing. In these activities, labour is hired. Production in this sector is organised by entrepreneurs and capitalists with the primary objective of earning profit. Lewis invoked the distinction drawn by Adam Smith between productive and un-productive labour. Further, as mentioned earlier, Lewis adopted the classical view that real wages in the modern sector is exogenously given. Then, employment and profits are determined by the demand for labour (and not supply) necessary to put to work the existing stock of fixed capital in the short run. It is in this sense that Lewis spoke of unlimited supplies of labour. In addition, he assumed in the tradition of classicals that capital accumulation is influenced by savings out of profits. He made an additional assumption that while all wages are consumed, all profits are saved. The growth rate in the model is equal to the product of the profit rate and the propensity to save out of profits as in Robinson-Kaldor model or von Neumann model.

The process of economic development was postulated by Lewis as the expansion of the modern sector relative to the traditional sector until such time as the reservoir of surplus labour in the traditional sector is exhausted and "an integrated labour market emerges with a neo-classically determined equilibrium real wage." Amartya Sen in his 1966 article "Peasants and Dualism with or without Surplus Labour" in the Journal of Political Economy provided a very sophisticated and strong theoretical defence of the dual economy model of Lewis.

Lewis's approach of postulating a perfectly elastic supply of labour over the relevant range at each instant at a given real wage rate is not inconsistent with a rise in real wage over time as a result of exogenous forces such as union pressure or intervention of government. In the Neo-classical model, however, a rise in the real wage occurs only because of excess demand for labour at the original real wage level. The experience of developing countries in having open urban unemployment, rising both absolutely as well as relatively to the size of the labour force, besides widespread underemployment in rural and urban areas, is not consistent with the Neo-classical postulate. A plausible explanation is that the rate of rise in real wage is equal to the rate of rise in productivity as a result of which the rate of profit remains unchanged. Findlay observes: "The extensive literature associated with the popular Harris-Todaro (1968) model of urban unemployment follows Lewis in postulating an exogenously fixed real wage in the urban sector, above alternative rural earnings, which induces a flow of migration equilibrated by the probability of unemployment in relation to the urban-rural wage differential."

The purpose of the model put forward by Lewis, in his own words, was to explain "the central problem in the theory of economic development" which for him "is to understand the process whereby a community which was previously saving and investing 4 or 5 percent of its national income or less converts itself into an economy where voluntary saving is running at about 12 or 15 per cent of the national income or more." This phenomenon was explained by Lewis's model as a result of an increase in profits consequent to the relative expansion of the capitalist sector rather than by an increase in the propensity to save out of any given category of income. Chenery and Syrquin, in their book Patterns of Development 1950-1970, state that a number of econometric studies yield results in support of the basic hypothesis that "saving rises relatively to the national income because the incomes of the savers increase relatively to the national income."

The conditions of unlimited supply of labour put forward by Lewis's model must come to an end eventually when the growth of the developing country is governed by the Neo-classical type model, characterised by an integrated labour market and rather than a fixed saving rate.

In this context, the perceptive comment of Findlay is worth quoting in full. " The two models in combination...yield the prediction of a 'long swing' in the rate of growth, rising from a level of near zero towards a lower bound determined by the natural rate, the Lewis model governing the first phase and the Neo-classical model the second. The cross section data conforms to this prediction, since growth rate plotted against per capita levels show an inverted U-shaped pattern, with low growth in the very poor countries such as Bangladesh, Burma and Nepal, very high growth rates in middle income countries such as Brazil, Korea and Taiwan and growth at around 3 or 4 per cent in the rich countries such as Germany and the U.S...."

5.2.3 NEXUS BETWEEN TRADE AND DEVELOPMENT

The 1954 paper of Lewis referred to earlier also contained seminal ideas on the relation between trade and growth in a brief section on the open economy. His ideas on this topic were presented in his other works including in his textbook on Development Planning. The ideas presented in 1954 paper were further developed in his 1969 Wicksell Lectures.

Lewis in his 1954 paper argued the case for protectionist policies of developing countries on the ground that workers' wages in industry are considerably higher than in agriculture. Lewis postulated that the "marginal product of labour in manufactures is equated with the average product in food, because of sharing within peasant families, whereas the social optimum requires it to be equal to the marginal product, which is less." It follows that the government has to intervene in the price mechanism in order to step up the output of manufactures and at the same time to effect contraction of the food output. Lewis, of course, did not discuss the question of the best way of intervention by the government. His analysis suggested that in such a situation, imposition of tariffs was better rather than leaving the price to be determined in the market.

In the same article, Lewis had presented another model, a simple Ricardo-Graham model which also he elaborated and developed further in his Wicksell lectures. The second model leads to a different policy recommendation. The Ricardo-Graham model contains two regions and three goods, with each region producing two goods, one of which is commonly produced by both countries. One of the two regions (Region I) produces two goods – Steel and Food – whereas the other region (Region II) produces Coffee and Food. It is assumed that both the regions consume all the three goods. The relative prices of Steel and Coffee are determined in the model in terms of Food, only from the supply side. As a consequence, the terms of trade between the two regions are determined purely by relative productivities of labour in Food. The demand conditions in the market for Food have no effect as the model assumes that each region has a linear transformation curve for the two goods it produces. Lewis explained the divergence of the double factorial terms of trade from unity in terms of the disparity in labour productivity in Food. This reflects the continuance of traditional methods in Region II whereas Region I adopts mechanisation and uses chemical fertilizers in the production of Food.

In the Wicksell lectures, Lewis demonstrated, on the basis of empirical data, that productivity in Steel increases more sluggishly than in Food in Region I, while in Region II productivity in Coffee rises faster than in Food. Therefore, the Steel price rises relative to the price of Coffee so that the commodity terms of trade as well as double factorial terms of trade turn against Region II. Lewis was thus able to provide a "rigorous and elegant argument for a modified form of the thesis of secular deterioration of the terms of trade, more familiarly associated with the names of Prebisch (1950) and Singer (1950)."

From the above analysis, Lewis came to a conclusion that the development of labour-intensive manufactured exports was not an appropriate long-term strategy for developing countries. Instead, he favoured a strategy, which aimed at raising productivity in Food, through investment in human and physical capital, using technological innovations and government assistance.

From his various writings, one can clearly gauge Lewis's scepticism about the effectiveness of trade as an engine of growth. He rather favoured for developing countries a strategy of balanced growth, which aims at development oriented towards the home market. In regard to this controversy (whether or not trade is an engine of growth for developing countries), Findlay expresses the view that "...in the context of today there is ample evidence of a positive association between trade and growth...."

5.2.4 EXPLANATION OF MODERN ECONOMIC GROWTH: APPROACH OF LEWIS AND NEO-CLASSICALS

As outlined earlier, the approach of Lewis and Neo-classicals in regard to the explanation of modern economic growth are complementary. They are not alternative models for explaining the same phenomenon. The complementarity of the two approaches was clearly recognised not only by Lewis himself but also by Solow, Swan, Meade and Hicks, among others.

The controversy regarding Lewis's model seems to have been generated because of the widespread impression that for the operation of the model it is necessary to have "disguised unemployment" in the rural sector; that is, zero marginal productivity of labour. It is, however, contended by economists like Findlay that what Lewis meant by "unlimited supplies" is an excess supply of labour at an exogenously given real wage.

A part of the criticism of Lewis's model comes from the impression that it makes the real wage in the "capitalist" sector endogenous, in the sense that real wage is determined as some function of the alternative earning opportunities present in the rural sector. A popular scenario is farming by peasant families owning land whose members equally share the aggregate farm output. In such a situation, the average product in peasant agriculture becomes the wage to the "Capitalist" sector. This can give rise to a perfectly elastic supply curve of labour if there is abundant land in the peasant sector, making average product equal to marginal product. Findlay observes: "In this case the Lewis model and the Neo-classical model of the labour market become identical. It is 'unlimited supplies of land' which creates 'unlimited supplies of labour' to the 'Capitalist' sector in this instance."

In the case of densely populated developing countries of the present, land in the rural sector is a scarce factor implying that marginal product is below the average product, with both average and marginal products declining in response to increase in labour input. Under such circumstances, the supply curve of labour to the Capitalist sector would be sloping upward if the wage is an endogenous variable whether determined by marginal or average productivity in agriculture. This holds true even if there were "disguised unemployment" in rural areas as any withdrawal of labour leaving the aggregate output unchanged would imply increase in the per capita share of the remaining labour. Thus, "it is clear that 'disguised unemployment' in agriculture, by itself, is neither necessary nor sufficient for the horizontal supply curve of labor to the 'Capitalist' sector though it is compatible with it." Findlay comments: "Though it is not essential to his model, Lewis is clearly a believer in the widespread existence of the phenomenon of zero marginal productivity of labour in the densely populated LDC's [developing countries]."

5.3 CONCLUDING OBSERVATIONS

In his Nobel lecture "The Slowing Down of the Engine of Growth," Lewis returned to his pet subject and stated: "For the past hundred years the rate of growth of output in the developing world has depended on the rate of output in the developed world.... The principal link through which the former (developed countries or MDCs) control the growth rate of the latter (developing countries or LDCs) is trade. As MDCs grow faster, the rate of growth of their imports accelerates and LDCs export more...the relationship was quantitatively the same over a hundred years.... The main link between MDC and LDC economies has been the MDC demand for LDC primary commodities.... The real problem is whether LDCs will persist in rapid growth despite the slowdown of the MDCs.... The problems tackled in this paper would not arise at all if MDCs were willing to allow LDCs a greater share of MDC markets.... Neither would these problems arise if the MDCs would return to the attack on mass poverty within their own borders which they launched so successfully in the 1950s and 1960s and have now abandoned; since what we really need is that world trade recapture its growth rate of eight per cent per year...."

Evaluating the contributions of Arthur Lewis to Economics, Findlay sums up: "Lewis's stature and authority as a student of the economic problems of the contemporary LDC's largely stems from the fact that he has always looked at these problems in the context of the evolution of the world economy as a whole." Referring to Lewis's contribution to the field of quantitative economic history, he says: "Though his name has never been associated with 'Cliometrics' he should certainly be regarded as a pioneer in this field...."

Findlay makes a special reference to Lewis's "acute theoretical insights, vast historical knowledge and painstaking labor in the collection and analysis of the statistical data" and comments, "The result is a combination of theory, history and statistics that only a Schumpeter could match." Reference is also made to Lewis's extraordinary ability to connect apparently isolated phenomena into a rationally coherent whole in which theory and history, past and present, illuminate each other.

Finally, Findlay sums up: "He [Lewis] alone has had the vision, the courage and the fortitude to devote a career, in an age of increasing specialization dedicated to the principle of discovering more and more about less and less, to no less a theme than the structure and evolution of the world economy during the last century."

5.4 SELECT BIBLIOGRAPHY OF WILLIAM ARTHUR LEWIS'S WORKS

5.4.1 BOOKS

1949 a Economic Survey 1919-1939, George Allen and Unwin, London.

b Principles of Economic Planning, George Allen and Unwin, London.

1950 Overhead Costs, George Allen and Unwin, London.

1955 Theory of Economic Growth, George Allen and Unwin, London.

1966 Development Planning, George Allen and Unwin, London.

1969 Aspects of Tropical Trade,1883-1965 (Wicksell Lectures) Almqvist and Wicksell, Stockholm.

1971 (ed.) Tropical Development,1883-1913,George Allen and Unwin, London.

1974 a Dynamic Factors in Economic Growth, Tata Memorial Lectures, Orient Longman, New Delhi.

b The University in Less Developed Countries, International Council for Educational Development, New York.

1978 a Growth and Fluctuations 1870-1913, George Allen and Unwin, London.

b The Evolution of International Economic Order, Janeway Lectures, Princeton University Press, Princeton, NJ.

c LDC's and Exchange Stability, Per Jacobson Lecture, IMF, Washington D.C.

5.4.2 ARTICLES

1945 "Competition in Retailing," Economica, Vol.12, No. 48.

1954 "Economic Development with Unlimited Supplies of Labour," Manch Sch, Vol.22, May.

1959 "Sponsored Growth: Challenge to Democracy," in Problems of Economic Growth, M. K. Haldar and E. Ghosh (ed.), Delhi.

1965 "A Review of Economic Development," (Richard T. Ely Lecture), AER, Vol.55, No. 2.

1979 "The Dual Economy Revisited," Manch Sch, Vol. 47, No. 3.

1980 "The Slowing Down of the Engine of Growth," (Nobel Lecture), AER, Vol. 70, No.4.

1988 "The Roots of Development Theory," in Handbook of Development Economics, H.B. Chenery & T. N. Srinivasan (eds.) Edition 1, Vol.1., Elsevier, Amsterdam.

5.5 WORKS OF OTHERS

Chenery, H.B., and M. Syrquin (1975), Patterns of Development, 1950-1970, Oxford University Press for the World Bank.

Findlay, R (1980), "On W. Arthur Lewis Contributions in Economics," ScandJE, Vol. 82, No.1.

Lewis W. Arthur (1987), The New Palgrave: A Dictionary of Economics, Macmillan, London.

Gensovitz, M. et.al (eds.) (1982), The Theory and Experience of Economic Development: Essays in Honour of W. Arthur Lewis, George Allen and Unwin, London.

Gersovitz, M. (ed.). (1983), Selected Economic Writings of W. Arthur Lewis, New York University Press, New York.

Sen, A. K. (1966), "Peasants and Dualism with or without Surplus Labor," JPE, Vol. 74, Oct.

CHAPTER 6

LAWRENCE ROBERT KLEIN

(1920 – 2013)

Professor Lawrence Robert Klein, University of Pennsylvania, U.S.A., was awarded the 1980 Alfred Nobel Memorial Prize in Economic Sciences for the "creation of econometric models and their application to the analysis of economic fluctuations and economic policies." The award announcement by the Royal Swedish Academy of Sciences notes: "During the last three decades, Lawrence Klein has become the leading researcher in the field of economic science which deals with the construction and analysis of empirical models of business fluctuations." He started his career in this field by publishing a paper in 1950 presenting his attempts to numerically specify some models of the U.S. economy during the inter-war period. In the following years, he continued his research in this field. He constructed several new models, among which, the one constructed in collaboration with Arthur Goldberger became the most famous.

Klein's model-building marks a renewal of the attempts at econometric macro-analysis initiated in 1930s by Jan Tinbergen. However, significant differences between the two attempts should be noted here. Klein used a different economic theory and a separate statistical technique and his aim also was different. While Tinbergen mainly aimed at analysing business conditions and price movements, Klein primarily desired at creating an instrument for forecasting the development of business fluctuations and for studying the effects of economic policy measures.

His early publications are mainly of a methodological character. Later, however, his work has been marked by efforts to formulate and make use of the models for practical purposes. After World War II, Klein used his model to correctly predict, contrary to prevailing expectations, that there would be an economic upturn rather than a depression. Likewise, he correctly predicted a mild recession at the end of the Korean War. During the course of 1950s, Klein's models of the U.S.A. became firmly established as successful instruments for short-term forecasting. He also collaborated with other economists in constructing econometric models in several countries, such as Canada and United Kingdom. Specifically, he developed a model of the United Kingdom known as the Oxford model in association with Sir James Ball. At the Institute of Statistics, he helped in the creation of British Savings Surveys. At the start of the 1960s, Klein became the leader of a large and extensive research project, "The Brookings-Social Science Research Council (SSRC) Project." The aim of this far-reaching project was to construct a detailed econometric model and employ it for forecasting short-term development of the American economy.

Sometime later, Klein set out to construct another model, 'The Wharton Econometric Forecasting Model' – a model which is considerably smaller than the Brookings model. For this purpose, at Wharton School of Finance and Commerce of the University of Pennsylvania, he founded Wharton Econometric Forecasting Associates or WEFA (now IHS Global Insight). The Wharton model has gained a very good reputation for its analysis of business conditions. It has been used regularly for forecasts of fluctuations in national product, investments, consumption and exports, among others. It also studied the effects on those variables of policy changes, such as taxation, public expenditure, rising oil prices and so on. Under the leadership of Klein, it has become a continuous research project with systematic follow-up of forecasts and successive revisions.

At the end of the 1960s, a new large research project called LINK was started in which Klein had played a central role, as initiator as well as an active research leader. This project has the aim of coordinating econometric models in different countries, which hopefully, will improve the possibilities of analysing the diffusion of business fluctuations among different countries in order to facilitate forecasts of international trade and international capital movements. A second objective of the project is the study of the economic effects of political measures in one country spreading to other countries and, may be, after some timelag have repercussions on the first country's economy.

The importance of the LINK project is its opening up, in empirical macroeconomic research, a completely new line of development which is of great theoretical and practical value. It has also been influential in promoting the construction of econometric models in the participating countries. The countries participating in the project include most of the OECD countries, as also socialist nations and some developing countries. LINK, which is now operated by the United Nations, still has regular meetings; it had a meeting at Bangkok in October 2009.

The award announcement refers specially to Klein's leadership role. Through his publications and extensive guidance to groups of research workers in different countries including India, Klein had stimulated research on econometric forecasting models and on the possibilities of making use of such models for practical analysis of economic policies. Furthermore, thanks to Klein's contributions, the construction of econometric models has attained wide-spread, if not universal, use. Econometric models can be found throughout the world, not only in scientific institutions, but also in large business enterprises, public administration and political organisations. Few, if any, researchers in the field of economic science have had so many successors and such a large impact as Lawrence Klein.

6.1 A SHORT BIOGRAPHICAL SKETCH: LAWRENCE KLEIN

Lawrence Robert Klein was born in Omaha, Nebraska, U.S.A. on September 14, 1920. He had his early education in the public school system. He acknowledged the benefits he had from the high school training in mathematics, English, foreign languages and history. He said: "Although I was not aware of it at the time, the experience of growing up during the Great Depression was to have a profound impact on my intellectual and professional career." The teachings of mathematics faculty at Los Angeles City College provided him with great stimulus and the onset of World War II made great impression on his thoughts about "socio-politico-economic inter- relationships."

After completing undergraduate studies at the University of California, Berkley, he studied at Massachusetts Institute of Technology (MIT). Klein stated: "A chance to study at MIT under the rising star of the period – Paul A. Samuelson – was an unforgettable experience." After completing his Ph.D. dissertation under Samuelson, he joined the econometrics team at the Cowles Commission of the University of Chicago, where its Director, Jacob Marschak, gave him "the challenging assignment of reviving Jan Tinbergen's early attempts at econometric model building for the United States." At Chicago, he was in the midst of a veritable galaxy of stars: Trygve Haavelmo, Tjalling Koopmans, Kenneth Arrow, Herbert Simon, Leonid Hurwicz(all Nobel Laureates), Don Patinkin, Herman Chernoff, among others. Klein admitted: "I completed my first of a series of macroeconomic models, solidified my understanding of econometrics, learned...about the functioning of the economy, and got started on several theoretical paths such as aggregation, demand systems, and prediction."

In 1948, he joined the staff of National Bureau of Economic Research (NBER), New York, as a post-doctoral fellow. He joined the staff of the Survey Research Center, University of Michigan in 1950. At Michigan, he started his work on macro econometric model building. With his student, Arthur Goldberger, Klein put together a new model of the U.S. economy (Klein-Goldberger model). The New York Times reports: "During his study days in Chicago, Klein joined the Communist Party, a move that later haunted him. Though he left the party in 1947, while teaching at the University of Michigan in 1954, his past association came up during the House Un-American Activities Committee hearings, and the university denied him tenure. Klein then went to England and taught at Oxford for four years. An invitation from Wharton School of the University of Pennsylvania brought him back to U.S.A." He was Research Officer at the Oxford University Institute of Statistics during 1954 and 1955 and Reader in Econometrics between 1956 and 1958.

Klein returned to America in 1958 to join the faculty of the University of Pennsylvania (Penn), Philadelphia, which has been 'my professional home' ever since. At Penn, he was Professor of Economics 1958-1964, University Professor of Economics, 1964-1967, Benjamin Franklin Professor, 1968-1985 and Benjamin Franklin Professor, Emeritus since 1985. He was a visiting Professor at a number of Universities and Institutes including City University of New York, Princeton University, Stanford University, University of California, Berkley, Institute of Advanced Studies, Vienna, University of Copenhagen and the Hebrew University, Jerusalem. He taught at the University of Penn for 33 years. He rejected an offer to join the Carter administration.

In 1959, Klein was awarded John Bates Clark Medal. He was elected President of the Econometric Society as well as of the American Economic Association. He was a founding trustee of Economists for Peace and Security. Klein served as a thesis advisor for numerous well-known economists including E Roy Weintraub.

Lawrence Klein died at his home on October 20, 2013 (aged 93) Gladwyne, Pennsylvania.

6.2 A BRIEF SUMMARY OF LAWRENCE KLEIN'S CONTRIBUTIONS

The contributions of Klein have been spread over a broad professional spectrum. R J Ball evaluates: "Few people have straddled the subject matter and techniques of economics in such an impressive way. It is difficult to find a leading economist who has made so many distinct contributions in so many different compartments of the profession." While it would be too ambitious to attempt a reasonably satisfactory summary of all of his numerous contributions, we should at least summarise his contributions to three major fields.

1. Economic/Econometric Model Building;
2. Economic Theory; and
3. Statistical Analysis.

6.2.1 ECONOMIC / ECONOMETRIC MODEL BUILDING

While there is no doubt that Tinbergen was an early pioneer in the field of economic model building, he did not exert much influence on the work in the field in other countries because of various factors, such as data difficulties and 'cool' reception by contemporary stalwarts like Keynes. In contrast, Klein's work has influenced economic model builders in a large number and wide variety of countries – developed countries, developing countries, socialist countries, etc. There can be no two opinions that Klein's own work has shaped the developments in the field quite uniquely and has significantly influenced model builders in other countries. It is said that Klein's 'unique' achievement lay in his combining economics of Keynes with the new theoretical developments in statistics.

Despite very important limitations, Klein's early work in economic model-building is considered to have served as a paradigm for subsequent model-builders for a long time since then. In the words of R. J. Ball: "Perhaps the original reaction to the work was somewhat that of Dr. [Samuel] Johnson who observed that the proper response to a dog dancing on its hind legs was not to observe that he did it badly, but that it is remarkable that he did it at all."

In the face of scepticism and doubt regarding the extent of usefulness of statistical models for the purpose of forecasting and in the matter of providing tools to help policy making, Klein not only steadfastly continued his work of model-building but also encouraged others to follow his lead. Klein stated, "From the beginning of my tenure at [the University of] Pennsylvania and the Wharton School, I set out to build a model of the American economy." He started the first generation of Wharton models using quarterly data and including some expectational "magnitudes." The shift of the Wharton model to a quarterly time frame was with the objective of emphasising interest in short-run business cycle movements. In the models, he stated all the accounting identities in current prices to correct a specification deficiency of the Klein-Goldberger model.

Recognising the importance of institutional setting in constructing economic models, Klein, in the model-building for the developing countries, had specifically taken into account the special features of the economy concerned. He also turned his attention to the development of growth and medium-term models. The Wharton medium-term model of the American economy is a good example of this genre. The Social Science Research Council planned in 1959 the creation of a new, enlarged, short-run forecasting model, (later called The Brookings Quarterly Econometric Model of the United States). Klein was one of the principal investigators of the project. In his lecture at Trinity University, San Antonio, Texas, Klein listed the real developments that emerged from the joint efforts of the project team:

"(1) a detailed monetary sector that drew on Federal Reserve talent and was the pre-runner of important monetary sectors in many subsequent models, thus repairing a defect of the Klein-Goldberger model;

(2) an explicit input-output sector of inter-industry flows that was tied consistently with the traditional macro models of final demand and income determination;

(3) the preparation of a <u>databank</u> for the systematic accounting of all the data used in the system; and

(4) automation of the computing for the project with a remarkable breakthrough in the ability to solve large systems of non-linear equations." (emphasis in the original)

In association with a group of international model builders from leading OECD Countries, Klein launched in 1968 a new project to model the international transmission mechanism – "a truly group endeavour." Out of this effort, there spawned project LINK – The International Linkage of National Economic Models. The launching of the LINK Project exemplifies the degree of Klein's influence on the economic model-building activity all over the world. LINK- compatible model-building work in Taiwan, Manila, Bangkok and New Delhi (Delhi University) - has furthered the effort to have good LINK models for the whole of Far East. Besides, bringing together model builders from many countries in an organised way to know each other's developments, it has provided a forum for continuous interaction with regard to problems of international linkage.

6.2.2 ECONOMIC THEORY

Klein's primary contributions to economic theory essentially relate to "specifying and extending" the basic ideas of J. M. Keynes. R. J. Ball ranks Klein's paper on alternative theories of effective demand (published in the <u>Journal of Political Economy</u>) along with J. R. Hicks's "Keynes and the Classics," and Franco Modigliani's 1948 paper. Klein differed with many economists like Modigliani with the view that the central argument of Keynes was wage and price inflexibility. He asserted that the important feature or crucial argument lay in the specification of liquidity preference function and the manner in which money wages are determined. Keynes's argument was that "the specification of speculative demand for money and the presence of money illusion in the setting of money wage introduced inhomogeneities into the system such that the marginal productivity equation was essentially a price determining equation so that, since the demand and supply for labour determined the money wage, the quantity of money completed the system with regard to the interest rate rather than the price level." This is part of Klein's The Keynesian Revolution. There are, of course, some economists who argue that this interpretation is valid only for relatively short periods of time.

Klein had also made contributions to other parts of the theory of Keynes. In this context, it is necessary to recall his earlier work, on the specification of the investment function and his attempt at resolving the stock-flow debate in macroeconomics. Another notable contribution of Klein is concerned with the Keynesian consumption function. In a 1958 paper in Econometrica on consumption function dealing with "Friedman-Becker Illusion," he had shown that Friedman's approach to consumption function is consistent with Keynesian version of that function in which household consumption depended on the Koyck type of distributed lag function of the household's disposal income.

In addition to the contributions outlined above, Klein had made other contributions in the field of macroeconomics, two of which stand out prominently. One of them is concerned with the problem of measuring capacity and the theory of capacity measurement and utilisation. In an important paper in 1960 Econometrica, he discussed significant theoretical problems connected with measurement of capacity. Reference is also to be made to his contributions, which resulted in the formulation and empirical verification of the Wharton Capacity Index for the U.S.A. though this work does not reflect the thinking of Klein as revealed in the Econometrica article.

Another contribution is related to Klein's belief that macroeconomic behaviour does reflect the underlying rational behaviour of individual decision-making units as can be seen in his 1946 Econometrica paper entitled "Macroeconomics and the Theory of Rational Behavior." This led to his publishing another paper in the same year in the same journal dealing with the general problem of "aggregation."

6.2.3 STATISTICAL ANALYSIS

Besides contributions mentioned above in the areas of economic model-building and macroeconomics, Klein had contributed to the statistical background of econometrics, "as an expositor and publicist." R. J. Ball in a critical review of Klein's work remarked: "...it is difficult to associate Klein with original contributions in this field [statistics] that approach those made by Haavelmo, Anderson and Rubin, Wold, Henri Theil or, in later years, by Arnold Zellner."

His association with the Cowles Commission had resulted in his belief of the need of simultaneous, as opposed to single, equation estimators and in careful empirical estimation of economic relationships. To substantiate his argument that Klein was basically an expositor and publicist of other people's work, Ball makes reference to Klein's

1955 Metroeconomica paper, interpreting Theil's proposed two-stage least squares method for estimating economic relationships and Klein's essay on the efficiency of estimation in econometric models, included in a volume brought out in honour of Harold Hotelling.

However, Klein's 1958 Econometrica paper relating to the problem of estimating distributed lag functions (referred to above) and his 1960 paper jointly with Dhrymes and Stiglitz go beyond this and "reflect different aspects of his work as an economic scientist."

6.3 CONCLUDING OBSERVATIONS

Klein was of the opinion that "at all levels of teaching...there should be close touch with daily news. The stock market crash and its monitoring provide more insight into the workings of financial markets and the economy than ordinary text book paragraphs." He expressed the view that the only satisfactory test of Economics is the "ability to predict." As regards good research, he emphasised the importance of motivation. He underlined the need and rationale for his preference for large econometric models. He stated: "...economic life is enormously complicated and that the successful model will try to build in as much of the complicated interrelationships as possible." He further stated: "Given...that the true economy is large, detailed and complicated, it is only natural that a team approach be used." In regard to the debate on the relative importance of real and monetary sectors in understanding the working of the economic process, Klein categorically expressed his view: "In a true sense, both are important, and one cannot meaningfully exist without the other.... Over the years...I have come to appreciate, more and more, the role of money and of the whole monetary sector. I think that monetarism is fundamentally flawed and dangerous when used as a doctrinaire policy approach, but I do believe now that money matters; it is not everything, but it does matter...." (emphases in the original).

Klein's important achievement was in pioneering an activity in economic model building "which has required foresight, persistence and great technical skill and which has been translated into a paradigm of research activity that has spread wherever statistical economics is taught and where models are built." He had attempted what others would not undertake because of inherent insurmountable difficulties connected with information and interpretation. The achievement of lifting the practice of large-scale econometric model-building to a position of great importance and high professional respectability testifies to his intellectual quality as well as entrepreneurial character.

Even though his book The Keynesian Revolution is an important work, it cannot be compared to such outstanding and original works as Hicks's Value and Capital, or Samuelson's The Foundations of Economic Analysis, or Joan Robinson's Theory of Imperfect Competition. Klein's enormous influence on the economics profession is not a result of only published work or by his model- building activity. It is widely acknowledged that his research projects have served for many years as training ground for young econometricians from all over the world to learn the 'trade'. His wide influence can be essentially gauged from this observation: "His model-building activities were essentially changing laboratories to which came students and government officials from all over the world to study applied econometrics and, in particular, to participate in the model-building projects, and many of the students have returned to carry on the work in their own countries in the distinctive style he taught...through example and through active cooperation...serious applied econometrics cannot be learned from books and published work. The professional...can learn only by doing, and in this respect Klein has always given generously of himself in advancing the work through his apprentices."

In the final analysis, we can do no better than ending this note with a tribute by Klein's student and later a collaborator of distinction. "Without his influence, the profession would have been inestimably poorer and the integration of economic theory, statistical technique and practical economic decision-making could not have advanced in the way that it has."

6.4 SELECT BIBLIOGRAPHY OF LAWRENCE KLEIN'S WORKS

6.4.1 BOOKS

1947 The Keynesian Revolution, Macmillan, New York.

1950 Economic Fluctuations in the United States, 1921-1941, Wiley, New York.

1953 A Textbook of Econometrics, Row, Peterson& Co., Evanston, Ill.

1955 (with A. S. Goldberger) An Econometric Model of the United States, 1929-1952, North Holland, Amsterdam.

1961 (with R. J. Ball et. al.,) An Econometric Model of the United Kingdom, Basil Blackwell, Oxford.

1965 (with J. Duesenberry et.al.,) The Brookings Quarterly Econometric Model of the United States, Rand McNally, Chicago, Ill.

1967 a (with R. Summers) The Wharton Index of Capacity Utilization, Wharton School of Finance and Commerce, Philadelphia, Pa.

b (with A. Phillips and O. E. Williamson eds.) Wage and Price Determination in Macro econometrics, Prices: Issues in Theory, Practice and Policy, University of Pennsylvania Press, Philadelphia, Pa.

1968 a (with M. K. Evans) The Wharton Econometric Forecasting Model, Wharton School of Finance and Commerce, Philadelphia, Pa.

b (with K. Ohkawa ed.) Economic Growth: The Japanese Experience Since the Meiji Era, Irwin, Homewood, Ill.

1969 a (with J. Duesenberry et.al.) The Brookings Model: Some Further Results, Rand McNally, Chicago, Ill.

b (ed. in 3 volumes) Essays in Industrial Economics, Wharton School of Finance and Commerce, Philadelphia, Pa.

1971 An Essay in the Theory of Economic Predictions, Yrjo Jahnsson Foundation (2nd Enlarged Edition), Markham, Chicago, Ill.

1975 (with G. Fromm) The Brookings Model: Perspective and Recent Developments, North Holland, Amsterdam.

1980 a (with R. M. Young) An Introduction to Econometric Forecasting and Forecasting Models, D. C. Heath Lexington, MA.

b (with M. Nerlove et al.) Quantitative Economics and Development: Essays in Memory of Ta-Chung Liu, Academic Press, Salt Lake City, UT.

1991 Comparative Performance of U.S. Econometric Models, Oxford University Press, Oxford.

6.4.2 ARTICLES

1943 "Pitfalls in the Statistical Determination of the Investment Schedule," Econometrica, Vol. 11, July-Oct.

1946 a "Macroeconomics and the Theory of Rational Behavior," Econometrica, Vol.14, Apr.

b "Remarks on the Theory of Aggregation," Econometrica, Vol. 14, Oct.

1947 a "The Use of Econometric Models as a Guide to Economic Policy," Econometrica, Vol.15, Apr.

b "Theories of Effective Demand and Employment," JPE, Vol.LV, Apr.

1947-48 (with H. Rubin) "A Constant-utility Index of the Cost of Living," RES, Vol. XV, No. 2.

1950 "Stock and Flow Analysis in Economics," Econometrica, Vol. 18, July.

1951 a "The Life of John Maynard Keynes," JPE, Vol.LIX, Oct.

b "Estimating Patterns of Saving Behavior from Sample Survey Data," Econometrica, Vol.19, Oct.

c "Studies in Investment Behavior," Conference on Business Cycles, NBER, New York.

d (with J. N. Morgan) "Results of Alternative Statistical Treatments of Sample Survey Data," JASA, Vol. 46, Dec.

e "Assets, Debts and Economic Behavior," Studies in Income and Wealth, Vol.14, NBER, New York.

1953 (with H. W. Mooney) "Negro-White Savings Differentials and the Consumption Function Problem," Econometrica, Vol. 21, No.3.

1954 a (with H. J. Berger) "A Quarterly Model of the United States Economy," JASA, Vol. 49, Sep.

b "Empirical Foundations of Keynesian Economics," Post-Keynesian Economics, K. Kurihara(ed.) Rutgers University Press, New Brunswick, NJ.

1955 a "On the Interpretation of Theil's Method of Estimating Economic Relationships," Metroeconomica, Vol. VII, Dec.

b (with T.P. Hill and H. K. Straw) "The Savings Survey 1953 – Response Rates and Reliability of Data," Bulletin of the Oxford University Institute of Statistics, Vol.17, No.1.

c "Patterns of Savings – The Surveys of 1953 and 1954," Bulletin of the Oxford University Institute of Statistics, Vol.17, No.2.

d "Major Consumer Expenditures and Ownership of Durable Goods" Bulletin of the Oxford University Institute of Statistics, Vol.17, No.4.

1957 "The Scope and Limitations of Econometrics," Applied Statistics, Vol.VI, pp. 1-18.

1958 a "The British Propensity to Save," JRRS, Series A (General) Vol.121, pp.60-96.

b "The Friedman-Becker Illusion," JPE, Vol.66, pp.539-545.

c "Econometric Forecasts for 1959," Bulletin of the Oxford University Institute of Statistics, Vol.21, No.1.

d "The Estimation of Distributed Lags," Econometrica, Vol.26, Oct.

1960 a "Some Theoretical Issues in the Measurement of Capacity," Econometrica, Vol.28, Apr.

b "Entrepreneurial Saving," Proceedings of the Conference on Income and Saving, Vol.II, I. Friend and R. Jones (eds.) University of Pennsylvania Press, Philadelphia, Pa.

c "The Efficiency of Estimation in Econometric Models," Essays in Economics and Econometrics, R.W. Pfouts (ed.). University of North Carolina Press, Chapelhill, NC.

1961 "A Model of Japanese Economic Growth: 1878-1937," Econometrica, Vol.29, July.

1962 (with M. Nakamura), "Singularity in the Equation Systems of Econometrics: Some Aspects of the Problem of Multicollinearity," IER, Vol.III, Sep.

1963 (with Y.Shinkai) "An Econometric Model of Japan; 1930-1959," IER, Vol. IV. Jan.

1964 a "A Post-war Quarterly Model: Description and Applications," Models of Income Determination, Studies in Income and Wealth, Vol. 28, Princeton University Press, Princeton, NJ.

b (with R. G. Bodkin), "Empirical Aspects of the Trade-offs Among Three Goals: High Level Employment, Price Stability and Economic Growth," Inflation, Growth and Employment, Commission on Money and Credit, Prentice-Hall, New York.

c (with S. Ichimura et al.) "A Quarterly Econometric Model of Japan, 1952-1959," Osaka EP, Vo. XXII, Mar.

1965 a "Stocks and Flows in the Theory of Interest," The Theory of Interest Rates, F. H. Hahn and F.P.R. Brechling (eds.), Macmillan, London.

b (with G. Fromm) "The Brookings-SSRC Quarterly Econometric Model of the U.S.: Model Properties," AER, Vol. LV, No.2.

c "What Kind of Macro-Econometric Model for Developing Economies," The Indian Economic Journal, Vol. XIII, pp.313-324.

1967 a (with R. S. Preston) "Some New Results in the Measurement of Capacity Utilization," AER, Vol.LVII, No.1.

b (With R. G. Bodkin) "Non-Linear Estimation of Aggregate Production Functions," REStat, Vol. XLIX, Feb.

1968 "Simultaneous Equation Estimation," International Encyclopaedia of the Social Sciences, Macmillan and Free Press, New York.

1969 a "Estimation of Interdependent Systems in Macro-econometrics," Econometrica, Vol. 37, Apr.

b (with D. W. Katzner) "On the Possibility of General Linear Economic Model," Economic Models: Estimation and Risk Programming, (K. A. Fox, J. K. Sengupta and G.V.L. Narasimham, eds.) Springer-Verlag, Berlin.

1971 "Forecasting and Policy Evaluation Using Large Scale Econometric Models: The State of the Art," Frontiers of Quantitative Economics (M.D. Intriligator, ed.), North-Holland, Amsterdam.

1972 a "The Treatment of Uncertainty in Econometrics," Uncertainty and Expectations in Economics, (C.F. Carter and J. L. Ford, eds.), Blackwell, Oxford.

b (with M. K. Evans and M. Saito) "Short Run Prediction and Long-run Simulation of the Wharton Model," Econometric Model of Cyclical Behaviour, (B. G. Hickman ed.), Columbia University Press, New York.

c (with G. Fromm and G. R. Schink) "Short-and Long-Term Simulations with Brookings Model," Econometric Models of Cyclical Behavior, (B. G. Hickman ed.), Columbia University Press, New York.

d (with E. Phillip Howrey) "Dynamic Properties of Non Linear Econometric Models," IER, Vol. 13, Oct.

1973 a (With Gary Fromm) "A Comparison of Eleven Econometric Models of the United States," AER, Vol. LXIII, No.2.

b (with A. Van Peeterssen), "Forecasting World Trade with Project Link," The International Linkage of National Economic Models, R. J. Ball (ed.), North Holland, Amsterdam.

1974 a "Econometrics," Encyclopaedia Britannica, 15th edition.

b "Issues in Econometric Studies of Investment Behavior," JEL, Vol.12, No.1.

c (with H. N. Johnston and K. Shinjo) "Estimation and Prediction in Dynamic Econometric Models," Econometrics and Economic Theory, W. Sellekaerts (ed.) Macmillan, London.

1976 "Five-year Experience of Linking National Econometric Models and of Forecasting International Trade," Quantitative Studies of International Economic Relations, H. Glejser (ed.), North Holland, Amsterdam.

1977 a "Econometrics of Inflation, 1965-1974: A Review of the Decade," Analysis of Inflation: 1965-1974, Studies in Income and Wealth, Vol.42, J. Popkin (ed.), Ballinger for NBER, Cambridge, MA.

b "Economic Policy Formation Through the Medium of Econometric Models," Frontiers of Quantitative Economics, IIIB., M. Intriligator (ed.) North Holland, Amsterdam.

1980 "Some Economic Scenarios For the 1980's," Nobel Memorial Lecture, Nobel Lectures, Economics 1969-80, Assar Lindbeck (ed.), World Scientific Publishing Co., Singapore.

1983 (with E. Friedman and S. Able), "Money in the Wharton Quarterly Model," JMCB,Vol.16,No.1.

1985 "New Developments in Project Link," AER, Vol.75, No.2.

1988 "The Statistical Approach to Economics," Journal of Econometrics, Vol.37, No.1.

1992 "Some Tendencies in Modern Econometrics," Indian Economic Review, Vol.27, pp.5-14.

1993 "Irving B. Kravis: Memoir of a Distinguished Fellow," JEP, Vol.7, No.3.

1999 (with V. G. Duggal and C. Saltzman), "Infrastructure and Productivity: A Non-linear Approach," Journal of Econometrics, Vol.92, No.1.

2005 The Adam Smith Award Address, 2004, Business Economics, Vol.40, No.1.

2007 (with S. Ozmucur), "The Wealth Effect: A Contemporary Update to the Age of Affluence," JPM, Vol.29, No.4.

2009 "Measurement of a Shift in the World's Center of Economic Gravity," JPM, Vol.31, No.4.

2010 (with S. Ozmucur), "The Use of Consumer and Business Surveys in Forecasting," Economic Modelling, Vol.27, No.6.

6.5 WORKS OF OTHERS

Ball, R. J. (1981), "On Lawrence R. Klein's Contributions to Economics," ScandJE, Vol.83, No. 1.

CHAPTER 7

JAMES TOBIN

(1918 – 2002)

The Royal Swedish Academy of Sciences has awarded the 1981 Alfred Nobel Memorial Prize in Economic Sciences to Professor James Tobin, Yale University, U.S.A., "for his analysis of financial markets and their relation to consumption and investment expenditure decisions, employment, production and prices."

The Award announcement refers to Tobin's achievements covering a broad spectrum of economic research. His substantial contributions encompass various areas such as macroeconomics and monetary theory, the theory of household and firm behaviour, strictly formalised risk theory, econometric methods and applied analysis of economic policy.

Tobin's significant contributions were based on a theory which described how individual households and firms determine the composition of their financial and real assets. He was one of the foremost originators of this theory, which has become well-known as portfolio selection theory. Later, he had developed these ideas into a general equilibrium theory of financial and real assets and succinctly analysed it, as each component in this analysis concerns the study of transmission mechanisms that transfer changes on financial markets to real markets through expenditure decisions of households and firms. The Award announcement states that this classic problem in economic research had "thus far" not been tackled satisfactorily and conclusively. Tobin's studies constitute an important breakthrough in the integration of real and financial conditions in the core economic theory.

Tobin had used his portfolio selection theory to study decisions of individual households and firms to hold different financial and real assets and simultaneously incur debts by weighing the associated risk and expected rate of return. It is clear that, Tobin, unlike many other theorists in the subject, did not confine his analysis solely to money, but widened the choice to include the whole spectrum of assets and debts.

Other economists, who have contributed to portfolio selection theory like Markowitz, have singularly focussed their attention on indicating rules that govern rational investment decisions. Tobin's aim in developing portfolio analysis was to provide a basis for understanding how decision-makers actually behave when they choose different assets with different degrees of risk and associated expected rates of return and incur debts. His main interest in doing this was to find out the crucial components that have been absent in the analysis of impulses from financial markets to real markets.

Tobin underlined the effects of financial events on investment demand (demand for real assets) and consumer demand. In this context, he focussed his attention on the analysis of two fundamental issues. The first issue related to the transmission mechanism – how measures of monetary policy and fiscal policy, such as central bank purchases and sales of government bonds and treasury bills and changes in tax rates, affect the country's national income. The second issue concerned with the factors that determine how a change in nominal national income brought about through measures of monetary and fiscal policy will be distributed among changes in the volume of output and in general price level. For the purpose of answering the second question, Tobin had to enquire into the problem of wage formation. He accepted the rigidity of wages in the short run. Due to the phenomenon of rigidity of wages, changes in demand on the commodity and labour markets lead to variations in employment rather than changes in the price level and the rate of inflation. Furthermore, in the face of rigid wages, households and firms find it difficult in practice and in the short run to adjust their plans in line with the new information. Hence Tobin was highly critical of rational expectations hypothesis, which is based on the possibility for this kind of adjustment.

By examining a broad spectrum of assets and debts, Tobin's analysis of the transmission mechanism extended the channels of contact between financial markets and real expenditure decisions. Tobin's analysis suggested that the effects arise through the entire financial structure rather than through the level of "general" interest rate. He took into consideration various institutional conditions. He specifically took into account (neglected by many earlier and contemporary researchers) the condition where the financial system comprised numerous and diverse institutions following different policies of portfolio selection rather than a system consisting primarily of banks.

Tobin through the extension of the channels of contact between financial markets and real expenditure decisions, had indicated both theoretically and empirically the effects of changes in the real value of financial assets on the volume of consumption. He successfully reformulated an earlier hypothesis that real investment decisions of firms are strongly affected by the relation between the market value of the existing real capital and the acquisition cost of corresponding newly produced real capital. If the prices of existing real capital decline when the acquisition costs of new real capital are given or rising, then the investments are counteracted.

On the basis of his examination of the financial system and transmission mechanisms, Tobin had carried out thorough analyses of economic conditions and stabilisation policy during 1960s and 1970s. The significance of his portfolio selection theory and analyses of financial markets was heightened by the fact that the analysis of balance of payments and exchange rates during the 1970s had partly used Tobin's model.

7.1 A SHORT BIOGRAPHICAL SKETCH: JAMES TOBIN

James Tobin was born in Champaign, Illinois, on March 5, 1918. His early study was in a high school run by the University of Illinois in the twin city, Urbana. He was a bright student. He stated: "I was so unfailing an 'A' student that it was boring even to me." One month before he was scheduled to enrol at the University of Illinois, he was offered and he accepted a Connate Prize Fellowship at Harvard. Harvard at that time was the leading academic centre of economics in North America; only Columbia and Chicago were close competitors. In 1939, he received (B.A.) degree from Harvard University and M.A. degree from the same university in 1940. In economics, Harvard, the "center of the intellectual ferment of the day, was enjoying a golden age." Joseph Schumpeter, Alvin Hansen, Seymour Harris, Edwin Chamberlin, Edward Mason, Gottfried Haberler, and Wassily Leontief were the professors who meant most to him. There was a superb young faculty and graduate students including Paul Samuelson, Paul Sweezy, J. K. Galbraith, Richard Musgrave, Abram Bergson and Richard Goodwin.

Tobin left Harvard in 1941 for a job in Washington D.C. After the United States entered the war, he joined the Naval Reserve and returned to Harvard to complete his Ph.D. in 1946-1947. In 1947, in his doctoral dissertation, on the determinants of household consumption and saving (written under the supervision of Joseph Schumpeter), he developed a theoretical analysis of inter-temporal choice. He tried to 'marry' cross-section data from family budget surveys with aggregate time series, in order to better estimate effects of income, wealth and other variables. Tobin became Harvard Junior fellow for three years, spending the last year as a visitor to Richard Stone's Department of Applied Economics in Cambridge, England. In 1950, he moved to the Economics Department at Yale, with which his name has become synonymous. He was Associate Professor of Economics, Yale University, 1950-1955, and Professor of Economics, 1955-57. He became Sterling Professor of Economics in 1957 (continued for over three decades) and had served two terms as department chairman, 1968-1969 and 1974-1978. He became Research Director of the Cowles Foundation for Research in Economics in 1955, succeeding Tjalling Koopmans. He functioned as Director of Cowles Foundation during 1955-1961 and 1964-65. In 1961-62, he was a member of President Kennedy's Council of Economic Advisors. Tobin became Sterling Professor of Economics, Emeritus, Yale University, 1988-2002.

Among the honours and distinctions received by him, mention may be made of J. B. Clark Medal (1955) and his services to the American Economic Association in various capacities including President in 1971. He served on the Board of Governors of the Federal Reserve System. He also functioned as Chairman of a Committee, which examined Puerto Rico's economic problems in 1974-1975.

James Tobin died on March 11, 2002.

7.2 A BRIEF SURVEY OF JAMES TOBIN'S CONTRIBUTIONS

Tobin was a prolific writer and his contributions range over the entire spectrum of modern economics. He made significant and fundamental contributions to pure economic theory. He was widely known for his writings on monetary theory and macroeconomics and for his suggestion of a tax on foreign exchange transactions-'Tobin tax'-to curb speculation in the international currency markets.

He had also made important contributions to the theory and practice of stabilisation policy. Besides, these he had contributed to other areas, such as developing new statistical techniques to deal with discrete and limited dependent variables, pioneering in the use of pooled time series and cross-section data, analysing the informal content of survey data and their use for forecasting, and on the issue of poverty which are rated very high and treated now as "classics," besides writing widely in the popular press on numerous contemporary issues of political economy and economic and social policy.

Out of the varied and important contributions to economics by Tobin, we primarily summarise those, which fall under the following three broad heads.

1. His contributions to monetary theory including his outstanding work on portfolio balance and risk, his most important contribution;
2. His writings in macroeconomic theory, such as those on determination of wages, transmission mechanism and the writings on money and economic growth; and
3. His papers on Stabilisation Policy, which include his active participation in the debate on "Monetarism."

7.2.1 MONETARY THEORY, PORTFOLIO BALACE APPROACH ETC.

Tobin in his Nobel lecture stated how "John R. Hicks's 1935 article [A Suggestion for Simplifying the Theory of Money] has been an inspiration and challenge to me and to many other monetary economists. It stimulated us to look for the properties and functions of money, and promises to pay money in future, that underlie people's willingness to hold these assets. Understanding these foundations, we could seek the observable determinants of demand for money and money substitutes. This quest for the micro foundations of monetary theory has motivated inventory-theoretic models of the demand for transaction media...and models of portfolio choice. It is still unfinished."

The theory of demand for money, following the ideas of Keynes in the General Theory regarding motives for holding money, was generally divided into two categories – those theories that deal with the transactions motive or transactions demand for money and those that are concerned with risk-related speculative/precautionary motives or precautionary and speculative demand for money. Tobin contributed to both, though the second one relating to speculative/precautionary demand for money is widely regarded as seminal.

Pre-Keynesian ideas of the role of money in an economy were embodied in the equation of exchange – either Fisherian transactions version or Marshallian/Pigovian Cambridge version. The Cambridge k approach transformed the traditional equation of exchange into a theory of demand for money. The traditional equation of exchange approach did not have an explanation as to why economic agents hold cash balances. Even if currency or cash balances have to be used for effecting transactions, it would pay to hold interest-bearing financial assets and convert them into cash as and when the need arises to make transactions. By introducing the concept of transaction costs, Tobin tried to provide a rationale for public holding money. When the need arises for the use of cash for transaction purposes, one has to consider the trade-off between earning interest and bearing "brokerage" costs. Thus, economic agents have to make a non-trivial choice as to how to hold their wealth. "The key proposition is that even in a mechanical model with exogenous transactions, the possibility of economizing on cash balances emerges, rendering the demand for such balances interest-elastic." Thus, Tobin concluded that a rational, maximising economic unit will have an interest-elastic transactions demand for cash.

Keynes's analysis of demand for money in General Theory resulted in his putting forward the precautionary and speculative motives for holding money by economic agents. However, it was realised by many economists that there were serious deficiencies in Keynes's formulation of the problem. Keynes's emphasis on the short-run speculative motive as the source of interest-elasticity in liquidity preference resulted in households holding specialised portfolios – either cash only or bonds only. Further, William Fellner argued that Keynes's liquidity preference was an equilibrium phenomenon on the "logical ground" that speculators could not be assumed to expect higher interest rates to prevail indefinitely than those experienced.

Tobin's seminal article "Liquidity Preference As Behavior Towards Risk" repaired both these deficiencies, in the process "re-establishing the intellectual respectability" of Keynes's theory of liquidity preference, besides providing a satisfactory explanation as to why individuals hold fiat money when other assets bearing positive interest rate are available in the market. His paper also provided a fresh explanation for the observed phenomenon of the negative relationship between the quantity of cash demanded by economic agents and the yield on interest-bearing alternative assets. The most important theorem that Tobin established in this paper is what has come to be known as "separation" theorem or "mutual fund" theorem – a centrepiece of the theory of finance. In Tobin's words: "The term concerns portfolios, in which one safe asset is mixed with 'n' risky assets. The composition of the "mutual fund" of risky assets is independent of the degree of risk aversion of the investor. It depends only on the investor's estimates of the variances, co-variances, and expected returns of the assets. Differences in risk aversion are reflected not in the composition of this fund but in the proportions in which the investor divides his wealth between the fixed-weight fund on the one hand and the safe asset on the other." This result is central to Lintner's and Sharpe's Capital Asset Pricing Model

(CAPM) and the market-line analysis. The main implication is that the asset prices adjust so that in equilibrium the market portfolio is the efficient portfolio.

Tobin was able to show that individual economic units choose an optimum portfolio of both money and other assets by an assumption of uncertainty about the future behaviour of interest rates and specifically assuming the interest rate expectations in terms of a probability distribution. The individual economic unit's liquidity preference or demand for speculative balances is a response to the risk associated with the dispersion of the probability distribution. Those who are risk averse would diversify their portfolios between money (a safe asset with a zero nominal yield) and a basket of risky assets giving an expected positive net rate of return. Further, Tobin also demonstrated that the share of money in the portfolio of assets would decline if the expected return on the risky asset rises. An increase in the share of the risky assets in the portfolio causes a rise both in the expected mean return on the portfolio as also the variance of that return. In order to posit the analysis in terms of the two parameters, mean and variance, Tobin had argued that the utility function of the economic agent is quadratic or the probability distribution of portfolio returns has to be fully described by the knowledge of the first two moments of the probability distribution.

The original work in the field of portfolio analysis or mean-variance analysis is that of Harry Markowitz, which Tobin had employed with modifications. In addition, Tobin had made use of expected utility hypothesis put forward by John von Neumann and Oscar Morgenstern. Tobin made clear the distinction between Markowitz's work and his work in a footnote in Volume 1 of his Essays in Economics: "Harry Markowitz...treats the general problem of finding dominant sets and computing the corresponding opportunity locus, for sets of securities all of which involve risk. Markowitz's main interest is prescription of rules of rational behavior for investors; the main concern of this paper is the implications for economic theory, mainly comparative statics, that can be derived from assuming that investors do in fact follow such rules." The implications that Tobin mentioned here refer to negative interest elasticity of speculative demand for money, the separation theorem (explained above), the role of co-variance in the benefits of diversification and, above all, the measurement of risk.

Tobin by his paper "Liquidity Preference as Behavior Towards Risk" is generally considered as having sparked off the new field of the Theory of Finance. His influence in the discipline of Finance is underlined by Cowles Foundation monograph papers ("Risk Aversion and Portfolio Choice," "Studies of Portfolio Behavior," among others) authored by him along with his students and collaborators.

A distinction that is central in the discussions relating to monetary theory is the division of financial intermediaries into banks and non-bank financial intermediaries. Banks and non-bank financial intermediaries have liabilities, which are close substitutes for fiat money. While some of these liabilities of financial intermediaries are included in some definitions of money as they are close substitutes for fiat money, others are not included.

Generally, the exclusion is arbitrary and as such open to criticism and controversy. Tobin was critical of the models, which ignore the fact that there is no clear dividing line between "money and non-money." He was critical of simplistic money-multiplier models of credit expansion in which an arbitrary distinction is drawn between commercial banks and other non-bank financial intermediaries. The liabilities of banks are included in the definition of money while those of the latter are not (for example, Tobin's article "Commercial Banks as Creators of Money.") In later papers, written jointly with William Brainard, Tobin asserted that the presence of uncontrolled banks does not vitiate monetary policy nor does the presence of non-bank intermediaries imply that control of commercial banks is without effect. He, however, conceded the argument that substitutions into uncontrolled sectors do diminish the impact of a given change in the supply of currency.

Donald Hester in a review article in the Journal of Economic Literature on "Contributions and Growth in Tobin's Economic Essays" mentions Tobin's important result that raising an interest rate ceiling on bank deposits can be expansionary; it results in a reduction in the rate of return required on capital and through it to an increase in investment. Thus interaction between the demand and supplies of money-substitutes is an important insight of the Tobin's GE [General Equilibrium] approach.

7.2.2 MACROECONOMIC THEORY

In Macroeconomics, the key issues are generally grouped under three heads: (i) Issues relating to aggregate supply: factors determining the distribution of a given change in aggregate nominal income into changes in the real output level and into changes in the price level; (ii) Issues concerning transmission mechanism and the linkages between the monetary and real sectors of the economy; that is, how changes in the level of national income are brought about by exogenous factors and policy-induced disturbances; and (iii) Theory of macroeconomic growth and the relationship between short-run fluctuations and long-term growth.

7.2.2.1 ISSUES RELATING TO AGGREGATE SUPPLY

Keynes, in his General Theory of Employment, Interest and Money, had made a controversial statement (in contradistinction to Classical view) that a cut in money wages would not mitigate the type of severe unemployment experienced in developed countries during the Great Depression. Tobin addressed himself to this issue in his first published paper. This is of no surprise as he observed later: "To begin with, the General Theory is not just the ritual piety economists of my generation owe the book that shaped their minds." Tobin enquired into the issue whether a cut in money wages would exert an independent influence on the level of total employment other than through its influence on interest rates. He noted that Keynes's use of the concept of "money illusion" on the part of labour implies a denial of the "homogeneity postulate" for only one relationship in the system.

Douglas Purvis observes that "the focus on formal analysis of wages gave way over the next fifteen years to the development of his ideas in monetary economics...although his interest in the supply side shows up in his work on Negative Income Taxes and on the pressing social problem of poverty. During that period professional interest in the Phillips curve grew, and it had taken a central place in mainstream macroeconomics." Tobin had contributed significantly to the raging debate on Phillips curve. His Presidential address to the American Economic Association was devoted to the analysis of wages and aggregate supply and to put forward his response to the "influential Phelps-Friedman natural rate hypothesis."

In his 1971 Presidential address, Tobin contended that there was nothing optimal, efficient, or even natural about the zero-inflation rate of unemployment. Further, he observed that the point of natural rate of unemployment would be an inefficient position to operate the economy, in the sense that at that rate, the marginal product of labour would be higher than the marginal value of leisure. He also suggested that the macro economy had to be viewed as a multi-market economy with a number of heterogeneous types of labour rather than a single market for homogeneous labour and suggested a "theory of stochastic macro equilibrium."

In his articles of 1977 and 1980, Tobin had taken the view that inflation is "inertial" in nature. He defined inertial inflation as: "... the self-replicating pattern of wage and price inflation with which we have all become familiar. Whatever the historical origins of the inflation, once it is built into the system in a consistent manner it continues very much on its own...firms and employees relate their wage increases to recent settlements in other markets and to recent price trends...." His analysis of inertial nature of inflation implied that changes in aggregate demand in an economy show up basically in changes in output rather than prices.

7.2.2.2 THE TRANSMISSION MECHANISM

Tobin's doctoral dissertation, as mentioned earlier, was on consumption function. Tobin thought Keynes's psychological law of consumption and saving "should be interpreted to refer to the relation of lifetime consumption to lifetime income, not to a relation between these variables year by year. The same considerations implied that wealth, not just current income, determines consumption in the short run." Tobin's work on wealth-consumption relationship also took specifically into account capital-market imperfections. By including imperfect capital markets into his model, Tobin got an important conclusion: many households in real world situation are constrained in their consumption decisions by liquidity factors. In his consumption analysis, Tobin drew specific distinction between what he called the static wealth-spending relationship (exogenous increase in wealth) and the dynamic wealth-spending relationship (endogenous rise in wealth as a result of prior saving).

Another notable contribution of Tobin in regard to transmission mechanism is to be noted. In Keynes's model, the transmission of changes in the financial sector to the real sector is through the "eventual" effect of the interest rate on private investment. Tobin devoted a good part of his work on macroeconomics to include a much richer financial structure and studying the relative importance of different channels in regard to the transmission of financial impulses to the real variables in the system.

Tobin stated that "the ultimate gauge of expansion or deflation of monetary tightness or ease [in an economy] is the rate of return that the community of wealth-owners require in order to absorb the existing capital stock (valued at current prices), no more, no less, into their portfolios and balance sheet. This rate may be termed the supply price of capital." This concept is an important part of Tobin's macroeconomic model. The supply price of capital is determined in the asset market by conditions of overall portfolio equilibrium which, in turn, determines the desired flow of investment expenditure. When only two assets – money and capital – are available, the choice is simple – households hold either money or capital. But when we introduce government interest-bearing debt as a third asset into the model, the analysis gets complicated. Tobin, making use of the risk-diversification implications developed by him earlier, contended that bonds are likely to be a closer substitute for capital rather than for money. Under this analysis, an addition to the supply of government bonds tends to push up the supply price of capital, resulting in a reduced flow of investment. Tobin's 1969 paper "A General Equilibrium Approach to Monetary Theory," presented a complete model of asset market equilibrium explicitly presenting substitution relationships and balance sheet constraints. He connected the resulting equilibrium determination of yields on assets to investment flow.

In his Nobel lecture, "Money and Finance in the Macroeconomic Process," Tobin observed: "The aggregate stock of capital at any time...[is] valued continuously in the markets for goods themselves...and in markets for corporate securities or for entire businesses. These market valuations of old capital goods typically differ, up or down, from their replacement costs.... These deviations are, in turn, the incentives for rates of investment faster or slower than normal. When equity markets place high values on capital goods, the margin above replacement cost induces investors to speed up capital accumulation. This inducement is essentially what the great Swedish economist, Knut Wicksell, ascribed to a natural rate of interest higher than the market interest rate."

Thus, Tobin's 'q' theory of investment behaviour suggested that firms invest as long as the value of their shares exceeds the replacement cost of the firm's physical assets. As is clear 'q' refers to the ratio of two numbers: (1) the value of a firm to its share holders – equivalent to the present value of expected future profits of the firm; and (2) the replacement cost of the assets of the firm. If 'q' > 1, the firm should desire to expand as the expected profits from its assets are greater than the cost of its assets. Firms should invest or divest until 'q' is approximately equal to unity. Purvis remarks: "Tobin's q became the organizing principle for a number of empirical studies.... Tobin's q is also extremely valuable as an easy way to explain to students why the stock market matters!"

7.2.2.3 THEORY OF ECONOMIC GROWTH

The theory of economic growth received the attention of economists during 1950s and 1960s. Tobin made several notable contributions to this field. In the article "A Dynamic Aggregative Model," he integrated asset choice and the growth process – the key ideas of Keynes's short-run macroeconomic ideas to the growth theory developed by Hicks, Harrod and others. It is considered a forerunner to the literature on money and economic growth of the 1960s and 1970s.

Tobin, in his articles in this field, considered the contemporary important issue whether it is the level of capital stock or its rate of change that is related to the rate of interest. He had put forward a new investment theory replacing the investment theory of Keynes. His formulation stipulated that new investment in the economy takes place from growth in the desired capital stock. This led to the idea of stock or asset equilibrium "which was to evolve into the later development of the portfolio framework."

In Irving Fisher Lecture for Econometric Society meetings in 1964, Tobin's analysis of money and economic growth considered the role of government debt as an alternative store of value to physical capital. He argued that the presence of government debt might result in the economy choosing a lower capital stock than it would have had in its absence. Furthermore, an increase in the growth rate of money supply would result in a rise in the equilibrium inflation rate and prompt individuals to substitute capital for money in their portfolios.

7.2.3 STABILISATION POLICY

In his autobiographical note Tobin stated: "I studied economics and made it my career for two reasons. The subject was and is intellectually fascinating and challenging, particularly for someone with taste and talent for theoretical reasoning and quantitative analysis. At the same time it offered the hope, as it still does, that improved understanding could better the lot of mankind. For me, growing up in 1930s, the two motivations powerfully reinforced each other." Tobin, in line with his desire "to better the lot of mankind," had been a vocal participant in the professional and public discussions on economic policy. "In particular, he has carried on the Keynesian banner in numerous 'skirmishes' with monetarists, and in particular, with Milton Friedman." Of all branches of economics, macroeconomics has close links with issues of economic policy and it is not at all surprising that as a stalwart in the field of macroeconomics, Tobin had made outstanding contributions to the theory of stabilisation policy and was engaged in debates relating to the practical conduct of the policy. He stated, "macroeconomics has a strong and direct orientation to public policy."

Tobin's macroeconomic work, founded as it is on the economics of Keynes's General Theory, led him to consistently champion the policy of active demand management. In conjunction with this, he emphasised the necessity of pursuing incomes policies, negative income taxes and labour market policies, among others. In the debates on appropriate policy measures during periods of stagflation, Tobin was with the economists advocating policy of expansion for two reasons. First, it is based on the assessment of relative costs of unemployment and inflation. In his own words: "it takes a heap of Harberger triangles to fill an Okun's gap." Second, he believed that the self-correcting mechanisms work slowly (it is wasteful to wait for recessions to work themselves out).

Tobin had consistently opposed policies aimed at engineering recessions in order to curb inflationary pressures. In his address before the Royal Economic Society in 1980, Tobin found fault with the policy measures taken in each of the three recessions experienced in the United States in 1970s. His complaint "with these policy mistakes" was that they were inspired by the monetarist rallying-cry that "inflation is everywhere and always a monetary phenomenon." Tobin identified the 1973-74 double-digit inflation as caused by supply shocks, particularly OPEC oil price hike. According to him, the appropriate policy that should have been followed in that context was an expansionary rather than a contractionary policy, actually followed as a consequence of the monetarist demand-oriented analysis of inflation.

Tobin's participation in debates with monetarists, according to observers, had started with his review of Friedman-Schwartz's monumental work, A Monetary History of the United States. The review divided the Friedman- Schwartz analysis as concerning with two aspects: The first concerns the determination of the stock of money including the definition of money and second relating to determination of velocity. As regards the first aspect, namely determination of the stock of money in an economy, the crucial question is what is money? Or the definition of money. On this aspect Tobin had made a pertinent remark: "If money is so important, why is it hard to agree on a definition?" He found it unacceptable that in their analysis, Friedman – Schwartz fail to discuss alternative definitions of money. Friedman-Schwartz analysis of the determination of velocity elicited sharp criticism from Tobin. He did not accept on theoretical as well as on empirical grounds the explanation proffered by Friedman-Schwartz for the secular decline in velocity in terms of money being a luxury good, with an income elasticity of demand greater than unity. Tobin and Friedman had disagreement regarding many other issues, such as, stability and independence of velocity, the interpretation of monetary events surrounding the great depression, as also the general prognosis of and policy recommendations for monetary policy.

As regards the causal interpretation attached to Friedman-Schwartz and Friedman-Meisleman evidence on the correlation between money and income, Tobin presenting an extreme Keynesian model and an ultra-Friedman model drew a methodological point concerning "the dangers of accepting timing evidence as empirical proof of propositions about causation." The response of Friedman on the issue raised by Tobin evoked the following comment: "I am continually perplexed by Friedman's propensity in professional debate to evade by verbal quibbling the responsibility and the credit for the characteristic propositions of 'monetarism' associated with his name."

Purvis comments: "Friedman appears to have retired from the debate: his 'orthodox monetarist' approach has given way to the rational expectations' inspired 'new classical' economics arguing against policy activism and favouring Friedman-type k percent rules." Tobin, remarking that expectations are red-herring focussed on the assumed Walrasian, perfect price-flexibility, full employment assumptions inherent in their models had argued that "rigidities and inertias would support the use of stabilisation policy even in the face of rationally formed expectations."

7.3 CONCLUDING OBSERVATIONS

Besides the contributions outlined above, Tobin had contributed to other fields as well. His work provided highly original insights into the problems with which economists have been primarily concerned and "defining new areas and directions for scientific endeavour." Besides providing a framework of his own, he had effectively extended the work of other scholars. He is rightly considered an economists' economist.

His influence on other economists and the profession are impressive. His influence and effect of his writings on the subsequent literature is "profound." His influence on his own students, who are numerous and productive, was undeniably "pervasive." His work relating to general equilibrium approach is important and has influenced the profession. Tobin's application of techniques of comparative statics to problems of portfolio choice has set new standards for macroeconomic theorising. His development and application of statistical techniques and use of methods of simulation have added to the economists' tool kit.

It is remarked that Tobin's attacks on orthodoxy accompanied by the development of "original and plausible" alternatives are events that his teacher Joseph Schumpeter would have been exceedingly happy to call examples of the "process of creative destruction."

In the autobiographical account delivered by Tobin at Trinity University in 1985, he concluded his talk with the following reminiscent thought. "I have lived long enough to see the revolution to which I was an eager recruit fifty years ago become in its turn a mainstream orthodoxy and then the counter revolutionary attack. The tides of political opinion and professional fashion have turned against me. Many of my young colleagues in the profession are enthusiastic exponents of new classical macroeconomics as I and my contemporaries were crusaders against old classical macroeconomics in 1930s....The contesting factions are better equipped – our profession has certainly improved in mathematical, analytical and statistical tools. I do not despair over divisions of opinion in economics. Our subject has always thrived and advanced through controversy, and I expect a new synthesis will develop, may be even in my lifetime.... I still think and say that Keynesian ideas about how the economy works and what policies can make it better are relevant today – not just as Keynes wrote them, of course, but as they have been modified, developed, and refined over the last half-century."

7.4 SELECT BIBLIOGRAPHY OF JAMES TOBIN'S WORKS

7.4.1 BOOKS

1967 a (with D. Hester eds.) Risk Aversion and Portfolio Choice, Cowles Foundation Monograph No.19, Wiley, New York.

b (with D. Hester eds.) Studies of Portfolio Behavior, Cowles Foundation Monograph No.20, Wiley, New York.

1987-1996 Essays in Economics, Vols.1 to 4, MIT Press, Cambridge, MA.

1998 (with S.S. Golub) Money, Credit and Capital, Irwin/McGraw-Hill, New York.

7.4.2 ARTICLES

1941 "A Note on the Money Wage Problem," QJE, Vol.55, No.3.

1947 "Money Wage Rate and Employment," in S. E. Harris (ed.), The New Economics, McGraw-Hill, New York.

1955 "A Dynamic Aggregate Model," JPE, Vol.LXIII, Apr.

1956 "The Interest Elasticity of Transactions Demand for Cash," REStat, Vol.38, Aug.

1958 "Liquidity Preference as Behavior towards Risk," RES, Vol. XXV, Feb.

1960 (with H. W. Watts) "Consumer Expenditures and the Capital Account," Proceedings of the Conference on Consumption and Saving, Vol.2, Irwin Friend and R. Jones (eds.) University of Pennsylvania, Philadelphia, Pa.

1961 "Money, Capital and Other Stores of Value," AER, Vol.L1, No.2.

1963 a "An Essay on the Principles of Debt Management," Fiscal and Debt Management Policies, Commission on Money and Credit, Prentice-Hall, Upper Saddle River, NJ.

b (with W. C. Brainard), "Financial Intermediaries and the Effectiveness of Monetary Controls," AER, Vol. LIII, No.2.

1965 "Money and Economic Growth," Econometrica, Vol.33, Oct.

1967 a "Unemployment and Inflation, The Cruel Dilemma," in Price Issues in Theory, Practice and Policy, A Phillips (ed.), University of Pennsylvania Press, Philadelphia, Pa.

b "Life Cycle Saving and Balanced Growth," in Ten Economic Studies in the Tradition of Irving Fisher, W. Fellner (ed.), Wiley, New York.

1968 a (with W. C. Brainard) "Pitfalls in Financial Model Building," AER, Vol.LVIII, No.2.

b "Notes on Optimal Monetary Growth," JPE, Vol.76, Aug.

1969 "A General Equilibrium Approach to Monetary Theory," JMCB,Vol.1, No.1.

1970 "Money and Income: Post HOC Ergo Propter Hoc," QJE, Vol.LXXXIV, May.

1971 (with Walter Dolde), "Wealth, Liquidity and Consumption," in Consumer Spending and Monetary Policy: The Linkages, Federal Reserve Bank of Boston, Conference Series No.5.

1972 "Inflation and Unemployment" (Presidential Address at the Annual Meeting of American Economic Association, New Orleans), AER, Vol.LXII, No.1.

1976 (with W. Buiter) "Long Run Effects of Fiscal and Monetary Policy on Aggregate Demand," in Monetarism: Studies in Monetary Economics, Vol.1, J.L. Stein (ed.), North Holland, Amsterdam.

1977 a "How Dead is Keynes," Invited Address at Western Economic Association Annual Meetings, June, in Econ Inq, Vol. XV No.4.

b (with W.C. Brainard) "Asset Markets and the Cost of Capital," in Economic Progress : Private Values and Public Policy (Essays in Honor of William Fellner), R. Nelson and B. Balassa) (eds.), North Holland, Amsterdam.

1978 "Monetary Policies and the Economy – The Transmission Mechanism," SEJ, Vol.44, Jan.

1979 "Deficit Spending and Crowding out in Shorter and Longer Runs," in Theory of Economic Efficiency: Essays in Honor of Aba P. Lerner, (H.I. Greenfield et. al. eds.) MIT Press, Cambridge, MA.

1980 a "Are New Classical Models, Plausible to Guide Policy," JMCB, Vol. XII, No.4, Part 2.

b (with W. Buiter) "Fiscal and Monetary Policies, Capital Formation and Economic Activity," in The Government and Capital Formation, G.M. van Furstenberg (ed.), Ballinger, Cambridge, MA.

c (with J.B.de Macedo) "The Short-run Macroeconomics of Floating Exchange Rates: An Exposition," in Flexible Exchange Rates and the Balance of Payments, J.S. Chipman and C.P Kindleberger (eds.) North Holland, Amsterdam.

1981 "The Monetarist Counter-Revolution Today – An Appraisal," Paper given before the Royal Economic Society, July 1980, EJ, Vol.91, No.301.

1982 a "Money and Finance in the Macroeconomic Process," Nobel Lecture, JMCB, Vol.14, No.2.

b "The Commercial Banking Firm: A Simple Model," ScandJE, Vol.84,No.4.

1985 "Neoclassical Theory in America: J .B. Clark and Fisher," AER, Vol.75, No.6.

1986 a "The Monetary Fiscal Policy Mix: Long Run Implications," AER, Vol.76, No.2.

b "On the Welfare Macroeconomics of Government Financial Policy," Scand JE, Vol.88, No.1.

1989 a "Growth and Distribution: A Neo-Classical Kaldor-Robinson Exercise," Cambridge JE, Vol.13, No.1.

b (with W. Baumol) "The Optimal Cash Balance Proposition: Maurice Allais' Priority," JEL, Vol.27, No.3.

1992 (with W.C. Brainard) "On the Internationalization of Portfolios," OEP, Vol.44, No.4.

1993 "Price Flexibility and Output Stability: An Old Keynesian View," JEP, Vol.77, No.1.

2005 "Irving Fisher (1867-1947)," American Journal of Economics and Sociology, Vol.64, No.1.

7.5 WORKS OF OTHERS

Purvis, D.P. (1982) "James Tobin's Contributions to Economics," ScandJE, Vol. 84, No.1.

Myhrman, J. (1982) "James Tobin's Contributions to Economics," ScandJE, Vol.84, No.1.

CHAPTER 8

FRANCO MODIGLIANI

(1918 – 2003)

Professor Franco Modigliani, Massachusetts Institute of Technology (MIT), Cambridge, Massachusetts, U.S.A., was awarded the 1985 Alfred Nobel Memorial Prize in Economic Sciences for his pioneering analyses of saving and financial markets. The Royal Swedish Academy of Sciences' announcement of the award particularly refers to Modigliani's construction and development of the life-cycle hypothesis of household saving and formulation of the Modigliani-Miller theorems for valuation of firms and capital costs. These two contributions are closely related in that they deal with the "management of household property: one refers to total value, the other to its composition."

One of the cornerstones of Keynes's <u>General Theory</u> is the relationship between consumption and national income. Keynes had put forward a "psychological law" that "households increase their consumption as their income increases, but not as much as their income increases." One obvious consequence of this law is that the proportion of national income represented by saving increases during periods of economic growth.

While there was general acceptance of Keynes's theory by his contemporary economists, Simon Kuznets showed in 1942 that the empirical facts did not support the theory. He showed that the long-term saving-income ratio in the United States did not record any secular increase. This apparent paradox prompted economists to take up empirical studies during the years that followed and several new approaches to the theory of saving were presented. A rational and satisfactory explanation for the Keynes-Kuznets contradiction in the framework of a general well-defined theory of consumer demand over time was not given until 1957 when Milton Friedman put forward his Permanent Income Hypothesis (PIH). The characteristic feature of Friedman's hypothesis was that an individual consumer's income was supposed to consist of two parts (a permanent component and a transitory component) and that it is the permanent part that determines the decisions about consumption and saving. The contradiction surfaced as Keynes's original proposition was based on empirical observations of cross-section data referring to total income and not to permanent income. For several years, Friedman's Permanent Income Hypothesis was well received by economists and played a dominant role among the existing theories of aggregate saving.

However, three years before Friedman published his theory of consumption and saving, Franco Modigliani, in collaboration with Richard Brumberg, had already presented the life-cycle hypothesis (LCH). Like Friedman, Modigliani and Brumberg assumed that households attempt to maximise their utility of present as well as future consumption. The crucial difference between the two theories concerned with the length of the planning period. While for Friedman this period was infinite, for Modigliani and Brumberg, the period was finite. That is, Friedman's hypothesis implied that people save not only for themselves but also for their descendants, whereas Modigliani - Brumberg version implied that people save only for themselves. From the postulate of utility maximisation put forward by Modigliani and Brumberg, it followed that consumption was "evenly distributed over time" and this, in turn, implied that the individual built up a stock of wealth during the person's active period which he or she consumed in his or her old age.

The life cycle hypothesis is a purely microeconomic theory. In his later works – some of them singly and some in collaboration with others – Modigliani had shown that the hypothesis had a number of macroeconomic applications. A few of these are same as those of permanent income hypothesis; as, for example, that the long run aggregate saving ratio is constant and that consumption is affected only slightly by realised capital gains. However, some of the macroeconomic applications are largely different from those of the earlier theories. The most important of these is that aggregate national saving depends mainly on the rate of growth of the economy. Other (important) macroeconomic implications of the life cycle hypothesis include the following:

1. Aggregate saving is endogenously determined by not only economic factors but also demographic factors such as the population, age structure and life expectancy, and
2. An increase in the rate of economic growth entails a redistribution of income in favour of younger generations.

The life-cycle hypothesis has been widely used as a theoretical base for many empirical works; for example for the purpose of analysis of the effects of different pension systems. The analyses have indicated that the introduction of a general pension system results in a decline in private saving, which is in agreement with the Modigliani – Brumberg hypothesis.

While the underlying idea of the life-cycle hypothesis, namely, that people save in order to obtain financial security in their old age is not new, Modigliani was credited with the following two achievements in this context, which were important contributions to economic science.

1. He had rationalised the idea into a formal model and integrated in a well-defined and established economic theory; and
2. He had drawn significant macroeconomic implications from this model and performed numerous empirical tests of these implications.

The award citation mentions great impact of the life-cycle model on later theoretical and empirical research. The citation acknowledges that the life-cycle hypothesis "represents a new paradigm in studies of consumption and saving, and has become the basis for most dynamic models used in such studies."

We may now turn to Modigliani's significant and revolutionary contribution to another area – the field of Corporate Finance. While the life-cycle hypothesis concerns saving decisions of households, the Modigliani-Miller theorems concern decisions relating to the composition of the accumulated stock of savings.

Prior to early 1950's, the corporate finance literature consisted primarily of descriptions of institutions and methods, with very little theoretical analysis. It was not until Franco Modigliani and Merton Miller presented their famous theorem in 1958, and at about the same time James Tobin, Harry Markowitz and others started to develop the theory of portfolio selection, that a scientific theory emerged concerning the relationship between characteristics of financial markets and the financing of investments, debts, taxes etc. Once established, the theory of corporate finance developed extremely rapidly.

The first Modigliani-Miller theorem dealt with the issue of how the market value of a firm is affected by the volume and structure of its debts. Modigliani-Miller's first proposition provided a clear answer: neither the volume of debt nor the debt structure affects the market value of the firm under the assumptions of perfect financial markets, no taxes and no bankruptcy costs. The value of a firm is defined as the sum of the market value of its equity and the market value of its debts. Modigliani-Miller theorem stated that a firm's market value is equal to the discounted value of the flow of its expected future returns before interest, using the discount factor applicable to the same risk class. That is, the value of a firm is determined by this discount factor and by the return on existing assets and is independent of the mode of financing of these assets. There is a further implication of the theorem: the average cost of capital is independent of the volume and structure of debts and equal to the expected return on investment in shares of the firms in the same risk class.

In a later paper, Modigliani and Miller formulated another theorem which stated that for a given investment policy, the value of a firm was also independent of its dividend policy. These two theorems put forward by Modigliani and Miller hold regardless of individual differences between shareholders' valuations of risk, leverage effects and durability of loans. The logic of the theorems rests on the assumption of perfect financial markets; when the markets are perfect, a shareholder can compose his asset portfolio according to his preference through his own borrowing and lending and he can achieve his desired composition with respect to risk, leverage etc. without costs. For example, if there is an increase in the risk level of the assets of a firm, shareholders can neutralise this by lowering the risk of other assets in their portfolios.

The Modigliani-Miller theorems have had the following important implications for the theory of investment decisions:

Such investment decisions can be separated from the corresponding financial decisions.

A rational criterion for investment decisions by an investor is maximisation of the firm's market value; and the rational concept of capital cost refers to total cost and had to be measured as the rate of return on capital invested in shares of firms in an identical risk class.

The citation by the Royal Swedish Academy of Sciences observes: "The Modigliani-Miller theorems represent a decisive breakthrough for the theory of corporate finance and have had considerable impact on later research in this area. Thus, the scientific value of Modigliani- Miller's work...refers to a great extent to the introduction of a new analytical method within the discipline of corporate finance." Modigliani and Miller were the first to use the idea of "treating financial decisions as a market allocation problem for stringent analysis, thereby setting guidelines for further research in this area."

While the contribution of Modigliani to corporate finance is very briefly summarised in this chapter, Modigliani-Miller's work in the area of corporate finance will be covered in the chapter devoted to the work of Merton H. Miller.

8.1 A BRIEF BIOGRAPHICAL NOTE: FRANCO MODIGLIANI

Franco Modigliani was born in Rome, Italy, on June 18, 1918, the son of a leading paediatrician in the city. His school performance in the early years was 'good though not outstanding.' His father died when Modigliani was 13. He entered the University of Rome at 17 – 'two years ahead of the norm.' His family hoped that he would follow in his father's footsteps, entering a career in medicine. He decided against it because of "my low tolerance level for sufferings and blood. Instead, I chose law which in Italy, opens the way to many career possibilities." In his second year he decided to enter a national competition sponsored by a student organisation in the area of economics. Modigliani won first prize, although he "...would hesitate to recommend that first essay as a significant contribution to economics."

Modigliani received a Doctorate in Jurisprudence from the University of Rome in 1939. Shortly before the outbreak of World War II, he migrated with his family to the U.S.A., because of his Jewish origin and anti-fascist views, arriving in New York in August 1939. He did his graduate work at the New School for Social Research, where he had Adolph Lowe and Jacob Marschak as teachers. According to Modigliani, he owed a 'debt of gratitude beyond words' to Marschak, who helped Modigliani develop "solid foundation in economics and econometrics, some mathematical foundations, introduced me to the great issues of the day and gave me, together with his unforgettable kindness, constant encouragement. In particular, I owe to him that blend of theory and empirical analysis, theories that can be tested and empirical work guided by theory (that has characterized a good deal of my work)." Modigliani received a Doctorate in Social Science from the New School of Social Research in New York in 1944. In 1946, he became a naturalised citizen of the United States.

Modigliani worked at various institutions, including the Cowles Commission for Research in Economics at the University of Chicago, the University of Illinois, Carnegie Institute of Technology and North Western University, before joining the faculty of Massachusetts Institute of Technology (MIT) as Professor of Econometrics and Finance in 1962, where he remained till his death. In an autobiographical note, Modigliani stated that he had greatly benefited from his association with the Cowles Commission, "staffed and visited by people like Marschak, Koopmans, Arrow, Simon at a time when the profession was absorbing two important revolutions, one centering on the theory of choice under uncertainty initiated by von Neumann and Morgenstern, and the other on statistical inference from non-experimental observations, inspired by Haavelmo."

The first published article of Modigliani in English "Liquidity Preference and the Theory of Interest and Money" which is also "substantially" his doctoral dissertation and which he regarded as one of his major contributions appeared in the 1944 Econometrica. When he was at the University of Illinois, he "befriended a brilliant young graduate student, Richard Brumberg." With Brumberg's collaboration, Modigliani laid the foundations for what was to become the Life Cycle Hypothesis of Saving. It was elaborated in 1953 and 1954 in two research papers, one dealing with individual behaviour and the other with aggregate saving. The second paper ("aggregate" paper) was published in 1980 in Modigliani's Collected Papers because the shock of Brumberg's untimely death in 1955 "sapped my will to undertake the revisions and condensations that would have been required for publication...."

During the period of Modigliani's association with Carnegie Mellon, besides completing the two papers on the Life Cycle Hypothesis, he collaborated with Herbert Simon and others on a book dealing with the problem of optimal production smoothing, and wrote two essays with Miller on the effect of financial structure and dividend policy on a firm's market value. After joining the MIT, he pursued his interests in macroeconomics including criticism of the monetarist positions, generalisation of the monetary mechanism and empirical tests of the Life Cycle Hypothesis. In addition, he branched into new areas such as International Finance and the International payments system, effects of and cures for inflation, stabilisation policies in extensively indexed open economies and into various fields of finance like credit rationing, term structure of interest rates and valuation of speculative assets. Furthermore, Modigliani assumed a major responsibility for designing a large-scale model of the U.S. economy, MPS, sponsored by the Federal Reserve Bank.

Modigliani served on numerous advisory boards in the U.S. and Italy. He received a number of honours. He was President of the Econometric Society in 1962, President of the American Economic Association in 1976 and President of the American Finance Association in 1981. He also served as Honorary President of the International Economic Association. He was awarded James. R. Killian Faculty Achievement Award by MIT in 1985.

Franco Modigliani died on September 25, 2003.

8.2 A BRIEF SURVEY OF FRANCO MODIGLIANI'S CONTRIBUTIONS

It is commonly agreed that Franco Modigliani is one of the leaders of the post-war macroeconomics who had exerted a profound influence on the development of post-Keynesian economics, its empirical testing and its econometric modelling. His single most important contribution to macroeconomics is the life cycle hypothesis of consumption and saving. He had also significantly influenced the development of the theory of financial economics and empirical research work in the area. The Modigliani-Miller theorems relating to the market value of a firm had revolutionized the field and formed the basis of the bulk of modern theory of finance and gave theoretical and empirical direction to the work in the field. In addition, Modigliani had made path-breaking contributions to management science and had helped in advancing an understanding and knowledge of the channels through which financial markets and monetary policy influence the economic activity of a nation. He was also a leading and influential participant in what has come to be known as "monetarist controversy."

Space does not permit a complete or even a tolerably exhaustive survey of all Modigliani's writings. Instead, it is proposed to briefly review his work in and contribution to economics and finance under the following three broad heads.

1. Life Cycle Hypothesis of Consumption and Saving;
2. Macroeconomic Theory and Empirical and Theoretical Work on Macroeconomic Modelling; and
3. Corporate Finance.

8.2.1 LIFE CYCLE HYPOTHESIS OF CONSUMPTION AND SAVING

Economists have long been interested in studying individual thrift and aggregate saving and wealth as national saving is a source of supply of investment and capital which, in turn, influences the productivity of labour and secular growth of an economy. It was generally regarded that not only thrift is an individual virtue but also a socially beneficial act.

However, in the backdrop of the Great Depression and Keynes's interpretation of it in the General Theory, "saving came to be seen with suspicion, as potentially disruptive to the economy and harmful to social welfare." The argument was on the following lines: individual or household saving has the effect of reducing one component of aggregate demand, namely, consumption without a systematic and corresponding offsetting increase in another component, namely investment. As a consequence, the aggregate demand for the nation's output is "inadequate," or "deficient;" output and employment is lower than the capacity of the economy. "This failure was attributable to a variety of reasons including wage rigidity, liquidity preference, fixed capital coefficients in production and to investment controlled by animal spirits rather than by the cost of capital."

The great interest in the study of saving behaviour of the public since then owed not a little to the crucial role assigned by Keynes in the General Theory to the consumption function as a main determinant of aggregate demand and in particular by his well known "fundamental psychological law" to the effect that an increase in income leads to a smaller rise in consumption. Keynesian economics in 1940's and early 1950's was concerned with "over saving as a source of both cyclical fluctuations and long run stagnation." The general formulation of the consumption function is to express consumption as a linear function of income with a "substantial positive intercept." Modigliani in his Nobel lecture called these early efforts as "crudely empirical." No satisfactory explanation was provided as to why rational consumers would choose to allocate their current income to saving.

The important empirical work of Simon Kuznets (discussed in the chapter on Kuznets) and others dealt a severe and fatal blow to such simple view of the process of saving. Specifically, the empirical evidence showed that the saving-income ratio in the U.S.A. had not varied much since the middle of the 19th century, despite the large rise in per capita incomes. In a path-breaking contribution, Dorothy Brady and Rose Friedman demonstrated that the consumption function implied by the U.S. family budget data shifted in time as mean income increased in such a fashion that the saving rate was explained not by the absolute income of the family but rather by its income relative to overall mean income. They had thus provided reconciliation between Kuznets's time series results with the evidence from budget studies.

In 1949, James Duesenberry as well as Franco Modigliani had attempted separately at reconciling the cyclical variations of the savings ratio with its long run stability. Duesenberry postulated that current consumption is determined not just by current income but by its highest previous peak, giving rise to what is called a 'ratchet effect.' This explanation, however, failed to come to grips with the budget constraint in the case of "would-be dissavers below mean income." In his explanation, Modigliani laid particular stress on reasons for the pro-cyclical movement in the saving rate and on the fact that in an economy experiencing stable long run growth, the ratio of current income to highest previous income could be considered as a good measure of cyclical conditions. Modigliani in his Nobel lecture referred to Margaret Reid's unpublished "fundamental" contribution which provided a "totally different" explanation (that consumption was controlled by normal or "permanent," rather than current, income) and "was an important source of inspiration, both for the Life Cycle and roughly contemporaneous with Permanent Income Hypothesis (PIH) of Milton Friedman."

Modigliani in collaboration with Richard Brumberg had written two essays between 1952 and 1954 to show "that all the well-established empirical regularities could be accounted for in terms of rational, utility maximizing consumers, allocating optimally their resources to consumption over their life, in the spirit of Irving Fisher...." The hypothesis of utility maximisation coupled with perfect market implies that resources that a representative consumer allocates to consumption at any age depend not on current income but only on his life resources defined as the total of the present value of labour income plus bequests, if any. This, combined with the general observation that the representative consumer chooses to consume at a reasonably stable rate close to his anticipated average life consumption, leads to a conclusion that the size of an individual's saving is influenced by the extent to which current observed income varies from average life resources. While this conclusion is common to both Life Cycle Hypothesis (LCH), and Permanent Income Hypothesis (PIH) there is one vital difference. Friedman's PIH makes a simplifying assumption that individual's life is infinitely long whereas Modigliani's LCH explicitly recognises the finite life of households.

The explicit recognition of the finite life of households allows the LCH to focus on those systematic changes in income and in needs, which occur over the life cycle as a result of maturing and retiring and of changes in family size as also bequests and bequests motive. The LCH shows a number of implications, which were at that time "quite novel and surprising (almost counter-intuitive)." Modigliani's Nobel lecture lists the following implications.

1. A country's rate of saving is entirely independent of its per capita income.
2. Different national saving rates are consistent with identical life cycle behaviour.
3. Between countries with identical individual behaviour, the aggregate saving rate will be higher the higher the long run growth of the economy. It will be zero for zero economic growth.
4. The wealth-income ratio is a decreasing function of the growth rate, thus being largest at zero growth.

An economy can accumulate a very substantial stock of wealth relative to income even if no wealth is passed on by bequests. The main factor that controls the wealth-income ratio and the saving rate for given growth is the prevailing length of retirement.

The life cycle model has important implications for macroeconomic effects of fiscal and monetary policies that are significantly different from those derivable by standard Keynesian consumption function or refinements thereof.

In regard to short run stabilisation policy, the implications are the following:

The fact that wealth enters importantly in the short-run consumption function implies that monetary policy can affect aggregate demand not only through the traditional channel of investment but also through the market value of assets and consumption.

Attempts at restraining demand through transitory income taxes can be expected to have small effects on consumption and lowering saving because consumption depends on life resources which are little affected by transitory tax changes.

Modigliani listed out the following long run propositions of the Life Cycle Hypothesis.

A progressive tax on consumption is more equitable than one on current income because it more nearly taxes permanent income, quite apart from its incentive effects on saving.

As regards short and long run effects of deficit financing, Modigliani stated the following: Expenditures financed by deficit tend to be paid by future generations; those financed by taxes are paid by the current generation. The conclusion rests on the proposition that private saving, being controlled by life cycle considerations, should be nearly independent of the government budget situation and therefore private wealth should be independent of the national debt. It follows that the national debt tends to crowd out an equal amount of private capital at a social cost equal to the rate of return on the cost of capital (which is also approximately equal to the government interest bill).

The original formulation of the life cycle model assumed subjective certainty about the rates of return as also income. There have been several extensions of the analysis of inter-temporal choice to take into account uncertainty by Samuelson, Modigliani, Phelps, Merton, and Modigliani himself in collaboration with Dreze. Uncertainty that cannot be insured against introduced a third motivation for individual saving in addition to something of consumption over time and earning of interest. An increase in uncertainty about future income will increase saving for a risk-averse individual. An increase in uncertainty about rates of return may either increase or decrease saving. Uncertainty about expected rates of return does not change much the analysis of consumer's choice; however, "it is only for the special class of isoelastic utility functions that the proportionality hypothesis remains valid."

8.2.2 MACROECONOMIC THEORY AND MACROECONOMIC MODELLING

Modigliani's 1944 article "Liquidity Preference and the Theory of Interest and Money," is considered one of the best and most complete statements of the essence of static Keynesian macroeconomic theory. Many economists, such as Hicks, Lange and Lerner, had refined and developed the structure of the Keynesian model in the late 1930s. Modigliani's work, according to Kouri, goes beyond their writings in at least two respects. First, Modigliani showed the important point that liquidity preference plays an important part in the Keynesian system and the role of the very special assumptions about the supply of labour in it. The second contribution of the article concerned the explicit analysis of the short-run dynamics of the Keynesian model. "...in the short run the interest rate clears the money market...in the Keynesian medium run the level of output and the rate of interest are determined simultaneously to clear the financial and product markets."

The Modigliani model indicated that the money market clearing interest rate does not necessarily imply the equality of ex-ante saving and ex-ante investment. If the interest rate is too high, ex-ante saving is higher than ex-ante investment and the equilibrium is brought about through downward adjustment of production at the point of intersection of the IS and LM curves. The equilibrium is stable if the slope of the IS curve is algebraically smaller than the slope of the LM curve. Given the level of output, the marginal product of labour determines the real wage rate and price level in the economy. The Modigliani model postulated a constant nominal wage rate and a flexible price level, which adjusts to clear the product market at the intersection of the "notional supply curve with the effective demand curve."

Modigliani also considered a flexible wage model in which the real wage and the level of output and employment were determined by the demand for and supply of labour. In this model, the equilibrium rate of interest was determined by investors' demand for loanable funds and the supply of loanable funds by savers; the general level of prices was determined by equality of supply of money and demand for money. Furthermore, no role was assigned to liquidity preference in the determination of interest rate. In this (1944) paper, Modigliani took a position which stipulated that both monetary policy and fiscal policy can affect aggregate demand in contrast to the position taken by monetarists.

While there is very little difference between the short-run macroeconomic models then currently in use and the 1944 model of Modigliani, a number of significant developments had taken place since then in macroeconomic theory. They may be briefly summarised here in order to evaluate Modigliani's contribution in this field in the proper perspective. We may basically follow the attempt of Kouri.

(a) Refinement of the theoretical underpinnings behind various components of the Keynesian system; the refinement of the theory of the consumption function by Duesenberry, Friedman and Modigliani, among others. Modigliani's Life Cycle Hypothesis has been discussed in the earlier section. The development of the theory of investment by Jorgensen, Eisner and Bischoff; refinement of the theory of demand for money by Friedman, Tobin and Baumol among others; the development of the theory of supply of money by Brunner and Meltzer, Modigliani, de Leeuw and others; the general equilibrium formulation of financial markets, principally by Tobin; the theory of the term structure of interest rates by Hicks, Lutz, Culbertson, Meiselman, Modigliani, Sutch et al; the theory of credit rationing by Jaffee, Modigliani and others.

(b) Patinkin's reformulation of the neo-classical macro model.

(c) Estimation of various components of the Keynesian model as also the construction of complete macroeconomic models by Klein, Modigliani and many others, besides accumulation of empirical evidence in other ways, among others, by Friedman and Schwartz.

(d) A shift from comparative static analysis to explicit dynamic analysis of business cycles, growth and the interaction of unemployment and inflation.

(e) Development of 'micro-foundations of macroeconomics' and work on the dynamics of price formation and search unemployment by Phelps, Clower, Leijonhufvud, Barro, Grossman and others.

(f) Work on the theory of expectations by Muth and Lucas among others.

(g) Development of the macroeconomics and monetary theory of open economies by Mundell and others.

Cutting across the above classificatory framework, Kouri refers to the monetarist attack on Keynesian macroeconomic theory and policy; the monetary explanation of fluctuations in inflation and unemployment; the hypothesis of natural rate of unemployment and the acceleration hypothesis by Friedman and Phelps among others; and rational expectations revolution by Lucas and Sargent.

From the mid-1960's, Modigliani, in collaboration with Ando and others was engaged in constructing a large-scale macroeconomic model of the U.S. economy, which would incorporate "everything that is known in theory about macroeconomic relationships." The result is the construction of the FMP or MPS or MIT-PENN-FRB model. According to Kouri while the model is a team effort "there appears to be no doubt, however, that Modigliani is the 'brains' of the model (and Ando perhaps the engineer!)."

The MPS model has shown the various channels through which monetary policy influences aggregate demand. While the model has demonstrated that money is important, it refutes the claim of monetarists that fiscal policy is unimportant. Another contribution of the model relates to more satisfactory specification of some of the individual equations, such as incorporation of wealth effects in the consumption function, incorporation of the effects of credit rationing and formulation of the investment function in terms of a putty-clay vintage model.

8.2.3 CORPORATE FINANCE

In collaboration with others, particularly with Merton H. Miller, Modigliani made fundamental and significantly important contributions to the modern theory of corporate finance. However, the main results of the work of Modigliani and Miller have been subject to prolonged and intense controversy. These central results are referred to as the Modigliani-Miller "irrelevancy propositions." These propositions are best summarised in their own words:

"The market value of any firm is independent of its capital structure and is given by capitalizing its expected return at the rate that is appropriate to its class and...the current valuation is unaffected by differences in dividend payments in any future period and thus...dividend policy is irrelevant for the determination of market prices given investment policy."

Modigliani and Miller used partial equilibrium analysis in the proof of the theorem. Their proof basically rested on the assumption of the presence of arbitrage opportunities in the market and the assumption of no bankruptcy. Later on, other economists like Stiglitz, employed the assumption of perfectly competitive financial markets in the proof of the validity of Modigliani-Miller theorem.

The theorems have two important implications. First, it is possible to separate a firm's production and investment decisions from its financial decisions. Second, a firm in taking an investment decision has to use the criterion whether the decision will result in maximising its market value and the appropriate cost of capital to be used is aggregate capital cost, irrespective of the source of funds for financing the investment project.

The issue is whether the debt-equity ratio of the firm is important, in the absence of taxes.

Further discussion and elaboration of the model and the dividend policy of a firm and its effect on the market value of a firm is covered in the chapter on Merton H Miller.

8.3 CONCLUDING OBSERVATIONS

Besides the three broad fields in which Modigliani's contributions to economics have been outlined above, he had enriched many other fields with his theoretical and empirical work. He co-authored along with Holt, Muth and Simon a book devoted to some aspects of management science. The path-breaking volume attempts at developing quantitative decision methods for firms in planning tasks relating to production, inventories and work force. The authors put forward an inter-temporal quadratic function that is to be minimised subject to various constraints.

Modigliani had also worked on the anticipations of business firms in regard to future. His work on term-structure of interest rates along with others contained a very important idea – that individual investors possess different "preferred habitats" in accordance with their needs resulting in well-defined demand functions for bonds of different maturity. In order to induce investors to hold bonds of maturity that is different from what they prefer, risk premium has to be paid for increasing the risk of their portfolio. Thus, Modigliani and his co-authors argued that the equilibrium term structure of interest rates is determined by interest rate expectations coupled with the pattern of risk premiums.

Modigliani's work in the field of international economics and international financial system profess some important ideas such as the relation between foreign trade and levels of economic activity in various countries participating in international exchange. In his later work, Modigliani had advocated 'Crawling Peg' exchange rate system and a purchasing-power-guaranteed medium of international transactions.

Before concluding this write up, we cannot miss referring to his work in the field of credit rationing, a perceptive survey article on the theory of oligopoly, his article in the area of national debt and his work on consumption-saving choice under conditions of uncertainty. Modigliani worked till his death. He completed the last paper, "The Chinese Saving Puzzle and the Life-Cycle Hypothesis" on September 24, 2003. On September 25, he did not wake up as Francesco Franco writes. Kouri pays a tribute with which we close this note: Modigliani has taken us a long way and his life work will be a source of inspiration and guidance for generations of students to come.

8.4 SELECT BIBLIOGRAPHY OF FRANCO MODIGLIANI'S WORKS

8.4.1 BOOKS

1956 Editor : Problems of Capital Formation: Concepts, Measurements and Controlling Factors, Studies in Income and Wealth, Vol.19, NBER, Princeton University Press, Princeton, NJ.

1960 (with C. C. Holt, J. F. Muth and H. A. Simon), Planning Production, Inventories and Work Forces, Prentice-Hall, Upper Saddle River, NJ.

1980 The Collected Papers of Franco Modigliani, (A. Abel and S. Johnson eds.) Vols.1, 2 and 3, MIT Press, Cambridge, MA.

1983 (with R. Hemming eds.), The Determinants of National Saving and Wealth, Proceedings of a Conference held by the International Economic Association at Bergamo, Italy, Macmillan, London.

1989 The Collected Papers of Franco Modigliani, (S. Johnson ed.) Vols. 4 and 5, MIT Press, Cambridge, MA.

1989 (with L. Papademos), "The Supply of Money and the Control of Nominal Income," in Handbook of Monetary Economics, Friedman, B. and F. Hahn (eds.), North Holland, Amsterdam.

1996 (with F. J. Fabbozzi), Capital Markets: Institutions and Instruments (Second edition) Prentice-Hall, Upper Saddle River, NJ.

2001 Adventures of an Economist, Texere, New York.

2002 (with F. J. Fabbozzi et al.), Foundations of Financial Markets and Institutions (Third edition), Prentice Hall, Upper Saddle River, NJ.

2004 (with A. Muralidhar), Rethinking Pension Reform, Cambridge University Press, Cambridge.

2005 The Collected Papers of Franco Modigliani, (F. Franco, ed.) Vol.6, MIT Press, Cambridge, MA.

8.4.2 ARTICLES

1944 "Liquidity Preference and the Theory of Interest and Money." Econometrica, Vol.12, No.1, Reprinted in Readings in Monetary Theory, American Economic Association, 1951.

1949 "Fluctuations in the Saving-Income Ratio: A Problem in Economic Forecasting." Studies in Income and Wealth, Vol.II, NBER, New York.

1954 (with R. Brumberg), "Utility Analysis and the Consumption Function: An Interpretation of Cross-section Data," in K. Kurihara (ed.) Post-Keynesian Economics, Rutgers University Press, NJ.

1955 a (with C. C. Holt and H. A. Simon), "A Linear Decision Rule for Production and Employment Scheduling," Management Science, Vol.2, No.1.

b (with O. H. Sauerlender), "Economic Expectations and Plans of Firms in Relation to Short Term Forecasting," in Short-term Forecasting, Studies in Income and Wealth by the Conference on Research in Income and Wealth, Vol.17, NBER, Princeton University Press, Princeton, NJ.

1957 a "Business Reasons for Holding Inventories and the Macro-Economic Implications," in Problems of Capital Formation: Concepts, Measurement and Controlling Factors, Studies in Income and Wealth, Vol.19, by the Conference on Research in Income and Wealth, NBER, Princeton University Press, Princeton, NJ.

b (with A. K. Ando), "Tests of the Life Cycle Hypothesis of Savings: Comments and Suggestions," Bulletin of the Oxford University Institute of Statistics, Oxford, Vol.19, No.2.

1958 a "New Developments on the Oligopoly Front," JPE, Vol.66, No.3.

b (with M. H. Miller), "The Cost of Capital, Corporation Finance and the Theory of Investment," AER, Vol.48, No.3.

1959 a (with A. K. Ando), "Growth, Fluctuations and Stability," AER, Vol.49, No.2.

b (with M. H. Miller), "The Cost of Capital, Corporation Finance and the Theory of Investment: Reply," AER, Vol.49, No.4.

1960 (with A. K. Ando), "The 'Permanent' Income and the 'Life Cycle' Hypothesis of Saving Behavior: Comparison and Tests," in Consumption and Saving, Vol.2, Wharton School of Finance and Commerce, University of Pennsylvania, Philadelphia, Pa.

1961 a (with M. H. Miller), "Dividend Policy, Growth, and the Valuation of Shares," JB, Vol.34, No.4.

b "Long run Implications of Alternative Fiscal Policies and the Burden of the National Debt," EJ, Vol.71, No.284.

1963 a "The Monetary Mechanism and Its Interaction with Real Phenomena," REStat, Vol.45, NO.1, Part II, Supplement.

b (with A. K. Ando), "The 'Life Cycle' Hypothesis of Saving; Aggregate Implications and Tests," AER, Vol.53, No.1, Part I; Reprinted in Readings in Business Cycles, Vol. X, R. A. Gordon and L. R. Klein (eds.) American Economic Association, R. D. Irwin, Chicago, Ill.

c (with M. H. Miller), "Corporate Income Taxes and the Cost of Capital: A Correction," AER, Vol.53, No.3.

1964 a (with M. H. Miller), "Dividend Policy, Growth, and the Valuation of Shares: A Reply," JB, VOl.36, No.1.

b (with A.K. Ando), "The 'Life Cycle' Hypothesis of Saving: Aggregate Implications and Tests: A Correction," AER, Vol.54, No.2, Part I.

c "Some Empirical Tests of Monetary Management and of Rules Versus Discretion," JPE, Vol.72, No.3.

1965 a (with A.K. Ando), "The Relative Stability of Monetary Velocity and the Investment Multiplier," AER, Vol. 55, No.4.

b "Rejoinder" (to "Reply" by M. Friedman and D. Meiselman), AER, Vol.55, No.4.

1966 a (with R. Sutch), "Innovations in Interest Rate Policy," AER, Vol.56, No.2.

b "The Life Cycle Hypothesis of Saving, the Demand for Wealth and the Supply of Capital," Social Research, Vol.33 No.2.

c (with M.H. Miller), "Some Estimates of the Cost of Capital to the Electric Utility Industry, 1954-57," AER, Vol.56, No.3.

d (with P.A. Samuelson), "The Pasinetti Paradox in Neo-classical and More General Models," RES, Vol.33, No.4.

1968 "Liquidity Preference," in International Encyclopaedia of the Social Sciences, Vol.9, D.L.Sills (ed.) Cromwell, Collier and Macmillan Inc., New York.

1969 a (with A.K. Ando), "Econometric Analysis of Stabilization Policies," AER, Vol.59, No.2.

b (with D.K. Jaffee), "A Theory and Test of Credit Rationing," AER, Vol.59, No.5.

1970 a (with R. Rasche and J.P. Cooper), "Central Bank Policy, and the Money Supply, and the Short-term Rate of Interest," JMCB, Vol.2, No.2.

b "The Life Cycle Hypothesis of Saving and Inter-country Differences in the Saving Ratio," in Induction, Growth and Trade: Essays in Honour of Sir Roy Harrod, (W.A. Eltis et al.eds.) Clarendon Press, Oxford.

c "Monetary Policy and Consumption: Linkages via Interest Rate and Wealth Effects in the FMP Model," in Consumer Spending and Monetary Policy: The Linkages, Conference Series No.5, Federal Reserve Bank of Boston, June.

1971 (with H. Askari), "The Reform of the International Payments System," in Essays in International Finance, No.89, International Finance Section, Department of Economics, Princeton University, Princeton, NJ.

1972 a (with G. Pogue et al.), "Efficiency in European Capital Markets and Comparison with the American Market," in The Stock Exchange: How to Make it an Instrument of Economic-Social Progress in Europe and the World, Proceedings of the First International Conference of Stock Exchanges, Milan, Mar.

b "The Dynamics of Portfolio Adjustment and the Flow of Savings through Financial Intermediaries," in Savings Deposits, Mortgages and Housing, E.M. Gramlich and D.M. Jaffee (eds.) Studies for the Federal Reserve-MIT-Penn Econometric Model, Chapter 3, Lexington Books, Boston, MA.

c (with J. Dreze), "Consumption Decisions under Uncertainty," JET, Vol.5, No.3.

1973 (with R.J. Shiller), "Inflation, Rational Expectations and the Term Structure of Interest Rates," Economica, Vol.40, No.157.

1974 a (with G. Pogue), "An Introduction to Risk and Return: Concept and Evidence," Part I, Financial Analysts Journal, Mar/Apr. Part-II, Financial Analysts Journal, May/June.

b (with A.K. Ando et al.), "On the Role of Expectations of Price and Technological Change in an Investment Function," IER, Vol.15, No.2.

1975 a (with G.A. Pogue), "Alternative Investment Performance Fee Arrangements and Implications for SEC Regulatory Policy," Bell JE, Vol.6, No.2.

b "The Channels of Monetary Policy in the Federal Reserve-MIT-University of Pennsylvania Econometric Model of the United States," in Modelling the Economy, G.A. Renton (ed.), Social Science Research Council Conference, July 1972, Heinemann Educational Books Ltd., London.

c "The Life Cycle Hypothesis of Saving Twenty Years Later," in Contemporary Issues in Economics, M. Parkin (ed.) Manchester University Press, Manchester.

d (with A.K. Ando), "Some Reflections on Describing Structures of Finance Sectors," and (with K. Shell) "Appendix," in The Brookings Model: Perspective and Recent Developments, G. Fromm and L.R. Klein (eds.) North Holland/Elsevier, New York.

1976 a (with A.K. Ando), "Impact of Fiscal Actions on Aggregate Income and the Monetarist Controversy: Theory and Evidence," in Monetarism, Studies in Monetary Economy, J.L. Stein (ed.) North Holland, Amsterdam.

b "Models of the Economy and Optimal Stabilization Policies," in Mathematical Models in Economics, Papers and Proceedings of a US-USSR Seminar, Moscow, NBER, New York.

1977 a (with C. Steindel), "Is a Tax Rebate an Effective Tool for Stabilization Policy," BPEA-1. Washington D.C.

b "The Monetarist Controversy or, Should We Forsake Stabilization Policies?" Presidential Address delivered at the American Economic Association, Sep 1976, AER, Vol.67, No.2.

1979 (with R.A. Cohn), "Inflation, Rational Valuation and the Market," Financial Analysts Journal, Mar/Apr.

1982 "Debt, Dividend Policy, Taxes, Inflation and Market Valuation," Presidential Address Delivered at the American Finance Association, December 1981, JF, Vol.37, No.2.

1985 a (with R. Cohn), "Inflation and Corporate Financial Management," in Recent Advances in Corporate Finance, E.I. Altman and M.B. Subrahmanyam (eds.) R.D. Irwin, Chicago, Ill.

b "Life Cycle, Individual Thrift, and the Wealth of Nations," Nobel Prize Lecture, AER, Vol.76, No.3.

1988 a "The Role of Intergeneration Transfers and Life-Cycle Saving in the Accumulation of Wealth," JEP, Vol.2, No.2.

b "MM-Past, Present, Future," JEP, Vol.2, No.4.

c "Reagan's Economic Policies: A Critique," OEP, Vol.40, No.3.

2004 (with S.L. Cao), "The Chinese Saving Puzzle and Life Cycle Hypothesis," JEL, Vol.42, No.1.

8.5 WORKS OF OTHERS

Kouri, P.J.K. (1986), "Franco Modigliani's Contributions to Economics," ScandJE, Vol.88, No.2.

CHAPTER 9

ROBERT MERTON SOLOW

(1924 –)

The Royal Swedish Academy of Sciences has awarded the 1987 Alfred Nobel Memorial Prize in Economic Sciences to Professor Robert M. Solow, Massachusetts Institute of Technology, Cambridge, MA, USA, for "his contributions to the theory of economic growth."

As important feature of economic research for many years has been an extensive study of factors that help growth of output and enhance welfare of the people in an economy. The 1987 Nobel Memorial Award to Robert Solow recognises his "exceptional contributions" in this area. Intuitive reasoning suggests that growth in per capita output in a country is the result of a greater stock of real capital, such as a large number of machines and more factories. But it is plausible that increased production may be due to technical development which is embodied in improved machines and employment of more efficient methods of production. In addition, increase in productivity may have been brought about by improved education and training of people as also by use of improved methods of organising production in the country. Moreover, the discovery of natural resources or improvements in a country's position on global markets may provide opportunities for higher living standards. Solow is widely acknowledged as having created a theoretical framework that can be used to discuss the factors which promote economic growth in quantitative and technical terms. This framework can be and has actually been used in empirical estimation of contributions of different factors of production to a nation's economic growth.

Solow's growth model was presented in 1956 in a widely-read and well- known article entitled "A Contribution to the Theory of Economic Growth." The paper contains a mathematical model in the form of a differential equation, explaining how increased capital stock generates greater per capita production. Solow makes a number of assumptions; specifically, that society saves a given constant share of its income, that population and supply of labour grow at a constant rate and that capital per worker or capital intensity can be varied and is determined by wage rate or prices of production factors. However, because of the operation of diminishing returns, additions to capital or increasing capital intensity will make smaller contributions to production. The long-run implication of this phenomenon is crucial. The economy in the long run will approach a state of identical growth rates for labour, capital and total production, in the absence of any technological progress. That is, the economy approaches a long run situation where per capita output and real wage rate no longer increase. He comes to a conclusion that an increase in a nation's saving-income ratio cannot bring about a permanent increase in the growth rate of output.

But an economy with a higher saving-income ratio can have higher per capita production and, thus, a higher real wage. In the absence of technological progress, however, the rate of growth will be the same and equivalent to growth rate in labour supply, regardless of the saving ratio. Therefore, Solow's model underlines the crucial importance in the long run of technological development as the fundamental pre-requisite for a country's economic growth. In his model, if continuous technological progress is assumed, then growth in real wages will be determined by technological progress.

The press release by the Nobel Foundation announcing the award makes reference to the early empirical work relating to the measurement of the contribution of factors to total production using time series data on supply of labour and the stock of capital. Neither of these aggregates is non-controversial. Solow participated actively in exhaustive discussions, particularly about the measurement of aggregated capital stock (the so-called "capital controversy" of the 1960's and 1970's). In his 1960 article "Investment and Technical Progress," Solow presented a new method for studying the role of capital formation in economic growth. His main assumption is that technical progress is "built into" machines and other capital and that this must be taken into account in empirical measurements of the importance of capital. This idea has evolved into the so-called "vintage" approach. This approach assumes that at every point in time, new investments are characterised by the most modern technology and that the capital formed as a result does not change qualitatively during its remaining lifetime. Investment decisions restrict future technology to some extent through the technological knowhow tied up in physical capital. The formulation of a mathematical model by Solow based on these ideas enabled him to develop a theory that permitted empirical estimation. In a way, and more importantly, his model established a new way of aggregating capital stock of different ages. As compared to earlier approaches, the empirical results obtained by Solow assigned much greater significance to capital formation in explaining the increase in per employee output.

The most significant aspect of the above-mentioned article of Solow is his method of analysis of "Vintage Capital," but not the empirical results. The concept of Vintage Capital has found many other applications since then. Many numerical models of general equilibrium adopt Solow's approach "to make realistic studies of the sensitivity of economies to certain types of disturbances." The vintage approach is found to be highly useful from a theoretical point of view and in applications such as analyses of the development of industrial structures.

The award citation also refers to Solow's work 'in many vital areas' of economic theory. Theories of economic growth assume that the only factors limiting growth are labour, capital and technology. In recent years, the role of natural resources in influencing economic growth of nations has attracted considerable attention. Solow has published important contributions in the economics of natural resources. Can we conceive of continued economic growth when we know that natural resources are finite? According to Solow, the key to this problem is connected with assumption about elasticity of substitution between capital and inputs of natural resources. Solow has also studied environmental consequences in other contexts.

Over the last decade and a half, Solow has devoted his research efforts to macroeconomic issues involving unemployment, inflation and economic policy.

9.1 A BRIEF BIOGRAPHICAL NOTE: ROBERT SOLOW

Robert M .Solow was born in Brooklyn, New York, U.S.A., on August 23, 1924, the oldest of three children. His parents were themselves the children of immigrants. They had to earn a living as soon as they finished the secondary school. So his sisters, his cousins and Solow himself were the first generation of his family to attend a university.

Solow was educated— "well educated" – in the neighbourhood public schools of New York City. He won a scholarship to Harvard College. His first studies at Harvard were in Sociology and Anthropology as well as "elementary economics." By the end of 1942, when he had turned 18, "it seemed that there were more urgent and exciting matters" than what he was doing. So, Solow left the university and joined the U. S. Army.

Upon returning to Harvard in 1945, when he was discharged from the army, Solow chose "almost casually" to go on with economics. Solow says: "By a piece of good luck, Wassily Leontief became my teacher, guide and friend. I learned from him the spirit as well as the substance of modern economic theory." Leontief was also responsible for Solow's introduction to empirical work: as Leontief's research assistant, Solow produced the first set of capital coefficients for the input-output model.

He became interested in statistics and probabilistic models. According to Solow, "In those days, the teaching of statistics at Harvard was, to put it kindly, eccentric." Therefore, in 1949-1950, he spent a fellowship year at Columbia University, in the lectures of Abraham Wald, Jacob Wolfowitz and T. W. Anderson. During that year, he also worked on his Ph.D. thesis, an exploratory attempt to model change in the size distribution of wage income using "interacting Markoff processes" for employment-unemployment and wage rates. The thesis was awarded the Wells Prize at Harvard, which offered publication in book form and $500 (in 1951 prices!) upon completion. Solow observes: "When I reread the thesis, however, I thought that I could do it better. But I never returned to that work and the thesis remains unpublished (and the check uncashed)." He received his doctorate from Harvard University in 1951.

Just before going off to Columbia, Solow was offered and accepted an Assistant Professorship in the Economics Department at MIT. He remarks: "I have never had or wanted any other job. MIT hired me primarily to teach courses in statistics and econometrics. In the beginning I fully intended to make my career along those lines. It did not turn out that way, probably for a geographical reason. I was given the office next to

Paul Samuelson's. Thus began what is now [1987] almost 40 years of almost daily conversations about economics, politics, our children, cabbages and kings. That has been an immeasurably important part of my professional life. I suppose it was inevitable that I should drift back into 'straight' economics, where I discovered an instinctive macroeconomist struggling to get out."

Solow became Professor of Economics at MIT in 1957, retiring in 1995. By 1995 there was no compulsory retirement age, but "I thought the Department would be better off with another young teacher and researcher." His association with MIT continued even after retirement, when he has become Institute Professor Emeritus.

Solow was recipient of a number of awards and honours. He was elected to membership in the National Academy of Sciences in 1972. He has been also a member of the American Philosophical Society and the American Academy of Arts and Sciences and a Fellow of the British Academy. He served as President of the Econometric Society in 1964 and President of the American Economic Association in 1979. Robert Solow has received a number of honours. He received John Bates Clark Medal, American Economic Association, in 1961 and National Medal of Science, 1999. He served as a member and Chairman of the Board of Directors of the Federal Reserve Bank of Boston. He received honorary degrees from over two dozen schools, including the University of Chicago, University of Paris, Warwick University, Yale University, University of Helsinki, Harvard University, University of Buenos Aires, New York University and University of Geneva in Switzerland. Solow was a member of President Kennedy's Council of Economic Advisers.

Robert Solow remained active even after retirement. He is currently Chairman of the Manpower Demonstration Corporation, a non-profit research group that has done "pioneer work in the rigorous experimental testing of policy interventions that aim at improving the employment and earning power of disadvantaged groups like high school drop-outs, welfare mothers etc." More recently, he has succeeded the great sociologist Robert K. Merton as Foundation Fellow of the Russell Sage Foundation. Solow's first project at Russell Sage Foundation was an attempt to account for the extraordinary success of the U.S. economy during the years 1995-2000. This has resulted in a book The Roaring Nineties edited by him jointly with Alan Krueger.

9.2 A BRIEF SUMMARY OF ROBERT SOLOW'S CONTRIBUTIONS

Solow has made outstanding contributions to the field of growth theory and the field has blossomed after his contributions in the 1950s. In addition to his work in the area of Growth, Capital and Technical Progress, Solow has made contributions to other fields such as Inflation, Unemployment, Stabilisation Policy, Urban Economics and Exhaustible Resources. The main focus of this summary is on Solow's work in the broad area of growth theory and related topics; his contribution in other fields are briefly reviewed in a separate section.

1. Growth Theory.
2. Other contribution of Robert Solow.

9.2.1 GROWTH THEORY

Robert Solow in the 1950's was to follow a trail that had been marked out by Sir Roy Harrod and by Evsey Domar and also by Arthur Lewis "in a slightly different context." In his Nobel lecture, Solow states that he was "trying to track down and relieve a certain discomfort that I felt with their work" (the wobbly "Knife-edge" economic growth paths rigidly governed by capital and labour). He later wrote that if they were accurate all one could expect to find on earth was "the wreckage of a capitalism that had shaken itself to pieces long ago." Economic history was, however, a record of economic fluctuations, as well as of growth, but most business cycles were observed to be self-limiting. "Sustained, though disturbed, growth was not a rarity."

According to Solow, growth theory, like much else in macroeconomics, was a product of the depression of the 1930's and of the War that finally ended it. Harrod and Domar, independently, were answering a question: When is an economy capable of recording steady growth at a constant rate? Their answer was: the national saving rate has to be equal to the product of the capital-output ratio and the rate of growth of the labour force. Solow's discomfort was caused by the assumption of Harrod and Domar that all three of the key ingredients of steady growth, namely, the saving rate, growth rate of labour force and the capital-output ratio, were given constants, "facts of nature." Solow, however, felt: the saving rate was a fact about preferences, the growth rate of labour supply was a demographic-sociological fact, the capital-output ratio was a technological fact.

All the three ingredients are capable of changing from time to time, but "sporadically and more or less independently." In that case, however, the possibility of steady growth would be a miraculous stroke of luck. As such, "most-economies, most of the time, would have no equilibrium growth path." Harrod's writings also suggested that steady growth in any case is a case of unstable equilibrium. Furthermore, another implication of the Harrod-Domar model seemed to Solow to be unsound. If the achievement of steady growth is contingent upon the equality of the savings rate and the product of the growth rate of employment and capital-output ratio, then a labour surplus economy can hope to double its growth rate by simply doubling the savings rate, perhaps through government budget. It is common knowledge in the 1950s (in the light of the discussion relating to ex-ante and ex-post concepts of savings and investment) that doubling the ex-ante savings rate would not double the ex-post savings rate unless "something were taking care of the ex-ante investment rate at the same time." The recipe sounded implausible to Solow.

Solow, therefore, started tinkering with the theory of economic growth in an effort to improve upon the Harrod-Domar model. He decided to replace first the assumed constant capital-output and labour-output ratios by "a richer and more realistic representation of the technology." His argument is: "... even if technology itself is not so very flexible for each single good at a given time, aggregate factor-intensity must be much more variable because the economy can choose to focus on capital- intensive or labour-intensive or land-intensive goods."

By introducing a reasonable degree of technological flexibility, Solow was able to achieve two important things. First, the existence of a feasible path of steady growth turned out "not to be a singular event" A spectrum of states is possible and the spectrum may be wide, depending upon the range of aggregative factor-intensities to choose from. Second, Solow's model showed that the equilibrium rate of growth is independent of the saving/investment rate and not proportional to the saving/ investment rate. In other words, the permanent rate of output growth per unit of labour input is independent of the saving/investment rate and depends solely on the rate of progress of technology.

The model of economic growth presented by Solow in his 1956 paper "A Contribution to the Theory of Economic Growth" may be outlined here. It assumes constant returns to scale aggregate production function, permitting substitution between capital and labour inputs. The model is completed by making an assumption that a constant fraction of national output is invested. The model is as given below:

$$\dot{K} / sY \tag{1}$$

Where:

$\dot{K}$: rate of increase of the capital stock

s : fraction of output saved is a constant

$$Y = F(K, L) \tag{2}$$

Where:

$L(t)$: rate of labour input

Inserting Eq. 2 into 1, we get:

$$\dot{K} = sF(K, L) \tag{3}$$

Population growth is assumed to be exogenous. Then the labour force increases at a constant relative rate *n*. In the absence of technical change, *n* is Harrod's natural rate of growth.

Thus,

$$L(t) = L_0 e^{nt} \tag{4}$$

In Eq. 3, L stands for total employment; in Eq. 4 L stands for available supply of labour. Assuming full employment is perfectly maintained and inserting Eq. 4 in Eq. 3 we get:

$$\dot{K} = sF(K, L_0 e^{nt}) \tag{5}$$

Eq. 5 gives the basic equation that determines the time path of capital accumulation that must be followed if all available labour is to be employed. Alternatively, Eq. 4 can be looked at as a supply curve of labour.

In an equally brilliant paper "Technical Change and Aggregate Production Function" (1957), Solow used his neo-classical growth model to explain the growth in the U.S. economy. Solow says in his Nobel lecture: "The main result of that 1957 exercise was startling. Gross output per hour of work in the U.S. economy doubled between 1909 and 1949, and some seven-eighths of that increase could be attributed to 'technical change in the broadest sense' and only the remaining eighth could be attributed to conventional increase in capital intensity or in per-worker tangible capital."

As aptly observed by Solow, his "Neo-classical model of economic growth" started a small industry. It stimulated hundreds of theoretical and empirical articles by other economists. It quickly found its way into text books and into the fund of common knowledge of the profession. The influence of the model has spread far beyond the study of growth, into many areas such as public finance and business cycle fluctuations. David Cass in his article relating to the problem of optimal growth addressed himself to the question: what determines the savings rate? His solution "effectively endogenized the savings decisions since for this economy the optimal allocation is the competitive equilibrium allocation." Another important finding is implied in the endogenous savings decision. It is that "the equilibrium path converges to the balanced or steady state growth path. At that point, the marginal product of capital equals the steady-state rental price of capital" which depends in an explicit way on the features of the tax system. According to Edward C. Prescott "...the neo-classical growth model led to steady-state analysis, which is among the most important constructs in public finance."

In addition, steady-state analysis is the theory underlying much of the development literature as argued by Robert Lucas in his 1986 Marshall Lectures. Likewise, the theory developed by Solow is found to be useful in organising and understanding business cycle fluctuations.

In his Prize lecture, Solow recalls as to how much effort went into broadening the technological framework of growth theory in the articles he wrote in 1950's and 1960's. He tried to ensure that the model accommodates introduction of new technology with the use of newly designed and produced capital equipment, that factor proportions can be altered only when the gross investment is made and not after capital equipment has taken a particular form and that enough flexibility could be achieved with discrete activities.

Solow spells out the main reasons for this special orientation. First, it is the introduction of technological flexibility that has opened up growth theory to a wider variety of real world facts and to a closer link with general economic theory. The second reason is the empirical work which he was doing at that time using an aggregate production function "with apparently meaningful and clearly surprising results." Even though he was sceptical about its use, Solow wanted to demonstrate that the method is capable, "at least in principle, of dealing with the first few doses of realism."

Solow candidly admits that there was one bad by-product of the exclusive focus on the description of technology (that is, paying very little attention to the problems of effective demand). "To put it differently: a theory of equilibrium growth badly needed (and still needs) a theory of deviations from the equilibrium growth path." It is dealt with in the 1956 article in a perfunctory way with the implications of rigidity of real wages and with the possibility of a liquidity trap. He says, however, that he is "proud" of a paragraph included in the 1956 paper which contains a message that growth theory gives a framework within which one can seriously discuss macroeconomic policies "that not only achieve and maintain full employment but also make a deliberate choice between current consumption and current investment, and therefore between current consumption and future consumption."

The early discussions of Harrod-Domar growth theory were marked by talk of inherent instability of equilibrium growth. Instability could and did mean two different things. First, that well-behaved equilibrium paths are surrounded by badly-behaved equilibrium paths, so that "a small sideward step could lead to eventual disaster." Secondly, instability could mean that it applies to disequilibrium behaviour, so that "an economy that once strays from equilibrium growth would not <u>automatically</u> find its way back to any equilibrium growth path." (Emphasis in the original). The Harrod-Domar model appeared to be subject to both the difficulties.

Solow's neo-classical growth model took the sting out of the first sort of instability. The second sort of instability involves integration of growth theory and business cycle theory, of short-run and long-run macroeconomics. Solow puts the unsolved problem (the second type of instability) in the following words in his Prize lecture: One of the achievements of growth theory was to relate equilibrium growth to asset pricing under tranquil conditions. The difficult part of disequilibrium growth is that we do not have (and it may be impossible to have) a really good theory of asset valuation under turbulent conditions.

Growth theory, which is meant to systematically explain and compare equilibrium paths for the economy, has failed to come to grips adequately with the problem of the right way of dealing with deviations from equilibrium growth. It will not be correct, Solow argues, to claim as some economists do, that economic fluctuations are not deviations from equilibrium growth, but examples of equilibrium growth. It is difficult to accept that the equilibrium growth path is not affected by the short to medium-run economic fluctuations. According to Solow, the quantum and direction of capital formation would be definitely affected by the business cycle, may be through gross investment in new equipment or through the accelerated scrapping of old equipment. Therefore, a simultaneous analysis of trend and fluctuations involves an integration of long-run and short-run, or equilibrium and disequilibrium.

An economy which has deviated from the equilibrium growth path may eventually return to an equilibrium path, perhaps because prices are flexible. In the long run, it will not return, according to Solow, to the continuation of the equilibrium path it was on before it slipped off. The new equilibrium path will crucially depend on the amount of capital accumulation that has taken place during the disequilibrium period, and probably also on the amount of unemployment, especially long-term unemployment, that has been experienced. Solow surmises: "Even the level of technology may be different, if technological change is endogenous rather than arbitrary." Investment function plays an important role in this regard (investment decision-making in real firms may be influenced by profitability as emphasised by Malinvaud).

In the course of the Nobel Prize lecture, which surveys the goals and achievements of growth theory, Solow refers as much to the work of others like Denison, Hickman, Prescott and others as to his own. In his words, it is more than mere modesty. He is of the view that any successful line of economic analysis is a "group product" (ideas usually worked out and critically refined by a research community). In the concluding part of his lecture, Solow quotes Robert Frost: "Most of the change we think we see in life is due to the truths being in and out of favor."

9.3 ROBERT SOLOW'S OTHER CONTRIBUTIONS

In his other writings, Solow singly or in collaboration with other authors developed the ideas of the papers of 1956 and 1957 in a number of directions. In R.C.O. Matthews's words: "...he [Solow] dealt with 'embodiment' from a theoretical and empirical point of view...and with the distribution of income (including the concept of 'Solow-neutral' technical progress) and the relation of growth theory to capital theory...." Matthews was rather critical of Solow's work on capital theory in the 1960's. "A fair amount of the work on capital theory in the 1960's was of a defensive character, responding to the iconoclastic criticism of Joan Robinson and her associates. Like Solow's writings, this is intelligent, ingenious, and sensible, but because of the nature of the criticisms not much of interest really emerged (in my opinion) and it was perhaps unfortunate that Solow's energies were diverted to it."

The concept of optimal rate of capital accumulation was introduced by Solow and his collaborators in "Balanced Growth under Constant Returns to Scale" and in Chapter 12 of the book Linear Programming and Economic Analysis. The latter contained the first exposition of the turnpike theorem; "many economists would be proud to be known for this alone."

An important contribution of Solow in the area of Public Finance and Fiscal Policy is the paper co-authored with his student Alan Blinder entitled "Does Fiscal Policy Matter?" The study on the effects of the size of the government on "crowding out" is considered pioneering. It has demonstrated that the relative magnitude of the "opposing effects of the increase in private wealth on demand – via consumption and via the demand for real balances – had implications for the long run stability of the system." Furthermore, they have shown that in some cases, public expenditure is more expansionary if financed by government bonds than if financed out of taxation.

9.4 CONCLUDING OBSERVATIONS

Robert Solow's main claim to the Nobel Memorial award is clearly on account of his early work on growth and capital theories. It is the view of many of his peers in the profession that his subsequent work, taken by itself, would have made him a major figure in economics. Prescott refers as to how Solow's neoclassical growth model has become the "organizing structure" in macroeconomics as a result of which graduate students at the leading macro research centres focus on this model and spend little, if any, time on the IS-LM mechanism which it has replaced.

Solow is considered an "unrepentant Keynesian" with strong views on the desirability of government leadership in the economic sphere. In this context, reference needs to be made to the issue as to why Keynesian ideas and methods survived for over seventy years despite their "theoretical weaknesses and analytical crudities." Solow, in his work "Monopolistic Competition and Macroeconomic theory," asserts that "most of the viable macro models used for forecasting and policy analysis are recognizably Keynesian in structure, if not in every detail." According to him, "things are not the way that standard competitive theory claims that they are." The contrast is clearly strong in recessions; it can be clearly seen most of the time.

Solow provides two main reasons for the persistence of Keynesian ideas. He states: 1) Keynesian ideas survive because "the usual alternatives ask us to believe things that appear not to be true. The basic Keynesian building blocks ...seem rather close to every day observation. At least economists still estimate consumption functions, demand for money equations, and slow price-adjustment relations that are refinements, more or less, of these simple ideas. 2) The second point is that the <u>General Theory</u> itself is built formally on the assumption of competition in the goods market. So much the worse for Keynes."

Solow remarks that Keynes seemed to have realised early that his theory would make "more sense" without it. He states that "explicit modeling of imperfect competition in the product market will be good for macroeconomics. First, it facilitates the accurate description and analysis of modes of behavior that correspond better to what we see in the course of macroeconomic fluctuations. Second, macroeconomics can be built on more realistic micro foundations, so consciences can rest easier...." Specific reference is made by Solow to attempts made to incorporate monopolistic competition into aggregative models, such as Dixit-Stiglitz formalisation of the demand for a group of goods that are systematically imperfect substitutes for one another. In his view, this formulation "deserves the attention it gets; it works very neatly."

In an interview in 2002, he provides further elaboration of the underlying reasoning. There are two polar perspectives which can be taken about a modern capitalist economy. One view is that the system works so well. Markets clear all the time. Imperfections work themselves out. Competition eventually triumphs, especially "if the state keeps its paws off things." The alternative perspective is to say that the whole thing is hopelessly flawed. "There are asymmetries of information (By the way, nobody in the world today, after Enron and Arthur Andersen and all that, is ever going to be able to argue that information gets around. It does not.) There are substantial elements of monopoly. Even international trade does not necessarily clear that up." And there are inflexibilities, rigidities in the price and wage mechanism. Capitalism cannot be made to work well, and therefore we might as well have the state or some other agency run everything. Solow states: "I...stand squarely in the common-sensical center.... My view is that we know no better way of running an economy than market capitalism.... But there are many ways in which a market capitalist economy malfunctions. And one of the ways it malfunctions – and now I'm getting very close to Keynes – is it can have excess supply of goods in general and not be able to fix that by itself...there are periods of time when we have persistent excess supply or excess demand, and it is a function of the government to repair the malfunction." Solow does not, of course, believe that governments work beautifully. He advocates use of monetary policy and strengthening the mechanism of automatic stabilisers.

In regard to controversy surrounding globalisation and the opposition to it from some sections in the third world countries, Solow observes that open-economy partisans tend to look at overall progress and flush off the fact that a lot of people lose in this process. He further states that a society in which a small number of people get very rich and a large number of people get very poor is not really progressing, "even if when you add it up and average it, it appears to show rapid progress."

One of the by products of Solow's involvement in the work on projects at Manpower Demonstration Research Corporation, Russell Sage Foundation, and others is a "reinforced scepticism" about the way that labour and product markets are handled by the currently fashionable style in the macroeconomics of the short and medium run. "The traditional assumptions are sometimes useful, or even necessary, but have to be treated 'very gingerly' and not simply given the benefit of the doubt."

Solow is credited to have one of the sharpest intelligences, perhaps the sharpest intelligence--according to R.C.O. Matthews--among economists of the present time. Nobody better understands economics, both its limits and its possibilities, than Solow. Any gathering of economists or any collection of papers is enlivened by his participation. He has not sought fame and influence by adopting extreme positions on policy matters. His wit and clarity of expression are well known. He once quipped: "The best thing that you can say about Reaganomics is that it happened in a fit of inattention." Dismissing a rival's theory he said: "Intellectually soft as a grape."

9.5 SELECT BIBLIOGRAPHY OF ROBERT SOLOW'S WORKS

9.5.1 BOOKS

1963 Capital Theory and Rate of Return, Oxford University Press, New York.

1964 Sources of Unemployment in the U.S., Oxford University Press, New York.

1969 Growth Theory: An Exposition, Oxford University Press, New York.

1970 a Price Expectations and the Behavior of the Price Level, Oxford University Press, New York.

b (with R. Dorfman and P.A. Samuelson), Linear Programming and Economic Analysis,McGraw-Hill, New York.

1995 (with J. B. Taylor), Inflation, Unemployment and Monetary Policy, Alvin Hansen Symposium Series on Public Policy, Harvard University Press, Cambridge, MA.

1998 Monopolistic Competition and Economic Theory, Frederico Caffe Lectures, Cambridge University Press, Cambridge.

2002 (with A.B. Krueger eds.), Roaring Nineties: Can Full Employment Be Sustained? Russell Sage Foundation, New York.

2005 (ed.) Structural Reform and Economic Policy, International Economic Association, Palgrave Macmillan, London.

9.5.2 ARTICLES

1951 a "A Note on Dynamic Multipliers," Econometrica, Vol.19, July.

b "Some Long Run Aspects of the Distribution of Wage Incomes," Econometrica, Vol.19, July.

1952 "On the Structure of Linear Models," Econometrica, Vol.20, Jan.

1953 a "A Note on the Price Level and Interest Rate in a Growth Model," RES, Vol.21, No.1.

b (with P. A. Samuelson), "Balanced Growth under Constant Returns to Scale," Econometrica, Vol.21, No.3.

1954 a "A New Survey of Demand Analysis," REStat, Vol.36, Feb.

b "The Survival of Mathematical Economics," REStat, Vol.36, Nov.

1956 "A Contribution to the Theory of Economic Growth," QJE, Vol.70, No.1.

1957 "Technical Challenge and the Aggregate Production Function," REStat, Vol.39, No.3.

1960 "Investment and Technical Progress," in Mathematical Methods in the Social Sciences, (K.J. Arrow et al.eds.) Stanford University Press, Stanford, Ca.

1966 (with J. Tobin et al.eds.), "Neoclassical Growth with Fixed Factor Proportions," RES, Vol.34, Apr.

1987 "Growth Theory and After," Nobel Lecture, AER, Vol.78, No.3.

2000 "Toward a Macroeconomics of the Medium Run," JEP, Vol.14, No.1.

2007 "The last 50 years in Growth Theory and the Next 10," Oxford Review of Economic Policy, Vol.23, No.1.

9.6 WORKS OF OTHERS

Cass, D. (1965), "Optimum Growth in an Aggregate Model of Capital Accumulation," Econometrica, Vol.34, No.4.

Matthews, R.C.O (1988), "The Work of Robert M. Solow," ScandJE, Vol.90, No.1.

Prescott, E.C. (1988), "Robert M. Solow's Neoclassical Growth Model: An Influential Contribution to Economics," ScandJE, Vol.90, No.1.

CHAPTER 10

ROBERT EMERSON LUCAS Jr.

(1937 –)

The Royal Swedish Academy of Sciences has awarded the 1995 Nobel Memorial Prize in Economic Sciences to Professor Robert Emerson Lucas, Jr., University of Chicago, U.S.A., for having developed and applied the hypothesis of rational expectations and thereby having transformed macroeconomic analysis and deepened our understanding of economic policy.

Robert Lucas is one of the economists who have had significant influence on macroeconomic research since 1970. This work has brought about a swift and radical development in the following directions: application of the rational expectations hypothesis, rise of an equilibrium theory of business cycles, insights into the impediments in using economic policy for controlling the economy, and the prospects of sound evaluation of economic policy using statistical methods.

Expectations about the future are prominently important to economic decision-making by households, firms and organisations. A number of examples can be cited. For instance, wage formation where expectations about the inflation rate and future demand for labour influence the contracted wage level which, in turn, affects future actual inflation. Likewise, many other economic variables are to a large extent governed by expectations about future conditions. Lucas is credited to have won the Prize for work on how people form their expectations that overturned the basis for governmental fine-tuning.

Despite the major importance of expectations, economic analysis has for a long time not paid serious attention to the issue. During 1970's, it was not common to assume arbitrarily specified or even static expectations, as for example, assuming that the future price level will be the same as the current price level. If not static expectations, adaptive expectations were assumed – that is, the expected future price level was mechanically adjusted to the deviation between today's price level and the price level expected earlier.

Rational expectations are genuinely forward-looking. The rational expectations hypothesis postulates that economic agents utilise available information without making systematic mistakes implied by earlier theories. The information is constantly updated and reinterpreted in order to form expectations. Sometimes the consequences of rational expectations are striking, as in the case of economic policy. John Muth was the first economist to make precise formulation of the rational expectations hypothesis in 1961.

However, it has not gained much prominence until the 1970's when Lucas extended it to models of the aggregate economy. In a number of path-breaking articles, Lucas has shown the far-reaching consequences of rational expectations formation, specially relating to the effects of economic policy and the appraisal of these effects using econometric methods (that is, statistical methods particularly adopted for studying economic relationships). In addition to macroeconomics, Lucas has applied the rational expectations hypothesis to several other fields.

A particularly relevant and outstanding example of Lucas's contributions concerns the change in our understanding of the Phillips curve (displaying a positive relation between inflation and employment in an economy). Impressive empirical support was shown for the Phillips curve in the late 1960's. It was widely regarded as one of the more stable relations in economics. It was interpreted that government authorities have an option to increase employment by pursuing an expansionary economic policy, which raises inflation. This interpretation was criticised by Edmund Phelps and Milton Friedman; they argued that the expectations of the general public would adjust to higher inflation and stand in the way of achieving an enduring increase in employment. As a result, while the short-run Phillips curve is sloping, the long-run curve is vertical. This criticism was not entirely convincing as both Phelps and Friedman assumed adaptive expectations. As critics were quick to point out, such expectations imply a permanent increase in employment if only inflation is allowed to increase over time.

Using the rational expectations hypothesis, Lucas in a study published in 1972 "Expectations and the Neutrality of Money" provided the first theoretically satisfactory explanation of a short-run sloping and long-run vertical Phillips curve. He formulated an "ingenious theoretical model" which generates time series characterised by positive correlation between inflation and unemployment. Lucas has also shown in the paper that any attempt to exploit the Phillips curve and permanently increase employment by pursuing an expansionary economic policy would be futile and would only result in higher inflation. This is the result of agents in the model adjusting their expectations and wage and price formation to the new expected policy. Experience during 1970's and 1980's, when Central Banks and governments allowed inflation to rise in a number of countries, has shown that no permanent gain in employment could be achieved. This insight into the long-run effects of stabilisation policy has gained wide acceptance. It is now the foundation for monetary policy in a number of countries in their endeavours to achieve and maintain a low rate of inflation.

The shortcomings of uncritically depending upon statically estimated macro econometric models to draw conclusions about the changes in economic policy are illustrated by the short-run sloping and long-run vertical Phillips curve. In a study entitled "Econometric Policy Evaluation: A Critique," Lucas demonstrated that relations which had been interpreted as "structural" in econometric analysis were, in fact, influenced by past policy. In 1970's, practically all macro econometric models included relations which could be shown to depend on the fiscal and monetary policy carried out during the estimation period. It is clear that the same relations cannot be used in the simulation exercises designed to predict the effects of another fiscal or monetary policy, the way the models were often used.

The critique voiced by Lucas has had decisive influence on economic policy recommendations. Variations in economic policy often lead to a different outcome if the agents adapt their expectations to the new policy stance. While evaluating the consequences of economic policy shifts (such as, a new exchange rate system, a tax reform, a new monetary policy regime), it has now become common to consider changes in the behaviour of economic agents owing to revised expectations.

Lucas calls for a new research programme, the objective of which is to construct macro econometric models whose relations are not sensitive to policy variations – the models have to be "equilibrium models" characterised by rational expectations. That is, all important variables in the model have to be determined within the system on the basis of interactions among economic agents who are rational and have rational expectations operating in a well-specified economic environment. Furthermore, the models should be formulated in such a way that they only include parameters that are policy-independent; that is, those coefficients which describe the relations of the models. This presupposes sound microeconomic foundations. The parameters are estimated using econometric methods developed for the purpose. Innovative attempts to derive and estimate such models have subsequently been tried in a number of areas, such as asset pricing on financial markets and empirical analysis of consumption, investment and employment with mixed success.

The employment of powerful and operational methods in order to draw conclusions from models with rational expectations helped rapid development of macroeconomic analysis and has gradually become part of the standard tool box. Without the development of these methods, it would have been almost impossible to make clear-cut statements in specific situations. Rational expectations have now been accepted as the natural basis for further studies of expectation formation with respect to limited rationality, limited computational capacity and gradual learning.

Lucas has also pioneered new areas of research such as equilibrium theory of business cycles where the effects of real and monetary disturbances on the business cycle are studied. Initially, the equilibrium theory of business cycles depended upon the assumption of completely flexible prices and immediate adjustment to equilibrium on commodity and labour markets with perfect competition. It is pointed out, however, that Lucas's methodological approach is not inconsistent with sticky prices and various market failures such as imperfect competition and imperfect information. These imperfections and frictions should be introduced as explaining decisions by rational agents and interactions in a well-specified choice situation. This approach seems a satisfactory method and has led to greatest advances in modelling frictions and market imperfections.

Lucas's work has given rise to a new field of econometrics – rational expectations econometrics. In this field, to which other researchers have made important contributions, rational expectations hypothesis is used to determine the most efficient statistical methods for estimating economic relations where expectations are the key component.

Besides his work in macroeconomics, Lucas has made remarkable contributions to financial economics, international finance, monetary theory, investment theory, dynamic public economics and the theory of economic growth. In these areas, Lucas has carried out studies which had a significant impact, thus generating extensive new literature.

10.1 A BRIEF BIOGRAPHICAL OUTLINE: ROBERT LUCAS

Robert E. Lucas Jr was born on September 15, 1937 in Yakima, Washington, U.S.A., the oldest child of Robert Emerson Lucas and Jane Templeton Lucas. He attended Seattle Public Schools, graduating from Roosevelt High School in 1955. He joined University of Chicago on a scholarship. He received his B.A. Degree in 1959, majoring in History. Having obtained a Woodrow Wilson Doctoral Fellowship, Lucas did his graduate work in the University of Chicago. In his autobiographical note, Lucas states: "In the fall of 1960, I began Milton Friedman's price theory sequence. I had been looking forward to this famous course all summer, but it was more exciting than anything I had imagined." He also admitted: "Friedman's course ended my long career as a conscientious, near-straight A student. Now if a course did not promise to be a life-changing experience, I lost interest and attended only sporadically. I accumulated many C's, but also a lot of time to pursue what I found interesting." He received his Ph.D. in economics from the University of Chicago in 1964.

Lucas began his academic career as Assistant Professor of Economics at Carnegie Institute of Technology (now Carnegie-Mellon University), where he became Associate Professor in 1967 and Professor of Economics in 1970. In 1974 he returned to Chicago as a faculty member. He has held a professorship in Economics at the University of Chicago since 1975. In 1980, Lucas became the John Dewey Distinguished Service Professor at Chicago, the position he has been holding since then. His graduate teaching and research has been in monetary theory, international trade, fiscal policy, and economic growth ("all the basic topics in macroeconomics").

Lucas has been awarded a number of Fellowships and has been bestowed various honours. He received Brookings Fellowship (1961-1962), Ford Foundation Faculty Fellowship (1966-1967), Guggenheim Fellowship (1981-1982), Fellowship of Econometric Society (1975), Membership of the American Academy of Arts and Sciences (1980) and Membership of the National Academy of Sciences (1981). Lucas served as Vice Chairman (1975-1983), and Chairman, Department of Economics, University of Chicago, Associate Editor of Journal of Economic Theory and Journal of Monetary Economics and Editor of Journal of Political Economy. He was an Executive Committee member and Vice-President of the American Economic Association and Council Member and Senior Vice- President of

Econometric Society (1997) and President, American Economic Association (2002). Lucas delivered numerous Invited Lectures of which mention may be made of Marshall Lectures, Cambridge, England (1985), Yrjo Jahnsson Lectures, Helsinki, Finland (1985), Lionel McKenzie Lecture, University of Rochester (1987), Hicks Lecture, Oxford University (1989), Harry Johnson Lecture, Royal Economic Society (1991) and Fisher-Schultz Lecture, Econometric Society, Cambridge, England (1991).

10.2 A BRIEF SUMMARY OF ROBERT LUCAS'S CONTRIBUTIONS

Robert Lucas has made outstanding contributions to several areas of economics, though he is best known and most influential for his work in macroeconomic theory and policy. His early work was on the theory of investment and labour supply and wage-price dynamics. His later work included building up of a unified general equilibrium model of asset pricing under uncertainty by integrating ideas from economics and finance, discussing the issue of time-consistent optimal fiscal and monetary policy in a dynamic exchange economy and contributions to growth theory by formulating endogenous growth models.

The survey attempted here is organised under the following heads:

1. The Rational Expectations Hypothesis;
2. An Equilibrium Theory of Business Cycles;
3. Macro econometric Evaluation of Economic Policy; and
4. Other important Contributions.

10.2.1 RATIONAL EXPECTATIONS HYPOTHESIS

Stanley Fischer observes that the field of macroeconomics – both Keynesian and monetarist – was ripe for reform and improvement by 1970's. By the beginning of 1970's, Keynesian macro models were basically founded on Hicks's IS-LM framework with a Phillips curve and mark up equations tagged on to generate wage and price dynamics. Demand functions in these models were formulated, as Fischer points out, using sophisticated microeconomic theory, such as life cycle consumption function, neoclassical theory of investment demand, demand for money on the lines suggested in Baumol-Tobin's inventory theoretic approach and term-structure interest rate relationship. The development of aggregate supply function was far from satisfactory, though in the opinion of Fischer it was quite sophisticated as in the MIT-Penn-SSRC model. The models generally embraced the adaptive expectations approach. No specific formulation was made though there was awareness of the differing responses from consumers and investors to tax changes that were transient and those that were permanent.

It was realised by many economists by mid-1960's that the Phillips curve explanation was "theoretically inadequate." The robust empirical support to the absence of long-run trade off between inflation and unemployment put forward by Phelps and Friedman had lent credibility to this point of view. On the other hand, the viewpoint that there exists no exploitable short-run trade off has not been established. Further, a view has gained ground that implementation of a systematic monetary policy has real effects.

Lucas, in his Prize lecture, states that no one at the time considered the situation in regard to the field of macroeconomics as healthy. "Everyone paid lip service to the idea of unification of micro and macro economics or of discovering the microeconomic 'foundations' of macroeconomic theories and a vast amount of creative and valuable economics focused on inter-temporal decision problems, was inspired by this goal. The macroeconomic modelling in 1960's involved combining into a single model the individual or sector models arising out of inter-temporal theorising. However, models of individual decisions over time invariably involve expected future prices. Many current decisions are importantly influenced by economic agents' expectations about the future which, in turn, determine to a considerable degree the development of the economy. A common example is wage formation. Expectations about future inflation and expected future demand for labour influence the wage agreements for the period of the wage contract. These wage agreements strongly determine the realised inflation (expected inflation influencing the agreed-upon wages). Likewise, market interest rates vary with expected future inflation; expected future dividends and capital gains influence corporate share prices; and so on."

Despite their importance, a very superficial and unsatisfactory treatment was given to the issue of expectations for a long time. Some microeconomic analyses treated the future prices as known. Some analysts introduced 'exogenous or even static expectations' such that the expected future price level was equal to today's price level. In some cases, expectations of the future were approximated as an arbitrary function of observed variables. The assumption of adaptive expectations was considered an improvement. Such expectations are retrogressive in a mechanical fashion. Lucas comments: "The 'Church Supper' models assembled from such individual components implied behavior of actual equilibrium prices and incomes that bore no relation to, and were in general grossly inconsistent with, the price expectations that the theory imputed to individual agents." This modelling inconsistency came to be recognised when it was realised how important and explicit a role inter-temporal elements and expectations have come to play. This inconsistency was brought out by John Muth in his 1961 article "Rational Expectations and the Theory of Price Movements" and showed "how it could be removed by taking into account the influences of prices, including future prices, on quantities and simultaneously the effects of quantities on equilibrium prices." The formulation of rational expectations by Muth forced the modeller towards "a market equilibrium point of view."

L. Svensson explains how "rational expectations are forward looking and imply a much more sophisticated, and more realistic way of forming expectations; agents learn from their mistakes, use their intellectual capacity to understand the way the economy works and exploit available information in an efficient way." The rational expectations hypothesis is interpreted as extension of the assumption of rational behaviour of individuals and firms in dynamic situations characterised by uncertain future, imperfect information and positive cost of information collection. It does not assume possession of identical information set by all economic agents nor does it assume that all economic agents know the true economic model. The only assumption implied is that economic agents use in the best way possible all available information and seek more information making a cost-benefit analysis.

By early 1970's it was clear that there was an imperative need to put macroeconomics on a general equilibrium basis that incorporated rational expectations. Lucas in his Prize lecture says that by the 1960's, two closely related general equilibrium frameworks were readily available "for thinking about economic dynamics." One model was the mathematical model of general equilibrium developed by Hicks, Arrow, Debreu and Mckenzie, in which the commodity vector is defined to include dated claims to goods, "possibly made contingent on random events." The second general equilibrium framework that was available was developed by Samuelson and seemed better suited to the study of monetary questions. It is an overlapping generations model in which money is the only asset with no direct use in either consumption or production. People live for two periods only and work and save when young and consume in both periods.

Lucas used the latter model in his 1972 paper "Expectations and the Neutrality of Money" in an attempt to show how neutrality of money might be reconciled with the appearance of a short-term stimulus from a monetary expansion. He presents in his Prize lecture a simple version of the model. In the model, the economy is populated by two age cohorts, one young and the other old and there is a constant population. At the end of each year, the old die, the young become old and a new young group arrives. Other assumptions of the Lucas model include absence of a family structure implying no inheritances, bequests and no financial support by one cohort for another. It is also assumed that only the young work and produce goods while old only consume goods and further that goods cannot be stored for future consumption. In this society, young must be induced to produce for the consumption of their "contemporary old." An institution, such as a social security system or as Samuelson noted, a monetary system, may be able to achieve this outcome. Assuming that money in the hypothetical economy will circulate forever, being exchanged over and over again for goods in a single competitive spot market, an equilibrium price will be established. If the money supply remains constant, and evenly distributed over the old, the equilibrium price will be constant. Lucas shows that if money supply is "somehow" increased once-and-for-all, the equilibrium price level will be increased in the same proportion, and quantities of labour and production will not be affected at all, as argued by Hume and quantity theorists. That is, money is neutral.

To show how the issue of neutrality of money becomes more complicated, Lucas in his model replaces the assumption of once-and-for-all constant money supply change with the assumption that the quantity of money grows at a constant percentage rate. As regards the way the new money gets introduced into the system, Lucas explicitly assumes that each young person receives an equal share of the newly created money, in between his youth and old age, and that the size of this addition to his cash is independent of the amount he earns by working. A rational expectations equilibrium for this model yields a price level that increases between periods at exactly the rate of growth of the money supply. Furthermore, the faster the money grows, the more important is the "overnight transfer" relative to the cash accumulated through working, leading to the money transfers diluting the return from working. As the inflation rate rises, production of goods declines, making everyone worse off. Lucas concludes: "This is a non-neutrality of money, a real effect of a money change...a kind of tax" – inflation tax.

To get the inflation tax out of the picture, Lucas now makes an assumption that the fiscal transfers through which money supply expands are made in proportion to the balances one has earned through working. He demonstrates that it is not adequate simply to introduce uncertainty into the model in order to get an output effect from a monetary shock. Lucas states: "we need to imagine that the exchange of money for goods takes place in some manner other than in a centralized Walrasian market." In the above cited 1972 article, Lucas has made an assumption that exchange occurs in two markets, each with a different number of suppliers of goods. In such a situation, Lucas argues that a given increase in price can indicate to a supplier that the money transfer is large, in which case there would be no output effect or it can signal that there are only a few suppliers in the market, in which case the supplier responds by increasing his output. The best the individual producer can do, given his limited information or imperfect information, is to hedge. The increase in production that has come about is because of lack of complete information. Thus, Lucas in his 1972 article reconciles the long-run neutrality of money with a short-run trade off and concludes "...anticipated money changes will not stimulate production and that at least some unanticipated changes can do so."

The central lesson of the theoretical work of the 1970's by Lucas and others is the importance of drawing a distinction between anticipated and unanticipated changes in money as the effects in each case are different. The important conclusion of the work is that any rapid growth of money would produce only high inflation under conditions of perfect information but would produce both inflation and increased output under imperfect information. The Phillips curve relationship results are entirely from the economic agents' imperfect information about the current state of the economy. But it could not be used by policymakers. Fischer summarises: "At the technical level, Lucas claimed to establish, under certain restrictions, the existence of unique rational expectations equilibrium in which the price function on which agents based their expectation was the actual equilibrium price function. Furthermore, he argued, any change in the money supply process would change this function in such a way that the systematic part of monetary policy would not affect output."

Apart from the impact the article has had on macroeconomics, it has supplied a model that illustrates the information-conveying role of prices. For example, in the theory of finance, an efficient market is defined as one in which the prices reflect all relevant information available in the market.

Another paper of Lucas that is related to the field of rational expectations is his "Some International Evidence on Output-Inflation Trade-offs" which brings out important implications. For example, it shows that any systematic monetary policy has no real effects; another implication is that the slope of the Phillips curve is a function of the variability of the money stock.

The two papers together constitute the essence of Lucas's analytic contribution to the rational expectations equilibrium approach. According to Fischer, Lucas's achievement is to construct a rigorous model in which "all markets clear and all agents optimize in which (1) a Phillips curve is implied by imperfect information about the current state of the economy, (2) the policy ineffectiveness result holds, and (3) apparently structural parameters of the economy are policy dependent. The rational expectations assumption is essential to the latter two results."

10.2.2 AN EQUILIBRIUM THEORY OF BUSINESS CYCLES

Lucas made equally outstanding contribution to the area of equilibrium theory of business cycles. After the Second World War, economists treated business cycles as disequilibrium phenomena and business cycles research was primarily dominated by Keynesians. The research in the area assumed that key variables in the analysis are exogenously fixed – that is, not determined within the model. The implication of this assumption is that supply of goods and labour in the respective markets can be rationed. An alternative formulation that was made was that key variables such as wages and prices are "mechanically adjusted" to clear the excess supply in each of the markets. That is how Phillips curve approach attempted at explaining wage inflation as a decreasing function of the rate of unemployment in the economy. No adequate theoretical explanation was proffered for such postulated relations. Critics were dissatisfied with this lack of rigour and their critique carried particularly special weight "since it showed that the Keynesian approach, in effect, assumed agents to behave consistently against their own best interests."

Despite its unsatisfactory theoretical underpinnings, Phillips curve approach received considerable empirical support by the end of the 1960's. As mentioned above, Phelps and Friedman, taking into consideration the effects of expectations (assuming adaptive expectations) argued against the existence of a long-run trade-off between inflation and unemployment. They emphasised that the long-run Phillips curve would become vertical and the "natural rate of unemployment would be independent of inflation." A short-run sloping and long-run vertical Phillips curve was for the first time presented by Lucas based upon satisfactory theoretical formulation. In the model of Lucas, as outlined earlier, economic agents do not have perfect information as to whether a rise of prices of goods in the market is caused by an increasing demand for their product or is a general increase in the price level as a result of augmentation of money supply. Thus, Lucas's analysis is an equilibrium analysis. All the variables are endogenously determined; the agents set the variables controlled by them in line with their objectives and the agents possess rational expectations regarding the future development of the variables in the model. Svensson remarks: "Lucas formulated the model's equilibrium as a functional equation for the functions describing the responses of the model's endogenous variables to exogenous random disturbances, and he also solved the functional equation.... This was the first example of a rigorous equilibrium business cycle model with endogenous rational expectations. The model's main importance eventually derived from its role as a methodological example."

Lucas's 1977 paper "Understanding Business Cycles" outlines the rational expectations approach to business cycle theory. In a later work he states the objective: "One would like a theory which accounts for the observed in quantities (employment, consumption, investment) as an optimizing response to observed movements in prices." According to Fischer, the theory that Lucas sketches "starts from the Lucas supply function, emphasizing the role of inter-temporal labour substitution. Capital and inventories are then added, followed by aggregate shocks associated with money growth." As Lucas and Sargent observe, the equilibrium business cycle models are econometrically tractable and hold considerable promise. "Our intent is...to extend the equilibrium methods which have been applied to many economic problems to cover a phenomenon which has so far restricted their application: the business cycle." In the 1975 paper "An Equilibrium Model of the Business Cycle," Lucas shows that the propagation mechanism for the business cycle is provided by capital accumulation and slow diffusion of information.

In the beginning, Lucas's development of equilibrium business cycles analysis is made under the assumption of fully flexible prices and instantaneous realisation of equilibrium on goods and factor markets. However, it was realised later that his approach is not inconsistent with market imperfections, frictions and sticky prices. The model only requires that such imperfections and frictions have to be explained as resulting from agents' decisions and interactions in their environment and be not introduced in an arbitrary fashion. This approach is explained by Lucas while discussing models with prices fixed during a specific contract period as follows: "If...contract length is viewed as emerging from a decision problem solved by agents, then these models, so elaborated, would be equilibrium models."

Lucas's pioneering contribution to equilibrium business cycles has generated much research activity. A number of followers, such as Prescott, in the real business cycle literature, have focused on real disturbances in productivity rather than disturbances on the monetary front as a cause of business cycle variations. In recent years, there is a noticeable revival of interest in the role of monetary disturbances in generating equilibrium business cycles.

10.2.3 MACRO ECONOMETRIC EVALUATION OF ECONOMIC POLICY

In the 1975 paper entitled "Econometric Policy Evaluation – A Critique," Lucas has made an outstanding contribution to macro econometric evaluation of economic policy that has enormously influenced the profession. In it, he suggested that the estimated parameters that are considered as "structural" in econometric analysis of economic policy really depend on the economic policy followed during the estimation period. For example, in an analysis of Phillips curve, the variance of unobserved disturbances in money supply and money demand may influence the slope of the curve. As such, the parameters may vary as a result of shifts in the pursued policy which has an important bearing on economic policy decisions. The consequences of shifts in economic policy are many a time different if the economic agents adjust their expectations to the new policy than if they do not adjust. Because of Lucas's work, we notice that these days the effects of changing expectations are taken into consideration while evaluating the consequences of new policy measures – a tax reform, or a new monetary policy, or a new exchange rate system.

Before the work of Lucas, macro econometric models usually contained behavioural functions in the reduced form. The estimated parameters in those functions might implicitly depend on the policy regime. Svensson observes: "Parameters estimated under a particular policy regime were used in simulations with other policy rules, for the purpose of predicting the effect on crucial macroeconomic variables. With regime-dependent parameters, the predictions could turn out to be erroneous and misleading." Therefore, what is required to obviate this problem is a good understanding of the relationship between the standard behavioural functions in macroeconomic models and the result of dynamic optimisation in microeconomic models of economic behaviour. In the words of Svensson: "...Lucas could theoretically convince his contemporaries as well as later economists that three crucial building blocks of traditional macro models, the consumption function, the investment function and the Phillips Curve, had parameters that were regime dependent."

The work of Lucas is also a call to researchers in macroeconomics, particularly macro econometric model-builders, to construct models in terms of policy independent parameters to facilitate evaluation of alternative policies. Then, the parameters are estimated, employing specially developed econometric methods – rational expectations econometrics.

This principle has been fruitfully used by researchers since then. For example, dependence of labour supply on wages, unemployment benefits and taxes; similarly, dependence of the behaviour of consumers on taxes and transfers and so on. It is appropriate to point out that some of the early contributions using rational expectations econometrics were brought together in a volume edited by Lucas in collaboration with Sargent in Rational Expectations and Econometric Practice.

10.2.4 OTHER IMPORTANT CONTRIBUTIONS

Another significant contribution of Lucas concerns asset pricing. He constructed a theoretical model for the determination of asset prices under conditions of uncertainty. Before him, the finance literature contained partial equilibrium models of asset prices such as Sharpe, Lintner and Mossin's the Capital Asset Pricing Model (CAPM). In 1973, Merton extended the CAPM (a two- period model) to a more general inter-temporal setting. He has studied the relation of asset prices to economic environment as described by a finite vector of state variables (instead of the original CAPM in which individual preferences were defined only over the mean and variance of asset returns). In his 1978 paper, Lucas formulated a model showing the relationship between real activity in the economy, preferences for consumption goods and asset prices in a general equilibrium with rational expectations.

Lucas's model assumes a single representative consumer, a random quantity of non-storable consumption good produced by numerous identical production units, exogenous output following a Markov process with a time-invariant transition function. An asset is defined as a claim to the stochastic stream of output or dividends from a productive unit. It is postulated that consumption of the good and ownership of assets are determined each period in competitive stock markets. Each consumer is assumed to hold one unit of each asset and consumes all dividends each period. He derives the asset prices that support a rational expectations competitive equilibrium.

Robert Hall opines: "It [Lucas's paper] bridged a gap between the treatment of optimal consumption behavior in economics and the asset pricing models used in finance.... Few papers today address issues in equilibrium asset pricing without referring to Lucas's seminal work."

Yet another significant contribution of Lucas is in the area of economic growth. He was critical of the basic neo-classical growth model, particularly in regard to its prediction that incomes, growth rates and returns to the capital will be equalised across countries in contrast with the observed reality – huge and persistent differentials in international growth rates and real wages and small capital flows from rich to poor countries. He put forward two endogenous growth models. Human capital accumulation with an externality in human capital drives the growth process in one of the models, while the other model is driven by learning by doing in purely external form. It is to be noted that Lucas's first model produces growth even in the absence of the human capital externality. He recognises that human capital, as opposed to physical capital, is not internationally mobile. However, his human capital externality model explains the "strong incentive for individuals of all skill levels to migrate from less developed to developed countries." Lucas's second model of endogenous growth focuses on the interaction of growth and trade rather than on the details of growth. Through this model, he shows how increasing returns can negate the general presumptions about the positive welfare effects of trade. Hall remarks: "This provocative model has helped spawn a whole school of papers on the interaction between growth and trade in models with increasing returns and externalities."

10.3 CONCLUDING OBSERVATIONS

It is generally agreed that Robert Lucas's work had had the greatest impact on the development of macro economics and macro econometrics since 1970. According to Karl Shell, then editor of the Journal of Economic Theory in which Lucas's initial Rational Expectations article was published, after rejection by leading journals: "Lucas's contribution was built on three giant predecessors--the notion of rational expectations itself, which has been introduced by John Muth; the overlapping generations model of

Paul Samuelson; and an early use of the idea of asymmetric information from the island model of Edmund Phelps." There are a number of economists like Fischer who are of the view that "over time, it has become clear while rational expectations has been the most important contribution to the analysis of economic policy, the equilibrium approach is the more important contribution to macroeconomic analysis." Lucas's work "transformed macroeconomic analysis and deepened our understanding of economic policy" as the citation remarks. The success of the revolution is also ascribed to the work of economists, some of them co-authors, such as Thomas Sargent, Edward Prescott, Robert Barro, Neil Wallace and John Taylor.

Robert Hall particularly emphasises Lucas's contribution to economic dynamics. In his opinion, Lucas contributed to the transformation of the theory and practice of economic dynamics by supplying new tools and providing new ways of thinking about dynamic problems. It is also said that Lucas has been immensely successful in capturing the essence of important economic issues in his abstract and rigorous models.

In his Presidential Address to the American Economic Association in January 2003, "Macroeconomic Priorities," Lucas states:

Macroeconomics was born as a distinct field in the 1940's, as a part of the intellectual response to the Great Depression. The term then referred to the body of knowledge and expertise that we viewed would prevent the recurrence of that economic disaster.

In his opinion, macroeconomics in this original sense has succeeded in the sense that its central problem of prevention of depression has been solved. However, there remain important gains in welfare from better fiscal policies. Lucas argues that these are "gains from providing people with better incentives to work and to save, not from better fine tuning of spending flows." On the basis of U.S. experience of fifty years, he observes: "the potential for welfare gain from better long-run supply side policies exceeds by far the potential from further improvements in short-run demand management."

Lucas at the end of his Prize lecture remarks as to how his and other researchers' work has shown the way the general equilibrium can add discipline to the study of an economy's distributed lag response to shocks, as well as to the study of the nature of the shocks themselves. As to how the macroeconomic theory of the future will develop, he concludes: "...the progress will result from the continued effort to formulate explicit theories that fit the facts and that the best and most practical macroeconomics will make use of developments in basic economic theory."

10.4 SELECT BIBLIOGRAPHY OF ROBERT LUCAS'S WORKS

10.4.1 BOOKS

1981 a (co-editor with T. J. Sargent), Rational Expectations and Econometric Practice, University of Minnesota Press, Minneapolis.

b Studies in Business Cycle Theory, MIT Press, Cambridge, MA.

1987 Models of Business Cycles, Yrjo Jahnsson Lectures, Basil Blackwell, Oxford.

1989 (with N. L. Stokey and E.C. Prescott), Recursive Methods in Economic Dynamics, Harvard University Press, Cambridge, MA.

10.4.2 ARTICLES

1962 (with Z.Griliches, G.S.Maddala and N.Wallace), "Notes on Estimated Aggregate Quarterly Consumption Functions," Econometrica, Vol.31, no.3.

1967 a "Optimal Investment Policy and the Flexible Accelerator," IER, Vol.8, No.1.

b "Adjustment Costs and the Theory of Supply," JPE, Vol.75, Aug.

1969 a (with L. A. Rapping), "Real Wages, Employment and Inflation," JPE, Vol.77, Sep/Oct.

b (with L. A. Rapping), "Price Expectations and the Phillips Curve," AER, Vol.59, No.3.

1970 a (with E. C. Prescott), "Investment Under Uncertainty," Econometrica, Vol.39, No.5.

b (with L.A. Rapping), "Real wages, Employment and Inflation," in E.S. Phelps et al. (eds.) The New Microeconomics in Employment and Inflation Theory, W. W. Norton, New York.

1972 a (with E. C. Prescott), "A Note on Price Systems in Infinite Dimensional Space," IER, Vol.13, No.2.

b "Expectations and the Neutrality of Money," JET, Vol.4, Apr.

c (with L. A. Rapping), "Unemployment in the Great Depression: Is there a Full Explanation?" JPE, Vol.80, No.1.

d "Econometric Testing of the Natural Rate Hypothesis," in O. Eckstein (ed) The Econometrics of Price Determination Conference, Washington.

1973 "Some International Evidence on Output-Inflation Trade-Offs," AER, Vol.63, No.3.

1974 (with E. C. Prescott), "Equilibrium Search and Unemployment," JET, Vol.7, Feb. Reprinted in P. A. Diamond and M. Rothschild (eds.), Uncertainty in Economics: A Book of Readings.

1975 a "Econometric Policy Evaluation: A Critique," in K. Brunner and A. Meltzer (eds.), The Phillips Curve and Labor Markets, North-Holland, Amsterdam.

b "An Equilibrium Model of the Business Cycle," JPE, Vol.83, Dec.

1977 "Understanding Business Cycles," in K. Brunner and A. Meltzer (eds.), Stabilization of the Domestic and International Economy, North-Holland, Amsterdam.

1978 a "Asset Prices in an Exchange Economy," Econometrica, Vol.46, Dec.

b "Unemployment Policy," AER, Vol.68, No.2.

1979 (with T. J. Sargent), "After Keynesian Macroeconometrics," in After the Phillips Curve, Federal Reserve Bank of Boston, Conference Series No.19.

1980 a "Rules, Discretion and the Role of the Economic Advisor," in Stanley Fischer (ed.) Rational Expectations and Economic Policy, University of Chicago Press for NBER, Chicago, Ill.

b "Methods and Problems in Business Cycle Theory," JMCB, Vol.12, No.4.

1981 a "Distributed Lags and Optimal Investment Policy," in Rational Expectations and Econometric Practice, R.E. Lucas and T. J. Sargent (eds.), University of Minnesota Press, Minneapolis.

b "Optimal Investment with Rational Expectations," in Lucas and Sargent, op. cit.

c "Tobin and Monetarism: A Review Article," JEL, Vol.19, No.2.

1983 (with N. L. Stokey), "Optimal Fiscal and Monetary Policy in an Economy without Capital," JME, Vol.12, No.1.

1984 a (with N. L. Stokey), "Optimal Growth with Many Consumers," JET, Vol.32, No.1.

b "Money in a Theory of Finance," in K. Brunner and A. Meltzer (eds.). Essays on Macroeconomic Implications of Financial and Labor Markets and Political Processes, North-Holland, Amsterdam.

1986 "Principles of Fiscal and Monetary Policy," JME, Vol.17, No.1.

1987 (with N. L. Stokey), "Money and Interest in a Cash-in-Advance Economy," Econometrica, Vol.55, No.3.

1988 "On the Mechanics of Economic Development," JME, Vol.22, July.

1990 a "Liquidity and Interest Rates," JET, Vol.50, Apr.

b "Why Doesn't Capital Flow from Rich to Poor Countries?" AER, Vol.80, No.2.

c "Supply Side Economics: An Analytical Review," OEP, Vol.42, No.2.

1992 "On Efficiency and Distribution," EJ, Vol.102, No.411.

1993 "Making a Miracle," Econometrica, Vol.61, No. 2.

1994 Review of Milton Friedman and Anna J. Schwartz's 'A Monetary History of the United States, 1867-1960,' JME, Vol.34, No.1.

1995 a "Efficiency and Equality in a Simple Model of Efficient Employment Insurance," JET, Vol.66, No.1.

1996 "Monetary Neutrality," Nobel Lecture, JPE, Vol.104, No.4.

2000 a "Inflation and Welfare," Econometrica, Vol.68, No.2.

b "Some Macroeconomics for the 21st Century," JEP, Vol.14, No.1.

2001 (with F. Alvarez and W. E. Weber), "Interest Rates and Inflation," AER, Vol.91, No.2.

2003 "Macroeconomic Priorities," AER, Vol.93, No.1.

2004 "Life Earnings and Rural-Urban Migration," JPE, Vol.92, Feb.

2007 a (with F. Alvarez), "General Equilibrium Analysis of the Eaton-Kortum Model of International Trade," JME, Vol.54, No.6.

b (with M. Golosov), "Menu Costs and Phillips Curves," JPE, Vol.115, No.2.

2009 a "Trade and the Diffusion of Industrial Revolution," American Economic Journal: Macroeconomics, Vol.1, No.1.

b "Ideas and Growth," Economica, Vol.76, No.301.

2011 "What Economists Do?" Journal of Applied Economics, Vol.0, No.1.

10.5 WORKS OF OTHERS

Fischer, S. (1996), "Robert Lucas's Nobel Memorial Prize," ScandJE, Vol.98, No.1.

Hall, R.E. (1996), "Robert Lucas, Recipient of the 1995 Nobel Memorial Prize in Economics," ScandJE, Vol.98, No. 1.

Svensson, L.E. (1996), "The Scientific Contributions of Robert. E. Lucas, Jr." ScandJE, Vol.98, No.1.

CHAPTER 11

ROBERT ALEXANDER MUNDELL

(1932 –)

The Royal Swedish Academy of Sciences has awarded the 1999 Bank of Sweden Prize in Economic Sciences in Memory of Alfred Nobel to Professor Robert A. Mundell, Columbia University, New York, U.S.A. "for his analysis of monetary and fiscal policy under different exchange rate regimes and his analysis of optimum currency areas."

Mundell's work has laid the foundation for the theory which dominates practical policy considerations of monetary and fiscal policy in open economies. Generations of researchers have been inspired and influenced by his writings on monetary dynamics and optimum currency areas. Mundell's contributions remain outstanding and valuable and constitute the core of teaching in the field of international macroeconomics.

The research work of Mundell has had a far-reaching and lasting influence since it combines formal, but still accessible, analysis, intuitive interpretation and results that have immediate implications for policy. Most important of all, Mundell has shown a knack of choosing problems for his analysis "with uncommon (almost prophetic accuracy) in terms of predicting the future development of international monetary arrangements and capital markets." The Royal Swedish Academy specifically mentions that Mundell's contributions serve as a superb reminder of the significance of basic research. At a given point in time, academic achievements might appear rather esoteric; not long afterwards, they may take on great practical relevance and importance.

Robert Mundell has reshaped macroeconomic theory for open economies by posing and answering questions such as the following: How are the effects of monetary and fiscal policy related to the integration of global capital markets? How do these effects depend on whether a country fixes the value of its currency or allows it to float freely; that is, whether the country has a regime of fixed exchange rates or floating exchange rates? Should a country even have a currency of its own?

His most important contributions to the field were made in the 1960's. During the latter half of that decade, Mundell was one of the intellectual leaders in the creative research environment at the University of Chicago. Building on the foundation work of Mundell, many of his students from this period have become successful researchers in the field of macroeconomic theory for open economies.

Mundell's scientific contributions are original. Yet they quickly transformed the research in international macroeconomics and attracted increasing attention in the practically-oriented discussion of stabilisation policy and exchange rate system. A brief stint at the research department of the International Monetary Fund (IMF) during 1961-1963 apparently stimulated Mundell's choice of research problems. It also gave his research additional leverage among economic policy- makers. In several papers published in the early 1960's, Mundell developed his analysis of monetary and fiscal policy – rather stabilisation policy in open economies.

A pioneering and influential article of Mundell analyses the short-run effects of monetary and fiscal policy in an open economy. In the paper, Mundell introduced foreign trade and movements of capital into the IS-LM model of a closed economy developed by 1972 Economics Nobel laureate, Sir John Hicks. While the analysis is simple, the conclusions are numerous, clear and robust. In the paper, Mundell demonstrates that the effects of stabilisation policy crucially depend upon the degree of international capital mobility. Specifically, he has shown that under a regime of floating exchange rates, monetary policy becomes powerful and fiscal policy powerless, whereas the converse is true under a system of fixed exchange rates.

Mundell's research, however, did not stop at short-run analysis. Monetary dynamics is a key theme in several of his important papers. His contributions on dynamics proved to be a watershed for research in international macroeconomics. The contributions introduced a meaningful dynamic approach, based on a clear-cut distinction between stock and flow variables, as well as an analysis of their interaction during the adjustment of an economy to a stable long-run equilibrium. Mundell's work also initiated the much-needed rapprochement between Keynesian short-run analysis and Classical long-run analysis.

Mundell in his article "A Theory of Optimum Currency Areas" raised an important question which, at that time, seemed radical: when is it advantageous for a number of countries/regions to give up their monetary sovereignty in favour of a common currency?

Mundell has made many other contributions, particularly in macroeconomics and international trade theory.

11.1 A BRIEF BIOGRAPHICAL NOTE : ROBERT MUNDELL

Robert A. Mundell was born in Canada in 1932. After completing his undergraduate education at the University of British Columbia, he began his postgraduate studies at University of Washington in Seattle. He felt it was not the right place for his Ph.D. He went to Massachusetts Institute of Technology (MIT) and continued his doctoral work there and at London School of Economics. At London School, he decided to write his thesis for Massachusetts Institute of Technology (MIT) under James E. Meade, the 1977 Nobel

Laureate jointly with Bertil Ohlin. Mundell received his Ph.D. from MIT in 1956 with a thesis on international capital movements. He was a post-doctoral fellow in Political Economy at the University of Chicago in 1956-1957.

He taught at Stanford University and the Johns Hopkins Bologna Center of Advanced International Studies before joining the staff of the International Monetary Fund in 1961. From 1966 to 1971 he was a Professor of Economics at the University of Chicago and Editor of the Journal of Political Economy. From 1965 to 1975, Mundell was (Summer) Professor of International Economics at the Graduate Institute of International Studies in Geneva, Switzerland. Since 1974 he was Professor of Economics at Columbia University, New York. For 1997-1998 Mundell was the AGIP Professor of Economics at the John Hopkins University.

Mundell worked as an adviser to a number of international organisations and agencies including the United Nations, the International Monetary Fund, the World Bank, the European Commission, the Federal Reserve Board, the U.S. Treasury, several governments in Europe and Latin America and the Government of Canada. In 1970 he was a consultant to the Monetary Committee of the European Economic Commission and in 1972-1973 a member of its study group on Economic and Monetary Union in Europe.

The writings of Mundell include over a hundred articles in scientific journals and about ten books. He presented the Frank Graham Memorial Lecture at Princeton University in 1965, the Marshall Lectures at Cambridge University in 1974 and the Ohlin Lectures in 1998. He was the first Rockefeller Research Professor of International Economics at the Brookings Institution in 1964-1965, the Ford Foundation Research Professor of Economics at the University of Chicago in 1965-66, the Repap Professor of Economics at McGill University in 1989-1990 and the Richard Fox Professor of Economics at the University of Pennsylvania, Philadelphia in 1990-1991. He has been associated with Chinese University of Hongkong since 2009.

Mundell was recipient of a number of prizes and fellowships including a Guggenheim Fellowship (1971), the Jacques Rueff Medal and Prize (1983) and the Distinguished Fellow Award from the American Economic Association (1997). He was made a fellow of the American Academy of Arts and Sciences in October, 1998.

11.2 A BRIEF SUMMARY OF ROBERT MUNDELL'S CONTRIBUTIONS

Mundell's contributions are conveniently divided under the following two heads.

1. Stabilization Policy In Open Economies
2. Optimum Currency Areas

11.2.1 STABILIZATION POLICY IN OPEN ECONOMIES

In his Prize lecture titled "A Reconsideration of the Twentieth Century," Mundell states: "I want to bring out the role of the monetary factor as a determinant of political events.

Specifically, I will argue that many of the political changes in the [Twentieth] Century have been caused by little understood perturbations in the international monetary system; while these in turn have been a consequence of the rise of the United States and mistakes of its financial arm, the Federal Reserve System." Mundell's analysis of the U.S. macroeconomic policy identifies the problems affecting the international monetary system. He categorically states: "Until 1960's, U.S. macroeconomic policy was based more on closed economy principles than on the requirements of an international monetary system. Monetary and fiscal policies were directed at the needs of the internal balance and the balance of payments was all but ignored.... The problem of the appropriate mix for monetary and fiscal policy came to the foreground...during 1961."

Mundell, when he had joined the Research Department at the IMF, was asked to look into the theoretical aspects of monetary-fiscal policy mix. Three schools of thought about the policy mix have surfaced at that time among economists. Keynesians pushed for easy money and an increase in government spending. A policy mix of fiscal constraint and tighter money was advocated by the chambers of commerce. The Council of Economic Advisers, following the Samuelson-Tobin neoclassical synthesis argued for low interest rates to spur growth and a budget surplus to siphon off excess liquidity and prevent inflation. In his analysis, Mundell demonstrated that none of the three policies would work and, in fact, would lead the economy away from equilibrium. He advocated a policy mix of lower taxes to spur employment and following of a tight monetary policy to protect the balance of payments.

In a very important article "Capital Mobility and Stabilization Policy under Fixed and Floating Exchange Rates" published in 1963, Mundell has dealt with the short-run effects of monetary and fiscal policy in an open economy. In most practical applications, the exchange rate and international trade are important to short-run fluctuations. Mundell employs in his paper Hicksian IS-LM model of a closed economy and extended it by introducing foreign trade and capital movements. The simplest assumptions about capital movements are that there exist no barriers to capital movements and that investors are risk-neutral; that is, the assumption of perfect capital mobility is made, a good approximation. Regarding exchange rate expectations, the simple assumption to make is that investors do not expect the exchange rate to change. These simple assumptions about capital mobility and exchange rate movements are the hallmark of the well-known Mundell-Fleming model.

Mundell demonstrates the vital importance for the results of the regime of exchange rate that is assumed. He shows that under a fixed exchange rate regime, fiscal policy is powerful while monetary policy is powerless; under the assumption of a floating exchange rate, he demonstrates that monetary policy is powerful while fiscal policy is powerless. He has also shown that when there is high capital mobility and assuming that the exchange rate is expected to remain unchanged, domestic and foreign interest rate are equal. Under a regime of fixed exchange rate, a country's central bank has to intervene in the currency market for the purpose of satisfying the domestic demand for foreign currency at this exchange rate. When this happens, money supply is no longer under the control of the central bank; the money supply passively adjusts to meet the domestic liquidity requirements. The monetary policy becomes ineffective; for example, in such a situation if the central bank attempts to follow an independent monetary policy, say, through a policy of open market operations, it will be able to influence neither the interest rate nor the exchange rate. The only policy option available for the country is to implement fiscal policy measures (as, for example, by stepping up government expenditures). Such fiscal policy measures will lead to increase in national income and the level of domestic economic activity.

Under a system of flexible exchange rates, where central bank's intervention in the currency market is ruled out, monetary policy will be effective while fiscal policy will be powerless. With no change in monetary policy, any increase, say, in government expenditures results in an augmented demand for liquidity with a resultant tendency towards higher interest rates. With the assumption of high capital mobility and inflows of capital, there will be a tendency for hardening of the exchange rate. The strengthening of the exchange rate will have such an adverse impact on net exports, that the entire expansive effect of the fiscal policy change of increased government expenditure is eliminated. But a monetary policy change of expansion of the money supply results in lower interest rates, leading to outflows of capital and a weaker exchange rate. A downward pressure on exchange rate tends to expand the economy through higher net imports.

In the 1960's, when Mundell presented his analysis, as almost all countries were following a system of fixed exchange rates under the Bretton Woods system and with extensive capital and exchange rate controls, his analysis must have seemed like an "academic curiosity." It is now generally accepted that Mundell's far-sighted analysis became increasingly relevant over the next ten years, as Bretton Woods system broke down and international capital movements became increasingly important. At the time of Mundell's work, Marcus Fleming also presented similar research on stabilisation policy in open economies. As a consequence, this model is referred to as Mundell-Fleming Model. In terms of depth, range and analytical power, Mundell's contribution is considered superior and, as such, predominates. The Mundell-Fleming model suffers from some serious limitations, such as assumption of short-run price rigidity and simplified assumptions regarding expectations of public in the financial markets, which were remedied by later researchers.

A key theme in several important papers of Mundell is his focus on monetary dynamics. He underlined the differences in the speed of adjustment on goods and assets markets – referred to as "principle of effective market classification." Before Mundell's work, the general approach researchers adopted in regard to the analysis of deficits and surpluses in a country's balance of payments was to use static models, emphasise real economic factors and concentrate on flows in foreign trade. Taking a cue from David Hume's work, Mundell formulated dynamic models to analyse how prolonged imbalances in the balance of payments arise and how they could be eliminated. He showed that as the money holdings and wealth of the private sector change in response to surpluses or deficits in the balance of payments, the economy adjusts slowly over time. Under a regime of fixed exchange rates, when capital movements are sluggish, an expansive monetary policy tends to reduce interest rates and boosts domestic aggregate demand. The subsequent deficit in the balance of payments will result in outflows of money which, in turn, reduces domestic demand until equilibrium is attained in the balance of payments. This approach has come to be known as the monetary approach to the balance of payments. The insights from the analysis using monetary approach to the balance of payments have been found useful for practical economic policymaking, particularly by IMF economists.

Another significant aspect of the theory of stabilisation policy put forward by Mundell has to be noted here. Mundell employed a simple dynamic model to examine how each of the two instruments of stabilisation (monetary and fiscal policy) should be directed towards either external balance or internal balance to bring the economy nearer to these objectives over time. He is in favour of entrusting the responsibility for fiscal policy instrument to government and monetary policy instrument to central bank. Mundell's conclusion is important. To prevent creating instability in the economy, the linkage has to be in line with the relative efficiency of instruments. Monetary policy is linked to external balance and fiscal policy with internal balance. He anticipated the idea that the central bank should be entrusted with the task of maintaining price stability.

The short-run and long-run analysis attempted by Mundell arrives at the following conclusion:

"(i) with free capital mobility, monetary policy can be oriented towards either (ii) an external objective-such as the exchange rate, or (iii) an internal (domestic) objective – such as the price level but not both at the same time" – the so called incomparable trinity."

11.2.2 OPTIMUM CURRENCY AREAS

While international monetary system was characterised by fixed exchange rates in early 1960's, some discussion took place about the advantages and disadvantages of floating exchange rates. However, there were no two opinions regarding the essentiality of a national currency. Mundell questioned this opinion in his 1961 paper on optimum currency areas. His article recounts the advantages of a common currency, such as reduction in transaction costs in trade and less uncertainty about relative prices. However, he discusses at length the major drawbacks of a common currency such as difficulty of maintaining domestic employment in the face of demand changes or other "asymmetric shocks." In order to offset such disturbances, Mundell stresses the importance of high labour mobility.

He characterises an optimum currency area as "a set of regions among which the propensity to migrate is high enough to ensure full employment when one of the regions faces an asymmetric shock." Other researchers supplied some other criteria, such as capital mobility, regional specialisation and a system of common taxes and transfers. With significant changes in international monetary scenario in the recent decade or so, many observers view a currency union or a floating exchange rate (about which Mundell discussed in his article) as the most appropriate alternative. Mundell's analysis attracted attention, particularly in connection with the common European currency – Euro.

11.3 CONCLUDING OBSERVATIONS

Mundell's other contributions include those relating to macroeconomic theory. He has demonstrated that higher inflation can induce investors to economise on their holdings of cash balances in favour of increased investment. As a result, even expected inflation might have a real economic effect, came to be known as the Mundell-Tobin effect. He has pointed out how international mobility of factors, say labour and capital, tends to equalise commodity prices among countries, even in the face of trade barriers. This is considered as "the mirror image" of the well-known Heckscher-Ohlin-Samuelson result that free trade of goods tends to bring about equalisation of rewards to labour and capital among countries, even if international capital movements and labour migration are limited. His results prompt an important prediction: trade barriers stimulate international mobility of labour and capital, while erection of barriers to migration and capital movements stimulate trade in goods.

Mundell concludes his Nobel lecture with the following: "There are...two pieces of unfinished business. The most important is the dysfunctional volatility of exchange rates that could sour international relations in times of crisis. The other is the absence of an international currency. The [twentieth] Century closed with an international monetary system inferior to that with which it began, but much improved from the situation that existed only two-and-a-half decades ago. It remains to be seen where leadership will come from and whether a restoration of the international monetary system will be compatible with the power configuration of the world economy. It would certainly make a contribution to world harmony."

11.4 SELECT BIBLIOGRAPHYOF ROBERT MUNDELL'S WORKS

11.4.1 BOOKS

1968 International Economics, Macmillan, New York.

1968 Man and Economics: The Science of Chice, Macmillan, New York.

1971 Monetary Theory: Interest, Inflation and Growth in the World Economy, Good Year, Pacific Palisades, CO.

11.4.2 ARTICLES

1957		"International Trade and Factor Mobility," AER, Vol. 47, No.3.
1960		"The Monetary Dynamics of International Adjustment under Fixed and Flexible Exchange Rates," QJE, Vol. 84, No.2.
1961	a	"A Theory of Optimum Currency Areas," AER, Vol. 51, No.4.
	b	"The International Disequilibrium System," Kyklos, Vol. 14, No.2.
1962		"The Appropriate Use of Monetary and Fiscal Policy for Internal and External Stability," IMF Staff Papers, Vol. 9 No.1.
1963		"Capital Mobility and Stabilization Policy Under Fixed and Floating Exchange Rates," Canadian Journal of Economics and Political Science, Vol. 39 No.4, Nov. Reprinted in R. Caves and H. Johnson (eds.) Readings in International Economics for the American Economic Association, Richard D. Irwin, Inc. Burr Ridge, Ill, 1967.
1995		"The International Monetary System: The Missing Factor," JPM, Vol. 17, No.5.
1997	a	"Updating the Agenda for Monetary Reform," in Optimum Currency Areas, (M. I. Blejer et al. eds.), IMF, Washington, D.C.
1997	b	"The International Monetary System in the 21st Century: Could Gold Make a Comeback?" Center for Economic Policy Studies, St. Vincent College, Latrobe, Pa.
2000	a	"The Case for Intervention in the Dollar-Euro Market," JPM, Vol. 23, No.3.
	b	"A Reconsideration of the Twentieth Century," Nobel Lecture: AER, Vol. 90, No.3.
	c	"Currency Areas, Exchange Rate System and International Monetary Reform," Journal of Applied Economics, Vol. 0, Nov.
2001	a	"Currency Areas and International Monetary Reform at the Dawn of a New Century," Review of International Economics, Vol. 9, No.4.
	b	"Debt, Growth, and Poverty in the International Monetary System," The Pakistan Development Review, Vol. 40, No.4.
2002		"The Significance of the Euro in the International Monetary System," Zagreb Journal of Economics, Vol. 2, No. 2.
2003		"Prospects for an Asian Currency Area," Journal of Asian Economics, Vol. 14, No.1.
2005		"The Case for a World Currency," JPM, Vol. 27, No.4.

2007 "Dollar Standard in Dollar Area," JPM, Vol. 29, No.5.

2009 "The World Economy: Quo Vadis," JPM, Vol. 31, No.4.

2012 "U.S. and China in the World Economy: The Balance of Payments and the Balance of Power," JPM, Vol. 34, No.4.

11.5 WORKS OF OTHERS

Dornbusch, R. (2000), "Robert A. Mundell's Nobel Memorial Prize," ScandJE, Vol. 102, No.2.

CHAPTER 12

FINN ERLING KYDLAND & EDWARD CHRISTIAN PRESCOTT

(1943 –)&
(1940 –)

Finn E. Kydland of Carnegie-Mellon University, Pittsburgh, Pa, and University of California, Santa Barbara, CA,U.S.A and Edward C. Prescott, Arizona State University and Federal Reserve Bank of Minneapolis, U.S.A., have been jointly awarded the Bank of Sweden Prize in Economic Sciences in Memory of Alfred Nobel for the year 2004. The award was made to them for their contributions to dynamic macroeconomics: the time consistency of economic policy and the driving forces behind business cycles.

Macroeconomic analysis during the early post-war period was greatly influenced by the legacy of J. M. Keynes and the Great Depression. In this view, short-run fluctuations in employment and output are primarily caused by variations in aggregate demand – consumers` willingness to spend on consumption and investors` willingness to undertake investment activity. Further, to avoid recurrent fluctuations in output and employment, it is suggested that macroeconomic stabilisation policy should systematically control aggregate demand. This line of thinking was predicated upon the experience during the Great Depression when the developed world passed through deep continuous fall in aggregate output, combined with falling employment and capital utilisation. The macroeconomic researchers interpreted these phenomena as failure of the market system to coordinate aggregate supply and demand and thus requiring government intervention to remedy the situation. Charles Plosser's remarks are pertinent in this context: "The 1960's were a time of great optimism for macroeconomists. Many economists viewed the business cycle as dead. The return of the business cycle in 1970s, after almost a decade of economic expansion [in the Western World], and the accompanying high rates of inflation, came as a rude awakening for many economists.

Thus, while this line of reasoning appeared to be satisfactory in explaining the observed malaise in the economy of short-run macroeconomic fluctuations during the 1970's, it became quite clear that stabilisation policies followed by Western countries based on existing economic theory failed to achieve the objectives of economic policy. During the mid-1970s, Western economies were characterised by simultaneous inflation and unemployment which came to be called stagflation. It seemed that the phenomenon of stagflation was closely linked to shocks on the supply side of the economy, specifically rising oil prices and perceived slowdown of productivity growth worldwide. Such supply side shocks which played a subordinate role in the Keynesian framework appeared important for the business cycle. Moreover, monetary and fiscal policy measures appeared to make matters worse in many countries by accommodating private sector expectations of high prices and wage increases. This occurrence was contrary to stated objectives of governments and central banks to achieve low and stable inflation.

Another important development in early and mid-1970s was Robert Lucas's research which highlighted the drawbacks of approach taken in Keynesian models. Lucas's main contention was that the relationships between macroeconomic variables are likely to be influenced by economic policy itself. Because of this influence, policy analysis based on the relationships governing the important economic variables, such as output, unemployment, inflation and consumption, as attempted by Keynesian models, might turn out to be faulty. Lucas contended that the effects of macroeconomic policy could not be appropriately analysed without explicit foundations in microeconomics. He advocated appropriate modelling of the behaviour of individual agents – consumers and firms. He believed that such careful modelling would only yield robust conclusions regarding responses of the private sector to economic policy. According to him, the analysis must be in terms of consumers` preferences, technologies employed by firms and structure of markets which would be robust to economic policy changes.

Yet another crucial development was the Philips curve explanation of the relationship between level of unemployment and inflation rate in an economy. In the late 1950s and early 1960s, there was a consensus that unemployment in an economy can be lowered by allowing higher inflation. In the late 1960s and 1970s, however, several researchers had questioned this view, the prominent among them being Milton Friedman and Edmund Phelps. They both demonstrated that there exists a long-run equilibrium level of unemployment independent of the rate of inflation. Unemployment can be brought down below this equilibrium level through higher inflation but only in the short-run; In the long run, inflationary expectations and wage rises adjust to actual inflation when unemployment returns to its equilibrium level.

Because of various developments, some of which are outlined above, a need was felt to develop an alternative and operational macroeconomic framework which, at the same time, is based on strong microeconomic foundations. The new framework had to provide an integral role to economic policy and perception of economic agents as to how economic policy is determined. In the press release, the Royal Swedish Academy notes how the award-winning contribution by Kydland and Prescott took vital steps forward in this direction.

One of the key insights of their work is that many policy decisions are subject to a fundamental "time consistency" problem. Kydland and Prescott show how government's inability to make binding commitments regarding future policies will generate a credibility problem. They advocate designing of appropriate institutions that mitigate the time consistency problem. They attempt integration of the analyses of long-run economic growth and short- run economic fluctuations, by maintaining that a key determinant of long- run living standards, that is, growth in technology, can also generate short-run cycles. They thus argue that technology shocks should be taken seriously as a cause of business cycles. Kydland and Prescott's business cycle model depends on standard microeconomic mechanisms whereby prices, wages and interest rates facilitate clearing of markets instead of the Keynesian emphasis on inability of markets to coordinate supply and demand.

Before summarising Kydland and Prescott's contributions, it is proposed to give a brief biographical sketch of the awardees.

12.1 A BRIEF BIOGRAPHICAL NOTE

12.1.1 FINN KYDLAND

Finn Erling Kydland was born at Gjesdal, Norway, on December 1, 1943. His father was a truck owner. The students in elementary school in which he studied met twice a week in the first three years and three times a week during the remaining ones. The education was not especially "active." He was the only one in his class to go to beyond elementary school. As a 15-year old, he went off to Bryne to attend the nearest high school after passing an entrance examination. He had chosen concentration, emphasizing mathematics and physics. The education was termed "exceptional;" Kydland sometimes claimed that he knew more mathematics at the end of high school than a typical American business or economics major knows at the end of college. He states in his autobiographical note: "As a consequence of my personal experience through my first 12 years of schooling, my bias has been to pooh-pooh the need for intensive education in elementary school, believing it is better to allow the pupils more time for play while they're kids, and instead to emphasize the importance of great high-school education."

Kydland thought that with his school grades, theoretical physics was the only field unavailable to him. He admits that he was wrong. His application for admission into business education at the Norwegian School of Economics and Business Administration (abbreviated NHH in Norwegian) was rejected. He took a supplementary examination to make his high school education equivalent to that in the business orientation, completed one-year mandatory service and got admitted to NHH in mid-1965. Four years later, i.e., in 1969 he was off to the United State to pursue further studies. His formal status at Graduate School of Industrial Administration (GSIA) at Carnegie-Mellon University was visiting student. About a month into the semester, Kydland had realised that to make it in research he needed a doctoral degree. He got admitted into the doctoral programme with financial support from NHH.

In the doctoral programme, besides other courses, he took the most "unusual" course, Economic Fluctuation by Robert Lucas. In the initial lectures of Lucas, Kydland later realised, they had seen his paper "Expectations and the Neutrality of Money" (for which he [Lucas] was to get the Nobel Prize) being developed right there in front of their eyes. In his autobiographical note, Kydland sates: "GSIA was (and is) unusual in at least two ways. One was the small class size, which promoted a cooperative environment among the students. Also there was relatively little course work. Most of the material taught was foundational; with emphasis on tools to put the student right on the research frontier. Important requirements were the first- and second-year summer research papers." Kydland's first year paper was entitled "Durability in Fractional Programming" which was his first serious publication in Naval Research Logistics Quarterly. His second-year summer paper also involved dual prices, which was published in Management Science.

For his Ph.D. thesis work, Kydland selected an economic problem--- "the assignment problem." In his words: "The idea was, within the system of equations framework dominating macroeconomics at the time, that fiscal policy was more effective at achieving certain goals and monetary policy was effective at others. If the right instruments were assigned to the right targets, the economy would function quite well, while if the wrong assignment was chosen, the economy would function poorly and could, in the worst case, even be unstable." The problem he has set up represented an alternative to the symmetric non-cooperative Nash solution, and was an application of dynamic game theory.

In his autobiographical note, Kydland mentions that he met his co-author and the joint winner of the prize, Edward Prescott at GSIA and the latter "had insisted on becoming the chairman of my [Ph.D. Dissertation] Committee. Thus started,in earnest, years of productive and much appreciated interaction with Prescott."

After graduating in 1973, Kydland joined NHH. His first year at NHH was "frustrating" as modern macroeconomics was not the school's strength. In his Ph.D. thesis, Kydland suggested three different situations to the dominant player game, the recursive without commitment, the commitment solution in policy space and the commitment solution in sequence space. However, he provided computed examples of only the first, namely, recursive without commitment solution. When he was at NHH he calculated profits of a dominant firm on the assumption that it could commit to its optimal policy – the other two solutions, "it turned out those profits beat the use of the otherwise time-consistent outcome by an astounding margin. Further, in association with Prescott he completed a paper on rules vs discretion and submitted the paper to the Journal of Political Economy."

Kydland had gone on leave for the academic year 1976-77 to the University of Minnesota never to return, as it turned out, to Norway for any permanent position. During 1976-77, he was offered an associate professor position by Carnegie-Mellon University, which he accepted. Kydland and Prescott started their work on business cycles at that time. Their first real business cycle paper was included in the 1980 NBER conference volume, titled Rational Expectations and Economic Policy, edited by Stanley Fischer. Another paper on real-business cycle topic was published by Econometrica in 1982. Kydland's research works immediately after 1982 Econometrica article revolved around the labour market. As regards real business cycle research Kydland observes: "A breakthrough in Ed's [Edward Prescott's] and my continuing business cycle research was the realization that we could start with basic growth model with both production and utility functions in exponential forms...." In the two business cycle papers Kydland and Prescott wrote, they found that inclusion of money made 'very little difference' to the model outcomes. More importantly, they found that all the "action" came from the technology shocks and they fitted well with the data. The 1982 paper also revealed to them that inter-temporal labour substitutability was a way to produce more labour input volatility in the model.

In his autobiographical note, Kydland tries to clear a "prevalent misunderstanding" in the early 1980s that they (Kydland and Prescott) put forward their 1982 model as a way to "fit" the data. He stated that the question before them was, if technology shocks were the only source of impulse to post-war U.S business cycles, what portion of the cycle would remain? Their answer, on the basis of the model, was "over 50 percent." He observes: "Importantly, this measurement was based on a calibrated model that was explicit about the dynamic decision process faced by the model's people and businesses."

Throughout his academic career he worked with many "eminent" researchers, besides Prescott. He held professorship at the University of Texas and at the University of California at Santa Barbara, besides being adjunct professor at NHH.

12.1.2 EDWARD CHRISTIAN PRESCOTT

Edward Christian Prescott was born to German immigrant parents on December 26, 1940 in Glen Falls, New York, where he lived throughout most of his childhood. His father graduated as industrial engineer from Penn State University. By his own admission, Edward Prescott was a "shy" and "not very social child." In 1958, he joined Swathmore college because it was less intimidating and somewhat less expensive, than the Ivy League Universities. From his father, Prescott learned a lot about the way businesses operated. This was one reason why he liked the microeconomics course, the other reason being the text book used in the course-- Samuelson's Principles of Economics. He liked the simple and clear way Samuelson laid out the theory in his text book. When Prescott returned from the college in the summer, he worked with a local paper mill, which "paid well." He states: This helped pay for college, but more importantly, I got to know like, and respect my fellow workers who didn't have the opportunities I had. In the junior year, Prescott had taken an advanced seminar with the mathematics honours student (which he liked) and a "fascinating" course in engineering economics by the "charismatic" professor Sam Carpenter. This led him to enrol in graduate school in Operations Research at Case Tech (which later became Case Western University). Given his financial position, Prescott worked "intensively" and completed two-year master's programme in 15 months. What he had learnt in the Operations Research programme there, like recursive methods in Queuing Theory course and some probability theory proved to be of great value in subsequent years.

After earning Master's degree, Prescott had decided to go to the Graduate School of Industrial Administration (GSIA) at Carnegie Tech (now Carnegie Mellon University) in Pittsburgh, Pennsylvania. He says "If MIT had offered aid, I would have gone there. But they didn't." He enjoyed his graduate school days. In the same year, Robert Lucas Jr. arrived there as freshly minted assistant professor. Prescott specifically mentions Michael Lovell (who became his dissertation supervisor) from whom he learnt how to help students in that very difficult transmission from student to researcher. He states: "I think a number of my students have developed from interacting with me. I know I have benefited greatly from interacting with them. When my former students contribute to the advancement of economics, I take great pleasure in their success." With Lovell, Prescott wrote two joint research papers; one of them was on developing a business cycle model.

After three years at GSIA, he joined the faculty at the University of Pennsylvania (Penn) in Philadelphia. His Penn years were "good ones," though he had a fear that he would not make it as a professor. He says the junior faculty members there were bright and talented. He states that he benefited greatly from interaction with Lawrence Klein and even more from Edmund Phelps (both Nobel laureates), who had the vision of providing the economic foundations for macro econometric models. Phelps ran the famous conference on the "Micro Foundations of Wage and Price Determination" at Penn in 1969. In the same year, Prescott in collaboration with Lucas wrote a research paper "Investment under Uncertainty" for the summer Econometric Society meetings. According to Prescott, writing this paper "transformed" him into an economist; before that he was more a statistician than an economist.

In 1970, he was on leave as a Brookings Economic Policy Fellow. When he returned to Penn, Penn had two young faculty members, Stephen Ross and Thomas Sargent, both of whom he came to admire greatly. He admits: "With colleagues like this, Penn was a very good place for me to be, but I was worried that I might not be granted tenure." When GSIA at Carnegie Mellon made an attractive offer, he accepted it.

Upon arriving at GSIA he met two advanced graduate students, one of whom was Finn Kydland. Prescott became his dissertation advisor. Prescott spent 1974-75 at NHH, Norway, where he and Kydland returned to the problem of policy selection in dynamic, uncertain environments and found that the principle of optimality fails. They realised that macroeconomic policy is a game, not a control problem as they earlier thought. After returning from Norway, Prescott decided to leave Carnegie Mellon as he found economics much more exciting. In 1978-79, he visited the University of Chicago as a Ford Foundation Research Professor. The following year, he was visiting professor at North Western

University, where he received an offer from the University of Minnesota. He accepted as at that time Minnesota had the "best graduate program and was the leading producer of new assistant professors." Prescott began his association with Federal Reserve Bank of Minneapolis in the fall of 1981, having joined the Minnesota faculty in the fall of 1980.

The Minnesota economics department had no required courses, a principle that served well since its founding. The students chose the courses. If no one signed up for your graduate course, the course was dropped. Prescott remarks: "Having this rule mitigates a time consistency problem." He states that he was fortunate to have worked with a large number of outstanding students. He further observes that Minnesota graduates have done more than any group to advance macroeconomics. Prescott spent one year at University of Chicago; he had more interaction with the faculty there. He particularly valued his interaction with Gary Becker and James Heckman (both Nobel laureates).He returned to Minnesota next year.

At the FRB, Minneapolis, Prescott co-authored a paper in which he derived the implications of the neoclassical growth model for the value of the stock market. The theory worked for predicting the value of the stock market as it had worked for predicting the magnitude and nature of business cycle fluctuations. Prescott observes that the integration of the stock market into macro models has important ramifications for understanding the boom in employment and output in the U.S during the late 1990s.

12.2 A SUMMARY OF CONTRIBUTIONS OF FINN KYDLAND AND EDWARD PRESCOTT

Macroeconomic research in early 1970s and the late 1960s turned its attention to the problem of expectations formed by private agents since it was recognised that economic outcomes are importantly determined by expectations. In this respect, first to be mentioned is the work of Edmund Phelps and Milton Friedman--both had formulated expectations-augmented Phillips curve, postulating that the relationship between actual inflation and unemployment crucially depends upon expected inflation. The next important step was the work of Robert Lucas's analysis of rational expectations hypothesis. According to him, economic agents make the best possible forecasts of future economic events on the basis of available information, including knowledge of how the economy functions. The best possible forecast is based on the presumption that other agents also follow the same principle, now and in the future. In the world of rational expectations, an economic equilibrium is achieved when private decisions are optimal and mutually consistent and a policy rule spells out the setting of policy instruments for each state of the economy. A policy rule is necessary because, in its absence it is not possible to predict expectations of private economic agents regarding future policy. As a consequence, the economic equilibrium would be incomplete. Lucas posits that for specifying economic equilibrium, it is necessary that the normative policy is evaluated in order to compare alternative policy rules, considering in what way each rule impacts expectations of private agents.

Here rationality has a very particular connotation. Rational private agents would not believe any policy rule. Some policy rules are more credible than others. Expectations of private agents are formed after considering the process of policy formation as well as government incentives. As Guido Tabellini and other economists point out, private agents will be rational in a game-theoretic sense, not in a "statistical" sense. Tabellini observes: "The more stringent requirement of rationality shifts attention from the positive question of how policy rules are selected." This necessitates examination of how policy rules are decided as also constraints and incentives of policy makers. Besides, we have to understand how the incentives are viewed by private agents and how far decisions of private agents are optimal and mutually consistent. For this purpose, it is necessary to study the institutions that are important in making decisions.

12.2.1 TIME INCONSISTENCY OF ECONOMIC POLICY

The advanced information provided by the Royal Swedish Academy states that the analysis of economic policy design provided a new angle to expectations formation. Kydland and Prescott's 1977 pioneering paper treated the policy maker as a single decision-maker with an objective of maximising a social welfare function; that is, endogenisation of government decision-making. They, of course, go along with Lucas in assuming private agents' expectations about future government policies are rational. At the same time, they assume that those expectations are vital determinants of economic outcomes in line with the work of Phelps and Friedman. Under these assumptions, Kydland and Prescott show that government policy making is subject to what they term as "time consistency" problem.

The policy maker makes the choice, not once and for all but period by period. The analysis of Kydland and Prescott concerns the credibility of alternative policy rules. They argue that policy rules that are optimal from the perspective of initial date may be "time – inconsistent." Time consistency implies lack of credibility as policy rules may not be self-enforcing. Moreover, if policy rules are believed by private agents, there may be an incentive even for a benevolent policy-maker to deviate from such rules at a later stage. That is, if private agents' expectations about future policy choices are rational, some economic outcomes cannot be achieved under discretionary policy. They also demonstrate the policy outcomes that would result, if both private agents and policy makers act rationally. They have shown that equilibria, which are time-consistent without government commitment to policy rules, are characterised by lower welfare than those with government commitment. They, therefore, argue in favour of more or less unalterable policy rules. This gave rise to discussion of institutional design involving creation of commitment mechanisms that increase the set of feasible outcomes and raise economic welfare. One important outcome of their work is the transformation of the way in which economic policy is discussed. According to Tabellini "...a crucial step in the evolution of this line of research was the idea that optimal policy rules may lack credibility if they are chosen sequentially. It was here, with the notion of "time inconsistency" of optimal policy rules, that the foundations were laid for all subsequent research on endogenous macroeconomic policy, credibility and politics."

The press release of the Royal Academy gives a simple example to understand the basic idea of time consistency. The same example is used here. Let us take two time periods, t-1 and t. In t-1, a government wants to achieve an optimal outcome for economic agents in period t. As outlined above, economic outcomes in period t depend on the policy undertaken in period t; they are also determined by decisions made by private sector in period t-1; for instance, consumption/savings or wages in period t. Decisions made by private sector in period t-1, depend upon its expectations about the period t policy. The expectations are rationally formed. That is, in period t-1, private sector economic agents make the forecasts on the understanding and knowledge of the determinants of government policy in period t. The model rules out uncertainty; rational expectations imply perfect foresight on the part of private sector agents.

In the case with commitment to policy, the government chooses its period t policy in period t-1, with no option to change this policy later. In such a case, the optimal choice of period t policy has to consider the effect of the policy on private sector decisions in period t-1, since the equilibrium period t policy has to consider the effect of the policy on private sector decisions in period t-1. Since the equilibrium period t policy pins down the expectations in period t-1 as to what this policy will be, it influences decisions made by private sector in period t-1 that affect period t economic outcomes.

The more realistic case is policy without commitment, i.e., discretionary policy. In this case, in period t-1, the government cannot make binding decisions over policy in period t until period t arrives. So, the period t policy choice will not take into account how private sector decisions are made in period t-1, as when this policy choice is undertaken, private decisions in period t-1 would have already been made and can no longer be influenced. Hence, this will generally lead to different period t policy than in the commitment case resulting in economic outcomes that will lead to lower welfare than under commitment. This is a consequence of perfectly anticipating policy in period t because of rational expectations. However, because of the time-sequencing of decision making, the government is not able to influence these expectations. When making policy decision in period t, the government thus solves an optimisation problem that does not take into account all the effects of its policy choice.

In the above example, the way the time-inconsistency comes about can be illustrated by an example. A government that cannot make commitments in period t-1 proclaims its intention to continue the same period t policy as the optimal policy it would hypothetically have selected under commitment. This announcement would not be credible anyhow, as when period t arrives and the government has to make its actual policy choice, it could find that it is optimal to go back on its announcement.

This kind of government's policy problem cannot be treated as an optimal control problem as is usually done in traditional macroeconomics. In the conventional optimal control problem, the optimiser selects a control variable sequence that maximises a constrained objective function. However, in Kydland-Prescott model, the constraints are endogenous since private behaviour depends upon rational private expectations about government's policy. These constraints explain relations between current policy and current economic outcomes that are influenced by future policy choices through expectations of the private sector. For determining equilibrium outcomes, it becomes necessary to use game-theoretic methods. In their paper Kydland and Prescott use different equilibrium concepts in different models and examples such as Nash equilibrium and similar to Selten's sub-game perfect equilibrium. They also show the use of recursive methods in a model example with an infinite time horizon. It is observed that such methods are especially useful for defining a special type of equilibria – the so-called Markov-perfect equilibria.

Kydland and Prescott pinhole a number of examples of time inconsistency which are referred to in the press release of the Nobel Foundation. These examples show that a successful government policy must impact private sector expectations but time inconsistency would prevent this from happening. An interesting example relates to provision of government assistance in case of natural disasters such as earthquakes and floods, that may be optimal ex-post but may not be optimal ex-ante. Assume that a uninhabitated area that is subject to high risk of exposure of tropical storms. From an ex-ante perspective it is not socially desirable for the population to settle in that area as protective assistance is very costly which only the government can undertake. If, however, people, in fact, settle in that area what action would the government take? The government can help settlers in constructing protective devices to mitigate losses in the event of a storm or it may not do so. When it is socially desirable to give protection ex-post, there is a time consistency problem. If the government makes a commitment to not providing such assistance in case people settle in that area, the citizens will refrain from settling there leading to the attainment of a socially desirable outcome. In case the government cannot commit to not providing such assistance, but citizens still settle there in the understanding that government will provide assistance and protection, then a socially less desirable outcome is obtained. Here is a moral hazard problem. To discourage this, an optimal government policy should promise only limited relief in the event of a natural disaster. However, this promise is not credible. A sub-optimal outcome emerges where private agents undertake excessive risks and eventually the government is forced to retract its policy.

In their paper, Kydland and Prescott not only present an abstract general model but also formally analyse two specific cases - one regarding government's tax policy and the other inflation policy or stabilisation policy. In the case of government's tax policy, they show that the time-consistent solution when both government and private agents are rational, the outcome with no commitment on the part of the government is worse than the outcome under commitment in that the tax rates are higher and consumers' utility is lower. As regards the issue of stabilisation policy, they show that discretionary monetary policy yields higher inflation without lower unemployment.

To show the above result, let us consider an expectations-augmented Phillips curve model (a la Phelps-Friedman) with sticky nominal wages. In such a case, monetary policy can bring down unemployment below NAIRU (non-accelerating inflation rate of unemployment) or natural rate, only if it creates an inflation rate higher than expected. Thus, policy makers who would put premium on a policy to reduce unemployment, ignoring its impact on inflation rate, would end up without lower unemployment but higher inflation than those with a stronger preference for low inflation relative to low unemployment. This striking result is a consequence of policy-maker's lack of commitment. Where there is commitment, the ex-post temptation to inflate the economy is absent, and rational expectations ensure the same outcome irrespective of the preference parameters. The press release's observation in this context is that Kydland and Prescott's contribution offered a politico-economic explanation as to why many countries found themselves in a process of self–generating inflation despite repeated promises to combat it. Barro and Gordon carried the analysis further and demonstrated that inflation is higher when equilibrium unemployment is higher relative to the unemployment target that politicians try but are unable to achieve. Their basic conclusions remain unchanged even when they introduce supply shocks and stabilisation policy into the model. The issue whether time-consistency problem could be resolved is a challenging one in research as well as in practice. One solution that some researchers have put forward is when monetary policy-makers "invest in a good reputation" by controlling inflation, they influence private sector expectations regarding future inflation rates. There are other researchers who turned their attention on institutional reforms that would help improve the performance of discretionary policy-making. In this context, reference is to be made to Rogoff's suggestion to entrust monetary policy to an independent and conservative central banker who could and would achieve a proper balance between credibility of policy of low inflation and flexible stabilisation. Such a banker is expected to be more inflation-averse than general public and hence can be expected to achieve better welfare outcomes.

12.2.2 REAL BUSINESS CYCLES

In 1960s, many economists expressed the view that business cycle is dead. A decade of economic expansion in the U.S accompanied by high rates of inflation brought about a rude awakening among economists who were of the view that there was a return of business cycle in the 1970s. Traditionally, macroeconomic analysis considered short-term fluctuations in output, employment, prices and financial conditions as business cycle while long term trends in output and living standards were treated as economic growth. As Prescott observes in his Prize lecture, many economists falsely concluded that business cycle fluctuations were not in large part equilibrium responses to real shocks. Factually, 1980s and 1990s have seen fundamental changes in the theory and practice of business cycle research and more generally in the prevailing views on business cycle phenomena. Keynesian analysis basically relied on a set of relationships among aggregate variables-reduced forms – that were meant to sum up the interaction between various structural relationships. As Charles Plosser observes, the prime defect in the Keynesian interpretation of macroeconomic phenomenon was the absence of a consistent foundation that lay in the choice of the theoretic framework of microeconomics. While the structural relationships in the Keynesian analysis are based on microeconomic theory of consumer and firm behaviour, it was not explicitly derived from such theory. More importantly, different macroeconomic relationships were not based on a common microeconomic structure when used together in applied macroeconomic analysis.

It was common in 1960s and early 1970s to use estimated versions of business cycle models mentioned above in practical forecasting and policy-oriented evaluations of monetary and fiscal policy interventions. However, serious limitations to this approach have been highlighted, particularly by Robert Lucas in his 1976 article "Econometric Policy Evaluation: A Critique." Estimated reduced from relationships could not be expected to be robust to changes in policy regimes or in the macroeconomic environment. As Prescott points out, in the 1970s after the development of dynamic economic theory, it was obvious that the system of equations approach has to be abandoned and macroeconomics was to be integrated with the rest of economics. Furthermore, seemingly stable macroeconomic relationships based on historical data, appear to have broken down in the 1970s. Particularly, the prevalent Phillips curve explanation postulating a stable negative relationship between the rates of inflation and unemployment was found to be wanting and unacceptable in view of latest macroeconomic developments--high unemployment combined with high inflation, the so called situation of stagflation. The predominant idea that business cycles are caused mainly by demand factors has not been vindicated by experience of the 1970s. Supply shocks such as steep rises in oil prices in 1973-1974 and 1979 appeared to be the important factor that characterised contemporary macroeconomic fluctuations. Another factor that appeared to have been responsible for the macro fluctuations was global slowdown in productivity growth in the mid-1970s.

Lucas has advocated formulating a new macroeconomic theory based on an explicit microeconomic structure, which should include assumptions regarding consumers and their preferences, firms and the technologies they employ, information set these agents possess and the specific markets in which they operate. Changes in fiscal or monetary policies or in the macroeconomic conditions would impact behaviour of consumers and firms but are unlikely to affect consumers' preferences and firms' technologies. Lucas did not agree with formulating or specifying expectations in an ancillary fashion. Instead, formulation of expectations must be considered as rational in the sense in which Muth suggested in his 1961 Econometrica article. It is argued that quantitative analysis founded on satisfactory microeconomic theory is likely to be more robust to changes in monetary and fiscal policy regimes and would therefore be found to be more useful in policy analysis than the models based on historical aggregate relationships as was the practice till then.

An analysis of business cycle facts has revealed, according to Prescott that two-thirds of business cycle fluctuations are accounted for by variations in the labour input and one-third by variation in total factor productivity (TFP). He found that variations in the capital service input did not contribute anything to business cycle fluctuations. He also found that while per capita labour input shows no secular trend, per capita output has a strong secular upward trend. Other business cycle facts Prescott's analysis revealed include pro-cyclical trend in consumption and, in percentage terms, investment varying ten times as much as does consumption. He, therefore, observes that investment is a disproportionate part of cyclical output variation. It is, therefore, surprising to many economists as to why total factor productivity and other real shocks were ruled out as being significant contributors to business cycle fluctuations. 1970s witnessed a flurry of activity to conjecture as to why the economy fluctuated as it did. In Prescott's view, most conjectures were concerned with finding a propagation mechanism that resulted in Lucas's monetary surprise shocks having persistent real effects. That is, economists searched for what Frisch called a "propagation mechanism" for the effects of monetary surprises.

In his Prize lecture, Prescott, while giving the back ground for his joint work with Kydland, mentions that macroeconomics of the 1970s largely ignored capital accumulation. Economic growth was considered as something that can be studied independently of economic fluctuations. Growth theory was taken to be concerned with the long term movements in the economic aggregates, whereas macroeconomics was concerned with the short term movements. He contends: "Virtually no connection was made between the then-dormant growth theory and the dynamic equilibrium theories of business cycles." In this context, it is pertinent to quote what Hicks had to say in his <u>Capital and Growth</u>. "The distinction between trend and fluctuation is a statistical distinction; it is an unquestionably useful device for statistical summarizing.... But this gives no reason to suppose that there is anything corresponding to it on the economic side which is at all fundamental. We have no right to conclude, from the mere existence of the statistical device, that the economic forces making for trend and for fluctuations are any different, so that they have to be analyzed in different ways." Following this line of reasoning, Kydland and Prescott have attempted integrating business cycle theory and growth theory. The Nobel Foundation release of advanced information provides other reasons for their approach. Since Kydland and Prescott considered technology shocks as potentially important sources of short run output fluctuations, it seemed natural to use Solow's neo-classical growth model. Further, it is taken that long run, by necessity, is a sequence of short runs. Another reason for the use of the growth model is the fact that most variables of interest in growth theory and business cycle theory coincide.

Kydland and Prescott use a closed economy dynamic, stochastic general equilibrium model with perfect competition and with no market frictions. They use the aggregate production function of Solow and Swan; Prescott, in his Prize lecture, presents the model that is given below.

The function, Ft, is the period t aggregate production. It shows the output that is produced as a function of inputs – labour service input (l) and capital service input (k)

$$F_t(k_t, l_t) = Y_t = C_t + X_t \quad .....(1)$$

where Y is output, C is consumption and X is investment. One unit of capital provides one unit of capital services. It is assumed that capital depreciates geometrically at rate δ.

Thus,

$$k_t + 1 = (1 - \delta)\, k_t + X_t \quad .....(2)$$

The shock propagation mechanism is provided by a multi- period requirement for building new capacity. The household maximises the expected value of

$$\Sigma_{t=0}^{\infty} \beta^t \mu(C_t, 1 - h_t) \quad .....(3)$$

where C is consumption and 1 – h is leisure. Eq (3) shows competitive equilibrium, representing maximisation of weighted average of individual utilities.

Prescott states that for studying business cycles it is necessary to treat consumer durable expenditures as an investment. This increases investment share of output and has consequences for the cyclical behaviour of the economy. The U.S growth data show that consumption and investment shares of output are roughly constant, as are labour and capital cost shares. While labour supply and the return on capital are roughly constant, all other variables and the real wage grow over time. Capital output ratio and rental price of capital are constant. Kydland and Prescott use a Cobb-Douglas production function. Making certain assumptions they postulate the following period utility function.

$$\log C + g(l - 1) \quad .....(4)$$

Prescott admits that the nature of the g function is important. He states that the growth facts do not tie down the elasticity of substitution between consumption and leisure and this parameter turned out to be crucial for deriving the prediction of the growth model for business cycle fluctuations.

Kydland and Prescott take some more steps (need not be gone into here) before computing the recursive competitive equilibrium stochastic process to generate a time series realisation of the model economy. Then, a comparison is made between the key business cycle statistics for the model and the actual economy.

The results as given in the Nobel Foundation advanced information may be conveniently summarised.

A positive technology shock in period t represents a higher than average growth rate of total factor productivity, leading to rise in wages. Since workers find work more profitable than leisure, labour supply in period t increases. Thus, the direct effect of higher productivity reinforced by the indirect effect of labour supply results in raising period t output. There is an increase in the return to capital as well; however, the capital stock in period t is predetermined. The higher level of output in period t has dynamic consequences. Part of the increase in output is consumed and the balance is saved and invested. The division between consumption and saving is determined by preferences of consumers and the expected persistence of the productivity shock. As consumers are known to prefer smoothing of consumption over time, the portion of a temporary output increase that is saved is determined by their preference for smoothing. Furthermore, it will be more profitable to save and invest the longer the productivity shock is expected to persist. The data on technology growth series that Kydland and Prescott employ show significant positive autocorrelation. This raises the t+1 period capital stock while technology is still above the trend because of autocorrelation. Moreover, as incentives for higher than normal labour supply continue and if there is a large increase in capital stock and if technology shocks are sufficiently auto correlated, labour supply as also investment in period t+1, would be higher than trend in period t.

The dynamic effects sketched above are what are termed by the authors as the model's propagation mechanism – an impulse of a temporary technology shock determining the path of future macroeconomic variables. The mechanism is shown to be stable. The model yields time series for macroeconomic variables broadly consistent with data pertaining to actual economy. The economy experiences booms and busts. One important aspect of their approach needs to be mentioned here. Instead of developing models capable of conventional econometric testing, Kydland and Prescott have developed what is referred to as a "calibration" method in which the simulated results of their model (when impacted by random shocks) in terms of important macroeconomic variables are compared with the actual behaviour of the economy. Kydland points out in his Prize lecture: "The question for which this frame work was first put to use by Ed Prescott and me can be stated as follows: if technology shocks were the only source of impulse, what portion of business cycle fluctuations would still have remained? The model produced a preliminary answer to that question: well over one half and that answer has pretty much been confirmed to be somewhere around 70 percent. The model provided measurement."

In his Prize lecture, Prescott reiterates that "if elasticity of labour supply is 3 and TFP shocks are highly persistent and of the right magnitude, then business cycles are what the neoclassical growth model predicts. That is, the model predicts the amplitude of output fluctuations, the serial correlation properties of cyclical output, the relative variability of consumption and investment, the fact that capital stock peaks and bottoms out later than does output, the cyclical behavior of leisure, and the cyclical output accounting facts". Kydland and Prescott also find that TFP shocks are the major contributors to fluctuations in the period 1954-1981 in the United States, once elasticity of labour supply is close to 3. They also report that introduction of monetary factors did not alter this crucial finding.

12.2.3 CRITIQUE OF REAL BUSINESS CYCLE THEORY

As outlined above, the real business cycle school posits that business cycles are essentially caused by real or supply side shocks rather than demand side shocks to the economy. The approach is considered to be fraught with a number of deficiencies and has proved to be highly controversial. One of the severest critics was Lawrence Summers. He observes that Prescott's argument (in "Theory Ahead of Business Cycle Measurement") is unpersuasive at four levels. First, Prescott's claim that Kydland and Prescott have parameterized their real business cycle model on the basis of well established microeconomic and long-run information is not "sustainable." Summers does not agree with the share of time devoted by labour to market activities as also with Prescott's assumption regarding the inter-temporal elasticity of substitution in labour supply. Summers remarks: "Prescott's growth model is not an inconceivable representation of reality. But to claim that its parameters are securely tied down by growth and micro observations seems to me a gross over statement."

Second, a more crucial objection relating to the real business cycle is the absence of any independent supporting evidence for the existence of technological shocks. No direct evidence exists of large technological shocks and those shocks accounting for large movements in measured total factor productivity.

Third, Summers objects to the model not taking into account prices; the model's economic analysis is completely price-free. It is an exercise in price-free economics. The model does not consider factors other than productivity shocks as causal elements of cyclical fluctuations.

The fourth major objection to the real business cycle model is its ignoring the breakdown of exchange mechanism as a causal factor for economic fluctuations. Break down in credit markets is an important example of the failure of exchange process. Summers's conclusion is trenchant: "... real business cycle models... have nothing to do with the business cycle phenomena observed in the United States or other capitalist economics." He further contends: "Nothing could be more counterproductive in this regard [in improving the track record of macroeconomics] than a lengthy professional detour into the analysis of stochastic Robinson Crusoes."

12.3 CONCLUDING OBSERVATIONS

Kydland in his Prize lecture makes some useful suggestions for learning macroeconomics. He states that the interesting macroeconomic phenomena are dynamic and inter-temporal. However, dynamic macro is difficult for beginners to learn. That is perhaps the main reason for the widening gap between macroeconomic text books and macroeconomic research. He offers important suggestions for bridging this gap.

The real business cycle approach, though highly controversial, is considered to have raised vital questions relating to the meaning, characteristics and significance of economic fluctuations. Guido Tabellini observes that Kydland and Prescott, with two path-breaking contributions – time inconsistency of optimal policy rules and analysis of business fluctuations-- have transformed the field of macroeconomics. Sergio Rebelo goes further and asserts that Kydland and Prescott have introduced three revolutionary ideas in their 1982 paper. The first idea is that business cycles can be studied using dynamic general equilibrium models. The second idea relates to the possible unification of business cycles with growth theory. The third idea concerns calibrating models with parameters drawn from microeconomic studies and the economy in long run properties. Such calibrated models can then be used to generate artificial data that can be compared with actual data. It is also observed that the research agenda in macroeconomics has been influenced by the work of Kydland and Prescott.

12.4 SELECT BIBLIOGRAPHY OF WORKS OF FINN E. KYDLAND AND/OR EDWARD C.PRESCOTT

12.4.1 BOOKS

1987 Prescott C. E. and N Wallace eds. Contractual Arrangements for Inter-temporal Trade, University of Minnesota Press, Minneapolis, Minn.

1989 Prescott C. E., N. Stokey and R. F. Lucas Jr. Recursive Methods in Economic Dynamics, Harvard University Press, Cambridge, MA.

12.4.2 ARTICLES

1971 Prescott E.C and R.E Lucas Jr, "Investment under Uncertainty," Econometrica, Vol.39, No.6.

1975 Kydland, F.E, "Non-cooperative and Dominant Player Solutions in Discrete Dynamic Games," IER, Vol.16, No.2.

1977 a Kydland, F.E and E.C Prescott, "Rules rather than Discretion: The Time Inconsistency of Plans," JPE, Vol.85, No.2.

b Kydland F.E, "Equilibrium Solutions in Dynamic Dominant Player Models," JET, Vol.15, No.2.

1980 a Kydland, F.E and E.C. Prescott, "Dynamic Optimal Taxation, Rational Expectations, and Optimal Control," Journal of Economic Dynamics and Control. Vol.2, No.1.

b Prescott, E.C. and R. Mehra, "Recursive Competitive Equilibrium: The Case of Homogeneous Households," Econometrica, Vol.48, No.5.

1982 Kydland, F.E. and E.C. Prescott, "Time to Build and Aggregate Fluctuations," Econometrica, Vol.50, No.6.

1984 a Prescott E.C. and R.M. Townsend, "Pareto Optima and Competitive Equilibria with Adverse Selection and Moral Hazard," Econometrica, Vol.25, No.1.

b Prescott, E.C. and R.M Townsend, "General Competitive Analysis in an Economy with Private Information," IER, Vol.25, No.1.

1985 Prescott, E.C and R. Mehra, "The Equilibrium Puzzle," JME, Vol.15, No.2.

1986 Prescott, E.C, "Theory Ahead of Business Cycle Measurement," Carnegie-Rochester Conference Series on Public Policy, Vol.25.

1988 Kydland, F.E and E.C Prescott, "The Work week of Capital and its Cyclical Implications," JME, Vol.21, No.2-3.

1990 Kydland, F.E and E.C Prescott, "Business Cycles: Real Facts and a Monetary Myth," Federal Reserve Bank of Minneapolis Quarterly Review, Vol.14.

1991 a Kydland, F.E and E.C Prescott, "Hours and Employment Variation in Business Cycle Theory," Economic Theory, Vol.1, No.1.

b Kydland, F. E, "Infllation, PersonalTaxes, and Real Output: A Dynamic Analysis," JMCB, Vol.23, No. 3.

c Kydland,F. E, "The Econometrics of General Equilibrium Approach to Business Cycles," ScandJE, Vol.93, No.2.

1992 a Kydland, F.E, D. K. Backus and P. Kehoe, "International Business Cycles," JPE, Vol.100, No.4.

b Kydland, F. E, "On the Econometrics of World Business Cycles," EER, Vol.36, No.2-3,

1993 Prescott, E.C and H. Andreas, "The Firm and the Plant in General Equilibrium Theory," in General Equilibrium, Growth and Trade II: The Legacy of Lionel Mckenzie (R. Becker et al. eds.), Academic Press, San Diego, Ca.

1994 Kydland, F.E, D. K. Backus, and J. Patrick, "Dynamics of the Trade Balance and the Terms of Trade: The J-Curve?" AER, Vol.84, No.1.

1995 a Kydland, F.E., "Business Cycles and Aggregate Labour Market Fluctuations," in Frontiers of Business Cycle Research, T. F. Cooley (ed.) Princeton University, Princeton, NJ.

b Prescott, C.E. and T. F. Cooley, "Economic Growth and Business Cycles," in Frontiers of Business Cycle Research, T. F. Cooley (ed.),Princeton University, Princeton, NJ.

1996 Kydland, F. E. and C. E. Prescott, "The Computational Experiment: An Econometric Tool," JEP, Vol.10, No.1.

1998 a Kydland, F.E., and D'Ann M. Petersen, "Does Being Different Matter" Economic Review, (Third Quarter), Federal Reserve Bank of Minneapolis.

b Prescott, E.C. and R.J. Hodrick, "Post-war U.S. Business Cycles: An Empirical Investigation," JMCB, Vol.29, No.1.

1999 Kydland, F. E. and W. T. Gavin, "Endogenous Money Supply and Business Cycle," Review of Economic Dynamics, Vol.2, No.2.

2000 Kydland, F.E, and E. C. Scott, "Monetary Aggregates and Output," AER, Vol.90, No.5.

2002 a Kydland, F.E., and C.E.J.M. Zarazaga, "Argentina's Lost Decade," Review of Economic Dynamics, Vol.5, No.1.

b Prescott, C. E., "Prosperity and Depression," AER, Vol.92,No.2.

c Prescott, E.C and K. Shell, "Introduction to Sunspots and Lotteries," JET, Vol.107, Nov.

d Prescott, E.C and H. Fumio, "The 1990s in Japan: A Lost Decade," Review of Economic Dynamics, Vol.5, No.1.

e Prescott, E.C and T.J. Kehoe, "Introduction to 'Great Depressions' of the 20th Century," Review of Economic Dynamics, Vol.5, No.1.

f Prescott, E.C., T.J. Kehoe,and D. K.Levine, "Lotteries, Sunspots and Incentive Constraints," JET, Vol.107, Nov.

2003 Prescott, E.C., and R. Mehra, "The Equity Premium in Retrospect," in Handbook of the Economics of Finance, Constantinides, G. et al. eds., Elsevier, Amsterdam.

2004 a Prescott, E.C., "Why Do Americans Work So Much More Than Europeans?," Federal Reserve Bank Minneapolis Quarterly Review, Vol.28, July.

b Kydland, F.E., "Quantitative Aggregate Theory," Nobel Prize Lecture, Prix Nobel, The Nobel Prizes, 2004, T. Frarigsmyr (ed.), Nobel Foundation, Stockholm, 2005.

c Prescott, E. C., "The Transformation of Macroeconomic Policy and Research," Nobel Prize Lecture, Prix Nobel, The Nobel Prizes, T. Frarigsmyr (ed.), Nobel Foundation, Stockholm, 2005 .

2005 a Prescott, E. C., and E.R. Mc Grattan, "Taxes, Regulation and the Value of U.S and U.K Corporations," RES, Vol.72, July.

b Prescott, E.C and E. R. Mc Grattan, "Productivity and the Post-1990 U.S Economy," Federal Reserve Bank St.Louis Review, Vol.87, July/Aug.

c Prescott, E.C and G.D. Hansen, "Capacity Constraints, Asymmetries and the Business Cycle," Review of Economic Dynamics, Vol.8. No.

2006 Kydland, F. E., "Quantitative Aggregate Economics," AER, Vol.96, No.5.

2007 Kydland,F. E.,W. T. Gavin and M. R. Pakko, "Monetary Policy, Taxes, and the Business Cycle," JME, Vol.54, No.6.

2010 Kydland, F. E. and E. Henriksen, "Endogenous Money, Inflation and Welfare," Review of Economic Dynamics, Vol.13, No.2.

12.5 WORKS OF OTHERS

Lucas, R. E. Jr (1976), "Econometric Policy Evaluation: A Critique," JME, Supplement, Vol. 5, No.1.

Lucas, R. E. Jr. (1977), "Understanding Business Cycles," in Stabilization of the Domestic and International Economy, Brunner, K. and A.H. Meltzer (eds.) North Holland, Amsterdam.

Plosser, C .I. (1989), "Understanding Real Business Cycles," JEP, Vol.3, Summer.

Rebello, S. (2005) "Real Business Cycle Models: Past, Present, and Future," ScandJE, Vol.107, No.2.

Rogoff, K. (1985), "The Optimal Degree of Commitment to an Intermediate Target," QJE, Vol.100, No.4.

Summers, L.H. (1986), "Some Skeptical Observations on Real Business Cycle Theory," Federal Reserve Bank of Minneapolis Quarterly Review, Fall, Reprinted in A Macroeconomic Reader , Snowdon, B. and H. R. Vane (eds.), Routledge, London and Newyork, 1997.

Tabellini, G. (2005), "Finn Kydland and Edward Prescott's Contribution to the Theory of Economic Policy," ScandJE, Vol. 107, No.2.

CHAPTER 13

EDMUND STROTHER PHELPS Jr.

(1933 –)

The Sveriges Riksbank Prize in Economic Sciences in Memory of Alfred Nobel 2006 has been awarded to Professor Edmund S. Phelps of Columbia University, USA. The Royal Swedish Academy of Sciences announcing the award makes specific reference to Phelps's "analysis of the inter-temporal trade-offs in macroeconomic policy." The central goals of economic policy in any country consist of ensuring full employment, stability of price level and rapid economic growth. However, it is not possible to achieve all the goals at the same time as policy is always exposed to difficult goal conflicts that need to be reconciled. One of the goal conflicts relates to the balancing of inflation and unemployment in an economy. Another issue that needs to be addressed concerns the acceptable trade-off between the consumption of current generation and future generations.

Before presenting a summary of Phelps's contributions to economics, a brief biographical note is presented.

13.1 A SHORT BIOGRAPHICAL SKETCH: EDMUND PHELPS

Edmund Strother Phelps Jr. was born in Evanston, Illinois, U.S.A. on July 26, 1933, "at the bottom of the great Depression." His parents moved in 1939 to New York, settling down in Hasting, a suburb up the Hudson River, where he attended a public school until graduation in 1951. He joined Amherst College "without a predetermined course of study and without even a career goal." Cajoled by his father, Phelps took a course in Economics in the second year of B.A. His lecturer at the college was James Nelson, an economist from Harvard who captivated "a succession of students – Pollak and Stiglitz, for example. The new text book in use, by Paul Samuelson, was brilliant." Phelps admits that even at that time he had "a vague sense that microeconomics taught in one set of courses was not communicating with the macroeconomics in the other courses!" He found that a reading of Hansen's and Haberler's surveys of the "dissonant views in macroeconomics makes one aware of this problem."

For graduate work Phelps went to Yale University where he developed close contact and rapport "with two of the most brilliant economists at Yale, the Americans James Tobin and Thomas Schelling" (both Nobel Laureates). He was grateful to them for their "lucid teaching" and amazed at their "high competence and ability to make everything look easy."

Other economists at Yale who influenced Phelps include Arthur Okun, William Fellner and Henry Wallich. The last two were from Europe, Fellner from Hungary and Wallich from East Germany. In his autobiographical note, Phelps observes that Okun was "a model of braininess and relevance..." who supervised Phelps's dissertation. As regards Fellner and Wallich, with their experience in Central Europe, they emphasised the role of expectations of inflation, prices and wages. Phelps comments: "It would not be going too far to say that they intuited the idea of natural rate of unemployment."

In 1959 Phelps joined his first job as Economist at the Rand Corporation – then devoted mostly to Air Force work. He realised that "the absence of a broad academic stimulus and sounding board was a serious disadvantage of Rand". Therefore, he shifted in 1960 to a research position at Yale's Cowles Foundation with reduced teaching at Yale. Phelps observes: "The five and a half years at the Cowles Foundation formed a distinctive phase of my research, and a necessary stage in my professional development". While he wrote a number of research papers while at Yale including golden rule of national saving and vintage models of investment, he admits "I felt these papers were not as deep as I was capable of, however, and compensated by writing a great many of them."

Phelps received an invitation to visit MIT in 1962-63, where he had "unforgettable conversation" with Paul Samuelson. He also got to teach a course in Capital Theory with Robert Solow. "... who clarified the subject as much for me as for the students". Franco Modigliani ".... was also hugely stimulating. Within a few short years I became an internationally known economist." Phelps moved to University of Pennsylvania, Philadelphia, as Professor of Economics in 1966. He shifted to Columbia University in 1971. At Columbia University, Phelps was designated in 1982 as McVickar Professor of Political Economy. He founded Columbia's Center on Capitalism and Society in 2001.

Phelps received numerous awards and honours. Among them, particular mention may be made of the Fellowship of Econometric Society, 1966, Fellowship of Guggenheim Foundation, 1978 and Vice-presidentship of American Economic Association, 1983. He was conferred honorary doctorate by his old Alma meter, Amherst College, in 1985. Phelps was elected Distinguished Fellow of the American Economic Association in 2000.He was elected to the American Academy of Arts and Sciences in 1980 and to National Academy of Sciences n 1981. In 2008, Phelps received Pico Della Mirandola prize and Global Economy Prize. Since 1976, he was Senior Advisor, Brookings Panel on Economic Activity, Brookings. He was also Visiting Professor at a number of Universities and Institutions. In 2003, Princeton University published in his honour a 600 page Festschrift Volume, Knowledge, Information and Expectations in Modern Macroeconomics edited by Joseph Stiglitz et al.

13.2 A SUMMARY OF EDMUND PHELPS'S CONTRIBUTIONS TO ECONOMICS

The main goals of stabilisation policy have traditionally been keeping unemployment in an economy at a low level and containing inflation at a relatively low rate. The choice of macroeconomic policy hinges upon the relationship between inflation and unemployment and the trade-off between the welfare of current and future generations. These issues which concern trade-offs between different policy objectives have been for long the focus of macroeconomic research. The research centred on a few key questions as put forward by Phelps, such as: How can involuntary unemployment exist in an economy, specifically in conditions of equilibrium in the expectational sense? How could the rate of unemployment remain below its natural level, however briefly? In such an infra-natural state, what is the process by which nominal wages go on rising upward? There are other questions which call for an explanation such as: How should fiscal and monetary policy attempt to resolve the conflict between the goals of low unemployment and low inflation? How should society resolve the conflict between present consumption and future consumption? Or, putting it in another way, how much should the society save in order to increase future consumption?

Before we survey Phelps's contribution to the resolution of these issues, it may be in order to outline the macroeconomic framework that was in vogue in 1950s.

In the literature, broadly two schools of macroeconomics are basically distinguished, namely Classical school and the Keynesian school with respect to the school's faith in the "invisible hand" put forward by Adam Smith. The Classical school believed the optimisation of private economic actors, the adjustment of relative prices to equate supply and demand and the efficiency of free and unfettered markets. The Keynesian school, on the other hand, emphasised that understanding economic fluctuations requires appreciating the possibility of "market failure on a grand scale" but not just studying the intricacies of general equilibrium.

A central idea of the analysis of Keynes was his emphasis of the inherently unstable character of the capitalist market economies which tend to come to rest in a chronic condition of sub-normal activity for a considerable period without any marked tendency, either towards recovery or towards complete collapse. This instability is mainly ascribed to fluctuations in aggregate demand. As a consequence, reflecting the state of deficient aggregate demand, there arises "involuntary" unemployment in the economy. In Keynes's view, market mechanism cannot bring about equilibrium and stabilise the economy at full employment in the absence of active government intervention through fiscal and monetary policy measures. Keynes believed that limited government intervention could be the remedy for the shortcomings in the operation of the invisible hand.

The IS-LM model of Hicks, as is well known, is viewed as an approach for studying the determination of aggregate demand. The aggregate demand curve is a downward sloping curve in P-Y (price-income) space. However, one requires a good theoretical frame for obtaining an aggregate supply curve, as aggregate demand and aggregate supply curves determine, among other things, the equilibrium price level. Early discussions of inflation were conducted in terms of shifts in these aggregate demand and aggregate supply curves. Demand-pull inflation is explained as a result of an exogenous upward shift in the aggregate demand curve -- increasing both equilibrium output and equilibrium price. Likewise, an exogenous upward shift in the aggregate supply curve results in cost-push inflation by reducing equilibrium output and increasing equilibrium price. The upward shift in the aggregate supply curve is explained as the result of increased costs.

The interaction between demand-pull and cost-push effects is recognised in the traditional discussion of inflation. When there is an exogenous rise in aggregate demand resulting in higher price level, workers would be prompted to seek higher nominal wages; if the firms concede workers' demand for higher wages, costs would rise leading to an upward shift of the aggregate supply curve. The higher wages for workers would mean higher income for labour. As a result, workers' demand for products and services would increase, leading to further upward shift in the aggregate demand curve. Further price increases would result and this cycle would be repeated.

13.3 THE PHILLIPS CURVE

However, while orthodox Keynesians had a good theory of aggregate demand they had no good theory of aggregate supply. The absence of a good theory of aggregate supply is underlined by their ready and enthusiastic acceptance of the Phillips Curve which postulated the existence of a stable negative relationship between inflation and unemployment. In 1958, A.W. Phillips discovered the existence of an inverse empirical relationship between the percentage rate of change of money wages on the one hand and the unemployment rate in an economy on the other. The inverse relationship that Phillips obtained was for the United Kingdom over the period 1869-1957.

The simple Phillips curve can be written as

$$\dot{W} = \frac{W_t - W_{t-1}}{W_{t-1}} = f(U) \qquad (1)$$

$$f'(U) < 0$$

Where

W_t = level of money wages in time period t

W_{t-1} = level of money wages in time period (t-1)

$\dot{W}$ = percentage rate of change of money wages, i.e., the rate of money wage inflation.

U = rate of unemployment.

While a linear relationship for 'f' is convenient to assume, a hyperbolic relationship, such as the following is indicated by much of the empirical evidence.

$$\frac{W_t - W_{t-1}}{W_{t-1}} = a_0 + a_1 U^{-1} \tag{2}$$

$$a_1 > 0$$

In this case, the trade-off relationship between money wage inflation and the rate of unemployment becomes steeper the lower the unemployment level as illustrated below.

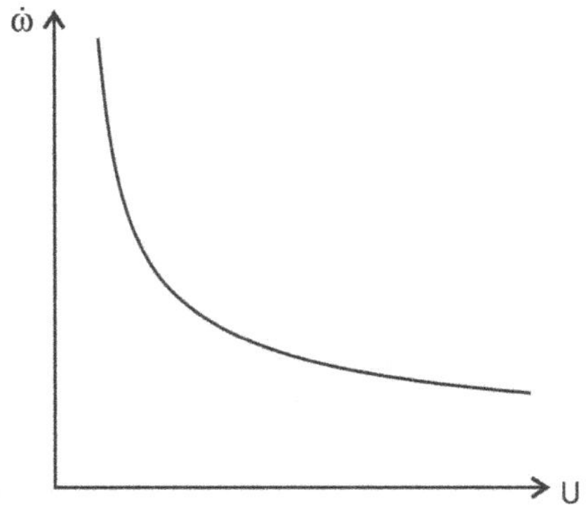

Fig. 13.1 The Phillips curve

The term Phillips curve is more commonly used to describe the relationship between the rate of change of prices and unemployment rather than the rate of money wage inflation and unemployment. The relationship between the two, namely the rate of money wage inflation and the rate of inflation can be shown by assuming the following simple pricing relationship.

$$P = m(ULC) \tag{3}$$

where

P = Price of output,

m = mark up factor, assumed to be constant ≥ 1,

ULC = unit labour costs.

Here price is assumed to be set as a mark-up on unit labour costs where

$$ULC = \frac{WN}{Y} \tag{4}$$

where

N = employment of labour,

Y = total output

W is defined earlier

Taking percentage changes of equations (3) and (4) gives the rate of price inflation. If average labour productivity (Y/N) grows at a rate, say, r, equation (3) and (4) can be combined to derive the following equation:

$$p = w - r \tag{5}$$

Equation (5) implies the rate of price inflation/unemployment trade-off. The relationship is given below:

$$p = f(U) - r \tag{6}$$

The reasons that prompted orthodox Keynesian economists to quickly adopt Phillips curve may be recounted here. First, the hypothesis furnished a satisfactory explanation of price determination and inflation. Within the Hicks-Hansen IS-LM framework or neo-classical synthesis, the price level is assumed to be at less than full employment. As such, changes in aggregate demand affect only the level of employment and output. Money wages are taken to be fixed and not responsive to changes in aggregate demand up to full employment level. The Phillips curve permitted orthodox Keynesian economists to link their theory of determination of output and employment to a theory of wage and price inflation.

Second, the Phillips curve provided strong empirical evidence of a stable relationship between level of unemployment and inflation rate for almost a century. Third, in the face of the problem policy makers face of simultaneously achieving high levels of employment and price stability in an economy, the Phillips curve interpretation by orthodox Keynesians as implying a stable long run trade-off between wage inflation and unemployment, offered the authorities a menu of possible inflation-unemployment combinations for policy choice. In the words of Snowdon and Vane "... up to at least the mid-to-late 1960s the prevailing Keynesian consensus in macroeconomics was one in which the IS-LM model was used to explain the determination of output and employment, while the Phillips curve enabled policymakers to predict the rate of inflation which would result from different target levels of unemployment being attained by activist demand-management policies." (However, we must recall that some of the prominent followers of the economics of Keynes like Professor Sidney Weintraub of University of Pennsylvania did not accept this approach).

There were several problems associated with the wage-unemployment trade-off as presented by Phillips though this relationship was "apparently confirmed" by empirical work done in several countries. It was purely a statistical relationship with no convincing link to microeconomic theories about the behaviour of individual firms and households. One common interpretation was that unemployment could be seen as a proxy for excess demand (supply) in the labour market, so that the Phillips curve is considered as an equation describing how the price (wage) level responds over time to an imbalance between demand and supply. A second problem concerns the view inherent in the hypothesis that higher employment could be permanently achieved by accepting higher inflation; it goes contrary to the assumption in the economic theory that real rather than nominal forces determine the real variables in the economy in the long run. Further, there was no theory about the socalled frictional unemployment level though there is general agreement that the rate of unemployment could not be reduced to zero through economic policy measures. There was, however, no clear understanding of what unemployment level was compatible with labour market equilibrium.

Several attempts were made in 1960s to providing the Phillips Curve relationship with some theoretical underpinnings. Notable among them were those by Lipsey, Eckstein, Eckstein and Wilson and Perry. By about the middle of the 1960s, however, the simple Phillips curve appeared to be breaking down. The degree of explanatory power of the Phillips curve tended to decline. Furthermore, the empirical estimates employing the Phillips curve framework were found to be typically unstable.

13.4 CHALLENGE OF PHELPS

In the late 1960s, Edmund Phelps challenged the postulated relationship between inflation and unemployment. He has attempted rectification of the theory of inflation and unemployment by explicitly modelling the wage and price-setting behaviour of firms, specifically introducing expectations of agents into the analysis. Phelps distinguishes between expected and unexpected inflation and explored its macroeconomic implications. He has argued that inflation does not only depend on unemployment but also on the expectations of firms and employees about price and wage increases. He analyses the determination of wages and prices by taking into account problems of information in the economy. According to him, individual economic agents have incomplete knowledge about the actions of others and must base their decisions on expectations. He has argued that it is the difference between expected and actual inflation and not inflation per se that is related to unemployment. Phelps thus has posited that current inflation depends on unemployment as well as inflationary expectations. He argues that wages and prices are adjusted only infrequently and as such the adjustments that are effected are based on forecasts of inflation. Thus, the higher the anticipated rate of inflation the higher the unemployment required to reach a certain actual inflation rate.

Phelps formulated the first model of what has come to be known as the expectations-augmented Phillips Curve, according to which inflation depends on both unemployment and expectations of inflation. The relationship is expressed in the following equation.

$$p = f(U) + p^e \qquad (7)$$

where,

p = actual rate of inflation,

p^e = expected rate of inflation, and

$f(U)$ = a decreasing function of unemployment, U

According to equation (7), actual inflation depends on both unemployment rate and the expected rate of inflation. The equilibrium rate of unemployment is obtained as the outcome of an expectational equilibrium with $p = p^e$; that is, when current rate of inflation is equal to the expected rate of inflation. The equilibrium rate of unemployment, U* is given by f(U)* = 0. If expectations are based on observations of inflation in recent past or based on adaptive expectations, inflation will be increasing so long as U < U* and decreasing as long as U > U*. This is commonly referred to as the "accelerationist hypothesis." The equilibrium rate of unemployment is referred to as non-accelerating inflation rate of unemployment or NAIRU or natural rate of unemployment according to Friedman. Phelps's formulation says that for a given unemployment rate, a one percentage point increase in expected inflation leads to a one percentage point in actual inflation. He contends that in setting prices and negotiating wages and salaries, firms and employees base their decisions on their beliefs about the development of prices and wages in general. The inter-temporal perspective that is thrown up by Phelps's work is that current inflation expectations impinge on the future trade-off between inflation and unemployment.

The hypothesis advanced by Phelps (and Friedman independently at about the same time) has received overwhelming support in subsequent empirical research. One exception, however, was recognised: The impact of expectations of inflation on actual inflation may be smaller at very low rates of inflation. Phelps's hypothesis implied that there was no long run trade-off between inflation and unemployment because there could be no permanent discrepancy between expected rate of inflation and actual inflation rate. His analysis was at variance with the earlier view that inflationary demand policies could permanently achieve higher employment.

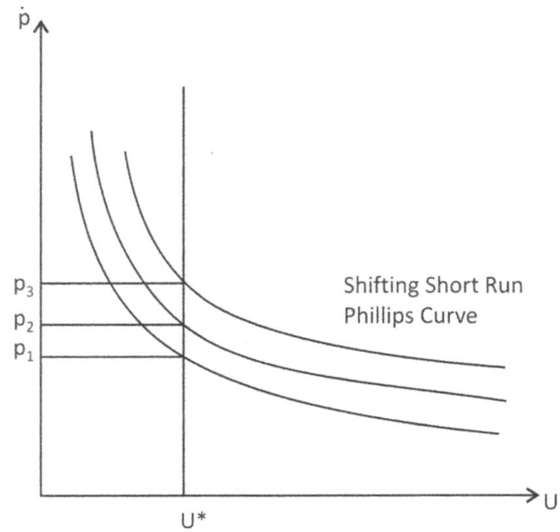

Fig. 13.2 The Long Run Phillips Curve

His hypothesis of a vertical long run Phillips curve at the equilibrium rate of unemployment (U^*) is "one of the most influential ideas in macroeconomics over the past 50 years." It has important policy implications. A notable result of this work is that the long run rate of unemployment in an economy cannot be influenced by monetary or fiscal policy affecting aggregate demand, thus identifying crucial limitations on what demand management policies can achieve.

In Phelps's view the task of demand management policy is not to solving a static optimisation problem of achieving the best attainable combination of unemployment and inflation at a given point in time. The issue of trade-off between inflation and unemployment is basically inter-temporal. As mentioned earlier, Phelps was the first to supply the analysis of the determinants of the equilibrium unemployment rate. The influence of his analysis on the conduct of monetary policy by modern central banks (essentially of developed countries) can be seen in that they make decisions on interest rates on the basis of estimates of the equilibrium unemployment rate. It has now become standard practice for the central banks to take Phelps's inter-temporal approach to monetary policy. Low current inflation can be taken as an investment in low inflation expectations. An important result of this is a more favourable inflation–unemployment trade-off in the future. This perspective of Phelps is natural to him as it is in the line of his earlier work on capital formation.

Phelps put forward an explicit model of an imperfect labour market with frictions, job search behaviour and wage-setting firms that is helpful in explaining the determinants of equilibrium unemployment. This is a significant contribution which has provided for the first time microeconomic foundations to mainstream macroeconomic theory, especially to employment and inflation theory. He has derived aggregate wage setting behaviour of firms from detailed modelling of the behaviour of individual agents.

He has explained how market interactions take place and how wages and prices are determined. Jobs and workers are heterogeneous and there is imperfect and asymmetric information on both demand and supply sides of the labour market. Though markets are assumed to be atomistic, there is no Walrasian auctioneer who sets wages and prices that clear all markets. Instead, wages are set by firms that are able to exercise temporary monopsony power. Workers and firms meet randomly at a rate dependent upon the number of searching unemployed workers and the number of vacancies according to what is now referred to as matching function. The gross rate of hiring at any point of time in the economy is determined by the matching function. "Neither demand nor supply determined the quantity of labor traded; instead the market would typically be characterized by the simultaneous existence of vacant jobs and unemployed workers, thanks to the frictions encapsulated in the matching function."

He has also developed a formal model of so called efficiency wages embedded in macroeconomic framework. The implication of efficiency wage models is that a firm finds it profitable to set its wage above the level of market-clearing wage. The efficiency wage improves worker morale, reduces labour turnover which is costly or improves the quality of the pool of job applicants.

Phelps also made significant contribution to the theory of price-setting in microeconomic theory. In collaboration with Sidney Winter, he developed a model which shows why prices need not fully reflect short-term fluctuations in marginal costs. This is based upon the argument that firms enjoy transitory monopoly power (due to phenomenon of asymmetric information and slow diffusion of price information) and costly search on the part of customers. As a consequence, firms would face a dynamic trade-off between more profit today and more future profits because of more customers. The idea that business fluctuations give rise to changes in the relationship between prices and marginal costs is "commonplace" nowadays in macroeconomics. Howitt remarks "[It is] one of the systematic explanations of why prices do not always mirror marginal costs even in a world of 'atomistic' competition." In a 1969 paper Phelps has made another important contribution to the development of micro foundations of macroeconomic theory. In that paper, he presented the well-known "island" parable that demonstrates how imperfect information can result in price stickiness leading to generation of real effects of monetary policy. Such real effects arise in an economy where there are no constraints – either physical or regulatory – on price adjustment, where all participants behave rationally and where gains from trade are fully realised. Howitt argues that "this... parable was the explicit foundation of Lucas's (1972) paper on 'Expectations and the Neutrality of Money,' one of the most influential contributions to twentieth century economics."

13.5 PHELPS'S EARLY WORK ON CAPITAL ACCUMULATION AND INTER-GENERATIONAL TRADE-OFFS

Phelps's early significant contribution was contained in his 1961 article which puts forward the Golden Rule of Capital Accumulation. A key issue that became important in 1950s and early 1960s, in view of the fact that the aggregate U.S. savings rate was considered too low, concerned as to how society should trade-off the consumption of current citizens against that of future citizens. Phelps, underlining the main objective of inter-generational fairness, asked what rate of capital formation (both in the form of physical capital and human capital) was desirable. The prime question is what fraction of national income of a country should be consumed now and how much should be saved and invested in order to augment the capital stock with a view to boosting future production and consumption. In regard to distribution of consumption and welfare across generations, this issue becomes quite important.

To answer this question, Phelps using a Solow-Swan neo-classical growth model, has obtained the golden rule of capital accumulation – the return to capital should equal the growth rate of output. The golden rule prescription specified a savings rate that was of the same order of magnitude as that in the U.S. data. In his later work, Phelps has argued that rates of savings higher than the golden rule are not beneficial for any generation. He suggested the possibility of dynamic inefficiency implying overaccumulation of capital, constituting market failure in the sense that resources are simply left "on the table." In such a situation, lowering of the savings rate increases consumption in the short run and, if the initial capital stock is above the golden rule level, will also increase consumption in the long run. This is so, as the golden rule by definition maximises longrun consumption. To conclude: "the striking conclusion... is that regardless of which inter-generational utility perspective is adopted, a savings rate above the goldenrule rate is too high." Phelps has later carried the analysis further in a joint paper with Robert Pollak suggesting government intervention in private consumption decisions. This argument has been employed to justify active government role in old-age savings plans.

13.6 OTHER CONTRIBUTIONS BY PHELPS

Phelps has also generalised the golden rule in his analysis of the role of investment in education and research and development. In a joint work with Nelson, he has demonstrated how poorer countries easily "catch up" with richer countries by educated work force in the former countries facilitating the dissemination of new technology. Their analysis provided a plausible explanation for the phenomenon of high return to education noticed in periods of rapid technological change.

His later contributions also include elaborate non-synchronous models of wage-setting and price-setting which have paved the way for development of the New Keynesian School. The models of the New Keynesian School show that the general price or wage level does not jump to the final adjustment level even in the face of the macro shock because firms have overlapping or staggered price or wage commitments. He also made attempts at completing the "structuralist" model of unemployment determination in which the path of equilibrium unemployment rate constantly approaches a steady rate that is a "moving target" – "a variable natural rate adjusting to the evolution of the economy's state variables" [such as foreign oil shocks and shifts in unemployment compensation].

Finally, we have to refer to his work related to developing a theory of expectations and consequent macroeconomic behaviour. Phelps's emphasis in this work is that while it is possible to justify assumption of rational expectations on pragmatic grounds, there is no epistemological basis for such an assumption. This view is based on his contention that there exists a pluralism of models. If expectations are rational according to A's model, they cannot be rational in B's contrary model.

It is easily seen that in this short note no attempt is made to cover even briefly all his scientific work that spans over forty-five years. He also made significant contributions to public finance, social choice, entrepreneurship, etc.

13.7 CONCLUDING OBSERVATIONS

Phelps contributions to macroeconomics have not only enriched the literature but also continue to have an important influence on the economics profession. Critics have also noted the "depth of his ideas." Specifically, mention is made of Phelps's island parable providing "the basic conceptual framework by Lucas's 1972 paper 'Expectation and the Neutrality of Money' and Prescott and Kydland's analysis of monetary policy in their 1977 paper in the Journal of Political Economy using the framework put forward by Phelps in his 1967 Economica article." In this context a reference may be made to Howitt's observation that "... Phelps even played a big role in laying the foundations of the real business cycle analysis [of]...Kydland and Prescott." Howitt also notes Phelps's role in gathering researchers together, encouraging them and publishing their findings. Furthermore, Howitt specifically mentions as to how Phelps has taken macroeconomics as a social science, tackling important contemporary social issues such as unemployment, inflation, technological change, fiscal policy and social justice. "This is why his ideas stay with us in the long run". We may close this note with Axel Leijonhufvud's comment reviewing Phelps's Festschrift volume Knowledge, Information and Expectations in Modern Economics: "Phelps was the one to provide a micro founded model with the natural rate property. Macroeconomics has not been the same since.... Aggregate demand management lost any theoretical rationale. Macro policy has to be supply-side policy... the remarkable thing about this Festschrift is that all of its papers have strong links to the contributions of Ned Phelps.... the volume... should be an eye opener to many readers who have not been aware of the full range and long-lasting influence of his contributions."

13.8 SELECT BIBLIOGRAPHY OF EDMUND PHELPS'S WORKS

13.8.1 BOOKS

1965 Fiscal Neutrality Toward Economic Growth, McGraw-Hill, New York.

1966 Golden Rules of Economic Growth, W. W. Norton, New York.

1970 (with A.A. Alchian, C.C. Holt et.al.), Microeconomic Foundations of Employment and Inflation Theory, W. W. Norton, New York.

1972 Inflation Policy and Unemployment Theory, W. W. Norton, New York.

1974 Editor and Contributor, Economic Justice, Penguin, Hammondsworth, England.

1975 Editor and Contributor, Altruism, Morality and Economic Theory, Basic Books, New York.

1979 Studies in Macroeconomic Theory: Volume 1 - Employment and Inflation, Academic Press, New York.

1980 Studies in Macroeconomic Theory: Volume. 2 - Redistribution and Growth, Academic Press, New York.

1983 (with R. Frydman), Contributor and Editor, Individual Forecasting and Aggregate Outcomes: Rational Expectations Examined, Cambridge University Press, Cambridge.

1985 Political Economy: An Introductory Text, W. W. Norton, New York.

1988 (with J.P. Fitoussi), The Slump in Europe: Open Economy Theory Reconstructed, Basil Blackwell, Oxford.

1990 Seven Schools of Macroeconomic Thought: The Arne Ryde Lectures, Oxford University Press, Oxford.

1991 Recent Developments in Macroeconomics, 3 Volumes, Edward Elgar, Oxford.

1994 Structural Slumps: The Modern Equilibrium Theory of Employment, Interest and Assets, Harvard University Press, Cambridge, MA.

13.8.2 ARTICLES

1961 a "A Test for the Presence of Cost Inflation in the U.S. Economy, 1955-57, "Yale Economic Essays, Vol.1, Jan.

b "The Golden Rule of Accumulation: A Fable for Growth men," AER, Vol.51, No.4.

1962 a "The Accumulation of Risky Capital: A Sequential Utility Analysis," Econometrica, Vol.30, Oct.

b " The New View of Investment: A Neoclassical Analysis," QJE, Vol.76, Nov.

1965 a "Anticipated Inflation and Economic Welfare," JPE, Vol.73, No.1.

b "Second Essay on the Golden Rule of Accumulation," AER, Vol.55, No.4.

1966 "Models of Technical Progress and the Golden Rule of Research," RES, Vol.33, Apr.

1967 "Phillips Curves, Expectations of Inflation and Optimal Unemployment over Time," Economica, Vol.34, Aug.

1968 a (with R.A. Pollak), "On Second-Best National Saving and Game-Equilibrium Growth," RES, Vol.35, Apr.

b "Money-Wage Dynamics and Labor-Market Equilibrium," JPE, Vol.76, Aug, Part 2, Revised version in E.S. Phelps et al., Microeconomic Foundations of Employment and Inflation Theory, W.W. Norton, New York.

1969 a "The New Microeconomics in Inflation and Employment Theory," AER, Vol.59, No.2, Revised version in E.S. Phelps et al., Microeconomic Foundations of Employment and Inflation Theory, W.W. Norton, New York.

b (with K. Shell), "Public Debt, Taxation and Capital Intensiveness," JET, Vol.1, Oct.

1970 (with S.G. Winter Jr.), "Optimal Price Policy under Atomistic Competition," in E.S. Phelps et al., Microeconomic Foundations of Employment and Inflation Theory, W.W. Norton, New York.

1971 (with E. Burmeister), "Money, Public Debt, Inflation and Real Interest," JMCB, Vol.3, May.

1972 "Money, Public Expenditure and the Labor Supply," JET, VOL.5, Aug.

1977 (with J.B. Taylor), "Stabilizing Powers of Monetary Policy under Rational Expectations," JPE, Vol.85, No.1.

1978 "Ralwsian Growth," RES, Vol.45, Feb.

1983 "The Trouble with Rational Expectations and the Problem of Inflation Stabilization," in (E.S. Phelps and R. Frydman et al.), Individual Forecasting and Aggregate Outcomes: Rational Expectations Examined, Cambridge University Press, Cambridge.

1987 "Distributive Justice," The New Palgrave: A Dictionary of Economics, Macmillan, London.

1991 "The Effectiveness of Macro Policies in a Small Open-Economy Dynamic Aggregative Model," in Money, Macroeconomics and Economic Policy, MIT Press, Cambridge, MA.

1992 "Macroeconomic Shocks in a Dynamized Model of the Natural Rate of Unemployment," AER, Vol.82, No.4.

1998 (with G. Joega), "Natural-rate Theory and OECD Unemployment," EJ, Vol.108, May.

2000 a "Lessons in Natural-rate Dynamics," OEP, Vol.52, No.1.

b (with M. Francesconi et. al), "Education and Natural Rate of Unemployment," OEP, Vol 52, No.1.

2005 (with A. Petrucci), "Capital Subsidies versus Labor Subsidies: A Trade-Off Between Capital and Employment," JMCB, Vol.37, No.5.

2006 a (with H.T. Hoon), "Future Fiscal and Budgetary Shocks," JET, Vol.143, No.1.

b "Prospective Shifts, Speculative Swings: 'Macro' in the Twenty First Century in the Tradition Championed by Paul Samuelson," in Samuelson Economics and the Twenty First Century, M. Szenberg (ed.), Oxford University Press, Oxford.

2007 "Macroeconomics for a Modern Economy," Nobel Prize Lecture, AER, Vol.97, No.3.

2011 (with Sinn eds.), "Perspectives on the Performance of the Continental Economies," MIT Press, Cambridge, MA.

2012 "Refounding Capitalism," in The Oxford Handbook of Capitalism, D. C. Mueller (ed.), Oxford University Press, New York.

13.9 WORKS OF OTHERS

Friedman, M. (1968), "The Role of Monetary Policy," AER, Vol.58, No.1.

Hayek, F. A (1968), "Competition as a Discovery Procedure," Reprinted in F. A. Hayek, New Studies in Philosophy, Economics and History of Ideas, University of Chicago Press, Chicago, Ill.

Howitt, P. (2007), "Edmund Phelps: Macroeconomist and Social Scientist," ScandJE, Vol.109, No.2.

Kydland, F. E. and E. C. Prescott (1977), "Rules Rather than Discretion: The Inconsistency of Optimal Plans," JPE, Vol.85, No.3.

Lucas Jr R. E. (1972), "Expectations and the Neutrality of Money," JET, Vol.4, No.2.

Phillips, A.W. (1958), "The Relation Between Unemployment and the Rate of Change of Money Wage Rates in the United Kingdom, 1861-1957," Economica, Vol.25, No.100.

Rao, B.S.R. (2007), Edmund S. Phelps: Recipient of 2006 Nobel Memorial Prize in Economic Sciences (Unpublished lecture at Economics Department, Osmania University, Hyderabad).

CHAPTER 14

PAUL ROBIN KRUGMAN

(1953 –)

Paul Robin Krugman, Professor of Economics and International Affairs at Princeton University, U.S.A. and an OP-ED Columnist for the New York Times, was awarded the 2008 Nobel Memorial Prize in Economic Sciences "for his research on international trade and economic geography." The Prize, of course, is for his academic research in Economics, specifically, as the press release announcing the award says, "for his analysis of trade patterns and location of economic activity." Patterns of trade and location of economic activity have invariably been crucial issues in the economic debate. For a long time, the analysis of foreign trade had been grounded in a well-established theory – David Ricardo's comparative advantage. The theory provided satisfactory answers why some countries export certain goods and import others.

There are questions, however, for which economists are called upon to provide approximate answers. How are the countries and populations affected by globalisation? In regard to rapid urbanisation witnessed in a large number of countries in the twentieth century, the crucial question is why do increasing numbers of people flock to large cities, while rural areas become depopulated? For answering these and similar questions, the need for a sound theoretical foundation had been felt. Furthermore, after World War II, it became quite clear that the traditional foreign trade theory was found wanting in explaining the patterns of trade that had emerged. In 1979, Paul Krugman put forward a new model which provides a better explanation for the observed foreign trade patterns. Krugman's theory was intended to explain the intra-industry trade. His theory has assumed presence of scale economies in the manufacturing industry, which resulted in mass production leading to diminished cost per unit of output. The Nobel Foundation notes: "The basic idea is rather self-evident, but the step from speculation to a stringent and cohesive theory is substantial – and this was precisely the step Krugman took... in 1979."

Besides economies of scale, Krugman's new theory has made an additional crucial assumption: that is, consumers like diversity in their consumption. Though this concept was considered new at that time, it seemed to correspond to reality. The real life situation attests to growing supply of available commodities and the luring of consumers by a continuous proliferation of new brands. In this connection, a reference has to be made to the 1977 article of Avinash Dixit and Joseph Stiglitz which analysed consumers' preferences for product diversity. They show that each producer, operating under increasing returns to scale, became more or less a monopolist in terms of his own branded product, though his product faces stiff competition in the market from other brands.

The information supplied for the public by the Royal Swedish Academy observes that such a model (the model of Dixit and Stiglitz referred to above) can be used to demonstrate that foreign trade will occur not only between countries which are different as in traditional theory but also between countries identical in terms of factor endowments and access to technology. Furthermore, it can be shown that extensive intra-industry trade will take place. As each country takes effective advantage of economies of scale, consumers globally will benefit from increased welfare as a consequence of greater diversity of consumption products at lower prices. This can be contrasted with each country producing only to satisfy its domestic market demand, with no international trade.

While Krugman's brief article of 1979 initially did not attract much attention, perhaps owing to its simplicity, economic researchers in international economics have later realised its importance as it has "pointed to vital mechanisms in the economy." The theory has been fortified with greater realism over time with subsequent articles and books by Krugman as well as other researchers. It is now generally accepted that the "basic mechanisms specified by Krugman constitute an important complement to the traditional Heckscher-Ohlin theory" encompassing features of both theories. Krugman's "new" theory has inspired vast volume of research, which is, the press release of the Nobel Foundation observes, usually a reliable indication of theoretical quality.

Krugman's approach to explain foreign trade, particularly his assumption of economies of scale in production and consumers' preference for product diversity in consumption, is found to be useful for analysis of issues in economic geography. Economic geography is concerned with the distribution of factor resources, say labour and capital, over countries and regions and not merely with what and where goods are produced. Krugman has been able to "integrate two disparate fields" into a unified model--called the "new economic geography." In the last part of 1979 article, Krugman poses questions as to what would happen if foreign trade cannot take place owing to excessively high transport costs or other obstacles. His reasoning is as follows. If two countries are completely alike, welfare will be the same in both countries. But if the countries are exactly alike but one country has a slightly larger population than the other, then the country with larger population can successfully exploit economies of scale resulting in lower consumer prices and/or greater diversity in the supply of goods, and the labour will enjoy a higher real wage. This, in turn, increases the welfare of consumers in the country with larger inhabitants encouraging labour to move to it. In the next round real wages and the supply of goods will further increase in that country, giving rise to further migration, and so on. Krugman formulated these concepts clearly in his 1991 article which was devoted to developing a comprehensive theory of location of labour and firms. In this article, he assumes that although trade is possible, it would not occur because of high transport costs. There can be free movement of labour to the country or region where real wages are high and there is diversity in supply of goods. The location decisions of firms are crucially determined by the trade-off between utilising economies and saving on transport costs.

The press release states that the "core-periphery" model that emerged from the above-mentioned considerations, results in either concentration of communities or their decentralisation depending upon the relation between transport costs and economies of scale. The forces which facilitate concentration of communities will prevail under certain conditions leading to regional imbalances and concentration of population in a "high technology core." A small minority of population will live in the periphery dependent on agriculture. It is noted that "such a mechanism could underlie the explosive urbanisation witnessed today throughout the world with rapidly growing mega cities surrounded by increasing depopulated rural areas." An alternative possibility namely decentralisation can occur at other times in terms of Krugman's model.

14.1 A BRIEF BIOGRAPHICAL NOTE: PAUL KRUGMAN

Paul Krugman, who was the only child of David Krugman and Anit, was born in New York, U.S.A and brought up in Long Island, New York. Paul Krugman's father was a middle manager in the insurance industry. Krugman did his graduation from John F. Kennedy High School in Baltimore. He has a bachelor's degree from Yale University in 1974 and a doctorate from MIT in 1977. He returned to Yale in 1977 and worked there as assistant professor till 1980 when he joined there as associate professor. During 1980-83, Krugman served as a Senior International Economist at the Council of Economic Advisors of President Reagan. Since 1984 until 2000, he taught at MIT as Ford International Professor of Economics. He taught at Stanford University between 1994 and 1996 and at University of California at Berkeley. Since 2000, he has been teaching at Princeton University, Princeton, New Jersey, where he is Professor of Economics and International Affairs.

Krugman is a Fellow of Econometric Society, Fellow of the American Academy of Arts and Sciences (1992), a research associate of the National Bureau of Economic Research and a member of the Group of Thirty – a group of economists that "aims to deepen understanding of international economics and financial issues." He has served as a consultant to the Federal Reserve Bank of New York, the World Bank, the International Monetary Fund, the United Nations as well as a number of countries including Portugal and the Philippines. He has won Adam Smith Award in 1995 and William Alonso Memorial Prize in 2002 for his innovative work in Regional Science. Krugman received honorary doctorate from a number of academic institutions.

Krugman is the author or editor of 23 books and more than 200 professional journal articles, many of them on International Trade and Finance. In recognition of his work, the American Economic association awarded him its John Bates Clark medal, a prize given every two years (prior to 2009) to "that economist under forty who is adjudged to have made a significant contribution to economic knowledge." He follows a long list of Clark medal recipients (in fact, he is the twelfth) who have gone on to win Nobel in Economic Sciences, including Paul Samuelson and Joseph Stiglitz.

14.2 A SUMMARY OF PAUL KRUGMAN'S CONTRIBUTIONS

14.2.1 NEW TRADE THEORY

Traditionally, David Ricardo's theory of comparative advantage remained a cornerstone of international trade theory. In his Principles of Political Economy and Taxation, Ricardo stated that "it [foreign trade] will very powerfully contribute to increase the mass of commodities, and therefore the form of enjoyments." Schumpeter in his History of Economic Analysis commented: "Needless to say, this is an essential part of Ricardo's free trade argument; foreign trade increases indeed the ' happiness of mankind' by improving the allocation of resources and by giving 'incentives to saving and to the accumulation of capital'- ' by the abundance and cheapness of commodities' which it bring[s] about ...." Ricardo took international productivity differences as given. The next significant development in the subject was the recognition in the early twentieth century by Heckscher and Ohlin of differences in factor endowments as a major source of comparative advantage. After "definitive formalisation" of the view by Samuelson and R.W.Jones, the theory continued to dominate the field of international trade.

In the 1970s, economists have realised that factor endowments or the theory founded upon comparative advantage was not able to explain the empirical data in foreign trade. These theories predicted that trade between countries should be exchange of different goods and the essential basis of this trade was in differences in the relative production possibilities. As J.F Neary notes, most of the voluminous growth in trade since World War II was in relatively similar goods, particularly manufactures between relatively similar countries--developed countries. That is, the growth was more in intra-industry as opposed to inter-industry trade. Krugman in his Prize lecture remarks: "...there was an undercurrent of dissatisfaction with conventional trade theory. I used to think of the propagation of this dissatisfaction as the counterculture." He makes reference to "underground classics," such as S.B Linder's An Essay on Trade and Transformation (1961) which argued that exports tend to reflect the characteristics of the home market. He also makes a reference to empirical work of Balassa and Grubel and Lloyd that "cried out" for a theoretical framework. Krugman wondered as to why trade counter-culture prevailed even though there was general agreement about the "apparent completeness" of traditional trade theory. It may be called a "similar-similar" problem. That is, exchange of similar products between similar countries as envisaged by huge two-way trade in automotive products between the United States and Canada. The Royal Swedish Academy's information for the public gives another example. "A country such as Sweden, for example, exports and imports cars. This would not be compatible with the theory of comparative advantage unless the production of Volvo cars required a wholly unique technology, or a completely different combination of labor and capital than, for instance, production of BMW cars. But this appears highly unlikely."

Neary provides another reason for the dissatisfaction with the comparative advantage theories. Those theories predict that the countries have to undergo hardship in the process of adjusting to trade liberalisation. Liberalisation could necessitate factors of production to move out of sectors in which a country has comparative disadvantage and move into expanding sectors. The theory envisages a smooth movement of factors along a production possibility frontier; however, "factor specificities" and "factor-price rigidities" may make the adjustment painful. He cites the smooth integration of basically similar economies of Western Europe form the European Economic Community (EEC) as belying the theoretical prediction. Krugman also refers to research work of Balassa and others which showed that this process of adjustment "proceeded with surprisingly few costs of adjustments." Specialisation appeared to be, once again, intra-industry, rather than inter-industry.

Krugman, in his Prize lecture, furnishes empirical evidence to demonstrate that trade "in the first age of globalisation-- the age made possible by steam engines and telegraphs-- was mainly dissimilar-dissimilar: trade in dissimilar goods between dissimilar countries." In the empirical work using British trade data, Krugman shows that the pattern of trade on the eve of World War I "made perfect sense in terms of classical comparative advantage." Britain exported manufactured goods and imported raw materials. However, comparable British data for 1990 offers "no comparably easy interpretation: Britain both imported and exported mainly manufactured goods. He also shows that trade after World War II took place largely between similar countries. Before World War I, Britain traded remarkably little with its neighbouring countries. By 1990, however, Britain was a constituent of European economy in which "nations seemingly made a living by taking in each others' washing, buying goods that they could and... did produce for themselves." In this context, Krugman in his lecture refers to Balassa's work in the rise of intra-industry trade in Europe where Balassa points out that each country produced only part of the range of potential products within each industry, importing those goods it did not produce. Balassa rationalised this phenomenon thus as quoted by Krugman: "because specialization in narrower ranges of machinery and intermediate products will permit the exploitation of economies of scale through the lengthening of production runs."

Thus, the situation was ripe for a theoretical breakthrough. There was a need for integrating both increasing returns to scale and product differentiation. Chamberlin's model of monopolistic competition was eminently appropriate. In this context, Neary, recalling Harry Johnson's observations that the theory of Chamberlin's monopolistic competition has had virtually no impact on the theory of international trade... comments: "What was needed was a tractable specification of preferences and costs which would make it possible to apply Chamberlin's insights at the global level, and the technical tools for doing just that were assembled by Dixit and Stiglitz (1977)." An identical view has been expressed by Krugman in his Nobel lecture. He observes: "Then came the new monopolistic competition models" and refers to the work of Spence and Lancaster, in addition to the work of Dixit and Stiglitz (referred to by Neary). These papers focused on the classic welfare questions regarding whether monopolistic competition resulted in inefficient scale of operations or to production of a wrong product mix. Krugman has realised that models of monopolistic competition could be employed to deal with international trade issues, bypassing the traditional models based on comparative advantage. Krugman outlines his approach: "...countries that were identical in resources and technology would nonetheless specialize in producing different products, giving rise to trade as consumers sought variety." The theory of comparative advantage can be brought in as a natural extension by assuming that "all the differentiated products within an industry were produced with the same factor proportions; one could then explain inter-industry trade in terms of Heckscher-Ohlin model, with an overlay of intra-industry specialization due to increasing returns" (emphases in the original). Thus, a satisfying explanation of similar-similar trade could be given. Countries which have little comparative advantage to each other can nevertheless have good intra-industry trade as a result of economies of scale.

Krugman's model assumes that the firm enjoys internal economies of scale so that its average cost decreases when production is expanded. As a consequence, markets cannot be perfectly competitive. He assumes that there are different goods and that consumers desire to have variety. It is expressed by the following utility function:

$$U = \sum_{i=1}^{n} v(C_i) \tag{1}$$

where C_i is consumption of the ith good ,and

where v (.) is an increasing concave function.

Concavity denotes the taste for variety. Assuming that there is no price difference between goods, the consumer would spread his expenditure evenly across as many goods as possible.

Assume further that v (.) takes the following specific form

$$v(c_i) = \frac{c_i^{\gamma}}{\gamma}, 0 < \gamma < 1 \tag{2}$$

Equations (1) and (2) representing consumer preferences are referred to as Dixit-Stiglitz preferences.

Krugman assumes that labour(*l*) is the only factor of production (by definition all countries use identical factor proportions) and that all goods are produced by identical cost functions. As increasing returns to scale are assumed to be present, the labour requirement for production of good i is given by

$$l_i = \alpha + \beta x_i,\ \alpha,\ \beta > 0 \tag{3}$$

where X_i is the output of good i, and α denotes a fixed cost. The market is composed of monopolistically competitive firms, with free entry of firms, clearing of all markets indicating zero profits for all firms in equilibrium.

The model can be solved for the three unknowns: the price of each good relative to wage rate of labour, p_i/w (where w is the wage rate), the output of each good, X_i, and the total number of goods produced in the economy that is n. It is seen that consumers maximise their utility subject to their budget constraint:

$$\sum_{i=1}^{n} p_i c_i = w$$

It can be shown that the consumer's marginal rate of substitution between two goods i and j equals relative price. The following first order condition can be derived.

$$v'(c_i)/p_i = v'(c_j/p_j) = \lambda$$

for any two goods i and j where λ denotes the shadow value of income. An individual consumer's demand function for good i is

$$c(p_i) = (\lambda p_i)^{1/(y-1)}$$

Indirect utility is proportional to $(w/\overline{p})\Upsilon$

where $\overline{p}$ = is a price index across goods.

The real wage in this economy is w/p.

Profits by the firm which is a monopolistic competitor are maximised by setting the price so that MR = MC. With L total consumers in the economy, the firm's total revenue is

$$P_i L_c(p_i)$$

Its total costs are

$$\alpha + \beta L_c(p_i)w$$

Further, we can verify that when MR = MC, the monopolistically competitive firm chooses a constant mark-up over MC. New firms enter the market, augmenting product varieties until profits of each firm equal zero.

Since profits equal $p_i x_i - [(\alpha + \beta x)w]$ and all goods are symmetric and produced in equal quantity, equilibrium output is given by

$$X_i = (\alpha/\beta)y/(1-y) = \overline{x}$$

With above expression giving the quantity produced of each good, the variety of goods produced, n, is determined by

$$L = (\alpha + \beta\overline{x})n$$

since the L aggregate consumer-workers have to allocate their labor supply to n different goods.

Let us now turn our focus to determine how the size of the economy, given by L, influences the equilibrium. First, given the shape of the utility function explained earlier, the output of each good, $\overline{x}$, is unaffected. However, the number of goods (variety) increases proportionately with L. Second, since cL = $\overline{x}$, per-capita consumption of each good decreases. Third, welfare per consumer increases with L since, as product variety increases, real wages rise. This is easily seen as increasing returns to scale operate as the large economy implies production of more varieties of goods. Further, in the analysis of Krugman, increasing returns to scale leads to larger output of each good and lowering unit cost of each good.

Neary in his 2009 article explains the features of Krugman's 1979 paper and demonstrates the condition for goods market equilibrium, labour market equilibrium, the equilibrium of the model in that each firm maximises profits where MR= MC and that profits are driven to zero by free entry and exit of firms. He observes that as consumers demand all varieties, there is an increase in trade, all of which is intra-industry that is consistent with empirical evidence. Neary concludes: "Krugman's landmark 1979 paper was thus the first to present a coherent general equilibrium analysis of the kind of trade that in the words of the Nobel Memorial Prize committee, 'enables specialization and large-scale production which results in lower prices and a greater diversity of commodities.' It was arguably also the last, since most of the subsequent literature has concentrated on a special case in which only the final prediction, a great diversity of goods consumed, remains true." Krugman himself in his 1980 article and in later papers and many subsequent writers on monopolistic competition and trade obtained results that de-emphasised the implications of increasing returns and highlighted the range of varieties of goods available to consumers. Specifically, Krugman built in his 1981 paper, a special version of the emerging style of model to "encapsulate Balassa's insight that trade expansion had taken the form of intra-industry specialisation rather than inter-industry specialisation. The fears expressed in various member countries of [European] common market concerning the demise of particular industries have not been realized. There are no examples of declining manufacturing industries in any of the member countries." In particular, in the words of Krugman "What the model showed was that the classic Stolper-Samuelson result, in which trade liberalization hurts scarce factors, <u>can</u> emerge – but only if comparative advantage is strong and/or economies of scale weak. In the reverse case, which seemed to describe the growth of trade among industrial countries, trade was win-win." (Emphasis in original):

In his Nobel lecture, Krugman also refers to the significant insight he got from the application of Dixit–Stiglitz-based models to trade. That is, increasing returns to scale encourages concentration of production of any one product in a single location. By the firm choosing a location close to the large domestic market, transport costs are minimised and the firm would be encouraged to export to other markets. That is, countries tend to export goods for which they have a large domestic market. This is how Krugman has provided analytical precision to what is referred to as the "home market effect" discussed earlier by Corden. The key elements of the new trade theory are provided by Krugman in association with Helpman in his 1985 book. The definitive statement put forward by them integrates the following earlier work: factor price equalization theorem demonstrating how goods trade integrates factor markets globally, the Rybczynski and Hecksher-Ohlin theories linking factor endowments to production and trade patterns respectively and the Stolper-Samuelson theorem, connecting changes in goods prices to variations in real factor rewards. Krugman in his Prize lecture observes that increasing returns ordinarily reinforce, rather than call into question, the argument that there are gains from trade. He adds: "By the mid-1980s ...the 'new trade theory' had integrated increasing returns more or less seamlessly into our understanding of international trade. The impossible complexity that had previously daunted economists contemplating a major revision of trade theory had vanished, replaced by a surprisingly simple and elegant structure." This task was accomplished by the use of new models of monopolistic competition and the shift of the focus of trade economists to system-level or aggregate descriptions of the trade patterns from the effort of giving detailed predictions regarding which country produces each specific good.

Krugman is also credited with making "essential contributions" to the approach which used oligopolistic models (as opposed to monopolistic competitive models) of small group competition to issues of trade, employing Cournot's duopoly model, where two firms produce identical products, one located in the home country and the other in the foreign country. Brander, assuming zero transport costs and segmentation of national markets, predicted two-way trade or cross hauling of identical products even where both firms and markets were identical. Neary observes: "Moving from autarky to free trade in effect means moving from monopoly to duopoly, and the resulting fall in price and increase in sales raises consumer surplus by more than enough to offset the loss in profits by the home firm and to raise domestic welfare overall." Krugman in association with Brander showed in his 1983 paper that the basic results do not undergo any change even when transport costs are included. The paper reaches the conclusion that the home firm absorbs part of transport costs in its export price and spreading a lower profit margin on its export sales; that is, it is dumping in the foreign market. Neary observes that: "Since the foreign firm is doing exactly the same in the home market, the Cournot equilibrium with transport costs exhibits 'reciprocal dumping' by both firms." The effect on welfare of the level of transport costs is, however, complicated and crucially depends on the response of profits on home sales.

14.2.2 NEW ECONOMIC GEOGRAPHY

Traditionally, a major challenge for economists was combining space and competitive equilibrium. Taking that heterogeneity of space is exogenously determined, trade literature analysed the emerging trade patterns based on differences in factor proportions and technology. Further, starting with Alfred Marshall, bulk of regional analysis posited that economies of scale drive the agglomeration of economic activity. In addition, it was assumed that economies of scale are external to the individual firm while internal to the industry or region or city. It is, therefore, contended that it is consistent with perfect competition. However, there was no enquiry into the nature of external scale economies, making measurement of these economies difficult, preventing empirical verification of the theory. The absence of microeconomic foundations might have led to limited impact of the literature that had relied on the assumptions of external economies of scale.

Historically, the later major development in trade theory is the general agreement that factor mobility and trade function as substitutes for one another. Any trade restrictions would result in difference in factor prices, encouraging migration of labour and capital. Mundell in his 1957 paper analysed this phenomenon. Krugman in his 1969 paper on trade dealt with the issue of factor mobility in a situation of monopolistic competition and differentiated products. The inducement for factors to migrate, when there is no trade, is provided by the higher welfare the inhabitants of the larger region enjoy, because of the availability of a greater variety of products. If no restrictions on factor migration are imposed, in the limit, the whole population migrates to the region that is largest at the outset. It was argued that even if labour productivity differed in the regions, there would still be concentration of population in the region with low labour productivity.

It is to the credit of Krugman that he broke with the traditional approach of external scale economies and perfect competition. He assumed internal scale economies and imperfect competition. In this model agglomeration of activity is driven by "pecuniary externalities" mediated through market prices as a large market permits greater product variety and lower costs. Any transaction in the market by a consumer/household or by a firm, impacts other economic agents through its effect on price. Thus, in the work of Krugman, the presence of internal economies of scale and monopolistic competition are combined. This approach has been helpful in concentrating on increasing returns and product differentiation as the factors giving rise to intra-industry trade. His model launching the new economic geography is referred to as "core- periphery" model. The prevailing pattern which he tried to explain is that more than half of the global population lives in well – developed urban regions (called the core) while a minority remains in a predominantly agriculture hinterland (called the periphery). It is assumed that two types of products are produced; food, which is homogeneous and produced under constant return to scale and a large number of varieties of manufactured goods, each of which is produced under increasing returns to scale and marketed in monopolistically competitive markets. Consumer preferences are expressed by a Cobb-Douglas function in food and the substitutability of manufactured goods, the latter given by a Dixit- Stiglitz utility function with a constant elasticity of substitution [cf. eq (2)].

Assume that there are two regions with identical consumer preferences and production functions and goods can be exported from one region to the other. While agricultural goods are costlessly traded, manufactured goods bear transport costs which are proportional to the quantity of goods shipped (called ice-berg type). Further, assume that there are two types of individuals – manufacturing workers free to migrate to the region which offers highest utility level and peasants who do not migrate. Location choices of individuals and firms dictate the allocation of economic activity and population between the two regions. Now, consider a situation where initially the population is divided equally in the two regions and the two regions are identical which is an equilibrium. Now, if it is assumed that by chance the equilibrium is disturbed by migration of workers so that one region becomes larger than the other. Further migration to the larger region is stimulated if real wage effect together with the home market effect is sufficiently strong causing a cumulative process of increase in market size, further rise in the real wage leading to even more migration and so on. Then the new equilibrium will be distinctly different from the initial one. It may be recalled that this model of the process of circular causation was earlier discussed by Gunnar Myrdal and Alfred Hirschman.

However, one cannot ignore the presence of counteracting forces. Carrying the argument further, when all firms were concentrated in one region alone, it may be profitable for a single firm to move to the periphery, act as a monopolist in the market for manufacturing goods there. Welfare of the workers in the smaller region is influenced by wages paid by the firm, the price of consumption goods the firm produces (which is relatively low since the good bears no transport cost) and the price at which they purchase imported goods which bear transport costs. The combined effect of all these may offer an incentive for more firms to locate in the smaller region, something in a decentralised equilibrium. The final outcome would depend, of course, on the relative strength of each of these forces and their interaction. There may also be other factors such as rising land price or congestion costs in the larger region that may determine whether dispersal or concentration will ultimately result. Comparative static analysis would lead to an understanding of why urbanisation and the move towards a centre-periphery structure would tend to emerge as a result of decrease in transport costs or greater use of technologies with increasing returns. Perhaps, such trends were significant during the industrialisation process. Krugman's model can also explain "catastrophic" change in locational patterns and tendencies for agglomeration may suddenly become strong at a certain point of development.

Economic analysis of special issues has been stimulated by the core-periphery model, leading to integration of economic geography with main stream economics. Krugman, in his Nobel lecture, draws essentially two insights from his work on new economic geography.

"1. A self-sustaining concentration of production in space can occur if economies of scale (F/S) [Fixed costs/fixed sales] are large, transport costs low, and enough production is mobile.

2. Which location gets the concentration of production is arbitrary, and can be presumed to be a function of initial conditions or historical accident."

The empirical strength of new economic geography has been verified by many researchers and a large amount of literature has grown which has been surveyed and presented by Head and Mayer in the Hand book of Regional and Urban Economics.

14.3 PAUL KRUGMAN'S OTHER CONTRIBUTIONS

Krugman has also contributed papers on trade using models of perfect competition. In addition, his best-known work is international macroeconomics and international monetary economics including currency crises. He has shown how fixed exchange rate targets were susceptible to speculative pressure. He has also demonstrated that in target zones regime (that is, in a system in which exchange rate fluctuates within a band), however, the exchange rate is less volatile provided the target zone is credible.

Before the summary of Krugman's contributions is concluded, it is essential to refer to his "non- scientific writings," particularly a regular column for the New York Times. This is considered as Krugman's "transition from academic superstar to public intellectual." He is one of the very few economists who have tried to explain economic principles to a wider audience and thus educate the larger public.

14.4 CONCLUDING OBSERVATIONS

One of the newspapers reporting the announcement of the Nobel Memorial award remarked: "Paul Krugman has at least three jobs; he is professor of economics and international affairs at Princeton University, Centenary Professor at the London School of Economics, and , perhaps, his best known job as Op - Ed columnist for the New York Times." In recognition of his influence, The Washington Monthly called him the most important political columnist in America. Martin Wolf of Financial Times (London) observes that Krugman is both the "most hated and the most admired" columnist in the U.S. Foreign Policy named Krugman one of its 2012 Top 100 "Global Thinkers" for "wielding his acid pen against austerity."

Paul A. Samuelson, a previous winner of the Nobel Prize in Economics Sciences said: "I praise today's prize as being deserving and even overdue.... [He] is the only columnist in the United States who has had it right on almost every count from the beginning." Avinash Dixit observes in this connection that Krugman is "best known outside the profession for a [popular] book [The Age of Diminished Expectations] that disseminates ideas from frontier economics to the general public." In Dixit's words "If Krugman is rare among economists in the originality and elegance of his theoretical thinking, he is almost unique in the simplicity and clarity of his expository writing.... His clear and simple explanations of quite complex economic issues and ideas in a few sentences have to be read to be believed." Peter Neary praises Krugman's achievements thus: "Taking new theoretical tools and adapting them to explain empirical anomalies which Krugman did in international trade, is the essence of scientific progress." His evaluation is: "Everything he [Krugman] has touched he has adorned."

14.5 SELECT BIBLIOGRAPHY OF PAUL KRUGMAN'S WORKS

14.5.1 BOOKS

1985 (with E. Helpman), Market Structure and Foreign Trade: Increasing Returns, Imperfect Competition and International Economy, MIT Press, Cambridge, MA.

1986 (ed.) Strategic Trade Policy and the New International Economics, MIT Press, Cambridge. MA.

1988 Exchange Rate Instability, MIT Press, Cambridge, MA.

1989 (with E. M Graham), Foreign Direct Investment in the United States, Institute for International Economics, Washington D.C.

1989 (with E. Helpman), Market Structure and Trade Policy, MIT Press, Cambridge, MA.

1990 The Age of Diminished Expectations, MIT Press, Cambridge, MA.

1991 Geography and Trade, MIT Press, Cambridge, MA.

1992 (with M. Miller, eds.), Exchange Rate Targets and Currency Bands, Cambridge University Press, Cambridge, MA.

1994 Peddling Prosperity: Economic Sense and Nonsense in the Age of Diminished Expectations, W. W. Norton, New York.

1997 a Development, Geography, and Economic Theory, MIT Press, Cambridge, MA.

b Pop Internationalism, MIT Press, Cambridge, MA.

1998 (with M. Obstfeld), International Economics: Theory and Practice, Pearson Education, Upper Saddle River, NJ. (8 th Edition, 2009).

2000 Geography and Trade, MIT Press, Cambridge, MA.

2001 (with M. Fujita and A. Venables), The Spatial Economy: Cities, Regions, and International Trade, MIT Press, Cambridge. MA.

2007 The Conscience of a Liberal, W.W. Norton, New York.

14.5.2 ARTICLES

1978 a "Purchasing Power Parity and Exchange Rates: Another Look at the Evidence," JIE, Vol.8, No.3.

b (with L. Taylor), "Contractionary Effects of Devaluation," JIE, Vol.8, No.3.

1979 a "A Model of Balance of Payments Crises," JMCB, Vol.11, No.3.

b "A Model of Innovation, Technology Transfer, and the World Distribution of Income," JPE, Vol. 87, No.2.

c "Increasing Returns, Monopolistic Competition, and International Trade," JIE, Vol. 9, No.4.

1980 "Scale Economies, Product Differentiation, and the Pattern of Trade," AER, Vol.70, No.5.

1981 a "Trade, Accumulation, and Uneven Development," JDE, Vol.8, No.2.

b "Intra-industry Specialization and the Gains from Trade," JPE, Vol. 89, No.5.

1983 a "New Theories of Trade among Industrial Countries," AER Vol. 73, No.2.

b (with J. A. Brander), "A 'Reciprocal Dumping' Model of International Trade," JIE, Vol.15, No.3-4.

1984 "Import Protection as Export Promotion: International Competition in the Presence of Oligopoly and Economies of Scale," in Monopolistic Competition in International Trade, H. Kierzkowski (ed.), Oxford University Press, Oxford.

1985 (with T. Persson and L E. Svensson), "Inflation, Interest Rates, and Welfare," QJE, Vol.100, No.3.

1987 a (with R. Baldwin), "The Persistence of the U.S. Trade Deficit," BPEA, Vol.18, No.1.

b "Is Free Trade Passé?" JEP, Vol.2.

c "The Narrow Moving Band, the Dutch Disease, and the Economic Consequences of Mrs. Thatcher: Notes on Trade in the Presence of Dynamic Economies of Scale," JDE, Vol.27, No.1-2.

1988 a "Increasing Returns and the Theory of International Trade," in Advances in Economic Theory, Fifth World Congress, (T. Bewley, ed.), Cambridge University Press, Cambridge, MA.

b (with R. Baldwin), "Market Access and Competition: A Simulation Study of 16K Random Access Memories," in Empirical Studies of International Trade, R. Feenstra (ed.) MIT Press, Cambridge, MA.

1989 a "Market-based Debt Reduction Schemes," in Analytics of International Debt, (J. Frankel, ed.), IMF, Washington D.C.

b "Industrial Organization and International Trade," in Handbook of Industrial Organization, R. Schmalensee and R. Willig (eds.), North-Holland, Amsterdam.

	c	(with R. Baldwin), "Persistent Trade Effects of Large Exchange Rate Shocks," QJE, Vol.104, No. 4.
1991	a	"History vs. Expectations," QJE, Vol.106, No.2.
	b	"Increasing Returns and Economic Geography," JPE, Vol. 99, No.3.
	c	"Target Zones and Exchange Rate Dynamics," QJE, Vol. 106, No.3.
1993	a	"On the Relationship Between Trade Beyond Location Theory," Review of International Economics, Vol. 1, No.2.
	b	"The Narrow and Broad Arguments for Free Trade," AER, Vol. 83, No.2.
1994		"The Myth of Asia's Miracle," Foreign Affairs, Vol.73, Nov-Dec.
1995	a	"Growing World Trade: Causes and Consequences," BPEA, Vol. 26, No.1, 25th Anniversary issue.
	b	(with M. Fujita), " When is the Economy Monocentric?: von Thunen and Chamberlin Unified," Regional Science and Urban Economics, Vol.25, No.4.
	c	(with A.J Venables), "Globalization and the Inequality of Nations," QJE, Vol.110, No. 4.
1998		"Two Cheers for Formalism," EJ, Vol. 108, No. 451.
2000		"Technology, Trade and Factor Prices," JI, Vol. 50, No.1.
2008		"Trade and Wages Reconsidered," BPEA, Vol.39, No.1.
2009		"The Increasing Returns Revolution in Trade and Geography," Noble Lecture, AER, Vol.99, No.3.

14.6 WORKS OF OTHERS

Balassa, B (1966), "Tariff Reduction and Trade in Manufactures among the Industrial Countries," AER, Vol.56, No.3.

Balassa, B (1967), Trade Liberalization among Industrial Countries, McGraw –Hill, New York.

Corden, W.M (1970), "A Note on Economies of Scale, the Size of the Domestic Market and the Pattern of Trade," in Studies in International Economics, A. M. McDougall and R. H. Snape (eds.) North- Holland, Amsterdam.

Dixit, A. K. and Stiglitz J.E (1977), "Monopolistic Competition and Optimum Product Diversity," AER, Vol. 67, No.3.

Grubel, H. G. and P. J. Lloyd (1975), Intra-Industry Trade: The Theory and Measurement of International Trade In Differentiated Products, Macmillan, London.

Head, K. and T. Mayer (2004), "The Empirics of Agglomeration and Trade," in Hand Book of Regional and Urban Economics, Vol. 4, J. V. Henderson and J. F. Thisse (eds.) Elsevier North Holland, Amsterdam.

Hirschman, A.O. (1958), The Strategy of Economic Development, Yale University Press, New Haven, Ct.

Johnson, H.G (1967), "International Trade Theory and Monopolistic Competition Theory," in Monopolistic Competition Theory: Studies in Impact; Essays in Honor of Edwin H. Chamberlin, Kuenne, R. E. (ed.) John Wiley, New York.

Jones, R.W. (1965), "The Structure of General Equilibrium Models," JPE, Vol. 73.

Linder, S.B. (1961), An Essay on Trade and Transformation, John Wiley, New York.

Mundell, R. (1957), "International Trade and Factor Mobility," AER, Vol.47, No.3.

Myrdal, B. (1957), Economic Theory and Underdeveloped Regions, Duckworth, London.

Neary, J.P (2009), "Putting the 'New' into New Trade Theory: Paul Krugman's Noble Memorial Prize in Economics," ScandJE, Vol.111, No.2.

Samuelson, P. A. (1949), "International Factor Price Equalization Once Again," EJ, Vol.59, No. 234.

CHAPTER 15

PETER ARTHUR DIAMOND, DALE THOMAS MORTENSEN & CHRISTOPHER ANTONIOU PISSARIDES

(1940 –),

(1939 – 2014) &

(1948 –)

The 2010 Nobel Memorial Prize in Economic Sciences was awarded to Peter Diamond, Dale Mortensen and Christopher Pissarides "for their analysis of markets with search frictions." Diamond says in his Nobel lecture: "Economics education starts with the abstraction of an ideal market demand, supply, and a price that clears the market. This is an extremely valuable starting place – it shows some of the effects that are present in pretty much all markets." In this classical view of the market in which buyers and sellers find one another immediately, at no cost, and have perfect information about the prices of all goods and services, prices are determined so that supply equals demand and there are no supply and demand surpluses and there is full utilisation of resources. This is not what happens in real world markets. The structure of real world markets differs from the idealised version. For example, buyers may find difficulty in finding sellers because of search costs; even if sellers are located, the goods they have may not correspond to the buyers' "requirements." The buyer may consider the seller's price too high or the seller might not be willing to sell the good as the buyer's bid is considered too low. In all such cases, no transaction will take place and with parties-buyers and sellers-will have to continue the search operations. In essence, the process of finding the "right outcome" is not "without frictions." A number of such markets may be cited such as labour market, housing market-where searching and finding suitable counterparties are needed and where transactions (or trade) takes place by pair-wise matching of buyers and sellers.

An important characteristic of this process is the element of time involved. In this context Diamond appropriately quotes Alfred Marshall: "The element of time is a chief cause of those difficulties in economic investigations which make it necessary for man with his limited powers to go step by step; breaking up a complex question, studying one bit at a time, and at last combining his partial solutions into a more or less complete solution of the whole riddle.... The more the issue is thus narrowed, the more exactly can it be handled but also the less closely does it correspond to real life. Each exact and firm handling of a narrow issue, however, helps towards treating broader issues, in which that narrow issue is contained more exactly than would otherwise have been possible. With each step...exact dimensions can be made less abstract, realistic discussions can be made less inexact than was possible at an earlier stage." The prime difference between the classical analysis of demand and supply and the search theory for which the award has been made basically consists of the treatment of time-- "the use of time as well as resources to learn about opportunities."

The essential idea in search theory is that market participants make an attempt to identify cooperative partners for the purpose of implementing joint projects. Examples include simple cases of a buyer and a seller of a product or more complex cases involving worker seeking a job and an employer hiring a worker or relations between firms and their suppliers.

As is known, some researchers had started employing mathematical models to understand the best possible way in which a buyer can find an acceptable price for the good he intends to buy. The first mentioned and widely quoted attempt was by Peter Diamond. In his 1971 pioneering article, Diamond examined the issue of price formation in a market where buyers are looking for the best possible price and sellers at the same time set their best price while taking search behaviour of buyers into account. His study revealed that once search costs are included, the result would not be competitive result. He has shown that, even small search costs would generate a radically different outcome. More importantly, equilibrium prices in such a setting are equal to monopoly price; that is, the price which a monopolist would set on a corresponding market with no search costs. This surprising finding which has been labelled "Diamond Paradox" attracted wide attention and led to a flurry of research work on search markets.

A substantially important issue to be considered is whether or not search markets yield efficient outcomes in that whether there is too much or too little search. As it is clear that in search markets there will be unexecuted trade and some resources are unemployed, can the outcome be regarded as necessarily inefficient? But there is a crucial question: whether the comparison is appropriate; that is, comparing an economy with frictions with an economy without frictions. Further, if the economy cannot avoid frictions, the appropriate issue is whether the economy can be considered as "constrained efficient;" that is, given the constraint, can the outcome be termed best? Since search is costly, the aggregate welfare is not necessarily higher. The question of efficiency was examined by Diamond, Mortensen and Pissarides and provided significant insights. "A generic result is that efficiency cannot be expected and policy interventions may therefore become desirable."

In a significantly important and influential paper, Diamond has put forward a model containing multiple steady-state equilibria and has contended that an environment of search and matching can lead to macroeconomic unemployment problems because of difficulties in coordinating trade. His model suggests that a search externality (a searching worker does not internalise all the benefits and costs to other searchers) is the rationale for the management of aggregate demand to conduct the economy to the best possible equilibrium. An important insight that is provided by the work is that an unregulated search market does not yield an efficient outcome. This research work of Diamond gave impetus to research in a number of applied areas, such as housing and monetary economics.

While the research on search and matching theory raises many significant issues relevant for many applied contexts, the theory has its deepest impact on issues within labour economics. A central and very important issue in economics concerns the reasons for existence of unemployment in an economy and the policy interventions that are required to redress it. There is a widespread impression that the labour markets do not appear to "clear" in that there are unemployed workers who search for work and at the same time there exists firms that look for workers to fill the job vacancies. It has been found difficult to construct a fully specified equilibrium market that generates both unemployment and vacancies. The economics viewpoint on the determinants of unemployment in an economy and more generally on the workings of labour markets has been shaped by the research work of the laureates of this year.

Diamond, Mortensen and Pissarides developed a new framework for the analysis of labour markets for both "normative and positive purposes in a dynamic general equilibrium setting." The press note containing the scientific background on markets with search frictions states that the resulting class of models have come to be known as the Diamond-Mortensen–Pissarides Model (or DMP Model). It adds: "The DMP model allows us to consider simultaneously (i) how workers and firms jointly decide whether to match or to keep searching; (ii) in case of a continued match, how the benefits from the match are split into a wage for the worker and a profit for the firm; (iii) firm entry, i.e., firm's decisions to 'create jobs;' and (iv) how the match of a worker and a firm might develop over time, possibly leading to agreed-upon separation."

The DMP model proved to be quite versatile and further theoretical and applied research work has been undertaken by the profession. The model has been employed to analyse the process of transmission of aggregate shocks to the labour market that would result in fluctuations in unemployment, job vacancies and employment flows. Besides, the search and matching theory has been used to study also issues in consumer theory, monetary theory, industrial organisation, public economics, financial economics, urban economics and family economics.

The contributions to the search and matching theory will be summarised after presenting brief biographical sketch of each of the three laureates.

15.1 A BRIEF BIOGRAPHICAL NOTE: PETER DIAMOND

Peter A. Diamond was born on April 29, 1940, in New York. His grandparents were immigrants to the U.S. His parents were born and grew up in New York, and "never lived outside the metropolitan area." Both his mother and father finished high school and went to work. After high school education in New York, Diamond went to Yale University. He first considered majoring in engineering, but finally chose mathematics. He learned how to do a rigorous mathematical proof from Shizuo Kakutani. He had proved a fixed-point theorem that plays a key role in some economic analysis. Having interested in economics (he took two courses), Diamond took the graduate mathematical economics course taught by Gerard Debreu based on his newly published Theory of Value. Diamond states: "Debreu was an outstanding teacher, and my early and thorough grounding in general equilibrium theory has stood me in good stead ever since, shaping my thinking about economics." At the same time he started studying game theory in a seminar.

Diamond's first job "as an economist (sort of)" was as a research assistant for Koopmans for the summer of 1960. He was hired to help with the mathematics. He documents his progress: "When asked to produce an example of a function with certain properties, I found it easier to produce a class of functions with the desired properties.... That led Koopmans to reorient his research plan, giving this class of functions a central role, and to promote me to a co-author for my first publication (appearing in 1964)." Diamond confesses in his autobiographical note: "I had had no idea that the class of functions would be interesting, and have come to recognize that an important part of education is learning to recognize the value of what you stumble over, as well as choosing research topics with a sense of how valuable possible findings might be." Diamond acknowledges: "I have always viewed this splendid economist [Koopmans] and splendid person as a role model for how to do economics and how to relate to people."

Diamond joined MIT for graduate work. He enjoyed economic theory and as an economist "I have always been more interested in working on models generating new insights...." A key part of the normal two-year course load for Diamond was the public finance class taught by E. Cary Brown. In his autobiographical note Diamond states: "We worked through everything in the newly published The Theory of Public Finance by Richard

Musgrave, an outstanding scholar who had written an exceptional book. Musgrave's drive to put public finance on a general equilibrium basis was important for my development and fitted well with the general equilibrium orientation that I had acquired from the class with Debreu. This background played a central role in my later work on optimal taxation."

Robert Solow was Diamond's thesis supervisor. According to Diamond "Solow was and is an outstanding economist, a splendid person and a good friend. He has supervised a large fraction of MIT dissertations. He and Koopmans have been my role models." Diamond has a high opinion of MIT which "was (and is) a terrific place to be a graduate student, to get an outstanding and broad education, while having a good time."

Diamond joined as an assistant professor in the University of California at Berkeley in September 1963. McFadden was one of his colleagues there. His teaching of the public finance course helped him explore topics and introduced him to the experience of "discovering results leading to good papers as part of developing material for a class of sharp, attentive students." Diamond's paper on public debt is a good example. He makes a very valuable and significant observation: "While many are concerned about the tension between teaching and research, my experience is that they reinforce each other. Indeed, the times when I had the most difficulty in finding good research topics have occurred when I did little teaching." Diamond joined MIT as associate professor in 1966 where he became full professor in 1980. He was designated there as Jennie S. MacDonald Professor in 1989. In 1992 he became the first holder of Paul A. Samuelson Chair which "pleased me greatly and seemed to please him [Samuelson]." Diamond observes: "Beyond being a great economist, as everyone knows, and together with Bob Solow, the creator and shaper of the MIT Economics Department, Paul has always been a true friend." Diamond became an Institute Professor in 1997, retiring in the year 2011.

Diamond's reflections at the end of the autobiographical note are worth reproducing: "I have worked in a large number of different areas. The kind of theoretical work I most enjoy is sorting out how to approach a problem to get insights, more so than refining models to shed further light on it." He explored new areas once he felt that he had hit diminishing returns in one area.

Diamond received a number of honours, awards and grants. They include Guggenheim Fellowship, Social Science Research Fellowship, MIT's Killian Award, Samuelson Award, Jean-Jacques Laffont Prize and Mahalanobis Memorial Award. He is a member of the National Academy of Sciences and founding member of the National Academy of Social Insurance. He is a Fellow of the Econometric Society and of the American Academy of Arts and Sciences. He was elected President of the American Economic Association (2003) and of the Econometric Society (1991). He was Associate editor of Journal of Economic Theory (1969-1971) and of the Journal of Public Economics (1971-1986). He served as co-editor and Advisory Editor of the latter. He had visiting appointments from a number of colleges and Universities including Churchill College, Cambridge, Nuffield College and Balliol

College, Oxford, Harvard University, Hebrew University, Jerusalem and University College, Nairobi.

Three of his articles (of which two are co-authored with James Mirrlees) are included in the Top 20 articles in 100 years of the American Economic Review (AER), the highest number of any single author.

15.2 A SHROT BIOGRAPHICAL SKETCH: DALE MORTENSEN

Dale Mortensen was born in 1939 of immigrant parents in Enterprise, Oregon, USA. His parents migrated in the war years to the Portland area. After the war, the family moved to the Hood River Valley where Dale and his brother grew up. Mortensen had his school education in the local Wy'east High School. He was a good student with mathematical ability and interests. In his last year at Wy'east, Mortensen became interested in American social history of the late 19th and early 20th centuries and the related literature, much of which is concerned with the industrialisation of America. He formed his own picture of the industrialisation and developed an understanding of how it had affected the lives of people for both better and worse. He admitted: "By the end of my senior year in high school, I faced a dilemma...how could I combine my interest in analytical problem-solving with a concern for social issues?"

Discussion with a high school friend and chance finding of the book, The Theory of Games and Economic Behavior in the local library helped Mortensen decide that by choosing economics he would perhaps be able to continue his two principal interests. He enrolled in Willamette University as the beneficiary of a full tuition scholarship, majoring in economics and mathematics. Mortensen went on to do graduate work at what was then the Carnegie Institute of Technology as he was offered "a more generous fellowship than either Stanford or Harvard." According to him, the programme at Carnegie was an innovative programme that emphasised an analytic as well as interdisciplinary approach to the study of economics and management. He was also attracted to Carnegie as "it was located in Pittsburgh, which had played central role in the industrialization of America."

In his autobiographical note Mortensen specially mentioned of the faculty there. Herbert Simon taught Ph.D. students "how to think about social phenomena and how to represent those thoughts in a mathematical model." He also taught them the application of the recently developed methods of linear, non-linear, and dynamic programming. The students were also instructed in the new behavioural approach to the theory of organizations in general by James March and Herbert Simon and the application of that theory to the analysis of the firm in particular by Richard Cyert and Jim March. Although Mortensen was interested in new ideas he turned to the more traditional economics and began a thesis in growth theory.

Mortensen reminisced: "Carnegie Tech was an amazing place at the time. New ideas of all kinds were in the air. They were not always consistent with each other, as in the case of the conflict between John Muth's suggestion about how to model expectations as 'rational' and Simon's notion of 'bounded rationality'. We students benefited from the lively debates among the faculty." He further stated: "In my last two years, I took courses from Robert Lucas and Oliver Williamson with fellow student Ed Prescott, all of whom are now Laureates. In retrospect, it was obviously a very special educational experience."

Mortensen joined as a member of the faculty at the North Western University in 1965 but completed his Ph.D. two years later. At North Western he was mentored by Robert Eisner, Robert Strotz and Robert Clower. He confessed: "I finally learned the foundations of economic analysis by teaching Hicks and Samuelson to first year Ph.D. students." Mortensen and his colleague Brent Stigum taught themselves dynamic control theory from the pages of Pontriagin's book. He became fully proficient in control theory and dynamic programming, "the tools that dominate macroeconomic theory to this day." A debate raged over the Phillips curve and its implications for economic policy in the mid-1960's, particularly the short run and long run influence of monetary policy on unemployment level. Edmund Phelps and Milton Friedman argued that the efficiency of the policy is "frustrated" in the long run as workers and employers as rational decision-makers see through what is happening. In essence, economic agents do not suffer from "money illusion." Phelps also complemented his assertions with a "new view" of how the labour market works. Particularly, he has contended that some positive unemployment level was "a natural outcome of the matching process" in the labour market.

At North Western, Mortensen developed the idea of modelling the consequence of search and matching friction in the labour market as the outcome of a sequence of random meetings between potentially interested parties. He developed his first major paper, "A Theory of Wage and Employment Dynamics" and presented it at a conference organised by Edmund Phelps at the University of Pennsylvania, his academic home at the time. The papers presented at the conference were published in 1980 known as the "Phelps Volume," Microeconomic Foundations of Employment and Inflation Theory which became a classic. In Mortensen's view, the message of the collection of papers in the Phelps volume was that "one could and should consider the dual macroeconomic problems of employment and inflation as the outcomes of market behavior of individual agents who act in their own interests as best they can in a market environment characterized by uncertainties and incomplete information. As a corollary, the papers argued that macroeconomics should be founded on microeconomic principles."

Mortensen developed a companion paper, "Job Search, the Duration of Unemployment and the Phillips Curve," which was published in the American Economic Review. It is an attempt to use his ideas about decentralised exchange in the labour market to provide an interpretation of the Phillips curve. In the model, "an unemployed worker samples sequentially from a known distribution of wage offers until one is found that exceeded an optimally chosen reservation wage." As this has suggested that the time spent searching was productive, the model offered an entirely new view of unemployment. His view that workers might rationally choose to be unemployed was not acceptable to Keynesians, as, according to them, unemployment arose because the real wage was too high.

The new area of information economics had seen developments in the 1970's. Search theory, which stressed the need to gather information, was joined by models that characterised asymmetric information. Mortensen stated in his autobiographical note: "Signaling, screening, moral hazard and adverse selection, terms never mentioned when I was a graduate student, became the new vocabulary of the analysis of market performance during these years. Search theory, particularly as it related to the phenomena of unemployment, continues to develop as well." The focus of the theory of unemployment got shifted, partly in response to research work by economists such as Diamond, from the problem of a worker seeking a more, remunerative job to the formation of "good job-worker matches."

The so-called matching problem (found in the labour, housing, and other markets) is one of "forming complementary pairs in a world in which individual workers and jobs are heterogeneous" and which takes time and resources to accomplish it. Mortensen and other researchers developed models which have been used by empirical labour economists, together with the statistical tools of duration analysis, to interpret both unemployment and job spell data. Further progress on the topic was facilitated by development of models by Mortensen besides Diamond and Pissarides. The model called DMP model of labour market is an equilibrium theory of unemployment determination that has significant implications for unemployment dynamics and for the effects of government policies on labour market outcomes. Further progress was the result of research work by many researchers. This will be covered below in the section devoted to the summary of the theory.

Mortensen referred to his association with other universities. Most of his teaching took place at his home base since leaving graduate school in 1965, namely North Western University; he also taught at Essex University, Cornell University, the California Institute of Technology, New York University, and more recently at Aarhus University. He stated that he has been fortunate to have excellent (undergraduate) students and that many Ph.D. students have been "at least as important in disseminating my research ideas and results as my published papers." Mortensen noted with great satisfaction the progress North Western University made during his association with it for 45 years "from a party school that catered to the children of the upper income professional classes of middle America to a first rate international center of learning and research."

Mortensen was elected Fellow of Econometric Society in 1979. He was President of the Society of Economic Dynamics, 1995-2000, and was a member of the Board of Editors of The American Economic Review, 1998-2000. Among lectures he had delivered, mention may be made of Klein Lecture at the University of Pennsylvania, 2004 and Marshall Lecture, European Economic Association Meeting, 2004. He was on the Advisory Board of the Tinbergen Institute, Amsterdam. He was a Research Associate of NBER, since 2005 till death.

Mortensen ended his autobiographical note with the following: "My colleagues have long noted that my research on search and matching deals with the formation and dissolution of relationships. How is it, they ask, that you have had the same job for 45 years and the same wife for 47? My response is simple: Both are excellent matches!"

Dale Mortensen died on Jan, 9, 2014 at Wilmet, U.S.A.

15.3 A BRIEF BIOGRAPHICAL SKETCH: CHRISTOPHER PISSARIDES

Christopher Pissarides was born in Nicosia, Cyprus, on 20 February 1948. His was a happy family and he had had a good upbringing. He has fond memories of the family evenings at home before television and summers on the coast of Kyrenia and the mountains and valleys of Agros village. He had his elementary school education in Cyprus which was "badly disrupted by the independence movement against British colonial rule." His parents, who valued education greatly, made Pissarides take lessons from tutors outside school, and he got on. In his autobiographical note Pissarides states: "Of the eleven years that I spent in schools in Nicosia, only three were not disrupted...." When he was in high school military conscription for young men started but as Pissarides finished school at 17, instead of the usual 18, he was considered too young to serve in the army and was allowed to leave to go abroad for degree studies. He went to London to study for a degree but his love at school was mathematics. He studied mathematics on his own and entered the A level (university entrance) examinations as a private student. Pissarides observes: "... it proved to be the most useful preparation for my economics degree."

Although Pissarides applied to six universities, he was accepted by the University of Essex-- a campus university which helped him integrate easily into British student life, and the standard of work there was "very high." The Economics department was also new and it was set up by young successful academics from the London School of Economics (LSE). Pissarides was particularly influenced in his early studies by Richard Lipsey, Michael Parkin and Chris Archibald. When Pissarides had to decide whether to end his studies with the first degree and return to Cyprus as planned, or go on to graduate school, he was advised to go to one of the top American schools. Further, he happened to meet Dale Mortensen at that time; he invited Pissarides to go to North Western to do a Ph.D. with him. However, he decided to move to the London School of Economics, since he felt he knew what to expect at LSE. This decision was helped by his father's promise that he would pay for all the costs of Pissarides's education if he needed it. Pissarides remarks: "I did not have to draw on that promise, but without it I couldn't have stayed in Britain."

As regards LSE's approach to doctoral research, Pissarides says it is a completely hands off and disorganised approach. Students have to find a topic and write a thesis. Pissarides had a helpful supervisor in Michio Morishima; however, he was not interested in search theory and unemployment, in which Pissarides got interested in at Essex. Morishima made Pissarides appreciate the classics. Pissarides read Keynes and Hicks under Morishima's guidance, but he spent most of his time reading articles and books on his own. He diligently read an enormous amount of literature. In the process, he stumbled on a paper by Samuel Karolin "Stochastic Models and Optimal Policy for Selling an Asset." Reading it Pissarides reasoned: "let's think of a worker's human capital as an asset that he sells in the labour market, where job outcomes are uncertain. I tried to work on the idea and it delivered." Within six months, Pissarides prepared thesis in search theory that was approved for the Ph.D. degree. Soon after, it was published as a book.

With the Ph.D. in hand, Pissarides had to decide whether to go back to Cyprus or apply for a university job. Though he returned to Cyprus and joined the research department of the country's central bank in February 1974, he decided to fly to Athens to accompany his girl friend to Cyprus. In his words "That decision turned out to be a pivotal event in my life." The flight he took out of Nicosia airport turned out to be one of the very last civilian flights out of the airport. He observes: "My life had changed forever. I was in Athens unable to get news of any kind...." With the promise of help from Michael Parkin, who found that two universities had one-year positions open, Pissarides borrowed a jacket and flew to England with no money. He was offered both the jobs on the spot. He took a one-year lectureship at the University of Southampton, teaching business economics to second year students. Pissarides recalls: "Life in Southampton was tough, having to borrow both money and clothes to get by, and worrying about events back home. Teaching was boring, being in an area that I knew nothing about and was not interested in. But I threw myself into work, finishing the book on search theory and writing papers whenever I could spare a few minutes. My lectureship was renewed for a second year, but in the meantime a position had opened at LSE and I applied for it. I was offered it and I moved to London in 1976. I have not moved since."

As a young lecturer, he found LSE as intimidating as he did when he was a Ph.D. student. However, one of his senior colleagues recommended Pissarides for a winter retreat in Germany organised by the Econometric Society for junior faculty. At the retreat he was given the first chance to present his new way of doing research: "a very early version of one of the papers cited by the Economics Prize committee." As he assumed away too many things in his research work he had difficulty publishing his first papers, unlike his papers in other branches of macroeconomics. Richard Layard, his colleague at LSE formed an informal group to work on topics of applied labour economics like social security, pensions and education which Pissarides had joined though he had never taught labour economics. He published some papers besides bringing "some good results." The group taught him to think of the empirical implications of the theoretical work and to think first of the big problem that required to understand before writing models about it.

Unemployment was the big problem in the late seventies and early eighties on which Mortensen wanted to do research. Pissarides received a one-year Ford Foundation fellowship at Harvard, to work on the economics of education. He found "Harvard a difficult place to visit. The facilities offered to visitors were basic and there was no effort to integrate visitors with the department." A few weeks after arriving, he despaired and started seriously thinking about returning to London when, by chance, he met Martin Feldstein, who invited Pissarides to leave the Harvard department and join NBER. Pissarides accepted the offer. At NBER he had the access to all the facilities and work in his own office. He loved it and "it rescued my visit." He had been going back to the NBER practically every year since then. At one of their seminars he met Peter Diamond who was presenting his early work on search theory. He very briefly met Diamond once again several years later; he did not meet him or communicate with him about "our work until we both went to Stockholm for the award ceremonies."

On his return from Harvard, Pissarides got deeply involved in research into search and matching theory. This time also marked the beginning of his most productive and innovative period, which lasted for about five years. In the mean time, Layard had secured funding for creating a research centre in labour economics at LSE and Pissarides became one of its first members and channelled his entire research output through it. The centre's research objectives were to understand European unemployment in the 1980's. The centre taught him what made a successful research group: "one that has people thinking along similar lines, with a common objective, and with a strong belief that the objective is important and they can make a difference."

In the late 1980s LSE, like other British universities, went through bad times as funding was cut and salaries fell behind. In 1990, Pissarides with the young family went to the University of California at Berkeley for the year. He states: "George Akerlof was instrumental in arranging it and making us feel welcome." During this visit, Pissarides undertook a short visit to North Western for a seminar and got to know Mortensen better. They started collaborative work which lasted ten years. They produced their best known paper, which sealed what was already known to some as the DMP model.

Back in London, Pissarides became head of the Economics department at LSE, from 1996 to 1999 to "make LSE the pre-eminent social sciences research centre in Europe." He travelled frequently to Cyprus to serve on the Interim Governing Board of its first university and later joined its Monetary Policy Committee as an external member. In 2008 his marriage abruptly broke down. Life returned to a "new normal," with his marriage to Rachel Ngai, a colleague, and more involvement with the University of Cyprus.

Pissarides had visiting positions, among others at Harvard University, NBER, Princeton University, Institute of Advanced Study, Vienna, Yale University, UCLA and Hong Kong University. He received a number of honours and awards besides Nobel Memorial Prize. They include elected Fellow Econometric Society, Vice-President (2010) and President (2011) of European Economic Association, elected Fellow Society of Labour Economists (2008) and Elected Member of the Council, Royal Economic Society (1996-2003). He was made Foreign Honorary Member of the American Economic Association (2011). He was also co-winner with Dale T. Mortensen of IZA Prize in Labour Economics.

15.4 A BRIEF SURVEY OF CONTRIBUTIONS OF DIAMOND, MORTENSEN, AND PISSARIDES

Prior to the late 1960s and early 1970s, economic theory used a paradigm in which the market was characterised by a large number of participants who trade at the same time. The access to the market place was free and all the relevant information needed for trading to take place was available to all economic agents at no cost. Specifically, all traders would trade at the same market price. However, in real world, buyers and sellers face difficulties in locating each other. As a result, markets may fail to clear at all points in time. Furthermore, buyers and sellers in the market may have to incur costs to locate each other (search) and meet pair-wise when they actually come into contact (the problem of matching). It is realised by economists that as a result, the crucial issue that needs to be answered is "how price formation works in a market with search frictions." More importantly, there is the question of quantum of price dispersion that is observed and how large are the deviations from competitive pricing. Mortensen observed in his Prize lecture: "The presence of search and matching costs has some important general implications for how markets perform their function of allocating goods and services to producers and consumers. They serve as hindrances to the process of efficient allocation not only because they reduce the gains from trade. The costs must be borne now but the returns come only in the future. Furthermore, a rule for stopping a sequential search is needed." As the future is uncertain, there is a need to form expectations of future, if only for evaluating the prospective benefits. Prominent markets of this type include labour market and housing market. Search and matching theory was developed to answer these and other related questions.

According to James Albrecht, search theory has its origins in the consensus that was reached in the late 1960's, as expressed, for example, in the "Phelps Volume" which underlined the need of a solid micro economic foundation for macroeconomics. Search theory employs tools of microeconomics for the purpose of analysing the determinants of aggregate unemployment in an economy, focussing in particular on the steady-state or natural rate of unemployment, as also for the inflation-unemployment trade-off. In this context Pissarides states: "Research in the economics of the labour market when there are search frictions started in the 1960's, with influential contributions from George Stigler (1962), John McCall (1970) and the papers collected in Edmund Phelps et al., (1970)." He also refers to insightful discussions of the role of frictions in labour market equilibrium in works of John Hicks (1932) and William Hutt (1939). However, Pissarides notes: "But it was not until the late 1960's that formal mathematical models of individual behaviour and labour market equilibrium appeared." Further, he refers to the claim of Axel Leijonhufvud (1968) that search theory could provide a micro foundation for Keynes's concept of effective demand: "The idea was that the job seeker could make her demand for goods effective only after she succeeded in locating a mutually acceptable job match."

The Royal Swedish Academy's Scientific Background Report on Markets with Search Frictions points out three important issues addressed by the early theoretical work on search and matching frictions. They are:

1. Price or wage dispersion-- That is, whether the traditional theory's single price or wage is expected to be true in markets with frictions.
2. Whether markets characterised by frictions are efficient.
3. Whether or not such markets generate macroeconomic coordination failures.

We may briefly survey the work on these three problems.

15.4.1 WAGE DISPERSION

The work that has addressed the first issue mostly focused adopting microeconomic approach. It examined the issue of workers' optimal search behaviour under conditions of imperfect information about wages such as McCall's and Mortensen's work. The work essentially dealt with the optimal rule for accepting job offers. Assume that unemployed worker searching for employment is aware of the distribution of wage offers across firms but is not aware of available wage offers at a single firm. The worker who has a reservation wage (it is a wage at which the worker is indifferent between accepting a job or continues to be unemployed) examines the wage offers by firms sequentially with a view to maximise the expected present value of future wage income. He tries to equate the value of unemployment (such as unemployment benefit) to the discounted present value of future wage income from the job (including the likelihood of keeping the job, any expected wage movements on the job and the discount rate). The Scientific background note remarks: "A fundamental question left unanswered in the early micro literature was whether the postulated distribution of... wages, could be rationalized as an equilibrium outcome."

In his 1971 paper, Diamond established what has come to be known as the "Diamond Paradox". The paradox was presented by Diamond using a product market context; the same is presented by James Albrecht in a labour-market setting. The latter is followed here. Assume a market in which unemployed workers search for vacant jobs. Workers are assumed to be homogeneous-- equally productive- incur the same time cost of search and have the same flow value leisure, b. Likewise, firms are assumed to be homogeneous. The distribution of wage offers by firms is given by F (w). It is also assumed that there are a large number of firms as also workers, so that "each agent is individually negligible." Workers have the same reservation wage, R. If all firms offer a wage R>b, then the distribution F(w), changes leading to the fall of workers reservation wage from R, to say, R'. The process will not stop till all firms offer same wage, b, i.e., "Diamond monopsony wage." Albrecht comments: "More precisely, the only Nash equilibrium in the wage-posting game is the symmetric one in which all firms post b. The situation is even worse if there is a monetary cost of search. In that case, unless the first search step is free—an assumption that is made in many equilibrium search models—no equilibrium exists." Diamond, in his article, has argued that even with small search costs and a large number of firms, an environment of search and matching would result in "a large departure from the outcome under perfect competition (that is, where there are no search costs)."

Diamond's 'surprising result' inspired further research into the problem. Mortensen co-authored with Burdett an article, making a key innovation, namely allowing for on-the job search and recognising the difference in reservation wage among employed and unemployed searchers. The heterogeneity in reservation wage lends support to equilibrium wage dispersion. It is possible for high wage firms to attract and retain more workers than low-wage firms. However, the rent per worker that high wage firms can obtain is relatively low. In addition, an appropriately set minimum wage can augment employment, as in traditional models of monopsony. The Scientific Background Note concludes: "One strand of arguments in the literature on wage dispersion suggests that models with quantitatively large wage dispersion require that workers can search for other jobs while employed."

In an article in 2010 AER, Mortensen, assuming that firms have many employees face diminishing returns in production and wages are the outcome of intra-firm bargaining, showed that a dispersed wage steady state equilibrium exists in the search and matching model. In addition, he showed existence of unique dispersed wage equilibrium with the property that more productive employers pay more, if employed workers are assumed to search. Also, in the dispersed wage equilibrium, the labour market tightness and aggregate employment are lower.

15.4.2 ISSUE OF EFFICIENCY

The second issue relates to the question of efficiency of the outcome. It is generally observed that frictional markets involve search externalities that may not be internalised by agents. The individual worker searching for a job may not reckon with two externalities. They are:

(a) ***Congestion Externality:*** The rates of job finding by other unemployed workers are reduced by workers searching hard.

(b) ***Thick Market Externality:*** Worker who is searching hard makes employers better off in that the rate at which they can fill their existing vacancies will increase. While these externalities are common in search and matching models, a priori, it is not clear whether "decentralized decisions on search and wage setting will internalize them."

The efficiency properties of markets with frictions have been studied by the three laureates, besides some other economists. There is no clear answer; some studies show that the equilibrium is "generically inefficient." A study by Hosios, however, shows that the equilibrium outcome is "constrained efficient."

15.4.3 COORDINATION FAILURES

In an article, Diamond has contended that search externalities can even generate macroeconomic coordination problems. Using an 'abstract' model, Diamond shows the possibility of multiple equilibria and equilibria involving a higher level of economic activity yielding higher welfare. Thus, there is "potentially a role for demand management, i.e., for government policy inducing higher activity so that the economy could move from a bad to a good steady state." However, proving that a good steady state is better than a bad steady state does not imply inefficiency. In a later paper, co-authored with Fidenberg, Diamond has established inefficiency, besides entirely "expectations driven" equilibrium multiplicity. They also showed that this economy "could feature business–cycle like fluctuations in output without fluctuations in the fundamental parameters." An important component of their model was the larger the number of traders, the lower is the search functions-- usually referred to as "increasing returns to scale." The appropriateness of this assumption has been questioned by many economists. They argue that labour markets with constant returns describe the reality better. With the assumption of constant returns the existence of multiple steady states is ruled out.

The importance of Diamond's contribution in this regard is clear from this quote from Royal Swedish Academy's Scientific Background note: "Diamond's (1982b) article is often viewed as defining a new approach, based on a careful analysis using micro economic foundations, to analyzing some of the central themes of Keynes's business cycle theory. Coordination problems were of central importance in Keynes's writings; they can be viewed as a way of allowing for 'sentiments' to influence the economy, such as Keynes's well-known parable of the 'animal spirits' of investors. If investors sense that other investors will be active and produce, they produce too, thereby leading to high economic activity ...."

15.5 LABOUR MARKET AND THE DIAMOND-MORTENSEN-PISSARIDES (DMP) MODEL

Unemployment signifies "missing opportunities" from the perspective of society and potential inefficiency of market outcomes. The early one-sided search models viewed the duration of unemployment as an issue concerning as to how many job offers an unemployed worker would reject prior to receiving an offer that is acceptable. Albrecht considers the early models as taking the labour supply side view of unemployment while the DMP model reverses the focus. The foundation for the analysis of labour market built on search and matching frictions was the result of systematic and partly overlapping contributions of Diamond, Mortensen and Pissarides (DMP). According to Albrecht the history of the DMP model is not very clear--who came up with which idea first. He is of the opinion that the idea of matching function seems to have first been suggested by Edmund Phelps in his 1968 JPE article. "Pissarides (1979) and Diamond and Maskin (1979) developed the idea more or less in the way it is used in the DMP model." The key idea of closing the model with a simple free-entry condition seems to originate in Pissarides. Albrecht opines: "The idea of applying the Nash bargaining solution to determine the division of surplus in a match between a worker and a firm seems to have first been made explicit in Diamond (1982b)...."

The DMP model has more or less become a corner stone of macroeconomic analysis of the labour market. An important concept in the DMP model is the matching function relating to the flow of new hires to the crucial inputs in the matching process, namely, number of job vacancies. This concept facilitated incorporating search friction into macroeconomic models. The DMP model was supposed to have been designed to understand equilibrium or natural rate of unemployment. Mortensen in his Prize lecture observed: "...the flow of matches is represented as increasing, concave, and linearly homogenous in its two arguments, the number of unemployed workers and the number of vacancies participating in the matching process." Given the specification, the expected meeting rates per unemployed worker can be expressed as

$$M = \frac{M(u,v)}{u} = M(1,\theta) = m(\theta) \tag{1}$$

where m(θ) is an increasing and concave function of the ratio of vacancies(v) to unemployed workers(u), θ = v/u , referred to as "labour market tightness."

Likewise, the rate at which a vacancy is contracted by an unemployed worker is

$$\frac{M(u,v)}{v} = \frac{M(u,v)}{v}\frac{u}{v} = \frac{m(\theta)}{\theta} \tag{2}$$

Assume that m (θ) is increasing and that m (θ)/θ is decreasing in θ.

Labour market tightness is determined by free entry of vacancies. θ increases as the firms post more vacancies and the expected profit from the vacancy posting decreases. It is clear that the tightness of the labour market has to adjust until the value of a vacancy equals zero.

When the matching of a worker and a firm takes place, a surplus will result, a surplus relative to what they would get, if no matching occurs. A key assumption of the DMP model is that Nash bargaining determines the surplus, which in turn, determines the wage of the worker. The model is closed by a steady–state condition.

Mortensen states: "... unemployment should tend over time toward the steady-state value."

$$u = \frac{s}{s + m(\theta)} \tag{3}$$

where s denotes separation rate, and

u, m and θ are as defined earlier.

Eq.(3) indicates that the steady state unemployment rate falls as the number of vacant jobs increases relative to the unemployed workers searching for jobs. It underlines that the fundamental equilibrium object in the model is labour market tightness.

In his Prize lecture, Pissarides defines a job as an asset owned by the firm. If the job is filled, it is producing for profit. On the other hand, if the job is vacant, it has some value since the firm can expect to recruit a worker and yield some profit in the future. He states that we can derive the equilibrium number of jobs from the stipulation that the value of a new job vacancy must be zero. Further, he states:

"When the zero-profit condition for new vacancies is combined with the Nash wage equation it gives an equilibrium wage rate and job creation rate that depend on the frictions contained as summarized in the matching function, and on all the other variables that influence labour market outcomes in the standard models, such as productivity and taxes." From this condition, Pissarides obtains θ representing the labour market tightness. He derives equilibrium unemployment by using the Beverigde curve which shows combinations of vacancies and unemployment that are consistent with equality between the entry into unemployment with the exit from it. According to Pissarides "this implies that once on the Beveridge curve, unemployment is not changing, unless one of the flows (in or out) changes because of an exogenous shock."

The aggregate matching function basically determines the shape and properties of the Beveridge curve shown in Fig. 15.1.

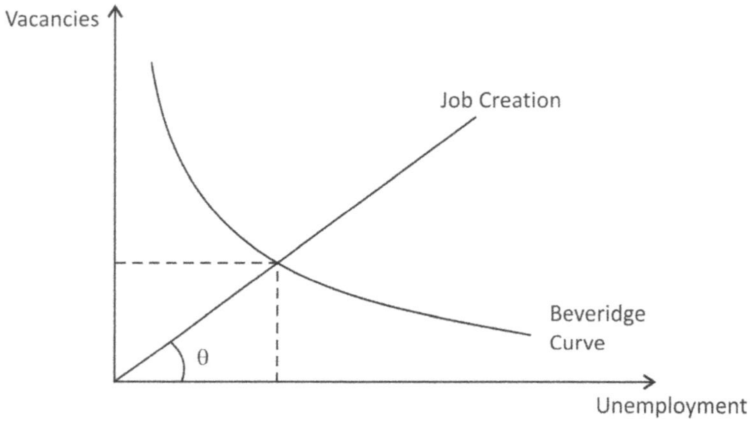

Fig. 15.1 Beveridge Curve and Equilibrium Vacancies and Unemployment

The convex shape of the curve is because of the constant returns satisfied by the aggregate matching function. Drawing a line through the origin with slope θ, we obtain the equilibrium point at the intersection of this line with the Beveridge curve. Frictions in the labour market keep Berveridge curve away from the origin. Pissarides provides a list of factors that could cause frictions in the labour market, such as institutional structure of the economy as regards transmission of information about jobs, locational differences and mismatch between the skill requirements of unemployed workers. It is obvious that an economy experiencing more frictions has a Beveridge curve further away from the origin than an economy with fewer frictions.

Pissarides clarifies further. In models that permit different labour productivities the position of the Beveridge curve is also influenced by the incentives the workers have to search for and accept jobs. In these models, two factors determine the matching rate, contacting a firm searching for workers and acceptability of the firm's offer. In an economy which follows a passive income support policy(an unemployment insurance system, which generously compensates workers without imposing pre-conditions in regard to quick acceptance of a job offer), the Beveridge curve lies further away from the origin. On the other hand, in an economy that has active income support policy, which supports the unemployed during search, and also provides incentives for more intensive job search, the

Beveridge curve shifts towards the origin and improve the performance of the labour market in matching workers to jobs.

The next issue is the determination of wage. As Mortensen observed bilateral bargaining process determines wage in the DMP model. Some share of the match surplus is received by the worker and the complementary share goes to the employer as future profit. However, in the model, the share of surplus that is claimed by labour depends on his "bargaining power," not explicitly modelled in theory.

As regards demand for labour, Mortensen remarked: "... a clear and simple statement of labour demand consistent with the search and matching framework was not fully articulated until Pissarides (1985)... introduced the 'free entry' condition; given that it takes time to fill a vacancy, the appropriate demand condition requires that the expected cost of posting a vacant job ... must be equal to the present value of the future profit that employees expect from a job –worker match. For any surplus value of a match, the model is complete." The expected surplus cannot be precisely estimated as it materialises in the future. Mortensen stated: "... exactly, what the future will bring in terms of both the market for the product of a particular match as well as the appropriate rates at which to discount the future surplus is fraught with uncertainty. How do participants in the labour market form these expectations? Is it possible to read the minds of human agents in our models?" Despite reservation about the hypothesis of rational expectations, Mortensen went along with others and adopted this hypothesis. However, he made two assumptions: i) Identical expectations by firms and workers, (ii) The common expectation can be represented by a single number. He showed that the reservation wage was linear and increasing in market tightness with an intercept determined by the unemployment benefit and a slope coefficient that reflected the cost of posting a vacancy and the relative share of future returns that flow to the worker. The reservation wage rises with labour market tightness (RE in Figure 15.2) and job creation curve (JC in Figure 15.2) is downward sloping as reservation wage is inversely related to search equilibrium labour market tightness. Fig. 15.2 depicts the intersection of RE curve and JC curve that gives the equilibrium.

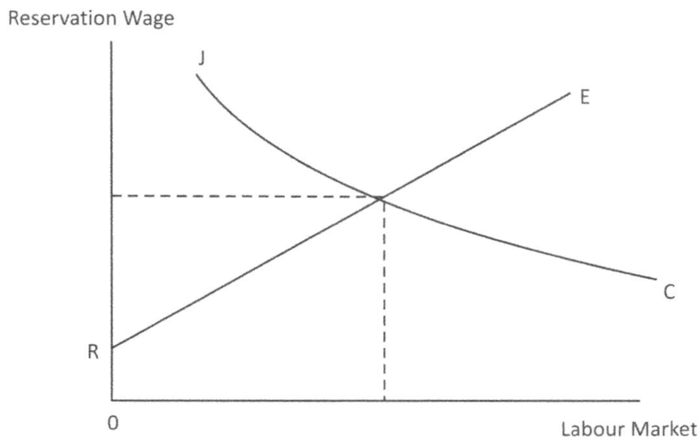

Fig. 15.2 Search Equilibrium

As shown in Fig. 15.2, Mortensen agreed that both labour market tightness (θ) and the reservation wage (R) were positive, if and only if, market product exceeded the unemployment benefit. In his Prize lecture, Mortensen provided empirical support (with the U.S data) that is consistent with the predictions of DMP theory. Pissarides, in his lecture says that the DMP model can be used "... to compare two economies, one with more frictions and passive policies with one with fewer frictions and active policies." He contends that the economy with more frictions would have more unemployment than the economy with fewer frictions but the two economies may have a similar level of vacancies. This conclusion, he says, can be contrasted with the comparison of two economies at different levels of aggregate economic activity, demand or supply. A lower level of aggregate economic activity suggests lower profitability from new jobs. Job creation falls, equilibrium unemployment increases and vacancies fall in response to the shock. Pissarides documents the results of empirical research into the reasons for different response of vacancies to more frictions and lower level of aggregate activity and rise in unemployment in different countries.

Dwelling on the nature of the matching function, Diamond observes that it is not a technologically given structural relationship but a reflection "at the aggregate level of a complex and varied pattern of hiring at the level of individual employers and workers." He, therefore, suggests examination of some of the details at a less aggregate level to see how "the current slump [in the U.S.] might be affecting the aggregate relationship." His examination and analysis of the data prompts him to conclude that the severity of the current recession in both severity and length has resulted in a great deal of long-term unemployment. As long-term unemployment imposes severe hardship on workers experiencing unemployment as also on their families and extended durations of unemployment would adversely affect the workers' behaviour, economists and policy makers have a reason to be specially concerned about how long the economy does badly. He states: "Historically, recovery is slow after financial crises. The impact of a slow recovery on the long–term unemployed emphasizes the importance of stimulating aggregate demand enough to speed up recovery. And it emphasises the importance of experimenting with programmes to help the long-term unemployed find and hold jobs." Diamond recommends the following policy inferences in his Prize lecture. He feels that what is important is what is to be done on the aggregate demand side.

1. Policies, providing more and better education and good retraining at a measurable cost for making the labour force more productive, need to be pursued.
2. He further observes: "Indeed a time of high unemployment is likely to be a time when further education is less socially costly by using time that would otherwise not be so well spent."
3. Even though there is some opinion that the current increase in aggregate unemployment is "structural" rather than deficit aggregate demand, there is "enough need" for stimulating aggregate demand.

4. Diamond is sceptical about the usefulness of attempts at separating cyclical from structural unemployment over a business cycle. It is because "... the willingness to hire for a given quality of match depends on expectations about the profitability of investing in a new worker and about the likely pool of future applicants."

He observes that "supporting current stimulus policies as very good for the economy is entirely compatible with taking care to avoid future inflation." He suggests that "for addressing unemployment, the model has to incorporate credit markets and non-Walrasian output markets, besides including nominal thinking and nominal contracting as well as a larger role for current income."

Diamond concludes his lecture with the following advice: "More inclusive modeling aside, I want to reiterate the perspective of Marshall quoted at the start. Understanding of the economy, and policy recommendations and decisions, should reflect analysis through multiple models. And they should incorporate insights that seem right even though they have not been modeled."

15.6 OTHER CONTRIBUTIONS

The Scientific Background note states that Mortensen's and Pissarides research careers essentially have centred on search and matching theory. They have been helpful in building foundations for labour market models featuring unemployment. Diamond has contributed, however, to a number of other areas in economics, though in a way they cover frictions in markets. Missing markets is viewed as an extreme form of frictions, particularly in the context of uncertainty. In the face of uncertainty, characterised by numerous possible states of nature, a large number of financial assets must be available to have a complete market structure. The existence of such a market structure enables economic agents to fully insure against all kinds of risks including risks that are specific to individual consumers or firms. In such an unrealistic scenario, life would be quite simple for market participants. Diamond contends that "a better description of how agents have to deal with uncertainty is one where insurance possibilities are limited or absent."

Diamond conducted research as to how absence of some insurance markets would affect resource allocation and economic efficiency and perhaps provide a rationale for government intervention. He has argued that "potentially useful government policy would not be able to directly overcome the lack of insurance markets by simply introducing them." Instead, government policy should be framed taking into account that the extant market structure is incomplete. This would facilitate a fair comparison between what markets and governments can do.

His most important early contribution is in the theory of public finance. His widely known contribution in this field relates to production efficiency his joint work with Mirrlees. The two articles by them are rated in the top 20 articles in 100 years of the American Economic Review. The committee which rated the articles observes: "This paper, in two parts, is the foundation of the theory of optimal taxation and public production in the presence of second–best limitations on redistribution and private production.... By subjecting tax systems to rigorous microeconomic analysis, this paper opened research on tax mechanism design and the minimization of the burden of taxes." Diamond's 1965 paper on public debt is also included in the top 20 papers by the committee. The committee refers to two fundamental contributions in this paper. (i) The paper shows that even in the absence of conventional market failures, competitive equilibria of infinite horizon overlapping generation models can be inefficient. (ii) He provides mechanisms through which "both external and internal debt can potentially reduce the capital stock. In classifying the general equilibrium effects of displacing physical capital with government debt in individuals' portfolios, it solved a long-standing debate concerning the feasibility of using internal debt to shift the burden of paying for public expenditures to future generations."

15.7 CONCLUDING OBSERVATIONS

Economists observe that DMP model has become "a work horse" in modern microeconomics. The research using the model shows that during periods of recession, wages do not show a tendency to fall adequately to clear the labour market. We may conclude by quoting from the Nobel Foundation's note. It identifies a number of ways in which search and matching theory by the three laureates has been used by researchers. They are the following.

1. The analysis of wage and price dispersion in search equilibrium.
2. The literature that has been developed relating to macroeconomic coordination problems.
3. "Fundamental work" on constrained efficiency in search and matching markets.
4. The model has been found to be useful in macroeconomic analysis and is considered helpful for policy making.

15.8 SELECT BIBLIOGRAPHY OF WORKS OF DIAMOND, MORTENSEN AND PISSARIDES

15.8.1 BOOKS

15.8.1.1 DIAMOND

1978 (with M. Rothschild, eds.), Uncertainty in Economics: Readings and Exercises, Academic Press, San Diego, Ca. (Revised edition 1989).

1984 A Search Equilibrium Approach to the Micro Foundations of Macro-Economics, MIT Press, Cambridge, MA.

1990 (ed.) Growth, Productivity, Unemployment: Essays to Celebrate Bob Solow's Birthday, MIT Press, Cambridge, MA.

1994 On Time: Lectures on Models of Equilibrium, Cambridge University Press, Cambridge, MA.

2010 (with N. Barr), Pension Reform: A Short Guide, Oxford University Press, Oxford.

15.8.1.2 MORTENSEN

2003 Wage Dispersion: Why are Similar Workers Paid Differently?, MIT Press, Cambridge, MA. (Paperback edition, 2004).

2011 (with C.A. Pissarides), Search Matching, Wage Dispersion and Unemployment, Oxford University Press, Oxford.

15.8.1.3 PISSARIDES

1976 Labour Market Adjustment: Microeconomic Foundations of Short–run Neoclassical and Keynesian Dynamics, Cambridge University Press, Cambridge.

1990/2000 Equilibrium Unemployment Theory, Basil Blackwell, Oxford, 2nd ed., MIT Press, Cambridge, MA.

2005 (with J. Frankel eds.), International Seminar on Macroeconomics, NBER, MIT Press, Cambridge, MA.

2009 (with J. Frankel eds.), International Seminar on Macroeconomics, 2008, NBER, University of Chicago Press, Chicago, Ill.

15.8.2 ARTICLES

15.8.2.1 DIAMOND

1964 (with T. C. Koopmans and R.E. Williamson), "Stationary Utility and Time Perspective," Econometrica, Vol. 32, No.1-2.

1965 "National Debt in a Neoclassical Growth Model," AER, Vol.55, No.5.

1967 "The Role of a Stock Market in a General Equilibrium Model with Technological Uncertainty," AER,Vol.57, No.4.

1970 "Incidence of an Interest Income Tax," JET, Vol. 2, No.3.

1971 a (with J.A. Mirrlees), "Optimal Taxation and Public Production, I &II," AER, Vol.61, No. 1 and 3.

b "A Model of Price Adjustment," JET, Vol. 3, No.2.

1973 (with J.A. Mirrlees), "Aggregate Production Function with Consumption Externalities," QJE, Vol.87, No.1.

1974 (with J.E. Stiglitz), "Increases in Risk and in Risk Aversion," JET, Vol.8, No.3.

1978 "Welfare Analysis of Imperfect Information Equilibria," BellJE, Vol. 9, No.1.

1980 (with E. Maskin), "An Equilibrium Analysis of Search and Breach of Contract, I: Steady States," BellJE, Vol.10, No.1.

1981 a "Mobility Costs, Frictional Unemployment, and Efficiency," JPE, Vol.89, No.4.

b (with E. Maskin), "An Equilibrium Analysis of Search and Breach of Contract II: A Non-Steady State Example," JET, Vol.25, No.2.

1982 a "Wage Determination and Efficiency in Search Equilibrium," RES, Vol.49, No.2.

b "Aggregate Demand Management in Search Equilibrium," JPE, Vol.90, No.5.

1984 "Money in Search Equilibrium," Econometrica, Vol. 52, No.1.

1987 "Search Theory," in The New Palgrave: A Dictionary of Economics, MacMillan, London.

1989 a (with O. Blanchard), "The Beveridge Curve," BPEA, Vol.20, No.1.

b (with D. Fudenberg), "Rational Expectations Business Cycles in Search Equilibrium," JPE, Vo.77, No.3.

1990 a "Pair-wise Credit in Search Equilibrium," QJE, Vol.105, No.2.

b (with J. Yellen), "Inventories and Money Holdings in Search Equilibrium," Econometrica, Vol.58, No.4.

1992 (with O. Blanchard), "The Flow Approach to Labor Markets," AER, Vol.82, No.2.

1994 (with O. Blanchard), "Ranking, Unemployment Duration and Wages," AER, Vol.84, No. 3.

1997 (with E. Shafir and A. Tversky), "Money Illusion," QJE, Vol.112, No.2.

1998 a "Optimal Income Taxation: An Example with U Shaped Pattern for the Optimal Marginal Rates," AER, Vol.88, No.1.

b "Managerial Incentives: On the Near Linearity of Optimal Compensation," JPE, Vol. 106, No.5.

2000 (with J.A. Mirrlees), "Adjusting one's Standard of Living: Two Period Models," in Incentives, Organization and, Public Economics, Papers in Honour of J. Hammond, (G.D. Myles et al. eds.), Oxford University Press, Oxford.

2006 "Reforming Public Pensions in the U.S. and the U.K.," EJ, Vol. 116, No.509.

2008 "Behavioral Economics," JPubE, Vol.92, No.8-9.

2011 a "Unemployment, Vacancies, Wages," Nobel Lecture, AER, Vol.101. No.4.

b (with J. Spinnewijn), "Capital Income Taxes with Heterogeneous Discount Rates," American Economic Journal: Economic Policy, Vol.3, No.4.

15.8.2.2 MORTENSEN

1970 a "A Theory of Wage and Employment Dynamics," in Microeconomic Foundations of Employment and Inflation Theory, (E.S. Phelps et al. eds.) Norton & Co, New York.

b "Job Search, the Duration of Unemployment and Phillips Curve," AER, Vol. 60, No.5.

1976 "Job Matching Under Imperfect Information," in Evaluating the Labor Market Effects of Social Programs, O. Ashenfelter (ed.), Princeton University Press, Princeton, NJ.

1977 "Unemployment Insurance and Labor Supply Decisions," Industrial Labor Relations Review, Vol.30, No.4.

1978 "Specific Capital and Labor Turnover," BellJE, Vol.9, No.2.

1980 (with K. Burdett), "Search, Layoffs, and Labor Market Equilibrium," JPE, Vol.88, No.4.

1982 a "The Matching Process as a Non Cooperative Bargaining Game," in The Economics of Information and Uncertainty, J. J. McCall (ed.), NBER, New York.

b "Property Rights and Efficiency in Mating, Racing and Related Games," AER, Vol.72, No.5.

1986 "Job Search and Labor Market Analysis," in Handbook of Labour Economics, Vol. 2, O. Ashenfelter and R. Layard (eds.), Elsevier, Amsterdam.

1988 "Matching: Finding a Partner for Life or Otherwise," American Journal of Sociology, Vol.94, Issue Supplement.

1992 "Search Theory and Macroeconomics: A Review Essay," JME, Vol.29, No.1.

1994 a (with C. Pissarides), "Job Creation and Job Destruction in the Theory of Unemployment," RES, Vo. 61, No.3.

b "The Cyclical Behavior of Job and Worker Flows," Journal of Economic Dynamics and Control, Vol.18, No.6.

c "Reducing Supply Side Distributions to Job Creation," in Restructuring Unemployment: Current Issues and Policy Options, FRB of Kansas City.

1998 a (with C. A. Pissarides), "Technical Progress, Job Creation and Job Destruction," Review of Economic Dynamics, Vol.1, No.4.

b (with K. Burdett),"Wage Differentials, Employer Size and Unemployment," IER, Vol.39, May.

1999 a (with C. A. Pissarides), "Unemployment Responses to 'Skill Biased' Shocks: The Role of Labor Market Policy," EJ, Vol. 109, April.

b "Equilibrium Unemployment Dynamics," IER, Vol.40, No.4.

c (with C. Pissarides), "New Development in Models of Research in the Labor Markets," in Handbook of Labor Economics, Vol.3, Part 2, O. Ashenfelter and D. Card (eds.), Elsevier, Amsterdam.

d (with C. Pissarides), "Job Reallocation, Employment Fluctuations and Unemployment," in Handbook of Macroeconomics, Vol.1, Part 2. M.Woodford and J.B Taylor (eds.) Elsevier, Amsterdam.

2002 (with R. Wright), "Competitive Pricing and Efficiency in Search Equilibrium," IER, Vol.43, No.1.

2003 (with C. Pissarides), "Taxes, Subsidies and Equilibrium Market Outcomes," in Designing Inclusion: Tools to Raise Low-end Pay and Employment in Private Enterprise, E.S. Phelps (ed.) Cambridge University Press, Cambridge.

2005 a "Growth, Unemployment and Labor Market Policy," Alfred Marshall Lecture, Journal of the European Economic Association, Vol.3, No.2-3.

b (with R. Lentz), "Productivity Growth and Worker Reallocation," IER, Vol.46, No.3.

2007 a (with R. Lentz), "More on Unemployment and Vacancy Fluctuations," Review of Economic Dynamics, Vol. 10, No.3.

b (with Nagypal), "Labor-Market Volatility in Matching Models, with Endogenous Fluctuations," ScandJE, Vol. 109, No.4.

2008 (with R. Lentz), "An Empirical Model of Growth Through Innovation," Econometrica, Vol. 76, No.6.

2009 "Island Matching," JET, Vol.144, No.6.

2010 "Wage Dispersion in the Search and Matching Model," AER, Vol.100, No.2.

2011 "Markets with Search Frictions and the DMP Model," Nobel Lecture, AER, Vol. 101, No.4.

15.8.2.3 PISSARIDES

1974 "Risk, Job Search, and Income Distribution," JPE, Vol. 82, Nov-Dec.

1976 "Job Search and Participation," Economica, Vol.43, Feb.

1978 a "Liquidity Considerations in the Theory of Consumption," QJE, Vol.92, May.

b "The Role of Relative Wages and Excess Demand in the Sectoral Flow of Labour," RES, Vol.45,Oct.

1979		"Job Matching with State Employment Agencies and Random Search," EJ, Vol.89, Dec.
1980		"Social Security and the Choice between Full-time Work, Part-time Work and Retirement," JPubE, Vol.14, Dec.
1982		"Job Search and the Duration of Layoff Unemployment," QJE, Vol.97, Dec.
1983		"Efficiency Aspects of the Financing of Unemployment Insurance and Other Government Expenditure," RES, Vol.50, Jan.
1984	a	"Search Intensity, Job Advertising and Efficiency," Journal of Labor Economics, Vol.2, Jan.
	b	"Efficient Job Rejection," EJ, Vol.94, No.376a, Supplement.
1985	a	"Taxes, Subsidies and Equilibrium Unemployment," RES, Vol.52, Jan.
	b	"Short-Run Equilibrium Dynamics of Unemployment, Vacancies and Real Wages," AER, Vol.75, No.4.
	c	"Dynamics of Unemployment, Vacancies and Real Wages with Trade Unions," ScandJE, Vol. 87, No. 3.
1986		"Trade Unions and the Efficiency of the Natural Rate of Unemployment," Journal of Labor Economics, Vol.4, Oct.
1987	a	"Mass Unemployment: A Review Essay", JME, Vol.20, June.
	b	"Search, Wage Bargains and Cycles," RES, Vol.54, July.
1988		"The Search Equilibrium Approach," AER, Vol.78, No. 2.
1989	a	"Unemployment and Macroeconomics," Economica, Vol. 56, Feb.
	b	"Unemployment Consequences of an Aging Population: An Application of Insider-Outsider Theory," European Economic Review, Vol.33, May.
	c	(with R. Jackman and R. Layard), "On Vacancies," Oxford Bulletin of Economics and Statistics, Vol. 51, No.5.
	d	(with J. Wadsworth), "Unemployment and the Inter-regional Mobility of Labour," EJ, Vol.99, Sep.
1990		(with I. McMaster), "Regional Migration, Wages and Unemployment: Empirical Evidence and Implications for Policy," OEP, Vol. 42, No.4.
1991		"Real Wages and Unemployment in Australia," Economica, Vol.58, Feb.

1992 "Loss of Skill during Unemployment and the Persistence of Employment Shocks," QJE, Vol.107, Nov.

1993 (with C. Bean), "Unemployment, Consumption and Growth," European Economic Review, Vol. 37, May.

1994 a (with D. Mortensen), "Job Creation and Job Destruction in the Theory of Unemployment," RES, Vol.61, July.

b "Search Unemployment with On-the-Job Search," RES, Vol. 61, July.

1997 "Learning by Trading and the Returns to Human Capital in Developing Countries," World Bank Economic Review, Vol.11, Jan.

1999 (with D. Mortensen), "Unemployment Responses to 'Skill-Biased' Technology Shocks: The Role of Labour Market Policy," EJ, Vol.109, Apr.

2001 (with B. Petrongolo), "Looking into the Black Box: A Survey of the Matching Function," JEL, Vol. 38, June.

2005 (with M. Amiti), "Trade and Industrial Location with Heterogeneous Labor," JIE, Vol.67, Dec.

2006 (with B. Petrongolo), "Scale Effects in Markets with Search," EJ, Vol.106, Jan.

2007 a (with C. Azariadis), "Unemployment Dynamics with International Capital Mobility," European Economic Review, Vol.51, Jan.

b (with L. R. Ngai), "Structural Change in a Multi-Sector Model of Growth," AER, Vol.97,Mar.

c (with G. Vallanti), "The Impact of TFP Growth on Steady-State Unemployment," IER, Vol.48, May.

2008 (with B. Petrongolo), "The Ins and Outs of European Unemployment," AER, Vol.98, No.2.

2009 "The Unemployment Volatility Puzzle: Is Wage Stickiness the Answer?" Walras-Bowley Lecture, Econometrica, Vol.77, Sep.

2010 "Why Do Firms Offer 'Employment Protection?" Econometrica, Vol.77, Oct.

2011 "Equilibrium in the Labour Market with Search Frictions," Nobel Lecture, AER, Vol.101, No.4.

15.9 WORKS OF OTHERS

Albrecht, J. (2011), "Search Theory: The 2010 Nobel Memorial Prize in Economic Sciences," ScandJE, Vol. 113, No. 2.

Hicks, J.R. (1932), The Theory of Wages, Macmillan, London.

Hutt, W. H. (1939), Theory of Idle Resources, Jonathan Cape, London.

Leijonhufvoud, A. (1968), On Keynesian Economics and Economics of Keynes: A Study in Monetary Theory, Oxford University Press, New York.

Marshall, A. (1948), Principles of Economics, 8th edition, Macmillan, New York.

SECTION - II

FINANCIAL ECONOMICS

CHAPTER 16

HARRY MAX MARKOWITZ

(1927 –)

Harry M. Markowitz shared the 1990 Nobel Memorial Prize in Economic Sciences with Merton H. Miller and William F. Sharpe for their pioneering work in the theory of Financial Economics. In the press release announcing the award, the Royal Swedish Academy of Sciences states: "Harry Markowitz is awarded the Prize for having developed the theory of portfolio choice; William Sharpe for his contributions to the theory of price formation for financial assets, the so-called Capital Asset Pricing Model (CAPM); and Merton Miller for his fundamental contributions to the theory of corporate finance." Financial economics as a sub-discipline of Economics has developed from 1950s. In fact, the first pioneering contribution in this field was Harry Markowitz's development of the theory of portfolio choice – a theory dealing with allocation of financial assets under uncertainty by households and firms. The theory analyses the manner in which wealth can be optimally invested in assets which differ in regard to their expected return and degree of risk, with a view to reducing the aggregate portfolio risk.

The award of Nobel Memorial Prize to Markowitz, Sharpe and Miller evoked the following comment from the New York Times: "Collectively, their theories are widely applied today. They influence the investment decisions of stock brokers, bankers, mutual fund managers and government agencies and millions of individuals." James Tobin's comment on the award: "They are all pioneers in finance theory which has been flourishing in recent years."

Assar Lindbeck, Chairman of the Prize Committee at the Royal Swedish Academy of Sciences noted that while the three did not collaborate, their work was a continuum. "Each one of them gave one building block for a unified theory of financial economics. This theory would have been incomplete if one of these pieces were missing."

While contributions of Markowitz are summarised in this chapter, those of Sharpe and Miller are presented in the next two chapters.

16.1 A BRIEF BIOGRAPHICAL NOTE: HARRY MARKOWITZ

Markowitz was born in 1927 and grew up as an only child in a middle class neighbourhood in Chicago, Illinois. During high school, Markowitz developed an interest in physics and philosophy, in particular the ideas of David Hume, an interest he continued to follow during his undergraduate years at the University of Chicago. The "exhilarating" intellectual environment at the University of Chicago in the late 1940's and early 1950's with Cowles Commission for Research in Economics located there induced Markowitz to apply to the University. He admits: "Becoming an economist was not a childhood dream of mine. When I finished the Bachelor's degree and had to choose an upper division, I considered the matter.... It was the 'Economics of Uncertainty' which interested me – in particular, the von Neumann and Morgenstern and Marshack arguments concerning expected utility; the Friedman-Savage utility function; and L.J.Savage's defence of personal probability. I had the good fortune to have Friedman, Marshack, and Savage among other great teachers at Chicago." After earning an undergraduate degree in Economics, Markowitz continued at University of Chicago for doing graduate work while serving as a Research Associate at Cowles Commission, which provided the opportunity to pursue his own research, write papers, present seminars, and attend seminars offered by distinguished in residence scholars or by visiting scholars. The Director of Research of the Cowles Commission at that time was a Dutch economist, Tjalling Koopmans, who developed an analytical method – linear programming or activity analysis – who shared Nobel Memorial Prize in Economics in 1975 for his work in the area. Markowitz was working in the field of linear programming. Markowitz states: "Koopmans's course on activity analysis with its definition of efficiency and its analysis of efficient sets was also a crucial part of my education."

When Markowitz had to choose his doctoral dissertation topic, he went to see Jacob Marschak. Waiting outside Marschak's office to meet him, Markowitz struck up a conversation with a stockbroker who urged Markowitz to write his thesis about the stock market, specifically applying the technique of linear programming to the investor's problems in the market. When Markowitz mentioned this suggestion to Marschak, the latter enthusiastically endorsed the suggestion, pointing out the pioneering work Cowles himself had done in that area. However, as Marschak did not feel qualified to guide Markowitz in the field, he referred Markowitz to Marshall Ketchum, then Dean of the Graduate School of Business and co-editor of the Journal of Finance, the official organ of the American Finance Association. Ketchum advised Markowitz to read John Burr William's The Theory of Investment Value (1938) what was then and still is an authoritative work on the valuation of financial assets.

The very first sentence in the book sets Markowitz thinking: "No buyer considers all securities equally attractive at present market prices...on the contrary, he seeks 'the best at the price.'" The book seemed to be suggesting that the investor should buy the one stock that had the highest expected return and "shun all the rest." Many years later, Markowitz said in a conversation with Peter Bernstein: "I was struck with the notion that you should be interested in risk as well as return." Markowitz's crucial insight is central to the process of investing as risk means that "more things can happen than will happen.... Variance came to mind as a measure of risk. The fact that portfolio variance depends on security covariances added to the plausibility of the approach. Since there were two criteria, risk and return, it was natural to assume that investors selected from the set of Pareto Optimal risk-return combination."

Markowitz left the University of Chicago, to join the RAND Corporation in 1952. At RAND he met George Dantzig. With the help of Dantzig, Markowitz continued to research on Optimization Techniques further developing the "critical line algorithm for identification of optimal mean-variance portfolios relying on what was later named the Markowitz frontier."

Markowitz's efforts resulted in publishing a fourteen-page article titled "Portfolio Selection" in June 1952 issue of the Journal of Finance. His attempt was to deal with the management of the investor's aggregate wealth--investor's portfolio. A fuller treatment of various aspects of the subject is contained in his book, Portfolio Selection: Efficient Diversification of Investments (based upon his Ph.D. thesis) published in 1959. This book was written principally at the Cowles Foundation at Yale on leave from the RAND Corporation, at the invitation of James Tobin. A reprint of this book including some new material was published in 1991. The presentation of the contribution made by Markowitz that revolutionised the subject and profession of investment management "by elevating risk to equal importance with expected return" is based upon ideas contained in all of Markowitz's work.

In 1989, he was awarded the von Neumann Prize in Operations Research Theory, citing his works of portfolio theory, sparse matrix techniques and the SIMSCRIPT programming language. Markowitz won the Nobel Memorial Prize while he was Professor of Finance at Baruch College of the City University of New York.

Presently Markowitz is an adjunct professor of Finance at the Rady School of Management at the University of California, San Diego (UCSD).

16.2 A SUMMARY OF HARRY MARKOWITZ'S CONTRIBUTIONS

A brief summary of his work that formed the basis for the award of Nobel Memorial Prize is attempted under the following heads.

1. Portfolio Analysis;
2. Portfolio Returns;
3. Measurement of Investment Risk;
4. Feasible Set of Portfolios;
5. Efficient Set Theorem;
6. Non-satiation and Risk Aversion; and
7. Investor's Selection of an Optimal Portfolio.

16.2.1 PORTFOLIO ANALYSIS

Markowitz observes that a good portfolio is more than a long list of good stocks and bonds. The investor's task is "Portfolio Selection" rather than "Security Selection." It is a balanced whole, providing the investor with protection and opportunities in the face of a wide range of contingencies. An investor has to build an integrated portfolio that best suits his needs. Information concerning individual securities is the first step in portfolio analysis, which ends with conclusions pertaining to portfolio as a whole. The purpose of the analysis is to identify portfolios which best meet the investors' objectives.

Markowitz emphasises uncertainty as a salient feature of investment in securities. A number of factors including economic and non-economic factors affect the security returns. "Only the clairvoyant could hope to predict the picture with certainty."

Markowitz assumes that an investor has a given sum of investible funds, which can be invested for a specific length of time – the investor's holding period. The investor commits the funds for investment in securities at the beginning of the period (t=0) and sells the securities at the end of the period (t=1). The proceeds realised by the sale of securities at period 1 will either be spent on consumption or reinvested in various securities or some of both will be done. Thus, the approach of Markowitz is viewed as a single period approach. The return on a security for a single period may be computed as follows:

(Closing price of the security at the end of the period - Closing price at the beginning of the period + Dividends during the period)/(Closing price at the beginning of the period).

That is,

$$R = [(P_1 - P_0) + D_1] / P_0$$

where

P_1 and P_0: A security's Closing and Opening price;

D_1: Dividends received during the year; and

R: Returns during the period.

Assuming that an investor purchased a share at a price of Rs. 110 on January 1, 2009 and sold the share at a price of Rs. 100 on January 1, 2010 after collecting a dividend of Rs. 4.50 during the year, the return during the year 2009 was

$$\frac{(100-110)+4.50}{110} = -5.5/110 = -0.05 \text{ or a loss of 5 percent}$$

Here, the implicit assumption is that a rupee of capital gain (realised) is exactly equal to a rupee of dividends (received), no better and no worse.

In making the investment decision at period 0, the investor, as mentioned above, should recognise that security return as well as portfolio returns over the one-year holding period are unknown and uncertain. Expected returns on various securities under consideration could, however, be estimated but not with certainty. While the typical investor wants returns to be "high," he also desires the returns to be "as certain as possible." Markowitz notes that a typical investor has two conflicting objectives, viz., maximisation of expected returns and minimising uncertainty or risk.

One period rate of return on a security could be calculated using the following formula:

$$\text{Rate of return} = \frac{(\text{End}-\text{of}-\text{Period Wealth})-(\text{Beginning}-\text{of}-\text{Period Wealth})}{\text{Beginning}-\text{of}-\text{Period Wealth}}$$

where beginning of period wealth (W_0) is the purchase price of one unit of the security at period 0 and end-of-the period wealth (W_1) represents the market value of the unit at period 1 along with the value of any cash and cash equivalents (such as dividend or interest) paid to the owner of the security between periods 0 (t_0) and 1 (t_1).

16.2.2 PORTFOLIO RETURN

A portfolio, as mentioned above, is a chosen or selected group of securities; its return, R_p, can be calculated in a similar manner.

$$R_p = \frac{W_1 - W_0}{W_0} \times 100 \qquad (1)$$

where

W_0: denotes the aggregate purchase price at t_0 of the securities included in the portfolio.

W_1: denotes the aggregate market value of the securities in the portfolio at t_1 along with the aggregate cash or cash equivalents received by the investor between t_0 and t_1 from owning these securities.

Equation (1) can also be expressed as

$$W_1 = W_0 (1 + R_p) \qquad (2)$$

where

W_0, W_1 and R_p are as defined earlier.

Thus, we can see that end-of-period wealth or terminal wealth of an investor is obtained by multiplying the beginning-of-period wealth with 1 plus the rate of return of portfolio.

However, the investor does not know what the value of W_1 will be, as the rate of return on portfolios under consideration of the investor is not known to him/her.

What is required for the investor is the expected rate of return, not the actual or realised rate of return in the past. Similarly, investor would like to know how stable the rate of return on various portfolios under consideration is. Therefore, the investor should consider the rate of return as, what in statistics is called, a random variable. It is also known that such random variables can be adequately described by the first two moments of their distribution, namely mean or expected value and variance or standard deviation of return representing risk.

Markowitz asserts that investors should make their portfolio decisions based exclusively on expected returns and standard deviations requiring the investor to estimate the expected return and standard deviation of each portfolio and then choose the "best" portfolio on the basis of the relative magnitudes of the expected return and standard deviation. It is clear while expected return is the reward associated with a portfolio, standard deviation can be considered as a measure of portfolio risk. The expected return of a portfolio and the standard deviation of the portfolio return depend on the expected return and the standard deviation of each security included in the portfolio, besides the amount invested in each security.

To understand the relationship between rate of return and standard deviation of individual securities contained in the portfolio as also the amount invested in these securities and the expected return and standard deviation of a portfolio, an illustrative example of a three-security portfolio given in below Table 16.1 will be of help. This example discussed in this and the subsequent sections (16.2.3 and 16.2.4) is adopted from Sharpe, W. F. et al., Investments (sixth edition, Prentice Hall of India, New Delhi, 2003).

Let us assume that the initial value of wealth (W_0) of an investor (on January 1, 2009) is Rs. 68,800. His initial market value, portfolio value is Rs. 68,800. The initial composition of the portfolio comprising (securities) shares A, B and C, the market price per share at the beginning of the period, January 1, 2009 and aggregate initial investment in each share are given here in Table 16.1.

Table 16.1 Computation of Expected Return on a Three-Security Portfolio

Security	Number of shares in the portfolio	Initial market price per share	Aggregate investment	Proportion of Initial Market value of portfolio
A	400	Rs. 40	Rs. 16,000	Rs. 16,000/Rs. 68,800 = 0.2325
B	800	Rs. 35	Rs. 28,000	Rs. 28,000/Rs. 68,800 = 0.4070
C	400	Rs. 62	Rs. 24,800	Rs. 24,800/Rs. 68,800 = 0.3605

Initial Market Value of Portfolio (W_0) = Rs. 68,800

Sum of Proportions = 1.0000

Assume, the investor expects a rate of return of 16.2 per cent for share A, 24.6 percent for share B and 22.8 per cent for share C. Using the expected return of each of the securities A, B and C, we can calculate the expected return on this portfolio as the weighted average of the expected returns on its component securities, A, B and C. The relative market values of the three securities in the portfolio are used as weights.

Table 16.2 Calculation of Expected Return for a Portfolio using Security Expected Returns

Security (1)	Proportion of Initial Market Value of Portfolio (2)	Security Expected Returns (3)	Contribution to Portfolio return (4 = 2x3)
A	0.2325	16.2%	3.77%
B	0.4070	24.6%	10.01%
C	0.3605	22.8%	8.22%

Expected Return on the Portfolio = 3.77% + 10.01% + 8.22%

$$R_p = 22.0\%$$

In general, for calculating the expected return on a portfolio comprising *n* securities [in the above example in Table 16.1, N is equal to (3)], the following formula can be used.

$$\tilde{R}_p = X_1\tilde{r}_1 + X_2\tilde{r}_2 + \ldots + X_n\tilde{r}_n \qquad (3)$$

$$\tilde{R}_p = \sum_{i=1}^{n} X_i\tilde{r}_i$$

where

$\tilde{R}_p$: expected portfolio return,

X_i : Proportion of the portfolio's initial value invested in security i,

r_i : expected return of security i, and

n : number of securities in the portfolio.

Note: We assumed that short sales of securities are not permitted. To calculate the expected return for any portfolio constructed from *n* securities, an expected return vector of the following form can be used

$$\begin{vmatrix} \tilde{r}_1 \\ \tilde{r}_2 \\ \tilde{r}_3 \\ \cdot \\ \cdot \\ \tilde{r}_n \end{vmatrix}$$

As can be seen, this vector consists of one column of numbers, where the entry in row i contains the expected return on security i. In the above example of three-security portfolio, the investor's estimated expected return vector is

$$\begin{vmatrix} 16.2\% \\ 24.6\% \\ 22.8\% \end{vmatrix}$$

showing expected returns for shares A, B and C.

Equation (3) shows that a portfolio's expected return is simply a weighted average of the expected returns of the securities included in it, weights being the proportionate share of each security in the initial market value of the portfolio (participation level of each security in the portfolio). If an investor desires to have the greatest possible expected return from his investment, equation 3 indicates that he can achieve this object by holding a security which, in his opinion, has the greatest or highest expected return. Very few investors do this. Investors, no doubt, want return to be high on their investment; they also want this return to be "dependable, stable, not subject to uncertainty." Markowitz observes: "The portfolio with highest 'likely return' is not necessarily the one with 'least' uncertainty of return.... The portfolio with the least uncertainty may have an undesirably small 'likely return.' Between these extremes would be portfolios with varying degrees of likely return and uncertainty (risk)." With the purpose of reducing risk, investors include more than one security in their portfolio---adopt Markowitz's suggestion of diversification.

16.2.3 MEASUREMENT OF INVESTMENT RISK: STANDARD DEVIATION OF RETURN

Having understood, the method of computing expected return on a portfolio, we may now turn our attention to the calculation of a measure of portfolio risk. The matter of defining risk in terms of a number is crucial. The measure of risk has to estimate the extent to which the actual outcome is likely to diverge from the expected outcome. In the absence of the magnitude of investment risk they face, investors cannot decide how much risk to take. Statistical measure of standard deviation of return provides an estimate of the likely divergence of actual return from expected return. When the probability distribution for a portfolio's returns can be approximated by the bell-shaped curve (normal distribution), standard deviation proves to be a very good measure of the degree of uncertainty. According to Levy and Markowitz, even if returns are not normally distributed, the use of standard deviation as a measure of risk is justified in an approximate sense, provided that there are small probabilities of extremely high and low returns. Furthermore, the assumption of normal distribution of returns is considered plausible for analysing returns on diversified portfolios when the investor's holding period is relatively short (say, a quarter).

The formula for calculating the standard deviation for the portfolio consisting of *n* shares/securities is given by

$$\sigma_p = \sqrt{\sum_{i=1}^{n} \sum_{j=1}^{n} X_i X_j \rho_{ij} \sigma_i \sigma_j} \tag{4}$$

where

σ_p : Standard deviation of the *n*-stock portfolio,

X_i : Defined earlier,

ρ_{ij} : Covariance between returns on securities i and j.

Covariance is a measure of how returns on securities i and j (the two random variables) move together. A positive covariance indicates a tendency for the security returns to move in the same direction. On the other hand, a negative value for covariance indicates a tendency for the returns to offset one another. That is, a worse-than-expected return for one security is likely to occur with a better-than-expected return for the other. Further, a zero value or a relatively small value for the covariance suggests that there is no or little relationship between the returns for the two securities.

The statistical measure of correlation is closely related to co-variance. In fact, the correlation between the two random variables times the product of their standard deviations yields the co-variance between those two random variables. The following formula establishes the relationship:

$$\rho_{ij} = [\text{Co-variance } (i, j)] / (\sigma_i \sigma_j) \tag{5}$$

Theoretically, the value of the correlation coefficient always lies between –1 and +1. The value of +1 indicates perfect positive correlation while value of –1 represents perfect negative correlation. When the correlation coefficient between two random variables is equal to zero, it denotes that the two security returns are uncorrelated.

We may note that in order to calculate the standard deviation of a portfolio comprising three securities, nine terms are to be added together; the number of terms to be added together (that is, 9 terms) is equal to the number of securities squared (3^2).

We may now derive a general formula for calculating the standard deviation for a portfolio consisting of n securities.

$$\sigma_p = [X_1^2 \sigma_1^2 + X_2^2 \sigma_2^2 + ... + X_n^2 \sigma_n^2 + 2 X_1X_2 \sigma_1 \sigma_2 \rho_{12} + ... + 2 X_1X_n \sigma_1 \sigma_n \rho_{1n} + .. + 2 X_{n-1}X_n \sigma_{n-1} \sigma_n \rho_{(n-1)n}]^{1/2} \tag{6}$$

Consider the following variance-covariance matrix for the portfolio consisting shares A, B and C (Continuing the example given above).

$$\begin{vmatrix} 146 & 187 & 145 \\ 187 & 854 & 104 \\ 145 & 104 & 289 \end{vmatrix}$$

Given the variance-covariance matrix and the proportions of investment (in shares A, B and C) given in Table 16.2, i.e. X_1 = 0.2325, X_2 = 0.4070 and X_3 = 0.3605, the standard deviation of the portfolio is:

σ_p = [(0.2325 x 0.2325 x 146) + (0.2325 x 0.4070 x 187) + (0.2325 x 0.3605 x 145) + (0.4070 x 0.2325 x 187) + (0.4070 x 0.4070 x 854) + (0.4070 x 0.3605 x 104) + (0.3605 x 0.2325 x 145) + (0.3605 x 0.4070 x 104)+ (0.3605 x 0.3605 x 289).

$$\sigma_p = \sqrt{27712} = 16.65\%$$

Notice that variance-covariance matrix is square---number of columns equals the number of rows; for n security portfolio, the number of cells equal n^2. Further, the variance of the securities appears on the diagonal of the matrix (in the above examples: 146, 854 and 289). Thirdly, it is a symmetric matrix, i.e. the number appearing in row i of column j also appears in row j of column i (in the above example, number 145 appearing in row 1 of column 3, also appears in row 3 of column 1). It is clear that covariance between first and third securities must be same as the covariance between third and first securities.

16.2.4 FEASIBLE SET OF PORTFOLIOS

Feasible set or opportunity set is the set of all portfolios that can be formed from the group of securities; say n securities, being considered by an investor. The feasible set generally will have an umbrella shape as shown in Figure 16.1. All possible portfolios that could be formed from a group of N securities lie either within or on the boundary of the feasible set. Points denoted 1, 3, 5 and 9 in the figure are examples of feasible portfolios.

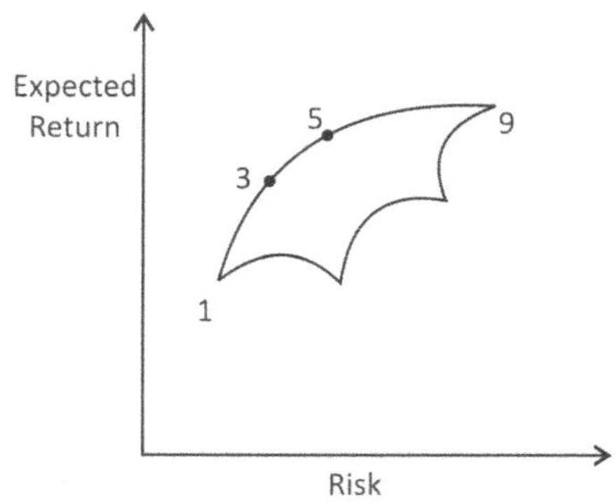

Fig. 16.1 Feasible Portfolio Set

16.2.5 EFFICIENT SET THEOREM

Efficient set of portfolios or Efficient Frontier has to satisfy the following two conditions:

(i) Offer highest expected return for varying risk levels; and

(ii) Offer lowest risk for varying levels of expected return.

This theorem when applied to the feasible set of portfolios yields efficient set. A look at Figure 16.1 reveals that there is no portfolio offering less risk than that of portfolio 1.

Further, there is no portfolio having more risk than that of portfolio 9. Thus, the set of portfolios lying on the northern boundary of the feasible set between points 1 and 9 offers maximum expected return for varying levels of risk.

Now let us consider the second condition specified above for identifying efficient set. Portfolio 9 offers maximum expected return as there is no other portfolio in or on the feasible set offering a greater expected return. Likewise, there is no other portfolio in or on the feasible set, which offers a lower expected return than 1. Thus, the set of portfolios lying on the western boundary of the feasible set offers minimum risk for varying levels of expected return. It is seen that only those portfolios lying on the northwest boundary between points 1 and 9 on the feasible set satisfy the above two conditions and thus form the efficient set from which the investor has to choose. All the other feasible portfolios are termed "inefficient" portfolios and can be ignored by the investor. As the investor goes up the scale of expected returns, he finds that risk is increasing. As he goes up the scale of risk, he finds that the expected rate of return is increasing at the same time.

16.2.6 NON-SATIATION AND RISK AVERSION

Once an investor identifies efficient frontier, how does she or he choose from among the portfolios on the efficient frontier? The answer rests on a pervasive feature of human behaviour--- risk aversion. In the portfolio selection problem of Markowitz, two assumptions are implicit. Markowitz assumes that investors, when given a choice, always prefer higher levels of terminal wealth to lower levels of terminal wealth – the non-satiation assumption. Thus, given two portfolios with the same risk or standard deviation, the investor will choose the portfolio, which offers a higher expected return. The question is what the investor will do when he/she has to choose between two portfolios having identical expected return but different degrees of risk or different levels of standard deviation.

Though investors are assumed to be risk averse, different investors possess different degrees of risk aversion. If taking on more risk is the price the investor has to pay for the opportunity to become richer, then he can use the concept of marginal utility in deciding which of the portfolios on the Efficient Frontier to select. The investor goes up the line toward higher expected return to the point where the additional risk required to gain an extra rupee of wealth is just too high a price to pay (see Figure 16.1). The precise relationship between utility and wealth is called the investor's utility of wealth function.

Markowitz contends: "When early mathematicians first formulated principles of behavior in chance situations, they assumed that the proper objective of the individual was to maximize expected money return. It was later found that this objective could be incredibly bad." (Classic example was provided by St. Petersburg Paradox). He proposes expected utility rule as a substitute for expected return rule. In support of this substitution Markowitz argues: "An investor who sought only to maximize the expected return would never prefer a diversified portfolio. If one security had greater expected return than any other, the investor would place all his funds in this security. If several securities had the same (greatest) expected return, the investor would be indifferent among portfolios, diversified or not, which contained only these securities. Thus, if we consider diversification as a sound principle of investment, we must reject the objective of simply maximizing expected return."

A utility map (three utility curves) is depicted below:

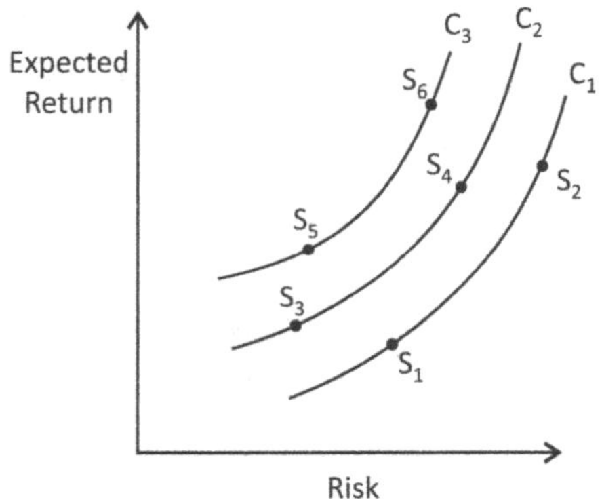

Fig. 16.2 Risk-Return Indifference Curves

The expected utility maximum points that the individual should act as if he attaches numbers, called their utility, to each possible outcome, and when faced with choice under conditions of uncertainty, he selects the one with the greatest expected value of utility.

If the investor's utility curve is of the shape shown in Figure 16.2, with increasingly greater returns adding less and less to utility, he will generally prefer a diversified portfolio.

If over the range of possible returns, an individual's utility (U) depends on the expected return, E(r), according to a formula of the form of

$$U = A - AE(r^2)$$

The investor will select one of the efficient portfolios after an analysis based on expected return and variance or standard deviation. The particular portfolio preferred by him depends on the value of the positive number A.

As outlined above, the Markowitz's portfolio selection function can be viewed as an effort to maximise the expected utility associated with the investor's terminal wealth. Each investor's utility of wealth (which is unique) gives the exact relationship between utility and wealth. Under the assumption of non-satiation, investor prefers more wealth to less wealth. That is, the utility function is positively sloped, irrespective of the wealth level of the investor. The function is concave indicating diminishing marginal utility of wealth. In an article "Portfolio Selection" in March 1952 issue of the Journal of Finance and another article, "The Utility of Wealth" in April 1952 issue of the Journal of Political Economy and in his 1959 publication, Portfolio Selection, Markowitz observes that a utility function need not be everywhere concave or everywhere convex. It may be concave at first, then convex, then concave again. Such a curve is consistent with insurance against losses, taking small bets and the diversification of the portfolio. As each investor has a unique utility of wealth function, the marginal utility of wealth may differ among investors. Moreover, the increment to utility of an extra rupee for an investor may depend on the level of wealth he possesses before receiving the extra rupee. A poor investor may value an extra rupee of wealth much more than a rich investor does.

It is generally assumed that investors experience diminishing marginal utility of wealth; that is, he is necessarily risk-averse. Risk-averse investors are willing to accept lower expected returns (or willing to forego some expected terminal wealth) in exchange for less risk; that is, investors are willing to trade off some expected return against risk in order to achieve a desired level of portfolio risk. Thus, various combinations of expected returns and risk will yield the same level of expected utility for an investor. The concept of indifference curves demonstrates this relationship.

An indifference curve represents a set of expected return and risk combinations that produce the same utility level for an investor. In other words, an investor is said to be indifferent between different risk-expected return combinations on the same indifference curve. A map of indifference curves where the horizontal axis measures the portfolio risk, as measured by standard deviation of the portfolio (σ_p) and the vertical axis indicates expected return of the portfolio ($\tilde{R}_p$).

We see from Fig. 16.2 that the investor finds portfolios S_1 and S_2 equally desirable, as they lie on the same indifference curve, C_1, despite the fact that they have different expected portfolio returns and standard deviations. Even though portfolio S_2 has a higher standard deviation compared to portfolio S_1, it offers a higher expected return than portfolio S_1. However, the investor prefers portfolio S_4 (on C_3) with a higher expected return than both portfolios S_1 and S_2, Portfolio S_4, though has a higher standard deviation than S_1, it has a sufficiently large expected return relative to S_1 that makes S_4 more desirable than S_1. The smaller standard deviation on S_4 compared to S_2 more than offsets its smaller expected return and makes it, on balance, more desirable than S_2.

In general, an investor has an infinite number of indifferent curves representing his preferences for expected returns and standard deviations. The twin assumptions of non-satiation and risk aversion cause indifference curves of the investors to be positively sloped and convex. Further, we may note that it is not assumed that all investors have identical degree of risk aversion. Some investors may be highly risk averse, some may be moderately risk averse while others may be slightly risk averse. The more risk averse an investor is, the more steeply sloped his indifference curves will be. Furthermore, he will find any portfolio that is lying on an indifference curve that is farther north-west to be more desirable in that it provides greater utility than any portfolio lying on an indifference curve that is not as far north-west.

While Markowitz makes a reasonable assumption that investors generally are risk averse, it is not necessary to make this assumption. It can be assumed that investors are either risk-neutral or risk- seeking. However, there is empirical evidence to suggest that investors, in general, are more accurately characterised as being risk-averse.

16.2.7 INVESTOR'S SELECTION OF AN OPTIMAL PORTFOLIO

Given the efficient set of portfolios or efficiency frontier, the investor has to choose his or her optimal portfolio. He should plot his indifference curve on the same figure as the efficient set in order to choose the portfolio that is most desirable. Such an efficient portfolio will correspond to the point at which an investor's indifference curve is just tangent to the efficient set as shown in Figure 16.3.

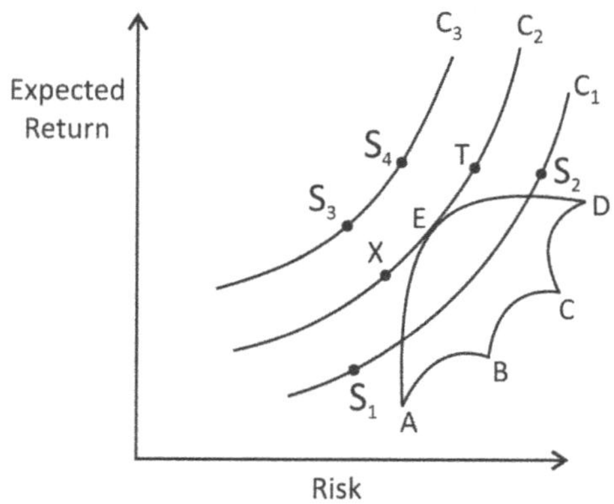

Fig. 16.3 The Efficient Portfolio

As can be seen in the figure, portfolio E on indifference curve C_2 is the optimal portfolio. Even though the investor would prefer a portfolio on C_3 (as C_3 is a higher indifference curve) no such portfolio exists in the market. Any portfolio on indifference curve C_1 is dominated in regard to $\tilde{R}_p$ by portfolios such as E as it is on an indifference curve that is farther north-west.

Similarly, we can show the choice of an optimal portfolio by a highly risk-averse investor (a portfolio that is close to X) and the one by a slightly risk averse investor (a portfolio that is closer to T).

As argued above, indifference curves for a risk-averse investor are positively sloped and convex while the efficient set is generally positively sloped and concave. These two properties will ensure that there will be only one tangency point between the investor's indifference curves and the efficient set. At the tangency point lies the optimal portfolio chosen by the investor. Rational investors select the portfolio that best suits their taste. Markowitz's approach combines "two clichés that investors learn early in the game: nothing ventured, nothing gained, but don't put all your eggs in one basket."

16.3 A BRIEF CRITIQUE OF PORTFOLIO SELECTION

While Markowitz's work (1952 article and 1959 book) revolutionised investment theory and the profession of investment management and laid the foundation for about all of theoretical work in finance that followed, there are a number of criticisms of the work. Some of the problems critics have raised are basically technical and mechanical which have been overcome in later works. We may briefly summarise here the substantive issues.

Firstly, the critics questioned the investors' rationality assumption. The debate relates to whether investors are sufficiently rational in their investment decision-making to follow Markowitz's presumption. "If intuition triumphs over measurement in investing, the whole exercise could turn out to be waste of time and a flawed explanation of market behaviour."

Another criticism relates to the measure of investment risk – whether variance or standard deviation is a proper and good proxy for risk. If investors perceive that some measure of risk other than variance might serve equally well, the consequences of another proxy for risk are less clear.

What are the consequences for portfolio choice if Markowitz's assumption that there is a positive relationship between risk and expected return does not survive empirical tests? What will be the investor's choice if "high returns are systematically available on low-risk securities?"

The technical problems in regard to portfolio selection arise from Markowitz's unquestioned assumption that it is not difficult for investor to estimate the required inputs – expected returns, variances and co- variances among all the individual securities. It is, of course, true that Markowitz expressed his concern about the difficulties that are present for the practical use of his ideas. The development on this front will be discussed in the chapter on William F. Sharpe.

Finally, another technical problem relates to Markowitz's assumption that a portfolio can be described adequately with only two numbers: expected return and variance or standard deviation. Dependence on expected return and standard deviation is appropriate, if and only if, security and portfolio returns are normally distributed.

16.4 CONCLUDING OBSERVATIONS

The contribution of Markowitz is rated as "immense." Bernstein observes: "...diversification has become a veritable religion among investors. Even the attacks on

Markowitz [some of which are noted above] have triggered new concepts and new applications that might never have come about without his innovative contributions." Particular mention may be made of attacks on concepts of rational behaviour and risk aversion and the gradual rise of behavioural finance. Some of these developments are discussed in other chapters. At this point, it is sufficient to note that a growing volume of research reveals that people succumb to inconsistencies, myopia and other forms of distortion in the process of decision-making.

It is said that Markowitz is the first to put a number on investment risk as von Neumann and Morgenstern had put a number on utility. In addition, in any study of the History of Modern Economic Analysis, we find that finance as a sub-discipline of Economics "barely existed" before Markowitz. Now we notice that methods of financial economics are finding increasing acceptance in other sub-disciplines of Economics.

We may conclude with a quote of Richard Brearley of the comment made by Blanchard and Mankiw in 1988:

"Twenty years ago, it was standard practice in describing macroeconomic behavior to build theoretical models assuming all current and future variables were known with certainty. When models were applied to the data, the only concession to the presence of uncertainty was more often than not the introduction of an unexplained error term in the regression. Ten years ago, under injunctions to 'take uncertainty seriously,' macroeconomists started introducing uncertainty explicitly at the model-building stage."

Much of the expanding interest in the economics of uncertainty is attributable to the work of Harry Markowitz.

16.5 SELECT BIBLIOGRAPHY OF HARRY MARKOWITZ'S WORKS

16.5.1 BOOKS

1959 Portfolio Selection: Efficient Diversification of Investments, Wiley, New York.

Yale University, New Haven, 1970.Basil Blackwell, Oxford, 1991.

1987 Mean-Variance Analysis in Portfolio Choice and Capital Markets, Basil Blackwell, Oxford.

2009 Harry Markowitz: Selected Works, World Scientific Publishing, Hackensack, NJ. Nobel Laureate Series, Vol.1.

16.5.2 ARTICLES

1952 a "Portfolio Selection," JF, Vol.7, No.1.

b "The Utility of Wealth," JPE, Vol.60, Apr.

1976 "Investment for the Long Run: New Evidence for an Old Rule," JF, Vol.31, No.5.

1981 "Portfolio Analysis with Factors and Scenarios," JF, Vol.36, No.4.

1983 "Nonnegative or Not Negative: A Question about CAPMs," JF, Vol.38, No.2.

1984 "Mean-Variance versus Direct Utility Maximization," JF, Vol.39, No.1.

1990 "Normative Portfolio Analysis: Past, Present, and Future," Journal of Economics and Business, Vol. 42, No.2.

1991 a "Individual Versus Institutional Investing," Financial Services Review, Vol.1, No.1.

b "Foundations of Portfolio Theory," Nobel Lecture, JF, Vol.46, No.2.

1996 a (with N. Usmen), "The Likelihood of Various Stock Market Return Distributions, Part 1: Principles of Inference," JR&U, Vol.13, No.3.

b (with N. Usmen), "The Likelihood of Various Stock Market Return Distributions, Part 2: Empirical Results," JR&U, Vol. 13, No.3.

2006 (with J. Hanqig and Z. Y. Xun), "A Note on Semi-variance," Mathematical Finance, Vol.16. No.1.

2010 a (with S. Das et al.), "Portfolio Organization with Mental Accountings," JFQA, Vol.45, No.2.

b "Portfolio Theory: As I Still See It," Annual Review of Financial Economics, Annual Reviews, Vol.2, No.1.

16.6 WORKS OF OTHERS

Bernstein, P. L. (1996), Against the Gods: The Remarkable Story of Risk, John Wiley & Sons, New York.

Bernstein, P. L. (2005), Capital Ideas: The Improbable Origins of Modern Wall Street, John Wiley & Sons, Hoboken, NJ.

Brealey, R.A. (1991), "Harry M Markowitz's Contributions to Financial Economics," ScandJE, Vol.93, No.1.

Williams, J. B. (1956), The Theory of Investment Value, North Holland, New York.

CHAPTER 17

WILLIAM FORSYTH SHARPE

(1934 –)

William F. Sharpe shared the 1990 Alfred Nobel Memorial Prize in Economic Sciences with Harry M. Markowitz and Merton H. Miller for pioneering work in the theory of financial economics. Specifically, the Royal Swedish Academy identifies his formulation of Capital Asset Pricing Model (CAPM) as the main contribution to award the prize. The preceding chapter has summarised the contribution of Harry Markowitz; the contribution of Merton Miller who shared the 1990 prize is covered in the next chapter.

17.1 A BRIEF BIOGRAPHICAL NOTE: WILLIAM SHARPE

William Sharpe was born on June 16, 1934, in Boston, Massachusetts, U.S.A. He had his early education in the Public Schools of Riverside, California. After enrolling in 1951 at the University of California at Berkley with a plan to major in science en route to a medical degree, Sharpe shifted in 1952 to the University of California at Los Angeles (UCLA) with a declared major in business administration, taking courses in the fields of Economics and Finance. He earned his B.A. in economics at UCLA in 1955 and his M.A. in economics the following year. Two professors at UCLA had a profound influence on Sharpe's career – J. Fred Weston, Professor of Finance in the Business School and Armen Alchian, Professor of Economics.

After a short stint in the Army, Sharpe joined the RAND Corporation (a think tank) in 1956 as an Economist while pursuing a Ph.D. degree in Economics at UCLA. In 1960, he began work on a dissertation concerning the economics of transfer prices. After writing some 60 pages of what he thought was "earth-shattering stuff," Sharpe showed his work to Jack Hirshleifer who had done previously work on the subject. Hirshleifer came back to him a week later and declared flatly "that there was absolutely no thesis there." Weston suggested that Sharpe talk with Markowitz who was then at RAND Corporation, having moved from the Cowles Commission in New Haven. Sharpe began to work closely with Markowitz on the topic "Portfolio Analysis." Sharpe completed a paper containing the full development of the ideas during 1961, the same year he was awarded his doctorate. He titled the paper "A Simplified Model for Portfolio Analysis" which was published in the January 1963 issue of Management Science, one of only two journals at the time that published articles on Operations Research. Although Markowitz was not on his Ph.D.

Committee at UCLA, he filled a role similar to that of dissertation advisor. Sharpe acknowledges: "My debt to him is truly enormous."

William Sharpe was associated at sometime or the other with the University of Washington, Seattle, University of California at Irvine and Stanford University's Graduate School of Business. He was Timken Professor of Finance at Stanford, Consultant to Merrill Lynch, Pierce, Fenner and Smith, and Consultant to Wells Fargo Investment Advisors. He was a founder of Sharpe-Russell Research. Sharpe was Timken Professor Emeritus of Finance at Stanford University and consultant to William F-Research Associates. He also served as Trustee of the College Retirement Equities Fund, Trustee for the Research Foundation of the Institute of Chartered Financial Analysts, a Committee Member for the Institute of Quantitative Research in Finance, a member of the Council on Education and Research of the Institute of Chartered Financial Analysts, Strategic Advisor for Nikko Securities Institute of Investment Technology and the Institutional Portfolio Management Division of the Union Bank of Switzerland. Sharpe received a number of awards from diverse constituencies including the American Assembly of Collegiate School of Business Award for outstanding contribution to the field of business education and Financial Analysts' Federation, Nicholas Molodovsky Award for outstanding contributions to the profession of Finance.

17.2 A SUMMARY OF WILLIAM SHARPE'S CONTRIBUTIONS

William Sharpe's notable contributions that are summarised here include the following.

1. A Simplified Model for Portfolio Analysis.
2. Capital Asset Pricing Model (CAPM).
3. Risk-free Asset.
4. Portfolio that includes Riskless Asset.
5. Lending and borrowing at Risk-free rate.
6. Capital market line and the Separation Theorem.
7. Security Market Line.

17.2.1 A SIMPLIFIED MODEL OR DIAGONAL MODEL FOR PORTFOLIO ANALYSIS

Sharpe's 1963 Management Science article "A Simplified Model for Portfolio Analysis" was only the third time he had appeared in print.

Though Sharpe terms his simplification of Markowitz's approach for Portfolio Analysis as "diagonal model," it is referred to in the literature as the single index model. He observes: "The major characteristic of the diagonal model is the assumption that the returns of various securities are related only through common relationships with some basic underlying factor." The underlying factor could be the GNP, some price index or the level of the stock market as a whole. However, it must be a factor considered the most important single influence on the security returns. Sharpe's suggestion would considerably reduce computations of calculating covariances between each pair of securities. The analyst has to calculate only the relationship of each of the securities to the dominant factor.

The single index model's big attraction is in the saving of the computing time. In his article, Sharpe points out that the time required for solving a 100 security example on a state-of-the art mainframe IBM Computer was reduced from 33 minutes with the full Markowitz programme to mere 30 seconds with the simplified model.

Sharpe's simplified model adopts separation theorem which was discussed in the Chapter on Tobin by incorporating borrowing and lending into Tobin's model. Sharpe's argument is that at some interest rate, money can be lent "with virtual assurance that both principal and interest will be returned." Some investors-- those who are conservative-–may not desire to put all their wealth into risky assets, such as stocks. They may lend; that is, buy bonds. On the other side of the spectrum, there may be aggressive investors, who desire to take more risk than any combination of stocks would provide; they may be willing to borrow funds in order to purchase even greater amounts of a portfolio than his own funds permit.

Sharpe demonstrates, like Tobin in his article "Liquidity Behavior....," that when investors have the facility of lending or borrowing, there exists a portfolio on the Efficient Frontier introduced by Markowitz whose trade-off between risk and expected return dominates all other portfolios. This portfolio on the Efficient Frontier is one portfolio that all investors should hold, irrespective of their appetite for risk, because it is optimal. Within a short time after the publication of the 1963 paper, Sharpe transformed his simplified model into a major breakthrough whose "theoretical ingenuity and practical importance" would rival those of Markowitz himself. Bernstein's remark in this regard is worth quoting: "Markowitz had launched William Sharpe, unaware that he (Sharpe) would soon rise so high that he too would go into orbit [like Alan Sheppard, American Astronaut, who first rode a missile in space]."

17.2.2 CAPITAL ASSET PRICING MODEL (CAPM)

Sharpe's major breakthrough came in 1964 with the Capital Asset Pricing Model (CAPM) which starts out from the basic idea of his single-index model that individual security returns are related only through common relationship with basic underlying factors but ending up "a long way from there."

Markowitz's approach to Portfolio Selection is prescriptive in nature in the sense that it tells what the investors should do. It thus belongs to normative economics. Sharpe's CAPM is considered as an exercise in positive economics. It presents a descriptive model of how assets are priced in the market assuming that all investors adopt Markowitz's approach to investing.

CAPM model makes the following assumptions, some of which are also behind the normative approach to investing.

Investors evaluate portfolios using expected return and standard deviation over a one-period time horizon. Furthermore, all investors are the same one-period investors.

Investors, when given a choice between two portfolios with identical standard deviation but different expected returns, will invariably choose the portfolio with the higher expected return. That is, investors are never satiated.

Investors are risk averse. That is, given a choice between two otherwise identical portfolios, they choose the one with lower standard deviation.

Assets are infinitely divisible; that is, an investor can buy a fraction of a share or security, if he so desires.

There exists a risk-free rate at which an investor may either lend (say, invest in bonds) or borrow money. Further, risk-free rate is the same for all investors.

Taxes and transaction costs are ignored.

Relevant information is freely and instantly available to all investors.

Investors have homogeneous expectations; that is, all investors have identical perceptions as regards expected returns, standard deviations and variances of securities.

Thus, we can see that CAPM assumes that securities' markets are perfect markets and they are in equilibrium.

17.2.3 RISK-FREE ASSET

The assumption of a risk-free asset in the economy is crucial in developing portfolio theory into Capital Market theory. Even though Sharpe is credited with the development of Capital Asset Pricing Model, John Lintner and Jan Mossin had developed similar models independently. Consequently, in the literature on the subject, we find references to Sharpe-Lintner-Mossin Capital Asset Pricing Model.

As mentioned earlier, a risky asset is defined as one from which future returns are uncertain, and such uncertainty is measured by the variance or standard deviation of expected returns. The return on a risk-free asset, on the other hand, is entirely certain, the standard deviation of its expected return is zero ($\sigma_{RF} = 0$). The rate of return on such an asset should be the risk-free rate of return (R_{FR}).

Recall from the earlier chapter (chapter on Markowitz) that covariance of return between security i and security j, σij is a measure of how returns on securities i and j move together. Because the returns for the risk-free asset are certain ($\sigma_{RF} = 0$), covariance of the risk-free asset with any risky asset or portfolio of risky assets will always equal zero.

Likewise, the correlation between any risky asset i and the risk free asset, would be zero (since ρ_{Rfi} = Covariance RFi /σ_{RF} σ_i).

17.2.4 RISK-RETURN COMBINATION FOR A PORTFOLIO OF RISKLESS ASSET AND RISKY ASSET PORTFOLIO

As both the expected return and the standard deviation of return for a portfolio consisting of the riskless asset and risky asset portfolio are linear combinations, it is a straight line between the two assets as shown in Figure 17.1.

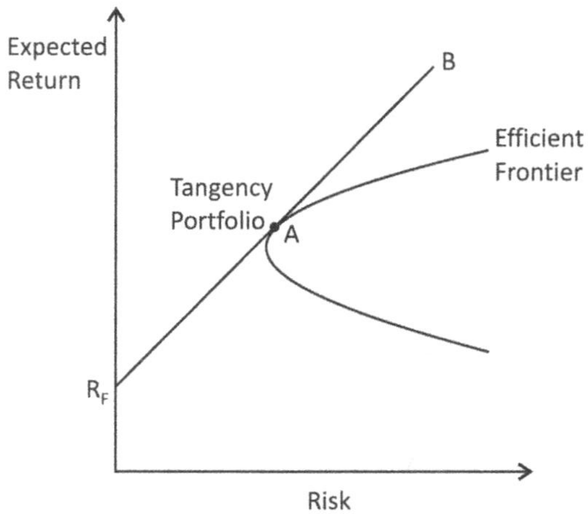

Fig. 17.1 Combination of Risk free Asset and Risky Portfolio on the Markowitz Efficient Frontier

The investor, at any point along the straight line R_FB, invests a portion of his portfolio in the risk-free asset, X_{RF}, and the remainder (1-X_{RF}) in the risky asset portfolio at point A on Markowitz efficient frontier. Note that all the risky asset portfolios on the efficient frontier below point A are dominated by the set of portfolio possibilities represented by A.

An investor, by accepting higher risk, may wish to attain a higher expected return. He may achieve his objective by investing in one of the risky asset portfolios on the efficient frontier beyond point A.

17.2.5 LENDING AND BORROWING AT RISK-FREE RATE

Portfolio theory as summarised earlier, states that when two assets are perfectly correlated, the set of portfolio possibilities falls along a straight line. That is, the investor invests part of his portfolio in the risk-free asset (lending at the risk-free rate, shown as R_F in Figure 17.2) and the remainder in the risky asset portfolio or he borrows funds at R_F and invests these funds in the risky asset portfolio, M. We can thus see that, in either case, all the variability of return emanates from the risky asset portfolio, M. The only difference in the two cases (alternative portfolios on the Capital Market Line or CML) is the magnitude of the variability arising from the difference in the proportion of the risky asset portfolio in the total portfolio.

As portfolio M lies at the point of tangency, it has the highest portfolio possibility line and every investor wishes to invest in portfolio M by borrowing or lending to be at some point on the CML. Portfolio M must, therefore, include all risky assets in the market. Furthermore, as Sharpe assumes that the capital market is in equilibrium, it is necessary that all risky assets are included in this portfolio in proportion to their market value. This portfolio that includes all risky assets is referred to as market portfolio. Market portfolio is defined as a portfolio consisting of all securities in which the proportion invested in each security corresponds to its relative market value. The relative market value of a security is equal to the aggregate market value of the security in question divided by the sum of the aggregate market value of all securities in the market. Further, the aggregate market value for the equity shares of a company is equal to the current market price of the share multiplied by the number of shares outstanding.

We may note that the slope of the Capital Market Line is equal to the difference between the expected return of the market portfolio and that of the risk free security, i.e. $E(R_M - R_F)$, divided by the difference in their risks, σ_M; in other words the slope is equal to

$$E(R_M - R_F) / \sigma_M$$

As the vertical intercept of the CML is R_F, the straight line characterising the CML has the following equation:

$$E(R_p) = R_F + \sigma_p \left[(R_M - R_F) / \sigma_M \right]$$

where

$E(R_p)$: expected return of an efficient portfolio

R_F : risk free rate

R_M : expected return of the market portfolio

σ_p: portfolio risk (standard deviation)

σ_M: risk of the market portfolio

Two key numbers characterise the security market equilibrium:

First, the vertical intercept of the CML – the risk-free rate or reward for waiting, which can be thought of as the price of time; and

Second, the slope of the CML – the reward per unit of risk borne by the investor, which can be thought of as price of risk.

We can thus view the security market as providing an arrangement for trading time and risk, with the price for each determined by the forces of supply and demand.

Because the market portfolio contains all risky assets (not only equity shares but also bonds, real estate, options, art, antiques, etc.), it is a completely diversified portfolio; that is, all the risk unique to individual assets is diversified away. A completely diversified portfolio would have a correlation with the market portfolio of 1.0. This unique or diversifiable risk is referred to as unsystematic risk. On the other hand, systematic risk is defined as variability in all risky assets caused by macroeconomic variables (such as variability of growth in money supply, volatility in interest rates, industrial production, corporate cash flows, and corporate earnings) and remains in the market portfolio. The systematic risk, measured by the standard deviation of expected returns of the market portfolio, can vary over time by changes in the macro variables that affect the valuation of all risky assets.

17.2.6 CAPITAL MARKET LINE (CML) AND THE SEPARATION THEOREM

The capital market line leads all investors to invest in the same risky portfolio – the market portfolio. The position of individual investors on CML depends upon their risk preferences as represented by their indifference curves. How an investor gets to a point on the CML depends on his financing decision. If an investor is relatively risk averse, he will lend some part of the portfolio at R_F by buying some risk- free securities, say government bonds, and investing the remainder in the market portfolio of risky assets. For example, an investor might invest in the portfolio combination at point A in Figure 17.2. A is an optimal portfolio with low risk comprising portfolio of securities and cash on investment in risk-free security. In contrast, an investor who is willing to take more risk, might borrow funds at R_F, invest the total funds (his capital plus the amount he borrowed) in the market portfolio – Point B in Figure 17.2. This financing decision of the investor provides greater expected returns than those on the market portfolio. Further, an investor who has a greater risk tolerance, may choose to invest in portfolio B, involving higher risk. (see Figure 17.2.)

Tobin calls this division of the investment decision from the financing decision the separation theorem (see chapter on Tobin). That is, the optimal combination of risky assets for an investor can be determined without any knowledge of the investor's preference towards risk and return.

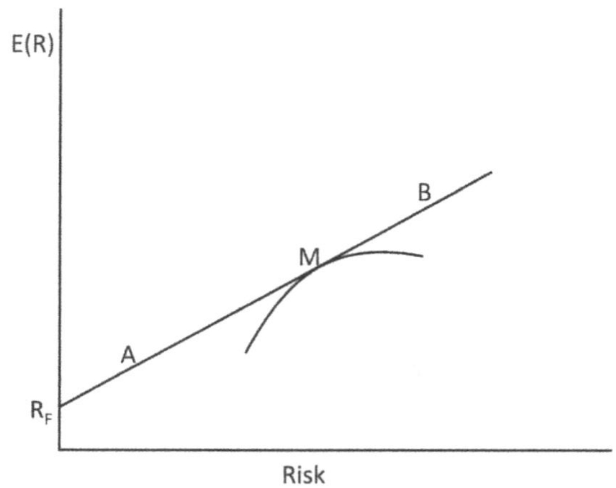

Fig. 17.2 Capital Market Line

17.2.7 THE SECURITY MARKET LINE (SML)

As explained earlier, CML represents the equilibrium relationship between the expected return and standard deviation for efficient portfolios. Individual risky assets always plot below the CML.

We know that the relevant risk measure for an individual risky asset (i) is its covariance with the market portfolio – Cov_{im}. Therefore, we can draw a security market Line (SML) representing an individual security's risk-return relationship with Cov_{im} as risk measure as shown in Figure 17.3. The return for the market portfolio (R_M) should be consistent with its own risk, which is the covariance of the market with itself (Cov_{MM}) or the variance of the market rate of return ($Cov_{MM} = \left(\sigma_M^2\right)$. Therefore, the equation for risk – return Line (Security Market Line – SML) depicted in Figure 17.3 is

$$E(R_i) = R_F + \beta_i \left[E(R_M - R_F)\right]$$

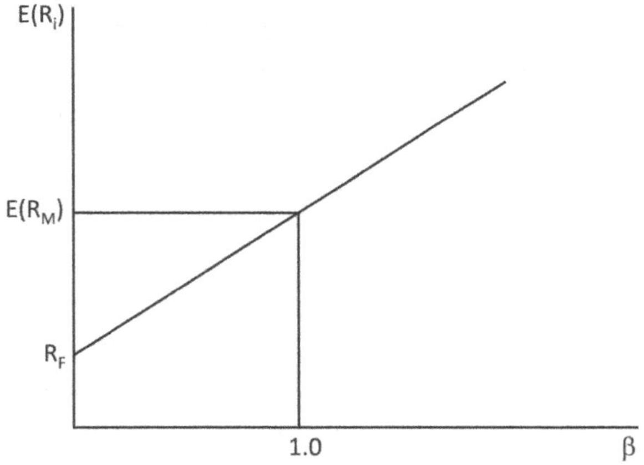

Fig. 17.3 Security Market Line

The term β_i is the beta coefficient or beta for security i, and is an alternative way of representing the covariance of a security. Beta can be viewed as a standardised measure of systematic risk. It is a standardised measure of risk because it relates the covariance of any asset i with the market portfolio σ_{iM} to the variance of the market portfolio σ^2_M. As a result, the market portfolio has a beta of 1.0. Therefore, if the σ_i for any asset or security is above 1.0, the asset or security has higher normalised systematic risk than the market; that is, it is more volatile than the overall market portfolio. We have shown earlier that the expected return of a portfolio is a weighted average of the expected returns of its component securities, where the proportions invested in the securities are weights. Every portfolio, therefore, plots on SML because every security plots on SML. We can therefore conclude that while all efficient portfolios plot on both the CML and SML, inefficient portfolios plot on the SML but below the CML.

Another point of interest is to be noted. The SML must go through the point representing the market portfolio itself.

17.3 OTHER CONTRIBUTIONS OF WILLIAM SHARPE

While William Sharpe's greatest legacy to the finance profession in the words of Litzenberger is the Capital Asset Pricing Model (CAPM), there are other contributions as well of Sharpe. We have to mention, without any discussion of his 1966 "landmark work" on mutual fund performance, wherein he has demonstrated that portfolio performance of mutual funds is inversely related to the transaction costs associated with portfolio turnover. Reference may also be made here to Sharpe's development of an efficient algorithm for calculating the mean-variance frontier, his Presidential Address to the American Finance Association in 1981 that outlines incentive structures that allow portfolio managers specialising in different segments to make decisions that are consistent with the overall portfolio objective, his work on binomial option pricing that has helped in enhancing the level of competition among market- makers in the options markets, thereby lowering bid/ask spreads and improving the operational efficiency of the capital market and his work on bank capital adequacy, deposit insurance and security values which made an important recommendation that deposit insurance premium should reflect the risk of bank assets.

17.4 CONCLUDING OBSERVATIOS

While investment managers and academic economists had long recognised the need to weigh potential returns against risks, Markowitz provided a formula to do so. Sharpe used Markowitz's theory to develop a model for explaining how securities' prices are established in the market to reflect risks and potential returns. His theory--CAPM--is now widely used by investment firms to predict, for instance, how a stock will perform in relation to the overall market.

In Bernstein's words "... CAPM combines so many strands of theoretical innovation that it remains the keystone in investment theory, theories of market behavior, and the allocation of capital in both private and public enterprises. Moreover, its theoretical significance is equaled if not surpassed by its widespread use in business and finance." Sharpe's work has had and continues to have "a major influence on scholarly research, the practice of portfolio management, and corporation finance." The Royal Swedish Academy of Sciences in its announcement of the award to Sharpe observes that the CAPM is considered the backbone of modern price theory for financial markets. It cites important examples of areas where CAPM and its beta coefficients are used routinely that include calculations of costs of capital associated with investment and takeover decisions and estimates of costs of capital as a basis for pricing in regulated public utilities. Along with Markowitz's portfolio model, Sharpe's CAPM has also become the framework in textbooks on financial economics throughout the world.

To recall:

Sharpe is credited with the development of

1. Sharpe Ratio for Risk-adjusted Investment Analysis;
2. Development of Binomial Method for Valuing Options;
3. Gradient Method for Asset Allocation Optimisation;
4. Return-based Style Analysis for Evaluating the Style; and
5. Performance of Investment Funds.

In his Princeton lectures (published under the title "Investors and Markets: Portfolio Choices, Asset Prices and Investment Advice") Sharpe states: "Mean-Variance analysis [of Markowitz] provides the foundation for many of the quantitative methods used by those who manage investment portfolios or assist individuals with saving and investment decisions". [Kenneth Arrow has suggested] that an investor should consider alternative outcomes and the amount of consumption obtained in each possible situation. [Most of the published work of Sharpe] is in the first category.... This is not entirely happy state of affairs. There are strong arguments for viewing mean/variance analysis as a special case of more general asset pricing theory (albeit a special case with many practical advantages). Sharpe is of the view that it is preferable to teach...both general asset pricing and the special case of mean/variance analysis. Sharpe further observes: "Furthermore, portfolio choice and asset pricing,...cannot be adequately understood in isolation, for they are inextricably intertwined.... Asset prices are determined as part of the process through which investors make portfolio choices. Moreover, the appropriate portfolio choice for an individual depends crucially on available expected returns and risks associated with different investment strategies, and these depend on the manner in which asset prices are set...."

17.5 SELECT BIBLIOGRAPHY OF WILLIAM SHARPE'S WORKS

17.5.1 BOOKS

1970 Portfolio Theory and Capital Markets, McGraw-Hill, New York.

1973 Introduction to Managerial Economics, Columbia University Press, New York.

1978 Investments, Prentice Hall, Englewood-Cliffs, New York, N.J.

2006 Investors and Markets: Portfolio Choices, Asset Prices and Investment Advice, Princeton Lectures in Finance, Princeton University Press, Princeton, Nj.

2012 Selected Works of William F Sharpe, World Scientific, Nobel Laureate Series, Vol. 2.

17.5.2 ARTICLES

1963 a "A Simplified Model for Portfolio Analysis," Management Science, Vol.9, No.2.

b "Mathematical Investment Portfolio Selection – Some Early Results," University of Washington Business Review, Apr.

1964 "Capital Asset Prices – A Theory of Market Equilibrium under Conditions of Risk," JF, Vol. XIX, No.3.

1965 "Risk Aversion in the Stock Market- Some Empirical Evidence," JF, Vol. XX, No.3.

1966 "Mutual Fund Performance," JB, Vol.XXXIX, No.1, Part II.

1967 "Portfolio Analysis," JFQA, Vol.2, No.2.

1970 "Computer–Assisted Economics," JFQA, Vol.5, No.3.

1971 "A Linear Programming Approximation for the General Portfolio Analysis Problem," JFQA, Vol.6, No.5.

1974 "Imputing Expected Security Returns from Portfolio Composition," JFQA, Vol.9, No.3.

1976 "Corporate Pension Funding Policy," JFE, Vol.3, No.3.

1978 a "Bank Capital Adequacy, Deposit Insurance and Security Values," JFQA, Vol.13, No. 4.

b (with R. Lanstein), "Duration and Security Risk," JFQA, Vol.13, No.4.

1981 "Decentralized Investment Management," JF,Vol.36, No.2.

1991 "Capital Asset Prices with and without Negative Holdings," Nobel Lecture, JF, Vol.46, No.2.

1992 "Asset Allocation: Management Style and Performance Measurement," Journal of Portfolio Management, Vol.18, No.2.

17.6 WORKS OF OTHERS

Blume, M. and I. Friend (1973), "A New Look at the Capital Asset Pricing Model," JF, Vol. 28, Mar.

Lintner, J. (1965), "The Valuation of Risk Assets and the Selection of Risky Investments in Stock Portfolios and Capital Budgets," RES, Vol. 33, Feb.

Litzenberger, R H. (1991), "William F. Sharpe's Contributions to Financial Economics," ScandJE, Vol.93, No.1.

Mossin, J. (1966), "Equilibrium in a Capital Asset Market," Econometrica, Vol.34, Oct.

CHAPTER 18

MERTON HOWARD MILLER

(1923 – 2000)

Merton Howard Miller, University of Chicago, U.S.A., was awarded 1990 Alfred Nobel Memorial Prize in Economic Sciences, jointly with Harry M. Markowitz and William F. Sharpe for their pioneering work in the theory of financial economics and specifically to Miller for his fundamental contribution to corporate finance.

Markowitz's and Sharpe's contributions have been surveyed in the preceding two chapters; this chapter covers Miller's contribution.

18.1 A BRIEF BIOGRAPHICAL SKETCH: MERTON MILLER

Merton Howard Miller was born in Boston, Massachusetts, U.S.A. on May 16, 1923. After graduating from Harvard University in 1943, Miller spent the next few years in Washington, first as an Economist in the Division of Tax Research of the U.S. Treasury Department and subsequently in the Division of Research and Statistics of the Board of Governors of the Federal Reserve System. In 1949, Miller decided to return to Graduate School and chose John Hopkins University in Baltimore "primarily because Fritz Machlup was then a leading member of its small but very distinguished faculty." One of his college classmates was Robert M. Solow, Economics Laureate for 1987. Miller's first academic appointment after receiving his doctorate from John Hopkins in 1952 was visiting Assistant Lecturer at the London School of Economics for 1952-53. From there he went to Carnegie Institute of Technology (now Carnegie Mellon University). Among his colleagues at Carnegie were Herbert A. Simon and Franco Modigliani, both Nobel Laureates in Economics. With the latter, he published the first of the joint M & M (Modigliani and Miller) papers on corporate finance in 1958. Miller left Carnegie in 1961 for the Graduate School of Business at the University of Chicago. Except for a one-year visiting professorship at the University of Louvain in Belgium during 1966-67, he remained at Chicago. From 1961, he taught finance and economics at the Graduate School of Business. He served as Edward Eagle Brown Professor of Banking and Finance, and from 1981 to 1987, he was Leon Carroll Marshall Distinguished Service Professor. In 1987, he became Robert R. McCormick Distinguished Service Professor. Upon retirement in 1993, he became Professor Emeritus. Other positions he occupied include public director of the Chicago Board of Trade and of the Chicago Mercantile Exchange.

Miller received a number of professional awards and honours. He was a member of the American Economic Association becoming a Distinguished Fellow of the Association, 1990. He was elected Vice-President of American Finance Association, 1975, and its President in 1976. He was elected Fellow, Econometric Society, 1975. Miller was Fellow, American Academy of Arts and Sciences, 1989 and Senior fellow, American Association of Financial Engineers, 1992. Miller was closely associated with a number of professional journals – Associate Editor, Journal of Financial Economics, 1973-1983 and co-editor, Journal of Business, 1977-1989.

He had also received honorary degrees from nearly a dozen institutions in the United States and other countries.

Merton H. Miller died on June 3, 2000.

18.2 A SUMMARY OF MERTON MILLER'S CONTRIBUTIONS

A major part of Miller's work in the field of Corporate Finance was done in collaboration with Franco Modigliani.

The contributions of Miller (and MM) are covered under the following heads:

1. Cost of capital
    - 1.1 Proposition I;
    - 1.2 Proposition II;
    - 1.3 Proposition III;
2. Taxes and Capital structure; and
3. Irrelevance of Corporate Dividend Policy;
    - 3.1 MM's position

18.2.1 COST OF CAPITAL

While this chapter is devoted to covering the contributions of Miller, we refer all through (except where we deal with his individual contribution) to Miller and Modigliani or Modigliani and Miller or simply as MM (since they are known and referred to). MM in their 1958 article "The Cost of Capital, Corporation Finance and the Theory of Investment" raise an important question as to what the cost of capital to a firm is "in a world in which funds are used to acquire assets whose yields are uncertain and in which capital can be obtained by many different media, ranging from pure debt instruments...to pure equity issues.... This question has vexed at least three classes of economists: (1) the corporation finance specialist concerned with the techniques of financing firms as so as to ensure survival and growth; (2) the managerial economist concerned with capital budgeting; and (3) the economic theorist concerned with explaining investment behavior at both the micro and macro levels."

MM observed that the economic theorist had tended to "side-step" the cost of capital problem by proceeding as though physical assets could be regarded as yielding known, sure streams of cash, like bonds. Given this assumption, the economic theorist came to the conclusion that the cost of capital to the owners of a firm was simply the rate of interest on bonds and as such the firm acting rationally, would tend to push investment to the point where the marginal yield on physical assets is equal to the market-rate of interest. This proposition can be shown to follow from either of the two criteria of rational decision-making, which are equivalent under certainty, namely (1) profit maximisation; and (2) maximisation of the firm's market value. MM contended that "only recently" economists began to face up seriously to the problem of cost of capital under conditions of uncertainty. With the recognition of uncertainty the equivalence of the two criteria disappears. In fact, the criterion of profit maximisation is no longer even well defined.

The second approach based on maximisation of market value of a firm, however, can provide the basis for an "operational definition of the cost of capital and a workable theory of investment." Under this approach, any investment project and its concomitant financing plan must pass the following test: will the project, as financed, increase the market value of the shares of the firm? If yes, the project is worth undertaking; if not, it should not be undertaken, as its rate of return is less than the marginal cost of capital to the firm. It is important to note that such a test is independent of the tastes of the current owners of the firm because market prices of shares reflect not only the preferences of current owners but also all potential owners. If any shareholder disagrees with management in regard to the method of financing of the new project, he is "free to sell out and reinvest elsewhere but will still benefit from the capital appreciation resulting from the management's decision."

MM developed a cogent theory of the effect of financial structure on market valuation and of its implications for the problem of cost of capital. The following are the basic assumptions underlying the MM model.

Capital markets are perfect. There are no transaction costs and all securities are infinitely divisible. Information is free and readily available. Investors behave rationally.

A firm's average expected future operating earnings are represented by subjective random variables. The average value over time of the stream accruing to a given share is referred to as the return of the share and the mathematical expectation of this average as the expected return of the share. All investors are in agreement as to the expected return. Corporate income taxes are ignored. MM relax the assumption later.

Firms can be divided into equivalent return classes, which play a strategic role in the MM analysis. It implies that various shares within the same class differ, "at most, by a scale factor." It follows that all the relevant properties of a share are uniquely characterised by specifying (i) the class to which it belongs, and (ii) its expected return. This assumption permitted MM to classify firms into groups within which the shares of different firms are "homogeneous" perfect substitutes to one another. It follows that in any given class the price of every share must be proportional to its expected return.

Denoting this factor of proportionality for any class, say the kth class, by $1/\rho_k$, denoting the price of a share of the jth firm in class k by pj and the expected return of the share $\bar{X}_j$, we must have

$$P_j = \frac{1}{\rho_k}\bar{X}_j \qquad (1)$$

Or, equivalently

$$\bar{X}_j / P_j = \rho_k \text{, a constant for all firms j in class K} \qquad (2)$$

ρ_k (constant for each of the risk classes) can be interpreted as the expected rate of return of any share in the class. Additionally $1/\rho_k$ can be interpreted as the price, which an investor has to pay for a rupee's worth of expected return in the class k.

Now, imagine two firms that generate the same stream of operating income and different only in their capital structure – firm u is unlevered (no debt in its capital structure, only equity) and firm L is levered (that is, partly debt-financed). In the case of the first firm (u), the total value of its equity (E_u) is the same as the total value of the firm (V_u). On the other hand, in the case of the second (levered) firm, the value of its stock is equal to the aggregate value of the firm less the value of debt: $E_L = V_L - D_L$, or $V_L = E_L + D_L$. MM assume that (1) all bonds (including any debts issued by households to purchase shares) yield a constant certain income per unit of time, and (2) bonds, like equity shares, are traded in a perfect market. It follows that all bonds are perfect substitutes upto a scale factor and they must yield the same rate of return, r. r can be interpreted as the rate of return or, equivalently, as the capitalisation rate for sure income streams.

They put forward the following two basic propositions in regard to the valuation of securities in companies with different capital structures.

18.2.1.1 PROPOSITION I

The market value of any firm is independent of its capital structure and is given by capitalising its expected return at the rate ρ_k appropriate to its risk class. Equivalently, the average cost of capital to any firm is completely independent of its capital structure and is equal to the capitalisation rate of a pure equity stream of its class.

This proposition can be shown as given below.

Consider any company j and let $\bar{X}_j$ represent the expected return on the assets owned by the company (that is, its expected profit before deduction of interest on debt). Let D_j stand for the market value of the debts of the company and S_j for the market value of its equity shares. The market value of the firm is

$$V_j = S_j + D_j$$

Proposition I asserts that, in equilibrium, we must have

$$\begin{aligned} V_j &= S_j + D_j \\ &= \bar{X}_j/\rho_k, \text{ for any firm j in class k} \end{aligned} \qquad (3)$$

Equivalently

$$[\overline{X}_j /(S_j + D_j)] = (\overline{X}_j / V_j) = \rho_k \text{ for any firm j, in class k} \quad (4)$$

MM demonstrated that "as long as relations (3) or (4) do not hold between any pair of firms in a class, arbitrage will take place and restore the stated equalities." MM's position is based on the idea that as a firm's aggregate investment value is dependent on its underlying profitability and risk, it is invariant to relative changes in the firm's financial capitalisation. The investment value of the firm is conserved – an idea first put forward by John Burr Williams in his The Theory of Investment Value. This basic idea is conveyed by an analogy: "the value of a pie does not depend on how it is sliced." The MM's position is based on the idea that in a perfect capital market investors are able to substitute home-made leverage for corporate leverage, thereby replicating any capital structure the corporation might undertake. Therefore, two firms similar in every respect except capital structure must have the same aggregate value. If not, arbitrage will cause the two firms to sell in the market at the same total value.

Miller once gave a simple and colourful analogy that gives a clear insight. The same as given by the Encyclopaedia of Economics (EEE) is reproduced here.

Think of the firm as a gigantic tub of whole milk. The farmer can sell the whole milk as it is. Or he can separate out the cream, and sell it at a considerably higher price than the whole milk would bring. (Selling cream is the analog of a firm selling debt securities, which pay a contractual return.) But, of course, what the farmer would have left would be skim milk, with low butter-fat content, and that would sell for much less than whole milk.(Skim milk corresponds to the levered equity.) The Modigliani-Miller proposition says that if there were no cost of separation (and, of course, no government dairy support program), the cream plus skim milk would bring the same price as the whole milk.

18.2.1.2 PROPOSITION II

From Proposition I, MM derived the following proposition relating to the return on equity shares in firms whose capital structure includes some debt.

The expected rate of return on the equity shares of a levered firm increases in proportion to the debt-equity ratio (D/S), expressed in market values. More specifically, the expected rate of return or yield on equity shares of any company j belonging to the kth class is equal to the appropriate capitalisation rate, ρ_k for a pure equity stream in the class, plus a premium related to financial risk equal to the debt-to-equity ratio times the spread between ρ_k and r (where r is defined as the rate of interest, or, equivalently as the capitalisation for sure streams).

That is,

$$i_j = \rho_k + (\rho_k - r)\, D_j / S_j \quad (5)$$

To establish proposition II, note that by definition, the expected rate of return, i, is given by

$$i_j = \frac{\bar{X}_j - r\,D_j}{S_j} \tag{6}$$

From Proposition I (equation 3), we know that

$$\bar{X}_j = \rho_k\,(S_j + D_j)$$

Substituting in (6) and simplifying we obtain equation (5)

$$i_j = \frac{\rho_k (S_j + D_j) - r\,D_j}{S_j}$$

$$i_j = \rho_k + (\rho_k - r)\,D_j / S_j \tag{7}$$

This proposition can be illustrated with a numerical example. Let the operating income of a firm be Rs. 15 crore and market value of all its securities before deciding to borrow was Rs. 100 crore. In such a situation, the expected return on the equity shares of the firm, which is also equal to, expected return on assets, is

$$i_j = \rho_k = \frac{\text{Rs.15 crore}}{\text{Rs.100 crore}} = 0.15 \text{ or } 15\%$$

If the firm borrows Rs. 15 crore at an interest rate of 10 percent the expected return on assets, i_j, is still 15 per cent. The expected return on the firm's equity is

$$i_j = \rho_k + (\rho_k - r)\,D_j / S_j$$

$$= .15 + (.15 - .10)\,\text{Rs.15 cr} / \text{Rs.15 cr}$$

$$= .20 \text{ or } 20 \text{ percent}$$

The general implications of MM's Proposition II are shown in Fig.

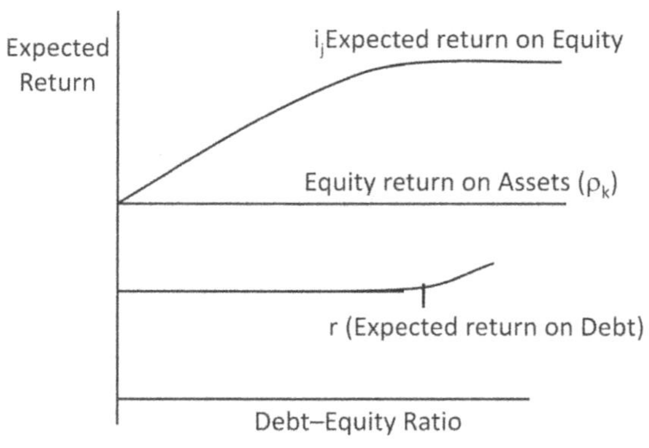

Fig. 18.1 MM's Proposition II

It is assumed that the firm's debt securities are risk-free at lower levels of debt. Thus r is independent of D/E at low debt levels and i_j increases linearly, upto a level, as D/E increases. As the firm's debt level increases, the default risk increases and the firm is required to pay higher rates of interest. Proposition II predicts that when this occurs, the rate of increase in return on equity slows down. The implication is that the holders of risky debt bear some of the firm's business risk – transfer of business risk from shareholders to bond holders.

Combining Propositions I and II provides an insight into the risk-return trade off. When financial leverage does not affect the wealth of shareholders and when the firm's debt-equity ratio enhances the rate of return the firm's shareholders expected to receive, then why should shareholders be indifferent to increased leverage? The answer lies in the fact that any increase in expected return is exactly offset by an increase in risk and thus in the rate of return required by shareholders.

At this point, we have to note that MM's proof of the proposition I that leverage is irrelevant for the firm's value does not depend on the two firms belonging to the same risk class. Van Horne observes: "this assumption was invoked for easier illustration of the arbitrage process. However, equilibrium occurs across securities of different companies on the basis of expected return and risk. If the assumptions of the Capital Asset Pricing Model hold, as they would in perfect capital markets, the irrelevance of (the firm's) capital structure can be demonstrated using the CAPM."

On the basis of Propositions I and II with respect to cost of capital and financial structure (neglecting taxes), MM derive Proposition III – a simple rule for optimal investment policy by the firm.

18.2.1.3 PROPOSITION III

If a firm in class k is acting in the best interest of shareholders at the time of the decision, it will accept an investment opportunity if and only if the expected rate of return on the investment, say ρ^* is as large as or larger than ρ_k. In other words, regardless of the financing used, the marginal cost of capital to a firm is equal to the average cost of capital, which in turn is equal to ρ_k (the capitalization rate for an unlevered stream in the class to which the firm belongs). MM point out that Proposition III states the irrelevance of the type of instrument used for financing an investment but say nothing about whether or not the investment is worthwhile.

18.2.2 TAXES AND CAPITAL STRUCTURE

MM's proposition regarding the irrelevance of capital structure on the firm's valuation and cost of capital rests on the absence of market imperfections. One of the important imperfections is the presence of taxes – corporate taxes and personal income taxes. The advantage of debt when corporations are levied taxes on their profits is that interest payments on debt are deductible as an expense. In contrast, dividends or retained earnings associated with equity shares are not deductible for purposes of tax. They recognise the value of corporate interest tax shields. The greater the amount of debt, the greater the tax shield and the grater the value of the firm, ceteris paribus.

In the context of corporate and personal taxes, the firm's objective is to minimize the present value of all taxes (including personal taxes paid by bond holders and equity holders) paid on corporate income. Equivalently, the firm's objective should be to arrange its capital structure so as to maximise its after tax income (or where the tax is least).

How does capital structure affect firm value when investors have different taxes? The model to answer this question was put forward by Miller in his 1976 presidential address to the American Finance Association. Assuming that all equity comes from in the form of unrealised capital gains and nobody pays any tax on equity income, T_{PE} is zero for all investors. But the rate of tax on interest income depends upon the investor's tax bracket. Tax-exempt institutions do not pay any tax; T_{PE} is zero for them. Rich people belonging to highest-tax-bracket pay tax at the prevailing highest rate on interest income from bonds. Most of the investors fall anywhere between these two extremes.

Assuming that firms are initially financed entirely by equity and assuming further that T_{PE} is zero, the firm has to take into account only corporate taxes. This will create a strong incentive for corporate borrowing, as debt financing is cheaper than equity financing. As firms begin to borrow, some investors have to be persuaded to hold corporate debt rather than equity shares in their portfolios. There exists no problem in inducing tax-exempt investors to purchase debt securities to be held in their securities portfolio. Thus, the initial impact of borrowing is to leave personal income taxes unchanged, saving corporate taxes at the same time. However, as corporates borrow more, the tax-paying investors have to be persuaded to purchase debt securities instead of shares. Such investors need a higher interest rate on their bonds as an inducement for migrating from equity shares to bonds. The migration to bonds will stop at the point when T_{PE} (personal income tax rate of the investor who wishes to acquire bonds instead of equity shares) equals the corporate tax rate (T_c).

The equilibrium in the financial market determines the aggregate amount of corporate debt but not the amount of debt issue of any individual firm. Thus, the debt-equity ratio for the corporate sector as a whole depends on the corporate tax rate and the funds at the disposal of individual investors in various tax brackets. There is therefore no optimal debt equity ratio for any single firm. No single firm can influence the total amount of debt while the market is only interested in it.

Miller through his model had illustrated how corporate tax and personal income tax in an economy could cancel out and leave the value of the firm independent of capital structure. Modern tax systems in many countries favour corporate borrowing. Miller's paper showed that, in reality, aggregate supplies of corporate debt and equity shares should so adjust as to minimise the sum of corporate and personal taxes. In practice, while there is a moderate tax advantage to corporate borrowing, the corporate tax spilled on debt is not constant, irrespective of the amount borrowed. The Miller tax equilibrium shows how MM's original leverage irrelevance theorem can work with taxes as well.

18.2.3 IRRELEVANCE OF CORPORATE DIVIDEND POLICY

One of the major decisions of a firm is its dividend policy – the percentage of earnings it pays (in cash) to its equity shareholders. The immediate consequence of the dividend payout is the reduction in the amount of earnings retained in the firm and has an impact on the total amount of internal financing. Therefore, the dividend policy/retained earnings policy is to be considered in relation to overall financing decision of a firm's investment. As specified earlier, the dividend policy of a firm has to be evaluated in the light of the firm's objective, viz., maximising the value of the firm to its shareholders.

18.2.3.1 MM's Position

MM argued that the dividend-payment ratio is a mere detail, once the investment decision of a firm is made. The shareholders' wealth is not affected by the dividend policy. The value of the firm is determined by the earning power of the assets of the firm or its investment policy. The value is not affected by the manner in which the stream of earnings is split between dividends and retained earnings. Their position is contrary to the general belief at that time that even under idealised assumptions, increased corporate dividends made shareholders better off; the notable exceptions include J. B. Williams and J. Lintner. The position of MM is contained in the article "Dividend Policy, Growth and the Valuation of Shares" that appeared in the October 1961 issue of the Journal of Business.

They made the following assumptions:

1. It is assumed that capital markets are perfect, investors are rational, securities are infinitely divisible and transaction costs are absent.
2. Taxes are ignored.
3. There are no flotation costs on securities issued by the firm.
4. The firm's investment policy is given and unchanged.
5. All investors have perfect certainty in regard to future investments and profits of the firm. (This assumption is relaxed later).

The irrelevance of dividend policy to the valuation of the firm is shown here.

Assume that the market price of an equity share of a corporate at the beginning of a period (period 0) is defined as equal to the present value of the dividend paid at the end of the period (period 1) plus the market price of the share at the end of the period (period 1) thus

$$P_0 = \frac{1}{(1+\rho)}(D_1 + P_1) \tag{8}$$

where

P_0 : Market Price per share at time 0,

ρ : Capitalization rate for firm in that risk class assumed to be constant throughout time,

D_1 : Dividend per share at time 1,

P_1 : Market price per share at time 1

Now, let 'n' be the number of equity shares outstanding at time 0 and let 'm' be the number of new shares sold by the firm at time 1 at a price of P_1. Equation (8) can be rewritten as

$$nP_0 = \frac{1}{(1+\rho)}(nD_1 + (n+m)P_1 - mP_1) \tag{9}$$

That is, aggregate value of all outstanding equity shares at time 0 is the present value of the total dividend payments at time 1 on those shares (n) plus the total value of all equity shares outstanding at time 1 (n + m shares), minus the total value of the new equity shares issued. We know that the total sources of funds of a firm must equal total uses; or equivalently, net profit or earnings of the firm plus the proceeds from the sale of new equity shares must equal dividends plus new investments. This can be shown as

$$mP_1 = I - (X - nD_1) \tag{10}$$

Where

I : Total new investment during period 1,

X : Aggregate net profit or earnings of the firm for the period. The total amount of financing by the sale of new equity shares is determined by the aggregate amount of investment in time period I not financed by the firm's retained earnings.

By substituting Eq (10) into Eq (9), we obtain

$$nP_0 = \frac{1}{(1+\rho)}((n+m)P_1 - I + X) \tag{11}$$

We find that nD_1 term does not appear in Eq (11). As X, I, $(n+m)P_1$ and P are assumed to be independent of D_1, MM conclude that the current value of the firm is independent of its current dividend decision. MM argued that what is gained by the "old" shareholders is offset exactly by the decline in the terminal value of their equity shares. In other words, there is a transfer of value from the old shareholders to new equity shareholders. MM also demonstrated that nP_0 (the firm's value) is unaffected not only by current dividend decisions but by future dividend decisions as well. Under the assumption of perfect certainty by all investors (assumption 5), the share price in the market at time 1 time 2, and time n is solely determined by Eq (11). We, therefore, conclude that a firm's equity shareholders are indifferent between retention of profits in the firm and dividend payments (and concurrent share financing) in all future periods. In other words, shareholder wealth is not affected by dividend decisions – current and future; it depends entirely on the firm's expected future earnings stream.

Even when assumption (5) that all investors possess complete certainty in regard to the firm's future investments and earnings is relaxed, dividend payout would be a matter of irrelevance for shareholders in a world of perfect capital markets and the absence of taxation. This argument involves the same reasoning that is employed to show the irrelevance of capital structure. Investors are able to replicate any dividend stream the firm might pay. The investors will be able to manufacture "home-made" dividends in a way similar to the devising of "home-made" leverage in capital structure decisions.

Corporate income taxes can be shown to have no bearing on dividend relevance unlike the capital structure decision. Corporate tax is generally levied on the firm regardless whether or not a dividend is paid to the shareholders. It is only profit (after corporate taxes are paid) that is divided between dividends and retained earnings.

Myers highlights the following three important ideas in MM's 1961 Dividend Policy Paper. They are

1. The proof that shareholders' wealth is not affected by a firm's dividend policy in perfect and efficient capital markets.
2. The information content of dividends for investors.
3. Specification of the impact of the firm's growth opportunities on its current share price in the market.

In his Nobel lecture "Leverage," Miller stated categorically that he was not the co-inventor of the leveraged buyout – "the transaction that perhaps more than any other has come to symbolize the supposed financial excesses of the 1980's." Leveraged Buyouts (LBO's) are those transactions in which the active mangers of corporate unit borrow funds to buy its contributing shares from its retired founder or from his estate. He observes that it is "doubly ironic" since the central message of M&M Propositions was that the value of the firm was independent of its capital structure. No one could hope to enhance the shareholder value merely by leveraging up. As argued by M&M in their 1958 article investors would not pay a premium for corporate leverage because they could, if they so choose, leverage up their own holdings by borrowing on personal account.

The qualification to the M-M value invariance proposition, as outlined earlier, concerns the tax deductibility of interest payments. Miller pointed out that tax savings alone cannot "plausibly account for the observed LBO premiums" (in 1980's). The academic research studies (such as the one reported by S. N. Kaplan in his article in the June 1989 issue of the Journal of Financial Economics) show that the LBO entrepreneurs achieved substantial real efficiency gains by "re-concentrating corporate control" and "redeploying" the corporate assets. His reply to the public fears expressed against LBO's such as that the real efficiency gains, if any, will be more than offset by the "collateral damage" from the financial leveraging used to bring about the restructuring of the taken over firm were the main focus of Miller's Nobel lecture.

Miller's reply to the so-called problems of corporate leveraging basically contained four points

1. Miller disputed the charge that the U.S. became over leveraged in the 1980's as evidenced, as some contend, by the defaults of many junk-bond issues in late 1989. He argued that all the buyers of junk bonds, save the most hopelessly gullible, were aware that the expected yields on them were "below the normal or promised yields." The high promised yields that might be earned during good years are to be considered essentially as risk premiums for the possible bad years in time. In finance theory defaults (as occurred in the case of junk bonds in late 1989) represent bad outcomes ex post rather than systematic misperception of the true ex ante odds.
2. Secondly, Miller disputed the argument that increased leveraging by corporations implied increased risk for the economy as a whole. He observed: "M & M propositions are the finance equivalents of conservation laws. What gets conserved in this case is the risk of the earning stream generated by the firm's operating assets. Leveraging or de-leveraging the firm's capital structure serves merely to partition that risk among the firm's security holders." –equity and debt holders. He further observed: "From a bloodless finance perspective, a default signifies merely that the stock holders have now lost their entire stake in the firm. Their option, so to speak, has expired worthless," in terms of derivatives market terminology.
3. The third point of Miller was that the financial distress suffered by some highly leveraged firms involves mainly private costs, not social costs. Human and capital resources of bankrupt firms will eventually be reemployed. However, one cannot ignore the personal costs of "disemployment." All modern economies take steps to ease the pains involved in transferring human resources to other and better uses.
4. That the capital markets have built-in controls against overleveraging is the final point Miller made. According to him whether we are talking of automobiles or leveraged equity or high-yield bonds, the market's response to changes in tastes or to changes in products or technology is limited and self-regulating. In the financial markets, if the public's demand for junk-bonds is overestimated by take-over entrepreneurs, the higher interest rates they must offer to junk bond buyers will eat into the gains from the deals, eventually slowing down the process of leveraging or even reversing it.

Miller therefore advised against worrying about "largely self-correcting problems like financial leveraging."

18.3 CONCLUDING OBSERVATIONS

Miller in his 1988 article in the Journal of Economic Perspectives stated: "Our proposition I holding the value of the firm to be independent of its capital structure (that is, its debt/equity ratio) is accepted as an implication of equilibrium in perfect capital markets." He further argued that "...our Proposition II...showed that when Proposition I held, the cost of equity capital was a linear increasing function of the debt/equity ratio.... Our propositions implied that the weighted average of these costs of capital to a firm would remain the same no matter what combination of financing sources the firm actually chose." (Emphasis in the original). In the same article Miller dealing with the other MM invariance proposition – that the value of the firm was independent of its dividend policy – observed: "Managerial decision on dividends...might affect the cash component of an investor's return; but they would not affect the total return of cash plus appreciation, and the total is what mattered. In practice...even changing the cash-dividend component often seemed to matter a great deal.... Management initiated actions on dividends...might...serve, by implication, to convey to outside market information not yet incorporated in the price of the firm's securities" (Emphasis in the original).

Joseph Stiglitz, in an article in the same issue of the Journal, acknowledges the great importance of the MM contribution in these words: "The 1958 paper by Franco Modigliani and Merton Miller has been justly hailed as a landmark in the modern theory of finance. What has not been sufficiently emphasized is the importance of the paper to the development of economic theory and practice." As regards the critical unstated assumption in the MM theorem that all market participants have full and equal information concerning the returns to the firm, Stiglitz states that the existence of asymmetric information gives rise to two problems: "...current owners may wish to convince potential borrowers that the firm is worth more; and managers can take actions which affect the returns to those who provide capital. Because of...differences between debt and equity, a firm's choice of financial structure may convey information about the firm's prospects to potential lenders and purchasers of equity." Stigliz contends that problems of adverse selection and moral hazard arising as a result of the existence of asymmetric information may make the financial structure of firms relevant. He observes: "Theories of optimal financial structure can be derived, with the optimal structure depending on the nature of the information problems being faced."

Stiglitz concludes his article by stating that Modigliani and Miller "in their brilliant papers have set forth a research agenda which will occupy economists for decades to come. The direction which Modigliani and his co-authors suggest... a systematic exploration of market 'irrationalities' seems among the most fruitful for enhancing our understanding of these hitherto unexplained quandaries."

Critics admit that MM were the first to integrate the analysis of corporate financing with personal portfolio decisions of investors as evidenced by their concept of homemade leverage as a substitute for corporate debt. In the words of Myers "their proof of the irrelevance of financial leverage is a separation theorem, in which shareholders can unanimously direct the firm to maximize market value and not in any way shade its financing decisions to account for different shareholders' preferences for security type or for their degree of aversions to financial risk.... They established the major tenets of corporate finance (their) papers were the first to show the equivalence of market value maximization and cost of capital minimization and also the first to develop risk and tax-adjusted hurdle rates for capital investment decisions." (Emphasis in the original). It is also recognized that MM's proof of irrelevance of capital structure is the benchmark from which all subsequent theory starts.

Corporate financial practice has accepted MM's argument that the earnings-price ratio (E/P ratio) of a firm understates investors' expected return when firms have valuable growth opportunities. Furthermore, few finance mangers now accept the argument that corporate diversification undertaken solely to reduce the variance of earnings increases firm value. Amalgamating or combining or merging different businesses into a single corporate entity does in no way increase value unless synergies or real economies are achieved.

It is widely admitted that a firm's dividend decisions are generally mixed up with its other financing and investment decisions. The dividend is a by-product of a firm's capital budgeting decisions when its management's optimism about the firm's future leads to retaining a significant share of its earnings for expansion and therefore pay low dividends. In contrast, another firm might decide to finance its investment projects largely by borrowing. In this case, dividend payment by a firm is essentially a by-product of its borrowing decision. Furthermore, dividends give a clue to the investors to distinguish marginally profitable firms from good profitable firms since dividends anticipate future earnings of the firm. Manager's minds cannot be read by investors but the former's actions can to an extent reveal their minds. Thus, investors value the information content of dividends.

Before the publication of the MM's article on Dividend Policy there was discussion whether a firm's dividend decision changes the value of its equity shares rather than providing a signal of stock value. MM's theoretical paper demonstrated the irrelevance of corporate dividend policy for the value of the firm in a world without taxes, transaction costs and other market imperfections. The most obvious and serious market imperfection is the different tax treatment of dividends and capital gains in many countries.

At the end, we have to note that this essay does not cover Miller's contribution on a number of topics such as leasing, firm's demand for money, natural resources valuation and volatility and market microstructure.

18.4 SELECT BIBLIOGRAPHY OF MERTON MILLER'S WORKS

18.4.1 BOOKS

1991 *Financial Innovation and Market Volatility*, Blackwell, Cambridge.

1997 *Merton Miller on Derivatives*, Wiley, New York.

18.4.2 ARTICLES

1958 (with F. Modigliani), "The Cost of Capital, Corporation Finance and the Theory of Investment," *AER*, Vol. 48, No.3.

1959 (with F. Modigliani), "The Cost of Capital and the Theory of Investment: A Reply," *AER*, Vol. 49, September.

1961 (with F. Modigliani), "Dividend Policy, Growth, and Valuation of Shares,"*JB*, Vol.34, Oct.

1963 a (with F. Modigliani), "Dividend Policy and Market Valuation: A Reply," *JB*, Vol.36, Jan.

b (with F. Modigliani), "Taxes and the Cost of Capital: A Correction," *AER*, Vol. 53, June.

c "The Corporation Income Tax and Corporate Financial Policies," Report to the Commission on Money and Credit, in *Stabilization Policies*, Prentice-Hall, Englewood Cliffs, NJ.

1968 (with D. Orr), "The Demand for Money by Firms: Extension of Analytic Results," *JF*, Vol.23, No.5.

1976 (with C. W. Upton), "Leasing, Buying, and the Cost of Services," *JF*, Vol.31, No.3.

1977 "Debt and Taxes," *JF*, Vol.32, No.2.

1978 a (with R. W. Branz), "Prices for State-Contingent Claims: Some Estimates and Applications," *JB*, Vol.51, No.4.

b (with M.S. Scholes), "Dividends and Taxes," *JFE*, Vol.6, No.4.

1980 "The Precautionary Demand for Narrow and Broad Money," *Economica*, Vol.47, No.188.

1982 "Dividends and Taxes: Some Empirical Evidence," *JPE*, Vol.90, No.6.

1985 a (with C. W. Upton), "A Test of the Hotelling Valuation Principle," *JPE*, Vol.93, No.1.

b "Dividend Policy under Asymmetric Information," *JF*, Vol.40, No.4.

1986 a "Behavioral Rationality in Finance: The Case of Dividends," JB, Vol.59, No.4.

b "Financial Innovation: The Last Twenty Years and the Next," JFQA, Vol.21, No.4.

1988 a (with S. J. Grossman), "Liquidity and Market Structure," JF, Vol.43, No.3.

b "The Modigliani – Miller Propositions after Thirty Years," JEP, Vol.2, No.4.

1989 (with B. Malkiel et al.), "Stock Index Futures and the Crash of 87," JACF, Vol.1, No.4.

1990 (with D. A. Hsieh), "Margin Regulation and Stock Market Volatility," JF, Vol.45, No.1.

1991 a "International Competitiveness of U.S. Futures Exchanges," JACF, Vol.3, No.4.

b "Leverage," Nobel Lecture, JF, Vol.46, No.2.

c "Tax Obstacles to Voluntary Corporate Restructuring," JACF, Vol.4, No.3.

1992 "Financial Innovation: Achievements and Prospects," JACF, Vol.4, NO.4.

1994 (with J. Muthuswamy and R. E. Whaley), "Mean Reversion of Standard & Poor's 500 Index Basis Changes: Arbitrage-Induced Statistical Illusion?" JF, Vol.49, No.2.

1995 a "Do We Really Need More Regulation of Financial Derivatives?" Pacific-Basin Finance Journal, Vol.3, No.2-3.

b "Do the M&M Propositions Apply to Banks?" Journal of Banking and Finance, Vol.19, No.3-4.

1996 "The Social Costs of Some Recent Derivatives Disasters," Pacific-Basin Finance Journal, Vol.4, No.2-3.

1997 "The Future of Futures," Pacific-Basin Finance Journal, Vol.5, No.2.

1998 a (with C. L. Culp and A. M. P. Neves), "Value at Risk: Uses and Abuses," JACF, Vol.10, No.4.

b "M&M Propositions 40 Years Later," European Financial Management, Vol.4, No.2.

c "Financial Markets and Economic Growth," JACF, Vol.11, No.3.

2000 "The History of Finance: An Eyewitness Account," JACF, Vol.13, No.2.

2004 "Challenges to Demand Management," Fiscal Studies, Vol.25, No.3.

18.5 WORKS OF OTHERS

The Concise Encyclopaedia of Economics (CEE), 2nd edition.

Myers, S. C. (1991), "Merton H. Miller's Contributions to Financial Economics," ScandJE, Vol.93, No.1.

CHAPTER 19

ROBERT C MERTON & MYRON SAMUEL SCHOLES

(1944 –) &
(1941 –)

The Royal Swedish Academy of Sciences has awarded the Bank of Sweden Prize in Economic Sciences in Memory of Alfred Nobel for the year 1997 jointly to Professor Robert Merton, Harvard University, Cambridge, MA, and Myron Samuel Scholes of Stanford University, Stanford, CA, for developing a new method for determining the value of a derivative. The announcement adds that Merton and Scholes, with the late Fischer Black, developed a pioneering formula for the valuation of stock options. The methodology developed by them paved the way for economic valuation in many areas. It has also generated new type of financial institutions and facilitated more efficient societal risk management.

In a market economy, economic units are exposed to various types of risk and it is necessary for them to choose an appropriate level of risk in their transactions. This takes place in financial markets which redistribute risks to those agents who are able and willing to assume them. Options and derivative markets are important in that agents who anticipate revenues or payments can ensure a profit above a certain level or insure themselves against loss above a certain level. Options by giving the right but not the obligation to buy or sell a certain security in future at a pre-specified price protect against one-sided risk. However, such financial instruments need to be correctly valued or priced for efficient risk management. The announcement declares: "A new method to determine the value of derivatives stands out among the foremost contributions to economic sciences over the last 25 years."

Merton and Scholes developed this new method for determining the value of derivatives in close collaboration with Fischer Black, who died in his mid-fifties in 1995. The problem on which the three worked was on option valuation. Tracing the development of the new method, the press release cites the publication in 1973 by Black and Scholes of what has come to be known as Black--Scholes formula. The citation states: "Thousands of traders and investors now use this formula every day to value stock options in markets throughout the world." Robert Merton has suggested an alternative method to derive the formula that turned out to have wider applicability. He has also generalised the formula in many directions.

Historically, many attempts were made to value derivatives. As far back as 1900, a French mathematician, Louis Bachelier, reported perhaps one of the earliest attempts in that direction. In his doctoral dissertation on the theory of speculation, he derived a formula, which was found to be flawed in several ways. A number of attempts were made thereafter by researchers who studied movements of share prices and interest rates. They were more successful; however, there remained a fundamental shortcoming. Risk premia were not dealt with in an accurate way.

Before discussing the method of valuation of options by Black, Merton and Scholes, it may be in order to discuss briefly the essential features of derivative financial instruments.

19.1 DERIVATIVES

Financial innovation in the last quarter of twentieth century was rapid and extensive. One of the most remarkable developments was the growth in the use of derivatives or synthetic securities to manage financial risk. A derivative is defined as an asset that has no value of its own; its value is derived from the value of some other asset; for example, an option or a future. Derivatives are a system of side bets. The side bets may be on commodity prices, share prices, interest rates, exchange rates and so on.

We may distinguish here a primary financial instrument and a derivative instrument. A primary financial instrument, such as an equity share or bond or debenture evidences a direct claim against some other party or counter-party. These instruments are generally traded in the spot markets with the prices determined by forces of supply and demand. In contrast, a derivative security derives its value from an underlying primary security. As the derivatives derive their value from the value of some other (underlying) asset, they serve well to hedge the risk of unexpected price fluctuations. They hedge risk in owning things like quintals of wheat or paddy, U.S. dollars, government bonds or equity shares in a corporation—in short, any asset whose price is volatile. However, one thing is to be noted. Derivatives cannot reduce the risks that go with owning volatile assets; they can determine who avoids the risk and who takes on the risk. Derivatives have value in an environment of price volatility.

Derivatives generally come in two flavours: as futures-contracts for future delivery at pre-determined prices; and as options that allow one to buy or sell an object, usually a security, at a future date for a guaranteed price. Trade in such contracts allows contracting parties to insure against the risk of future price movements. Further, in contrast to futures contracts, options need not be exercised. Options are widely used in management of risk by banks and non –financial corporations. They enable firms to control their exposure to the volatility of asset prices. The two most basic types of options contracts are known as calls and puts. Standard option contracts are traded on many exchanges around the world and are known as exchange traded options. Many such contracts are also created privately—that is, off exchange or over- the – counter. Privately created put and call options typically involve financial institutions or investment banking firms on one side and their clients on the other side.

19.2 CALL OPTION

A call option grants the holder the right (but not the obligation) to buy ("call away") a specified quantity of an asset, say, a specified number of shares of a specific company from the option writer at a designated purchase price on or before a specific date. An option contract specifies four items.

1. The asset (say, the company whose shares) that is proposed to be bought.
2. The quantity of an asset (say, the number of shares) that is to be bought.
3. The purchase price for the asset (say, the share price), known as strike price or striking price or exercise price.
4. The date when the right to buy expires, known as expiration date.

Options may be European options or American options. In the case of European options, options can be exercised only on their expiration dates. In the case of American options, options can be exercised at any time during their life.

A simple hypothetical example illustrates the concept. Assume that investors K and P decide to sign a call option contract. The contract allows K to buy 200 shares of XYZ Company from P for Rs: 60 per share (exercise price) at any time during the next three months (American option). Currently, the share of XYZ Company is selling for Rs: 50 per share on National Stock Exchange (NSE).

The buyer of a call option (K in the example) will have to pay to P (the option writer) a premium (option price is a more appropriate term) in order to get the writer sign the option contract. This is because P is running a risk by signing the contract--- share price of XYZ Company may rise above Rs: 60 per share. In such a situation, P will have to buy the shares at the market price, say Rs: 70 per share, and then turn them over to K for the contract price of Rs: 60 per share. Consequently, P will have incurred a loss of Rs: 2,000 (purchasing 200 shares at the rate of Rs: 70 per share; that is spending Rs: 14,000 and receiving from K Rs: 12,000--- 200 shares at the rate of Rs. 60 per share). Assuming, the option premium to be paid to P by K for the former to write the call option contract is Rs: 5 per share. Thus, P receives Rs.1,000 (200* Rs 5) as option premium from K. Thus, the net loss P incurs on account of the call option contract is Rs: 1,000. The attraction of purchasing call option, instead of outright purchase of shares of XYZ company, is that investor K can apply a high degree of leverage; only Rs: 5 per share needs to be spent in order to purchase the option, instead of immediately spending Rs: 10,000 (200 * Rs 50) to make an outright purchase of shares.

K, the option buyer enters into a contract as he believes that the price of the share of XYZ Company would rise significantly over the next three months. Investor P, the option writer or option seller, has a different opinion. He expects or believes that the price of XYZ company's share will not rise above Rs: 60 over the three-month time period; in fact, he believes it may be Rs: 60. As K, option buyer, has the right but no obligation to buy the shares contracted, he will not exercise the option in case the share price falls below Rs: 60. Then, he will lose only the option premium he has paid to P, namely Rs: 1,000. On the other hand, if the share price increases, say, to Rs: 70 and the option buyer, K , exercises the option within the stipulated period of three months or on the day on which the three—month period ends, P has to purchase 200 shares at the market price of Rs: 70 per share and deliver them to K. P's net loss from this transaction is Rs:1,000 (P receives Rs: 12,000 and spends Rs: 14,000 in the purchase of shares, implying a loss of Rs: 2,000. Setting off Rs: 1,000 option premium received by P, the net loss suffered by him on account of the transaction amounts to Rs: 1,000).

19.3 PUT OPTION

A second type of option contract is the put option. The buyer of the put option has the right (with no obligation) to sell (" to put away") an asset or a specific number of shares of a company to the option writer at a pre-fixed selling price at any time up to and including a specific date. The put option contract specifies four items that are given below.

1. The asset or shares of the company that are contracted to be sold.
2. The quantity of an asset or the number of shares of the company that is intended to be sold.
3. The selling price for the asset or for those shares (exercise price or striking price).
4. The date when the right to sell expires or expiration date.

The concept can be illustrated with a simple example. Assume that K and P, investors, decide to sign a put option contract, which allows K to sell 100 shares of ABC Company to P at the rate of Rs: 40 per share at any time during the next three months. The current market price of a share of ABC Company on NSE is Rs: 45. P, potential option buyer, anticipates a significant rise in the share price over the next three months. On the other hand, K, the potential put option writer, expects that the share price of ABC Company would decline below Rs: 40 over the same time-period.

In this case, P would be exposed to risk by signing the contract; as such, he could demand compensation for undertaking the risk of the fall of the share price of the company to below Rs: 40. If, for instance, the share price declines to Rs: 30, P, will have to buy from K the shares contracted. While the shares are now worth only Rs: 3,000, the purchase cost for P is Rs: 4,000. He would have incurred a loss of Rs: 1,000. K would have made a profit of Rs: 1,000, purchasing 100 shares of the ABC company for Rs: 3,000 and selling them to P for Rs: 4,000.

As in the case of call option, the writer of a put option has to pay a premium to the put option buyer for assuming the risk. Both call options and put options may be closed out or offset by the buyer and writer by entering into an offsetting transaction.

As outlined above, the value of an option to buy or sell an asset or a share crucially depends on the uncertain developments in the market regarding the price of the asset or share price (that is, the underlying asset) till the date of maturity of the contract. Earlier researchers on the subject, therefore, assumed that valuation of an option requires taking a view on which risk premium to use. This is similar to determining which risk premium to use when computing present value in evaluating an investment project with future uncertain returns. Nevertheless, in the absence of information on investor's attitude towards risk, it is rather difficult to assign a risk premium. While an investor's attitude towards risk can be strictly defined in theory, it is almost impossible to observe it in reality.

The Royal Swedish Academy's press release observes that Black, Merton and Scholes made a significant contribution by demonstrating that it is, in fact, not necessary to use any risk premium while valuing an option. Risk premium does not disappear; it is embedded in the share price or the price of the asset.

Assume that an European call option that gives the right to buy one share in a certain firm at a strike price of \$50, three months from now. The value of the option depends not only on the strike price but also on today's price. The higher the share price today, the greater the probability that it will exceed \$50 in the three- month period, in which case it is advantageous to exercise the option. As a simple example, assume that the share price goes up by \$2 today; the option goes up by \$1. Assume further that an investor owns a number of shares in the firm in question and wishes to lower the risk of change in the share price. He can completely eliminate that risk by selling (writing) two options for every share that he owns. Since the portfolio thus created is risk- free, his investment has to pay interest, say on a three – month Treasury bill. If this were not the case, arbitrage trading would begin to eliminate the possibility of making a risk-free profit. As the time to maturity approaches, however, the share price changes and the relation between the option price and the share price also changes. It follows that to maintain a risk-free option stock portfolio, the investor has to make gradual changes in its composition.

By using this argument and making certain technical assumptions, one can write down a partial differential equation. The solution to the equation is the Black-Scholes formula, which is presented later in the chapter. It may be noted that valuation of other derivative securities can be done along similar lines.

A brief biographical note on each of the laureates—Robert Merton and Myron Scholes is given below.

19.4 A SHORT BIOGRAPHICAL SKETCH: ROBERT MERTON

Robert Merton was born in New York City on July 31, 1944. His father, born in Philadelphia, the son of immigrant parents, was a reputed professor of sociology at Columbia University, New York. His father was awarded the National Medal of Science for founding the sociology of science and for his contributions to sociological knowledge, such as the self-fulfilling prophecy and the focus group. Young Merton grew up in Hastings-on Hudson, a village outside the city of New York. He was educated in the local public school which "provided a fine education opportunity." In his autobiographical note Merton states that he took mathematics through the calculus and five years of science. He was a good student but not at the top of his class. Merton further adds that mathematics was his favourite subject. His passion for cars began around age 11. Merton thought he would be an automobile engineer when he grew up.

Merton reminisces: "Both of my parents played important roles in my early life of learning. My father introduced me to baseball, poker, magic, and the stock market.... Books of every kind were everywhere.... By self-exemplification, he [Merton's father] set the standards for work effort and for clarity of thought and expression." His mother taught him caring and sensitivity towards the feelings of others.

Merton's arrival at college marked the beginning of serious focus on academic matters. Just one day after entering Columbia College, he switched to the Engineering School. There he took several undergraduate and graduate mathematics courses. He also took one introductory course in economics (using Samuelson's Economics text). In 1966, he received B.S. degree in Engineering Mathematics from Columbia University. After Columbia, Merton went west to pursue a Ph.D. in applied mathematics at the California Institute of Technology (Cal Tech). His brief one year stay there added "significantly" to his stock of mathematics. He states: "Even more valuable to me was its creed of placing students from the outset in a research framework, 'playing' with their subject instead of merely passively learning the material." Merton received M.S. degree in Applied Mathematics from California Institute of Technology in 1967. Sometime during the year, he decided to leave Caltech and mathematics to study economics. He applied to half a dozen good departments, but only one, M.I.T, accepted him, and gave him a full fellowship.

The decision of Merton to leave applied mathematics for economics was "... in part to the widely-held popular belief in the 1960s that macroeconomics had made fundamental inroads into controlling business cycles and stopping dysfunctional unemployment and inflation." He, therefore, felt that working in economics could "really matter" and that potentially one could affect millions of people. Merton learned early on that the "institutional rigidities," often postulated as inviolate in academic financial modelling, can be more flexible and permeable in their real world counterparts.

At MIT, Merton was advised to take Paul Samuelson's mathematical economics course. He did. According to him "Not only did I get to interact with Paul Samuelson, but I met the then second-year students, Stanley Fischer and Michael Rothschild." Merton learned economics from Samuelson's Foundations and wrote a term paper on an optimal growth model with endogenous population changes which was later published in 1969. Samuelson hired him as his research assistant that spring, which evoked the following remark from Merton: "Quite a yield from a single course!."

Discovering shared interests and some common knowledge about the stock market, warrants and convertible securities Samuelson and Merton began in the summer of 1968, a joint effort to advance Samuelson's theory of warrant pricing (published later in 1969). Samuelson asked Merton to present their paper at the inaugural session of the MIT-Harvard Mathematical Economics seminar at which were present Arrow, Leontief and Houthakker. Merton remarks: "... It was surely a memorable baptism." His joint work with Samuelson introduced Merton to the expected utility maxim and its application to optimal portfolio selection. He "attacked" the problem of dynamic portfolio theory in a continuous-time framework. For this work, he learned stochastic dynamic programming and Ito calculus. The work on dynamic portfolio theory was published in 1969.

Despite having a galaxy of reputed teachers including Samuelson, Modigliani and Solow (all Nobel Laureates), Merton's focus was more on research "...than classes from the beginning (and my course grades reflected that). However, no one could have had a better introduction to economics than I did, with these great teachers and the opportunity to live in Paul Samuelson's office as his assistant for two and a half years." Three of the five chapters of his doctoral thesis were published prior to the submission of the thesis. A fourth one, "Optimum Consumption and Portfolio Rules in a Continuous-Time Model," was presented at the Second World Congress of the Econometric Society in August 1970 and was published in 1971. During the days of graduate study, Merton worked on the core of his later papers on the inter-temporal Asset Pricing Model, the Rational Theory of Option Pricing, and the Pricing of Corporate Debt. In 1969-1970, he worked as Instructor, Department of Economics, MIT. At the invitation of his teacher Modigliani, Merton started teaching Finance at the Sloan School of Management. He developed close relationship with Modigliani and developed deep respect and affection for him over years. He also met Myerson Scholes at MIT.

Merton was appointed as Assistant Professor of Finance (1970-1973), became Associate Professor (1973-74) and Professor (1974-1980), at Sloan School of Management, MIT. At Sloan School, Merton felt it was a stimulating and happy place to do research. He expresses his great debt to his "brilliant" colleagues there and from the economics department. Merton observes: "The tenure and the tenor of the finance area varied considerably and it was small, rarely having more than half a dozen members at a time. But the quality of mind, diversity of thought, devotion to the subject of finance, and genuine affection for one another were reliable constants throughout those years."

In his autobiographical note, Merton states that his research interests fit into three regimes of roughly equal lengths across time: 1968 to 1977, 1977 to 1987, (a reflective year 1987-1988) and 1988 to the present. His focus of research in the first decade (1968 to 1977) was on development of dynamic models of optimal life-time consumption and portfolio selection, equilibrium asset pricing and contingent claim pricing. In the next decade, i.e. the period of 1978 to 1987, his focus shifted to applications of those models. The reflective year (1987-1988) is considered by Merton as a water-shed for his research and for where it would take place. He tried to understand the financial system with special emphasis on the dynamics of institutional change. Specifically, he started studying the role of financial technology and market design, the management of financial service firms and the regulatory and accounting systems. Merton claims: " There is...continuity of this line of inquiry with the past: Fischer's, Myron's and my derivative-security research provided much of the foundation for the contract and security-design technology that is central to the extraordinary wave of real-world financial innovation of the past two decades." This turn in his research interests significantly influenced his decision to move from MIT to the Harvard Business School in 1988. At the School, he was George Fisher Baker professor of Business Administration (Dean's Chair), 1988-1998 and John and Natty McArthur University Professor, Graduate School of Business Administration since 1998 until his retirement in 2010. He is currently the School of Management Distinguished Professor of Finance at MIT's Sloan School of Management.

In his autobiographical note, Merton rightly emphasises the need to integrate finance theory with finance practice. He observes: "Throughout the last 30 years of academic research, I have been involved in finance practice. The vast bulk of my research has been in mathematical finance theory, but I believe that my involvement in practice has shaped that research and in turn has been shaped by it, this interplay to the benefit of both."

Besides Nobel Memorial Prize in Economic Sciences, Merton received numerous awards, prizes and honours. He is past president of the American Finance Association, elected Fellow of Econometric Society, a member of the National Academy of Sciences and fellow of the American Academy of Arts and Sciences. He received honorary doctorates from a number of universities including University of Chicago, University of Lausanne, National Sun Yat-Sen University and University of Paris—Dauphine. He was awarded Kolmogorov Medal by University of London. In 1993 the International Association of Financial Engineers conferred on him Financial Engineer of the year award. He was inducted (1998) into Derivatives Hall of Fame by the Derivatives Strategy Magazine.

19.5 A BRIEF BIOGRAPHICAL NOTE: MYRON SCHOLES

Myron Scholes was born in Timmins, Ontario, Canada, on July 1, 1941. His father was a dentist and his mother with her uncle established a chain of small department stores in Timmins. The death of her uncle resulted in a family dispute, exposing Scholes for the first time to agency and contracting problems. At the age of ten the family moved to Hamilton in Ontario where Scholes pursued his studies. He was a good student, ranking near the top of his class. He developed an eye disease which prevented him from reading for extended periods of time. Sholes states in his autobiographical note: "I learned to think abstractly and to conceptualize the solution to problems." He became a good listener, out of necessity. A successful cornea transplant at the age of twenty-six improved his vision.

During his teenage years, Scholes traded extensively among his friends; he gambled to understand probabilities and risks. He invested in the stock market while in high school and university. Scholes attended McMaster University for his undergraduate studies, where he majored in Economics. One of the professors at McMaster, a graduate in economics from University of Chicago, directed Scholes to read and understand the works of George Stigler and Milton Friedman. He was "impressed."

Sholes states in his autobiographical note: "Intuitively, I knew that if I wanted to grow and achieve my potential, I should attend a school where I could learn from and work with those who were the best and who could bring out the best in me. And that has become a cornerstone of my career." During his first year in Chicago, Scholes had a few classmates, Michael Jensen and Richard Roll, who became life-long friends. He observes that he learned a "tremendous amount" of knowledge over the years. Jack Gould helped him "clarify many of the finer points of economic reasoning."

The summer after first year of graduate study, Scholes secured a junior computer-programming position at the school. He spent the next four and one-half months falling in love with computers. He declares: "I must have been one of the first computer nerds.... By the end of that summer, I was becoming a computer wizard."

During that summer, he became intensely interested in economics and economic research. This was "empowering." He observes: "Either because of my scholastic qualities or because he did not want to lose me as a programmer, Merton Miller suggested that I enter the Ph.D. program. I did and I came to love economics and its young new branch, which has come to be called Financial Economics." He further observes: "Chicago provided me with a wonderful learning environment. Miller and Fama were blazing ahead in financial economics. Stigler was leading the way in information economics. Friedman was fighting on in the macroeconomic front.... I will never get over the joy and excitement those professors had about their work."

At this time, Scholes became interested in relative asset prices and the degree to which arbitrage prevented economic agents from earning abnormal profits in security markets. According to Peter Bernstein, Scholes's doctoral dissertation was an "original and powerful piece of theoretical and empirical research that supported the efficient market hypothesis. He took as his subject the impact on the market of large sales of stock by major holders." Scholes reasoned that the characteristics of risk and return distinguish one security from another; the extent of the market was far greater than that of individual security. New information brings about a change in the price of a security, information that was signalled by a large sale by an informed trader.

In a paper with Merton Miller, Scholes worked on measures of risk and the effect of differential risk on security returns. In the fall of 1968, Scholes became an Assistant Professor at the Sloan School of Management at MIT after finishing his Ph.D dissertation. Paul Cootner, Franco Modigliani and Stewart Myers became his colleagues. Scholes struck a fruitful and productive relationship with Fischer Black, who was working then as a consultant for Arthur D. Little in Cambridge, MA. Modigliani influenced Scholes's thinking on macroeconomics and asset pricing models while Myers influenced him in the area of corporate finance.

Scholes had many interactions with Robert Merton, and Fischer Black in regard to asset pricing and derivative pricing models. They extended the field of contingent-claims pricing. In his autobiographical note Scholes reminisces: "During my years at the Sloan School, I worked on testing the Capital Asset Pricing Model (CAPM) with Fischer Black and Michael Jensen, and developing the option pricing technology with Fischer Black, while continuing to work with Merton Miller." Scholes returned to the Graduate School of Business at the University of Chicago in 1974 where Black accepted Professorship in 1972. However, Black left Chicago for Boston in 1974. During his Chicago years, Scholes started to work on the effects of taxation on asset prices and incentives. Between the years 1973 - 1980 he became heavily involved with the Center for Research in Security Prices at the University of Chicago. In collaboration with Joe Williams, he wrote a paper on the estimation of risk parameters employing non-synchronous data.

Scholes visited Stanford University in 1981 and became a permanent faculty member in the Business School and the Law School in 1983. According to him, the period at Stanford was a time of significant learning for him. William Sharpe and James Van Horne were some of his close colleagues in the Business School. Scholes wrote several papers on pension planning jointly with Jeremy Bulow and wrote several articles together with Mark Wolfson on investment banking and incentives. They together developed a new theory of tax planning under uncertainty and information asymmetry.

While still conducting teaching and research at Stanford University, Scholes became a special consultant to Salomon Brothers Inc. In 1994, he joined Merton and others to become a principal and co-founder of a hedge fund called Long-Term Capital Management (LTCM). According to Merton "...seven of the eleven founders [of LTCM] ... were either graduates or their faculties or both [of MIT and Harvard Business School]." Many commentators are of the view that LTCM experience characterises Merton's theme of the productive interaction of finance theory and finance practice. In this context Peter Bernstein's observations are worth quoting: "As one might expect from a fund with Merton and Scholes as partners, LTCM had in place an elaborate set of risk management controls." Four years after LTCM opened business, i.e. in 1998, its supposedly safe portfolios "imploded." One pertinent remark was "In five weeks, the professors went from mega–rich geniuses to discredited failures." The consequences of a possible LTCM failure were considered serious; the Federal Reserve Bank of New York organised a bailout to prevent its collapse. In this connection, it is pertinent to quote from the dust jacket of Roger Lowenstein's book When the Genius Failed: The Rise and Fall of Long – Term Capital Management: "Lowenstein explains not just how the fund made and lost its money, but also how the personalities of Long Term's partners, the arrogance of their mathematical certainties, and the cultures of Wall Street in the late [nineteen] nineties contributed both to their rise and fall."

Scholes was the recipient of a number of awards and honours. He was a Research Associate, National Bureau of Economic Research (NBER), Senior Research Fellow, Hoover Institution and Member American Economic Association and American Finance Association. He is the Frank E Buck Professor of Finance, Emeritus, at the Stanford Graduate School of Business and Chairman of Platinum Grove Asset Management. He is also on the Board of Directors of Dimensional Fund Advisors. Scholes has received honorary doctoral degrees from University of Paris - Dauphine, McMaster University and Katholicke Universiteit Leuven.

19.6 A BRIEF SURVEY OF MERTON'S AND SCHOLE'S CONTRIBUTIONS

Darrell Duffie of Stanford University says that finance is a large, richly interwoven, widely applied and extremely active area of economics. In the words of Merton: "the special sphere of finance within economics is the study of allocation and deployment of economic resources, both spatially and across time, in an uncertain environment. One of the key issues within the area of finance is the valuation of future cash flows. A current basic paradigm for valuation in both academia and practice is that of competitive market equilibrium." Merton in his Nobel lecture, 'Application of Option – Pricing Theory: Twenty – Five Years Later' states that for capturing the influence and interaction of time and uncertainty effectively, requires sophisticated mathematical and computational tools.

Duffie expresses the following view in his sum up. "With this year's award to Merton and Scholes, three important contributions to the theory of financial valuation founded on the market equilibrium paradigm have now received Nobel Memorial Prize. That is:

1. Modigliani and Miller's renowned theory dealing with the irrelevance of capital structure or dividend policy for the market value of a corporation presented in 1958 article;
2. William Sharpe's 1964 work on the Capital Asset Pricing Model (CAPM);
3. And now Black – Scholes- Merton's Option Pricing Theory."

After tracing the modern finance theory to Louis Bachelier's 1900 work, Merton observes in his Nobel lecture that prior to the pioneering work of Markowitz, Modigliani, Miller, Sharpe, Samuelson, Lintner and Fama, finance theory was "little more than a collection of anecdotes, rules of thumb and shuffling of accounting data." Academic finance research of the 1960's did influence finance practice; however, Merton is of the view that the speed of adoption and the intensity of that influence was not comparable to the influence of the option model. He puts forward a hypothesis that the manifest need determined that difference. According to him in the 1960's, especially in the U.S., financial markets experienced low volatility; there was a steady rise in share prices, relatively stable interest rates and fixed foreign exchange rates. On the other hand, in the 1970's, there were structural changes and large increased market volatility. There was a shift to floating foreign exchange rates, oil price shocks, higher interest rates and double–digit inflation in the U.S and a sharp decline in real return in the U.S. stock market. Merton notes that as a consequence, increased demand for risk management in a volatile and structurally "different" economic environment contributed to a marked success of derivative security exchanges established in the 1970's to trade listed options on shares, futures on major world currencies and futures on fixed – income instruments. This gave impetus to embrace quantitative financial models to help value options and evaluate risk exposures.

In his Nobel lecture, Scholes states that three strands of financial economics set the tone for his research. They are the concept of arbitrage and the notion of substitutes, efficient market hypothesis and the Capital Asset Pricing Model. These strands provided a mathematical basis to the models of finance in the general equilibrium framework. Further, the capital structure models, the efficient market hypothesis and the Capital Asset Pricing Model have the common central themes of arbitrage and market equilibrium. Arbitrage profits are washed away as securities with similar economic risk have to exhibit similar returns. This principle applies to all types of securities-- be they equity, bonds or physical instruments. It was Modigliani and Miller who gave a general equilibrium model for corporate finance. Scholes acknowledges the profound effect Modigliani and Miller's arbitrage arguments had on his thinking and the way he analysed and modelled many problems in economics. His thinking on the dynamics of asset prices and how markets adjust to news was influenced by Fama's and Samuelson's efficient market hypothesis. As Scholes observes, it set the stage for empirical testing of how information was incorporated into security prices. He used the concept of efficient markets and arbitrage to test the extent to which security prices were influenced by the size of sales of large blocks of securities or by changes in the information set. The basis for measuring the risk of a security is supplied by capital asset pricing model— a general equilibrium model of asset prices under uncertainty.

The origin of option pricing technology was outlined by Peter Bernstein. He refers to Aristotle who credits the development of "a financial device which involves a principle of universal application" to Thales, the Milesian. Bernstein's comment: Aristotle's anecdote about Thales and his device is the first recorded mention of the instrument that has come to be known as an option. Further, Bernstein says: "A 1688 treatise on the working of Amsterdam Stock Exchange by Joseph de la Vega reveals options and similar type of securities in common use today were already dominating the trading activities at the time. This is significant, as Amsterdam Exchange was the most sophisticated and important financial center of the seventeenth century, even more important than London.... Louis Bachelier, in the course of writing his thesis in Paris in 1900, was attracted to the problem of valuing options."

Bernstein summarises the functions options perform-- an almost endless variety of functions. The primary function, however, is to provide some control over how market changes affect investors' portfolios. Buyers of options can limit losses, for a cost, with almost no limit on their profits. Investors can also use options to give them time to appraise the market movements before committing their full capital. Sellers of options, who expect little change in the market prices, can pocket an extra premium. In short, needs of both hedgers and speculators are satisfied by options. As mentioned earlier, options basically are divided into call options and put options. Call options cover situations in which asset values are likely to rise; put options, on the other hand, are attractive in situations in which asset values are likely to decline.

While reconnecting the story of the development of the option price technology and the Black-Scholes model, Bernstein observes that in mid- 1960's "... a theory to establish the scientific principles for valuing options was just then becoming a hot topic among the finance and economics faculty at MIT. This was heady business for mathematically inclined economists." It was necessary to consider the fact of uncertainty besides time, interest rates, the current price of the stock and the exercise price specified in the option contract. Samuelson set the ball rolling with a paper published in 1965, "Rational Theory of Warrant Pricing." Warrants are essentially similar to options. His paper "almost succeeded in solving the valuation problem;" but- uncharacteristically he did not quite get there on this particular occasion. Bernstein quotes Samuelson who had noted that "the results of the paper were not obvious... [I] was not sure how they would come out until the work was done."

According to Bernstein again, the prime movers in bringing the theory of option pricing to fruition were Fischer Black, a young mathematician in Boston who would end up on the MIT faculty, and Myron Scholes, "a fledgling member of the MIT faculty." Black received his Ph. D at Harvard in 1964 in applied mathematics. A year after that, Black decided his studies had been abstract; deciding to join the world of business, he took a job at Arthur D. Little. Bernstein makes an insightful observation: "Black's decision to switch career paths is another example of how the study of financial markets seem to pull students into its orbit. Bachelier was lured from mathematics, Sharpe from medicine, Osborne from astronomy, Working and Kendall from statistical theory and Treynor from physics and math."

Black worked on the Capital Asset Pricing Model because "he wanted the truth ... the cruel truth." He posits: "To get higher expected gains, you must take more risk. If you wish to climb a tall mountain, you must be prepared to suffer from pain." Market is propelled toward the equilibrium by the linkage between gain and pain. He states: "when people are seeking profits, equilibrium will prevail." Black had applied Capital Asset Pricing Model to warrants than options as warrants were being traded on the New York and American Stock Exchanges and the market for warrants was more efficient than the market (over–the–counter) for options.

19.7 The Black – Scholes Formula

The press release of the Royal Swedish Academy of Sciences gives the following formula for a European Option.

$$C = SN\,(d) - Le^{-n}N(d - \sigma\sqrt{t}) \tag{1}$$

where the variable d is defined as

$$d = \frac{\ln\frac{S}{L} + \left(r + \frac{\sigma^2}{2}\right)t}{\sigma\sqrt{t}} \tag{2}$$

The explanation of the formula is given below.

The value of the call option C, is given by the difference between the expected share value (the first term on the right-hand side) and the expected cost (the second term on the right – hand side), if the option is exercised at maturity. Further, the option value (C) is higher the higher the share price today (S), the higher the volatility of the share price (measured by its standard deviation), σ, the higher the risk-free interest rate, r, the longer the time to maturity, t, the lower the strike price or exercise price, L, and the higher the probability that the option will be exercised. The probability that the option will be exercised is evaluated by the normal distribution function, N. The key insight in Black-Scholes approach is their assumption that the price of an option is a function of the stock price and time.

Darell Duffie giving the history of the development of the Black – Scholes formula, narrates: "Fischer Black ... began with the idea of applying the Capital Asset Pricing Model (CAPM), at each instant of time, for investment over infinitesimally small periods of time. This allowed him to derive a partial differential equation (PDE) for the option price... for that would apply at any time... and at any stock price... for that time.... Black had found this PDE by 1969 or earlier but could not initially solve it. He did note, however, the solution could not allow any role for the... expected rate of return on the stock! With this in mind Black and Scholes teamed up at MIT.... They noted that since the PDE did not involve... [the expected rate of return on the stock] any expected return for the stock would generate the same option price, including the risk-less rate of return. Then they noted that if the stock could be treated as having a risk-less rate of return, then, by applying the CAPM instant by instant so could the option, because (under the assumption that the option price is a smooth function of the stock price) changes in the option and stock prices over infinitesimal periods of time are perfectly correlated. The solution they derived satisfied the PDE. "

Black in his 1989 article said: "...As we [Black and Scholes] worked on the paper we had long discussions with Robert Merton, who was also working on option valuation.... He [Merton] made a number of suggestions that improved our paper. In particular, he pointed out that if you assume continuous trading in the option or stock, you can maintain a hedged position between them that is literally riskless. In the final version of the paper, we derived the formula that way, because it seemed to be the most general derivation." The simple assumption of no arbitrage is adequate to derive the solution which appeared in the final published form of Black – Scholes Model.

In his autobiographical note, Scholes states: "To our dismay, when we submitted a version of our [Black – Scholes] paper entitled 'A Theoretical Valuation Formula for Options, Warrants and Other Securities' (October 1970) to the Journal of Political Economy (JPE), it was rejected without review. The Review of Economics and Statistics [RE Stat], also rejected the paper.... With the help of Merton Miller and Eugene Fama, who took an interest in the paper and stepped in on our behalf... [the JPE] agreed to consider the paper if we revised it and broadened its applicability.... The final version of the paper was published in 1973 in... [the JPE] under the title "The Pricing of Options and Corporate Liabilities."

Stephen Schaefer of London Business School notes three discoveries that are contained in Black – Scholes – Merton papers. They are the following.

1. Assuming frictionless trading and that asset prices follow Ito processes, they demonstrated that a perfect hedge between an option and an underlying asset could be created. More importantly, they realized that because the position was riskless, the required rate of return on the hedged position must, therefore, be riskless rate of interest. These two results lead directly to a valuation equation (a differential equation) which the option price must satisfy.
2. The second discovery was the option pricing formula itself which relates the price of an option to the price of the underlying asset.

$$C = SN(d_1) - PV(E)N(d_2) \tag{3}$$

where:

$$d_1 = \frac{\ln(S/PV(E))}{\sigma_S\sqrt{T}} + 1/2\,\sigma_S\sqrt{T} \tag{4}$$

$$d_2 = d_1 - 1/2\,\sigma_S\sqrt{T} \tag{5}$$

C: Value of the call option

S: Stock Price

PV (E): Present Value of the Exercise Price

N (.): Cumulative Normal Density

T: Time to Expiration of the option

σ_S: Standard deviation of the rate of return on the underlying asset.

The above formula is the solution to the valuation equation for the European options.

3. Black – Scholes-- Merton demonstrated that options permeate financial contracting. Many familiar types of contract, such as warrants, corporate debt and equity itself could be considered as options of one kind or another and could be valued along similar lines.

The theory of option pricing depends on the main economic principle that in a competitive market, no opportunities exist for pure arbitrage profits. To examine the implication of the absence of arbitrage, Black and Scholes used the argument involving hedging. The approach taken by them was to combine one risky asset i.e., option and combine it with another asset, the underlying share or stock to produce a perfectly hedged or riskless position. The approach taken by Merton is to show how the cash flows at time 'T' on an asset, e.g., an option, may be exactly "replicated" in all states of the world by a dynamically managed portfolio which is also "self – financing" over the time interval [0, T]. Self- financing is defined that over (0,T), the replicating portfolio "neither generates, nor consumes cash, other than what is necessary to replicate any cash flows generated by the option itself in this period. If such a self–financing portfolio can be constructed, it's initial cost must be equal to the price of the option or costless arbitrage would be possible."

In his Nobel lecture, Merton says that his principal contribution to the Black-Scholes option pricing theory was to show that in a situation of costless continuous trading, following their dynamic trading strategy using the underlying traded asset and the riskless asset would exactly replicate the pay-off on the option. He asserts: "... in a continuous trading financial environment the option price must satisfy the Black-Scholes formula or else there would be an opportunity for arbitrage profits." Merton's 1973 Bell Journal paper extended the applicability of the Black- Scholes model to allow for stochastic interest rates on the riskless asset, dividend payments on the underlying asset, a changing strike price or exercise price, American type early exercise of the option and other "exotic" options. He also notes that the subsequent research in the field was concerned with the application of the technology to other than financial options, empirical testing of the pricing formula using a sample from over-the-counter data and weakening the assumptions used in the derivation.

From 1973 to 1985, there was phenomenal growth of both the derivative exchange industry and derivative academic industry. The prime factor which led to growth of the option-pricing technology is that it reduced transaction costs. Besides, the spread of option-valuation technology was rapid once the Chicago Board Options Exchange launched its first contracts on listed securities. The model has been used to infer the implied volatility that the market is using to price the option, given the rate of interest, the share price, the dividend yields, the strike price and the maturity date of the option. Even today, options are described in terms of implied volatility. Scholes, in his autobiographical note, states: "we always stressed the role of options as insurance."

In his Nobel lecture, Scholes emphasises the key role of advances in financial theory in recent years in enabling financial services firms to meet the complex public needs effectively and at low cost. He further elaborates that till now the growth of derivatives has been helped by the pronounced noticeable trend towards securitisation and the increasing understanding of the role derivatives can play in unbundling, packaging and transferring of risks. Moreover, with information asymmetries between clients and their financial service providers, Scholes is of the view that it would be prohibitively expensive for a client to develop close relations with many financial services firms. Creating customer-tailored solutions strengthens relations between the financial services firms and their clients. Given the scenario of global competition in financial markets, Scholes expects the disappearance of inefficient financial services firms. Their clients, however, are expected to obtain more value-enhancing and less costly services from the surviving firms.

Scholes notes that the available data show that the OTC market in derivatives has grown much faster than the exchange market between 1986 and 1996 and expects the same trend to continue in future. He also notes that many regulators, market commentators and the public suspect the role of derivatives whenever the stock market declines sharply or when entities announce unanticipated financial losses. Their suspicion is based partly on the novelty of derivatives and partly because of their explosive growth during the decade mentioned above. The market losses in 1990s were attributed to derivative trading. Scholes does not think that we have seen the end of derivative failures. He surmises that, in all probability, the extent of these losses could have been mitigated if efficient risk management policies had been followed.

The option pricing methods of Black, Merton and Scholes are widely taught to most graduate students in economics and in almost every business school, particularly in the west and Japan. Around the world most of the newspapers contain a financial or business section devoted to reporting the prices of exchange–traded derivative securities, both options and futures exchange markets along with the OTC derivative market trade futures and options on individual shares, stock index and mutual fund portfolios, on bonds and other fixed income securities of different maturities, on currencies and on commodities including agricultural products, crude oil, refined products, metals and even electricity. In Western countries particularly, many investors and major corporate units use these methods for "planning, purchasing, pricing or accounting purposes." Corporations also use the models to value executive stock compensation plans, real productions, warrants, convertibles etc. It is noticed that for many of these applications, the methods are sometimes applied "inappropriately."

It may be recalled that options were seen as rather "arcane" and specialised financial instruments when the research resulting in Black-Scholes Model was under way. However, all the three, Black, Merton and Scholes, recognised early that the approach used to price options could be applied to a variety of other valuation problems. Merton observes in his Nobel lecture that perhaps the first major development in this regard was the pricing of corporate liabilities, the left hand side of a firm's balance sheet. The option pricing approach provided a unified theory for pricing a firm's liabilities—or various instruments used to finance firms. He remarks: "Because application of the pricing methodology does not require a history of trading in the particular instrument to be evaluated, it was very well suited for pricing new types of financial securities issued by corporations in an environment of financial innovation. Development of option pricing theory has propelled stupendous research effort in its application."

As mentioned earlier, put option is a basic option that gives its owner the right to sell the underlying asset at a specified strike price on or before a given expiration date. When the put option is purchased by the owner of the underlying asset, it is "functionally equivalent to an insurance policy, protecting against loss consequent to a decline in the value of the asset below the strike price, where the term of the insurance policy corresponds to the expiration date. Therefore, the theory of option pricing is applicable to value insurance contracts." An early insurance application of Black-Scholes model was by Merton. This was for pricing of guarantees and deposit insurance. So also was the application of option pricing theory to credit derivatives and valuation of catastrophic insurance reinsurance contracts and bonds.

Option model has been used in the case of many legal and tax issues involving policy and behaviour of economic agents. Merton in his 1995 and 1997 papers examined the prospective application of derivative-security technology to enhance central bank stabilisation policies in respect of interest rates and currencies. In his Nobel lecture, Merton mentions the application of option analysis to get new insights into optimal government policies in developing countries despite less efficient financial markets in those countries.

It is clear that a number of option pricing applications do not involve financial instruments; they are referred to as "real" options. An important area for application of real options relates to a firm's investment decisions. Merton provides a number of examples of valuation of project investments. They include option to initiate or expand, the option to abandon or contract and the option to wait, slow- down or speed up development, valuing product development in pharmaceutical industry, power plant construction to use a single fuel or use one of two fuels or use a least–cost fuel or decision about making a sequel to a movie.

The past twenty–five years or so have shown as to how wide ranging are the applications of new financial technologies for pricing and measuring risk of derivatives. Nevertheless, Merton notes intense uneasiness among managers, regulators, politicians, the press and the public over these new derivative–security activities and their perceived risks to financial institutions. This widespread uneasiness is attributable to instances of individual costly events, such as, the failure of Barings Bank and losses of Proctor and Gamble on interest rate contracts. Merton is of the view that these are "relatively isolated events—unfortunate pathologies rather than indicators of systemic flaws."

Attempting to predict the future for derivatives, Scholes expresses his opinion that financial innovation will continue, may be, "at an accelerating pace" as derivatives have become an essential mechanism in the tool kit of financial innovation. Merton argues that the functions of a financial system change far less than the institutions. More importantly, most financial instruments are derivative contracts in one form or another. Specifically, contracts of corporate debt and equity are derivatives to underlying investments. Scholes contends as Merton does that a firm's investment decisions are better understood by using an option framework rather than the more conventional framework of present value analysis. Scholes also predicts that time will continue to blur the distinction between debt and equity.

It is well accepted that a firm's managers should act as if the firm is risk- neutral. Three reasons are advanced as to why a firm might hedge its cash flows, all reasons being linked to the cost of financial distress. They are

1. Convexity of the tax schedule;
2. Bankruptcy costs associated with high levels of debt; and
3. Owner- managers in small firms might not be able to diversify their holdings.

As such, hedging the firm's cash flows might be a low cost alternative. Of course, corporate use of derivatives is not limited to hedging. They are also being used to beat the market using highly leveraged strategies, which, in Scholes's opinion, have been the cause of the reported financial losses, some of which were referred to earlier. Nevertheless, the future is expected to find many new solutions to solve corporate problems. Specifically, Scholes predicts that corporations will increasingly use techniques of risk management, in order to reduce their level of equity capital. While equity capital is an all purpose risk cushion, hedging is targeted risk control. As the costs to hedge decline relative to the costs of equity, firms will have an incentive to substitute hedging for equity. He predicts that the evolution of option technology will open up entirely new financial institutional structures. Scholes concludes his Nobel lecture saying: "In a world of information asymmetries, derivative instruments provide lower cost solutions to financial contracting problems in a dynamic environment and these lower–cost solutions enhance economic efficiency."

Merton, however, is less sanguine about the scenario. He refers specifically to the knowledge base now required to manage and oversee financial institutions which differs greatly from the traditional training and experience of many financial managers and government regulators. He makes a pertinent comment: "Dealing with this knowledge gap offers considerable challenge to private institutions and governments as well as considerable opportunity to schools of management and engineering and to university departments of economics and mathematics." At the end of his lecture, Merton sounds an appropriate warning: "At times we can lose sight of the ultimate purpose of the [mathematical] models when their mathematics becomes too interesting. The mathematics of financial models can be applied precisely, but the models are not at all precise in their application to the complex real world.... The models should be applied in practice only tentatively, with careful assessment of their limitations in each application..."

Merton's forebodings and his emphasis on the caution to be exercised in practical applications, have come out to be true in the case of Long-Term Capital Management, a hedge fund, in which he and Scholes were partners and founders.

19.8 OTHER CONTRIBUTIONS

Merton's work on solving the problems of optimal consumption and portfolio choice in a continuous time setting is rated as path- breaking. Though Mirrlees is credited with the first use of stochastic continuous time model in economics, it is Merton who employed the model, for instance, to develop the inter- temporal Capital Asset Pricing Model. Stephen Schaefer remarks: "For many in academic finance profession, their introduction to the methods of continuous time and Brownian motion came from the work of Robert Merton." Darrell Duffie mentions some of Merton's important extensions of the Black-Scholes formula. They include his work on American Options and on options on stock paying dividends and his extensions to the case of discontinuous stock price processes.

Scholes's ideas and papers go well beyond the development of Black-Scholes formula. His other important contributions to the development of finance theory or financial markets may be briefly mentioned. Scholes did significantly important work on dividends and their impact on the value of the common stock of a corporation in collaboration with Fischer Black and Merton Miller. Scholes, in collaboration with J. Williams, shows how to estimate betas in the CAPM approach from non-synchronous data, a reference to which has been made earlier. This study is an important and widely cited contribution to empirical methods in finance. Scholes is considered one of the leading experts on employee stock compensation plans. He co-authored a number of papers on the subject, the first of its kind, in "a critical and understudied" area of finance.

19.9 CONCLUDING OBSERVATIONS

It is observed that the most striking feature of Black- Sholes result is that though options are clearly risky instruments, their value relative to underlying asset does not depend in any explicit way on the risk aversion of investors. Specifically, the expected return on the share does not appear in the formula. This result has had significant consequences for theory and practice. A paper by Cox and Ross implies that convenient choice for the risk premium on the underlying share and therefore on the option is zero, which would be true only if investors were risk–neutral. The risk–neutrality approach has become standard in financial economics and is extensively used in practice to obtain numerical solutions to complex valuation problems.

As regards the influence of the Black-Scholes- Merton model on the development of derivative markets, Stephen Schaefer states: Factors such as the increase in volatility in exchange rates and interest rates, the consequent demand for risk management tools combined with the cost of managing these risks in other ways, have had a major impact on the demand for derivatives. He further observes: If current proposals from the Bank for International Settlements (BIS) are implemented, option pricing models will be central to the way bank capital requirements are determined in the future. Schaefer's observation about the Black-Scholes-Merton formula is worth quoting: "There is nothing about the solution they came up with. Only casual acquaintance is necessary to identify it immediately as a thing of beauty: generations of economists will be grateful to them for that alone."

Peter Bernstein's critical assessment of the importance of the development of what he calls the universal financial device in practice bears particular mention. He states: "...the three scholars [Black, Scholes and Merton] at MIT had turned Thale's financial device into an instrument of great power and overwhelming importance. Options enable investors to control risk and to shape the outcomes they face: at a cost, losses can be limited while upsides can be magnified. This is the most attractive feature of options.... Options were incorporated into the entirely new and complex debt instruments that blossomed during the 1980's.... Seldom has the marriage of theory and practice been so productive. Every time an institution uses these instruments, a corporation issues them, or a house owner takes out a mortgage, they are paying their respects, not just to Black, Scholes and Merton but to Bachelier, Samuelson, Fama, Markowitz, Tobin, Treynor and Sharpe as well."

Schaefer offers the following comment: "Few people in 1973, and one suspects that this would include Black, Scholes and Merton themselves,would have predicted either the dramatic growth in options (or, more generally derivatives) markets or how great an impact the Black-Scholes- Merton model would have on practice in the financial services industry. This is underlined by Merton's 1973 paper in which he could write that options were "specialized and relatively unimportant financial securities." The situation is entirely different now. It is reported that derivatives are a global business representing for a number of banks, good sources of earnings as well as risk. From a report of 1993 by the Group of Thirty, Schaefer gives the estimate that the total notional amount of the OTC derivatives on interest rates and currencies worldwide at around $30 trillion. He comments that the model was not only a major innovation in economic theory, it also broke new ground for economics in terms of the extent to which the theory has been applied in practice. He remarks that it may well be true that the BSM [Black-Scholes-Merton] model is the "most widely applied in the history of economics.... Generations of economists will be grateful to them for that."

We may conclude this chapter by quoting Samuelson's high tribute to Merton. Samuelson said: "Among connoisseurs, Robert C. Merton is known as an expert among experts, a giant who stands on shoulders of such giants as Louis Bachelier.... I am proud to have figured in the Mertonian march to fame.... One of the great pleasures of academic life is ... the rare sight of the companion at arms who forges ahead of you as you were able to do at the inflection point of your own career."

19.10 SELECT BIBLIOGRAPHY OF MERTON'S AND SCHOLES'S WORKS

19.10.1 ROBERT MERTON'S WORKS

19.10.1.1 BOOKS

1990 Continuous-Time Finance, Basil Blackwell, London, (Revised Edition: 1992).

1995 a (with S. Mason, et al.), Cases in Financial Engineering: Applied Studies of Financial Innovation, Prentice-Hall, Englewood-Cliffs, NJ.

b (with D. Crane et al. (eds.), The Global Financial System: A Functional Perspective, Harvard Business School Press, Cambridge, MA.

1997 (with Z. Bodie), Finance, Prentice-Hall, Englewood- Cliffs, NJ.

19.10.1.2 ARTICLES

1969 a (with P. A. Samuelson), "A Complete Model of Warrant Pricing That Maximizes Utility," Industrial Management Review, Vol.10, Winter.

b "Lifetime Portfolio Selection Under Uncertainty: The Continuous-Time Case," REStat, Vol. 51, Aug.

1971 "Optimum Consumption and Portfolio Rules in a Continuous-Time Model," JET, Vol.3, Dec.

1972 "An Analytical Derivation of Efficient Portfolio Frontier," JFQA, Vol.10, Sep.

1973 a "Theory of Rational Option Pricing," BellJE, Vol.4, No.1.

b "An Inter-temporal Capital Asset Pricing Model," Econometrica, Vol. 41, No.5. Reprinted in Bicksler, J. and I Friend (eds.), Studies in Risk and Return, Ballinger, Cambridge, MA.

1974 a (with P. A. Samuelson), "Generalized Mean-Variance Tradeoffs for Best Perturbation Corrections to Approximate Portfolio Decisions," JF, Vol.29, No.1.

b (with P. A. Samuelson), "Fallacy of the Log-Normal Approximation to Optimal Portfolio Decision Making Over Many Periods," JFE, Vol. 1, May.

Reprinted in Bicksler, J. and I Friend (eds.) Studies in Risk and Return, Ballinger, Cambridge, MA.

c "On the Pricing of Corporate Debt: The Risk Structure of Interest Rates," JF, Vol.29, No.2.

1975 a "An Asymptotic Theory of Growth Under Uncertainty," RES, Vol.42, July.

b "Theory of Finance From the Perspective of Continuous Time," JFQA, Vol.10, Nov.

1976 a "Option Pricing When Underlying Stock Returns are Discontinuous," JFE, Vol.3, Jan- Feb.

b "The Impact on Option Pricing of Specification Error in the Underlying Stock Price Returns," JF, Vol. 31, No. 2.

1977 a "A Re-examination of the Capital Asset Pricing Model," in Bicksler, J. and I. Friend, (eds.), Studies in Risk and Return, Ballinger, Cambridge, MA.

b "An Analytic Derivation of the Cost of Loan Guarantees and Deposit Insurance: An Application of Modern Option Pricing Theory," Journal of Banking and Finance, Vol.1, June.

c "On the Pricing of Contingent Claims and the Modigliani-Miller Theorem," JFE, Vol.5, Nov.

1978 a (with M. S. Scholes and M. L. Gladstein), "The Returns and Risk of Alternative Call Option Portfolio Investment Strategies," JB, Vol. 51, April.

b "On the Cost of Deposit Insurance When There Are Surveillance Costs," JB, Vol.51, July.

1980 "On Estimating the Expected Return on the Market: An Exploratory Investigation," JFE, Vol.8, Dec.

1981 a "On Market Timing and Investment Performance Part I: An Equilibrium Theory of Value for Market Forecasts," JB, Vol.54, July.

b (with R.D. Henriksson), "On Market Timing and Investment Performance Part II: Statistical Procedures for Evaluating Forecasting Skills," JB, Vol.54, Oct.

1982 a (with M. S. Scholes and M.L. Gladstein), "The Returns and Risk of Alternative Put Option Portfolio Investment Strategies," JB, Vol. 55, Jan.

b "On the Microeconomic Theory of Investment Under Uncertainty," in Handbook of Mathematical Economics, Volume II, (Arrow, K. and M. Intriligator, (eds.)), North-Holland, Amsterdam.

c "On the Mathematics and Economic Assumptions of Continuous-Time Financial Models," in Financial Economics: Essays in Honor of Paul

Cootner, (Sharpe, W.F., and C. M Cootner, (eds.)), Prentice Hall, Englewood-Cliffs, NJ.

1983 "Financial Economics," in Paul Samuelson and Modern Economic Theory, Brown, E.C and R.M. Solow, (eds.), McGraw-Hill, New York.

1984 (with S. Fischer), "Macroeconomics and Finance: The Role of the Stock Market," in Essays on Macroeconomic Implications of Financial and Labor Markets and Political Processes, K. Brunner and A.H. Meltzer (eds.), Vol. 21, North Holland, Amsterdam.

1985 a (with S. Mason), "The Role of Contingent Claims Analysis in Corporate Finance," in Recent Advances in Corporate Finance, Altman, E. I. and M. G. Subrahmanyan, (eds.), Richard D. Irwin, Homewood, Ill.

b "Implicit Labor Contracts Viewed as Options: A Discussion of 'Insurance Aspects of Pensions'," in Pensions, Labor, and Individual Choice, Wise, D.A (ed.), University of Chicago Press , Chicago, Ill.

1986 (with T. A. Marsh), "Dividend Variability and Variance Bound Tests for the Rationality of Stock Market Prices," AER, Vol. 76, No.3.

1987 a (with T. A. Marsh), "Dividend Behavior for the Aggregate Stock Market," JB, Vol. 60, Jan.

b (with Z. Bodie and A. J. Marcus), "Pension Plan Integration as Insurance Against Social Security Risk," Issues in Pension Economics, Bodie, Z. et al., (eds.), University of Chicago Press , Chicago, Ill.

c "On the Current State of the Stock Market Rationality Hypothesis," in Macroeconomics and Finance: Essays in Honor of Franco Modigliani, (Dornbusch, R, S. et al.(eds.)), MIT Press, Cambridge, MA.

d "A Simple Model of Capital Market Equilibrium With Incomplete Information," JF, Vol. 42, July.

e (with Z. Bodie and A. J. Marcus), "Defined Benefit Versus Defined Contribution Pension Plans: What Are the Real Tradeoffs?" in Pensions in the U.S. Economy, Shoven, J. B. and D. Wise (eds.), University of Chicago Press, Chicago, Ill.

f "In Honor of Nobel Laureate, Franco Modigliani," JEP, Vol.1, Fall.

g "Continuous-Time Stochastic Models," in The New Palgrave: A Dictionary of Economic Theory and Doctrine, MacMillan, London. Revised in The New Palgrave Dictionary of Money and Finance, MacMillan, London, 1992.

	h	"Options," in The New Palgrave: A Dictionary of Economic Theory and Doctrine, MacMillan, London. Revised in The New Palgrave Dictionary of Money and Finance, MacMillan, London, 1992.
1989		"On the Application of the Continuous-Time Theory of Finance to Financial Intermediation and Insurance," Twelfth Annual Lecture of the Geneva Association, The Geneva Papers on Risk & Insurance, Vol.14, July.
1990	a	"The Changing Nature of Debt and Equity: A Discussion," in Are the Distinctions Between Debt and Equity Disappearing? R. W. Kopeke and E. S. Rosengren, (eds.), Conference Series, No.33, Federal Reserve Bank of Boston, Boston.
	b	"Capital Market Theory and the Pricing of Financial Securities," in Handbook of Monetary Economics, B. Friedman and F. Hahn, (eds.) North-Holland, Amsterdam.
	c	"The Financial System and Economic Performance," Journal of Financial Services Research, Vol.4, Dec.
1992	a	"Financial Innovation and Economic Performance," JACF, Vol. 4, Winter.
	b	(with Z. Bodie and W. Samuelson), "Labor Supply Flexibility and Portfolio Choice in a Life-Cycle Model," JEDC, Vol.16, July-Oct.
	c	(with Z. Bodie), "On the Management of Financial Guarantees," in Financial Management, Vol. 21, Winter.
1993	a	(with Z. Bodie), "Deposit Insurance Reform: A Functional Approach," in Carnegie-Rochester Conference Series on Public Policy, A. Meltzer and C. Plosser, (eds.), Vol.38, June.
	b	(with A. Perold), "Management of Risk Capital in Financial Firms," in Financial Services: Perspectives and Challenges, S.L. Hayes III, (ed.), Harvard Business School Press, Boston, MA.
	c	(with A. Perold), "Theory of Risk Capital in Financial Firms," JACF, Vol.5, Fall.
	d	(with Z. Bodie), "Pension Benefit Guarantees in the United States: A Functional Analysis," in The Future of Pensions in the United States, R. Schmitt, (ed.), Pension Research Council, University of Pennsylvania Press, Philadelphia, PA.
1994		"Influence of Mathematical Models in Finance on Practice: Past, Present and Future," Philosophical Transactions of the Royal Society of London, Series A, Vol.347, June.
1995	a	"Financial Innovation and the Management and Regulation of Financial Institutions," Journal of Banking and Finance, Vol.19, July.
	b	"A Functional Perspective of Financial Intermediation," Financial Management, Vol.24, Summer.

	c	(with M. Scholes), "Fischer Black," JF, Vol.50, Dec.
1997		"A Model of Contract Guarantees for Credit-Sensitive, Opaque Financial Intermediaries," European Finance Review, Vol.1, No.1.
1998		"Applications of Option-Pricing Theory: Twenty-Five Years Later," Nobel Lecture, AER, Vol.88, No.3.
2002		(with Z. Bodie), "International Pension Swaps," Journal of Pension Economics and Finance, Vol.1, No.1.
2005		(with P. Hancock and R.G Mendoza), "A Proposal for Expensing Employee Compensatory Stock Options for Financial Reporting Purposes," JACF, Vol.17, No.3.
2006	a	(with J. Li and Z. Bodie), "Do a Firm's Equity Returns Reflect in Risk of its Pension Plan?" JFE, Vol. 81, No.1.
	b	"Allocating Shareholder Capital to Pension Plans," JACF, Vol.18, No.1.

19.10.2 MYRON SCHOLES'S WORKS

19.10.2.1 BOOKS

1991		(with Mark A. Wolfson), Taxes and Business Strategies: A Planning Approach, Prentice-Hall, Englewood-Cliffs, NJ.

19.10.2.2 ARTICLES

1967		(with H. Theil), "Forecast Evaluation Based on a Multiplicative Mean Square Error Pattern," Econometrica, Vol.35, No.1.
1970		(with W. Beaver and P. Kettler), "The Association Between Market Determined and Accounting Determined Risk Measures," Accounting Review, Vol. XLV, No. 4.
1972	a	(with F. Black and M. Jensen), "The Capital Asset Pricing Model: Some Empirical Tests," in Studies in the Theory of Capital Markets, Jensen, M.J. (ed.), Praeger, New York.
	b	"The Market for Securities: Substitution Versus Price Pressure and the Effects of Information on Share Prices," JB, Vol. 45, No. 2.
	c	(with M. H. Miller), "Rates of Return in Relation to Risk: A Re-examination of Some Recent Findings," in Studies in the Theory of Capital Markets, Jensen, M.J (ed.), Praeger, New York.
	d	(with F. Black), "The Valuation of Options Contracts and a Test of Market Efficiency," JF, Vol.27, No.2.
1973		(with F. Black), "The Pricing of Options and Corporate Liabilities," JPE, Vol.81, No. 3.

1974 a (with F. Black), "The Effects of Dividend Yield and Dividend Policy on Common Stock Prices and Returns," JFE, Vol.1, May.

b (with F. Black), "From Theory to a New Financial Product," JF, Vol.19, No.2.

1976 "Taxes and the Pricing of Options," JF, Vol.31, No.2.

1977 (with J. Williams), "Estimating Betas from Nonsynchronous Data," JFE, Vol.5, No. 3.

1978 a (with R.C. Merton and M.L. Gladstein), "The Return and Risk of Alternative Call Option Portfolio Investment Strategies," JB, Vol.51, No.2.

b (with M. Miller), "Dividends and Taxes," JFE, Vol.6, No.4.

1980 (with G. Constantinides), "Optimal Liquidation of Assets in the Presence of Personal Taxes: Implications for Asset Pricing," JF, Nov.35, No. 2.

1981 a (with M. H. Miller), "Executive Compensation Taxes and Incentives," in Financial Economics: Essays in Honor of Paul Cootner, (W.F. Sharpe and C.M. Cootner (eds.)) Prentice-Hall, Englewood-Cliffs, NJ.

b "The Economics of Hedging and Spreading in Futures Markets," Journal of Futures Research, Vol.1, No.2.

1982 a (with R.C Merton and M.L. Gladstein), "The Return and Risk of Alternative Put Option Portfolio Investment Strategies," JB, Vol.55, No.1.

b (with M.H. Miller), "Dividends and Taxes: Some Empirical Results," JPE, Vol.90, No. 6.

1983 a (with J. Bulow and P. Menell), "Economic Implications of ERISA," Financial Aspects of the U.S. Pension System, NBER, University of Chicago Press, Chicago, Ill.

b (with J. Bulow), "Who Owns the Assets in a Defined Benefit Pension Plan," Financial Aspects of the U.S. Pension System, NBER, University of Chicago Press, Chicago. Ill.

1985 (with R. S. Hamada), "Taxes and Corporate Financial Management," in Recent Advances in Corporate Finance, (E. Altman and M. Subrahmanyan, (eds.)), Richard D. Irwin, Homewood, Ill.

1987 a (with R. J. Gilson and M. A. Wolfson), "Taxation and the Dynamics of Corporate Control: The Uneasy Case for Tax Motivated Acquisitions," in Knights, Raiders and Targets: The Impact of the Hostile Takeover, (J. C. Coffee, Jr, et al. (eds.)), Oxford University Press, Oxford.

b (with M. A. Wolfson), "Issues in the Theory of Optimal Capital Structure," in Frontiers in Modern Finance, (S. Bhattacharya and G. Constantinides, (eds.)) Rowman and Littlefield, Totowa, NJ.

1988 (with M.A. Wolfson), "The Cost of Capital and Changes in Tax Regimes," in Uneasy Compromise: Problems of a Hybrid Income-Consumption Tax, J. A. Pechman, (ed.) The Brookings Institution, New York.

1989 a (with E. Terry and M. Wolfson), "Taxes, Trading and the Value of Real Estate," Journal of Accounting, Auditing and Finance, Vol. 4, No.3.

b (with M. A. Wolfson), "Decentralized Investment Banking: The Case of Discount Dividend-Reinvestment and Stock-Purchase Plans," JFE, Vol.24, No.1.

1990 a (with M. A. Wolfson), "The Effects of Changes in Tax Laws on Corporate Reorganization Activity," JB, Vol.63, No.1, Part.2.

b (with M. A. Wolfson), "Employee Stock Ownership Plans and Corporate Restructuring : Myths and Realities," Financial Management, Vol.19, Spring.

c (with M. A. Wolfson), "Converting Corporations to Partnerships through Leverage: Theoretical and Practical Impediments," in Debts, Taxes and Corporate Restructuring, (J. B. Shoven and J. Waldfogel (eds.)), Brookings Institution, New York.

d (with P. Wilson and M. A. Wolfson), "Tax Planning, Regulatory Capital Planning, and Financial Reporting Strategy for Commercial Banks," Review of Financial Studies, Vol. 3, No.4.

1991 a (with M.A. Wolfson), "Employee Stock Ownership Plans and Corporate Restructuring: Myths and Realities," The Battle for Corporate Control, (A. W. Sametz, ed.), Business One, Irwin, Homewood, Ill.

b (with M. A. Wolfson), "The Roles of Tax Rules in the Recent Restructuring of U.S. Corporations," in Tax Policy and the Economy, (D. F. Bradford, ed.), NBER/MIT Press, Cambridge, MA.

c "Stock and Compensation," JF, Vol.46, No.3.

1995 a "The Future of Futures," in Risk Management Problems & Solutions, (W.H. Beaver and G. Parker, eds.), McGraw-Hill, New York.

b (with R.C. Merton), "Fischer Black," JF, Vol.50, No.5.

1996 "Global Financial Markets, Derivative Securities and Systemic Risks," in Journal of Risk and Uncertainty, Vo. 12, No. 2-3.

1998 "Derivatives in a Dynamic Environment," Nobel Lecture, AER, Vol.88, No.3.

2000 "Crisis and Risk Management," AER, Vol.90, No.2.

2001 "Merton H. Miller: Memories of a Great Mentor and Leader," JF, Vol.56, No.4.

2004 "The Future of Hedge Funds," Journal of Financial Transformation, Vol.10, pp. 8-11.

19.11 WORKS OF OTHERS

Bernstein, P.L (1992), Capital Ideas: The Improbable Origins of Wall Street, The Free Press, New York.

Duffie, D. (1998), "Black, Merton and Scholes—Their Central Contributions to Economics," ScandJE, Vol. 100, No.2.

Schaefer, S.M. (1998), "Robert Merton, Myron Scholes and the Development of Derivative Pricing," ScandJE, Vol. 100, No.2.

Section - III

New Methods of Economic Analysis: Econometrics etc

CHAPTER 20

RAGNAR ANTON KITTEL FRISCH

(1895 – 1973)

The first Nobel Prize in Economics – The Sveriges Riksbank Prize in Economic Sciences instituted in memory of Alfred Nobel-- was awarded in the year 1969 jointly to Ragnar Frisch of Norway and Jan Tinbergen of The Netherlands for "having developed and applied dynamic models for the analysis of economic processes." The Royal Swedish Academy of Sciences in its citation, announcing the award, makes reference to the most salient feature in the development of economics in "recent decades," namely, the emphasis on mathematical statistical descriptions of precision of the economic processes involved. The earlier more 'literary' descriptions of economic processes, coupled with vague discussions about the possible courses of crises, unemployment, inflation and so on, have in increasing measure been replaced by attempts to use mathematical precision in arranging the developments in model systems, and in associated efforts to test systematically the hypotheses proposed in relation to empirical reality. While this trend is noticeable in many areas of Economic Science, this development is particularly marked "in the analysis of market conditions and growth and in the theory of economic policy."

The pioneering contributions of Frisch and Tinbergen were made in the above domains. The citation refers to Frisch as a "leading pioneer in the realm of theory and method development." It notes his development of mathematically specified dynamic models for the purpose of analysing economic courses of events and his demonstration of how a combination of equations, giving hypothetic connections to consumption, capital accumulation and money supply generates in an economy cyclical fluctuations that can be maintained by random disturbances.

The citation also acknowledges that the fundamental work of Tinbergen gives the theory of economic evolution a form that facilitates empirical quantification and statistical testing of the formulated hypotheses. It makes specific reference to his pioneering work in econometrics concerning the analysis of economic development of the United States during the period 1919-32.

Both Frisch and Tinbergen pioneered mathematical formulation of economic problems and succeeded in giving a "new and more exact content to the means-end problems in economic policy." In the field of problems of long-term growth and planning, which was the focus of economic research in later years, Frisch and Tinbergen had contributed significantly to the construction of new models. These contributions have been very important "for the development of the method, in particular for the planning of the economic evolution of the developing countries."

The major contributions of Ragnar Frisch to Economic Science are covered in this chapter while those of Tinbergen were summarised in the next one.

20.1 A BRIEF BOIGRAPHICAL NOTE: RAGNAR FRISCH

Ragnar Frisch was born in 1895. He graduated in Economics from the University of Oslo in 1919, "although as a son of goldsmith, he 'supplemented' this by finalising his apprenticeship as a goldsmith in 1920." He studied in France from 1921 to 1923 and in Britain in 1923. He was an associate at the University of Oslo from 1925 and received his doctorate in 1926 in mathematical statistics. Further studies in the U.S.A, France and Italy during 1927-1928 were followed by an associate professorship at the University of Oslo (1928) and a full professorship in 1931. At the age of 36, Frisch became Professor at Oslo University. From the beginning of the 1930s, he was Director of the then newly established Institute for Social Economy at the University till his retirement in 1965. At the Institute, he inspired and led a large number of theoretical investigations concerning dynamic processes, theory of production, national accounting, economic planning, and mathematical programming among others. He had a number of eager and successful students who have come to constitute a school. Frisch was visiting Professor at a number of universities after the end of the Second World War. He also advised a number of countries on economic planning in developing countries including India. Frisch was one of the founders of the Econometric Society and the driving force behind its creation. He was the Chief Editor of the journal of the Society, Econometrica, for over two decades, from 1933 to 1955.

He received honorary doctorates from a number of universities including Stockholm and Cambridge. Frisch was the first recipient of the Schumpeter Prize (1955). He was a visiting professor/guest lecturer of a number of universities including Yale, Minnesota and Paris. Ragnar Frisch died in 1973.

20.2 A SUMMARY OF RAGNAR FRISCH'S MAJOR CONTRIBUTIONS

Ragnar Frisch's scientific work extended across many areas of economics. However, an underlying thread in his contributions is his conscious effort to make economics an exact and quantitative science, which has been expressed repeatedly by him. At the same time, he had invariably aimed at real practical tests and applications of the theories he had formulated and the method he had espoused. Frisch, of course, was aware of the danger inherent in "mathematization" of economics that could result in empty, formalistic theories.

While it would not be possible to review the voluminous work of Frisch, given the space constraint, following the approach of Leif Johansen we propose to cover three main areas in economics to which Frisch had made notable contributions;

1. Quantification of Economics,
2. Theories and Methods for Economic Policy and Planning, and
3. Development of Economic Dynamics.

20.2.1 QUANTIFICATION OF ECONOMICS

Quantification of the subject of economics, according to Frisch, presupposes that theory and measurement have to be viewed as part of a whole. Under this broad head are covered the major topics of Theory of Consumer Behaviour or Demand Theory and Production Theory from Microeconomics, Macroeconomics and Econometric Methodology.

20.2.1.1 DEMAND THEORY

In one of his early publications (1926), Frisch derived the existence of a utility function by constructing a system of basic axioms that are simple and easily comprehensible. It is generally accepted that Frisch was the first to employ the axiomatic method, which was later employed by a number of writers in the areas of utility, demand theory and welfare economics. Frisch employed measurable or cardinal concept of utility. Though his approach was subject to criticism (such as by Herman Wold in his Demand Analysis), one cannot deny the importance of Frisch's work "as a model of the axiomatic approach" in the theory of consumer behaviour.

While formulating consumer's utility functions employing axiomatic approach, Frisch did not neglect the empirical application of the theory. He connected the theory to empirical studies devoted to measuring the major characteristics of the consumer's utility structure. The later development of Frisch's ideas in utility analysis is to be found in his 1959 Econometrica article, "A Complete Scheme for Computing all Direct and Cross Demand Elasticities in a Model with Many Sectors." This article presents a complete scheme for computing all direct and cross demand elasticities in a model with many sectors. This approach is particularly useful in models of extensive planning. For the purpose of ease of estimation, Frisch had to make a dubious assumption of independent utilities; that is, the utility functions can be written as a sum of functions of each of the goods consumed by the consumer. P.N. Rasmussen observes: "It is a tribute to his work that it has in fact been used in practice, for example in Norwegian Planning."

20.2.1.2 PRODUCTION THEORY

In the area of theory of production, Frisch had made important contributions such as, formulating the theory in a strict mathematical form to render the theory exact, which can also be applied to concrete problems. One of the early attempts in this direction was his 1935 study – "The Principle of Substitution: An Example of its Application in the Chocolate Industry."

However, Frisch's contribution to the development of production theory is difficult to document as most of his works in this field were in the form of mimeographed lecture notes in the 1930s and remained unpublished till early 1960s. Nevertheless, the main results of his work have been known internationally through the works of eminent economists, such as, Hicks, Schneider and Carlson. In this context, a reference to what Schumpeter said in his A History of Economic Analysis is particularly relevant: "The term isoquant (equal product curve) was introduced by Frisch...." One can assess how advanced and important Frisch's contribution was in relation to others by a reference to Kenneth Boulding's survey article on "The Theory of the Firm" in his 1942 paper in the American Economic Review wherein he states that "the use of isoquants to describe the production function did not develop to any great extent until the thirties (1930s)." Boulding makes references to Norwegian accounts of Frisch's lectures. It is stated by Johansen that Frisch's lectures from the 1920s and 1930s have inspired and influenced books that have become classics in the area of production theory.

20.2.1.3 MACROECONOMIC THEORY

During the 1930s, influenced by the then economic crisis, Frisch turned his attention to macroeconomic problems. Rasmussen states: "... in the theory of macroeconomics, Frisch was at the front, even, it can be argued, ahead of Keynes.... He shows convincingly, how a capitalist economy may go into a deadlock when, to put it in a simple way the tailor cannot sell to the shoemaker because the shoemaker cannot sell to the tailor." In Schumpeter's words "...Aggregative Analysis or as it is sometimes called macro analysis (This term is due to Professor Ragnar Frisch)...." For the purpose of constructing quantifiable theories in macroeconomics, it is necessary to have a system of national accounts. A simple system of national accounting was suggested in his article contributed to a volume of Essays in Honour of Gustav Cassell (1933) entitled "Propagation Problems and Impulse Problems in Dynamic Economics" (The terms microeconomics and macroeconomics were used for the first time by Frisch, according to Schumpeter and others). Frisch jointly presented with Odd Aukrust and Petter Jacob Bjerve a much more detailed system of national accounting in 1948 in a mimeographed paper "A System of Concepts Describing the Economic Circulation and Production Process." While talking of pioneers in the development of the theory of national accounting, Ragnar Frisch is mentioned along with Irving Fisher, Richard Stone (who was a recipient of Nobel Memorial Prize for Economic Sciences, 1984), Erik Lindahl and Wassily Leontief(Nobel Prize winner,1973). In 1934 Econometrica article, Frisch outlined (even before Leontief) an input-output analysis. In retrospect, his contributions in these areas are considered path- breaking.

Frisch's contributions to other aspects relating to the area of macroeconomics are discussed below in the discussion on economic dynamics.

20.2.1.4 ECONOMETRIC METHODOLOGY

Frisch's interest in statistical methodology is widely known as also his awareness of the problems connected with the application of statistical methods while quantifying economic relationships. His first foray into this field was his 1929 essay "Correlation and Scatter in Statistical Variables" followed by "Statistical Confluence Analysis by Means of Complete Regression Systems" (1934) and "Statistical versus Theoretical Relations in Economic Macro Dynamics." Rasmussen's assessment in this regard is worth quoting: "...in general, he enriched our methodological vocabulary by a number of precise concepts: macro versus micro analysis, statics versus dynamics, exogenous versus endogenous variables, the concept of autonomous relations, the problem of identification of relations, confluent relations, decision models, conjectural behavior (by firms)...." It is notable that while he 'created' econometrics in the modern sense of the word, he repeatedly warned against misuse of the new tools. In his own words: "...I have stressed that econometrics must have relevance to concrete realities – otherwise it degenerates into something which is not worthy of the name econometrics, but ought rather to be called playometrics."

Frisch is generally recognised as the first econometrician who squarely faced the problem of errors in variables. In his "Statistical Confluence Analysis by Means of Complete Regression Systems" (1934), he attempted at decomposing observed variables into a systematic part and a random disturbance part. Though he could not satisfactorily resolve the problem of errors in variables, he is credited with raising fruitful questions connected with the problem.

Frisch was highly sceptical of sampling theory and significance tests in econometrics. His objection to the use of significant tests was based on his concern with the problems of multicollinearity and measurement errors which he believed afflicted all economic variables observed under non-controlled experimental conditions. By drawing attention to the fictitious determinateness created by random errors of observations, Frisch severely attacked regression and correlation analysis which is valid even now. With characteristic clarity Frisch stated: "As a matter of fact I believe that a substantial part of the regression and correlation analyses which have been made on economic data in recent years is nonsense because of random errors."

20.2.2 THEORIES AND METHODS FOR ECONOMIC POLICY AND PLANNING

The economic crisis of the 1930's, besides stimulating Frisch's interest in macroeconomics, had led him to focus attention on developing economies and in formulating economic policy for the purpose of developing those economies. In this context, reference has to be made to Frisch's 1934 Econometrica articles "Circulation Planning." The papers mainly discuss the problem of restarting production and circulation processes in an economy passing through depression arising out of deficient aggregate demand. These papers help explain the economic crisis of the 1930's by adopting a disaggregated method in contrast to the Keynesian – type aggregative models.

This work of Frisch did not receive the attention it deserved because of the arbitrary assumptions that he had made, as also because of the sharp focus he laid on technical problems connected with the computational methods. A modern reader, however, locates in the paper important ideas closer to what has come to be known later as closed input-output model and the type of inequalities in terms of a modern mathematical programming problem. It is also pointed out by critics that Frisch had introduced in the "Circulation Planning" articles, a function for balancing between the wishes of different groups which can be regarded as a preference function of the type used in modern literature on economic planning. This formulation is regarded very similar to the one used, in particular by Professor Theil in recent years.

During the later part of 1950's and thereafter, Frisch started developing comprehensive programming models, a pioneering work in this field. His models are more comprehensive than most other models developed by other economists at that time. A notable feature of his work on programming models relates to the studies he had made based on planning problems of developing countries, such as India and Egypt. Special mention must also be made of the interaction between short-run decisions and the analysis of long-run economic development in the models constructed for Indian planning -- Planning for India: Selected Explorations in Methodology (1960).

In the context of Frisch's work on Planning Models, two aspects of this work are specially referred to by critics as of great significance. First, his development of methods for constructing preference functions by conducting systematic interviews with politicians and other authorities entrusted with making policy decisions.

The second notable aspect relates to development of techniques of computing. Frisch had addressed himself to the complex and extensive computing problems posed by planning models when put to practical use. We may refer here to his development of various computing methods for solving programming problems – the logarithmic potential method, the multiplex method and the non-Plex method.

20.2.3 DEVELOPMENT OF ECONOMIC DYNAMICS

In the development of dynamic economic theory, it is widely acknowledged that Frisch is a pioneer. His 1929 article in a Scandinavian language "Statics and Dynamics in Economic Theory" is reported to have elucidated a number of concepts relating to the subject and provided specific examples of dynamic economic analysis. Schumpeter acknowledged Frisch's contribution to the dynamic analysis in these words. "Dynamic means exclusively analysis that links quantities pertaining to different points of theoretic time...and not the theory of evolutionary processes that run their courses in historic time; it is practically co-extensive with sequence analysis and includes period analysis as a special case, but it is not co-extensive with the theory of economic growth or development or progress." In a footnote to this statement Schumpeter admitted, "The chief authorities for our terminology are Frisch and Hicks."

Frisch's contribution to the area of economic dynamics has become internationally known from his 1936 article "On the Notion of Equilibrium and Disequilibrium." We can judge the importance of this contribution by Paul Samuelson's use of Frisch's concepts and terminology of economic dynamics in his monumental work Foundations of Economic Analysis. Frisch's contributions to the theory of business cycle are profound. We may cite his articles "The Relation between Primary Investment and Reinvestment" (1927), and articles in The Journal of Political Economy (1931, 1932) putting forward the concept of Acceleration Principle and its role in providing explanation of the trade cycle.

Frisch constructed an original and mathematically complete trade cycle theory in his well-known paper "Propagation Problems and Impulse Problems in Dynamic Economics," which were contributed to Economic Essays in Honor of Gustav Cassell. As Robert Gordon and Lawrence Klein remark in their introduction to Section II on Methodology to American Economic Association Readings in Business Cycles. "...Mathematical formulation of theory and an econometric approach to empirical work are probably the two outstanding (and interrelated) developments in the recent business cycle literature. Frisch's paper...charted as early as 1933 the course that was to be followed by future builders of aggregate dynamic models. It combines an internal mechanism, which may be cyclical by itself with external shocks which may be either random or autonomous." Paul Samuelson underscores the importance of this paper of Frisch in the context of the explanation of his "Correspondence Principle." He states in his Foundations: "An understanding of this principle is all the more important at a time when pure economic theory has undergone a revolution of thought – from statical to dynamical models. While many earlier foreshadowings can be found in the literature, we may date the upheaval from the publication of Ragnar Frisch's Cassel Volume essay."

Frisch observed that the majority of economic oscillations, can be explained "most plausibly as free oscillations." The characteristic feature of the free oscillations, according to him, is that the length of the cycles and the tendency towards dampening are determined by the intrinsic structure of the swinging system, while the intensity (amplitude) of the fluctuations is determined primarily by the exterior impulse. Frisch argued further: "If a cyclical variation is analysed from the point of view of a free oscillation, we have to distinguish between two fundamental problems: first, the propagation problem; second, the impulse problem." Given an initial situation in which the system starts, the propagation problem attempts at explaining the character of the swings the system experiences with the help of the structural properties of the swinging system. This needs to be done by the use of a dynamic theory, explaining how one situation shows out of the earlier one. In such an analysis, we consider a set of magnitudes in a given point of time, study the interrelations between the magnitudes as also magnitudes of certain of the variables in different points of time. Also, we introduce certain equations, which "embrace at the same time several of these magnitudes belonging to different instants." One point to note here, which is in contrast to a Walrasian system of equations, is that all variables in the system belong to the same point of time. Like the Walrasian system, this dynamic system has, of course, to be determinate – as many equations as there are unknowns. Frisch contended that when we engage in the study of business cycles, a truly dynamic analysis demands distinction being drawn between micro-dynamic analysis and macro-dynamic analysis. While there are examples of the former, he observed, "as far as I know no determinate macro-dynamic analysis is yet to be found in the literature. In particular no attempt seems to have been made to show in an exact way what the relations between the propagation analysis and the impulse analysis are in this field." He developed simplified systems in which the variables exhibit a secular trend but no oscillations. Oscillations could be produced in such a system in a number of ways; for example, distinguishing between savings and investment (a la Keynes), by introducing debt into the system which affects the behaviour of both producers and consumers (a la Irving Fisher's approach to the business cycle problem), and by introducing the Marxian idea of a bias in the distribution in the economy of the purchasing power etc.

However, when an economic system gives rise to oscillations such as those mentioned above and others, these will most frequently be damped. In contrast, the cycles we observe in reality are generally not damped. Then how does one explain the maintenance of swings in a business cycle? Frisch argued that the theoretical dynamic laws must not be taken as an immediate explanation of the observed oscillating phenomena. They only form one element of explanation. They solve the propagation problem. But the impulse problem remains. This problem may be approached in several alternate ways. A fruitful and promising approach is to expose the dynamic system "to a stream of erratic shocks that constantly upsets the continuous evolution and then introducing into the system the energy necessary to maintain the swings."

In this connection, Frisch acknowledged the important work of Knut Wicksell in this area. He stated: "Knut Wicksell seems to be the first who has been definitely aware of the two types of problems in economic cycle analysis – the propagation problem and the impulse problem – and also the first who formulated explicitly the theory that the source of energy which maintains the economic cycles are erratic shocks. He conceived more or less definitely of the economic system as being pushed along irregularly, jerkingly. New innovations and exploitations do not come regularly he says, but...these irregular jerks may cause...regular cyclical movements. He illustrates...'If you hit a wooden rocking-horse with a club, the movement of the horse will be very different to that of the club.'" Johan Akerman took up Wicksell's idea and had discussed how small fluctuations may be able to generate larger ones. Frisch traced the further development of the idea of how irregular fluctuations get transformed into business cycles by making reference to the works of Slutsky, Yule and Hotelling.

While no doubt the idea of erratic shocks is an essential part of the impulse problem in economic cycle analysis, Frisch also made use of Schumpeterian theory of innovations as a factor in maintaining oscillations – the idea of "auto – maintained" oscillation.

While concluding this section dealing with Frisch's contribution to economic dynamics, a reference is warranted to Arrow's opinion that Frisch's work on the polypoly theory and his analysis of the phenomena of "economic pressure" as important contributions to economic dynamics.

20.3 OTHER MAJOR CONTRIBUTIONS

Besides the three main areas to which Frisch made significant contributions, he had done important work in many other different areas. On the occasion of Frisch's 65th birthday, Kenneth Arrow wrote an article "The Work of Ragnar Frisch, Econometrician" in the April 1960 issue of Econometrica, in which he lists 119 items as Frisch's most important publications up until 1959. Leif Johansen's article in the 1969 issue of Swedish Journal of Economics, extends the list to 150. No attempt is made here to summarise even his main contributions; some of the important works will be referred to before closing the essay. His well-known contribution to the important issue of cost of living indices is contained in "Annual Survey of General Economic Theory: The Problem of Index Numbers" (Econometrica, 1936). Another work which deserves greater attention is Frisch's 1940 paper "On Optimum Population," considered as "one of the clearest and most complete theoretical treatment of the problem." Two other articles of Frisch, which belong to the genre of History of Economic Analysis and which cannot be missed are his 1950 Quarterly Journal of Economics article "Alfred Marshall's Theory of Value" and his article on "Wicksell" in The Development of Economic Thought edited by Henry William Spiegel. It is said that "both studies belong to the most profound interpretations of Marshall and Wicksell and they pursue the analysis in original ways."

20.4 CONCLUDING OBSERVATIONS

One of the secrets of the success of Frisch as an economist lies in his method of formulating problems which was done clearly and in a fruitful way. In addition to the great influence Frisch enjoys in the profession, his work remains "a rich source for future research." Many of his original and important ideas and profound analyses have not yet become known globally "due to the modes of publication used and to the fact that Frisch is never guided by what is 'fashionable' in the discipline."

By common consent, Frisch's life work is highly impressive as also the man himself. He had felt a strong social responsibility as evidenced through his work on the economic problems of the 1930s experienced by developed countries as well as "by his consciousness" towards the less developed countries. We cannot do better than close this essay by quoting from Rasmussen's tribute to Frisch in the New Palgrave: A Dictionary of Economics.

"He could at times be a bit harsh on his colleagues who do not live up to his own standards for serious work. At the same time he was extremely kind and helpful to students doing their best. He never failed to encourage. And few will forget when his strong blue eyes were shining with joy."

20.5 SELECT BIBLIOGRAPHY OF RAGNAR FRISCH'S WORKS

20.5.1 BOOKS

1932 New Methods of Measuring Marginal Utility, Tribingen.

1933 Pitfalls in the Statistical Construction of Demand and Supply Curves, Hans Buske Verlag, Leipzig.

1934 Statistical Confluence Analysis by Means of Complete Regression Systems, University Institute of Economics, Oslo.

1960 Planning in India: Selected Explorations in Methodology, Indian Statistical Institute, Calcutta.

20.5.2 ARTICLES

1929 "Correlation and Scatter in Statistical Variables," Nordic Statistical Journal, Vol.1, pp.36-102.

1930 "Necessary and Sufficient Conditions Regarding the Form of Index Which Shall Meet Certain of Fisher's Tests," JASA, Vol.25, Dec.

1931 "A Method of Decomposing an Empirical Series into its Cyclical and Progressive Components," JASA, Vol.26, March Supplement.

1932 a "The Interrelation between Capital Production and Consumer-Taking," JPE, Vol. XXXIX, No.5.

b "New Orientation of Economic Theory: Economics as an Experimental Science," Nordic Statistical Journal, Vol.4, Parts 1-2.

1933 a (with F.V. Waugh) "Partial Time Regressions as Compared with Individual Trends," Econometrica, Vol.1, No.4.

b "Propagation Problems and Impulse Problems in Dynamic Economics," Economic Essays in Honor of Gustav Cassel, Allen and Unwin, London, Reprinted in Readings in Business Cycles, R.A. Gordon and L.R. Klein (eds.), Allen & Unwin, London, 1966.

1934 a "Circulation Planning," Econometrica, Vol.2, No.3-4.

b "More Pitfalls in Demand Supply Curve Analysis," QJE, Vol. XLVIII, No.4.

1936 a "Annual Survey of General Economic Theory: The Problem of Index Numbers," Econometrica, Vol.4 No.1.

b "On the Notion of Equilibrium and Disequilibrium," RES, Vol. III, No.2.

1939 "A Note on Errors in Time Series," QJE, Vol.LIII, Aug.

1946 "The Responsibility of the Econometrician," Econometrica, Vol.14, No.1.

1947 a "Tribute to Irving Fisher," JASA, Vol.42, No.237.

b "Irving Fisher at Eighty," Econometrica, Vol.15, No.2.

1950 "Alfred Marshall's Theory of Value," QJE, Vol.LXIV, No.4.

1952 "Frisch on Wicksell," The Development of Economic Thought, H.W.Spiegel (ed.), John Wiley &Sons, Inc., New York.

1954 a "Some Basic Principles of Price of Living Measurements," Econometrica, Vol.22, No.4.

b "Linear Expenditure Functions," Econometrica, Vol.22, No.4.

1955 a "Market Price versus Factor Cost in National Income Statistics," Sankhya, Vol.15, March, Parts 1 & 2.

b "From National Accounts to Macroeconomic Decision Models," Paper read at the Meeting of the International Association for Research in Income and Wealth, Rome, September 1953, Income and Wealth Series IV, London.

1957 "The Multiple Method of Linear Programming," Sankhya, Vol.18, Sep, Parts 3 & 4.

1959 a "A Complete Scheme for Computing all Direct and Cross Demand Elasticities in a Model with Many Sectors," Econometrica, Vol.27, No.2.

b "On Welfare Theory and Pareto Regions," International Economic Papers, No.9, pp. 39-92, London.

1960 "Market Prices vs. Factor Costs and the Constancy of Production Coefficients," in Essays in Economics and Econometrics, A Volume in Honour of Harold Hotelling, North Carolina University, Chapel Hill, NC.

1961 "A Reconsideration of Domar's Theory of Economic Growth," Econometrica, Vol.29, No.3.

1964 "Dynamic Utility," Econometrica, Vol.32, No.3.

1966 "Rational Price Fixing in a Socialist Society," Economics of Planning, Vol.6, No.2.

1970 "Econometrics in the World of Today" in Induction, Growth and Trade, Essays in Honour of Sir Roy Harrod, (W.A. Eltis et al.(eds.)), Clarendon Press, London.

20.6 WORKS OF OTHERS

Arrow, K. J. (1960), "The Work of Ragnar Frisch, Econometrician," Econometrica, Vol.28, Apr.

Johansen, L. (1969), "Ragnar Frisch's Contributions to Economics," Swedish JE, Vol.71, No.4.

Rasmussen, P. N. (1987) "Frisch, Ragnar Anton Kittel," in The New Palgrave: A Dictionary of Economics, Macmillan, London.

CHAPTER 21

JAN TINBERGEN

(1903 – 1994)

Jan Tinbergen shared the ***Sveriges Riksbank*** Prize in Economic Sciences instituted in memory of Alfred Nobel for the year 1969 with Ragnar Frisch for their pioneering work on econometric model building.

The award is considered as a 'method award.' While the award to Frisch was for the development of general methodology of dynamic and econometric analysis for Tinbergen it was for his pioneering work in the empirical application of such methodology.

Tinbergen's contribution is summarised here while the contribution of Frisch is briefly covered in the preceding chapter.

21.1 A BRIEF BIOGRAPHICAL NOTE: JAN TINGERGEN

Jan Tinbergen, a pioneer in the development of econometrics linking statistics and mathematics to economic theory, was born in The Hague on April 12, 1903. He was educated at the University of Leiden, where he earned a doctoral degree in Physics. He was from 1929 to 1945, with many breaks for other activities, an official of the Netherlands' Central Bureau of Statistics, the economic planning unit of the Dutch government.

Beginning in 1933, he was also an Extraordinary Professor of Economics at the Netherlands School of Economics at Rotterdam, an institution he served for his entire academic career. During the period 1936 to 1938, he was economic adviser to the League of Nations at Geneva for the specific purpose of the development of econometric analysis of market variations in the U.S.A. At the end of World War II, in 1945, Tinbergen was appointed by the Dutch government as Director of the newly created Central Planning Bureau of the Netherlands. He served as director from 1945 to 1955. On his retirement from the Directorship of the Central Planning Bureau in 1955, the Extraordinary Professorship was converted into a full Professorship with a focus on development problems of less developed countries, which he held till 1973. Since then, besides teaching and research, he served as an adviser and consultant to numerous governments, especially of developing countries. He served from 1966 as Chairman of the United Nations' Committee for Development Planning.

A number of Universities and institutions worldwide, had awarded him honorary degrees (twenty). Jan Tinbergen died in The Netherlands on June 9, 1994. The Tinbergen Institute has been established in Rotterdam in his honour.

21.2 A BRIEF SUMMARY OF JAN TINBERGEN'S CONTRIBUTIONS

Bent Hansen divides Tinbergen's activities and contributions to economics into three groups, representing consecutive periods of his professional career. During each period, he made pioneering contributions to economics and helped set economics on a new track, opening up new vistas for both economic theory and policy. The totality of his work exerted "a profound and lasting influence within the field to which he devoted his attention and energy."

His contributions are divided under three broad heads.

1. Contributions to Econometrics;
2. Foundation of Quantitative Short-term Economic Policy Planning; and
3. Planning for Economic Cooperation and Development of Developing Countries.

21.2.1 CONTRIBUTIONS TO ECONOMETRICS

From the end of 1920's to World War II Tinbergen, along with some well-known economists like Ragnar Frisch and Irving Fisher, helped in the establishment of Econometrics as a science. In 1930, these three economists took the initiative in the creation of the Econometric Society. The constitution of the society says that it is "an international society for the advancement of economic theory in its relation to statistics and mathematics." Its main objective as spelt out in the constitution is "to promote studies that aim at a unification of the theoretical-quantitative approach and the empirical quantitative approach to economic problems and that are penetrated by constructive and rigorous thinking similar to that which has come to dominate in the natural sciences."

Besides being one of the founders of the Econometric Society, Tinbergen made some of the most fundamental early contributions to the subject. Among his important contributions, mention has to be made of the well-known cob-web theorems, shipbuilding cycles and related contributions to dynamic economics and statistical testing of business cycle theories. In agricultural markets that are uncontrolled, it is usually found that product prices and quantities sold move in opposite directions. This phenomenon cannot be explained in terms of the usual demand and supply theory. For explaining such market behaviour, economists have to resort to artificial assumption of repeated shifts in supply and/or demand curves. In a celebrated article (1930), Tinbergen sought to explain this phenomenon (using the regular demand and supply curves) by postulating that supply or production of agricultural products responds to market prices with a time lag of one year. This mechanism (explaining by the market phenomenon through introduction of one period lag) is referred to in literature as cob-web theorem.

The cob-web problem was explained by Joseph Schumpeter in his History of Economic Analysis by means of the following illustration: When farmers observe current prices of e.g., pork and fodder, they will decide to produce more or less hogs according as hog production is or is not profitable at this current relation between the prices of pork and fodder. But this decision cannot take effect before a certain period has elapsed. The resulting supply of pork will then impinge on the market and change the pre-existing relation between the prices of pork and fodder. This will induce new decision by the farmers and so on.

Tinbergen's formulation of the cob-web theorem had facilitated improved understanding of the price formation in agricultural markets. This innovation in the theory of a single market had profound repercussions on economic theory in general. Even though Wicksell's and Richardson's monetary theories were examples of formulating theories in dynamic terms, economic theory till the time of Tinbergen's development of cob-web theorem ran almost exclusively in static terms. Attempts to formalise dynamic economic theories, explaining a process over time, were rather rare. Tinbergen's work thus can be considered as the first crucial step in the development of modern dynamic economic theory.

Tinbergen, displaying the phenomenon for durable goods, in his 1931 article on the shipbuilding cycle employed the mathematical technique of difference equations which, by the end of 1930s, had become a standard method of dynamic analysis. The importance of Tinbergen's contribution to dynamic analysis can be gauged from this comment by Schumpeter in his History: "...readers of Professor Tinbergen's paper will note with concern the formidable list of assumptions contrary to fact that they are asked to accept.... On the other hand, however, schemata of this kind are first step toward a more perfect dynamic theory and must therefore be listed as pioneer ventures of first order of importance.... Such work cannot at present claim to be more than exploratory. But it explores the ground on which a new structure will stand some day." A great insightful comment indeed!

Another significant contribution to the field of Econometrics by Tinbergen is related to his work on statistical testing of business cycles. His work published by the League of Nations, Geneva, was in two volumes: 1. A Method and its Application to Investment Activity, and 2. Business Cycles in the United States of America, 1919-32. The first volume contains Tinbergen's explanation of his method – a combination of classical multiple regression analysis and Frisch's confluence analysis – and three examples of the application of the method. Tinbergen's study of investments showed that while market rate of interest was the major determinant of investment in residential construction, rate of profit was the main factor influencing the railway rolling stock. He found very little empirical support in favour of the acceleration principle.

The second volume comprised a macro model developed by Tinbergen for the United Sates economy. The size of the model consisting of 48 difference equations and definitional relations was at that time a novelty. This work of Tinbergen was a departure from the past work in regard to theory of business cycles and macroeconomic policy making. As regards the first, he showed how the cycle "could and should be considered a unified, single phenomenon to be explained by the properties of a complete dynamic model rather than to view it in terms of various phases of the cycle and to search for the causes of each of the phases as was the practice of business cycle theorists until that time."

The second volume of Tinbergen's work published by the League of Nations also paved the way for describing an economy in quantitative terms in a fashion that not only facilitated better understanding of the past developments but did also help making forecasts of future developments and designing suitable economic policies in an attempt to modify future developments in a desired direction. Though Keynes derisively described the work contained in the two volumes as 'alchemy,' in retrospect we can see that it has opened up a new branch of economics, viz., empirical macroeconomics. The significant improvements witnessed in macroeconomic theory, the availability of primary statistical data since 1930's and the progress in the establishment of statistical methods required for dealing with estimation problems arising in models of this type are in no small measure due to Tinbergen's work.

21.2.2 FOUNDATION OF QUANTITATIVE SHORT-TERM ECONOMIC POLICY PLANNING

After accepting the Directorship of the Central Planning Bureau of The Netherlands, Tinbergen turned his attention to building econometric models, which would enable him make reliable short-term economic forecasts as well as discuss rational policy measures required for achieving the chosen policy targets. While it is not possible to identify Tinbergen's personal contribution to the "Dutch model" and the other achievements of the Central Planning Bureau since the publications are confidential government documents, it is an incontrovertible fact that Planning Bureau's models had "grown out" of Tinbergen's 1936 model. In addition, by the time Tinbergen left the Bureau in 1955, the Bureau's model which Tinbergen helped building up was considered by many as a model with better predictive abilities than any other extant model at that time. The credit for this must go to Tinbergen who played a leading and pioneering role.

At the same time as he was working on building short-term models, Tinbergen worked on the theoretical problems of policymaking. He published in 1952 an important work – The Theory of Economic Policy, followed two years later by Centralization and Decentralization in Economic Policy. The latter served as a basis for rational thinking and quantitative computation in economic policy. The importance of these works on economic policy can be gauged when we recall that till that time the usual approach was to discuss each type of economic policy – fiscal policy, monetary policy, labour market policy, foreign exchange policy, etc., – separately, and examine each one of them in relation to a particular policy target – income distribution, price level, employment and balance of payments. Even when economists were forced by actual developments in the economy to examine several targets simultaneously, such as maintaining price level stability and the period of full employment, they had no way to deal systematically with such multi-target problems in the face of the non-existence of any such method. In this context Sukhamoy Chakravarty's observation is worth quoting: "While the result on quality instruments and targets is widely known (a result which is valid only in the case of linear systems with boundary conditions), the important contribution was in identifying the basic structure of a policy problem that was generally the inverse of what he (Tinbergen) called the 'analytical problem.' H. Theil and H. A. Simon extended the policy model by introducing stochastic elements."

Tinbergen's precise formulation of the multi-target problem and his suggested solution by simultaneous and coordinated use of a sufficient number of appropriately chosen instruments was inspired by a memorandum titled "Price-Wage-Tax-Subsidy Policies as Instruments in Maintaining Optimal Employment" by Ragnar Frisch to the United Nations in 1949. According to the noted economist Bent Hansen, "(Tinbergen) dealt with both the case of absolute targets and the case of maximizing a given social preference function, and solved a number of problems related to the efficiency of policy instruments, centralization and decentralization of policy decisions....His discussion was confined to so-called quantitative changes in the economy whereas problems related to changes in the economic system as such were left aside.... Tinbergen's basic work today is considered the obvious starting point for any discussion on general macroeconomic policy problems...."

When Tinbergen's theory of economic policy is compared with the modern welfare economics, which received specific attention of Anglo-Saxon academics during 1940s and 1950s, we find the former, though simple, is concerned with the real world macroeconomic targets and was very much applicable to the then current economic problems. In contrast, the Anglo-Saxon work was concerned with Pareto-optimal situations. It dealt with perfectly competitive market situations, which have no counterpart in real world. While there is no doubt that the theory was elegant, it is difficult to apply it to real world policy problems. One perceptive commentator pertinently observes: "(Tinbergen) has never been very much interested in esoteric theorizing for theory's own sake. His pre-occupation has always been quantification and empirical application." Tinbergen's approach is to make a frontal attack of basic economic problems on a broad scale "by means of crude methods" rather than conducting intensive studies of small isolated problems "by means of highly refined methods." In this context, Bent Hansen makes an apt comparison. "In the childhood of the automobile, the French engineer Panhard once commented upon the newly invented manual (unsynchronised) gear box: 'It is brutal, but it works'." Although brutality is the last thing one could associate with Tinbergen, Panhard's comment certainly applies to Tinbergen's economic methods.

Besides theoretical studies on economic policy discussed above, Tinbergen also covered a large number of quantitative policy problems in his 1956 publication: Economic Policy : Principles and Design.

21.2.3 PLANNING FOR ECONOMIC COOPERATION AND DEVELOPMENT OF DEVELOPING COUNTRIES

Tinbergen got interested in problems of economic cooperation, specifically after the creation of the European Common Market (ECM). His interest in the development problems of poor countries had arisen out of sincere desire for ameliorating the economic conditions in those countries and his attempt at repairing some of the evils of colonialism and "pay off some of the debts of old colonial powers – including his own country." Tinbergen's work on the theory and practices of long-term economic planning for growth is quite simple as he was conscious of the paucity of needed statistical information in developing countries and the limited skills of economic planners, bureaucrats and politicians in those countries. That is why he did not concern himself much with nor made any significant contribution to the then fashionable topics such as optimal growth paths, turnpike theorems and dynamic economic efficiency. He was aware of little practical importance of such topics that are basically extensions of modern welfare theory.

Tinbergen's contributions in this field – theory and practices of long-term economic planning for growth of developing countries – are divided mainly into three types of models (i) Planning by stages (ii) Models that have close affinity to Frisch's repercussion models and are a combination of models of Harrod, Domar and Keynes and input-output models of Leontief, and (iii) Semi-input-output models. The first type of model is perhaps the most widely used for planning in developing countries. It consists of planning at four stages. The first stage works out the aggregate investments and savings envisaged for the plan period followed by the next stage in which is determined the sectoral distribution of total investments, using a small input-output model and capital-output coefficients of various sectors. The third stage operation consists of preparing a regional growth plan, wherever necessary and feasible. The selection of specific investment projects in each sector determined by the use of investment criteria chosen on the basis of the country's policy targets forms the fourth stage of the plan. The clear disadvantages to this type of model include its failure to ensure efficiency in the economic system and its failure to plan implementation in terms of policy instruments (such as tax policy, credit and monetary policy etc.,) to be employed, besides the difficulty in arriving at a consistent solution to the model, especially in regard to external trade.

The second type of model, akin to Frisch's repercussion model, integrates the first two stages of the first type of model, explicitly incorporating the policy instruments in the model's solution. This model, however, does not attempt at optimising neither the choice of commodities to be produced in the economy, in regard to commodities to be traded nor the choice of technique to be employed. These deficiencies were sought to be remedied in Tinbergen's third type of model, the so-called Semi input-output model. This model starts with micro plans, taking into account individual investment projects, appraises each project using shadow prices reflecting international prices for the purpose of evaluating its global competitiveness, from which the macro plan emerges. The main feature of this model from the viewpoint of developing countries is its requirement of minimum amount of data.

The third and final model is considered the most ingenious contribution of Tinbergen to economic planning, despite its theoretical deficiencies and practical drawbacks. Bent Hansen argues in favour of this type of model developed by Tinbergen: "Given the production frontier of the country quite apart from scarcity of capital, shortage of competent engineers and lack of information about technical possibilities may make the frontier far inside that of the developed countries – a country may simply not have the specialists...needed for finding the optimal point on its frontier. Lack of technical knowledge and inefficiency within the given technical knowledge are both of them characteristics of underdevelopment."

Whatever may be the drawbacks or deficiencies in the models of economic planning developed by Tinbergen for developing countries, one can hardly ignore his concern for the development of developing countries and the sincere efforts he had made for promoting planning in the Third World countries like India. There are critics of Tinbergen's planning models from Third World countries who argue that planning in general and his methods in particular have done more harm than good. However, those who support Tinbergen's efforts for promoting development in developing countries counter this criticism. Their reply runs on these lines: "The relatively disappointing performance of the Third World during the Development Decade has been caused much more by bad internal policies and implementation than by planning or external difficulties. Without people like Tinbergen, and their patient indefatigable efforts things would, however, have been worse than they are. Those people and their methods should not be blamed for the follies and imperfections of governments and politicians in underdeveloped countries."

21.3 OTHER CONTRIBUTIONS

Besides those discussed above, Tinbergen made contributions to a number of fields in the subject and contributed to the solution of many economic problems which the nations were facing. The fields in which he worked and made contributions include empirical determination of supply and demand, imperfect competition, issue of stability in economic systems, the question of non-linearities in cyclical models, national accounting, optimum problems in national savings, theory of interest, international commodity agreements, international factor price equalisation, problems relating to balance of payments, tariff unions and problems of education and growth.

21.4 CONCLUDING OBSERVATIONS

The selection of Ragnar Frisch and Jan Tinbergen for the award of the first Nobel Memorial Prize in Economics was widely welcomed by the economists. According to Assar Lindbeck "Frisch and Tinbergen were...instrumental in developing a formalized theory of the relation between instruments and targets of economic policy."

Paralleling Meade's analysis of similar issues, Frisch and Tinbergen gave these theories a form that was favourable for empirical quantification and statistical testing. Together and individually they contributed significantly to the development of the subject of Economics and have helped greatly in the subject's progress towards its being deserving the name of a science among all the branches of social sciences. Tinbergen's undisputed claim to the conferment of the first Nobel Prize in Economic Sciences can be buttressed by his pioneering work in modern development planning in developing countries and in modern economic dynamics, his efforts, along with others, in establishing econometrics, his founding of empirical macroeconomics, his decisive contributions to create modern techniques of forecasting and above all in founding the modern theory of economic policy. He is considered a "Schumpeterian" figure in economics. We may quote from Chakravarty's tribute: "His great quest has been always to use economics to determine the contours of a humane society. His research amply reflects this feature along with his scientific imagination and sense of empirical relevance." Tinbergen's work has provided the necessary stimulus for the extensive model-building that has taken place throughout the world in recent years.

It is of interest to note that four years after Jan Tinbergen was awarded Nobel Prize in Economic Sciences, his younger brother Nikolaas (Nico) Tinbergen was awarded the Nobel Prize in Physiology or Medicine jointly with Karl Von Frisch and Konrad Lorenz. According to one commentator "Two brothers with different natures seem to duplicate each other's fate. The adventurous Nico did not have brother Jan's quiet nature and love for study. Still both were rewarded for their individual efforts arrived at through different methods. They did share several factors: genes and family upbringing that encouraged intellectual curiosity and independent thinking. And they certainly got the same encouragement from their family to do what they liked best, and to do it well. Well enough to be given the highest accolade one can get for their respective fields. No matter what the critics may say."

21.5 SELECT BIBLIOGRAPHY OF JAN TINBERGEN'S WORKS

21.5.1 BOOKS

1939 Business Cycles in the United States, 1919-32, League of Nations, Geneva.

1951 Business Cycles in the United Kingdom, 1870-1914, North Holland, Amsterdam.

1952 On the Theory of Economic Policy, North Holland, Amsterdam.

1954 Centralization and Decentralization in Economic Policy, North Holland, Amsterdam.

1956 Economic Policy: Principles and Design, North Holland, Amsterdam.

1959 Selected Papers, North Holland, Amsterdam.

1962 (with H.C. Bos) Mathematical Models of Economic Growth, McGraw-Hill, New York.

1964 Essays in Regional and World Planning, National Council of Applied Economic Research, New Delhi.

1965 International Economic Integration, Elsevier, New York.

1967 (with J. Linemann and J. B. Pronk) Convergence of Economic Systems in East and West, Oslo.

1968 On the Theory of Economic Policy, North Holland, Amsterdam.

1969 (with L. B. M. Mennes and J. G. Waardenburg) The Element of Space in Development Planning, North Holland, Amsterdam.

1974 The Dynamics of Business Cycles: A Study in Economic Fluctuations, University of Chicago Press, Chicago, Ill.

1978 Economic Policy: Principles and Design, North Holland, Amsterdam.

1981 Centralization and Decentralization in Economic Policy, Greenwood, Westport.

21.5.2 ARTICLES

1946 "Unstable Equilibria in the Balance of Payments," in Economic Research and the Development of Economic Science and Public Policy, NBER, New York.

1947 "The Netherlands Central Economic Plan for 1947," Swiss Journal of Economics and Statistics, Vol.83, No.1.

1951 "Reformulation of Current Business Cycle Theories as Refutable Hypotheses," Conference of Business Cycles, NBER, New York.

1961 "The Spatial Dispersion of Production: A Hypothesis," Swiss Journal of Economics and Statistics, Vol.97, No.4.

1964 "Possibilities for Application of Operations Research to Problems of Development," Management Science, Vol.10, No.2.

1970 "A Positive and a Normative Theory of Income Distribution," Review of Income and Wealth, Vol.16, No.3.

1972 "The Impact of Education on Income Distribution," Review of Income and Wealth, Vol.18, No.3.

1974 a "Substitution of Graduates by Other Labour," Kyklos, Vol.27, No.2.

b "Ragnar Frisch's Role in Econometrics: A Sketch," European Economic Review, Vol.5, No.1.

1976 "The Demand-Supply Theory of Incomes Tested by 1970 Census Figures," Review of Income and Wealth, Vol.22, No.2.

1979 "How to Reduce the Incomes of the Two Labour Elites?" European Economic Review, Vol.10, No.2.

1980 "Two Approaches to Quantify the Concept of Equitable Income Distribution," Kyklos, Vol.37, No.1.

1981 a "Some Neglected Determinants of Welfare Functions," Journal of Economic Psychology, Vol.1, No.1.

b "The Use of Models: Experience and Prospects," Nobel Lecture, AER, Vol.71, No.6, Special Issue.

1991 "On the Measurement of Welfare," Journal of Econometrics, Vol.50, No.1-2.

1992 "Optimal Redistribution," Indian Economic Review, Vol.27, pp. 1-4.

1995 "The Duration of Development," JEvolE, Vol.5, No.3.

1996 "Is 0.7% Development Assistance Enough?" Social Indicators Research, Vol.39, No.3.

21.6 WORKS OF OTHERS

Bos, H.C. (1979). "Jan Tinbergen" in International Encyclopaedia of the Social Sciences, Vol.18, Biographical Supplement, Free Press, New York.

Chakravarty, S. (1977), "Tinbergen, Jan," The New Palgrave: A Dictionary of Economics, Macmillan, New York.

Hansen, B. (1969), "Jan Tinbergen: An Appraisal of His Contributions to Economics," Swedish JE, Vol. 71, No.4.

Klassen, L.H., Koyck, L.M., and Witteveen, H.J. eds. (1959), Selected Papers by Jan Tinbergen, North Holland, Amsterdam.

CHAPTER 22

WASSILY WASSILYOVICH LEONTIEF

(1906 – 1999)

Professor Wassily Leontief, of Harvard University, USA, was awarded the Nobel Memorial Prize in Economic Sciences for 1973 for the "development of the input-output method and its application to important economic problems." He was the sole and undisputed creator of the important innovation, namely the input-output technique. His innovation has provided economic science an empirically useful method to highlight the general interdependence in a society's production system. The method provides tools for a systematic analysis of the complex inter-industry transactions in an economy.

Input-output analysis describes the interdependence in a country's production system as a network of deliveries between various production sectors. For every production sector, technical coefficients define the quantities of intermediate products required per unit produced of each commodity.

The input-output model usually treats final demands of production for consumption, investment and exports as determined by conditions exogenous to the production system. The purpose of this exercise is to determine the increase in production in various sectors of the economy to meet a given planned increase in final demand for consumption, investment and exports. The increased production in each sector has to be adequate both for the changes in the final demand and the derived changes in demand for intermediate products in various production sectors.

The usefulness of the input-output system developed by Leontief is underscored by extensive use in forecasting and planning in short term as well as in the long run in quite different types of economic systems, including decentralised market economies, as well as centrally planned economies. It has been also found useful in studies of how cost and price changes are transmitted through various sectors of an economy.

The citation refers to the later extension of the method to include smoke, water pollution etc., thus studying the effects of production on a country's environment.

22.1 A SHORT BIOGRAPHICAL SKETCH: WASSILY LEONTIEF

Wassily Wassilyovich Leontief was born on 5th August, 1906 in St. Petersburg (now Leningrad), only child of an academic family. His father was a professor of economics. He entered the University of Leningrad in 1921. After studying philosophy, sociology and finally economics, Leontief received the degree of Learned Economist in 1925. He continued his studies at the University of Berlin and received the Ph.D. degree in 1928. While still working on his doctorate, Leontief was appointed as a research economist of the Institute for World Economics at the University of Kiel from 1927 to 1930. During this period, he was engaged in research on derivation of statistical demand and supply curves. This academic work was interrupted in 1929 by a year's stay in China as advisor to the Ministry of Railways in Nanking.

Leontief moved in 1931 to the National Bureau of Economic Research (NBER) in New York and to the Department of Economics at Harvard University in 1932 where he remained for the following forty-four years. He became Professor of Economics in 1946, organised the Harvard Economic Research Project in 1948, and served as the Project Director until 1973. He became Chairman of the Harvard Society of Fellow in 1965.

Leontief attained worldwide eminence, particularly for the development and application of input-output analysis. Prominent among the honours Leontief received during those years were two Guggenheim Fellowships and election as President of the American Economic Association, 1970. He was elected President of Econometric Society in 1954, Honorary Fellow, Royal Statistical Society, London, and member of the American Philosophical Society, American Academy of Arts and Sciences and International Statistical Institute. He received honorary doctorates from a number of universities including University of Pennsylvania, University of Paris (Sorbonne), Karl Marx University of Budapest, Hungary and University of Brussels.

Wassily Leontief died on February 5, 1999.

22.2 A SUMMARY OF WASSILY LEONTIEF'S CONTRIBUTIONS

Leontief's prime contribution – Input-Output Economics is covered under the following heads:

1. Input-output Analysis;
2. The input-output Model;
3. Two Major Theorems of Input-Output Analysis.

22.2.1 INPUT-OUTPUT ANALYSIS

The discovery and development of input-output analysis is widely recognised as Leontief's 'major life work.' Robert Dorfman observes: "whoever thinks of Wassily Leontief thinks of input- output and vice-versa.... But Leontief is not a one idea, one gadget economist....the discovery of input-output might well be regarded as the most inevitable result of the kind of economist that he is. He strongly believes that economics is an empirical and applied science and that the only litmus test of economic research is its empirical importance and its practical implications." Furthermore, Leontief had always emphasised that economic concepts are 'meaningless and misleading' unless they could be observed and measured.

Two characteristics of Leontief that standout in his career are strong training in mathematics which helped his 'adroitness' at mathematical expression and analysis and his consistent emphasis on the need for the theoretical concepts to be amenable for application in economic research. The interdependence of the various sectors of a country's economy, the essence of input-output analysis, has long been recognised and appreciated by economists. As a purely theoretical construct, it has had a long genealogy. It can be, in fact, traced from Richard Cantillon. In the 18th century, Francois Quesnay, a French economist and leader of the Physiocrats used his Tableau Economique (1758) to illustrate the relationships between agriculture and other sectors of the economy. By a similar two-sector table, Karl Marx, a century later, demonstrated the relationship between the capital goods sector and consumer goods sector of an economy. The most important predecessor of Leontief, however, was Leon Walras who developed "a closed system of functional relationships connecting the activity levels of all components of an economy." With Leontief's work, "the time-honored theory was lifted out of the text books and treatises and placed in the arena of applied economic analysis."

Leontief's outstanding contribution lies in cutting a Gordian knot of the complexity of the interactions and inter-relationships between various sectors of a modern economy. That is how Leontief translated the theoretical structure of the input-output model into a practical reflection of an actual economy, which could serve as the basis for recommendations of policy. His achievement was to see the solution of this problem in matrix algebra. Modern computers have helped translate input-output analysis into a practical proposition as input-output computations involve inverting large matrices.

Another difficulty in the way of practical application of the input-output model is the type of data required--namely coefficients specifying the amounts of various raw materials and intermediate products needed to produce one unit of output in each sector. Many of such coefficients are available in the U.S. Census of Manufactures and laborious efforts have to be put in to compile the rest.

Leontief started compiling coefficients for a 44-sector input-output table around 1933-1934 (about 2000 coefficients). The first result of this study "Quantitative Input and Output Relations in the Economic System of the U.S." appeared in 1936. In 1937, he published "Interrelation of Prices, Output, Savings and Investment." Leontief's definitive monograph, The Structure of the American Economy, 1919-1929 was published in 1941. The theoretical analysis in this monograph demonstrates the inspiration of Walras. Leontief's reformulation for empirical research work resulted in a shift in emphasis of the system. While Walras subordinated the issue of the intermediate goods, Leontief brought to the fore the purchases of various industries from each other in the production of final output.

The first version of the work of Leontief was what is called the 'closed' input-output system. The monograph established the usefulness of such tables for economic planning. Within a few years, the U.S. Bureau of Labor Statistics constructed a 400-sector input-output table for projecting post-war employment by major industries. Leontief worked as a consultant to the Bureau. Later, many other countries used this method to formulate economic development plans.

As Input-Output analysis became a major field of economic research activity, Leontief could establish the Harvard Economic Research Project for applying and extending such analysis. He became Founder Director of the Project and headed it for the next twenty-five years. His work at the center included development of inter-regional input-output analysis, and introduction of capital co-efficient matrices to obtain the implications for investment of changes in final demand. This work resulted in two publications, The Structure of American Economy 1919-1939 in 1951 and Studies in the Structure of the American Economy in 1953.

22.2.2 THE INPUT-OUTPUT MODEL

The model makes assumptions aimed at simplifying the linear multi-market analysis. Utility functions are omitted and consumer demands are usually treated as exogenous. Equilibrium of individual consumers is not explicitly considered. The unit of production is not the firm but industry. Each industry produces a single homogenous output using a single linear production activity. This restriction, of course, can be relaxed by interpreting this as a composite commodity, which consists of several items produced in fixed proportions. Each industry uses as inputs both produced and non-produced outputs. Another crucial assumption is that in any production process all inputs are used in fixed proportions. Further, the use of these inputs expands in proportion with the output level – a special case of an assumption of constant returns to scale but far more restrictive.

Essentially, the input-output analysis involves solution of a set of n-simultaneous linear equations in n-variables.

The following explanation of the analysis from the ECONOMIST's Dictionary of Economics is helpful in understanding the topic.

The output of a good or service in an economy is used either in the production of goods and services (including itself) or it goes into final consumption, e.g. households, exports, government. Each output in an economy can be represented by an equation, with output equal to its final consumption plus the sum of its inputs used in all production activity throughout the economy. The amounts used in production will depend on the production function for each. Consider the simplified model of two commodities Y_1 and Y_2

$$Y_1 = C_1 + a_{11}Y_1 + a_{12}Y_2$$

$$Y_2 = C_2 + a_{21}Y_1 + a_{22}Y_2$$

Y_1 and Y_2 are total outputs.

C_1 and C_2 are the final consumptions for each, and a_{11}, a_{12}, a_{21} and a_{22} are the input-output coefficients representing the amounts of Y_1 and Y_2 required to produce one unit of Y_1 and Y_2.

These equations may be put in the matrix form:

$$Y = C + AY$$

or

$$Y = (1-A)^{-1} C$$

where

Y is the vector Y_1, Y_2,

C is the vector C_1, C_2, and

A the matrix

$$\begin{bmatrix} a_{11} & a_{12} \\ a_{21} & a_{22} \end{bmatrix}$$

AY is the total of intermediate demands and A is the matrix of input-output coefficients or technology matrix.

By structuring the production functions of the economy in this way, it is possible to trace the effects of a change in final demand, or change in output of one good or service, throughout its inter-industry linked relationships so that the knock-on effects on other industries may be measured.

22.2.3 TWO MAJOR THEOREMS OF INPUT-OUTPUT ANALYSIS

22.2.3.1 THE SAMUELSON SUBSTITUTION THEOREM

One of the restrictive assumptions of the input-output analysis listed above is the premise that there are fixed technological coefficients to produce a unit of output and that no other input proportion is possible. The firm has no choice but to use the same input proportion dictated by technology. It cannot adopt, say, capital saving or labour saving devices.

Paul Samuelson had proved (in an article that appeared in Tjalling C. Koopmans(ed.) Cowles Commission Monograph Activity Analysis of Production and Allocation) that in certain circumstances this restriction is not serious. He had proved that even where variation in input proportion is possible it will never be advantageous for the firm to use provided that:

there are constant returns to scale;

there is only one scarce input (say labour, or capital); and

there are no joint products.

That is, the fixed input-output relation may be dictated by considerations of productive efficiency rather than technological requirements.

However, if there is more than one scarce factor of production, the substitution theorem no longer holds.

22.2.3.2 THE HAWKINS-SIMON CONDITIONS

The formulation of an input-output system does not guarantee that it has a general solution with all non-negative numbers. If the solution yields one or more negative numbers, the implication is that negative outputs of some commodities are required in order to achieve the final consumption targets, which is not meaningful.

Hawkins and Simon had derived mathematical conditions that provide us with mathematical requirements which must be met by any meaningful and acceptable input-output system. As such, Hawkins-Simon conditions can be used as a basis for further theoretical analysis.

There are a number of important applications of Leontief's input-output analysis some of which deserve to be mentioned here.

Leontief first applied his input-output analysis to the problems of international trade in an article "Exports, Imports, Domestic Output and Employment" published in the Quarterly Journal of Economics (1946). He returned to this application in 1954-56, in a couple of papers: "Domestic Production and Foreign Trade: the American Capital Position Re-examined" (1954) and "Factor Proportions and the Structure of American Trade: Further Theoretical and Empirical Analysis (1956)." Using the input-output technique, he estimated the relative capital and labour contents of American exports and imports and reached a 'surprising' conclusion that American exports are more labour-intensive than U.S. imports in the sense that the capital per person required to produce $ 1 million of exports was less than the capital per person required to produce $1 million in import substitutes. This seemed to go against the general belief that the US was abundant in capital compared with labour.

Leontief's finding was in contradiction to the received theory (The Heckscher-Ohlin-Samuelson model) of international trade with two factors of production and two commodities that it has been called 'Leontief Paradox.' In the words of Lerner, "it is difficult to find another empirical result that has had as great an impact on the intellectual development of the discipline." Among the explanations of the finding, the following are noteworthy.

1. High Productivity of US Workers;
2. Reversal of Factor Intensities;
3. Capital- biased US Consumption;
4. Abundance of Human Capital;
5. Abundance of Natural Resources;
6. Tariffs; and
7. Technological Differences.

The very simple theoretical foundation for the Leontief calculation was put forward by Leamer in his 1980 article in the Journal of Political Economy showing that Leontief's data in fact reveal the US to have been abundant in capital compared with labour.

Edward Leamer States: "The Leontief Paradox (1954) rests on a simple conceptual misunderstanding. It makes use of the intuitively appealing but none-the-less false proposition that if the capital per man embodied in exports is less than the capital per man embodied in imports, the country is revealed to be poorly endowed in capital relative to labor. This is a true proposition if the net export of labor services is of the opposite sign of the net export of capital services, but when both are positive, as in Leontief's data, the proper comparison is between the capital per man embodied in consumption. Leontief's figures, which produced the so-called result that the U.S. exports are less capital intensive than the U.S. competing imports, can also be used to show that U.S. net exports are more capital intensive than U.S. consumption, which infact implies that capital is abundant relative to labor. There is no paradox if the conceptually correct calculations are made."

It is in 1946 again that Leontief studied the input-output analysis of inflationary processes in his Quarterly Journal of Economics paper "Wages, Profits and Prices" in which he showed how wage and price increases emanating from different sectors of the economy get diffused throughout the price structure. As the problem of inflation continues to be important, the powerful methods initiated by Leontief continue to be employed for analysing inflationary processes.

The Harvard Economic Research Project under the leadership of Leontief had made numerous other applications of input-output analysis, including computations of the direct and indirect effects of U.S. defence expenditures on the individual sectors of the economy and methods for projecting sectoral growth paths in a developing economy and estimation of capital requirements for economic development. As input-output analysis has been found to be an essential component of economic development planning, a large number of nations (including India) – at least fifty as per one count – have been compiling input-output tables, for nations as also sub-national regions.

Though Leontief's interest was in basic static input-output tables, he later got interested in extending his studies to developing the theory of dynamic input-output models. For a number of reasons-- both theoretical and statistical – Leontief was not as successful; dynamic input-output analysis remained largely a text-book theory. Another area of extended interest to which he devoted some effort is the study of inter-regional and international trading relationships – a spatial extension.

Later in his career, Leontief turned his attention to a study of the problems of 'world-wide' economic growth, the impact of growth on environment, its demand on the natural resources of the world, and specially on its implications for relations between the economies of the first world and the third world countries. He had directed an extensive study under the auspices of the United Nations on the evolution of the world economy until the year 2000 based on a multi-regional input-output model consisting of 15 regions, each consisting of 45 sectors and linked by balanced trading relationships. The study brought out an important and illuminative finding that "under a wide range of plausible assumptions, little progress would be made in closing the gap between the industrial and the developing regions unless current policies concerning international trade and finance were changed drastically in the direction of increased multinational aid and an increased flow of imports from the third world to the first."

22.3 CONCLUDING OBSERVATIONS

Robert Dorfman summarising Leontief's contribution to economics makes a specific mention of Leontief's "extremely keen mind with a strong critical and empirical bent as also the great technical and logical skill." While Leontief contributed a major innovation, 'novelty and originality' are not what Leontief seems to strive for in his work. Though input-output analysis is, no doubt, a development in the art of applying economics to practical problems, it is not a progress in economic theory proper; "in some respects it is a retreat," according to Dorfman. To put Leontief's contribution in a proper perspective, Dorfman remarks that the nature of the contribution is illuminated by a "fortuitous coincidence." Piero Sraffa's publication, Production of Commodities by Means of Commodities: A Prelude to a Critique of Economic Theory presents "a very elegant independent discovery of the theoretical basis of input- output analysis." Dorfman comments: "Therein lies all the difference between an insightful contribution to economic theorizing and the discovery of a practical new tool of analysis.... Leontief was not content until he had showed how they could be measured...and presents some interesting and important logical relationships and confirmed empirically, and applied to practical problems. It is the implementation that makes the discovery significant."

Input-Output analysis, now called inter-industry analysis, is widely used.

Leontief's tables are commonly used by the World Bank, the United Nations and the U.S. Department of Commerce.

Throughout his life Leontief campaigned against "Theoretical Assumptions and Non-observed Facts," the title of the speech he delivered as President of the American Economic Association.

Assar Lindbeck comments: "....[Leontief's] is also well suited to an analysis of the short-term effects of shocks in one sector on the other sectors of the economic system. The candidacy of Leontief was greatly enhanced by the fact that he also pioneered in applying his method to empirical data. There is a parallel between Tinbergen's contribution to make macroeconomic theory empirically operational and Leontief's inter-industry operational."

Leontief Medal for 'Achievement in Economy' was established by the Russian Academy of Natural Science in 2002.

We could do no better than close the essay with a fitting tribute, again, by Dorfman. "To resort to a faddish word, he is and always been concerned with the 'relevance' of economics and with its application to 'relevant problems.' Herein lies his pre- eminence....

The discovery of input-output is a fitting capstone to his combination of scientific soundness and technical brilliance."

22.4 SELECT BIBLIOGRAPHY OF WASSILY LEONTIEF'S WORKS

22.4.1 BOOKS

1941 The Structure of the American Economy, 1919-1929: An Empirical Application of Equilibrium Analysis, Harvard University Press, Cambridge, MA.

1951 Second Edition of the Above, Oxford University Press, New York.

1953 (with H.B. Chenery et al.) Studies in the Structure of the American Economy: Theoretical and Empirical Explorations in Input-Output Analysis, Oxford University Press, New York.

1966 a Essays in Economics: Theories and Theorizing, Oxford University Press, New York.

b Input-Output Economics, Oxford University Press, New York.

22.4.2 ARTICLES

1933 "The Use of Indifference Curves in the Analysis of Foreign Trade," QJE, Vol.47, No.3.

1936 a "The Fundamental Assumption of Mr. Keynes's Monetary Theory of Unemployment," QJE, Vol.51, No.1.

b "Composite Commodities and the Problem of Index Numbers," Econometrica, Vol.4, No.1.

1937 a "Implicit Theorizing: A Methodological Criticism of Neo-Cambridge School," QJE, Vol.51, No.2.

b "Inter-relation of Prices, Output, Savings and Investment: A Study of Empirical Application of Economic Theory of General Interdependence," REStat, Vol.19, No.3.

1938 "The Significance of Marxian Economics for Present Day Economic Theory," AER, Vol.28, No.1.

1944 "Output, Employment, Consumption, and Investment," QJE, Vol.58, No.2.

1946 a "Exports, Imports, Domestic Output, and Employment," QJE, Vol.60, No.1.

b "Wages, Profits, and Prices," QJE, Vol.61, No.1.

1947 a "Introduction to a Theory of the Internal Structure of Functional Relationships," Econometrica, Vol.15, No.4.

b "Postulates: Keynes's General Theory and the Classicists," in (S. Harris ed.) The New Economics, A. A. Knopf, New York.

1953 "Domestic Production and Foreign Trade: The American Capital Position Re-examined," Proceedings of the American Philosophical Society, Vol.97, No.3.

1955 "Some Basic Problems of Empirical Input-Output Analysis" in Input-Output Analysis: An Appraisal, Studies in Income and Wealth, Vol.18, NBER, New York.

1956 "Factor Proportions and the Structure of American Trade: Further Theoretical and Empirical Analysis," REStat, Vol.38, No.4.

1958 "Theoretical Note on the Time-Preference, Productivity of Capital, Stagnation and Economic Growth," AER, Vol.48, No.1.

1960 "The Rise and Decline of Soviet Science," Foreign Affairs, Vol.38, Jan.

1963 (with A. Strout) "Multi-Regional Input-Output Analysis," in Structural Interdependence, Proceedings of an International Conference on Input-Output Techniques, Geneva, 1961, MacMillan-St. Martin's Press, New York.

1969 "Input-Output Analysis," International Encyclopaedia of the Social Sciences, MacMillan and the Free Press, New York.

1970 "Environmental Repercussions and the Economic Structure – An Input-Output Approach," REStat, Vol. LII, No. 3.

1971 "Theoretical Assumptions and Non-Observed Facts," Nobel Lecture, AER, Vol.61, No.1.

1974 "Structure of World Production: Outline of a Simple Input-Output Formulation," AER, Vol.64, No.6.

1993 (with A. Brody) "Money-Flow Computations," Economic Systems Research, Vol.5, No.3.

22.5 WORKS OF OTHERS

Dorfman, R. (1973), "Wassily Leontief's Contribution to Economics," Swedish JE, Vol.75, No.2.

Dorfman, R. (1987), "Input-Output Analysis," The New Palgrave: A Dictionary of Economics, Macmillan, London.

Leamer, E. E. (1980), "The Leontief Paradox, Revisited", JPE, Vol. 88, No. 3.

Lindbeck, A. (2001), "The Sveriges Riksbank Prize in Economic Sciences in Memory of Alfred Nobel 1969:2007," in The Nobel Prize: The First 100 Years, W. Levinovitz and N. Ringertz (eds.), Imperial College Press and World Scientific Publishing Co. Pvt. Ltd., Singapore.

Sraffa, Piero (1960), Production of Commodities by Means of Commodities, Cambridge University Press, Cambridge.

CHAPTER 23

LEONID VITALIYEVICH KANTOROVICH

(1912 – 1986)

The Royal Swedish Academy of Sciences has awarded the Nobel Memorial Prize in Economic Sciences for 1975 jointly to Professor Leonid Vitaliyevich Kantorovich of the then U.S.S.R. and Professor Tjalling C. Koopmans, U.S.A. for their contributions to the theory of optimum allocation of resources. The Award announcement makes specific mention that Kantorovich and Koopmans had both done their most important scientific work in normative economic theory; that is, the theory of the optimum allocation of resources. They both had studied the problem (fundamental to all economic activity) as to how available productive resources can be employed to the greatest advantage in production of goods and services. This field of enquiry covers questions such as what goods to be produced, what production methods to be used and how much of current output to be consumed and how much to be saved and invested to create new resources for future production and consumption.

Formulating the problem and outlining the connections between productive inputs and production results, Kantorovich and Koopmans had achieved highly significant results. Early in his research, Kantorovich applied the analytical technique of linear programming to show how economic planning in his country could be improved. Koopmans for his part had demonstrated, for instance, that on the basis of certain efficiency criteria, it is directly possible to make important deductions concerning optimum price systems.

Kantorovich made his first contribution in the field of economic research as early as 1939 when he wrote an essay on the meaning and significance of an efficient use of resources in individual firms. In a number of publications, such as his book, The Best Use of Economic Resources, Kantorovich had analysed similar efficiency conditions for the entire economy. He demonstrated, in particular, the connection between the resource allocation and the price system, both at a certain point of time and in an economy that is experiencing growth. An important element in this analysis is to show how the possibility of decentralising decisions in a planned economy depends on the existence of a rational price system, including a uniform accounting interest rate to serve as a basis for investment decisions.

On his part, Koopmans, in a series of works, primarily, Analysis of Production as an Efficient Combination of Activities, had developed what is called "Activity Analysis." Within this theory, novel ways of interpreting the relationship between inputs and outputs of a production process were used to clarify the correspondence between efficiency in production and the existence of a system of computing prices. This sheds a new and interesting light on the connection between normative allocation theory and general equilibrium theory. During the 1960's, Koopmans studied the problem of finding criteria for an optimum growth rate of an economy. In this context, he paid special attention to factors, such as technological advance and population growth which, in a more fundamental sense, determine the value individuals and society place on consumption at different times.

Besides his contribution to the normative theory of resource allocation, Koopmans has done distinguished work in the field of econometric methods.

The award committee sums up their contributions thus: Kantorovich and Koopmans – largely independent of one another – have renewed, generalized and developed methods for the analysis of the classical economic problem as regards the optimum allocation of scarce resources.

While Kantorovich's contributions to economics are surveyed in this chapter, the next chapter 24, summarises the contribution of Koopmans.

23.1 A BRIEF BIOGRAPHICAL SKETCH: LEONID KANTOROVICH

Leonid Vitaliyevich Kantorovich was born in Leningrad (Petersburg) on 19th January 1912. His father Vitalij Kantorovich died when Leonid was 10 years old. Leonid graduated in Mathematics from the University of Leningrad in 1930. In the 1930's, he taught mathematics at a technical university in Leningrad. Between 1932 and 1934, he was also a teacher at his alma mater and from 1934 a Professor at the same university. He received his doctoral degree in mathematics in 1935. At that time, he worked at the Leningrad University and in the Institute of Industrial Construction Engineering.

The Thirties was a time of intensive development of functional analysis. Kantorovich made a systematic study of functional spaces with an ordering defined for some of pairs of elements. He was co-author of a book Functional Analysis of Semi ordered Spaces in 1950. Another book, Functional Analysis in Normed Spaces was co-authored by him and published in 1959. From 1958 to 1964 he was a corresponding member of Academy of Sciences of the then U.S.S.R. and from 1964, a full member in the mathematics section.

Kantorovich in his autobiographical note stated: "The Thirties was also important for me as I began my first economics.... In 1938, as a Professor of the University, I acted as a consultant for the Laboratory of the Plywood Trust... it was a problem of distributing some initial raw materials in order to maximize equipment productivity under certain restrictions. Mathematically, it was a problem of maximizing a linear function on a convex polytope." In 1939, the Leningrad University Press printed Kantorovich's booklet titled The Mathematical Method of Production Planning and Organization which contained the main ideas of the theories and algorithms of linear programming. The work remained unknown for many years to scholars in the West. From the late 1950's, he had published a long series of works on methods of economic calculation and planning. In 1959 appeared The Best Use of Economic Resources containing a broad exposition of the optimal approach to such central problems of economics as planning, pricing, rent valuations, stock efficiency and decentralisation of decisions.

Besides working in Leningrad, Kantorovich had for a long period directed along with V S Nemchinov the Department of Mathematical Economic Methods at the Siberian Division of the Academy of Sciences of the then U.S.S.R. He was awarded the Lenin Prize in 1965. He received the order of Lenin in 1967 and was Elected Fellow of Econometric Society in 1972. He received honorary degrees from the universities of Glasgow, Grenoble, Nice, Helsinki and Sorbonne.

Leonid Kantorovich died on April 7, 1986.

23.2 A BRIEF SURVEY OF CONTRIBUTIONS OF LEONID KANTOROVICH TO ECONOMICS

Kantorovich's contributions are all directly or indirectly concerned with the core economic problem of the optimal use of a nation's resources. Most important of these were his contributions to the development of linear programming and the implied importance of prices in relation to resources allocation, choice of techniques of production and so on. It is proposed to survey Kantorovich's major economic contributions under the following heads.

1. Linear Programming and its Origins;
2. Computational Techniques and Resolving Multipliers;
3. Transportation Planning Problem;
4. National Economic Planning and the Price System; and
5. Investment Criteria.

23.2.1 LINEAR PROGRAMMING AND ITS ORIGINS

Linear programming technique is helpful in finding the extremum (i.e. maximum or minimum) of a linear function of a set of variables that are subject to certain constraints: namely, linear equations, non-negativity requirements and possibly more general inequalities. Three aspects are involved in the development of linear programming.

1. Formulation of the problem. This also involves demonstration that a wide range of problems in economics involving optimisation can be cast in this form either directly or after making some transformations.
2. For practical solution of such problems, it is necessary to develop methods of computation and algorithms.
3. Clarification of theoretical aspects and implications--that is, essentially the theory of the dual problem and its relation to the primal problem.

The technique of linear programming has found extensive use in economic research since a wide range of economic problems can be formulated as linear programming problems. Furthermore, the technique opened up the road for practical implementation of computations for the purpose of optimising the resource use in many different fields since algorithms that have been developed enable solution to such problems even when they are of very large size in terms of variables as well as in terms of conditions. As Leif Johansen observes: "...the theory related to linear programming and especially the theory of the relation between the dual and primal problem, has served to elucidate many central economic problems, such as within the fields of general equilibrium theory and the theory of international trade." The development of game theory in continuous contact with linear programming is another example of the profound influence of linear programming on economic theory.

A brief history of the development of the field of linear programming may be in order. Dantzig, who was a member of a group of economists and mathematicians working with the problems of allocation of resources for the United States Air Force during World War II, was credited with formulating a general linear programming problem and developing a method (simplex method) for solving such problems in 1947. It was included in the 1951 Cowles Commission Monograph No.13 (T C Koopmans (ed.), <u>Activity Analysis of Production and Allocation</u>) in which are included many other contributions to the linear programming theory. The paper of Koopmans in the volume "Analysis of Production as an Efficient Combination of Activities" is of special significance from the viewpoint of economic theory.

This is the "conventional history" of the development of linear programming until it came to be known that already in 1939 Kantorovich had developed a mathematical model for "organizing and planning production" which is essentially a linear programming model and, more importantly, it had contributed in all three directions mentioned at the beginning of this survey[(1), (2) and (3)]. Kantorovich's work from 1939 became known and available to the world outside the then Soviet Union when the journal, <u>Management Science,</u> carried an English translation of the work in 1960. The initiative for the translation and publication was taken by Koopmans.

Kantorovich's earlier work since 1939 was concerned with the treatment of planning problems at the micro level, mainly within the enterprise. The problem he formulated took the form of maximising a linear function which expresses the total number of complete articles (machine tools) as a function of variables which indicate the time each machine tool is used in order to produce each type of component. The maximisation takes place under certain given conditions in the form of equations expressing the fact that the total time a machine tool is used to produce different components should be equal to the total time available and the conditions in the form of inequalities that express the fact that the time a machine tool is used to produce a certain component cannot be negative. In his later work, Kantorovich introduced additional constraints. In the most general formulation, he introduced the possibility that a machine tool may perform several operations in order to produce different components at the same time.

Concerning the fields of applications to which Kantorovich exemplified in the Management Science paper, Koopmans said "that the wide range of applications perceived by the author makes his paper an early classic in the science of management under any economic system." Dantzig in his "Linear Programming and Extensions" characterises Kantorovich's contribution in the following manner: "Kantorovich should be credited with being the first to recognize that defined mathematical structures which, he believed, were amenable to practical numerical evaluation and could be numerically solved.... The report contains an outstanding collection of practical applications...." Johansen concludes: Kantorovich was "the first scholar to formulate the linear programming problem and to give a large and diversified set of examples of practical problems which can be dealt with and solved by this approach."

23.2.2 COMPUTATIONAL TECHNIQUES AND RESOLVING MULTIPLIERS

In his 1939 work, Kantorovich introduced certain variables which are called "resolving multipliers." He demonstrated that if the values of these multipliers were found for a certain problem, then the values of the original unknowns, namely, the variables which characterise production plans, transport plans and so on in physical units, could be found rather easily. Generally, the number of such resolving multipliers are smaller than the number of variables in the physical plan. For this purpose, Kantorovich developed an iterative procedure. After making preliminary estimates of the multipliers and computing the corresponding physical plan, a check is made whether that plan satisfies all the constraints of the problem. The multipliers are adjusted when there are discrepancies and new calculations of the corresponding physical plans are made. The next step is to carry out new tests to find out whether the revised physical plan satisfies all the constraints and so on. This step-by-step approach in the end will yield the optimal plan or a very good approximation of it.

However, the simplex method which was developed (in Western research) later by Dantiz is found to be superior to the above method of Kantorovich in that the former is more complete and easily programmed for computers. As a consequence, simplex method has become the standard method for solving linear programming problems. There exists, of course, certain kinship between the methods in that both methods are iteration methods and in both of them multipliers of the Lagrangean type play an important role. However, in this context, we may quote Johansen's comment: "Even if Western research on linear programming seems to have developed more efficient algorithms, it is accordingly possible that these early methods which were proposed by Kantorovich, but which never seem to have been completely developed, nevertheless contain ideas which may still prove to be of great importance."

The resolving multipliers have other uses as well. In the optimum solution to a linear programming problem, the resolving multipliers are the same as the dual variables. As pointed out above, Kantorovich demonstrated how the resolving multipliers could be used to give a criterion for whether or not a proposed solution is optimal. From this, theoretical property derived their usefulness in algorithms.

Multipliers indicate how marginal modifications of the conditions of the problem affect the value of the objective function. That is, the multipliers represent the marginal values of the limiting factors of the problem.

Later, there was some discussion as to how far Kantorovich interpreted his multipliers as 'shadow prices' or 'efficiency prices'. Koopmans said "...of greatest interest to the economist are the interpretations...of the dual variables of the linear programming, which the author [Kantorovich] calls resolving multipliers, and which have been called, among other names, efficiency prices in Western economic literature."

Charnes and Cooper suggest a careful and historical examination of the origin and development of the various ideas concerning linear programming and pertinently remark "when this has been done, it will then be possible to place Kantorovich's ideas in their proper perspective. We believe that the brilliance of his accomplishment will not lose any lustre if this kind of work is accurately and carefully done."

23.2.3 TRANSPORTATION PLANNING PROBLEM

One of Kantorovich's early papers published in the then U.S.S.R. was titled "On the Translocation of Masses." It is reported to be a brief, abstract mathematical paper, but it formulated in a general form a wide class of problems which Kantorovich by way of example specialised to a transportation planning problem. The essence of the problem is assigning places of consumption to places of production for commodities with the objective of minimising aggregate transportation costs. He posited necessary and sufficient conditions for optimum for this class of problems but did not develop efficient methods of computation for deriving such an optimum. However, critics have called it the 'locus classicus' for the abstract transportation problem.

Johansen is of the view that Kantorovich had continued to be especially interested in transportation problems and location of production facilities ever since. He also makes reference to a 1974 paper written by Kantorovich jointly with A. Zhuravel which illustrated empirically the great importance of the transport sector for the utilisation of economic resources and the great need of having a rational freight rate structure. The authors drew on empirical work on the cost structure, optimisation of transport and location plans and so on and argued for reforms in the freight rate system in the then U.S.S.R. Thus, it is seen that Kantorovich had contributed important papers in the two spheres (the very abstract 1942 paper and the very practice-oriented 1974 paper) managing "to retain the contact and fruitful interaction between the two spheres."

23.2.4 NATIONAL PLANNING AND THE PRICE SYSTEM

Besides his contribution at micro and enterprise level and to problems such as optimal planning of transportation and localisation, Kantorovich influenced macro issues such as ways of organising a socialist economy so as to achieve a high degree of efficiency in the utilisation of resources. He visualised a system of planning based on linear programming where, in addition to the main 'physical' aspects of the plan, shadow prices for the most important products and resources were obtained from the calculations. Kantorovich advocated using these as a basis for the price system in the economy. According to him, these prices could be a rational basis for decisions in regard to a large amount of choices in the economy. He also discussed the "relative stability" of shadow prices which were found by the solution of an optimisation problem. As such, shadow prices were associated only with those elements in the plan that were explicitly fed into the calculations carried out.

It appears that in the price system discussions in the then U.S.S.R., though Kantarovich's viewpoint received considerable support, it was not accepted as the sole basis for price fixation. It was because while Kantorovich's proposal was primarily concerned with the solution to the problem of resource allocation, the price system in an economy has many different functions.

23.2.5 INVESTMENT CRITERIA

Investment criteria and price problems are intimately related. Kantorovich argued for criteria based on his shadow prices or resolving multipliers. Similar to the role of interest rate in calculations of present value, the "normal efficiency of capital investment" has an important role. In economics literature in the West, investment criteria were generally discussed in an isolated fashion without taking a comprehensive view of optimisation in an economy as a whole. It is Johansen's opinion expressed in 1976 that Kantorovich's discussion on investment criteria is both lucid and constructive as Kantorovich derived his suggested criteria from the viewpoint of optimisation for the entire economy. He recognised the limitations of the investment criteria deduced from the linear programming formulation. He had also attempted computation of the norm by means of macroeconomic models. He discussed the numerical derivation of a norm of investment efficiency under different assumptions regarding forms of production functions and types of technological progress as also with a distinction between the roles of the consumption goods sector and investment goods sector.

23.3 CONCLUDING OBSERVATIONS

The work of Kantorovich outlined above and other works not referred to here establish him together with F.P Ramsey and J.von Neumann as the founders of the optimisation approach to the analysis of economic problems. He demonstrated the power of his method for analysis and improvement of the mechanism of economic management of a socialist economy. Kantorovich also proposed an 'original theory' of economic evaluation of technical ventures.

He was also a world-famous mathematician. He is reported to have made great contributions to a number of different branches of mathematics. He was author of about 300 scientific papers. In the opinion of Johansen: "Kantorovich is a distinguished mathematician but there is no doubt that we also have the right to include him among the ranks of the most outstanding economists of the last decades."

In his Nobel Prize lecture titled "Mathematics in Economics: Achievements, Difficulties, Perspectives" Kantorovich, after listing the achievements and outlining the difficulties encountered and expected, stated: "I am looking optimistically on the prospects of widespread use of mathematical methods, especially those of optimization, in economic science and in all-level economic control. It can give us a significant improvement of planning activity, better use of resources, increment of national income and living standards. The difficulties of modeling and data creation can be overcome like similar difficulties were overcome in the natural and technical sciences....The mathematicians, economists and practical managers have achieved a better mutual understanding."

23.4 SELECT BIBLIOGRAPHY OF LEONID KANTOROVICH'S WORKS (IN ENGLISH)

23.4.1 BOOKS

1965 The Best Use of Economic Resources, Pergamon Press, London & New York.

23.4.2 ARTICLES

1958 "On the Translocation of Masses," Management Science, Vol.5, No.1.

1960 "Mathematical Methods of Organizing and Planning Production," Management Science, No.4, July.

1964 a "Mathematical Methods of Production Planning and Organization," in The Use of Mathematics in Economics, A. Nove (ed.), Oliver & Boyd, Edinburgh & London.

b Further Development of Mathematical Methods and Prospects of their Application in Economic Planning, in "The Use of Mathematics in Economics," A. Nove (ed.), Oliver & Boyd, Edinburgh & London.

1974 (with A. Zhuravel) "The Role of the Transport Factor in the Location of Production," in Problems of Economic Transition, Vol. 17, No.7.

1975 "Mathematics in Economics; Achievements, Difficulties, Perspectives," Nobel Lectures, Economics. 1969-1980, Assar Lindbeck (ed.), World Scientific Publishing Co., Singapore, 1992.

23.5 WORKS OF OTHERS

1. Charnes A. and W. W. Cooper (1962), "On Some Works of Kantorovich, Koopmans and others," Management Science, Vol. 8, No. 3.
2. Dantzig, G.B. (1963), Linear Programming and Extensions, Princeton University Press, Princeton, NJ.
3. Johansen, L. (1966) "Soviet Mathematical Economics," EJ, Vol. 76, No. 303.

4. Johansen, L. (1967), "Review of L V Kantorovich: The Best Use of Economic Resources," EJ, Vol. 77, No. 305.
5. Johansen, L. (1976), "L. V. Kantorovich's Contributions to Economics," ScandJE, Vol.78, No.1.
6. Koopmans, T. C. (ed.) (1951) Activity Analysis of Production and Allocation, Cowles Commission Monograph No: 13, John Wiley & Sons, New York.
7. Koopmans, T. C. (1960), "A Note about Kantorovich's Paper, Mathematical Methods of Organizing and Planning Production," Management Science, Vol.6, No. 4.
8. Koopmans, T. C. (1962), "On the Evaluation of Kantorovich's work of 1939," Management Science, Vol.8, No.3.
9. Markorov, V. (1987) "Kantorovich, Leonid Vitaliyevich," The Modern Palgrave: A Dictionary of Economics, Macmillan, London.

CHAPTER 24

TJALLING CHARLES KOOPMANS

(1910 – 1985)

Tjalling Charles Koopmans shared the 1975 Prize in Economic Sciences in Memory of Alfred Nobel with Leonid Vitaliyevich Kantorovich of the U.S.S.R. The award was made for their contributions to the theory of optimum allocation of resources. While Kantorovich's contributions to the field have been summarised in the preceding chapter, Koopmans's contributions to Economic Sciences are covered in this chapter.

24.1 A BRIEF BIOGRAPHICAL NOTE: TJALLING KOOPMANS

T C Koopmans was born in 1910 in Cravelon in the Netherlands, the third son of Sjoerd Koopmans and Wijtske Vander Zee. Both parents were trained as school teachers. Koopmans studied physics and mathematics at the University of Utrecht. The great depression of 1930s (what Marxist economists described as the great crisis of capitalism) indicated to Koopmans that "...the economic world order was unreliable, unstable, and, most of all iniquitous." Karl Marx's Das Kapital, Vol. I, was the first book in economics that he studied. In Koopmans's own words: "While never accepting the labor theory of value, I was stirred by the famous chapter on the state of the English workers during the Industrial Revolution." From his explorations of Marxist thinking in his student years, Koopmans retained "a lifelong interest in the prior formulation of that fundamental part of economic theory that does not require specifying the institutional form of society to be used as a framework for the description and comparison of different economic systems."

Koopmans came to know from a friend in Utrecht that a new field called mathematical economics was being developed and that Jan Tinbergen was the leader in this field in the Netherlands. In 1933, Koopmans moved to Amsterdam where Tinbergen was then lecturing once a week. In the first half of that year, Koopmans had weekly tutoring from Tinbergen over lunch after his lecture. Koopmans was "deeply impressed by his [Tinbergen's] selflessness, his abiding concern for economic well-being and greater equality among all of mankind...his ingenuity in economic modelling and his sense of realism and wide empirical knowledge of economic behaviour relations."

Koopmans took his Ph.D. degree in mathematical statistics at the University of Leiden in 1936. The title of his Ph.D. dissertation is "Linear Regression Analysis of Economic Time Series." After teaching at the Netherlands School of Economics in Rotterdam, he was engaged as an economist at the League of Nations in Geneva in 1938. He moved to the United States in 1940 and first held a research post. Between 1942 and 1944, he worked as a statistician for the Combined Shipping Adjustment Board. He came to the University of Chicago in 1944, was appointed associate professor there in 1946 and professor in 1948. In the same year, he succeeded Jacob Marschak as Director of Research of Cowles Commission for Research in Economics (affiliated with the University of Chicago) for a six-year period.

In 1955, he moved, along with the Cowles Commission of which he was the research director at Yale University and became a Professor there. There was also another six-year stint as Director of the Cowles Foundation from 1961 to 1967. He was a member of the Economics faculty at Chicago from 1946 to 1955, and at Yale from 1955 to 1981.

His work had earned him great professional honours. He was elected President of the Econometric Society in 1950, Distinguished Fellow of the American Economic Association in 1971 and its President in 1978.

Koopmans died on February 26, 1985 at New Haven, U.S.A.

24.2 A BRIEF SURVEY OF TJALLING KOOPMANS'S MAJOR WORKS

Koopmans's major work on Activity Analysis is a deeper enquiry into the innermost content of the production side of resource allocation in an economy, simultaneously providing a new set of concepts and tools for understanding basic economic problems. The development of the field of Activity Analysis was linked to the development of linear programming and the modern theory of general equilibrium. In addition to the formulation of Activity Analysis, his initial efforts, until the beginning of 1950s, resulted in important contributions to the field of econometric principles and methods. During the late 1950's and early 1960's, Koopmans extended his work to a study of problems relating to inter-temporal resources allocation.

We propose to cover his contributions under the following three major heads.

1. Activity Analysis;
2. Inter-temporal Resources Allocation Theory; and
3. Econometrics

24.2.1 ACTIVITY ANALYSIS

The basic document, which presents a clear exposition of activity analysis by Koopmans is contained in Chapter III of Cowles Commission Monograph No.13 titled *Analysis of Production as an Efficient Combination of Activities*. The traditional theory of production was expressed in terms of production functions; in the process, analysing the management of production is ignored which implies that a large part of the actual process of resource allocation in an economy is outside the realm of economics.

Koopmans replaced the production function with a system of production in terms of the joint operation of a collection of separate activities, each characterised by fixed relations between inputs and outputs. In other words, he put forward a model of production involving, besides inputs and outputs of commodities, explicit recognition of the processes used in the course of production. We find this idea in Leontief's input-output analysis. Koopmans carefully distinguished various types of commodities, such as primary, intermediate and final. All the final commodities and some of the primary ones are desired; that is, being the object of consumption in activities outside the system. In Koopmans's formulation, each process was associated with a non-negative variable, which he termed the level of activity representing that process.

Koopmans's formulation is claimed to be more realistic than the traditional production function formulation. He argued: "Rare is the industrial firm that knows and charts its own production function as the economist defines it. The form in which knowledge of technological possibilities is kept and transmitted is usually quite different." Further, in real world, substitution generally occurs when levels of activities increase somewhere in the system and a decrease somewhere else. These important phenomena relating to production are captured by the activity analysis; they do not fit well into the production function approach.

Koopmans separated, in his work on activity analysis, the goals and optimising choices from the analysis of production itself; that is, the institutional framework in which production is carried out. He wanted to demonstrate "explicitly and clearly" the way in which efficiency is achieved. This follows from his acceptance of the principle of autonomy suggested by his teacher and colleague, Trygve Haavelmo.

In the general case, in which commodities of all categories are represented as infinite number (a set of commodities that is attainable in terms of technology as well as resources), Koopmans showed, that in a situation which is efficient, the prices are such as to make all activities actually carried out break even and all other activities unprofitable. The prices are positive for all final commodities and also for scarce resources. The prices are zero for primary commodities that are in excess supply, implying that they are free goods. In an efficient situation, intermediate commodities may command any price. In Koopmans's system, an interesting case arises related to commodities with negative price; that is, "no activity which allows the commodity to be disposed of without cost."

We can thus see that a perfectly competitive market system is characterised by prices and profitability outlined by the solution developed by Koopmans. As Werin aptly remarks "...the proof of the relation between efficiency and competitive prices had finally been put forth with perfect strictness; and remarkably, nothing else is needed except a description of technology and resources and an assumption as to which goods are the desired ones. ...his [Koopmans's] results just mean the price system is able to sustain an efficient situation once it is reached. Nothing is implied about the process by which such situations are arrived at."

One point that needs to be noted is that Koopmans, though he played an important role in the development of the field of linear programming, was 'reluctant' to apply linear programming to activity analysis proper. This may be because of his view that activity analysis "is, and should be a basic theory of production." By applying linear programming, the issue boils down to introducing a single maximisation which, in a decentralised economy, does not make any sense. As the idea of single maximisation in an economy is fundamentally false, under many circumstances it is "misleading or even dangerous" to use it. This unwillingness of Koopmans to introduce linear programming into the framework of activity analysis is an illustration of his keenness to maintain strict scientific standards.

24.2.2 THE THEORY OF INTER-TEMPORAL RESOURCE ALLOCATION

During the 1960's, the economics literature was enriched by articles that describe some path over time for the optimal use and pricing of scarce resources. There was indeed a breakthrough in the field of dynamic economic analysis and this development particularly started with contributions to the theory of capital and growth. There are a number of contributors of whom Koopmans was in the forefront. His contributions in three important fields, namely, efficiency in growth, optimality in growth and preference orderings of indefinite programs are specially to be mentioned. He is remembered in this field for his important theoretical contributions concerned with problems involving infinite horizon economies. Koopmans's papers published in 1965 and 1973 were devoted to the analysis of optimal economic growth (for example, "On the Concept of Optimal Economic Growth" and "Some Observations on 'Optimal' Economic Growth and Exhaustible Resources"). His papers written alone or in collaboration with others concerning preferences and their representation by real-valued utility functions over infinite horizon are of special interest making significant contribution to the field.

Optimal growth theory is concerned with analysing the level of economic growth that maximises social welfare. The basic article was by Frank Ramsey in 1928. According to Ramsey, given initial stock of capital, the optimal growth path imputed maximum satisfaction from the feasible consumption and investment over an infinite future. The starting point is the 'golden rule' (a concept similar to von Neumann's maximal growth) which, under a host of assumptions, shows that the optimal growth path will be the one that maximises consumption per worker over time. To assure determinateness, Ramsey employed an ingenious device; that is, the utility of consumption was constrained from above by bliss or production was satiated by capital at some finite level.

Koopmans attempted at developing the approach of Ramsey to the concept of optimal growth path. It was realised that Ramsey's restrictive assumption of bliss or saturation became necessary since in Ramsey's world population was constant and capital never depreciated. Once these assumptions are relaxed, a positive savings ratio is necessary for attaining a steady state of per capita consumption and per capita capital stock. The observations of Jungenfelt on this issue merit reproduction in toto. "Given the rates of population growth and depreciation, the steady state solution to per capita capital stock and per capita consumption can be affected only by changes in the savings ratio. With ordinary neo-classical production technologies, consumption per capita reaches its maximum in the golden rule path." Koopmans could abandon the concept of bliss of Ramsey with the help of golden rule. He then applied the turnpike theorems, which were already established, to a much simpler case.

Koopmans's 1964 joint paper with P. A. Diamond and R.E. Williamson demonstrated that it is possible to introduce a measure of time preference for a certain sub-class of utility functions which represent the given preference ordering. They formalised, what is termed, the concept of impatience (which was originally introduced by Bohm-Bawerk into the theory of the rate of interest). They demonstrated that impatience is a "necessary logical consequence of a set of postulates concerning utilities over infinite time horizons. The postulates include continuity and stationarity."

As regards contributions involving infinite time horizon, mention must be made of Koopmans's work on exhaustible resources and the problem of transition from exhaustible resources to renewable resources. It is also pertinent to refer to his work on modelling of alternative energy futures, a work Koopmans did for National Academy of Sciences, U.S.A.

24.2.3 ECONOMETRICS

Koopmans's doctoral dissertation "Linear Regression Analysis of Economic Time Series" (now a classic) is his earliest contribution to econometric methods. It is remarked that "in it [doctoral dissertation], he brought the insight of Frisch and the rigour of R.A. Fisher to linear regression when all variables are subject to errors of measurement." He proposed a synthesis of the errors-in-variables approach of Frisch and the errors-in-equation approach of R.A. Fisher, using the likelihood framework to the estimation of economic relations. Koopmans demonstrated the possibility of probabilistic characterisation of economic relations, even in circumstances where important deviations from the classical regression framework are necessitated by the nature of economic data.

Koopmans, in a paper titled "Measuring the Equation Systems of Dynamic Economics" co-authored with H. Rubin and R. B. Leipnik published in 1950, used the term 'identification' for the first time in econometrics. He also gave now familiar rank and order conditions for the identification of a single equation in a system of simultaneous linear equations. Koopmans obtained the solution to the identification problem in a case where there are a priori linear restrictions on the structural parameters.

Koopmans and his associates proposed the information-preserving maximum likelihood method, more commonly referred to as the Full Information Maximum Likelihood (FIML) method. These developments created a revolution in the theory and practice of econometrics. Subsequent work by associates of Koopmans led to what has come to be known as limited information maximum likelihood estimator, which is computationally much simpler. Later work by Theil, Zellner and others resulted in the development of still simpler Two Stage Least Squares (TSLS) estimator and Three-Stage Least Squares. In the words of Carl Christ and Leonid Hurwicz "Koopmans can fairly be said to be the father of simultaneous equation econometric methods, though it is clear that there were grandfathers and great grand fathers too."

24.3 CONCLUDING OBSERVATIONS

There is no doubt that, in addition to econometrics, Koopmans made outstanding contributions in several areas of economic analysis, both theoretical and applied some of which are summarised in the earlier part of the chapter. He made a number of contributions to the field of business cycles in his writings during 1940's. He had also shown interest in major macroeconomic issues such as inflation, in addition to business cycles.

Koopmans is widely recognised as a pioneer in the development of mathematical economics and econometrics. As head of the Cowles Commission from 1948 until 1967, Koopmans presided over a crucial period in the development of what is known as neo-Walrasian economics.

An important work of Koopmans is the "Three Essays on the State of Economic Science," which is referred to as a "pedagogical masterpiece." Besides containing less technical presentation of activity analysis, the book also deals with topics such as general theory of decentralised decision-making and of competitive equilibrium and its relation to Pareto efficiency as also some useful discussions on methodological problems. His review article on Burns and Mitchell's measuring business cycles titled "Measurement without Theory" is generally considered as Koopmans's most celebrated contribution to the debate on methodology. Koopmans concluded his review article by the categorical assertion that "the decision not to use theories of man's economic behavior, even hypothetically, limits the value to economic science and to the maker of policies, of the results obtained or obtainable by the methods developed."

In his Nobel lecture delivered on December 11, 1975, titled "Concepts of Optimality and their Use," Koopmans clarified: "According to a frequently cited definition, economics is the study of the 'best use of scarce resources.' The definition is incomplete. 'Second best' use of resources and outright wasteful uses, have equal claim to attention. They are the other side of the coin."

He concluded the lecture thus. "One final remark. The economist as such does not advocate criteria of optimality. He may invent them. He will discuss their pros and cons, sometimes before but preferably after trying out their implications. He may also draw attention to situations where overall objectives, such as productive efficiency, can be served in a decentralised manner by particularised criteria, such as profit maximisation. But the ultimate choice is made, usually only implicitly and not always consistently, by the procedures of decision making, inherent in the institutions, laws and customs of society. A wide range of professional competences enter into the preparation and deliberation of these decisions. To the extent that the economist takes part in the decisive phase, he does so in a double role, as economist and as a citizen of his polity: local polity, national polity, or world polity."

24.4 SELECT BIBLIOGRAPHY OF TJALLING KOOPMAN'S WORKS

24.4.1 BOOKS

1937 Linear Regression Analysis of Economic Time Series, De Erven F.Bohn, Haarlem.

1950 (ed.)Statistical Inference in Dynamic Economic Models, Cowles Commission Monograph No.10, Wiley, New York.

1951 (ed.)Activity Analysis of Production and Allocation, Cowles Commission Monograph No.13, Wiley, New York.

1953 (with W. C. Hood eds.) Studies in Econometric Method, Cowles Commission Monograph, No.14, Wiley, New York.

1957 Three Essays on the State of Economic Science, McGraw-Hill, New York.

1970 Scientific Papers of Tjalling C. Koopmans, Springer-Verlag, Berlin.

1980 Scientific Papers of Tjalling C. Koopmans, Vol.2, MIT Press, Cambridge, MA.

24.4.2 ARTICLES

1940 "The Degree of Dumping in Business Cycles," Econometrica, Vol.49, No.1.

1941 "The Logic of Economic Business-Cycle Research," JPE, Vol.49, pp. 157-181.

1942 "The Dynamics of Inflation," REStat, Vol.24, No.1. "Reply," REStat, Vol.24, No.4.

1945 "Statistical Estimation of Simultaneous Economic Relations," JASA, Vol.40, Dec.

1947 "Measurement without Theory" (Review Article of A F Burns and W.C. Mitchell, Measuring Business Cycles), Reprinted in Readings in Business Cycles, American Economic Association Readings (edited by R A Gordon and L R Klein) R D Irwin, Homewood, ILL.

1949 "Identification Problems in Economic Model Construction," Econometrica, Vol. 17, No.2.

1960 a "Stationary Ordinal Utility and Impatience," Econometrica, Vol.28, No.2.

b "A Note About Kantorovich's Paper 'Mathematical Methods of Organizing and Planning Production'," Management Science, Vol.6, No.4.

1964 (with P.A. Diamond and R E Williamson) "Stationary Utility and Time Perspective," Econometrica, Vol. 32, No. 1-2.

1967 a "Objectives, Constraints, and Outcomes in Optimal Growth Models," Econometrica, Vol. 35, No.1.

b "Inter-temporal Distribution and 'Optimal' Aggregate Economic Growth," Ten Economic Studies in the Tradition of Irving Fisher, Wiley, New York.

1972 a "Representation of Preference Orderings with Independent Components of Consumption," in Decision and Organization, A Volume in Honor of Jacob Marschak, C. B. Mcguire and R. Radner (eds.), North-Holland, Amsterdam.

b "Representation of Preference Orderings Over Time," in Decision and Organization, A Volume in Honor of Jacob Marschak, C. B. Mcguire and R. Radner (eds.), North-Holland, Amsterdam.

1973 "Some Observations on Optimal Economic Growth and Exhaustible Resources," in Economic Structure and Development: Essays in Honor of Jan Tinbergen, H. C. Bos et al. (eds.), North Holland, Amsterdam.

1974 "Is the Theory of Competitive Equilibrium With It?" AER, Vol.64, No.2.

1975 "Concepts of Optimality and Their Uses," Prize Lecture, Nobel Lectures, Economics, 1969-1980, Assar Lindbeck (ed.), World Scientific Publishing Co., Singapore, 1992.

1979 "Economics among the Sciences," Presidential Address to the American Economic Association, AER, Vol. 69, No.1.

24.5 WORKS OF OTHERS

Jungenfelt, K. G. (1976), Tjalling Koopmans's Contribution to Economics II, Koopmans and the Recent Development of Growth Theory, ScandJE, Vol.78, No.1.

Werin, L. (1976), "Tjalling Koopmans's Contribution to Economics, I: Activity Analysis, Methodology and Econometrics," ScandJE, Vol.78, No.1.

CHAPTER 25

SIR JOHN RICHARD NICHOLAS STONE

(1913 – 1991)

The Royal Swedish Academy of Sciences has awarded the 1984 Alfred Nobel Memorial Prize in Economic Sciences to Professor Sir Richard Stone, University of Cambridge, England, for his fundamental contributions to the development of systems of national accounts. Through these contributions, he greatly improved the basis for empirical economic analysis.

Economic reality can be seen as innumerable transactions between purchasers and sellers. For the purpose of surveying and analysing an endlessly detailed and complicated mass of transactions for a nation as an economic unit, it is useful and necessary to develop systematic methods in order to summarise and aggregate a reality, which, on the micro level, is cumbersome and infinitely complicated. A system of national income accounts facilitates simplification and helps in obtaining an overview of the picture.

Tracing the history of the development of systems in national accounts and the importance of such systems, the Royal Swedish Academy states that "this new analytical technique was introduced during World War II, primarily in the United Kingdom, where it was inspired by John Maynard Keynes." As an expert at the British Treasury, Keynes was concerned with the problems of financing the War. Keynes started from a balance between real gross national product on the supply side, and aggregate consumption, investment and expenditures on the demand side. In this task, Keynes was assisted by James Meade (1977 Nobel Laureate in Economics) and Richard Stone. Meade and Stone were assigned the work of collecting, processing and systematising the voluminous statistical material required by Keynes for his analysis of imbalances in the British national economy. The citation observes: "In this research environment (with all the stimulus provided by the prevailing tight economic situation and under the great personal influence of Keynes himself in regard to ideas and encouragement) the analytical technique emerged which is covered by the designation 'national' or 'social' accounts." The efforts involving experiments with systematic processing of overwhelmingly rich material contained in budget statistics caused Keynes to exclaim, "we are in a new era of joy through statistics."

Richard Stone has been recognised as a pioneer and the driving force in regard to both the theoretical underpinnings and practical application of different systems of national accounts. These accounts formed the basis for economic analysis of the imbalance of resources prevailing in Britain at that time and for making economic policy recommendations.

These days, computation and presentation of national accounts, with their rows of interconnected balance calculations for the different sectors of the economy (such as households, private business, government and the rest of the world), are regarded as a self-evident and required part of systematic reporting of countries' financial position and pattern of development. This is evident from the publications of the United Nations and the World Bank. The richness of details of accounts varies, of course, from country to country. However in early 1940's, reporting and analysis in the form of a logically linked system of national accounts constituted an "epoch-making innovation," the breakthrough of a "new methodology." Sir Richard Stone was primarily credited for this breakthrough.

Stone had found the system of double entry book-keeping useful as it provided a means of cross-checking the statistics for a large number of transactions. Each item of revenue or expenditure on one side of an account has to reappear as expenditure or revenue, respectively, in another account. Employing such an integrated system of accounts, covering household income and expenditures, disbursements of the business sector (as, for example, payment of wages and salaries), expenditures and revenues of the public sector, revenues for national savings and investments and payment balances towards the outside world, Stone showed a picture of interplay and interdependence of the whole economic system. In order to satisfy the requirements of the national accounts for empirical work, Stone had to pursue extensive statistical research.

At the end of World War II, Stone headed an international group of experts initially under the auspices of the League of Nations and later of the United Nations, for the preparation of standardised forms of national accounts, which could be applicable internationally. Stone's models for national accounts achieved wide international application, initially in a number of industrialised countries and later by a large number of developing countries. An excellent common basis was obtained for statistical comparisons between countries with respect to levels of economic activity and economic structures.

Stone perceived the theoretical analysis of problems of national economic balance as the starting point and justification for national accounts. While the system of double entry book-keeping served as a point of departure, a difficult and decisive question was how and to what extent an immense number of transactions in the system could be consolidated and aggregated in meaningful account summaries by sector and how to present the corresponding accounts. Stone was of the opinion that simple mechanical book-keeping methods would not serve the purpose. Instead, Stone's systems of national accounts were founded on economic theory, providing a systematic structure and facilitating economic analysis and forecasts and determination of economic policy.

Though the Keynesian revolution in economics had provided the primary impulse towards the construction of national accounts systems, these are now regarded as "neutral" from analytical and ideological points of view. The Nobel citation notes that the systems are being applied by all analytical streams within economic science and in all types of countries. National accounts have created a "systematic data base for a number of different types of economic analysis, including the levels of economic activity, inflation analysis, the analysis of economic structures, growth analysis and, particularly international comparison between countries in these respects."

Stone had also made important contributions to other fields, such as empirical growth research and demand analysis. However, it was his initiative and pioneering research in regard to systems of national accounts which represents Stone's central contribution in economic science.

25.1 A BRIEF BIOGRAPHICAL NOTE: RICHARD STONE

John Richard Nicholas Stone was born in London on 30th August, 1913, the only child of Gilbert and Elsie Stone. His father was a barrister. He had his schooling at Cliveden Place Preparatory School and at Westminster school. In 1930, Gilbert Stone was appointed a High Court Judge in Madras (now Chennai) and as a result, Richard Stone had a year's break in India between school and University.

From 1931 to 1935, Richard Stone was an undergraduate at Gonville and Caius College, Cambridge. After two years of law, Stone switched to economics, much to his father's disappointment. In Stone's own words: "At that time the World was in the depth of the great depression and my motive for wanting to change subject was the belief, bred of youthful ignorance and optimism, that if only economics were better understood, the world would be a better place."

As Stone's college did not have an economist among its fellows, he was sent to Richard Kahn at King's College for his "weekly supervisions." Stone considered this "a piece of great good fortune, as Kahn was not only a brilliant theorist but also a stimulating and encouraging supervisor." Another of his teachers was Colin Clark, a lecturer in statistics at that time. According to Stone's autobiographical note, "Finally, there was Keynes, who was in the habit of giving a short course of lectures on whatever book he happened to be writing; at that time, the book on the stocks was The General Theory." Stone was "invited" to become a member of Keynes's Political Economy Club. Keynes was kind to Stone as "he was to all young people." Later, Stone got to know Keynes well.

Stone took his degree in 1935 when his college offered him a research studentship. As he had only two years of economics and was not quite sure that he was ready for research and as his father was anxious to see Richard settled in a job, Stone did not take up his studentship. Instead, he joined the staff of Lloyds, a firm of brokers in London. Stone confessed: "I was never cut out for a business career but I did learn a great deal about life from my brief encounter with the insurance world."

Richard Stone, who joined the staff of the Ministry of Economic Warfare in 1939, was transferred in 1940 to the Central Economic Information Service of the Offices of the War Cabinet where James Meade was preparing the groundwork for a survey of the country's economic and financial situation. By December 1940, Meade and Stone completed a set of estimates, which they showed to Keynes, who was then at the Treasury. Through advocacy of Keynes, the estimates were published as the second part of a White Paper entitled, "An Analysis of the Sources of War Finance and an Estimate of the National Income and Expenditure" in 1938 and 1940. The estimates hardly amounted to a set of national accounts but it was a good beginning. Thanks to the encouragement by Keynes, whose assistant he had become, Stone continued to be responsible for national income estimation until he left the government service at the end of World War II.

At the end of the War in 1945, Stone was chosen to be the first director of the newly established Department of Applied Economics in Cambridge. Before joining the new job at Cambridge University, at the instance of the League of Nations, he prepared a memorandum on the problems of defining and measuring national income and related totals which was published as an appendix to Measurement of National Income and Construction of National Accounts, published by the United Nations in 1947. In late 1940's, the Organisation for European Economic Cooperation (OEEC) had set up a National Accounts Research Unit in Cambridge under the direction of Richard Stone. Several reports resulted from the activity. Of them, "A Simplified System of National Accounts" and "A Standardised System of National Accounts" were published by the OEEC in 1950 and 1952 respectively.

Concurrently with this work, Stone continued working on his main research interest, namely, analysis of consumer behaviour, at the Department of Applied Economics with the help of Deryck Rowe. This work, on the basis of which he read a paper "The Analysis of Market Demand" to the Royal Statistical Society, eventually resulted in publication of two large volumes, the first in 1954 and the second in 1967, under the title, The Measurement of Consumers' Expenditure and Behaviour in the United Kingdom, 1920-1938. At the time of the publication of the first volume, he wrote a paper on the "Linear Expenditure System."

During the early 1950's, Stone made a number of trips abroad in connection with the national accounts. Of particular interest to us is his visit to India in 1950 with Simon Kuznets and J.B.D. Dirksen to advise the National Income Committee on methods of estimation of national income. In July 1952, the U.N. Statistical Office, New York, had set up a committee of experts under the Chairmanship of Stone for the purpose of establishing a standard system of national accounts. The outcome of the committee's effort is the U.N. publication, A System of National Accounts and Supporting Tables (SNA) in 1952. A major revision of SNA started in 1964 and took four years for completion. The new system appeared in 1968 as A System of National Accounts. Stone wrote its first four chapters.

In 1955, when Stone was appointed P.D. Leake Professor of Finance and Accounting in Cambridge University, he gave up the directorship of the Department of Applied Economics. In collaboration with Alan Brown, Stone started building an econometric model of the British economy. This was the start of the Cambridge Growth Project. In

1962, Richard Stone and Alan Brown published their ideas in A Computable Model of Economic Growth, the opening volume in the series, "A Programme for Growth." Stone, in association with his third wife, Giovanna Croft-Murray, wrote two books, Social Accounting and Economic Models and National Income and Expenditure, besides editing the twelve volumes of "A Programme for Growth" which described the Cambridge Growth Model upto 1974.

In 1965, Stone started work on social demography and demographic accounting. He prepared a report under the title Demographic Accounting and Model Building for the Organization for Economic Cooperation and Development (OECD) which was published in 1971. In 1970, the U.N. Statistical Office became interested in developing an integrated system of social and demographic statistics, and invited Richard Stone as a consultant. He wrote a report which was published by the U.N. in 1975 under the title, Towards a System of Social and Demographic Statistics (SSDS). He was knighted in 1978.

In later years of life, Stone's interest was focussed on three subjects: social demography, improving national accounts and mathematical simulation models of economic growth and fluctuation, their stability and their control. Richard Stone retired from the Cambridge University post in 1980.

Stone received a number of awards and honours of which mention may be made of Emeritus Professorship at University of Cambridge, 1980, Honorary President of the Econometric Society, 1955, a number of Honorary doctorates from universities and honorary fellowship from Gonville & Caius College, Cambridge, 1976.

Richard Stone died on December 6, 1991 in Cambridgeshire, Cambridge.

25.2 A BRIEF SURVEY OF RICHARD STONE'S CONTRIBUTIONS

Stone's interest in national income studies started early in his life. The basis and rationale for this interest and the factors shaping the course of his research, become clear in the quote from one of his articles: "Anyone who believes in the maintenance of a social economy and the avoidance of the totalitarian direction of all aspects of economic life must be concerned...with the creation of an institutional framework which will permit a social economy, with the essential features of free markets, free choice of occupations and free choice in the spending of disposable income to function more in accordance with contemporary social ideals. In the achievement of this goal and in re-drafting the rules of the economic game in such a way that both laissez-faire and overall physical control are rejected as a basis for economic organization, national income and expenditure studies and their extension to the technique of national budgeting have, I believe, a great deal to offer." He emphasised the importance of contemporary social ideas, such as, stabilisation of economic activity, equalisation of income distribution and different forms of intervention in the competitive mechanism wherever necessary in order to ensure a more planned development of society.

As a prolific writer, Richard Stone had made contributions to a number of areas in economics, of which the following considered to be specifically important are covered here.

1. Development of National Accounts;
2. Methods for Demand Analysis and their Practical Applications; and
3. Development of Extensive Models for Economic Policy Analysis.

25.2.1 DEVELOPMENT OF NATIONAL ACCOUNTS

Richard Stone's early work on problems related to national income accounting, his work with James Meade on national income concepts and tables, his studies on the relation between national income estimates in the U.K. and the U.S.A. and his post-war work on the comparison of national income estimates between countries can be regarded as his preparation for his comprehensive study on the development of international standards for national income accounting. The most important work of Stone from this early period was the Appendix to a U.N. Publication, Definition and Measurement of the National Income and Related Totals. The material in the Appendix served as a guideline for the formulation of national income systems in a number of countries and has had a "profound effect" on the literature in the field. While these studies may not appear to be exciting, one cannot underrate the work necessary to get the idea of national income accounting accepted in practice. Further, there is no gainsaying the fact that any reader is impressed by Stone's "thoroughness, accuracy and perception of data possibilities and practical considerations." Even critics like Aukrust admitted that by virtue of his many influential studies, Stone had assumed "undisputed leadership in the field during the post-war years." One is also struck by Stone's perception of the accounts systems in the context of a more abstract and general model.

In regard to the logical structure of accounts systems, Leif Johansen makes a particular reference to Stone's 1948 article "Social Accounting, Aggregation and Invariance" in which was shown the equivalence between a matrix representation, a network representation and an accounting representation with the same fundamental structure, based on certain classification rules for the basic transactions. In this article, Stone had also introduced the general concept of invariance and also used it "in discussing the types of manipulations which can be performed on the basic entries without introducing arbitrary effects," demonstrating thereby how Stone had opened new vistas.

In regard to the question of the relevance of national income systems in practice, it is clear that Stone was aware of Jan Tinbergen's, Lawrence Klein's and others' constructions of macroeconomic models and the potential importance of national accounts in this context. In fact, in an article co-authored with E. F. Jackson, Stone considered as to how the use of macroeconomic models was helpful in the analysis of issues relating to economic policy. In his later work, Stone presented national accounts in the form of a "transactions matrix" and with its help constructed different types of models by comparing various kinds of restrictions on it and combining it with a "response matrix."

Besides linking national accounts to the construction of macroeconomic models, Stone explored the possibility of explaining the variation in the original economic variables, representing the components of a nation's total revenues and expenditures by a small number of derived variables constructed as linear combination of the original variables. Stone had shown, by using factor analysis, that variation in 17 different economic variables for the U.S.A. covering the period 1922-1938, could primarily be explained by three such variables or factors. Johansen is of the view that this method is important as "it documents the relevance of national income estimates when we want to arrive at 'explaining factors' which, as good approximations, can be taken to represent national income as well as its variations." Furthermore, in Stone's opinion, this technique was useful in connection with demand functions where the analysis can be made by including income, price of the good in question and a "summary index" of other prices as arguments in each demand function. In the construction of the summary index of other prices, we can use factor analysis. Stone had developed useful advanced ideas in the employment of sampling techniques to obtain data for national accounts, besides analysing the practical aspects of sampling surveys.

In his later work, Stone moved out from accounting formulations to the representation of national accounts in the form of a large "social accounting matrix" or "transactions matrix" and to explain the relations between input-output analysis and national accounts. These extensive and comprehensive transactions matrices include financial transactions, balances of financial assets and real assets and capital gains or losses on variations in the values of different kinds of assets. The transactions matrices also contained classification by sectors, useful in constructing ordinary input-output tables. This approach as well as his formulation of international standards for compilation of national accounts are available in U.N. Publications and in the project "A Programme of Growth."

With the growth in complexity of national accounts, there arose the serious problem of classification. Adopting a flexible approach, Stone suggested simultaneous use of several kinds of classificatory criteria in the same national accounts matrix. When multiple classification criteria are used and models are constructed that include production, consumption and investment structures, conversions were needed to be carried out among the different classifications. Stone recommended the use of the so-called classification constants. However, the assumption that the multipliers in classification converters are constant is of questionable validity.

In the context of national income accounts, Stone had done important work on the construction of indexes (specifically on the compatibility of a complete systems of price indexes, volume indexes and estimates in a system of national accounts where many definitional constraints have to be met). He was also instrumental in creating global standards. Furthermore, Stone was credited with extending the scope of national accounts to cover construction of regional accounts, incorporation of financial circulation into national accounts, programming models of financial markets and compilation of demographic data and descriptions of population development suitable for integrating demographic trends into economic models. Stone also applied these "accounting systems" to population flows through the education system which led to the construction of input-output models of the education system.

Johansen makes specific reference to Stone's article "The Social Accounts from a Consumer's Point of View" which, attempted at linking financial and demographic aspects to a survey and discussion of the U.N.'s (1968) new system of national accounts and comments: "...these accounting systems are very lucid and provide an appropriate system for structuring coherent and consistent data...." Johansen also opines that one of the most important analytical contributions of Stone was his "...use of Markov Chain method and related techniques...."

25.2.2 DEMAND ANALYSIS

Stone prepared a study of private consumption in England during the period 1920-1938, the first results of which were presented by him in 1945 in an essay "The Analysis of Market Demand," read to the Royal Statistical Society. He analysed demand for each commodity or group of commodities and the arguments in each demand function contained aggregate consumption expenditures, the price of the particular commodity, a variable to represent the price level of other goods, a selection of other relevant prices, trend variable etc. The main results of the work were presented in a "monumental two-part study," <u>The Measurement of Consumers' Expenditure and Behaviour in the United Kingdom, 1920-1938.</u>

The methodology employed in this study is considered importantly different compared to Stone's earlier studies in two respects – first, more thorough treatment of problems due to auto-correlated residuals in the demand functions through the use of several testing methods, such as Durbin-Watson test, and second, combining information from household budgets with time series data for many goods. Critics rate the work as "without a doubt one of the most serious, thorough and extensive econometric studies ever carried out.... It can hardly be surpassed by any other presentation in terms of the combination of insights into theory, data problems and methodological issues.... This study was received as a milestone in econometric research on demand relations and has become a standard reference." Commenting on Volume I of the study, R. G. D. Allen said: "This work of Mr. Stone and his colleagues is beyond adequate praise. The estimates are authoritative..." Even Lawrence Klein who was critical on several points remarks: "... [It] is a work of careful, painstaking research. There is no doubt of its enormous contribution to our basic fund of knowledge.... One cannot afford to overlook the details of this magnificent volume."

While Stone's early work was concerned with estimating individual demand functions separately, he was a pioneer in the simultaneous estimation of complete systems of demand functions. His first work along these lines was a well-known article on linear expenditure functions. Stone's main theoretical contribution in this area was to show that the sub-class of linear expenditure functions related to the construction of cost of living indexes (as in the works of Klein, Rubin and Samuelson) is the only class of such functions which satisfies the requirements of consumer demand theory based on the assumption of maximisation of utility.

Stone in his earlier work on demand analysis had mainly taken the dynamic aspects of the development of demand into account by means of trend components in the analyses. Later, he had also presented significant studies which included dynamic elements in a more satisfactory way. Foremost among such studies, it concerned durable goods. The approach he had adopted in these studies which includes the introduction of a "desirable" stock variable, drew a distinction between short-run elasticities in the demand structure, which reflect the effects of income and prices on purchases of durable goods during a period with given stocks and long-run elasticities reflecting the effects of income and prices on purchases in a comparison between alternative equilibrium situations. Purchases in the latter instance indicate those required to maintain equilibrium stocks of durable goods. Stone used the same model for individual goods separately as also to several commodity groups. The models used by Stone have had considerable impact on later research on dynamic demand functions, particularly for consumer durables.

In addition to the work related to private consumption expenditure, Stone had also made important contributions to econometric explanations of saving behaviour. His studies had aimed at improving the formulation of Keynesian consumption functions. His formulation of consumption functions was marked by inclusion of income and wealth as consumption–motivating factors and the differentiation between permanent and temporary components with respect to both these factors.

25.2.3 MODELS FOR ECONOMIC POLICY ANALYSIS

During 1960's, Richard Stone headed a project of the Department of Applied Economics at Cambridge University aimed at elucidating the prospects for more rapid growth in the British economy. Among the highly competent staff of the project was Alan Brown, who was instrumental in executing many phases of the project. The main publications which describe the project and present results appeared in a series under the joint title of "A Programme for Growth." The project was conceived mainly because of the "irregular and, on the average, relatively low growth rate in the economy of Great Britain in relation to many other comparable countries."

The philosophy behind and the rationale for undertaking the project was expressed by the authors headed by Stone as follows: "Whether we are interested in our own standard of living and that of our descendants, in our ability to help the poorer countries of the world to break the poverty barrier which has always enclosed them, or in the grosser forms of power politics, we cannot be indifferent to Britain's economic growth." The "environment" envisioned for the model was an economy with a competitive private sector and different forms of public intervention and control. Two alternative ways of guiding the economy to a higher growth path was identified. The first one was by employing appropriate public policy instruments, such as taxation and foreign exchange rate. The second method was by influencing expectations and plans in the private sector of the economy.

As regards the structure of the model, it has to be stated that the project was supposed to be carried out using two compatible models – a steady state model and a "transient" model. The latter or the second model was concerned with closer analysis of the time profile from the initial situation to that which prevailed when the first year of the balanced growth will start in line with the steady state model. However, the main body of work on the project focussed on the steady-state model. Reviewers of the work have rated it high despite many known weaknesses. The viewpoint is expressed well by Leif Johansen: "...the overall impression [is] that the project represents a very valuable and advanced research contribution which may well be regarded as one of the best examples of combined theoretical and empirical research concerning problems relevant to economic policy."

25.3 CONCLUDING OBSERVATIONS

Besides the above three areas to which he had made important and significant contributions, Stone had enriched input-output analysis, both theoretically and empirically. He also made notable contributions in the fields of demographic growth, education and the so-called social indicators. In addition to original scientific contributions, Stone had authored a number of valuable surveys, such as "Model Building and the Social Accounts," an article on "Statistics," and his lecture "Random Walk through the Social Sciences." He wrote a few original good text-books as well.

25.4 SELECT BIBLIOGRAPHY OF RICHARD STONE'S WORKS

25.4.1 BOOKS

1944 (with J. E. Meade), National Income and Expenditure, Oxford University Press, London.

1948 (with C. F. Carter and W. B. Reddaway), The Measurement of Production Movements, Cambridge University Press, Cambridge.

1954 (with D. A. Rowe et al.), The Measurement of Consumers' Expenditure and Behaviour in the United Kingdom, 1920-1938, Vol.1, Cambridge University Press, Cambridge.

1956 Quantity and Price Indexes in National Accounts, OEEC, Paris.

1961 (with Giovanna Stone), National Income and Expenditure, Fifth edition, Rewritten Tenth edition, 1977, Bowes & Bowes, London.

1962 a (with A. Brown), A Computable Model for Economic Growth, No.1 in A Programme for Growth, Chapman & Hall, London.

b (with A. Brown et al.), A Social Accounting Matrix for 1960, No.2 in A Programme for Growth, Chapman & Hall, London.

1966 a Mathematics in the Social Sciences and other Essays, Chapman & Hall, London.

b (with A. D. Rowe), The Measurement of Consumers' Expenditure and Behaviour in the United Kingdom, 1920-1938, Vol.2, Cambridge University Press, Cambridge.

1969 Demographic Accounting and Model Building, OECD, Paris, 1971.

1970 Mathematical Models of the Economy and Other Essays, Chapman & Hall, London.

25.4.2 ARTICLES

1936 (with W. A. Tweedle), "A Study of Costs," Econometrica, Vol.4 No.3.

1938 (with W. M. Stone), "The Marginal Propensity to Consume and Multiplier," RES, Vol. VI, No.1.

1939 (with W. M. Stone), "Indices of Industrial Output," EJ, Vol.XL1X, No.195.

1941 (with J. E. Meade), "The Construction of Tables of National Income, Expenditure, Savings and Investment," EJ, Vol. LI Nos.202-3. Reprinted in Readings in the Concept and Measurement of Income, R.H. Parker and G. Harcourt (eds.), Cambridge University Press, Cambridge.

1942 a "The National Income, Output and Expenditure of the United States of America, 1929-1941," EJ, Vol.LII, No.206-7.

b (with D.G. Champernowne and J.E. Meade), "The Precision of National Income Estimates," RES, Vol.IX, No.2.

1943 a "National Income in the United Kingdom and the United States of America," RES, Vol.X, No.1.

b "Two Studies in Income and Expenditure in the United States," EJ, Vol. LIII, No.209.

1945 "The Analysis of Market Demand," JRRS, Vol.108, Parts 3 & 4.

1946 (with E. F. Jackson), "Economic Models with Special Reference to Mr. Kaldor's System," EJ, Vol. LVI, No.224.

1947 a "Definition and Measurement of the National Income and Related Totals," Appendix to Measurement of National Income and Construction of Social Accounts, U.N., Geneva.

b "On the Interdependence of Block Transactions," Supplement to JRRS,Vol.IX,No.1-2.

c "Of Autoregressive Schemes and Linear Stochastic Difference Systems," Paper presented at the I S C, Washington, in Proceedings of the International Statistical Conferences, 1947, Eka Press, Calcutta, 1951.

d "The Measurement of National Income and Expenditure: A Review of the Official Estimates of Five Countries," EJ, Vol.LVII, No.227.

1948 a "The Analysis of Market Demand: An Outline of Methods and Results," Review of the International Statistical Institute, Vol.16, No.1/4.

b "The Theory of Games," EJ, Vol. LVIII, No.230.

1949 a "Functions and Criteria of a System of Social Accounting," Paper presented at the IARIW Conference, Cambridge, in Income and Wealth, Series I, Bowes and Bowes, Cambridge, 1951.

b (with J.E.B. Utting and J. Durbin), "The Use of Sampling Methods in National Income Statistics and Social Accounting," Paper presented at the ISI Conference, Berne, Review of the International Statistical Institute, Vol.18, No.1/2, 1950.

1950 (with J.E.B. Utting), "The Relationship between Input-Output Analysis and National Accounting," Paper presented at the first International Conference on Input-Output Techniques, Driebergen, in Input-Output Relations, H.E. Stenfert Kroese, Leiden, 1953.

1951 "The Use and Development of National Income and Expenditure Estimates," in Lessons of the British War Economy, Cambridge University Press, Cambridge.

1952 (with S.J. Prais), "Systems of Aggregative Index Numbers and their Compatibility," EJ, Vol.LXII, No.247.

1953 "Model Building and the Social Accounts: A Survey," Paper presented at the IARIW conference, Castelgondolfo, in Income and Wealth, Series IV, Bowes and Bowes, London, 1955.

1954 "Linear Expenditure Systems and Demand Analysis: An Application to the Pattern of British Demand," Paper presented at the Second International Conference on Input-Output Techniques, Varenna, EJ, Vol. LXIV, No.255.

1955 (with J.Aitchison and Alan Brown), "Some Estimation Problems in Demand Analysis," The Incorporated Statistician, Vol.5, No.4.

1957 (with D.A. Rowe), "The Market Demand for Durable Goods," Econometrica, Vol.25, No.3. Reprinted in, 1971. Consumer Behaviour, A.S.C.Ehrenberg and F.G.Pyatt (eds.), Penguin Books, Middlesex.

1958 (with D.A. Rowe), "Dynamic Demand Function: Some Econometric Results," EJ, Vol.LXVIII, No.270.

1960 a "Social Accounts at the Regional Level: A Survey," Paper presented at the OEEC Conference on Regional Economic Planning, Bellgio, in Regional Economic Planning: Techniques of Analysis, OEEC, Paris, 1961.

b (with D.A. Rowe), "The Durability of Consumers' Durable Goods," Econometrica, Vol.28, No.2, Reprinted in Readings in Economic Statistics and Econometrics, A. Zellner (ed.), Little, Brown and Co., Boston, 1968.

1961 (with A. Brown), "A Long-term Growth Model for the British Economy," Paper presented at the IARIW Conference, Tutzing, in Europe's Future in Figures, North Holland, Amsterdam, 1962.

1963 "Models of the National Economy for Planning Purposes," Operational Research Quarterly, Vol.14, No.1.

1964 a "Private Saving in Britain: Past, Present and Future," The Manchester School of Economic and Social Studies, Vol. XXXII, No.2.

b "The Changing Pattern of Consumption," in Problems of Economic Dynamics and Planning (Essays in honour of Michael Kalecki), Polish Scientific Publishers (PWN), Warsaw.

c "Transitional Planning," in On Political Economy and Econometrics (Essays in honour of Oskar Lange), Polish Scientific Publishers (PWN), Warsaw.

d "Models for Demand Projections," in Essays on Econometrics and Planning (in honour of P.C. Mahalanobis), Pergamon Press, Oxford, & Statistical Publishing Society, Calcutta.

1965 "The Social Accounts from a Consumer's Point of View," Paper presented at the IARIW Conference, The Review of Income and Wealth Series, Vol. 12, No.1, 1966.

1966 a "Mathematical Models in Educational Planning: A View of the Conference," Introduction to the Proceedings of a Meeting held by the OECD, Paris, in Mathematical Models in Educational Planning, OECD, Paris, 1967.

b "National Income," in Chamber's Encyclopaedia, Fourth Edition, London.

1968 "Demographic Input-Output: An Extension of Social Accounting," Paper presented at the Fourth International Conference on Input-Output Techniques, Geneva, in Contributions to Input-Output Analysis, Vol.1, North-Holland, Amsterdam, 1970.

1973 a "Personal Spending and Saving in Post-War Britain," in Economic Structure and Development (Essays in honour of Jan Tinbergen), North Holland, Amsterdam.

b "Demographic Variables in the Economics of Education," Paper presented at an International Economic Association Conference held at Valescure,

Published in Economic Factors in Population Growth, Macmillan, London, 1976.

1974 "Random Walk through the Social Sciences," Paper presented at the Sixth International Conference on Input-Output Techniques, Vienna.

1975 "The Expanding Frontiers of Input-Output Analysis," Paper presented at the 40th session of the International Statistical Institute, Warsaw.

1976 "Major Accounting Problem for a World Model," Paper presented at a Working Seminar on Global Opportunities and Constraints for Regional Development, Harvard University, in Problems of World Modelling, Ballinger, Cambridge, MA.

1978 "Input-Output Analysis and Economic Planning: A Survey," Paper presented at the International Symposium on Mathematical Programming and its Economic Applications, Venice, in Mathematical Programming and Its Economic Applications, Angeli, Milan, 1981.

1980 a "The Relationship of Demographic Accounts to National Income and Product Accounts," Paper presented to the SSRC Workshop on Social Accounting Systems, Washington DC, in Social Accounting Systems: Essays on the State of the Art, F. Thomas Juster and K.C. Land (eds.), Academic Press, New York, 1981.

b "Political Economy, Economics and Beyond," Royal Economic Society, Presidential Address, EJ, Vol.90, No.360.

1983 "Accounting Matrices in Economics and Demography," in Mathematical Models in Economics, F.van der Ploeg (ed.), Wiley, New York, 1984.

1985 "How Accurate are the British National Accounts?" in Specification Analysis in the Linear Model, M.L.King and D.E.A. Giles (eds), Routledge and Kegan Paul, London.

1986 "The Accounts of Society," Nobel Lecture, Journal of Applied Econometrics, Vol. 1, No.1.

25.5 WORKS OF OTHERS

Allen, R.G.D. (1954), "Studies in National Income and Expenditure," EJ, Vol.64, Mar.

Johansen, L. (1985), "Richard Stone's Contributions to Economics," ScandJE, Vol.87, No.1.

Klein, L (1954), "Book Review," AER, Vol.44.

CHAPTER 26

TRYGVE MAGNUS HAAVELMO

(1911 – 1999)

The Royal Swedish Academy of Sciences has awarded the 1989 Alfred Nobel Memorial Prize in Economic Sciences to Professor Trygve Magnus Haavelmo, Oslo, for his fundamental contributions to econometrics, and specifically for his "classification of the probability theory foundations of econometrics and his analyses of simultaneous economic structures." The field of econometrics is concerned with estimating economic relations and testing whether postulated relations conform fully with reality.

During the late 1920's and early 1930's, significant attempts were made under the leadership of Ragnar Frisch and Jan Tinbergen (both Nobel Laureates) to test economic theories empirically. The results of these attempts brought to the fore two fundamental problems associated with testing economic theories. First, postulated economic relations often refer to large aggregate of individuals or firms. Theories concerning such relations can never be expected to conform completely with available data, even when there are no measurement errors. The crucial and difficult question then is to determine what should be considered "sufficiently good" or "better" conformity.

The second problem that surfaced in the empirical testing of economic theories is this. Economists can seldom or never carry out controlled experiments in the same way as researchers in natural sciences. Available data representing observations of market outcomes etc., are results of a multitude of behavioural relations, which have mutually interacting effects. This gives rise to problems of interdependence; that is, difficulties in using observed data to identify, estimate and test the underlying relations in an unambiguous way.

In the Prize citation, the Royal Academy makes specific reference as to how Haavelmo in his 1941 dissertation and in a number of subsequent studies, was able to demonstrate convincingly that the two fundamental problems mentioned above could be solved satisfactorily if economic theories were formulated in probabilistic terms. Then, we can by applying methods of mathematical statistics, draw stringent conclusions about underlying relations from the "random sample" of empirical observations. Haavelmo had shown how those methods could be used to estimate and test economic theories and utilise them in making forecasts. He had also demonstrated that misleading interpretations of individual relations (due to) interdependence cannot be avoided in the absence of simultaneous estimation of all relations in the theoretical model.

Haavelmo's doctoral thesis had a swift and path breaking influence on the development of the field of econometrics. His programme of probability theory research attracted a number of economists and econometricians, such as Nobel Laureates, Koopmans and Klein. This gave rise to extraordinarily rapid development of econometric methodology, primarily during the 1940's. The foundation of modern econometric methods had been truly and firmly laid.

In the history of econometric research, we should first mention the U.S. economists Moore and Schultz who worked on econometric determination of supply and demand on individual markets. During the 1930's, Tinbergen and Frisch (teacher of Haavelmo) made the first attempts at applying corresponding methods to test various macro dynamic relations. These estimates touched on several problems which Haavelmo later analysed in his doctoral work.

Prior to Haavelmo's Ph.D. thesis, economic researchers did not have a common conceptual system for formulating, analysing and solving econometric problems. As few econometric methods were based on probability theory, statistical inference could not be utilised to draw conclusions from data. Simple statistical methods, primarily regression analysis, were employed in most cases, without any clear assumptions on probability theory. To the extent that calculations contained any random variations, they usually referred to measurement errors in the variables. During this period, most prominent economists, including J.M. Keynes, rejected extensive use of probability theory in empirical research because economic processes are irreversible. Even econometricians like Frisch were sceptical about the applicability of methods of statistical inference to economic data.

In his thesis, Haavelmo refuted these various objections and showed that in order for economic theories to be testable, probability theory formulation is not only a prerequisite, but also extremely reasonable. According to him, it is unreasonable to believe that economists could ever "fully" explain or predict millions of decisions individuals and firms usually make every day on the basis of necessarily simplified assumptions. Decisions are in fact affected by individual characteristics and continuously changing conditions. It is therefore always necessary that explanations of such decisions by economists encompass a stochastic term which summarises these different kinds of "disturbances." As economic theories in general do not refer to individual decisions but are concerned with numerous decision-makers, it is frequently possible to make relatively simple assumptions about the probability distribution of these aggregate relations.

Haavelmo also demonstrated that by formulating theories in terms of probability theory, methods of statistical inference could be applied to estimate and test economic theories and use them in forecasting.

The second issue he dealt with and analysed was concerned with interdependence in economic relations. Economic interdependence can be illustrated by the fact that in economic life every individual decision may be regarded as affecting all other decisions through a chain of market relations. This interdependence creates problems in empirical research as an observed market outcome is the result of a large number of simultaneous decisions or previous decisions and behavioural relations. As such, an underlying true relation can never be observed in isolation but only as conditioned by a multitude of other simultaneous relations and circumstances in the economy. Haavelmo had shown that such interdependence creates difficulties in specifying, identifying and estimating economic relations.

The difficulty in specifying economic explanatory models lies in choosing from a number of models or systems which might equally explain the observed market outcome. When the relations in the model are interdependent, then a set of model equations can be used in order to derive a multitude of other equation systems which produce the same observable result. Haavelmo stressed the importance of trying to choose a set of relations which are each as "autonomous" as possible; that is, which are not affected by changes in the other parts of the system. For example, if we would like to determine the effect on private consumption due to a decrease in household income consequent to fiscal policy changes, then obviously the estimate of the propensity to consume should not be conditioned by previous fiscal policy. The choice of autonomous relations in explanatory models is mainly a matter of adequate knowledge and intuition concerning the basic mechanism of the economy. However, Haavelmo had also discussed the need to conduct statistical invariance tests. Since then, researchers have developed a method whereby the autonomy in different relations can be tested statistically.

The fact that many different types and forms of explanatory models can explain observed data also gives rise to what is known as identification problem. For example, if a theory is intended to explain the observed relations between price and sales of a good in a market, the relations have to be sufficiently specified so as to be identifiable as supply and demand relations respectively, with some given form of probability distribution. Haavelmo was the first to provide an explicit mathematical formulation and solution of the identification problem. Later development of the criteria of identification has been based on his formulation.

Interdependence also gives rise to what Haavelmo called simultaneity problems in estimating models with several different structural relations. Since the combined relations limit the possible variation in the input variables, isolated estimates of individual relations can be highly misleading. Employing probability theory framework, Haavelmo suggested a generally valid formulation and method of measuring this bias in isolated estimates of individual relations in an interdependent system. He also showed that the problem could be obviated by using a method of simultaneous estimates of interdependence models. Haavelmo's analysis of simultaneity problems has had a "decisive influence" on later work with econometric models.

Haavelmo had also attempted to transform various components of economic theory so that the new econometric methods he had developed would be applicable. In his opinion, the pre-requisites for achieving this purpose are not only additional assumptions regarding probability distributions, but also in many cases a more dynamic theoretical formulation. In particularly two areas, namely economic development theory and theory of investment, Haavelmo's approach has resulted in influential and far-reaching contributions. Besides these, he had also made significant contributions in a number of other areas – from analysis of macroeconomic fluctuations and fiscal policy to price theory and the history of economic thought.

26.1 A BRIEF BIOGRAPHICAL SKETCH: TRYGVE HAAVELMO

Trygve Magnus Haavelmo was born in Skedsmo, Norway, on December 13, 1911. After he graduated in Political Economy from the University of Oslo in 1933, Ragnar Frisch hired him as a research assistant at the newly established Institute of Economics in the University of Oslo. During 1938-39, Haavelmo worked as lecturer in statistics at the University of Aarhus. At the outbreak of World War II, he travelled to the U.S.A. as a Rockefeller Fellow (1940-1942). He defended his thesis at Harvard University in 1941. Haavelmo's dissertation gained immediate recognition and paved the way for the econometric seminar set up by him and Jacob Marschak in 1941 in New York, where Haavelmo was employed by Norwegian Trade Commission. He worked as a statistician for Nortraship, New York, between 1942 and 1944. Haavelmo worked as a Commercial Attache, at the Norwegian Embassy, Washington D.C. in 1945.

In 1943, when Marschak was head of the Cowles Commission, he focussed the work at the Commission on extending and following up the research programme on simultaneous econometric structure formulated in Haavelmo's dissertation. Haavelmo was closely associated with the Cowles Commission and accepted a tenured position there in 1946, the year in which he was awarded Dr. Phil. from University of Oslo.

After returning to Norway in 1947, Haavelmo worked during 1947-48 as Chief of Section, Ministry of Commerce and Industry and Ministry of Finance, Oslo. In 1948 he became Professor of Economics at the University of Oslo. Afterwards, his research interests turned to economic theory. His 1954 book entitled A Study in the Theory of Economic Evaluation is recognised as a pioneering study of the factors that account for economic underdevelopment of a country in relation to other countries, long before economists became seriously interested in development research. Another valuable contribution was A Study in the Theory of Investment published in 1960. The book introduced theories on demand for real capital and sluggishness in the adjustment of real capital. It is noted by the prize committee that "numerous theoretical and empirical studies of investment behavior" have been inspired by his work.

Haavelmo received a number of honours and awards. He was elected Fellow of the Econometric Society (1944) and of the Institute of Mathematical Statistics (1946). He was made a member of the Norwegian Academy of Sciences in 1950. Haavelmo was a member of the Council of the Econometric Society for a number of years, between 1954 and 1958, during 1961-1963 and during 1966-1970. He was President of the Econometric Society, 1957. He was elected Honorary Member of the American Economic Association in 1975. In 1979 Haavelmo was made a member of the Danish Academy of Sciences and was given Fridtjof Nansen Award for outstanding research.

Trygve Haavelmo died on July 26, 1999.

26.2 A SUMMARY OF TRYGVE HAAVELMO'S CONTRIBUTIONS

Marc Nerlove suggests three criteria that can form the basis for evaluating a person's work in any field. These are: originality of the contribution, intrinsic quality of the work and influence of the work on the profession. Nerlove finds it difficult to assess the originality of Haavelmo's contribution because in the two main areas of work, namely, econometric methodology and the theory of capital, Haavelmo is strongly influenced by Ragnar Frisch who "was notorious for not writing down many of the best ideas, at least not in accessible form." Regarding Haavelmo's influence on the profession in general it is equally difficult to judge as he was disarmingly modest and was not been given to "extravagant claims about the novelty or importance of his results." With the exception of his famous 1944 supplement to <u>Econometrica</u>, "The Probability Approach in Econometrics," and a few articles, Haavelmo's work is not much cited by researchers in the field. However, no one can dispute the great influence he has exerted on the profession.

Haavelmo's contributions are summarised under two broad heads.

1. Contributions to Econometric Methods and Applications; and
2. Contributions to Economic Theory.

26.2.1 ECONOMETRIC METHODS AND APPLICATIONS

Haavelmo, in his 1938 article in <u>Econometrica,</u> had applied Frisch's method of confluence analysis to monthly stock price data for the period 1920-1926 relating to Norway and for the period 1903-1914 relating to the U.S.A. While there is no novelty in the method applied or surprises in the important results he obtained, Haavelmo's discussion of confluent relations versus structural relations "clearly foreshadows his great work of 1944." Nerlove observes: "The most interesting and, apparently, new point in the paper has to do with partial statistical analysis of a small number of structural relations in an economic system, what we would today call final form, reduced form or partially reduced form equations."

In his 1939 careful econometric work "A Dynamic Study of Pig Production in Denmark," Haavelmo studied a controlled market during the years 1936-1938 employing sophisticated econometric techniques. During the period of study, the production was controlled and the supply of hogs was distributed in Danish and British markets. While Haavelmo no doubt discussed the dynamics of the Danish market for slaughter hogs, he did not discuss the investment behaviour of Danish farmers nor did he bring out the capital-theoretic aspects involved in the supply of a livestock product.

Examining a few statistically determined confluent relations for the purpose of testing business cycle theories, Haavelmo demonstrated the difficulty of identifying a structural parameter from an estimated reduced form, final form or confluent relation. It is because an observed final form is compatible with more than one structural system. Here he drew an important distinction between introducing stochastic elements in the final form and introducing them from the beginning in structural relationships. The later work of Haavelmo dealt again with these questions in regard to problems of identification and the necessity of introducing stochastic elements from the beginning in the structural relationships.

In the 1943 paper "The Statistical Implications of a System of Simultaneous Equations," Haavelmo spelt out the implication of these ideas: "when one has to do with a system (of structural equations)...this system should, for statistical purposes, be considered as a system of transformation, by which to derive the joint probability distribution of the observable variables from the specified distribution of error terms." The paper categorically stated that for purposes of policy analysis, as distinguished from the objective of prediction, a structural estimate was essential.

"The Probability Approach in Econometrics" which appeared as a supplement to 1942 Econometrica is easily the most important and widely quoted work of Haavelmo on econometric method. In this paper, he comprehensively dealt with the statistical implications of the idea that economic observations are the outcome of a system of relationships operating on a sequence of random causes and exogenous factors. It further contained a clear exposition of the importance of specifically dealing with how and why stochastic elements enter and of spelling out the implications of such assumptions for the appropriate statistical procedures for estimation as well as hypothesis testing. Nerlove observes: "This work contains the first clear statement in the econometrics literature that I know of concerning the Neyman-Pearson theory of hypothesis testing. It also contains an early treatment of the difference between errors in variables models and models that introduce the stochastic elements as 'shocks' to the structural equations. The preoccupation of most econometricians until recently with stochastic structural-equation models to the exclusion of other stochastic formulation probably stems from Haavelmo's work, although, he himself, is quite clear that the former represent only rather special way of looking at the way in which economic observations may be generated."

Haavelmo's 1942 paper mentioned above influenced the work at the Cowles Commission. The paper by Koopmans, Rubin and Leipnik on full-information maximum-likelihood (FIML) estimation of the parameters of a system of simultaneous stochastic equations may be cited as "an extended development of the basic idea of Haavelmo." Haavelmo published four papers in 1947 which are an outcome of his participation in the Cowles Commission's activity. In his 1947 paper in Econometrica co-authored with Girshick, Haavelmo presented a simultaneous-equations model of demand for food that linked demand for a particular group of commodities to the way in which income is generated and prices are determined in the economy as a whole. This paper and the paper entitled "Quantitative Research in Agricultural Economics: The Interdependence between Agriculture and National Economy," which focused on the same issue are considered significant because "they represent a concrete working out of the idea of representing a full general equilibrium system in a sufficiently simple form to be manageable by means of 'partial confluent' relations."

26.2.2 ECONOMIC THEORY

A Study in the Theory of Economic Evolution is an important book of Haavelmo in economic theory. The book contains his presentation of a neo-classical one-sector growth model. He developed this model earlier than Solow and Swan whose contributions in the field are well-received and for which they received well-deserved recognition. In his work, besides presenting the basic model, Haavelmo introduced stochastic elements. The work has not received the recognition it deserved, "perhaps because Haavelmo becomes bogged down in technical details and in the solution of a variety of dynamic models."

On the subject of investment, before the publication of his book in 1961, Haavelmo wrote two papers- one in 1941 "The Effect of the Rate of Interest: A Note" and another in 1949, "A Note on the Theory of Investment." The first paper was mainly a critique of Tinbergen's 1939 formulation of investment demand. It focussed on the issue of inferring structural behaviour from an observed confluent relationship. The essence of the 1949 paper is Haavelmo's presentation of the view that capital has to be considered as a factor of production and the problem that needs to be addressed is the determination of demand for new investment. As investment is nothing but change in capital stock between two successive periods, and as capital stock is not instantaneously adjusted to the level of desired stock, the main question one has to address is the understanding of investment behaviour.

In the beginning of the book A Study in the Theory of Investment, Haavelmo identified the central problem of investment. "If only we knew more about the determinants of investment! But, unfortunately our knowledge in this direction is still very meagre. One might well ask, what is wrong with the theory of investment? Or, perhaps, what is wrong with the subject matter itself? For one thing – this variable, - the pivot of modern macroeconomics – has apparently lived somewhat a nomadic life among the various chapters of economic theory. Perhaps it has not stayed long enough in any one place. Perhaps, it has been ill-treated." In the book, he examined the implications of the neo-classical view that capital is a factor of production and investment as a derived demand for capital. He considered capital as a stock and investment as a flow term, that is the change in capital stock during a given period. While capital is measured at a point in time, investment can only be measured over a period of time. At the same time, he emphasized that a theory of optimum capital use does not in itself provide a theory of investment.

We can calculate the flow of investment in a period as the difference between the capital stock at the end of the period and the capital stock at the beginning of the period.

Thus the investment flow at time period t can be defined as

$$I_t = K_t - K_{t-1}$$

where, K_t is the capital stock at the end of period t, and K_{t-1} is the stock of capital at the end of period t-1 and thus at the beginning of period t.

Drawing a familiar distinction between working capital and fixed capital, Haavelmo argued that if all capital is circulating capital and completely used up within a period, the theory of capital and the theory of investment become one and the same thing. When fixed capital is present, two different decisions are involved. One is the desired level of capital stock. The other is about the desired rate of investment flow. The decisions governing one will inevitably affect the other, but it is not necessarily the case that one is reducible to the other.

There are principally two ways of thinking about investment. "Hayekian" perspective and "Keynesian" perspective. The Hayekian perspective conceives of investment as adjustment to equilibrium and thus the optimal quantum of investment is effectively a decision on the optimal speed of adjustment. A firm may decide it needs a factory (capital stock decision) but its decision on how fast to build it, how much to spend each month building it etc. – effectively the investment decision—is a separate consideration. Capital decision, of course, influences the investment decision. If the adjustment of the capital stock to a desired level can be accomplished "instantly," then there is no actual investment decision to speak of. However, if for some reason, instant adjustment is not possible, then the investment story begins to matter. How do we distribute the required amount of adjustment? There exist different patterns of approaching the desired amount of adjustment in capital stock and various considerations that enter into determining which adjustment pattern to follow is what lies at the heart of the Hayekian approach to investment theory. Some of the factors to be considered while deciding the most desirable adjustment process to follow include delivery costs, changing of prices by suppliers, fluctuating interest rates and financing costs.

The Keynesian approach puts much less emphasis on the "adjustment" nature of investment. Instead, writers adopting this approach have a more "behavioral take" on the investment decision. They contend that investment is nothing but what capitalists "do." The capital stock has been underplayed by Keynesians. They believe that the principal decision is the investment decision; the capital stock just "follows" from the investment decision. Thus, when firms make investment decisions, they do not have an "optimal capital stock" in the back of their mind. They are rather more concerned with what is the optimal amount of investment for a particular period. For Keynesians, according to Haavelmo, optimal investment is not about "optimal adjustment" but rather about "optimal behaviour."

Haavelmo is credited with clarifying the concept of capital, i.e. defining capital as a factor of production and emphasising the role of capital and time in the productive process. It is to be noted that the particular definition of capital adopted by Haavelmo has notable implications for understanding capital in an equilibrium framework, the role played by capital in economic growth and investment behaviour. He also considered the supply of capital and treatment of durability of capital as endogenous. The last part of the book is focused on the demand for and supply of investment goods in a market economy. In this part, Haavelmo expressed his view as to the central problem: "The fundamental difficulty about investment behavior is not only that its purpose is indirect in satisfying human wants, but that investment represents only the speed of adjustment from one economic situation to another." (Emphasis in original). The relative neglect of Haavelmo's work in the field of capital and investment by the profession has evoked the following insightful comment from Marc Nerlove: "Perhaps because it is so straight forward in its presentation, making its points sound obvious, Haavelmo's work on capital investment appears to have had little impact on the profession. It is seldom even cited."

26.3 CONCLUDING OBSERVATIONS

One well-known paper of Haavelmo, which is a clarification of a point "not original with him" is the 1945 Econometrica article "Multiplier Effects of a Balanced Budget." In elementary economics course, students learn that under conditions of less than full employment, increased government spending matched by an equivalent increase in taxes will have an expansionary effect exactly equal to the increase. The result and the reasons for this are derived in a neat mathematical form, which may perhaps explain the subsequent popularity of Haavelmo's version.

In his 1957 Presidential address to the Econometric Society, Haavelmo discussed the "interplay" between economic theory and econometrics and pleaded for greater use of economic theory in econometric formulations.

In Haavelmo's prize lecture "Econometrics and the Welfare State," he observed that it would be rather not meaningful "when an economic magnitude to be studied is determined by many different factors at the same time, some factors working in one direction, others in the opposite directions.... But what is the answer to the question of the total next effect of all the factors? This question cannot be answered without measures of the strength with which the various factors work in their directions." He acknowledges valuable contributions of Frisch and Tinbergen in this regard.

It is generally agreed that Haavelmo's fame finally rests on the work "The Probability Approach in Econometrics" which has had a major and far-reaching impact on the development of statistical technique appropriate to the analysis of econometric problems. The Nobel award significantly refers to this contribution of Haavelmo. It is a pity that his works on the theory of investment and the theory of economic growth which contain nuggets of wisdom have not received the recognition they ought to have.

26.4 SELECT BIBLIOGRAPHY OF TRYGVE HAAVELMO'S WORKS (IN ENGLISH)

26.4.1 BOOKS

1954 A Study in the Theory of Economic Evolution, North Holland, Amsterdam.

1960 A Study in the Theory of Investment, University of Chicago Press, Chicago, Ill.

26.4.2 ARTICLES

1938 "The Method of Supplementary Confluent Relations, Illustrated by a Study of Stock Prices," Econometrica, Vol.6, No.3.

1939 "A Dynamic Study of Pig Production in Denmark," Nordisk Tidsskrift for Tekmiskokonomi, Vol.5.

1940 "The Inadequacy of Testing Dynamic Theory by Comparing Theoretical Solutions and Observed Cycles," Econometrica, Vol.8, No.4.

1941 "The Effect of the Rate of Interest on Investment: A Note," REStat, Vol.23, No.1.

1943 a "The Statistical Implications of a System of Simultaneous Equations," Econometrica, Vol.11, No.1.

b "Statistical Testing of Business Cycle Theories," REStat, Vol.25, No.1.

1944 "The Probability Approach in Econometrics," Econometrica, Supplement, Vol.12, No.3.

1945 "Multiplier Effects of a Balanced Budget," Econometrica, Vol.13, No.4.

1947 a (with M. A. Girshick), "Statistical Analysis of the Demand for Food: Examples of Simultaneous Estimation of Structural Equations," Econometrica, Vol.15, No.2.

b "Methods of Measuring the Marginal Propensity to Consume," JASA, Vol.42, No.237.

c "Family Expenditures and the Marginal Propensity to Consume," Econometrica, Vol.15, No.4.

d "Quantitative Research in Agricultural Economics: The Interdependence Between Agriculture and the National Economy," Journal of Farm Economics, Vol.29, No.4.

1949 "A Note on the Theory of Investment," RES, Vol.16, No.2.

1950 "Remarks on Frisch's Confluence Analysis and its Use in Econometrics," in Statistical Inference in Dynamic Analysis, (T.C. Koopmans, ed.), Cowles Commission Monograph 10, John Wiley & Sons, New York.

1957 "Econometric Analysis of the Savings Survey Data," Bulletin of Oxford University Institute of Statistics, Vol.19, No.2.

1958 "The Role of the Econometrician in the Advancement of Economic Theory," Econometrica, Vol.26, No.3.

1968 "Business Cycles II: Mathematical Models," in International Encyclopaedia of the Social Sciences, D.L.Sills (ed.), The Macmillan Company and The Free Press, New York.

1969 "Stability of Absolute Prices in a Walrasian System," in Economic Models, Estimation and Risk Programming: Essays in Honor of Gerhard Tintner, K.A. Fox et al. (eds.), Springer-Verlag, New York.

1970 "Some Observations on Welfare and Economic Growth," in Induction, Growth and Trade, Essays in Honor of Sir Roy Harrod, W.A.Eltis et al. (eds.), Clarendon Press, Oxford.

1974 a "Ragnar A.K.Frisch (1895-1973)," Year Book of the American Philosophical Society, 1974.

b "What Can Static Equilibrium Models Tell Us?" Econ Inq, Vol.12, No.1.

1978 "Wicksell on the Currency Theory vs the Banking Principle," ScandJE, Vol.80, No.2.

1989 "Econometrics and the Welfare State," Nobel Prize Lecture, Nobel Lectures, Economics, 1981-1990, Karl-Goran Maler, World Scientific Publishing Co., Singapore, 1992.

2007 (with O. Bjerkholt), "The Nature and Logic of Econometric Inference: The 1942 Hillside Lecture," Econometric Theory, Cambridge University Press, Vol.23, No.5.

26.5 WORKS OF OTHERS

Koopmans, T.C. (ed.) (1950), Statistical Inference in Dynamic Economic Models, John Wiley & Sons, New York.

Nerlove, M. (1990), "Trygve Haavelmo: A Critical Appreciation," ScandJE, Vol.92, No.1.

Solow, R.M. (1956), "A Contribution to the Theory of Economic Growth," QJE, Vol.70.

Swan, T.W. (1956), "Economic Growth and Capital Accumulation," Economic Record, Vol.32, No.2.

CHAPTER 27

JAMES JOSEPH HECKMAN

(1944 –)

The Royal Swedish Academy of Sciences has awarded the Bank of Sweden Prize in Economic Sciences in Memory of Alfred Nobel for the year 2000 jointly to Professor James J. Heckman, University of Chicago, Chicago, U.S.A., and Professor Daniel Little McFadden, University of California, Berkley, U.S.A. In the field of micro econometrics, each of the laureates has developed theory and methods that are widely used in the statistical analysis of individual and household behaviour, within economics as well as other social sciences.

The citation of the Academy reads:

"...to James Heckman for his development of theory and methods for analyzing selective samples and to Daniel McFadden for his development of theory and methods for analyzing discrete choice."

Micro econometrics is an interface between economics and statistics. It comprises economic theory and statistical methods used for the purpose of studying microeconomic data – that is, economic information about individuals, households and business firms, such as decisions on labour supply, migration or occupational choice and consumption. Micro data appear either as cross section data or as longitudinal data. The former refer to conditions at the same point in time. Longitudinal data, also referred to as panel data, relate to the same observational units over a succession of periods, say years. During the last three decades and more, the field of micro econometrics has burgeoned owing to the creation of large data bases embodying micro data.

Greater availability of microeconomic data coupled with the development of increasingly powerful computers has facilitated empirical studies of many issues for testing microeconomic theory. The issues studied include: what determines whether an individual decides to work and, if so, how many hours? How do economic incentives impact choices of education, occupation or place of residence? What are the effects of labour market and educational programmes on an individual's employment and income?

The use of micro data has created fresh statistical problems or new econometric problems owing primarily to the limitations inherent in such non-experimental data. Since the researcher generally observes certain variables for particular individuals or households or firms, a sample selected by him or her might not be random and thereby not a representative sample. Even when samples are representative, some characteristics that affect behaviour of individuals remain unobservable, making it difficult or even impossible to explain some of the variation in behaviour among individuals.

The laureates of year 2000, James Heckman and Daniel McFadden have each shown how one can resolve some fundamental problems that arise in the statistical analysis of micro data. The methods developed by them have solid foundations in economic theory. These methods have, however, emerged in close interaction with applied empirical studies where new databases served as a definitive pre-requisite. The microeconomic methods developed by Heckman and McFadden are now part of the standard toolkit, not only of economists, but also of other social scientists.

Available microeconomic data involve selective samples. For instance, data on wages cannot be sampled randomly if only individuals, with certain characteristics unobservable to the researcher, choose to work or pursue education. If such selection is not taken into account, statistical estimation of economic relationships yields biased results. Such selection problems are legion in micro econometric studies. Heckman has developed statistical methods of handling selective samples in an appropriate way. He has also proposed tools for solving closely related problems with individual differences unobserved by the researcher. Such problems are common when evaluating social programmes or estimating how the duration of unemployment affects chances of getting a job and so on. He is considered a leader of applied research in these areas. His development of methodological contributions, in conjunction with applied empirical research, is particularly noteworthy in labour economics. Heckman's analysis of selection problems in micro econometric research has had profound implication for applied research in economics as well as in other social sciences.

Micro data often reflect discrete choices. For instance, data concerning individuals' occupation or place of residence or mode of travel reflect the choices they have made among a limited number of alternatives. In economic theory, traditional demand analysis presupposed that individuals' choice be represented by a continuous variable, thereby rendering it inappropriate for studying discrete choice behaviour. Prior to McFadden's contributions, empirical studies of such choices lacked a foundation in economic theory. The empirical research has been transformed by McFadden thanks to his developing a new theory of discrete choice as well as invention of appropriate statistical methods. McFadden's theory of discrete choice originates in microeconomic theory, according to which each individual chooses a specific alternative that maximises his utility. However, as the researcher cannot observe all the factors determining individual choices, he perceives a random variation across individuals with the same observed characteristics. On the basis of his new theory, McFadden developed micro econometric models that can be used, for example, to predict the share of a population that will choose different alternatives.

McFadden's micro econometric methods are eminently applicable in fields such as transportation, communications etc. His extensive application of his own methods includes the design of the San Francisco BART system, as well as investments in phone services and housing for the aged.

James Heckman's contributions are summarised in this chapter while Daniel McFadden's short biographical sketch and his contributions to economic science are provided in the next chapter.

27.1 A SHORT BIOGRAPHY: JAMES HECKMAN

James J. Heckman was born on April 19, 1944 in Chicago, U.S.A. His high school years were spent in Lakewood, Colorado, a suburb of Denver. He attended Colorado College, in Colorado Springs on a Boeltcher Foundation Fellowship majoring in mathematics. Heckman also took a course in economic development. After college, he briefly attended the University of Chicago in economics where he found Milton Friedman "fascinating" and also "enjoyed" the lectures of Harry Johnson.

Heckman joined Princeton University for his graduate studies and received Ph.D. in economics in 1971. During his graduate student days, there was an ongoing large scale empirical research on labour supply and projects on labour market models. He states: "These empirical projects were a major source of stimulation to my intellectual development. In addition, I was fascinated by the pioneering work of Richard Quandt on estimating travel demand–- a field that would later come to be called 'discrete choice theory' – and in particular the problem of using econometrics to estimate the demand for new goods." According to Heckman the ethos at Princeton at that time encouraged the application of economic theory and econometric methods to solve policy problems.

In his autobiographical note, Heckman traces the origin of his interest in labour economics and in developing new econometric methods. There was ferment in the air both at Princeton and elsewhere as many new sources of micro data became available to study the labour market. There was tremendous intellectual challenge in devising methods for creatively using these data. There was exciting new intellectual framework for analysing and interpreting the new microeconomic data in the works of modern labour economics as developed by Gary Becker (1992 Noble Laureate) and Jacob Mincer. Heckman states: "The scientific study of labour economics provided the opportunity for me to unite theory with evidence, my lifetime intellectual passion."

After serving as Assistant Professor at Columbia University, Heckman moved to the University of Chicago in 1973. He observes that at Columbia "it was from Kelvin Lancaster that I learned about problems with the representative consumer model and methods for dealing with them. Like Quandt, Lancaster was interested in the problem of estimating the demand for a new good." Since 1973, he has been Professor of Economics at University of Chicago. Since 1995 he is the Henry Schultz Distinguished Service Professor of Economics there. He was Director of the Economics Research Center, Department of Economics of the University of Chicago. He has been Director of the Center for Social Program Evaluation at the Irving B Harris Graduate School of Public Policy Studies at Chicago since 1991. Heckman has been professor of Science and Society at University College, Dublin, since June 2006. He is also professor of Law at the University of Chicago Law School. He is a

Senior Research Fellow at the American Bar Foundation since 1991. In 2004, Heckman was appointed as the Distinguished Chair of Micro econometrics at University College, London.

Heckman published over 280 professional articles and received numerous awards and honours for his work. The awards include John Bates Clark Award of the American Economic Association in 1983, the 2005 Jacob Mincer Award for Lifetime Achievement in Labor Economics, University College Dublin Ulysses Medal, 2005 and the Aigner award from the Journal of Econometrics, 2007 and 2008. He is a Fellow, Econometric Society (1980), Member, American Academy of Arts and Sciences (1985) and Member, National Academy of Sciences, 1992. He was awarded Guggenheim Fellowship (1978-1979). He is Fellow, Econometric Society (1980), the Society's First Vice-President, 2011-2012 and President-elect, 2013.

Since 1991, the American Bar Foundation has been supporting Heckman's work on the impact of law on the economy.

Heckman contributed policy analysis to Barack Obama's 2008 Presidential campaign. He became editor of the Journal of Political Economy (JPE) in 2011. His recent research is focussed on human development and lifecycle skill formation, with a special emphasis on the economics of early childhood education.

27.2 A SUMMARY OF JAMES HECKMAN'S CONTRIBUTIONS

Heckman, in his Nobel Prize lecture spells out the content and the rationale of the field of micro econometrics which has emerged in the past four decades or so "to aid economists in providing more accurate descriptions of the economy, in designing and evaluating public policies and in testing economic theories and estimating the parameters of well posed economic models." It links the theory of individual behaviour to individual data – individuals may be persons, households or firms. Research in micro econometrics, according to Heckman is "data driven" and is also "policy driven." His initial research effort focussed on the analysis of decision-making by households, particularly with regard to labour supply and consumption decisions. Two major contributions of this time are: "The Analysis of Female Labour Supply" and "A Study of Inter-temporal Labour Supply Choices." Through his work on labour supply, Heckman has achieved integration of consumer theory and the theory of labor supply, developed an empirical life-cycle perspective for labour supply and conducted statistical analysis of participation, labour supply and market wages. His studies covering labour supply, earnings of labour, duration of unemployment, evaluation of labour-market programmes, fertility and discrimination have led to the development of his research on:

1. Selection Bias and Self-selection;
2. Evaluation of Labour Market Programmes or Programme Evaluation; and
3. Labour Market Dynamics.

Heckman's major contributions are surveyed here under the afore mentioned three heads.

27.2.1 SELECTION BIAS AND SELF-SELECTION

Selection problems permeate in applied micro econometric research. Selection bias may crop up when a sample under study does not randomly represent the underlying population. Data on working hours or wages are available as they are observed only for those individuals who have chosen to work. Likewise, earnings of migrants are observed only for those who have opted to move. Similarly, earnings of university graduates are observed only for those who have completed university education and so on. Here, in these cases, selection bias arises when a sample under study does not randomly represent the underlying population. The selection problem can be construed as a problem of missing observations. We cannot observe wages and working hours of labour among non-working individuals, had they opted to work. Similarly, the non-migrant labour earnings are not observable to the analyst, had they chosen to migrate. Analogously, no information is available on the earnings of workers with a high school education had they pursued a university education. The problem facing the analyst is to estimate population parameters even in the face of a selective sample. Non-random sample selection may result from individual decisions by the economic agents under study or self-selection; it may also reflect administrative rules, or decisions on the part of analysts.

Hickman's approach to the selection problem is intimately associated to economic theory. He argues that observations are often missing as a result of conscious (self-selection) choices made by economic agents; for example the decision to work, to migrate or to pursue higher education. Thus, the relation between the reasons for missing observations and the nature of non-missing observations takes on "an intriguing theoretical structure." The solutions to selection problems suggested by Heckman can be well appreciated not only statistically but also in terms of microeconomic theory.

The Information Note put out by the Nobel Foundation provides an illustration of the selection problem, which may be adopted. Assume w denotes the wage of an individual (shown on the vertical axis) and x is a factor that affects this wage, such as the level of education of the individual (shown on the horizontal axis).

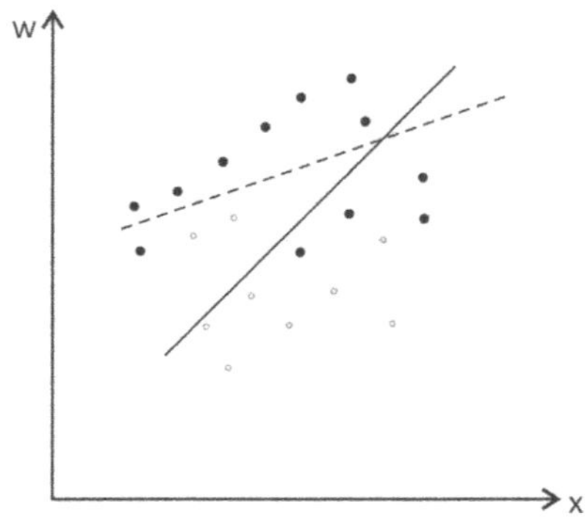

Fig. 27.1 Problem of Selection Bias

Each point in Fig. 27.1 represents individuals with the same education and wage levels in a large and representative sample of population. The same line depicts the statistical and true relationship that we would estimate if we could observe wages and education for all these individuals. Now assume, in accordance with economic theory, that only those individuals whose market wages exceed the threshold value (the reservation wage) choose to work. If this is the case, individuals with relatively high wages and relatively long education will be over represented in the sample we actually observe: the dark points in the figure. This selective sample creates a problem of selection bias in the sense that we will estimate the relation between wage and education given by the dashed line in the figure. We thus find a relationship weaker than the true one thereby underestimating the effect of education on wages.

Heckman's contributions to the econometrics of selective samples emerged concurrently with his studies of labour supply in the mid-1970's. In his work relating to male labour supply, Heckman was confronted with the economic problem of non-participation and the development of an analysis of reservation wage in the context of costs of child-care. In addition, as it was noticed that there was variation in hours worked among participants, the functional form employed had to be flexible. There was the issue of missing wage as well. He presented a model of married women's labour supply based on the utility maximisation hypothesis. The sample of working-women in his study is self-selected in that the hours of work are only observed for women with market wages higher than their reservation wages. Heckman derived a likelihood function for this problem, estimated equations for market wages, the probability for working and hours of work, and then used the structural parameters to predict the probability of working, hours of work, reservation wages and market wages. This paper is considered an excellent example of the way in which microeconomic theory can be combined with methods of micro econometrics to shed light on an important economic question.

Heckman's subsequent work provided computationally simpler methods for dealing with selection bias. Starting with an additive regression model, where the unobservables are additive with unconditional mean zero, he noted that, for normal distributions, the conditional mean for a selected sample involved a single additional term which itself was a function of the selection probability. This term or "control function" or "bias function" could therefore be estimated in a first step from the choice probability model. This well-known Heckman correction, which is also called the two-stage method, Heckman's lambda or the Heckit method has become part of the standard toolbox in applied micro econometric work.

The Advanced Information note of the Royal Swedish Academy of Sciences described Heckman's two-stage method with the following two equations:

$$w_i = x_{1i}\,\beta_1 + \varepsilon_{1i} \tag{1}$$

$$e^*_i = x_{2i}\,\beta_2 + \varepsilon_{2i} \tag{2}$$

The individual's market wage is determined by equation (1), while equation (2) is a "particular equation" describing the individual's propensity to work. Thus, w_i is the observed market wage for individual i if she works and ε_i, a latent variable that captures the propensity to work; x_{1i} and x_{2i} are vectors of 1 observed explanatory variables, such as age and education. ε_{1i} and ε_{2i} are mean-zero stochastic errors, representing the influence of unobserved variables affecting w_i and e^*_i. The parameters (vectors) of interest to us are β_1 and β_2.

The latent variable e^*_i is unobserved. Making use of a dummy variable approach, we can observe the market wage only if the individual works. It is likely that the unobserved terms ε_{1i} and ε_{2i} are positively correlated. Individuals with higher wages, given x_{1i} and x_{2i}, are presumably also more likely to work. If so, the sample of individuals observed as working will not accurately represent the underlying population, even in a large sample. Failure to recognise this fact of selectivity generally produces inconsistent estimates of the parameters in the wage equation [equation (1)].

Heckman suggested a simple method to deal with the selection problem or selection bias, which can be considered as a standard problem of omitted-variable bias. The problem is to find an empirical representation of the conditional mean of ε1i and include this variable in the wage equation. In his prize lecture Heckman states: "Much of the econometric literature on the selection problem combines discussions of identification (going from population generated by selection rules back to the source of population) with discussions, of estimation in solving the inferential problem of going from observed samples to hypothetical populations.... Understanding the sources of identification of a model are essential to understanding of how much of what we are getting out of an empirical model is a consequence of what we put into it."

As Richard Blundell comments: "The selection model and the two-step estimator were also much more generally applicable than in the normal distribution case and semi-parametric extensions were readily forthcoming for the additively separable model...this estimator not only became widely used in application, it also generated many important semi-parametric estimation and identification results."

Furthermore, Heckman's work has generated many empirical applications in economics as well as in other social sciences and applicable statistics concerned with non-randomly missing data. An early empirical application of this work is the 1978 study examining relative wage effects of union membership in the United States by Lung-Fei Lee. Lee's work is done recognising that union membership in the U.S. is not random but the outcome of individual self-selection. Another important work is 1979 paper by Willis and Rosen entitled "Education and Self Selection" examining the wage premium associated with higher education, taking into consideration, that endogenous educational choice is influenced by the perceived gains to education. In a later work, Heckman has shown in papers written in collaboration with co-authors that the aggregate and sector wage distributions are impacted when individuals self-select into the labour market and into sectors of the economy. The analysis in one of them includes an evaluation of how self-selection affects wage inequality.

Another work of Heckman which introduces what he calls the "principle assumption" is his 1978 Econometrica article "Dummy Endogenous Variables in a Simultaneous Equation System" which derives the conditions for a coherent econometric framework. The essence of the article as explained by Blundell: "If actions are a mixture of discrete and continuous variables – labour supply and consumption, for example – and are in addition simultaneously determined, then there will be a further condition [principle assumption] on the econometric model to guarantee that it provides a coherent statistical relationship between inputs and response.... This involved a jump parameter in the basic mean of the latent variable underlying the discrete choice."

27.2.2 PROGRAMME EVALUATION OR EVALUATION OF LABOUR MARKET PROGRAMMES

The classical problem of programme evaluation aims at determining how participation in a particular programme impacts individual outcomes, such as earnings or employment of labour, compared to non-participation. The greatest difficulty is to characterise the counterfactual situation; that is, the question that needs to be answered is; what would have happened if the individual had not participated in the programme? As it is not possible to observe an individual agent as both participant as well as non-participant, the information relating to outcomes of non-participants has to be used for this purpose. Since the assignment of individuals to programmes is rarely purely random, the participants' group becomes selected sample with observed and unobserved characteristics that may differ from those of overall population.

While Heckman's early research on issues in labour economics has the objective of measurement of the effects of policies, it is only in his work in mid-1980's that we see the comprehensive development of these ideas. The work was devoted to an examination of training programmes and marked the start of a large body of theoretical and empirical work that Heckman has produced on the problem of evaluation in association with his colleagues and students. His papers, particularly with Robb in 1985 and 1986, are considered very innovative. According to Blundell "[the papers] extend the control function approach for selection to the policy intervention framework.... These studies also develop the estimation of the treatment on the treated parameter in a random coefficient model for discrete programs – the heterogeneous response model – and point out to bias from standard instrumental variable procedures." They extend this to the repeated cross-section and panel data framework and develop conditions under which the fixed effect estimator recovers the treatment on the treated parameter. "The results relate to identification and estimation of the effects of social programmes." His work in this area, like his research on labour supply, makes use of a structural approach, grounded in microeconomic theory to guide the specification of the model and for interpreting the empirical results. We notice two principal components of evaluation: (i) a model of participation in programmes, and (ii) a model of programme outcomes.

This work was important and continues to be so, particularly in the context of increasingly widespread implementation of active labour-market programmes, such as training, job-search assistance and employment subsidies in most OECD countries. Such programmes are commonly targeted at individuals who are unemployed or have low skills or earnings. The importance of this type of work has become clear as greater emphasis was being put on the use of experimental design of evaluation programmes.

The availability of experimental data concerning policy interventions and especially the data developed for the purpose of evaluating participants in the Job Training Partnership Act gave impetus for appraising alternative approaches to valuation. The experimental data are employed to characterise the bias from depending on non-experimental econometric methods. In his 1998 Econometrica paper jointly authored with others, Heckman identified the biases in three popular non-experimental methods – matching, selection and difference-in-differences. "Selection adjusts for unobserved differences that are correlated with participation in the programme while matching adjusts for differences among observables. Difference-in-differences adjusts for unobservables – but only those that are time invariant – and it also requires repeated observations." The study is also helpful in regard to evaluation studies, which do not have access to experimental controls. The bias is due to the failure to directly measure the counterfactual impact of the programme on persons who did not receive it. With experimental data, this can be measured directly from the randomised control group.

The question of the efficacy of using the experimental data is an important one. In his later research work, Heckman has focused on this issue and has helped improve our understanding of the pros and cons of using experimental rather than non-experimental data in programme evaluation. These studies have also stimulated advances in theory in the use of matching methods as econometric evaluation estimators. These studies give an indication that Heckman, on balance, does not appear to be a strong supporter of the experimental approach. His argument boils down to a conclusion that social experiments are valid only under special statistical and behavioural assumptions. A main lesson seems to be that there exist no universally correct methods for evaluating programmes. Conclusions regarding the effects are often somewhat pessimistic. The Nobel Foundation's note observes: "A survey primarily of U.S. studies (Heckman, Lalonde and Smith, 1999) concludes that programs frequently have very small (sometimes negative) effects for the participants and do not appear to pass conventional cost benefit tests. On the other hand, there does seem to be substantial heterogeneity in program outcomes across participants and types of programs."

In his Prize lecture, Heckman observes: "Looking across countries and over time, most active labor market policies are ineffective in promoting long-term wage growth and employment. Application of very basic empirical methods shows that comparing post-program outcomes of trainees with program outcome measures – the common practice in many evaluation schemes – dramatically overstates the gains from participation in training." This occurs because trainees typically experience a decline in their employment prior to entering training and training is a form of job search. Much of the post program improvement in outcome measures would have occurred in the absence of any training program.

Another dimension to the programme evaluation work relates to its macroeconomic implications. The development of micro econometric methods is, no doubt, for evaluating a number of social programmes launched by the modern welfare state and for interpreting empirical economic relationships. However, many such programmes are national in character and are likely to have general equilibrium effects. Partial equilibrium methods, in their nature, cannot evaluate the complete impacts of large scale public programmes. Heckman recognises that the methodology developed for evaluating treatment effects or problem-specific parameters is ineffective in analysing programmes with universal coverage unless entire economies can be used for the treatment and control groups.

Heckman notes that the evidence from the microeconomic data has already had a significant effect on the development of macroeconomic theory which is "slowly abandoning the representative agent paradigm." He advocates a synthesis of macro and microeconomic approaches to analyse policies instituted at the national level with general equilibrium impacts and to interpret equilibrium pricing relationships such as earnings functions or asset pricing equations. He says: "...cross sectional variation cannot identify the effects of prices and interest rates that are common across persons. Yet accounting for the feedback of capital markets (borrowing costs) on human capital or physical capital investment decisions is essential in investigating the full effects of national policies on skill formation. Moreover, cross sectional variation in wages, prices, or interest rates is unlikely to be exogenous and this raises separate econometric issues."

27.2.3 LABOUR MARKET DYNAMICS

One of the more difficult issues in the macro econometrics facing a researcher using the panel data or longitudinal data concerns the separation of state dependence and heterogeneity. Heckman's 1980 World Congress address and his subsequent work, particularly 1991 article "Identifying the Hand of the Past: Distinguishing State Dependence from Heterogeneity" focusses on this issue. He has recognised that in the presence of heterogeneity, exogenous variables become endogenous. Permanent individual attributes of tastes or technology get reflected as unobserved heterogeneity in panel data. Since these attributes will be correlated with the past choices, variables that represent such past choices will be endogenous. They will be correlated with unobservables. Blundell states: "This includes historic outcomes of the dependent variable and explanatory variables related to those historic outcomes (predetermined or weakly exogenous variables).... Indeed, even if there is no direct state dependence in a process, unobserved heterogeneity can induce the appearance of state dependence, so that individual decisions may appear unduly habit forming and unemployment may appear to "cause" future unemployment even when it does not. Alternatively, true dependence on the past may be masked by offsetting effects of permanent heterogeneity."

Heckman's later work developed into the area of event history and duration analysis. The data that are available to a researcher in economics for the purpose of analysing labour market durations are not drawn from controlled experiments. As such, econometric analysis of duration data has to take into account the bearing that the sample plan has on the distribution of sample spells. The analysis of duration data, which has a long tradition in engineering and bio-medical research, has entered into economic and social science research for analysing a variety of problems. Duration models are used for studying the length of spells of unemployment, demographic events such as marriage, fertility, migration and mortality, issues relating to industrial relations such as duration of strikes and to political events as well such as dependence of the occurrence of government crises on the time elapsed since the last election. Consumer research has also been using duration models as, for instance, to study the timing of purchases of products. Macroeconomic research has started using duration models as, for example, for studying the duration of business cycles in an economy.

The information provided by the Royal Swedish Academy of Sciences while announcing the award makes a specific mention of the fact that in his work on econometric duration analysis, Heckman has been particularly preoccupied with the effects of unobserved heterogeneity, i.e. individual differences in unobserved variables that may impact the duration of employment or unemployment. Since unobserved heterogeneity in the context of duration data brings in specific selection problems, Heckman's work in this area conforms to his overall research agenda on sample selection. This may be illustrated by studies of how the exit from unemployment to employment unfolds over a spell of unemployment. One problem here is that persons with relatively weak prospects of employment seem to continue as unemployed to a higher degree than those with favourable characteristics. Thus, the "quality" of the stock of unemployed at each point in time is the consequence of a process of selection partly influenced by factors unobserved by the analyst. Overrepresentation of more "unemployment-prone" persons at long durations can easily lead to the conclusion of negative duration dependence. That is, the exit rate to employment declines over a spell of unemployment. However, what seems to be negative duration effect may simply be an effect of selection or sorting.

Blundell appraising the contribution of Heckman and his co-authors makes the following comments: "The conventional analysis of a single spell duration data remained based in a random effects approach with unobserved heterogeneity chosen from some parametric family. Although the parametric chosen was known to influence the resulting parameters, it was not until Heckman's Econometrica article with Singer...and subsequent studies...that it became apparent that the distribution of unobservables was non-parametrically identified."

Heckman's research work on labour market dynamics is quite extensive. Reference may be made to identification results for a class of duration models and further treatment of identification issues in his own work and his 1984 paper co-authored with Taber.

27.3 CONCLUDING OBSERVATIONS

Heckman has made outstanding contributions to economic science besides those that are briefly touched upon here. It is the opinion of researchers in the field that the "interaction between the economic behaviour of individuals and the micro data so generated was at the heart of Heckman's development of the selection model and has changed the way empirical microeconomics has been conducted since 1970's."

In regard to the research efforts of appraisal of labour-market programmes, James Heckman is widely accepted as the world's "foremost researcher" on econometric policy evaluation. According to Blundell a more robust approach to policy evaluation is being developed (for which substantial credit should go to Heckman) that will make policy analysis more objective and empirically rigorous.

Heckman is in no small measure responsible for the powerful challenge mounted to Alfred Marshall's theoretically fruitful motion of the "Representative Firm" and the "Representative Consumer," firmly rooted in economic theory. As he states in his Prize lecture "At its heart, economic theory is about individuals and their interactions in markets or other social settings. The data to test the micro theory are micro data." It is important to note in this context that the evolution of micro econometrics in the past more than thirty years can be described as in Heckman's words, "moving from answering the harder structural questions to the relatively easier treatment effect questions."

Heckman has also dealt with relevant contemporary developmental issues. As an example, we may refer to his argument that the most significant investments U.S. can make are in the first five years of a citizen's life and that they pay for themselves.

This note may conclude with Heckman's comment on the pleasures of academic life. "At Chicago, I have had close relationships with many students with whom I have co-authored numerous papers and from whom I learned much. One of the greatest pleasures of academic life is watching young tentative students form into finished mature scholars with well developed ideas."

27.4 SELECT BIBLIOGRAPHY OF JAMES HECKMAN'S CONTRIBUTIONS

27.4.1 BOOKS

1985 (edited with B. Singer), Longitudinal Analysis of Labor Market Data, Cambridge University Press, New York.

2003 (with A. Krueger), Inequality in America: What Role for Human Capital Policy?, MIT Press, Cambridge, MA.

2004		(edited with C. Pages), Law and Employment: Lessons from Latin America and Caribbean, University of Chicago Press for NBER, Chicago, Ill.
2001-2007		(edited with E.L. Leamer), Handbook of Econometrics, Vols.5, 6A and 6B, North Holland, Amsterdam.
2010		(edited with R. Nelson and L. Cabatingan), Global Perspectives on the Rule of Law, Routledge, New York.

27.4.2 ARTICLES

1974	a	(with O. Ashenfelter) "The Estimation of Income and Substitution Effects in Model of Family Labor Supply," Econometrica, Vol.42, Jan.
	b	"Life Cycle Consumption and Labor Supply: An Explanation of the Relationship between Income and Consumption over the Life Cycle," AER, Vol.64, No.1.
	c	"Shadow Prices, Market Wages and Labor Supply," Econometrica, Vol.42, June.
	d	"Effects of Child-care Programs on Women's Work Effort," JPE, Vol.82, No.2. Reprinted in T.W. Schultz (ed.), Economics of the Family: Marriage, Children and Human Capital, University of Chicago Press, Chicago, Ill.
	e	(with R. Willis), "A Stochastic Model of Reproduction: An Econometric Approach," Papers and Proceedings of the American Statistical Association, Social Statistics Section.
1976	a	"A Life Cycle Model of Earnings, Learning and Consumption," JPE, Vol.84, Aug.
	b	"Simultaneous Equation Models with both Continuous and Discrete Endogenous Variables with and without Structural Shift in the Equations," in Studies in Nonlinear Estimation, S. Goldfeld and R. Quandt (eds.), Ballinger, Cambridge, MA.
	c	"The Common Structure of Statistical Models of Truncation, Sample Selection and Limited Dependent Variables and a Simple Estimate for Such Models," Annals of Economics and Social Measurement, Dec.
1978	a	"A Partial Survey of Recent Research on the Labour Supply of Women," AER, Vol.68, No.2.
	b	"Dummy Endogenous Variables in a Simultaneous Equation System," Econometrica, Vol.46, July.
1979		"Sample Section Bias as a Specification Error," Econometrica Vol. 47, Jan.
1980	a	(with T. MaCurdy), "A Life Cycle Model of Female Labour Supply," REStat, Vol. 47, Jan.

	b	(with G. Borjas), "Does Unemployment Cause Future Unemployment: Definitions, Questions and Answers from a Continuous Time Model of Heterogeneity and State Dependence," Economica, Vol. 47, Aug.
	c	"Sample Selection Bias as a Specification Error with an Application to the Estimation of Labor Supply Functions," in J. Smith (ed.), Female Labor Supply: Theory and Estimation, Princeton University Press, Princeton. NJ.
1981	a	"Statistical Models for Discrete Panel Data," in Structural Analysis of Discrete Data with Econometric Applications, Manski, C. and D. McFadden (eds.), MIT Press, Cambridge, MA.
	b	"Heterogeneity and State Dependence," in Studies in Labor Markets, S. Rosen (ed.), University of Chicago Press, Chicago, Ill.
	c	(with T. Macrudy), "Current Theoretical and Empirical Studies of Labor Supply.: Second Generation Studies," Research in Labor Economics, JAI Press Inc., Greenwich, CT.
	d	(with C. Flinn), "Models for the Analysis of Labor Force Dynamics," in Advances in Econometrics, Bassman, R. and G. Rhodes (eds.), Vol. 1, Jai Press Inc., Greenwich, CT.
1984	a	(with B. Singer), "Econometric Duration Analysis," Journal of Econometrics, Vol. 24, No.1-2.
	b	(with B. Singer), "A Method for Minimizing the Impact of Distributional Assumptions in Econometric Models for Duration Data," Econometrica, Vol. 52, Mar.
	c	(with B. Singer), "The Identifiability of the Proportional Hazard Model," RES, Vol.51, No.2.
1985		(with G. Sedlacek), "Heterogeneity, Aggregation and Market Wage Function: An Empirical Model of Self-selection in the Labor Market," JPE, Vol. 93, Dec.
1986	a	(with T. Macurdy), "Labor Econometrics," in Griliches. Z and M. Intriligator (eds.) Handbook of Econometrics, Vol. 3, North Holland, Amsterdam.
	b	(with R. Robb) "Alternative Methods for Solving the Problem of Selection Bias in Evaluating the Impact of Treatment on Outcomes," in Weiner, H. (ed.), Drawing Inference from Self-selected Samples, Springer-Verlag, New York.
1987		"Selection Bias and the Economics of Self Selection," The New Palgrave: A Dictionary of Economics, Macmillan, London.
1989		(with B. Honore), "The Identifiability of Competing Risk Model," Biometrika, Vol. 89, June.

1990 a (with G. Sedlacek), "Self Selection and the Distribution of Hourly Wage Rates," Journal of Labor Economics, Vol. 8, Part 2, Jan.

b "Varieties of Selection Bias," AER, Vol. 80, No.2.

c (with B. Honore), "The Empirical Content of the Roy Model," Econometrica, Vol. 58, Sep.

1991 "Identifying the Hand of the Past: Distinguishing State Dependence from Heterogeneity," AER, Vol. 81, No.2.

1992 "Randomization and Social Policy Evaluation," in Evaluating Welfare and Training Programs, Manski, C. and I. Garfinkel (eds.) Harvard University Press, Cambridge, MA.

1993 "What Has Been Learned about Labor Supply in the Past Twenty Years?" AER, Vol. 83, No.2.

1995 (with J. Smith), "Assessing the Case for Social Experiments," JEP, Vol.9, Spring.

1996 (with H. Ichimura et al. eds.), "Sources of Selection Bias in Evaluating Programs: An Interpretation of Conventional Measures and Evidence on the Effectiveness of Matching as a Program Evaluation Method," Proceedings of the National Academy of Sciences, Vol.93, Nov.

1997 a "Instrumental Variables: A Study of Implicit Behavioral Assumptions used in Making Program Evaluation," Journal of Human Resources, Vol.32, Summer.

b (with Ichimura H. and P. Todd), "Matching as an Econometric Evaluation Estimator: Evidence from Evaluating a Job Training Program," RES, Vol.64, Oct.

c (with J. Snyder), "Linear Probability of Models of the Demand for Attributes with an Empirical Application to Estimating the Preferences of Legislators," RandJE, Vol. 28, Special Issue.

1998 a (with Lochner L. and C. Taber), "Explaining Rising Wage Inequality: Explorations with a Dynamic General Equilibrium Model of Labor Earnings with Heterogeneous Agents," Review of Economic Dynamics, Vol.1, No.1.

b (with Lochner L. and C. Taber), "General Equilibrium Treatment Effects: A Study of Tuition Policy," AER, Vol.88, No.2.

c (with Ichimura, H. et al.eds.), "Characterizing Selection Bias using Experimental Data," Econometrica, Vol.66, Sep.

d (with Vytlacil, E.), "Instrumental Variables Methods for the Correlated Random Coefficient Model: Estimating the Average Rate of Return to Schooling when the Return is Correlated with Schooling," Journal of Human Resources, Vol.33, Fall.

1999 a (with Vytlacil, E.), "Local Instrumental Variables and Latent Variable Models for Identifying and Bounding Treatment Effects," Proceedings of the National Academy of Sciences, Vol. 96, Apr.

b (with Lochner, L and C. Taber), "Evaluation of Education and Training Programs in a General Equilibrium Setting," in Trade, Growth and Development: Essays in Honor of T. N. Srinivasan, Ranis, G and L.K. Rant (eds.) Elsevier Science B.V., Amsterdam.

c (with Lalonde, R. and J. Smith), "The Economics and Econometrics of Active Labor Market Programs," in Handbook of Labor Economics, Vol.3, Ashenfalter, O. and D. Card (eds.), North Holland, Amsterdam.

2000 a "Casual Parameters with Policy Analysis in Economics: A 20th Century Retrospective," QJE, Vol.115, Feb.

b (with Vytlacil, E.), "Local Instrumental Variables," in Nonlinear Statistical Modeling: Proceedings of the Thirteenth International Symposium in Theory and Econometrics: Essays in Honor of Takeshi Amemiya, (Hsiao, C. et al. eds.), Cambridge University Press, Cambridge.

c (with Lyons, T. and P. Todd), "Understanding Black-White Wage Differentials," 1960-1990, AER, Vol.90, No.2.

d (with Browning, M. and L. Hansen), "Micro data and General Equilibrium Models," in Handbook of Macroeconomics, Taylor, J. and M. Woodford (eds.) North Holland, Amsterdam.

2001 a "The Dynamics of Educational Attainment for Blacks, Whites and Hispanics," JPE, Vol. 109, No.3.

b "Micro Data, Heterogeneity and the Evaluation of Public Policy," Nobel Lecture, JPE, Vol. 109,No.4.

c (with Vytlacil, E.), "Policy Relevant Treatment Parameters," AER, Vol. 91, No.2.

2002 a (with Vytlacil, E.), "Econometric Evaluation of Social Programs," in Handbook of Econometrics, Vol.6, Heckman, J. and E. L. Leamer (eds.), North Holland, Amsterdam.

b (with I. Ekeland and L. Nesheim), "Identifying Hedonic Models," AER, Vol.92, No.2.

c (with P. Carneiro), "The Evidence on Credit Constraints in Post-Secondary Schooling," EJ, Vol. 112, No.482.

2003 (with J. Abbring et al.), "Adverse Selection and Moral Hazard in Insurance: Can Dynamic Data Help to Distinguish?" Journal of the European Economic Association, Vol. 1, No.2-3.

2004 a (with S. Navarro), "Using Matching Instrumental Variables and Control Functions to Estimate Economic Choice Models," REStat, Vol.86, No.1.

b (with I. Ekeland and L. Nesheim), "Identification and Estimation of Hedonic Models," JPE, Vol.112, No.1.

2005 a (with F. Cunha and S. Navarro), "Separating Heterogeneity from Uncertainty in Measuring Income Inequality," OEP, Vol.57, No.2.

b (with E. Vytlacil), "Structural Equations, Treatment Effects and Econometric Policy Evaluation," Econometrica,Vol.73, No.3.

2006 (with S. Uzawa and E. Vytlacil), "Understanding Instrumental Variables in Models with Essential Heterogeneity," REStat, Vol.88, No.3.

2007 a (with F. Cunha), "The Technology of Skill Formation," AER, Vol.97, No.2.

b (with F. Cunha and S. Navarro), "The Identification and Economic Content of Ordered Choice Models with Stochastic Threshholds," IER, Vol.48, No.4.

2008 a (with F. Cunha), "A New Framework for Analysis of Inequality," Macroeconomic Dynamics, Vol.12, Supplement 2.

b (C. Taber), "The Roy Model," The New Palgrave: A Dictionary of Economics (2nd ed.), Palgrave Macmillan, New York.

c "Econometric Causality," International Statistical Review, Vol.76,No.1.

2009 (with L. Borgans et al.), "Gender Differences in Risk Aversion and Ambiguity Aversion," Journal of European Economic Association, Vol.7, No. 2-3.

2010 a (with P. LaFontaine), "The American High School Graduation Rate: Trends and Levels," REStat, Vol.92, No.2.

b "Building Bridges Between Structural and Program Evaluation Approaches to Evaluating Policy," JEL, Vol.48, No.2.

2011 (with P. Carneiro and E. Vytlacil), "Estimating Marginal Returns to Education," AER, Vol.101, No.6.

2012 "The Development Origins of Health," Health Economics, Vol. 21, No.1.

27.5 WORKS OF OTHERS

Blundell, R. (2001), "James Heckman's Contributions to Economics and Econometrics," ScandJE, Vol. 103, No.2.

CHAPTER 28

DANIEL LITTLE McFADDEN

(1937 –)

The 2000 Bank of Sweden Prize in Economic Sciences in Memory of Alfred Nobel was shared by Daniel McFadden and James Heckman. The information supplied by the Royal Swedish Academy of Sciences makes specific reference to the development by each of them of theory and methods that are extensively used in the statistical analysis of micro behaviour such as individual and household behaviour in economics as well as in other social sciences. They have made contributions of great importance to micro econometrics. McFadden's most notable contributions essentially relate to theory and methods applicable to analysis of discrete choice – choice among a finite set of alternatives – such as the choice of mode of transportation or occupational choice.

28.1 A BRIEF BIOGRAPHICAL NOTE: DANIEL McFADDEN

Daniel McFadden was born in 1937 in Raleigh, North Carolina, U.S.A., the eldest son of Robert Sain McFadden and Alice Little McFadden. Robert McFadden had only four years of formal schooling while Alice McFadden received a degree in architecture from the University of Minnesota and an MFA from Columbia University. The primary recreation for Daniel McFadden in his childhood was reading and he grew up planning to become a farm agent or a novelist. He attended rural North Carolina Public Schools. He was a good student. He received a B.S. in Physics with "highest honors" from the University of Minnesota. As an undergraduate, he got a job in which he was to programme card sorters that were being used to construct psychological tests. "This led to a great interest in psychological measurement."

He continued his studies in physics as a graduate student at Minnesota, but was greatly attracted to the study of human behaviour. At that time, the Ford Foundation sponsored "an ambitious" Behavioral Science Training Program at Minnesota designed to develop scholars in social sciences. In 1958, McFadden joined this programme and "embarked on a course of study that included the core Ph.D. courses in psychology, sociology, economics, anthropology, political science, mathematics and statistics, a total of more than 70 graduate-level courses." He chose economics as the lead field in the behavioural science programme and developed an interest in mathematical models of learning and choice. McFadden, during his graduate studies, was strongly influenced by John Chipman and

Leonid Hurwicz (2007 Nobel Laureate) in the Economics Department, particularly their emphasis on axiomatic development of economic theory and the power of formal models. Under the externship programme in summer of the Ford Foundation, he went to Stanford to work for Kenneth Arrow and Marc Nerlove. In his autobiographical note, McFadden observes: "While there, I had a brief interaction with Prof. Hirofumi Uzawa that proved to be a pivotal point in my research training, giving me a dissertation topic and, most importantly, a flash of understanding of how to use mathematics as a research tool."

McFadden received Ph.D. degree from the University of Minnesota in 1962. He then went to the University of Pittsburgh as a Mellon Post-doctoral fellow. In 1963 he joined the University of California, Berkley. He continued his interests in choice behaviour. He developed a new interest at that time, in the problem of linking economic theory and measurement. He says: "I benefited a great deal from interaction with my colleagues, Peter Diamond [2010 Nobel Laureate], Roy Radner, Dale Jorgensen and Gerard Debreu [1983 Noble Laureate]." In 1977 McFadden moved to the economics faculty at MIT. In those days, "Paul Samuelson, Robert Solow and Franco Modigliani [all three Nobel Laureates] were intensively active and intellectual life there was lively." His other academic appointments include Yale University, University of Chicago and California Institute of Technology. Since 1990, he is E. Morris Cox Professor of Economics at Berkeley. There he founded the Econometrics Laboratory which is devoted to statistical computation for economic applications.

In 2011, McFadden was appointed the Presidential Professor of Health Economics at the University of Southern California (USC) to examine "fundamental problems facing the health care sector, looking specifically at how consumers make choices about health care and medical services." He has joint appointment at the University of Southern California's School of Policy Planning and Development at the Department of Economics.

McFadden received numerous awards and honours of which the following may be mentioned. He was elected Fellow, Econometrics Society, 1969 and received John Bates Clark Medal of the American Economic Association, 1975. He delivered Hooker Lectures at McMasters University, 1984, Smith lectures at Brigham Young University, 1985, and Jahnsson Foundation Lectures, Helsinki, in 1985. In 1986, McFadden received Frisch Medal of Econometrics Society. He received Richard Stone Prize in Applied Econometrics, 2000-2001.

28.2 A SUMMARY OF DANIEL McFADDEN'S MAIN CONTRIBUTIONS

The most important contribution of McFadden is the integration of economic theory and econometric methodology for analysis of discrete choice data. He has successfully combined economic theory, statistical methods and empirical applications with the avowed objective of resolving social problems. Microeconomic data usually reflect discrete choices with regard to, for example, individuals' occupation, place of residence or mode of travel. Individuals make their choice from among a limited number of alternatives whereas traditional demand analysis posits that such choice be represented by a continuous variable. As such, for a study of discrete choice behaviour, the traditional microeconomic approach is clearly inappropriate.

In the traditional microeconomic theory, each individual chooses a specific alternative that maximises his utility. Since the researcher cannot observe all the factors affecting individual choices, he observes a random variation across individuals possessing the same observed characteristics. These differences were considered as an additive disturbance and are ascribed to data measurement errors rather than to unobserved factors within or across individuals. According to McFadden, classical economic theory argues that, for instance, consumers try to maximise their "self-interest" which broadly defined consistency properties across different decisions. He further observes: "The concept of rational consumer behaviour was given a much more specific meaning in the perfection of the classical theory by John Hicks and Paul Samuelson, where self-interest is defined in terms of stable, innate preferences, and in Herb Simon's words, 'The rational man of economics is a maximizer who will settle for nothing less than the best.'" Heterogeneous preferences were considered by later theorists but were ignored in empirical studies of market demand, employing a convenient device of a "representative consumer." Traditional consumer theory placed structural restrictions on mean behaviour, but the distribution of individual responses about their mean was not linked to the theory.

With the increasing availability of survey data on individual behaviour in 1960's, it has become possible to explain and model these variations in demand across individuals as an integral part of consumer theory rather than as ad hoc disturbances. This is particularly so in discrete choices, such as occupation choices or choice of mode of transportation. In a study of production functions for electricity, McFadden began his work on the problems of discrete choice. His familiarity with the work of psychologists on discrete choice was helpful in this regard. Another author, whose work was helpful in the development of McFadden's choice behaviour, was Jacob Marshack. Marshack's study of the theoretical implications for choice probabilities of maximisation of utilities that contained random elements called Random Utility Maximization (RUM) model is particularly relevant. So also is the work of R. Duncan Luce which introduced an axiom, Independence from Irrelevant Alternatives (IIA). This axiom helped simplification of experimental collection of data on choice by allowing inference of multinomial choice probabilities from binomial choice experiments. Marshack had shown that IIA implies RUM for a finite universe of objects.

In his Prize lecture, "Economics Choices," in which McFadden extensively discusses the microeconomic analysis of choice behaviour of consumers who face discrete economic alternatives, while tracing the development of his seminal classic contribution, "conditional logit model," an econometric version of the Luce model. The press release of the Royal Swedish Academy of Sciences gives the following description of the model. Suppose that each individual in a population faces a number (say, J), of alternatives. Let X denote the characteristics associated with each alternative and Z the characteristics of the individual that the researcher can observe in her data. In a study of the choice of a travel mode, for instance, where the alternatives may be car, bus or subway, X would then include information about costs and time, while Z might cover data on age, education and income. But, differences among individuals and alternatives other than X and Z, although the researcher cannot observe them, also determine an individual's utility-maximising choice. Such characteristics are represented by random "error terms," which, McFadden assumed, have a specific statistical distribution in the population. He terms this distribution as extreme value distribution. Under these conditions and making some technical assumptions, McFadden shows that the probability that an individual will choose alternative j can be written as

$$P_{ij} = \frac{e^{X_{ij}\beta + Z_i\delta_j}}{\sum_{k=1}^{j} e^{X_{ik}\beta + Z_i\delta_j}} \tag{1}$$

In this multinomial logit model (MNL model) e is the base of the natural logarithm, while β and δ are vectors of parameters. The researcher can observe the variables X and Z as well as the alternative the individual chooses. Consequently, the parameters β and δ can be estimated using the usual statistical methods. McFadden also developed a computer programme to estimate the MNL model by maximum likelihood. The model as developed by McFadden based on economic theory of population received immediate recognition as a "fundamental paradigmatic breakthrough." McFadden states: "The reason my formulation of the MNL model has received more attention than others that were developed independently during the same decade [for instance, by Theil or Quandt] seems to be the direct connection that I provided to consumer theory, linking unobserved preference heterogeneity to a fully consistent description of the distribution of demands...."

Models, such as the one developed by McFadden, are extremely useful and are found to be particularly appropriate in studies of urban travel demand, especially in traffic planning. There are other applications as well of such models; for instance, in studies of the choice of dwelling, place of residence and education. McFadden has used the methods developed by him in his analysis of numerous social issues, such as, housing for the aged, telephone services and demand for residential energy. In his Nobel lecture, McFadden specifically refers to close similarities between the travel demand problem and applications such as education and education choices, demand for consumer goods, and location choices. Consequently, the methods developed by him have been adopted in a variety of studies concerned with choice behaviour of firms as well as consumers.

McFadden in his 1974 article "Conditional Logit Analysis of Qualitative Choice Behavior" spells out the primary objective of his work: "This paper outlines a general procedure for formulating econometric models of population choice behavior from distributions of individual decision rules." He also states that the statistical procedure employed by him provides "...an analogue for qualitative dependent variables of the conventional linear statistical model." Charles Manski's comments on this article are worth quoting: "Perhaps the most striking characteristic of the article is its smooth progression from a conceptual contribution of great generality to a practical contribution of immediate usefulness. [It] is an extraordinary synthesis of basic economic theory, development of a general econometric approach, and embodiment of that approach in a particular form as practical as the conventional linear statistical model."

With a view to providing an appropriate framework for the empirical analysis of choice among finite set of alternatives (with each alternative characterised as a bundle of attributes a la Lancaster), McFadden developed econometric analysis of discrete choice. Charles Manski identifies four essential features in McFadden's vision of the appropriate framework. Manski's analysis may be summarised here.

1. The developed econometric analysis must be entirely consistent with the traditional utility theory. Recognising that the Random Utility Models (RUM) have "broad power" as a tool of econometric analysis, he (McFadden) is careful to state that the RUM idea is implicit in random coefficient models of classical consumer demand. In this context, he makes a reference to Richard Quandt's independent use of the idea in a discrete choice application. ("The Demand for Travel," 1970). His [McFadden's] main contribution lay in reinterpreting a decision-maker's selection of a utility function at random as arising from cross-sectional variation in utility functions across the population rather than from time-series variation within a given individual.

2. Econometric analysis should facilitate the researcher's forecast of individual's choice behaviour in new settings. More importantly, the researcher should be able to perform thought experiments to find out how population behaviour would change when existing alternatives cease to be available but new alternatives become available. The RUM is not meant to forecast behaviour in new settings; as such, it cannot be used to predict a decision–maker's behaviour when facing a different set of alternatives. It cannot also predict the behaviour of decision-makers in a different population. By mapping the qualitative differences in their attributes and assuming that each alternative j can be characterised through a vector of attributes xj and each decision-maker t can be characterised through a vector of attributes, McFadden saw the possibility of forecasting the decision-maker's behaviour. Then, the utility of alternative j to person t can be written in the following form.

$$u_t(j) = u(x_j, s_t) \tag{2}$$

Once the attributes are known and the mapping of the attributes of alternatives and decision-makers into utility values is done as given above, a researcher is enabled to determine the utility of any alternative to any decision-maker and also make prediction of the decision-maker's choice behaviour. For instance, a researcher into a transportation problem can predict how commuters with particular income and job attributes would choose among modes of travel with attributes of particular travel time and cost of travel. Manski succinctly sums up McFadden's contribution: "McFadden's explicit characterization of alternatives and decision-makers as attribute vectors marked a sharp departure from prevailing economic practice. In classical consumer demand, goods are qualitatively distinct and so are consumers. There is no way to predict the demand for a new good. Nor is there any way to predict the behavior of new consumers. A notable exception to the standard practice was the work of Lancaster (1966) which did recognize the value of attribute characterizations."

3. Econometric analysis has to reckon with the fact that the researcher's data are incomplete in regard to the attributes of decision-makers and the alternatives available to them. To get over this problem, McFadden assumes that the utility function of the individual decision-maker has the following linear-in-parameters separable form.

$$u(x_j, s_t) = v(x_{j0}, s_{t0})\beta + \varepsilon_{tj} \tag{3}$$

Here, x_{j0} and s_{t0} are the components of x_j and s_t which the researcher can observe and $v(x_{j0}, s_{t0})$ is a vector- valued function of those components using the available choice data.

The researcher can estimate the parameter vector β; the unobserved variable ε_{tj} expresses the contribution of unobserved attributes to utility. It is assumed that the cross-sectional distribution of these unobserved variables is known upto the value of a parameter vector α. He then derives choice probabilities conditional on the observed attributes. These conditional choice probabilities enable the researcher to estimate the parameters β and α using the data on the observed choices and attributes of a random sample of decision-makers and employing maximum likelihood method.

Manski finds some resemblance between McFadden's derivation of conditional choice probabilities from the RUM and Tobin's (1958) derivation of mixed conditional densities and probabilities from censored outcome data.

4. The fourth main feature of McFadden's vision of an appropriate approach concerns computational practicality of the econometric analysis. McFadden's concern was that the maximum likelihood estimation of the parameters β and α involves numerous computations of conditional choice probabilities and iterative search for the parameter value maximising the likelihood function. Making use of the earlier work of Marshack and others which showed that "... if the ε variables are assumed to be independently distributed, each according to the Type I extreme-value distribution, then the conditional choice probabilities have the multinomial logit form

$$P_i(S_0, X_0) = \frac{\exp[v(x_{i0}, s_0)\beta]}{\sum_{j\in C} \exp[v(x_{j0}, s_0)\beta]} \tag{4}$$

The distribution of $\left(\varepsilon_j, j\in C\right)$ having been fully specified, there are no α parameters to be estimated here, only the β parameters."

The most notable feature of McFadden's 1974 article is its "extraordinary synthesis of basic economic theory, development of a general econometric approach and embodiment of that approach in a particular form as practical as the conventional linear statistical model."

28.3 DISCRETE CHOICE MODELS AND ECONOMIC POLICY ISSUES

In his Nobel lecture, McFadden expands on the applications of discrete choice models to economic policy problems. Such applications call for estimation of Willingness-to-Pay (WTP) for policy changes. Referring to the theoretical result that any well-behaved RUM model can be approximated by mixed MNL (MMNL) model, McFadden demonstrates such a model's application to a study of trout fishing destination choice in Montana. The study sought to determine WTP for the increase in stocks of fish that would come from restoration of natural riparian conditions. In certain conditions, it is "much more burdensome" to compute exact Hicksian compensating variation. McFadden gives bounds that will sometimes be adequate for policy analysis and also develops Monte Carlo Markov chain methods for numerical calculation of exact WTP.

28.4 DYNAMIC MODELS OF DISCRETE CHOICE

McFadden, in his Nobel lecture, refers to Heckman's pioneering work concerning analysis of the dynamics of discrete choice in which Heckman recognises the crucial roles of initial values and recursive structure in well-specified dynamic models. Heckman is also credited with the development of appropriate econometric methods. A key feature in the analysis of the dynamics of discrete choice relates to the integration of expectations into choice decisions via dynamic optimisation and through interactions between agents. Dynamic discrete choice models are found to be useful in studies concerning issues of supply of labour and job status, timing of purchasing of new goods and life-cycle decisions like retirement.

28.5 PSCHOLOGY OF CHOICE BEHAVIOUR

McFadden dwells at length on the psychological theories of choice process. He states that "attitudes" play an important role in determining how consumers define the decision-making task and quotes from Kahneman's (2002 Nobel Laureate) work. "Economists have preferences; psychologists have attitudes." He then makes reference to psychologist Prelec's distinction between the psychologist's view of decision-making from economist's utility-maximisation models. After discussing the psychological view of decision-making as a theoretical alternative to the standard model of utility maximisation, McFadden asserts that there is now also substantial evidence that in a laboratory setting individuals sometimes make decisions that deviate "strikingly and systematically" from the predictions of the standard model. He cites experimental results of Kahneman and Tversky which forced economists to rethink the standard model. McFadden mentions the phenomenon of anchoring as one of the important cognitive phenomenon by cognitive psychologists and behavioural economists that appear to influence behaviour. Describing the two experiments which were conducted by McFadden jointly with others, he concludes that "...the anchoring phenomenon can introduce response bias that if unrecognized might seriously distort economic policy analysis." He opines that economists investigating consumer behaviour can learn substantially from a meticulous study of market research findings and marketing practice. Furthermore, there is a need for behavioural economists to move beyond stylised descriptions of choice behaviour; they should get involved in market research experiments that directly investigate the nature of the processes of economic choice.

28.6 DEVELOPMENT OF STATISTICAL METHODS

In the last part of his Nobel lecture, McFadden outlines the development of statistical methods as part of the research programme on economic choice behaviour. He observes that the micro econometric analysis of choice behaviour needs specific methods for parametric and non-parametric estimation. It is also necessary for testing hypotheses and for detection of specification errors that needed diagnostic tools. It is necessary to develop required system for producing disaggregate and aggregate forecasts and policy scenarios that track statistical accuracy. In the area of economic choice behaviour, reliance has been put in maximum likelihood methods and their large sample properties. McFadden notes that "there is increasing use of non-parametric estimates, bootstrap methods to refine asymptotic approximations, generalized method of moment's procedures for robustness and simulation methods to overcome problems that are intractable using conventional computation."

An attempt is made here to briefly summarise the developed methods.

Choice-Based Sampling: Statistical methods used for random samples will often be inconsistent or inefficient for use to choice-based samples. A choice-based sample is generated by stratification using as its basis the response behaviour, when the purpose is to explain such behaviour. Within each stratum, observations are collected on response and covariates. Statistical inference is made using conditional distribution of response, given explanatory variables. For example, an occupational choice study may be made by drawing a sample, stratified by occupation. Thus, the first stratum may be a sample of engineers while the second stratum may be a sample of educators and so on. Data may be collected on covariates or explanatory variables, such as, gender, use of training subsidies etc. The observations may be used to infer the impact of training subsidies on choice of occupation.

Thus, the analysis attempts to infer properties (such as, impact of training subsidies on occupational choices) of the conditional distribution of choices, given covariates or using observations that are drawn from the conditional distribution of explanatory variables, given choices.

It may be seen that the problem of choice-based sampling is closely related to the problem of analysis of self-selected samples to which Heckman's contribution is seminal as outlined in the preceding chapter.

Computation and Simulation: McFadden argues that the evaluation of choice probabilities that require numerical integration of moderately high dimension is computationally a tough problem. For such computationally difficult problems, use of simulation methods has proved to be handy. In his 1989 Econometrica paper, McFadden develops an approach and generalises simulators for the multinomial probit model first introduced by Manski and Lerman. Further research work has been done subsequently by many writers which helped researchers to work with quite flexible models, such as multinomial probit and mixed multinomial logit models. Statistical simulation is a powerful tool for comparison of models as also analysis of policy.

Specification Testing: IIA Tests: In the words of McFadden "The MNL (Multinomial logit model) is a powerful tool for analysis of economic choice behavior when its IIA (Independent from Irrelevant Alternatives) property is satisfied by an application, since it is easily estimated, allows drastic reduction of data collection and computation by sampling subsets of alternatives..., and gives an easy formula for forecasting demand for new alternatives. On the other hand..., the model can produce seriously misleading forecasts if IIA fails." There is, therefore, a need to develop specification tests that could be employed in order to detect failure of IIA. McFadden and other researchers such as Hausman have developed tests to tackle this problem.

Specification Testing: Mixing in MNL Models: One of the theoretical results of McFadden's work (referred to earlier) states that any well-behaved RUM model can be approximated by mixed MNL model. In the light of this, satisfaction of IIA property can be recast as a condition that there is no unobserved heterogeneity in the parameters of MNL. Therefore, a test for the validity of the IIA property, and specification test for the explanatory power may be added by introducing mixing, can be constructed using a Lagrange Multiplier approach. Following this method, the researcher has to set up test procedure requiring only estimation of basic MNL models, so that simulation estimators are not required; it can test against a battery of alternatives at the same time.

Market Research Data and Models: There has been in recent years marked interaction between economic choice analysis and market research. Market research uses experimental methods facilitating elucidation and measurement of the workings of the process of decision-making. Specifically, one can elicit what McFadden terms stated preference (SP) data as opposed to the revealed preference (RP) data obtained from observed choices. SP data uses variables and methods drawn from applied psychology. The method of conjoint analysis gives data that can augment the ability to predict consumer decisions. Dwelling on the major advantages of using experiments, instead of field surveys to collect data, McFadden remarks that the environment of hypothetical choice can be precisely specified, with a design that permits direct identification of effects. Further, large quantities of relevant data can be collected at moderate cost. Moreover, innovations in services can be studied.

However, for combining SP and RP data, an analytical frame is needed for the purpose of marketing and economic policy applications. Keeping this in mind, McFadden and other researchers have developed multiple-indicator, multiple-cause (MIMC) model. This was found to be a useful framework for integrating marketing data into forecasting problems.

28.7 CONCLUDING OBSERVATIONS

McFadden's research interests over the years included "a variety of topics in economics and choice theory, almost all having origins in applied problems." A common thread running through his research has been an emphasis on tightly binding economic theory and the problem of economic measurement and analysis, and "on developing theoretical and statistical tools that expand the options available to applied economists." In recent years, McFadden got particularly interested in experiments in cognitive psychology conducted by Tversky and Kahneman and their implications for economic analysis and the interpretation of economic data.

In his Banquet speech, McFadden bemoans the loss of practical side of the subject by economists. In this context, he quotes approvingly the statement of Keynes: "If economists could manage to get themselves thought of as humble, competent people, on a level with dentists, that would be splendid."

In his autobiographical note, McFadden announced his noble gesture to donate the prize money to the East Bay Community Foundation, and directed it to be used to promote arts and education.

28.8 SELECT BIBLIOGRAPHY OF DANIEL McFADDEN'S WORKS

28.8.1 BOOKS AND MONOGRAPHS

1974 (with M. Balch, and S. Wu (eds.), Essays on Economic Behavior under Uncertainty, North-Holland, Amsterdam.

1975 (with T. Domenich), Urban Travel Demand, North-Holland, Amsterdam.

1978 (with M. Fuss, (eds.), Production Economics: A Dual Approach to Theory and Applications, Vols. I and II, North-Holland, Amsterdam.

1981 (with C.F. Manski eds.), Structural Analysis of Discrete Data with Econometric Applications, MIT Press, Cambridge, MA.

1984 (with T. Cowing), Macroeconomic Modeling and Policy Analysis: Studies in Residential Energy Demand, Academic Press, New York.

1986 (with R.F. Engle eds.), Handbook of Econometrics, Elsevier, Amsterdam.

1990 Preferences, Uncertainty, and Optimality: Essays in Honor of Leonid Hurwicz, West View Press, Boulder, CO.

1994 (with R. Engle (eds.)), Handbook of Econometrics, Vol. IV, North-Holland, Amsterdam.

28.8.2 ARTICLES

1963 "Constant Elasticity of Substitution Production Functions," RES, Vol.30, No.2.

1967 "The Evaluation of Development Programmes," RES, Vol.34, No.1.

1969 a "On Hicksian Stability," In Value, Capital and Growth, J. N. Wolfe (ed.), University Press, Edinburgh.

b "On the Controllability of Decentralized Macroeconomic Systems: The Assignment Problem," in Mathematical Systems: Theory and Economics, Vol. 1, H. E. Kuhn and P. Szego (eds.),Springer-Verlag, New York.

1970 "On the Existence of Optimal Development Plans," in H. E. Kuhn(ed.), Proceedings of the Sixth Princeton Symposium on Mathematical Programming, Princeton University Press, Princeton, NJ.

1973 "On the Existence of Optimal Development Programmes in Infinite-Horizon Economies," in Models of Economic Growth, J. Mirrlees and N. H. Stern (eds.), Macmillan, London.

1974 a "The Measurement of Urban Travel Demand," JPubE, Vol.3, No.4.

b "Conditional Logit Analysis of Qualitative Choice Behavior," in Frontiers in Econometrics, P. Zarembka (ed.), Academic Press, New York.

1975 a (with F. Reid) "Aggregate Travel Demand Forecasting from Disaggregated Behavioral Models," Transportation Research Record: Travel Behavior and Values, No.534.

b "The Revealed Preferences of a Government Bureaucracy: Theory," Bell Journal of Economics and Management Science, Vol.6, No.2.

1976 a (with M. Majumdar and T. Mitra), "On Efficiency and Pareto Optimality of Competitive Programs in Closed Multisector Models," JET, Vol.13, No.1.

b "The Revealed Preferences of a Government Bureaucracy: Empirical Evidence," Bell JE,Vol.7, No.1.

c "The Mathematical Theory of Demand Models," in Behavioral Travel-Demand Models, P. Stopher and A. Meyburg (eds.), D. C. Heath and Co., Lexington, MA.

1978 "Quantitative Methods for Analyzing Travel Behaviour of Individuals: Some Recent Developments," in Behavioural Travel Modelling, D. Hensher and P. Stopher (eds.), Croom Helm, London.

1980 a "Econometric Models for Probabilistic Choice among Products," JB, Vol.53, No.3.

b (with M. Majumdar and J. Mitra), "Pareto Optimality and Competitive Equilibrium in Infinite Horizon," JMathE, Vol.7, No.1.

1982 "Qualitative Response Models," in Advances in Econometrics, W. Hildenbrand (ed.), Econometric Society Monograph, Cambridge University Press, Cambridge.

1984 a (with J. Dublin), "An Econometric Analysis of Residential Electric Appliance Holdings and Consumption," Econometrica, Vol.52, No.2.

b (with J. Hausman), "Specification Tests for the Multinomial Logit Model," Econometrica, Vol.52, No.5.

c "Econometric Analysis of Qualitative Response Models," in Handbook of Econometrics, Vol. II, Z. Griliches and M. Intriligator(eds.), Elsevier, Amsterdam.

1987 (with K. E. Train and A. Goett), "Consumer Attitudes and Voluntary Rate Schedules for Public Utilities," REStat, Vol.69, No.3.

1989 a "Testing for Stochastic Dominance," in Studies in the Economics of Uncertainty, T. Fomby and T. K. Seo, Springer, New York.

b "A Method of Simulated Moments for Estimation of Discrete Response Models without Numerical Integration," Econometrica, Vol.57, No.5.

1990 (with C. Ai et al.), "The Dynamics of Housing Demand by the Elderly: User Cost Effects," in Studies in the Economics of Aging, D. Wise (ed.), University of Chicago Press, Chicago, Ill.

1993 (with J.A. Hausman and G. Leonard), "Assessing Use Value Losses Caused by Natural Resource Injury, in Contingent Valuation: A Critical Assessment," J. Hausman (ed.), North-Holland, Amsterdam.

1994 (with A. Rudd), "Estimation by Simulation," REStat, Vol.76, No.4.

1996 (with K.E. Train), "Consumers' Evaluation of New Products: Learning from Self and Others," JPE, Vol. 104, NO.4.

1997 (with C. Ai), "Estimation of Some Partially Specified Nonlinear Models," Journal of Econometrics, Vol. 76, No. 1-2.

1999 a "Computing Willingness-to-Pay in Random Utility Models," in Trade: Theory and Econometrics: Essays in Honour of J. S. Chipman, (J. Moore et al. eds.), Routledge, London.

b "Rationality for Economists?" Journal of Risk and Uncertainty, Vol.19, No.1-3.

2001 a "Economic Choices," Nobel Lecture, AER, Vol.91, No.3.

b "On Selecting Regression Variables to Maximize their Significance," in C.Hsaio et.al (eds). Nonlinear Statistical Modelling, Cambridge University Press, Cambridge.

2003 (with P. Adams et al.), "Healthy, Wealthy and Wise? Tests for Direct Causal Paths Between Health and Socioeconomic Status," Journal of Econometrics, Vol.112, No.1.

2005 "Revealed Stochastic Preference: A Synthesis," Economic Theory, Vol.26, No.2.

2006 "Free Markets and Fettered Consumers," AER, Vol.96, No.1.

2010 (with W. Beckert), "Maximal Uniform Convergence Rates in Parametric Estimation Problems," Economic Theory, Vol.26, No.2.

2011 (with Lewbel and O. Linton), "Estimating Features of a Distribution from Binomial Data," Journal of Econometrics, Vol.162, NO.2.

28.9 WORKS OF OTHERS

Amemiya T. (1987), "Discrete Choice Analysis," in The New Palgrave: A Dictionary of Economics, Macmillan, London.

Coslett, S. (1981), "Efficient Estimation of Discrete Choice Models," in Structural Analysis of Discrete Data with Econometric Applications, (C. F. Manski and D. McFadden (eds.)), MIT Press, Cambridge, MA.

Manski, C. F. (2001), "Daniel McFadden and the Econometric Analysis of Discrete Choice," ScandJE, Vol.103, No.2.

CHAPTER 29

CLIVE WILLIAM JOHN GRANGER

(1934 – 2009)

Clive W. J. Granger shared the 2003 Nobel Memorial Prize in Economic Sciences with Robert F. Engle. Granger received the prize for developing methods for analysing and modelling non-stationary macroeconomic time series by introducing the concept of co-integration. Empirical research in macroeconomic time series is essentially based on time series. Since the work of Haavelmo, it has become a common practice to consider economic time series as realisation of stochastic processes. Since many macroeconomic time series are found to follow a stochastic trend, any temporary disturbance in the series, say GDP or consumption, has a long-lasting effect. Such time series are referred to as non-stationary. They are distinguished from stationary time series, which fluctuate around a given value but do not grow or decline over time. Granger demonstrated that the statistical methods used for stationary time series could yield quite misleading results when applied to the analysis of non-stationary data. His key discovery was that specific combinations of non-stationary time series may show stationarity, leading to incorrect statistical inference. Co-integration is the name given to this phenomenon by Granger. He suggested methods that have become highly valuable in systems where short-run dynamics are affected by large random disturbances and long-run dynamics are limited by economic equilibrium relationships. Examples include the relation between wealth, consumption and exchange rates.

29.1 A BRIEF BIOGRAPHICAL SKETCH: CLIVE GRANGER

Clive Granger was born in September 1934 in Swansea, Wales. His father was a commercial traveller for a firm producing some food products. When Granger was about one year old, the family moved from Wales to Lincoln in Eastern England. His father had left for service in the Second World War and his mother moved to Cambridge where Granger went to a local primary school, where he "did well in mathematics but not much else." His teacher told Granger's mother that he would "never become successful." Granger remarks in his autobiographical note: [It] illustrates the difficulties of long-run forecasting on inadequate data!

At the age of 11, Granger joined the Cambridgeshire High School for Boys where he "performed well but showed no particular activity." He reminisces: "At this stage of my life I had largely drifted through... I had no clear-cut ambition or long-run plan and that policy has generally continued. My career has largely been determined by a sequence of "lucky breaks." After the war in 1946, Granger's father took a job at Nottingham. Granger joined the West Bridgeford Grammar School. In sixth form, he concentrated on pure and applied mathematics and physics. He is appreciative of his mathematics teachers, their enthusiasm about the subject and their ability to pass on the enthusiasm and knowledge to the students.

Granger joined University of Nottingham for a joint degree in Mathematics and Economics. He was the first person anywhere in his family tree to go to University. At the end of the first year, he switched to a Mathematics degree. On completing his degree, Granger started work for Ph.D. in statistics. He chose Economic Time Series as his thesis topic, although he "knew very little about the topic." While doing research, he got selected for a junior lecturer's position in statistics at the age of 23. His candid statement in this regard: "I started the position in 1956 with what had to be a record of low knowledge of statistics and no established teaching ability." As the only person in the University calling himself a statistician, many researchers in other disciplines, such as Geography, Psychology, Chemistry and Economic History sought his help giving him a good opportunity to deal with data sets presenting unique problems. He remarked that it provided excellent training for a young statistician who would not get it these days with such emphasis on specialisation.

In 1959 Granger obtained a Ph.D. degree, his thesis topic being "Testing for Non-Stationarity." He received a Harkness Fellowship to go to the United States where he joined Oscar Morgenstern's "Time Series Project" at Princeton University with which project was associated M. Hatanaka, "an excellent econometrician who recently finished a book on 'Input-Output Analysis." Morgenstern, on the suggestion of von Neumann that economists should be using the Fourier methods with their data, had organised with John Tukey to teaching the members of the Time Series Project how to do it. The teaching was conducted for most of the academic year by which time Granger and his team mates "learnt a lot about filtering, the spectrum for a single series and the cross spectrum for a pair of series." On the basis of their work, Granger and Hatanaka published in 1969 a volume Spectral Analysis in Economic Time Series. When he was next at Princeton, Granger worked on stock market data for testing random walk theory using spectral methods and published two research papers. He also co-authored a book on commodity markets and another on stock market.

The work of Box and Jenkins, "Time Series Analysis: Forecasting and Control," prompted Granger to work in the area of forecasting as he knew "very little" about forecasting and "nothing" about control. Getting a research grant, Granger in collaboration with Paul Newbold, did intense research on forecasting which led to the publication of a volume, Forecasting Economic Time Series, in 1976. It was "widely used internationally in graduate courses." During this period, Granger, in association with Newbold, demonstrated that estimates of relationship between non-stationary variables could yield "nonsensical" results by erroneously indicating significant relationships between wholly unrelated variables.

In 1973, Granger was offered a Professorship at the University of California, San Diego (UCSD), which he accepted. He stated in his autobiographical note that the Department of Economics at UCSD was "already very strong but I was the only active research econometrician." In the same note, Granger referred to his earlier association with Engel on a committee and how Engel joined the University. Granger formed an econometric group, world ranked (top three) econometric group. The group worked on a variety of issues, including seasonal adjustment, aggregation and several new types of time series models. From his work, Granger observed that squares of white noise series were not always white noise which he discussed with Engel. Granger commented "... it might just have been the rolling pebble that much later produced the avalanche known as ARCH."

Granger retired from the University of California at the end of July 2003, at the age of almost 69, after about 48 years of teaching. He was visiting Professor at a number of Universities, including Oxford (Nuffield and All Souls), Cambridge (Trinity) and Australian National University. Granger was named Distinguished Fellow of the American Economic Association in 2003.

At the end of the autobiographical note, Granger gave a recipe for success which is worth reproducing. Do not start too high on the ladder, move to a good but not top University, work hard, have a few good ideas, choose good collaborations ("I had over eighty in my career"), attract some excellent students, wait twenty years or so, and then retire.

Granger died in San Diego, California, on 27th May 2009.

29.2 A SUMMARY OF CONTRIBUTIONS OF C. W. J. GRANGER

Marc Nerlove and Francis X. Diebold in their article, "Time Series Analysis" in the Palgrave's Dictionary of Modern Economics define time series as "any series of observations ordered along a single dimension, such as time." Another definition is time series is a "sequence of numerical data in which each item is associated with a particular instant in time." Many examples of time series from economics and financial economics can be given. Quarterly/annual series of gross domestic product (GDP), weekly/monthly measures of money supply –M_1, M_2, M_3, etc., daily closing prices of equity shares, share price indices, annual series of aggregate national savings and investment, daily foreign exchange rates, annual interest rates, and so on. Data relating to many important financial variables are known not only daily but can be found within seconds, if they change, such as highly traded equity share prices or exchange rates, called high frequency data. The emphasis in the analysis of time series is the examination of dependence among observations at different points in time. Univariate time series analysis refers to an analysis of a single series of data. Multivariate or multiple time series analysis is concerned with several sets of data for the same sequence of time series. For example, an analysis on the basis of annual data with intent of finding relationships among personal savings, personal disposable income, rate of interest, etc., falls under the latter category. The primary purpose of time series analysis is to study the dynamics or temporal structure of the data. The analysis attempts at studying the relationship over time. Many economic time series are non-stationary in the sense that the mean and variance depend on time. Further, they tend to deviate further from given value temporally or as time goes on.

Granger's major contributions are summarised under the following heads:

1. The Concept of Cointegration; and
2. Other Contributions.

29.2.1 METHOD OF CO-INTEGRATION

Macroeconomic research and empirical research in financial economics is to a large extent based on time series. As the Nobel Foundation's release of advanced information notes, the main objective of such empirical research is to test hypotheses and estimate relationships, derived from economic theory, among such aggregate macro variables. The statistical theory that was applied even till 1980s in building and testing large simultaneous-equation models was based on the assumption that the variables in these models were stationary. Many of these series were rather smooth moving with local trends or with long swings, but the swings were irregular. It is this relative smoothness that makes them unsuitable for analysis with standard statistical procedures which assume data to have a property known as "stationarity." Further, if the time series are an outcome of non-stationary processes, the statistical inference associated with stationary processes is no longer valid. Many series in economics, particularly in macroeconomics and financial economics do not have the stationarity property; they can be called "integrated" or sometimes incorrectly "non-stationary." Non-stationarity implies a variable that has no clear tendency to constant value or a linear trend. However, when expressed in terms of changes or rates of returns on, say assets, these derived series are seen to be closer to being stationary. Researchers, till 1980s, used to "manipulate" such series by using differencing, seasonal adjustments, etc., to reduce them to stationarity and to analyse the derived series as vector autoreggressions or with Box-Jenkins methods. This procedure was being used for analysis of short-run dynamics. However, this procedure was found to be unsatisfactory as it throws away potentially valuable information concerning long-run relationships about which economic theories have important propositions. The issue of integrating short-run dynamics with long-run equilibria was the focus of the theory of co-integration developed by Granger and Engel--the recipients of 2003 Nobel Memorial Prize for Economic Sciences. Granger had demonstrated that macroeconomic models containing non-stationary stochastic variables can be constructed in a manner such that the results are both economically meaningful and statistically sound. Besides, his work had furnished the underpinnings for modelling with rich dynamics among inter-related economic variables. By introducing the concept of co-integrated variables, he had fundamentally changed the approach to formulate empirical models of macroeconomic relationships.

The press release of Royal Academy mentions that for a long time it used to be assumed that time series have been generated by non-stationary stochastic processes and estimate equations involving non-stationary variables in macroeconomic models by straight forward linear regression. It was not generally appreciated that testing hypotheses about the coefficients using standard statistical inference might lead to spurious results. Granger, as a co-author of an influential paper, found fault with this procedure and argued that tests of such a regression may often indicate a statistically significant relationship between variables where none exists. This work suggested that many of the seemingly significant relationships between economic variables that are non-stationary in extant econometric models could as well be spurious. The press release emphasises that this work constituted a first step in Granger's research agenda of developing satisfactory methods for constructing more realistic and meaningful econometric models.

One of the solutions that was suggested to obviate the problem of spurious regression is to specify the economic relationships in first differences, instead of levels. The rationale for this suggestion is that differenced variables are generally stationary even when the original variables are not stationary. The difficulty with this approach is that economic theories are usually specified for levels of variables rather than for differences. As such, full use of these theories cannot be made. Another suggestion for solving the problem stipulates eliminating a linear time trend from the variables and formulating the empirical relationship between them, making use of detrended variables. This procedure is not without limitations either. Short-term dynamics of economic variables can be captured by dynamic econometric models using linear detrended variables; but such models cannot capture their long- run relationships. This deficiency is also true in case of models based on first differences.

While Box and Jenkins suggested methods to analyse a single integrated series, no method was available for the purpose of joint analysis of pairs or more of such series. Granger stated: It turns out that the difference between a pair of integrated series can be stationary and this property is known as co-integration. More formally, two smooth series, properly scaled, can move and turn, but slowly, in similar but not identical fashion, but the distance between them can be stationary.

Further for co-integration, a pair of integrated series must have the property that a linear combination of them is stationary. Once a pair of variables possesses the co-integration property, they possess some other properties as well. Granger explained: "... they must be co-integrated with the same hidden common factor. Further, they can be considered to be generated by what is known as the 'error-correction model,' in which the change of one of the series is explained in terms of the lag of the difference between the series, possibly after scaling, and lags of the differences of each series. The other series will be represented by a similar dynamic equation. Data generated by such a model is sure to be co-integrated." He noted that the error-correction model had greatly facilitated the practical application of the concept of co-integration, error-correction model.

To understand the concept of integration, let us take a time series, Y_t... Y_t is said to be integrated of order 1 or I(1) if ΔY_t is a stationary time series. A stationary time series is said to be I(0).

A special case of an I(1) series is a random walk. If Y_t is a random walk, ΔY_t is a random series or white noise which is a special case of stationary time series.

Suppose Y_t and X_t are time series and $Y_t \sim I(1)$ and $X_t \sim I(1)$. Then Y_t and X_t are said to be co-integrated if there exists a β such that $Y_t - \beta X_t$ is I (0). This is denoted as Y_t and X_t are [I(1, 1)]. That is, the regression equation

$$Y_t = \beta X_t + \mu_t$$

is meaningful since Y_t and X_t do not drift too far from each other over time and there is a long-run equilibrium relationship between them. If, on the other hand, Y_t and X_t are not co-integrated, that is

$$Y_t - \beta X_t = \mu_t$$

It means that Y_t and X_t can drift apart from each other more and more as time goes on and there is no long-run equilibrium between them. The above is also I(1).

The relationship that is obtained by regressing Y_t upon X_t is "spurious." By putting the question whether Y_t and X_t are co-integrated, we are asking whether there is any long-run relationship between the trends in Y_t and X_t.

The advanced information provided by Royal Swedish Academy gives a succinct presentation of Granger's solution to the problem which is presented here.

Assume a simple regression equation

$$Y_t = \alpha + \beta X_t + \Sigma_t \tag{1}$$

Where Y_t is the dependent variable,

X_t is the single exogenous regressor, and

Σ_t is a white-noise, mean-zero sequence.

To be meaningful, an equation has to be consistent. Granger uses the consistency test in the sense that "a simulation of the explanatory right hand side should produce the major properties of the variable being explained." That is, for instance, if Y_t is a seasonal variable, then X_t has to be seasonal, if Σ_t is to be white noise.

Granger developed the idea further by defining the concept of "degree of integration" of a variable. If a variable Z_t can be made approximately stationary by differencing it d times, it is called integrated of order d, or I(d). Weakly stationary random variables are thus I(0). Many macroeconomic variables can be regarded as I(1) variables. If $Z_t \sim I(1)$, then it is that I(1) variables dominate I(0) variables. Further, in a linear combination of variables, the variation of the former overwhelms the variation of the latter. To illustrate, if $Z_t \sim I(1)$ and $W_t \sim I(0)$, then $Z_t + W_t \sim I(1)$.

In eq(1), generally $Y_t - \beta X_t \sim I(1)$ as well. However, there is one important exception. If $\sum_t \sim I(0)$, then $Y_t - \beta X_t \sim I(0)$. That is, the linear combination $Y_t - \beta X_t$ has the same statistical properties as an I(0) variable. There exists only one such combination so that the coefficient β is unique. In this special case, variables X_t and Y_t are called co-integrated. This concept has been found to be very important in the analysis of non-stationary economic time series. We can further generalise to I(d) variables, where d is no longer an integer, in which case the linear combination of co-integrated variables has to be --$I(d - d_0)$, where $d_0 > 0$.

Yule, the famous statistician, was the first one to find out the misbehaviour of the conventional correlation coefficient when the low variables under study were integrated – be it I(1) or I(2) –and has given the name nonsense regression to such regressions. By formulating large econometric models, economic researchers had obtained "less accurate" forecasts than those researchers who employed time series models with no basis in economic theory. Granger in his work in association with Newbold pointed out in 1974 that econometric modellers' criteria for selection of equation were R^2, signs of coefficients and significances of regression estimates. Granger warned against accepting such spurious equations on expressing economic relationships. Hendry observes about the work: "...econometricians could not ignore the dynamic properties of the variables they analysed, especially when the time series are not stationary, emphasizing the importance of dynamic properties of economic relationships, during a time when econometric models were still essentially static, was a valuable contribution...." Besides, Granger and Newbold put forward a "positive" solution. That is, if researchers use first differences of variables instead of the levels, the severity of the problem is reduced – in fact practically non-existent. The relationship they suggested is of the following form:

$$\Delta Y_t = \alpha + \beta\, \Delta\, X_t + \mu_t \quad (2)$$

instead of the relationship usually postulated

$$Y_t = r + \theta\, Xt + \sum t \quad (3)$$

They emphasised the superiority of (2) above. If original variables as given in (3) were I(1), their differences [as in (2)] would be I(0) and non-sense regression problem would be removed.

However, the formulation in (2) creates a fresh problem. From the pure statistical viewpoint, it is all right to work with differencing variables, formulations in economic theory are in terms of levels. According to Hendry, Granger and Newbold suggested that statisticians who worked with differenced data and dynamic models have important lessons to teach economists who used simultaneous equation models based on the levels of variables forecasting.

Carrying forward his work, Granger specified the conditions under which co-integration could work-- what is referred to as the Granger representation theorem which has become the centrepiece of modern econometric analyses of integrated processes. In his 1981 path-breaking and extensively-cited paper, Granger suggested a neat solution. Suppose the dependent variable ΔY_t is I(0), first difference of the I(1) variable Y_t, where the right hand side of the equation like (2) contains level variables, Y_{t-1} and X_{t-1}, then Granger showed that the equation can be internally consistent, if and only if, a linear combination of the two level variables is I(0). Further, conversely if it is I(0) then both sides of the equation are stationary, and the formulation is internally consistent. A stationary linear combination of I(1) variables is a special case, but when it holds, such a pair of level variables is called co-integrated.

The concept of integration facilitates incorporation of relationships of level variables as put forward by economic theory into dynamic econometric equations in first differences. Hendry states: The stationary linear combination in levels may be integrated as an equilibrium long-run relationship, whereas the short-term adjustment process towards the equilibrium is characterized by differenced (and lagged) variables. Co-integration is perhaps the most important single innovation in time series econometrics since the probability foundations by Haavelmo (1944).

It is easy to see that Granger attempted at constructing consistent econometric equation containing both levels and first differences as variables. However, in the 1981 article he did not suggest statistical tests to find out whether or not a pair of non-stationary variables is co-integrated. To make the notion operational, he did this in 1983 article co-authored with A.A.Weirs. The suggested technique was founded on the same idea as the unit-roots prevalent at that time in econometrics. They also generalised the concept of co-integration to several variables, besides providing initial empirical examples in which a non co-integration test was applied to pairs and triples of economic time series.

The major milestone in this area of research is the work of Granger and Engle which in 1987 suggested a method of estimating equations with potentially co-integrated relationships. This article has generated new theoretical and applied work such as full maximum likelihood methods, techniques for correcting biases that would otherwise result and computing more efficient estimations. There were also efforts by researchers to generalise co-integration and stochastic roots. Hendry remarks: With feasible estimation methods, co-integration became enormously popular among applied econometricians. The importance of Granger and Engle's 1987 article can be gauged by the fact that it has been cited about 200 times per year since its appearance. David Hendry says that there are "in excess of 2800 citations" to this paper suggesting that Granger's research programme has received enthusiastic support of other researchers. It is reported that gradually revisions have been made in large simultaneous-equations models to have co-integrated linear combinations of level variables and required short-term dynamics in differences.

The Nobel Foundation's advanced information mentions some of the more important extensions of co-integration and also briefly covers application areas. Granger and Engel, with various co-authors have extended the concept of co-integration to seasonally integrated variables. The concept of multi-co-integration is defined, which can be a useful tool when modelling stock-flow relationships. In many cases deviations from equilibrium are explained by transaction and information costs. It was demonstrated how such costs may be incorporated into models with co-integrated variables and how they may result in a non-linear correction model.

As regards application area, co-integration has become a widely used econometric tool for empirical analysis in various areas where long-run relationships influence current observed values. For example, current consumption is affected by expected future income; current long-term interest rates are determined by expected short-term rates, etc. The traditional view, relying on econometric studies, was that an increase in wealth causes an upward movement in consumption in proportion to the real rate of interest. The magnitude of the effect may be acceptable in terms of the life-cycle model of consumption and savings. If it were true, the fluctuation in stock and farming markets would have strong impact on consumption. This wealth-consumption relationship is an example where the interplay between economic theory and practice is changing our view of the real world. It is now realised that we have to distinguish between temporary and permanent effects in wealth. Using the error-correction model, it is shown that stock market fluctuations have little effect on short-run as well as long-run consumption. To illustrate how co-integration may help transform empirical analysis and reveal ways of investigating old problems such as the study of exchange rates and prices, a number of researchers have used the basic proposition formulated by Gustav Cassel that exchange rates adjust so as to maintain purchasing power parity (PPP): The price of a bundle of goods, expressed in common currency should be the same across countries.

Another example where co-integration analysis has turned out to be especially valuable is in a system where short-term dynamics are affected by large random disturbances, while long-term changes are simultaneously contained by relationships of economic equilibrium such as the relationship between dividends and share prices. While share prices follow the developments in dividends in the long run, they exhibit substantially larger fluctuation in the short run.

29.2.2 OTHER CONTRIBUTIONS OF CLIVE GRANGER

One of the early important contributions of Granger related to spectral analysis. As mentioned earlier, he published a book on the subject in association with M. Hatanaka. In regard to the analysis of macroeconomic flow data with low frequency of observation – annual, quarterly or monthly, the standard statistical techniques were found to be adequate. However, for analysis of more disaggregated, micro level data observed at much greater frequency such as stock market data (generally daily observations) and data of movements in foreign exchange rates (almost on a continuous basis), the tools were found to be inadequate. Analysts have found the tools of spectral analysis and the frequency domain to be appropriate and started using the tools. William Greene observed: "In this framework, we view an observed time series as weighted sum of underlying series that have different cyclical patterns. For example, aggregate retail sales and construction data display several different kinds of cyclical variation, including a regular seasonal pattern and longer frequency variation associated with variation in the economy as a whole over the business cycle. The total variance of an observed time series may thus be viewed as a sum of the contributions of these underlying series which vary at different frequencies." Spectral analysis is applied to decompose the variance of time series. Hendry states that Granger and Hatanaka's book has since become a "citation classic." It contained a good discussion of non-stationarity and is considered a precursor to his development of causality.

Another important contribution of Granger concerned causal relationships between economic variables. The distinction between exogenous and endogenous variables in a model has generated considerable discussion, leading to build up of a large volume of literature. The classification, which in microeconomics seemed to be all right, has problem for use in macroeconomics. Granger found fault with the definitions of causality that have been employed. In an influential paper, Granger observed that the previous definitions of causality in econometrics were based upon the causal interpretation of simultaneous equation systems, usually "instantaneous" causality. A minor role was assigned to the notion of stochastic variables. Granger, on the other hand, assigned a central role in the definition to stochastic variables and the arrow of time! As Hendry observes Granger's definition of causality was founded on the concept of the prediction variance of a stationary time series. The definition became popular since it is easy to implement. He further states: "Granger's causality plays a pervasive role in econometrics."

Granger is also known for his valuable work on long-memory models. The processes with long memory, according to him, have the property that their auto-correlation function "decays" at a much slower rate than that of a linear autoregressive moving average (ARMA) process. He was credited with being one of the first econometricians to have done significant work in non-linear time series models, particularly in empirical macroeconomics. His early book on economic forecasting, particularly its role in the evaluation of econometric models, is the one that has enriched the field. In this context, his work in the field of applied finance in association with Oscar Morgenstern is considered an outstanding contribution and early classic in the area. In a later contribution, he was instrumental in extending economic analysis into cost-benefit framework of forecast errors.

29.3 CONCLUDING OBSERVATIONS

Granger was a titanic figure who had made significant contribution to the field of time series analysis. Economics and economic and econometric researchers have been immensely benefitted by his work. Granger and Engel together have been instrumental in developing a new area of financial econometrics. Their 1987 joint paper, which is considered seminal, is in the words of Francis Diebold, "the most cited paper in the history of econometrics, treating specification, representation, estimation and testing." Granger's work on the analysis of economic time series data was credited with improving the forecasting performance of the British Treasury and Bank of England. David Hendry's assessment of Granger's contributions and the tribute the former pays to the latter bear reproduction in full. In Hendry's words "[Granger's] unravelling of co-integration and common trends and their key properties is a major development, buttressed by many later important highlights. The wealth of citations, further advances and applications of his ideas, attests to his fecundity. It can be argued that Granger's work bears witness to one of the most successful research programmes in the history of econometrics, and will be a lasting contribution to our discipline."

29.4 SELECT BIBLIOGRAPHY OF CLIVE W. J. GRANGER'S WORKS

29.4.1 BOOKS

1964 (with M. Hatanaka), Spectral Analysis of Economic Time Series, Princeton University Press, Princeton, NJ.

1970 (with O. Morgenstern), Predictability of Stock Market Prices, D.C. Heath, Lexington, MA.

1977 (with P. Newbold), Forecasting Economic Time Series, Academic Press, New York.

1978 (with A .P. Anderson), Introduction to Bilinear Time Series Models, Vandenhoeck and Ruprecnt, Gottingen.

1991 (with R.F Engle, eds.), Long-run Economic Relationships, Oxford University Press, Oxford.

1993 (with T. Terasvista), Modeling Non linear Economic Relationships, Oxford University Press, Oxford.

1999 Empirical Modelling in Economics: Specification and Evaluation, Cambridge University Press, Cambridge.

29.4.2 ARTICLES

1963 (with O. Morgenstern), "Spectral Analysis of New York Stock Market Prices," Kyklos, Vol.16, No.1. Reprinted in P.H. Cootner (ed.) The Random Character of Stock Market Prices, MIT Press, Cambridge, MA.

1966 "The Typical Spectral Shape of an Economic Variable," Econometrica, Vol.34, No.1.

1969 a "Investigating Causal Relations by Econometric Models and Cross-Spectral Methods," Econometrica, Vol.37, No.3.

b (with J. Bater), "The Combination of Forecasts", Operations Research Quarterly, Vol.20, No.4.

1973 (with P. Newbold), "Some Comments on the Evaluation of Economic Forecasts," Applied Economics, Vol.5 No,1. Reprinted in T.C Mills (ed.) Economic Forecasting, Edward Elgar, Cheltenham, 1999.

1974 (with P. Newbold), "Spurious Regressions in Econometrics," Journal of Econometrics, Vol.2, pp.111-120.

1975 (with P. Newbold), "The Time Series Approach to Econometric Model Building," in (A. Simos (ed.), New Methods in Business Cycle Research, Federal Reserve Bank, Minneapolis, Minn.

1980 a "Long Memory Relationships and the Aggregation of Dynamic Models," Journal of Econometrics, Vol.14, No.2.

b (with R. Joyeux), "An Introduction to Long Memory Time Series Models and Fractional Differencing," Journal of Time Series Analysis, Vol.1, No.1.

1981 "Some Properties of Time Series Data and Their Use in Econometric Model Specification," Journal of Econometrics, Vol.16, No.1.

1983 a "Forecasting White Noise," in Applied Time Series Analysis of Economic Data, A. Zellner (ed.) Bureau of the Courses, Washington, DC.

b (with A.A. Weiss), "Time Series Analysis of Error-Correction Models," in Studies in Econometrics, Time Series, and Multivariate Statistics, (A. Kartin et al. eds.), Academic Press, New York,

1986 "Developments in the Study of Co-integrated Economic Variables," Oxford Bulletin of Economics and Statistics, Vol.48, No.3.

1987 (with R. F. Engel), "Co-integration and Error Correction: Representation, Estimation and Testing," Econometrica, Vol.55, No.2.

1989 (with T.H. Lee), "Investigation of Production, Sales and Inventory Relationships Using Multi Co-integration and Non-Symmetric Correction Models," Journal of Applied Econometrics, Vol.4, Supplement, pp. 145-159.

1990 (with S. Hylleberg et.al.), "Seasonal, Integration and Cointegration," Journal of Econometrics, Vol.44, No.1-2.

1991 (with T.H Lee), "Multicointegratoin," in Long- run Economic Relationships, (R. F. Engle and C. W. J. Granger eds.) Oxford University Press, Oxford.

1992 (with M. Deutsch), "Comments on the Evaluation of Policy Models," Journal of Policy Modelling, Vol.14, No.4.

1995 (with J. Gonjalo), "Estimation of Common Long-Memory Components in Cointegrated Systems," Journal of Business and Economic Statistics, Vol.13, No. 1, pp.27-35.

1996 (with N. R. Swanson), "Future Developments in the Study of Co-integrated Variables," Oxford Bulletin of Economics and Statistics, Vol.58, No.3.

1997 (with N. R. Swanson), "An Introduction to Stochastic Unit-root Processes," Journal of Econometrics, Vol.80, No.1.

2001 a "Evaluation of Forecasts," in Understanding Economic Forecasts, (Hendry, D. F. and N. R. Ericsson eds.) MIT Press, Cambridge, MA.

b "Spurious Regressions in Econometrics," in A Companion to Theoretical Econometrics,(Baltagi, B. H. ed.) Blackwell, Oxford.

2003 (with Poon, Ser.Huang), "Forecasting Volatility in Financial Markets: A Review," JEL, Vol.41, No.2.

2004 "Time Series Analysis, Co-integration, and Applications," Nobel Lecture, AER, Vol.94, No.3.

29.5 WORKS OF OTHERS

Greene, W.H. (2006), Econometric Analysis, Pearson Education, Delhi.

Hendry, D.F. (2004), "The Nobel Memorial Prize for Clive W.J. Granger," ScandJE, Vol.106, No.2.

Yule, G.U. (1926), "Why Do We Sometimes Get Nonsense – Correlations between Time–Series? A Study in Sampling and the Nature of Time Series," Journal of The Royal Statistical Society, Vol.89, No.1. Reprinted in The Foundation of Econometric Analysis, (Hendry, D. F. and M. S. Morgan eds.) Cambridge University Press, Cambridge.

CHAPTER 30

ROBERT FRY ENGLE III

(1942 –)

The Royal Swedish Academy of Sciences has awarded the Bank of Sweden Prize in Economic Sciences in memory of Alfred Nobel, for 2003, jointly to Clive W. J. Granger of the University of California at San Diego, U.S.A and Robert F. Engle of New York University, New York, U.S.A. While Granger was awarded the prize for deriving methods of analysing economic time series with common trends (co-integration), Engel got the prize for suggesting methods of analyzing economic time series with time-varying volatility (ARCH).

When estimating relationships and testing hypotheses from economic theory, researchers use data in the form of time series; that is, chronological sequence of observations. Such time series relate to gross domestic product (GDP), savings, investment, prices, interest rates, share prices and so on. During the 1980s, Granger and Engel developed new statistical methods for dealing with two important properties of many economic time series: non-stationarity and time-varying volatility.

Volatility or random fluctuations over time are especially important on financial markets. The value of financial instruments such as equity shares and options depends on their risk. Fluctuations can vary much over time. That is, turbulent periods with large fluctuations are followed by quiet periods with small fluctuations. In the absence of a better alternative, researchers, neglecting time varying volatility, used to explore statistical methods that assume constant volatility. Engle effected a breakthrough by discovering the concept of autoregressive conditional heteroscedasticity (ARCH) which accurately captures the properties of many time series. He also developed methods for statistical modelling of time-varying volatility. His ARCH models have become indispensable tools for researchers as also analysts on financial markets, employing them in asset pricing and in assessing portfolio risk.

30.1 A BRIEF BIOGRAPHICAL NOTE: ROBERT ENGLE

Robert Fry Engle III was born in Syracuse on November 10, 1942 in a Quaker family who emigrated from Cambridge, England in the 1600s. They left England to escape religious persecution and set up their lives in Pennsylvania with the other Quakers. His father, Robert Fry Engle Jr, a chemist, earned a Ph.D. in Chemistry from Cornell University. His mother, Mary Phillips was a student of Swarthmore College and University of

Pennsylvania, Philadelphia. The family moved back to the Philadelphia area in Swarthmore some time after Engle III's birth. Engle recalls that they had had a happy time. He was a very active child and as an adolescent, loved science, sports, music and friends. He attended Penncrest High School from where he graduated in 1960.

Engle studied at Williams College. His four years there were filled with "fun, growing up, and more science." He majored in Physics, joined the Beta, Theta, Pi fraternity. By senior year he was nominated to Phi Beta Kappa. Academically, he started with Physics and Mathematics at the sophomore level. According to his autobiographical note, "...a small event happened in my senior year that would have great consequences. I could take one more elective to finish out my courses.... I decided... to try Introductory Economics.... I loved the course.... Who could have predicted that this one elective would later serve as the catalyst that changed the course of my life?" Engle graduated from Williams Cum Laude with Highest Honors in Physics and went off to Ithaca, New York, for graduate studies.

In Cornell University, Ithaca, he worked in Professor Watt Webb's Laboratory. Engle realised that he did not like to spend the rest of his life as a physicist. He states: "After agonizing over the feelings... I approached... [the] Chairman of the Economics department at Cornell." Engel was admitted into the Ph.D. programme with a fellowship grant." Engle had to tell his father and Professor Webb. Both were supportive with "heavy hearts." At that point, according to Engle, neither his father nor he realised how important "all that scientific training would be in my contributions to Economics." He loved Economics.

The years Engle spent in graduate school passed quickly. A few summers were spent in Washington D.C at the Bureau of the Budget "doing program budgeting." He first tried to solve a cost-benefit problem for public transportation where he recognised that land use was endogenous in the long run and this was critical for the analysis. This was his first introduction to urban economics. As years passed his work became more focussed on time series econometrics. His advisor, Ta Chung Liu, suggested Engle try to theoretically analyse the relationship between the different time scales for economic modelling. Engel was able to use his skills in physics by formulating the problem in the frequency domain and applying Clive Granger's "typical spectral shape" for an economic time series which was his "first introduction" to Granger's work. Engle married Marianne Eger in August 1969. On the day of the marriage, Engle turned in his dissertation, received his Ph.D. They left Cornell to take up his first academic job at MIT.

MIT had many famous economists, "none of whom were particularly interested in times series." In 1970 summer, Engle attended the World Congress of Econometrics, where he met a number of economists including Clive Granger, Ken Walker and David Hendry who became lifelong friends and collaborators. When he was at MIT, he received an Outstanding Teacher of the Year Award from the graduate students. During the years at MIT, Engel was associated with Boston Redevelopment Project to build a model of the city of Boston. Other economists associated with the project included Franklin Fisher, Robert

Solow and Jerry Rothenberg. He became an urban economist, publishing very elaborate statistical models in a field "not known for its mathematical sophistication."

Engle was hired as an Urban Economist by UCSD (University of California, San Diego) and for years he taught urban economics course. Clive Granger was a Professor at the UCSD. According to the autobiographical note of Engel, "it was the beginning of a golden time for time series econometrics." He along with Granger started an econometric seminar series. In 1979, Engel took a sabbatical at London School of Economics. He was interested in Milton Friedman's "conjecture" that inflation uncertainty was a central cause of business cycles. Investors who did not know what prices and wages would be in the future might invest less. To test this, Engel wanted to develop a time series model with variances that could change over time. Two tools are needed to solve this problem. He states: "I had done a lot of work with the Kalman Filter and recognized that a one step predictive density would be sufficient to define a likelihood function. The second tool was a test Granger had proposed; a test for bilinear time series models." Granger suggested that Engel square the residuals and then fit an auto regression which he did and found that it was "quite significant." Engel later was to discover that it is the optimal test for ARCH and it is so called today. David Hendry named it Auto Regressive Conditional Heteroscedasticity (ARCH). They applied the ARCH model to UK inflation data and the ARCH model was launched. The paper was published in Econometrica.

In 1980, Engel became very interested in Granger's new concept of low frequency correlated, which Granger called co-integration. It seemed to Engel that Dickey-Fuller's unit roots tests could be extended to this case. Therefore, Engel constructed an econometric approach to estimation and testing of co-integrated systems. Engel, in collaboration with Granger, wrote two joint papers- one of which was published in Oxford Bulletin of Economics and Statistics and the other in Econometrica. Engel's student, Tim Bollersley created GARCH, by adding a moving average to the ARCH model. The GARCH model is an infinite order ARCH model with a geometrically declining set of weights. This extension made the model more useful. The profession rapidly developed a wide range of extensions of ARCH and GARCH models, like exponential GARCH model called EGARCH, TARCH etc.

Engel's interests gravitated more and more to finance. A central feature of financial analysis concerns the trade-off between risk and return. The ARCH model has a mechanism measuring this -- called the ARCH-M model. Engle, with co-authors, using a multivariate version of this, generalised the Capital Asset Pricing Model, CAPM. Options markets traded volatility and gave a "quantitative validation" of the ARCH models. Engel ran several conferences in San Diego on the ARCH model, designed for both academics and practitioners. Gradually this new area of research has come to be known as financial econometrics. It is the development of statistical tools, specifically designed for financial applications. The UCSD, under the leadership of Engel, has developed specialisation in Financial Econometrics. With support from collaborators, he introduced another idea into econometrics – common features. The objective is to simplify multivariate systems into a small number of variables that endow the system with its typical features that are common. The idea is to generalise factor analysis that has applications to co-integrated systems, multivariate ARCH models and many areas of economics. This simplified analysis is a way that is widely used in financial research. Engel, in his Nobel lecture states: I will be surprised if there aren't important research developments using common features in the next few years.

Later in collaboration with an associate, Engel developed a new approach to measuring the extremes of a distribution. The method quantifies the probability of large losses on a portfolio by predicting the future quantiles. The model called CAViaR- conditional autoregressive value at risk--uses the theory of regression quantiles in a time series context, an updating formula for the value at risk (extreme quantile) of a portfolio. Financial data often exhibit variation in trading rates, called duration clustering. Engel and an associate developed what is referred to as Autoregressive Conditional Duration (ACD) model for this purpose. It is a Poisson process with an intensity that is conditional on past information. ACD has the same structure as the GARCH model and recognises the close relation between trading intensity and volatility. Later in the Fisher Schultz Lecture, Engel combined the time between trades and the prices at which trades took place into an "ultra high frequency" or tick by tick GARCH model. In the Prize lecture, Engel states that he was convinced that the trading frequency measured a fundamental heart beat of financial markets. It reflects the information flow and also closely related to measures of liquidity.

In 1999, Engel spent a semester at New York University. He took a permanent position at New York University in 2000, retiring from UCSD and becoming an emeritus professor there.

30.2 A SUMMARY OF CONTRIBUTIONS OF ROBERT ENGLE

Engle's Prize lecture, a good summary of his and others' contributions to the subject, starts with a few introductory remarks. The knowledge of risks enables people to modify their behaviour to avoid them. People do not and cannot avoid all risks. Instead, they choose to take some risks since the rewards from taking them outweigh the possible costs. The central paradigm of finance suggests that optimal behaviour of people lies in taking risks that are worthwhile. In other words, people must take risks to obtain rewards but not all risks are equally rewarded. More importantly, both risks and rewards are in the future; the decision makers, therefore, are obliged to balance expectation of loss against expectation of reward; in particular, they achieve an optimal portfolio to maximise rewards and minimise risks. He then remarks that this simple concept has a hoary history in economics and in "Nobel citations." He refers to the work of Markowitz and Tobin who associated risk with portfolio variance. From the avoidance of risk, they derived optimising portfolio and banking behaviour. He then makes reference to Sharpe's CAPM which demonstrates a "natural relation" between expected returns and risk or variance. Next in line is the option pricing formula developed by Black, Scholes and Merton. Engle observes: "While the theory is based on option replication arguments through dynamic trading strategies, it is also consistent with the CAPM. Put options give the owner the right to sell an asset at pre-arranged price at a certain time in the future; hence they are thought of as insurance. Purchase of such put options enables an investor to completely eliminate the portfolio risk. The price of protection, that is, the cost of insurance, is determined by the risks which are measured by the variance of the asset returns. Financial economists are concerned with modelling volatility in asset returns; in other words, the covariance structure of asset returns.

The variances need to be estimated for those who desire to make use of the management strategies. Practitioners typically use the estimate of volatility which is taken as indicated by the square root of variance of returns. A simple approach which is widely used is the historical volatility. In this method, volatility is estimated by the sample standard deviation of returns over a short period. If a long period estimate is used, it may be inappropriate for use today. On the other hand, if the estimate is for too short a period, it will be "very noisy;" more importantly, future volatility is considered risk. As such, forecast of volatility of returns is required, besides a measure of volatility for today. The moot question is whether volatility remains unchanged from time to time. Historical volatility does not provide any satisfactory solution for these problems.

It is quite inappropriate to make an assumption that variance would be constant over time. There is, therefore, a need to have a theory of dynamic volatilities. The ARCH model developed by Engel and the many extensions of the original model by him and others foots the bill. The Royal Swedish Academy explicitly refers to "methods of analyzing economic time-series with time-varying volatility (ARCH)."

Engle's contributions are summarised under the following two heads:

1. Development of ARCH Model; and
2. Other contributions.

30.2.1 DEVELOPMENT OF ARCH MODEL

The background for the birth of the ARCH model was given by Engel in his Prize lecture. It was "invented" while he was on sabbatical at the London School of Economics in 1979. He was looking for a model that would examine the volatility of Milton Friedman's conjecture in his 1977 Prize lecture that the unpredictability of inflation was a critical cause for business cycles. According to Friedman, the problem was not the level of inflation. It was the uncertainty regarding future costs and prices which would hinder investment by entrepreneurs resulting in a recession. Engel thought that this could only be possible if the uncertainty were changing over time -- referred to as heteroscedasticity by econometricians.

Heteroscedasticity is generally viewed by economists as a cross-sectional phenomenon, not as a time-series one. A pertinent example is the estimation of Engel curve in microeconomics. In the estimation of Engel curve, the variance of the disturbances in expenditure equations tends to grow with income. It is realised by financial economists that the heteroscedasticity is pervasive in the time series estimates of returns on financial assets in which clustering of volatility (that is contiguous periods of high or low volatility) is noticed. Further, the marginal distributions of many asset returns are leptokurtic. They have thicker tails than the density of the normal distribution with the same mean and variance. Still, researchers modelled returns as independently and identically distributed over time. Further, in economic data, it is found that squared residuals often were auto-correlated though residuals themselves were not auto-correlated. The test for bilinear time series models developed by Clive Granger was based on dependence over time of squared residuals. Engel "suspected" that the test was detecting something besides bilinearity "but I didn't know what." In Engle's words, "The solution was autoregressive conditional heteroscedasticity or ARCH, a name invented by David Hendry." (Emphasis in the original).

The ARCH model describes the forecast variance in terms of current observables. It takes weighted averages of past squared forecast errors, a type of weighted variance. It is a simple generalisation of the sample variance. The big advance, according to Engel, was that the weights could be computed from historical data, though the true volatility could not be observed. Maximum likelihood procedure is adopted for estimating the optimal weights. After estimating the weights, this dynamic model of time varying volatility is employed in order to measure the volatility at any time as also to forecast it into the near and distant future. Granger's test for bilinearity turned out to be the optimal or Lagrange Multiplier test for ARCH and is widely used today. Engel remarks: While the trade-off between risk and return is an important part of macroeconomic theory, the empirical implications are often difficult to detect as they are disguised by other dominating effects, and obscured by the reliance on relatively low frequency data. In finance, the risk/return effects are of primary importance and data on daily or even intra-daily frequencies are readily available to form accurate variety of ARCH models developed.

Prior to the development of ARCH model, time-series econometric models were concerned with aspects of linear or non-linear conditional mean dependence. The question that needed to be answered was: What about conditional variance dependence or what about conditional heteroscedasticity. That is why Engel's modelling of time-varying volatility by way of autoregressive conditional heteroscedasticity is considered a genuine breakthrough.

The advanced information provided by the Royal Swedish Academy outlines the essence of the simple ARCH model which is given here.

In time series econometrics, model builders generally parametrise the conditional mean of a variable or a vector of variables. Suppose that at time't' a stochastic vector (Y_t, X^1_t) is observed where Yt is a scalar and Xt, a vector of variables, such that some of its elements may be logs of Yt. The following predictive model for variable Yt is implied.

$$Y_t = E\{Y_t/X_t\} + \varepsilon_t \qquad .....(1)$$

Here the conditional mean $E\{Y_t/X_t\}$ typically has a parametric form E{ε_t} = 0, and E{ε_t ε_s} = 0 for t≠s, that is, {ε_t} is a sequence of uncorrelated random variables with mean zero.

(The conditional mean may be a non-parametric function of Xt, in which case the focus is on estimating its functional form).

When estimating the parameters in $E\{Y_t/X_t\}$, it is generally assumed that the unconditional variance of the error term ε_t is constant or time-varying in unknown fashion.

In 1982, Engel in his just widely cited papers in the history of economics, considered the alternative assumption that, while the unconditional error variance, if it exists, is constant, the conditional error variance is time-varying. This step enabled Engel explain systematic features in the movements of variance over time and to estimate the parameters of conditional variance jointly with the parameters of the conditional mean. He parameterised the conditional variance of ε_t in eq.(1) such that large positive or negative errors ε_t were likely to be followed by another large error of either sign and small errors by a small error of either sign. More formally, Engel assumed that ε_t can be decomposed as ε_t = √Zt ht where {Zt} is a sequence of independently identically distributed random variable with zero mean and unit variance, and where

$$h_t = var(\varepsilon_t/F_t) = \alpha_0 + \sum_{j=1}^{q} \alpha_j \varepsilon_{t-j}^2 \tag{2}$$

In the above equation

$$\varepsilon_t = Y_t - E\{Y_t/X_t\}$$

and the information set

$$F_t = \{\varepsilon_t\text{-}j;\ j \geq 1\},\ \alpha_0 > 0, \text{ and } \alpha_j \geq 0,\ j = 1,\dots,q,$$

Eq.(2) defines the ARCH model introduced by Engel in his 1982 paper, where the conditional variance is a function of past values of squared errors. Further, he developed the estimation theory for the ARCH model, stipulated conditions for maximum likelihood estimators to be consistent and asymptotically normal and presented a Lagrange multiplier test for the hypothesis of no ARCH--equal conditional and unconditional variance – in the errors ε_t . Francis Diebold observes: “Interestingly, the serial correlation in volatility had been observed empirically decades earlier. In his classic analysis of returns on speculative markets Mandelbrot... was very clear, noting that ‘large changes tend to be followed by large changes – of either sign – and small changes tend to be followed by small changes.’ But Mandelbrot emphasised “the unconditional non-normality of returns, rather than their volatility clustering.”

To illustrate the use of ARCH models for financial applications, Engel provides an example in his Prize lecture. The example relates to the analysis of the Standard and Poor’s 500 Composite index representing the bulk of the value in the U.S. equity market. The analysis examined daily levels of the index from 1963 through late November 2003. He states that this gives a sweep of U.S. financial history which provides an ideal setting to discuss how ARCH models are used for risk management and option pricing. He finds a remarkable growth of equity prices during the reference period and the subsequent decline after the year 2000. He estimates that one U.S. dollar invested in 1963 would have become 16 U.S. dollars by November 21, 2003 (plus reinvestment of the possible stream of dividends). If the investor cleverly sells his position on March 24, 2000, it would have been worth 24 U.S. dollars. Hopefully, he was not so unlucky as to have purchased on that day.

Economists focus on returns, the relative price from the purchase point to the sale point. The data and the related diagram show that the most dramatic event is the crash of October 1987. It dwarfs all other returns in the size of the decline and subsequent partial recovery. The data series (before 1987) also show that the amplitude of the returns was changing. The magnitude of changes was sometimes large and sometimes small. Engel states that this is the effect that ARCH is designed to measure, called volatility. Further, it is clear that the volatility is higher when prices are falling. Volatility tends to be higher in bear markets. This is the asymmetric volatility effect that Nelson described with his EGARCH (Exponential GARCH) model.

An examination of the next sub-period after the crash of 1987 reveals a record low volatility of the middle-1990s. This was followed by a slow and steady growth of equity prices. However, this did not suggest the beginning of a new era of low volatility. In fact, the volatility began to rise as share prices got higher and higher, touching very high levels from 1998 on. It is clear that, judging by the pattern of observed volatility, the stock market was risky. However, investors were willing to take this risk because they were compensated by higher returns. Since 1998, the market continued to show high volatility till the official conclusion of the Iraq War. Then there was a substantial decline in volatility, which seemingly encouraged investors to return to the market which had experienced large price increases.

Engel in his lecture provides information on computed mean equity returns, standard deviations and skewness for the entire 40-year period and for the period since 1990. According to him, the remarkable feature is the kurtosis which measures the magnitude of the extremes. The value of kurtosis should be three, if returns are normally distributed. The computed value of kurtosis of the nineteen nineties is "substantial" at 6.8, while for the full period it is a "dramatic" 41. This is strong evidence that extremes are more substantial than would be expected from a normal random variable.

An examination of auto correlations shows the unpredictability of returns and clustering volatility. Engle's conclusions from the computations on the basis of the S&P 500 returns include:

(i) The return auto correlations are almost all insignificant;

(ii) The squared returns have all significant autocorrelations; and

(iii) The squared returns autocorrelations are all positive which is highly unlikely to occur by chance.

This is powerful evidence for both the unpredictability of returns and the clustering of volatility. Engel then turns to the issue of estimating volatility. He constructed estimates called historical volatility for 5 day, one-year and five-year windows based on rolling standard deviations of returns. As he could not get any true measure of volatility, Engel observes: it is difficult to pick from these candidates. The ARCH model provides a solution to this dilemma. He attempts at estimating volatility by using various models-- ARCH, GARCH (1,1), TARCH(Threshold ARCH)etc.-- and furnishes TARCH estimates of volatility in his Prize Lecture. He states: "... [the] example illustrates many of the features of ARCH/GARCH models and how they can be used to study volatility processes."

Engel, in his Prize lecture also dwells at some length on estimating Value at Risk (VAR) by financial services institutions and shows how ARCH and GARCH models can be used for this purpose. Here reference may be made to the advanced information provided by Royal Swedish Academy regarding a simple example of the use of GARCH models in the value-at-risk analysis. Assuming an investor with an S&P 500 index portfolio of one million U.S dollars (Daily returns for the period May 16, 1995 to April 29, 2003) and assuming further that he estimates GARCH(1,1) model with normal errors, the investor desires to estimate the amount below which his loss will remain with probability 0.99 the next day, when the stock exchange is open if he retains the portfolio. The maximum loss predicted from the GARCH model for September 2, 1995 equals $12,400 whereas the corresponding sum for August 1, 2002 is $61,500. The difference between the sums illustrates the importance of time-varying volatility and of ARCH as a tool in the value–at–risk analysis. Further, Engel demonstrates how the dynamic model can be used to value options. The pricing of options and other derivatives, where the variance of the underlying asset is a key parameter is an obvious area of application of ARCH, GARCH models. He also states in the concluding part of his lecture that there appears to be two important frontiers of research that are receiving a great deal of focus and have important promise for applications. These are high frequency volatility models and high dimension multivariate models. He concludes on a hopeful note: "It is safe to predict that in the next several years, we will have a set of useful methods for modelling the volatilities and correlations of large systems of assets."

30.2.2 OTHER CONTRIBUTIONS OF ROBERT ENGLE

Engle has made significant and valuable contributions in several areas of time-series econometrics. His collaborative work with Granger in developing tests for co-integration and techniques of estimation for models with co-integrated variables has been referred and summarised in the preceding chapter. Engel has done useful work on exogeneity which is an important concept in econometric modelling. A sizeable literature has grown using GARCH methods to measure and test hypotheses concerning risk premia in shares, bonds, commodities and foreign exchange markets. This is based on the phenomenon that when volatility of returns on financial assets varies, it may be that time-varying risk in premia may be present.

GARCH methods have been found to be eminently applicable for spot pricing of assets as also for pricing of derivatives. Since the important object in option pricing is a forecast of the underlying asset's volatility path over the option's life, GARCH models are found useful for improved pricing of options and other derivative products. Besides, GARCH methods have been applied for the purpose of hedging of option portfolios.

Cross-market transmission of shocks is a crucial concern in international finance. Engel's volatility models are applied in his studies investigating whether basics of volatility remain in that market or they tend to spread from market to market; that is, whether there is strong volatility across global equity markets (what Engel calls "heat waves, vs. meteor showers"). Extending the logic, research has spawned into cross-asset interaction in a single market, such as individual equity shares on an exchange.

These are some of the important extensions and applications of ARCH and GARCH, particularly in financial economics, which successfully has bridged academics and industry influencing modern asset pricing, portfolio allocation and risk management.

30.3 CONCLUDING OBSERVATIONS

Engel's total work is judged as a fine example of best-practice applied time-series econometrics. Francis Diebold tellingly summarises: "...he identifies important dynamic economic phenomena, formulates precise and interesting questions about those phenomena, constructs sophisticated yet simple econometric models for measurement and testing, and consistently obtains results of widespread substantive interest in the scientific, policy and financial communities." The blossoming of time-series econometrics from 1960's onwards is significantly due to the theoretical and empirical work of Engel and Granger. To this development, besides contributions of leading established econometricians around the world, one must acknowledge the contribution of Engel's graduate students. In Diebold's words: The Nobel Memorial Prize for Engel and Granger is a long awaited and well-deserved prize for time-series econometrics in general---appropriately paralleling the earlier Heckman-McFadden prize for micro econometrics---and for two of its most important contributions in particular: Models of volatility (ARCH)and common trends (co-integration). Of crucial importance is the fact that the Engel-Granger prize, like the Heckman-McFadden prize, is for economic research that is not only scientifically path-breaking, but also of great and immediate practical relevance.

30.4 SELECT BIBLIOGRAPHY OF WOKS OF ROBERT ENGLE-III

30.4.1 BOOKS

1994 (With D Fadden eds.), Handbook of Econometrics, Vol. iv, North Holland, Amsterdam.

1995 (ed.) ARCH: Selected Readings, Oxford University Press, Oxford.

30.4.2 ARTICLES

1973 "Band Spectrum Regression," IER, Vol.15, No.1.

1978 "Estimating Structural Models of Seasonality," in Seasonal Analysis of Economic Time Series, U.S., A. Zellner (ed.),Department of Commerce, Bureau of Census, Washington, D.C.

1982 "Autoregressive Conditional Heteroskedasticity with Estimates of the Variance of U.K Inflation," Econometrica, Vol. 50, No.4.

1983 "Estimates of the Variance of U.S Inflation Based on the ARCH Model," JMCB, Vol. 15, No.3.

1984 "Wald Likelihood Ratio and Lagrange Multiplier in Tests in Econometrics," in Handbook of Econometrics, Vol.2, Z. Griliches and M. Intrilligator (eds.) North Holland, Amsterdam.

1985 a (with D.F. Hendry and D. Trumble), "Small Sample Properties of ARCH Estimators and Tests," Canadian Journal of Economics, Vol.18, No.1.

b (with D. M. Lilien and M. Watson), " A Dymimic Model of Housing Price Determination," Journal of Econometrics, Vol.28, pp. 307-326.

1986 (with T. Bollersley), "Modeling the Persistence of Conditional Variances," Econometric Review, Vol.5, No.1.

1987 (with D. M. Lilien and R.P Robins), "Estimating Time- varying Risk Premia in the Term Structure: The ARCH-M Model," Econometrica, Vol.55, No.2.

1988 (with T. Bollersley and J. M. Wooldridge), "A Capital Asset-Pricing Model with Time Varying Co-variances," JPE, Vol.96, Feb.

1990 a (with T. Ito and W. Lin), "Meteor Showers or Heat Waves? Heteroskedastic Intra-daily Volatility in the Foreign Exchange Market," Econometrica, Vol. 58, No.3.

b (with V.K Ng and M. Rothschild), "Asset Pricing with a Factor-ARCH Covariance Structure: Empirical Estimates for Treasury Bills," Journal of Econometrics, Vol. 45, July-Aug.

1991 (with G. Gonzalez-Rivera), "Semi-parametric ARCH Models," Journal of Business and Economic Statistics, Vol.9, No.4.

1992 a (with R. Chou and A. Kane), "Measuring Risk Aversion from Excess Returns on a Stock Index," Journal of Econometrics, Vol.52, No.1-2.

b (with T. Ito and W. Lin), "Where Does the Meteor Shower Come From? The Role of Stochastic Policy and Coordination," Journal of International Economics, Vol.32, No.3-4.

c (with T. Rothschild, eds.), "ARCH Models in Finance," Journal of Econometrics, Vol.52, No. 1-2.

d (with C. Mustafa), "Implied ARCH Models from Options Prices," Journal of Econometrics, Vol.52, No.1-2.

1993 a (with V. K. Ng), "Measuring and Testing the Impact of News on Volatility," JF, Vol.48, No.5.

b (with T. Bollersley), "Common Persistence in Conditional Variances," Econometrica, Vol.61, No.1.

c (with C. H. Hong et al.), "Arbitrage Valuation of Variance Forecasts with Simulated Options," in Advances in Futures and Options Research, D. Chance and R. Tripp (eds.) JAI Press, Greenwich, CT.

d (with R. Susmel), "Hourly Volatility in International Equity Markets," Journal of Business and Economic Statistics, Vol.11, No.4.

1994 a (with A. Kane and J. Noh), "Forecasting Volatility and Option Prices of the S&P 500 Index," Journal of Derivatives, Vol.2, No.1.

b (with R. Susmel), "Hourly Volatility Spillovers Between International Equity Markets," Journal of International Money and Finance, Vol.13, No.1.

c (with T. Ito and W. Lin), "Do Bulls and Bears Move Across Borders?: International Transmission of Stock Returns and Volatility," Review of Financial Studies, Vol.7, No.3.

1995 (with J.V. Rosenberg), "Garch Gammas," Journal of Derivatives, Vol.2, No.4.

1997 (with J.R. Russell), "Forecasting the Frequency of Changes in Quoted Foreign Exchange Prices with Autoregressive Conditional Duration Model," Journal of Empirical Finance, Vol.4, No.2-3.

1998 (with J.R Russell), "Autoregressive Conditional Duration: A New Model for Irregularly Spaced Transaction data," Econometrica, Vol.66, Sep.

1999 (with A.D. Smith), "Stochastic Permanent Breaks," REStat, Vol.81, No.4.

2000 a (with J. V. Rosenberg), "Testing the Volatility Term Structure using Option Hedging Criteria," Journal of Derivatives, Vol.8, No.1.

b "The Econometrics of Ultra High Frequency Data," Econometrica, Vol.68, Jan.

2001 (with J. Lange), "Predicting VNET: A Model for the Dynamics of Market Depth," Journal of Financial Markets, Vol.4, No.2.

2002 a "Dynamic Conditional Correlation: A Simple Class of Generalized Auto-regressive Conditional Heteroskedasticity Models," Journal of Business and Economic Statistics, Vol.20, No.3.

b "New Frontiers for ARCH Models," Journal of Applied Econometrics, Vol.17, No.5.

2003 (with A. Lunde), "Trades and Quotes: A Bivariate Point Process," Journal of Financial Econometrics, Vol.1, No.2.

2004 a (with J.R. Russell), "Analysis of High Frequency and Transaction Data" in Handbook of Financial Econometrics, L.P. Hansen and Y. Ait Sahalia (eds.) North-Holland, Amsterdam.

b (with G.M. Gallo)," Risk and Volatility: Econometric Models and Financial Practice," Nobel Lecture, AER, Vol. 94, No.3.

2006 a (with F.X. Diebold et al.), "The Econometrics of Macroeconomics, Finance and the interface," Journal of Econometrics, Vol.131, No.1-2.

b (with C. Lorenzo and K. Sheppard), "Asymmetric Dynamics in the Correlation of Global Equity and Bond Returns," Journal of Financial Econometrics, Vol. 4, No.4.

2010 (with G.T. Bali), "The Intertemporal Capital Assets Pricing Model with Dynamic Conditional Correlations," JME, Vol. 57, No.4.

2011 "Long-Term Skewness and Systemic Risk," Journal of Financial Econometrics, Vol.9, No.3.

2013 (with E. Ghysels and B. Sohn), "Stock Market Volatility and Macroecomic Fundamentals," REstat, Vol. 95, No.3.

30.5 WORKS OF OTHERS

Diebold, F.X (2004), "The Nobel Memorial Prize for Robert F. Engle," ScandJE, Vol.106, No.2.

Friedman, M (1997), "Nobel Lecture: Inflation and Unemployment," JPE, Vol.85, No.3.

Mandelbrot, B. (1963), "The Variation of Certain Speculative Prices," JB, Vol.36, No.4.

Names of Journals: Abbreviations (Journal Index)

AER (American Economic Review)

Bell JE (Bell Journal of Economics)

BPEA (Brookings Papers on Economic Activity)

BPEA (Brookings Panel on Economic Activity)

Cambridge JE (Cambridge Journal of Economics)

Canadian JE (Canadian Journal of Economics)

Carnegie-Rochester (Conference Series on Public Policy)

Econ Dev & Cul Chang (Economic Development and Cultural Change)

EJ (Economic Journal)

GEB (Games and Economic Behavior)

HOPE (History of Political Economy)

IER (International Economic Review)

IJGT (International Journal of Game Theory)

JASA (Journal of American Statistical Association)

JDE (Journal of Development Economics)

JEBO (Journal of Economic Behavior and Organization)

JEDC (Journal of Economic Dynamics and Control)

JEH (Journal of Economic History)

JEL (Journal of Economic Literature)

JET (Journal of Economic Theory)

JEvolE (Journal of Evolutionary Economics)

JF (Journal of Finance)

JIE (Journal of International Economics)

JITE (Journal of Institutional and Theoretical Economics)

JLawE (Journal of Law and Economics)

JMathE (Journal of Mathematical Economics)

JMCB (Journal of Money, Credit and Banking)

JME (Journal of Monetary Economics)

JPE (Journal of Political Economy)

JPubE (Journal of Public Economics)

JRSS (Journal of the Royal Statistical Society)

OEP (Oxford Economic Papers)

QJE (Quarterly Journal of Economics)

Rand JE (RAND Journal of Economics)

RES (Review of Economic Studies)

REStat (The Review of Economics and Statistics)

RIE (Review of International Economics)

Scand JE (Scandinavian Journal of Economics)

SEJ (Southern Economic Journal)

WEJ (Western Economic Journal (later Economic Inquiry))

Name Index

C

D

E

F

G

H

I

J

K

M

N

O

P

S

W

X

Y

Z

Topic Index

A

B

C

D

E

F

N

Q

R

U

V

W

X

Y

www.ingramcontent.com/pod-product-compliance
Lightning Source LLC
Chambersburg PA
CBHW061151240926
51846CB00006B/981
9789395038942